# CALIFORNIA ARCHAEOLOGY

Pomo dancer in Bighead costume. (After Meighan and Riddell 1972: Figure 7; drawing by Don Meighan; courtesy of the Southwest Museum.)

# CALIFORNIA ARCHAEOLOGY

## Michael J. Moratto

*INFOTEC Development, Inc.*
*Sonora, California*
and
*California Academy of Sciences*
*San Francisco, California*

*with contributions by*

**David A. Fredrickson**      **Christopher Raven**      **Claude N. Warren**

*Sonoma State University*      *Desert Institute of Geography*      *University of Nevada, Las Vegas*
*Rohnert Park, California*      *Sacramento, California*      *Las Vegas, Nevada*

*with a foreword by*
Francis A. Riddell

1984

ACADEMIC PRESS, INC.
*Harcourt Brace Jovanovich, Publishers*

Orlando  San Diego  San Francisco  New York  London
Toronto  Montreal  Sydney  Tokyo  São Paulo

*The design on the front cover was adapted by Lesley Iura from petroglyphs photographed by Georgia Lee, Research Associate of the Institute of Archaeology of the University of California, Los Angeles, at site Iny-279 in the Renegade Canyon of the Coso Range. By permission of Lesley Iura and Georgia Lee.*

ACADEMIC PRESS, INC.
Orlando, Florida 32887

*United Kingdom Edition published by*
ACADEMIC PRESS, INC. (LONDON) LTD.
24/28 Oval Road, London NW1 7DX

Moratto, Michael J.
    California archaeology.

    (New world archaeological record)
    Includes index.
    1. Indians of North America--California--Antiquities.
2. California--Antiquities. I. Fredrickson, David A.
(David Allen) II. Title. III. Series.
E78.C15M665    1984        979.4'01        83-7141
ISBN 0-12-506180-3
ISBN 0-12-506182-X (Paper)

PRINTED IN THE UNITED STATES OF AMERICA

84 85 86 87    9 8 7 6 5 4 3 2 1

# NEW WORLD ARCHAEOLOGICAL RECORD

*Under the Editorship of*

**James Bennett Griffin**

Museum of Anthropology
University of Michigan
Ann Arbor, Michigan

*Published:*

**Michael J. Moratto, with contributions by David A. Frederickson,
Christopher Raven, and Claude N. Warren,** California Archaeology
**Robert E. Bell (Ed.),** Prehistory of Oklahoma
**James L. Phillips and James A. Brown (Eds.),** Archaic Hunters
and Gatherers in the American Midwest
**Dan F. Morse and Phyllis A. Morse,** Archaeology of the Central
Mississippi Valley
**Lawrence E. Aten,** Indians of the Upper Texas Coast
**Ronald J. Mason,** Great Lakes Archaeology
**Dean R. Snow,** The Archaeology of New England
**Jerald T. Milanich and Charles H. Fairbanks,** Florida Archaeology
**George C. Frison,** Prehistoric Hunters of the High Plains

*To Lynn,*
*whose patient confidence inspired me*
*to finish this work*

# Contents

# List of Figures

# List of Tables

# Foreword

California archaeology has benefited from the labors of a great number and variety of people, each generation building on the efforts of the past one. From this diversity of thought and action a man of considerable courage has attempted to bring some order to the great accumulation of archaeological data. When one considers the diversity of the researchers in professionalism, commitment, energy, and personality, and the immense prehistoric cultural and natural variability found in California, only a highly motivated person with outstanding ability and knowledge could take on such a task.

The author, Michael Moratto, has asked three other archaeologists to assist him in the individual preparation of three chapters. His selection was an act of brilliance in itself: he chose David Fredrickson, Claude Warren, and Christopher Raven, men whose areal specialization and high professionalism ensure that *California Archaeology* will be a landmark in the elucidation of the known record of California's prehistory.

Time has selected me as an elder statesman of the archaeology business in California. Looking back, from my first interest in archaeology at the age of six in the late 1920s, I had a keen interest in the human beings who seemed so carelessly to have left behind them evidence of their earlier presence near our ranch in northeastern California. Later, as a student at the Sacramento Junior College, I became closely associated with Jeremiah B. Lillard, president of that institution, and his student assistant, Franklin Fenenga—both pioneers in central California archaeology. In keeping with the times, collecting bodies of data through intensive fieldwork *was* archaeology. Interpretation and integration of the data we collected always seemed to lie in the future. Some of us were happily locked into this mode, this old strategy.

It is a pleasant and reasonably rewarding life to gather data and preserve it for the future, but, felicitously, new strategies have been invading the discipline of archaeology in California. Better planning for more complete data-gathering has largely replaced the collecting of data as an end in itself. Early on, our archaeological ranks were pitifully thin, but then the urgency was not so great. Fortunately our numbers greatly swelled in the post–World War II period to try to keep pace with the unbelievable changes being made to California's landscape with a concomitant loss of nonrenewable cultural resources. We are indeed fortunate that data are now collected more systematically and that they are used in a broad framework of more or less scientific theory to allow archaeologists to do what they really intended to do all along: to talk about those outstanding humans—the California Indians—who made California their home for the past twelve millennia or more. It is only through archaeology that their prehistory will be known. Archaeologists, working together with remaining California Indians, face the challenge of retrieving and interpreting what remains of our joint prehistoric patrimony in California.

*California Archaeology* serves as a rallying point, a highwater mark, that will allow us to gain a better grasp of the larger picture and then move forward to an even greater understanding of California's intricate and absorbing prehistoric past.

Francis A. Riddell
*State Archaeologist*

# Preface

"A book summarizing all California archaeology? It can't be done."
*Robert F. Heizer, 1975*

"He was right."
*M. J. M., 1982*

This book relates the story of California's early peoples and cultures, beginning with the Ice Age pioneers who first settled the area and ending with the Indian communities on the eve of history. In a word, this is a California prehistory—a synopsis of cultural developments, as known from archaeology, over a span of millennia. Beyond its role as a chronicle, this account seeks to define major themes in California prehistory, to explain important cultural events and patterns discovered archaeologically, and to show how California's past is relevant to a wider understanding of human behavior. Also provided is a history of archaeological work in California, although that is not the main focus of the book.

*California Archaeology* is designed first as an introduction to the topic for students and general readers, and next as a compilation of current knowledge for archaeologists who are not California specialists. The need was expressed by colleague from Oregon, who wrote: "I am wondering why you don't write a book on California archaeology to make sense of it for outsiders. Mostly we outsiders (speaking modestly for everyone without their authorization) find it an impenetrable maze" (Aikens 1975:1).

Indeed, even fanatic Californianists find their subject a bit overwhelming; but how could it be otherwise? During a hundred centuries and more, peoples of diverse origins migrated into California, often moved within it, and adapted to myriad coastal, desert, riverine, valley, and montane environments. In time California came to be the homeland of some 300,000 Indians speaking approximately 90 separate languages and belonging to perhaps 500 distinct ethnic groups. As one might expect, the archaeological record of these developments is both intricate and bewildering. Readers who join this expedition into the labyrinth of California's past will surely encounter the Minotaur of complexity. My job will be to hack away needless archaeological vines so as to improve the view of prehistory.

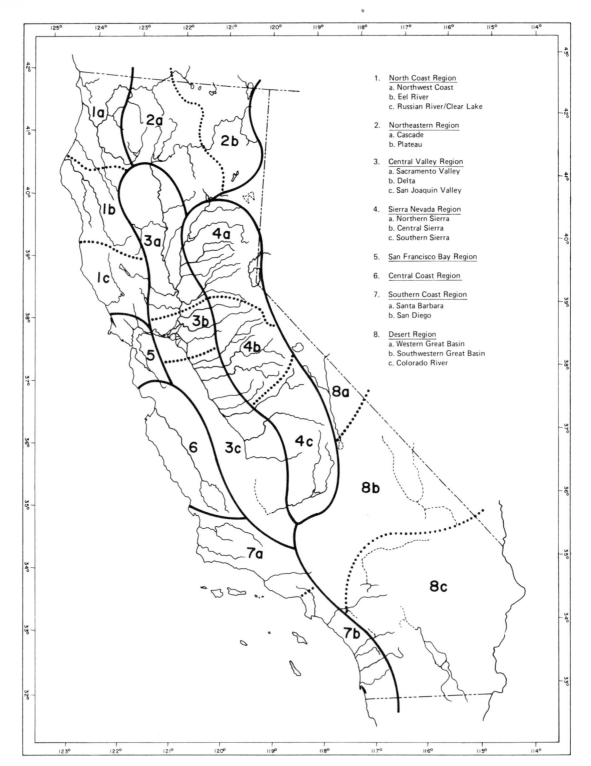

1. North Coast Region
   a. Northwest Coast
   b. Eel River
   c. Russian River/Clear Lake

2. Northeastern Region
   a. Cascade
   b. Plateau

3. Central Valley Region
   a. Sacramento Valley
   b. Delta
   c. San Joaquin Valley

4. Sierra Nevada Region
   a. Northern Sierra
   b. Central Sierra
   c. Southern Sierra

5. San Francisco Bay Region

6. Central Coast Region

7. Southern Coast Region
   a. Santa Barbara
   b. San Diego

8. Desert Region
   a. Western Great Basin
   b. Southwestern Great Basin
   c. Colorado River

**Figure 1** Archaeological regions and subregions of California. (Map by the author.)

This book is at once premature and long overdue—premature because California's archaeological testament is fragmentary, with key chapters still buried in the earth or lost forever, and overdue because no full-length synthesis has been published until now, even though a massive literature has accumulated during more than a century of research activity. Brief syntheses of California archaeology have been published (cf. Aikens 1978; Elsasser 1978b; Heizer 1964; Irwin 1975; Wallace 1978b; Warren 1973), but these differ from the present effort in scope and, in most cases, theoretical orientation.

Although the ken of this book is very wide, it does not extend to the domains of California historical archaeology (e.g., Schuyler 1978) or physical anthropology (e.g., Suchey 1975). Similarly, *California Archaeology* does not explicate archaeological method and theory; these too are topics better discussed elsewhere (e.g., Hole and Heizer 1973; Rathje and Schiffer 1982; Thomas 1979). Because this volume is intended for nonspecialists as well as for professional archaeologists, technical terms are kept to a minimum and those used are defined in the Glossary. Wherever possible, common names of plants and animals appear in the text, and scientific names are keyed in Appendix 1; exceptions are textual usage of *Haliotis* (abalone), *Olivella* (olive snail), and a few other scentific names—all of which enjoy wide colloquial usage in archaeology—and several scientific names lacking common equivalents.

Throughout this work, archaeological sites are designated by a county code and site number: DNo-99 thus refers to the ninety-ninth recorded site in Del Norte County. The locations of California's 58 counties are shown in Figure 3. County abbreviations are given in Appendix 2. For easy reference, maps of California's archaeological regions appear as Figures 1 and 2; Figure 4 shows a concordance of regional sequences. It is to be emphasized that the regions shown in Figure 1 are largely arbitrary and are intended more as organizational devices than as reflections of archaeological reality. For that matter, the state itself, bounded on the north and east by arbitrary lines, extends far beyond the natural and traditional culture areas of California. This book nonetheless deals with the entire political area of the state, including parts of the Great Basin and other areas adjoining the California heartland.

The architecture of this book consists of 11 chapters, the first 3 of which examine (1) California's historic and ancient environments, (2) evidence of Pleistocene (Ice Age) human activity, and (3) assemblages thought to be 8000–12,000 years old; the areal focus is statewide. Chapters 4–10 discuss cultural developments between ca. 6000 B.C. and A.D. 1750–1850 in eight archaeological regions (Figure 1). Each regional overview features environmental and enthnographic summaries, a brief history of archaeological studies, a detailed regional prehistory, and interpretive comments. The book concludes with a synthesis emphasizing the linguistic prehistory of California (Chapter 11).

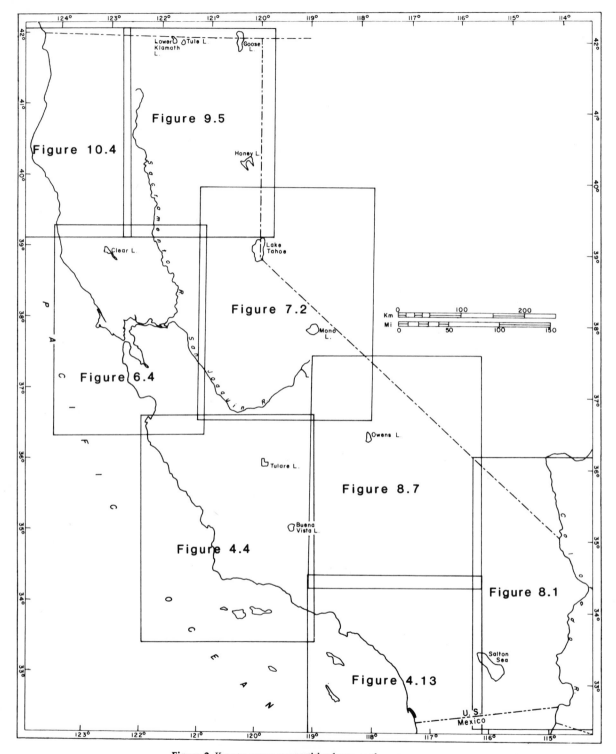

**Figure 2** Key to areas covered by large-scale maps.

xxx

**Figure 3** Counties of California, A.D. 1980.

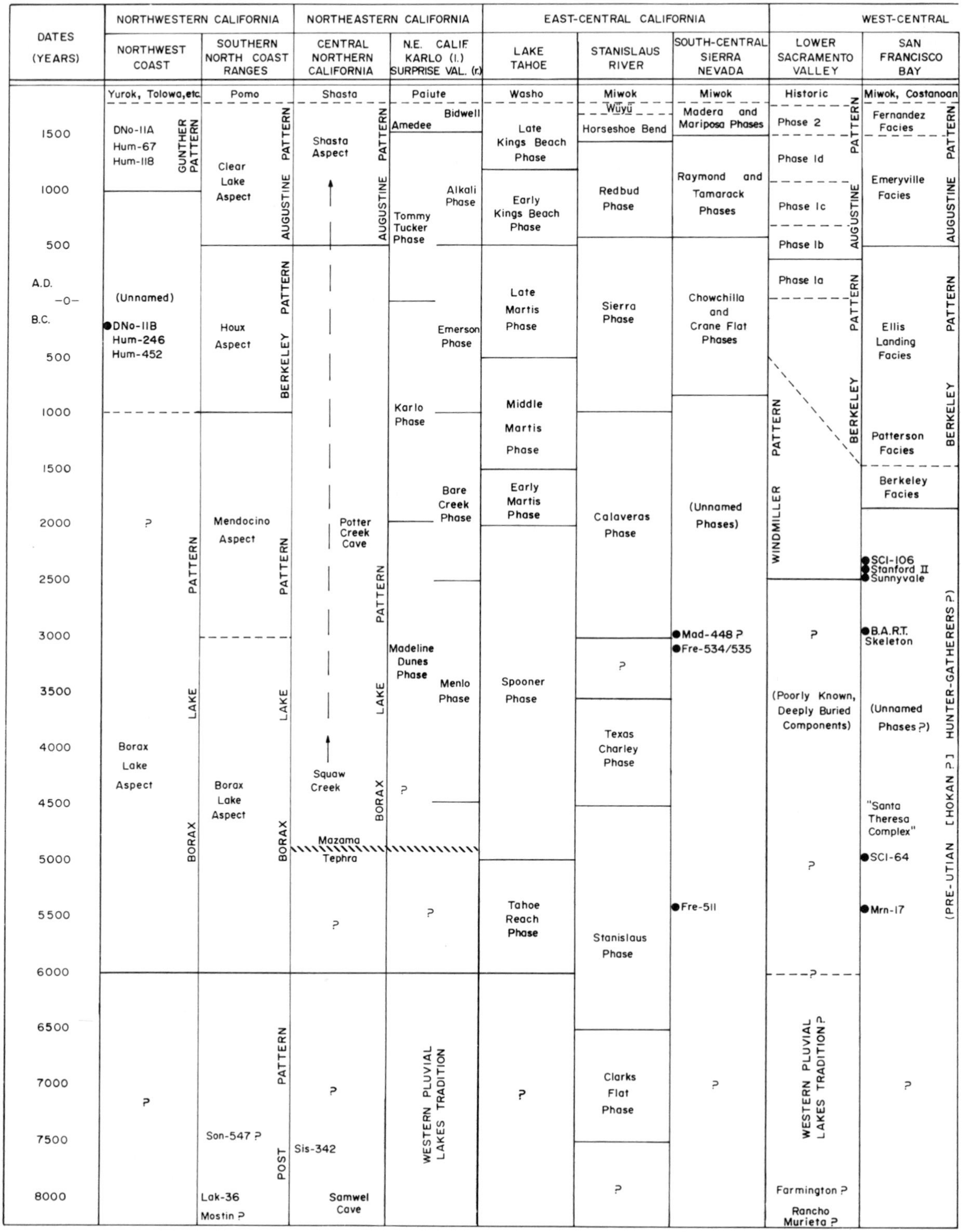
DATES (YEARS)
NORTHWESTERN CALIFORNIA
NORTHEASTERN CALIFORNIA
EAST-CENTRAL CALIFORNIA
WEST-CENTRAL
NORTHWEST COAST
SOUTHERN NORTH COAST RANGES
CENTRAL NORTHERN CALIFORNIA
N.E. CALIF. KARLO (l.) SURPRISE VAL. (r.)
LAKE TAHOE
STANISLAUS RIVER
SOUTH-CENTRAL SIERRA NEVADA
LOWER SACRAMENTO VALLEY
SAN FRANCISCO BAY
Yurok, Tolowa, etc.
Pomo
Shasta
Paiute
Washo
Miwok
Miwok
Historic
Miwok, Costanoan
1500
1000
500
A.D.
–0–
B.C.
500
1000
1500
2000
2500
3000
3500
4000
4500
5000
5500
6000
6500
7000
7500
8000
DNo-11A
Hum-67
Hum-118
GUNTHER PATTERN
(Unnamed)
DNo-11B
Hum-246
Hum-452
?
Borax Lake Aspect
BORAX LAKE PATTERN
?
Clear Lake Aspect
AUGUSTINE PATTERN
Houx Aspect
BERKELEY PATTERN
Mendocino Aspect
Borax Lake Aspect
BORAX LAKE PATTERN
POST PATTERN
Son-547 ?
Lak-36
Mostin ?
Shasta Aspect
AUGUSTINE PATTERN
Potter Creek Cave
Squaw Creek
BORAX LAKE PATTERN
Mazama Tephra
?
?
Sis-342
Samwel Cave
Bidwell
Amedee
Alkali Phase
Tommy Tucker Phase
Emerson Phase
Karlo Phase
Bare Creek Phase
Madeline Dunes Phase
Menlo Phase
?
?
WESTERN PLUVIAL LAKES TRADITION
Late Kings Beach Phase
Early Kings Beach Phase
Late Martis Phase
Middle Martis Phase
Early Martis Phase
Spooner Phase
Tahoe Reach Phase
?
Wüyü
Horseshoe Bend
Redbud Phase
Sierra Phase
Calaveras Phase
?
Texas Charley Phase
Stanislaus Phase
Clarks Flat Phase
?
Madera and Mariposa Phases
Raymond and Tamarack Phases
Chowchilla and Crane Flat Phases
(Unnamed Phases)
Mad-448 ?
Fre-534/535
Fre-511
?
Phase 2
Phase Id
Phase Ic
Phase Ib
Phase Ia
AUGUSTINE PATTERN
BERKELEY PATTERN
WINDMILLER PATTERN
?
(Poorly Known, Deeply Buried Components)
?
?
WESTERN PLUVIAL LAKES TRADITION ?
Farmington ?
Rancho Murieta ?
Fernandez Facies
Emeryville Facies
AUGUSTINE PATTERN
Ellis Landing Facies
Patterson Facies
Berkeley Facies
BERKELEY PATTERN
SCl-106
Stanford II
Sunnyvale
B.A.R.T. Skeleton
(Unnamed Phases ?)
"Santa Theresa Complex"
SCl-64
Mrn-17
(PRE-UTIAN [HOKAN ?] HUNTER-GATHERERS ?)
?

**Figure 4** Concordance of regional archaeological sequences in California.

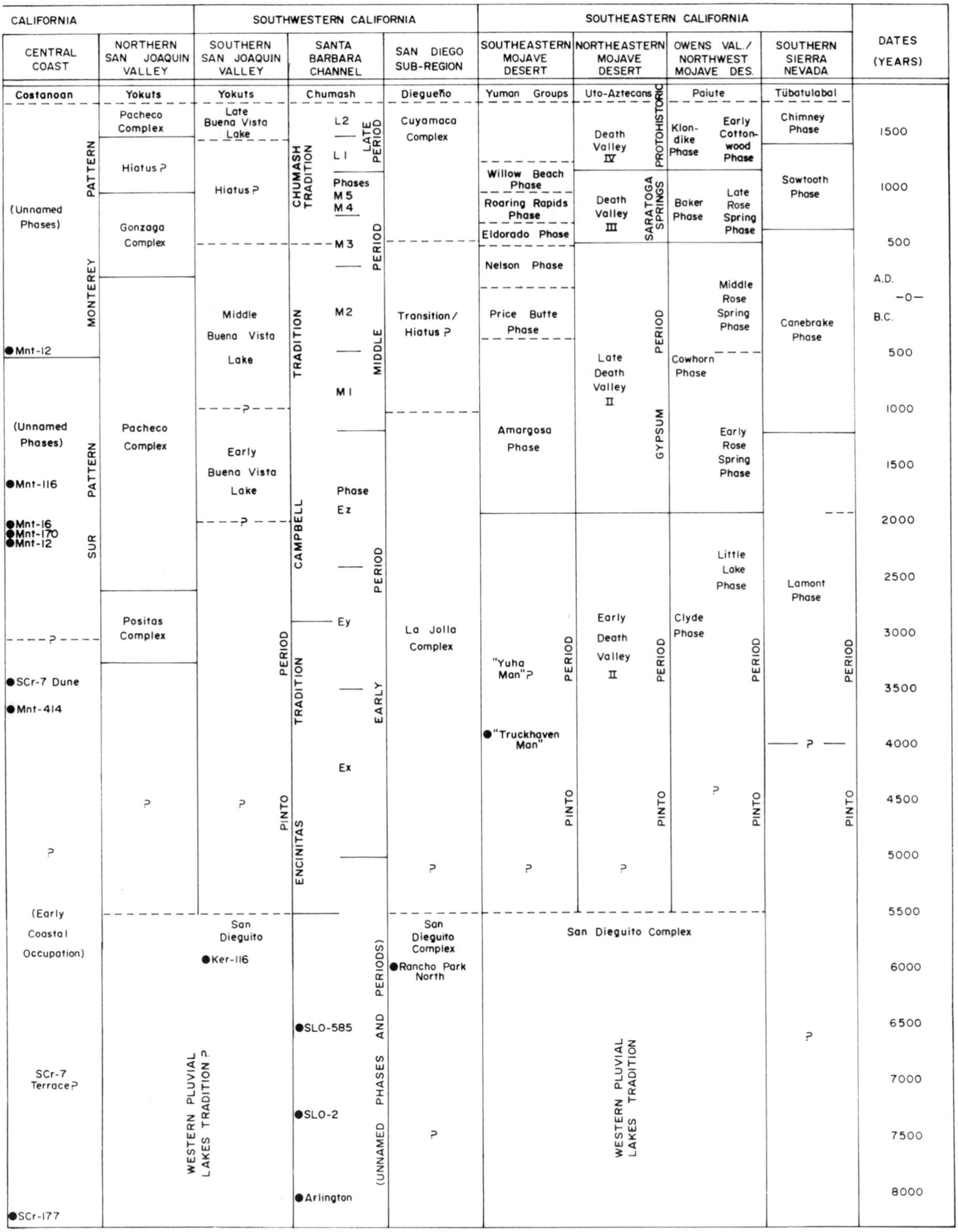

Figure 4. Chronological correlation chart of California archaeological complexes, phases, traditions, and periods.

| | CALIFORNIA | | SOUTHWESTERN CALIFORNIA | | | SOUTHEASTERN CALIFORNIA | | | | |
|---|---|---|---|---|---|---|---|---|---|---|
| | CENTRAL COAST | NORTHERN SAN JOAQUIN VALLEY | SOUTHERN SAN JOAQUIN VALLEY | SANTA BARBARA CHANNEL | SAN DIEGO SUB-REGION | SOUTHEASTERN MOJAVE DESERT | NORTHEASTERN MOJAVE DESERT | OWENS VAL./ NORTHWEST MOJAVE DES. | SOUTHERN SIERRA NEVADA | DATES (YEARS) |
| Ethnic group | Costanoan | Yokuts | Yokuts | Chumash | Diegueño | Yuman Groups | Uto-Aztecans | Paiute | Tübatulabal | |
| | | Pacheco Complex | Late Buena Vista Lake | L2 (Late Period) | Cuyamaca Complex | | Death Valley IV (Protohistoric) | Klondike Phase / Early Cottonwood Phase | Chimney Phase | 1500 |
| | (Unnamed Phases) | Hiatus? | Hiatus? | L1; Phases M5, M4 | | Willow Beach Phase; Roaring Rapids Phase | Death Valley III (Saratoga Springs) | Baker Phase / Late Rose Spring Phase | Sawtooth Phase | 1000 |
| PATTERN / MONTEREY | | Gonzaga Complex | (Chumash Tradition) | M3 | | Eldorado Phase; Nelson Phase | | | | 500 |
| | | | Middle Buena Vista Lake | M2 (Middle Period) | Transition / Hiatus? | Price Butte Phase | | Middle Rose Spring Phase | Canebrake Phase | A.D. –0– B.C. |
| | •Mnt-12 | | | M1 | | | Late Death Valley II (Gypsum Period) | Cowhorn Phase | | 500 |
| SUR / PATTERN | (Unnamed Phases) | Pacheco Complex | Early Buena Vista Lake | | | Amargosa Phase | | Early Rose Spring Phase | | 1000 |
| | •Mnt-116 | | | Phase Ez (Campbell Tradition) | | | | | | 1500 |
| | •Mnt-16 •Mnt-170 •Mnt-12 | | | (Early Period) | | | | Little Lake Phase | Lamont Phase | 2000 |
| | | | | | | | | | | 2500 |
| | ? | Positas Complex | | Ey | La Jolla Complex | "Yuha Man"? | Early Death Valley II (Pinto Period) | Clyde Phase | | 3000 |
| | •SCr-7 Dune | | | (Early) | | | | | | 3500 |
| | •Mnt-414 | | | Ex | | •"Truckhaven Man" | | | ? | 4000 |
| | ? | ? | ? | (Pinto / Encinitas Tradition) | | PINTO | PINTO | ? PINTO | PINTO | 4500 |
| | ? | | | | ? | ? | ? | ? | | 5000 |
| | (Early Coastal Occupation) | | San Dieguito •Ker-116 | | San Dieguito Complex | San Dieguito Complex | | | | 5500 / 6000 |
| | | | | | •Rancho Park North | | | | | |
| | | | | •SLO-585 | | | | | ? | 6500 |
| | SCr-7 Terrace? | WESTERN PLUVIAL LAKES TRADITION? | | | | WESTERN PLUVIAL LAKES TRADITION | | | | 7000 |
| | | | | •SLO-2 | ? | | | | | 7500 |
| | •SCr-177 | | | •Arlington | | | | | | 8000 |

Figure 4 (continued)

xxxiii

*California Archaeology* is chiefly a study of *culture history:* it is concerned mainly with reconstructing past lifeways—that is, determining what happened in prehistory. An understanding of culture history is basic to archaeological interpretation. At higher level, one may investigate *culture process*—the conditions and forces influencing cultures, and the dynamic relationships between cultures and their natural and social environments. The aim of process-oriented archaeology is to to explain *why* cultures developed as they did (cf. Binford 1968; Watson *et al.* 1971); by contrast, history- (*sensu lato*) oriented work describes *how* cultures developed. This book deals mostly with the "how" part of the question, but explanations are also attempted at the level of indicating why local settlement patterns seem to have changed at a particular time, or why certain economic practices apparently were successful under given conditions. Because such explanations relate to cultural ecology, much attention is devoted to the nature of paleoenvironments and how they might have influenced the course of California prehistory.

Also in terms of theoretical bias, this treatment may be characterized as *normative* insofar as it deals with culture classification and the typical or diagnostic traits of archaeological manifestations. In part, this normative focus results from the classificatory obsession of Californianists during the past 50 years. The pre-1970 archaeological literature of California is besotted with normative taxonomy. Still, one must classify to organize and describe what otherwise would be an impossibly large and diverse array of data. The trick is to minimize taxonomic structures so as to ensure that typologies reflect archaeological reality and do not unduly impose an order of their own. This I have tried to accomplish in *California Archaeology.* No new classificatory scheme is advanced; some old ones are discarded; and useful taxonomic devices are refined and retained for their heuristic value.

Several thousand published and manuscript sources were consulted during the research for this book. However, no attempt was made to comb the "gray literature" of mostly unpublished environmental impact reports, which run to 50,000 titles or more. Hence, although every effort was made to ferret out relevant material from both archives and libraries, the result should not be viewed as an exhaustive summary of archaeological work and findings in California.

This volume is not so much a definitive study as a working model to show how the pieces of California's past may fit together. Many are my colleagues who could have done a better job with this project but who, for various reasons, have not attempted it. Thus, it occurs to me that one useful function of this work will be to attract the critical comments of experts. Another will be to provide a systematic arrangement of data for comparison with the archaeology of neighboring areas. Finally, the book sets forth some hypotheses that, when tested, may lead to further advances in California archaeology.

# Acknowledgments

This book was written in fits and starts during a 7-year period, beginning in 1975. Because of heavy management and teaching commitments (i.e., earning a living), I found time to write only "after work" and on weekends, and there were some intervals of weeks or months when attention to the book simply was not possible. Over the years, however, *California Archaeology* remained my personal highest priority, consuming perhaps 200 weekends. Such a work schedule does not benefit family life. Thus, I am most appreciative to my wife, Lynn Riley, who sacrificed a great deal to support this endeavor.

By 1980 it was apparent that the manuscript was growing too slowly, so I invited three colleagues to join the writing effort. David Fredrickson, Christopher Raven, and Claude Warren surpassed all expectations with their chapters on the North Coastal, Northeast California, and Desert regions, respectively. I am grateful for their willingness to participate in this work as well as for the quality of their syntheses.

Others who assisted materially in the preparation of the book deserve special mention. Robert Bettinger, Michael Glassow, and James B. Griffin reviewed drafts and offered numerous helpful suggestions for improvement. Kenneth Whistler freely shared with me his impressive knowledge of California's linguistic prehistory, and Catherine Callaghan did the same with regard to parts of central California (the Miwok–Costanoan area). Personal notes of thanks are due to Keith Dixon, Roberta Greenwood, Tom King, and Russell Kaldenberg for their ideas, critical comments, and, most of all, their encouragement. Their friendship is much cherished.

Many others, whose names are listed below, contributed to this project by sharing information and insights, providing illustrations, or commenting on draft chapters. I am indebted to them all. Finally, I thank the staff at Academic Press for their support, forbearance, and publishing skills. It was they who transformed several reams of typescript into an attractive book.

## Technical Assistance

| | | |
|---|---|---|
| David Adam | Suzanne Baker | Gary Breschini |
| C. Melvin Aikens | Craig Bates | Fred Budinger, Jr. |
| Richard Ambro | Martin Baumhoff | Paul Chace |
| Keith Anderson | James Bennyhoff | Roger Cook |

| | | |
|---|---|---|
| Harvey Crew | Thomas L. Jackson | Lynn Riley |
| Emma Lou Davis | Joseph Jorgensen | William Roop |
| Stephen Dietz | John Kelly | Sally Salzman |
| Robert Edwards | Roger Kelly | Ruth Simpson |
| Albert Elsasser | Roger LaJeunesse | William Singleton |
| Katherine Flynn | Kelly McGuire | Sonia Tamez |
| David Fredrickson | Don Miller | R. E. Taylor |
| Alan Garfinkel | Randy Milliken | Dorothea Theodoratus |
| Bert Gerow | Kathy Moffitt | Rose Tyson |
| Susan Goldberg | John Moratto | Edward Von der Porten |
| Garland Gordon | L. Kyle Napton | Claude Warren |
| Trudy Haversat | Ann S. Peak | Tony Weber |
| Richard Hanes | Polly Quick | Wallace Woolfenden |
| Winfield Henn | Christopher Raven | Don Wren |
| Travis Hudson | Francis Riddell | |

Adán E. Treganza Anthropology Museum, San Francisco State
  University
Bureau of Land Management, California Desert District
California Academy of Sciences
California Department of Parks and Recreation
California Division of Mines and Geology
Interagency Archeological Services Division, National Park Service
R. H. Lowie Museum of Anthropology, University of California
San Bernardino County Museum
Sierra National Forest
Southern California Edison Company
Stanislaus National Forest
Theodoratus Cultural Research
University of California, Los Angeles, Institute of Archaeology
U.S. Forest Service, California Region
Western Archeological and Conservation Center, National Park Service
Yosemite National Park

## Illustrations

| | | |
|---|---|---|
| Jeffrey Bada | Emma Lou Davis | Paul Heuston |
| J. Barnes | Keith Dixon | Mary Hill |
| Bruce Bryan | Randall Engle | Travis Hudson |
| Clinton Blount | Joy A. Fox | Jesse D. Jennings |
| Fred Budinger, Jr. | Gerald R. Gates | John Johnson |
| Ernest S. Carter | Michael Glassow | Russell Kaldenberg |
| Allan Childers | C. Vance Haynes, Jr. | Clement Meighan |

George J. Miller
Frank Norick
Ann Odgers
James O'Connell
Phil C. Orr
Eugene R. Prince
Polly Quick

Christopher Raven
Shelly Raven
Francis Riddell
Eric Ritter
Rusty Rossman
Peter Schulz
John S. Shelton

Suzanne Sundholm
Nelson Thompson
Thad Van Bueren
Claude Warren
Barton Wright

California Division of Mines and Geology
Columbia State Historic Park
Commercial Photo and View Company
W. H. Freeman and Company
Great Basin Foundation
Imperial Valley College Museum
Modoc County Historical Society
Modoc County Museum
R. H. Lowie Museum of Anthropology, University of California, Berkeley
San Diego Museum of Man
Santa Barbara Museum of Natural History
Scripps Institution of Oceanography
Society for American Archaeology
Southwest Museum
University of California, Berkeley, Archaeological Research Facility
University of California, Santa Barbara, Department of Anthropology
University of Oklahoma Press
U.S. Geological Survey, National Cartographic Information Center
U.S. National Museum, Smithsonian Institution

# CALIFORNIA ARCHAEOLOGY

# 1. *A Goodly Ilande:* California's Natural Setting

*Sabed que a la diestra mano de las indias hubo una isla, llamada California, muy llegada a la parte del Paraiso Terrenal* (Know ye that on the right hand of the Indies there is an island, called California, very near to the Terrestrial Paradise)
*Garcirodriguez de Montalvo (1508)*

Sutter Buttes and Sacramento Valley, looking north. (U.S. Air Force photograph, courtesy of the U.S. Geological Survey.)

# Introduction

It is fitting to begin this archaeological study with an overview of California's geography and native cultures. Environmentally, California is diverse in the extreme. No other area of equal size in North America can match its range of climates, varied topography, wide array of rocks and minerals, or intricate patchwork of biotic communities. Within this setting prehistoric societies adapted in myriad ways to local conditions. Because the early Indians were dependent entirely on natural resources, their lifeways can be understood fully only with reference to the land and climate. A brief cultural survey at the outset will give perspective to the environmental overview.

# Native Cultures

## Numbers and Diversity

When Spanish colonization began in A.D. 1769, Alta California was the home of more than 300,000 Indians—a greater number than in any comparable area north of Mexico (Cook 1976). Population densities varied, largely according to local resources, from less than 0.20/km² in desert regions to more than 3.85/km² in places near the Santa Barbara Channel.

The Native Californians were by no means "primitive"; rather, they were singularly complex hunter–gatherers with social systems like "those of peoples with presumably greater technological advantages: e.g., horticulturalists and some agriculturalists" (Bean 1976:99). So diverse were the Indian life styles that no less than four major culture areas were represented in eighteenth-century California. Kroeber (1939) assigned southern California to the Southwest culture area; the eastern or trans-Sierran country to the Great Basin; the northwestern corner to the Northwest Coast; and the heartland, between the Sierran crest and the Pacific shore, to the central California area.

The linguistic picture was even more elaborate, with approximately 90 languages, including several hundred dialects, spoken in Old California (Figure 11.1). Also heterogeneous were physical types, among them the tallest (Mojave) and shortest (Yuki) Indians in America (Gifford 1926a; T. Kroeber and Heizer 1968). Such cultural, linguistic, and biological variations bespeak a long and rich prehistory in this part of the Far West.

## Subsistence

To sustain their populations, the California Indians pursued diverse economic strategies. Basic subsistence activities were gathering (acorns, roots, berries, etc.), hunting (deer, elk, sea mammals, and small game), fowling, collecting (mollusks, birds' eggs, insect foods), and both freshwater and marine fishing. Although only a half-dozen groups in southern California engaged in limited agriculture (growing maize, beans, gourds, and amaranth), many of California's transcendent hunter–gatherers achieved the status of "proto-agriculturalists": they sowed wild seeds; planted and/or tended native root crops, greens, and tobacco; pruned mesquite to stimulate growth; planted "vineyards" of wild grapes; irrigated desired plants; and used "quasi-agricultural" techniques to harvest acorns, grass seeds, yucca, mesquite, and pine nuts (Bean and Lawton 1973).

The advanced subsistence methods of the California Indians are further evinced by their

> invention of leaching for acorn and buckeye, grinding implements for hard seeds, canoes for acquiring marine mammals and fish, complex fishing and trapping gear, granaries for storing large supplies of food, hermetically sealed containers, artificial water-utilization methods such as digging wells and building reservoirs on the desert. (Bean and Lawton 1973: xxxvi)

The Native Californians managed their fish and wildlife resources in various ways. For example, among the Yurok, Hupa, and other northwestern groups, specialists controlled fishing and dam-building activities, regulated the opening of the salmon fishing season, and managed the use of the spawning runs to ensure a sustained, efficient harvest. The anadromous fishery was the most important and probably the most intensively manipulated food resource in aboriginal northwestern California (Swezey and Heizer 1977).

The Indians also widely managed their environment through the controlled burning of vegetation. Fire was used extensively to increase the yield of edible seeds, encourage the growth of desirable plants, flush and drive game, provide forage for deer and elk, and clear the ground below oaks and pines to facilitate nut harvests (Lewis 1973:41–44). Systematic

**Figure 1.1** Hupa woman leaching acorn meal in a basin of sand. Important in the acorn-processing technology were the burden basket (left), bowl (center), cooking basket (right), and hopper mortar basket (not shown). Note that the bowl is twined so tightly that it holds water. (Photograph by Pliny E. Goddard, 1902; courtesy of the R. H. Lowie Museum of Anthropology, University of California.)

burning was the single most important environmental modification by the California Indians, allowing them to control plant successions and, locally, to maintain biotic communities such as grasslands and oak savannas.

It is notable that early Spanish accounts describe not only Indian burning practices, but also certain edible seeds of grasses that may no longer exist. The historic cessation of burning, along with the spread of exotic plants and livestock, may have brought to extinction some floral species once important to the California Indians—an interesting problem for archaeology. Grass seeds likely were more significant in prehistory than has been thought and may have rivaled the acorn as a staple in the aboriginal diet (Bean and Lawton 1973) (Figure 1.1).

### Trade

To optimize the distribution of resources over large areas, California Indians developed sophisticated exchange systems. Trade in this area has considerable antiquity: a string of *Olivella* shell beads from the coast was found at Leonard Rockshelter, Pershing County, Nevada, in deposits nearly 8600 years old (Heizer 1978b). By late prehistoric times, Indians were transporting such items as acorns, salt, fish, shell artifacts, clothing, bows and arrows, baskets, and even dogs over a network of trails (J. T. Davis 1961; Sample 1950). The obsidian trade (Ericson 1977a,b) was central to this exchange system that allowed the unique or surplus resources of one group to be distributed to others. Trade feasts, such as those of the Pomo (Vayda 1966) and Chumash (C. King 1976), afforded a mechanism for neighboring groups to exchange surplus goods. Trade, coupled with the general use of money (e.g., clamshell disks), increased the potential size and stability of populations by diminishing the specter of starvation in the event of local, short-term failures of normal food resources (Chagnon 1970).

In the economic sphere the California Indians were by no means insulated. As early as A.D. 1800, and probably before, the Walla Walla were trekking from Washington to Santa Clara County to acquire cinnabar for use as a vermilion pigment; trade with the Great Basin was active for millennia; and lively commerce with the Southwest brought pottery, cotton blankets, stone axes, and other goods into California in exchange for shell and perhaps turquoise (J. T. Davis 1961; Heizer 1942b; Ruby 1970). There is also evidence that turquoise may have been mined in the Mojave Sink vicinity by Indians from the pueblos of northern Arizona (M. Rogers 1929a; see also Chapter 8).

## Social Organization

California Indian societies often were stratified, with individuals classed as elite, commoners, poor, slaves, or drifters. Recognized also were *bureaucrats* (chief's aides and managers) and religious functionaries who merited a notch above commoners. Presitge came as well to such craft specialists as expert traders, basket weavers, and bead makers. In the more complex societies, craft guilds controlled certain industries, for example, canoe building among the Chumash. Social preeminence was reserved for chiefs. Usually supported by their communities, chiefs lived in relative luxury with large houses, fancy clothing, stores of food, and money. Chiefs often married several women in order to strengthen alliances with the elite of other groups (Bean 1976:109–112).

The basic landholding group in much of the California heartland was the village community or *tribelet*—an independent social entity governed by a chief. As many as 500 such tribelets may have existed in precontact California (Kroeber 1925, 1954). Tribelets sharing the same language, culture, and history comprised nonpolitical ethnic groups. Individual tribelets held territories ranging in area from about 130 km² to as much as 15,500 km². Tribelet activities often focused upon a principal town that served as a political, ritual, and economic center to which nearby villages were tributary (Bean 1976:100–102).

Tribelets characterized the California culture area (Kroeber 1925, 1939), but not the adjoining regions. East of the cordillera were band societies of the Great Basin (Steward 1938). In northwestern California, families or individuals owned most land and valuables; status, prestige, and honor were derived from property, and competition instead of cooperation was emphasized among these "wealth-questing" peoples (Gould 1966b). Lacking chiefs, the northwestern societies kept flagrant individualism in check with strong laws and sanctions. In the northeast, the Modoc displayed a high measure of tribal solidarity, probably owing to their ties with Plateau cultures farther north. Similarly, the organized tribes of the Colorado River country manifested a degree of nationalism not found elsewhere in California (Kroeber 1925).

Beyond the tribelet or tribal units, higher-order alliances for trade, war, and ritual were found in many parts of California. These often linked members of diverse ethnic communities who had access to different resources (Bean 1976:104). At times, as many as several thousand Indians would convene in one place for rituals, trade fairs, or military ventures.

*Cultural Summary*

Although California's rich environment held enormous potential for hunter–gatherers, population growth and cultural elaboration were equally the result of social and economic institutions. Late prehistoric and ethnographic cultures were distinguished by (1) intensive and specialized mining, fishing, hunting, and gathering; (2) resource enhancement by controlled burning, fish and wildlife management, and protoagricultural methods; and (3) social mechanisms—alliances, ritual and kinship obligations, and banking—that effectively redistributed goods and services.

Native California seems to represent the upper limits of sociocultural integration possible without agriculture (Bean and Lawton 1973). Heizer (1958a:20) called attention to this many years ago when he cited "abundant and assured food supplies," dense populations, and stable settlements as evidence that Californian cultures belonged to the "Preformative Stage." Anthropologists are keenly interested in the processes by which California's largely nonagricultural societies evolved such intricate adaptations. As is seen in the following chapters, archaeology provides a means of tracing such developments through the expanse of prehistory.

## Environment: Scope and Purpose

Even though ranked highly among hunter–gatherers, the precontact California Indians were totally reliant upon natural resources for their survival and prosperity. They were intimately familiar with the habitats and ethology of game animals, the distribution of useful plants, and the sources of valuable rocks and minerals. As well, they knew about microclimates and how to site villages in dry, sheltered places selected for optimum solar gain and minimum cold-air accumulation. Nonetheless, the Indians depended upon the natural bounty of California, and their cultures were influenced strongly by the vicissitudes of nature. Thus, a knowledge of California's environmental setting is essential for understanding its human prehistory.

The following sections of this chapter explore various dimensions of the California environment: physiography, geology, climate, flora, and fauna. It is to be emphasized, however, that this book is not a primary study of natural history. The reader should look to specialists for current information about such topics as California's climate (e.g., Goodridge 1980, and cited references), geology and landforms (A. Howard 1979; Oakeshott 1971), soils (Soil Conservation Service 1960), vegetation (Barbour and Major 1977; Munz 1959), fauna (Ingles 1965; Moyle 1976), Pleistocene animals (Kurtén and Anderson 1980), and overviews of regional natural history (Gordon 1974; Jaeger 1965; Power 1980; S. Whitney 1979). The present summary, then, is to be viewed as a background for interpreting the archaeological record.

## Physiography and Geology

California's political boundaries are largely arbitrary, the only natural borders being some 2000 km of coastline and a 350-km stretch of the Colorado River. Hence the state does not coincide with any single topographic region. With a length of 1350 km and widths ranging from 260 to 405 km, California covers roughly 409,755 km² (or 157,207 mi²). This vast area embraces 11 geomorphic provinces, each with distinctive landforms, geology, and hydrology (Figure 1.2). The location and general character of these provinces are summarized below, and further details about regional environments are given in Chapters 4–10.

### Klamath Mountains

The rugged Klamath Mountains occupy about 31,000 km² in northwestern California (Figure 1.2). This ancient landmass—a potpourri of

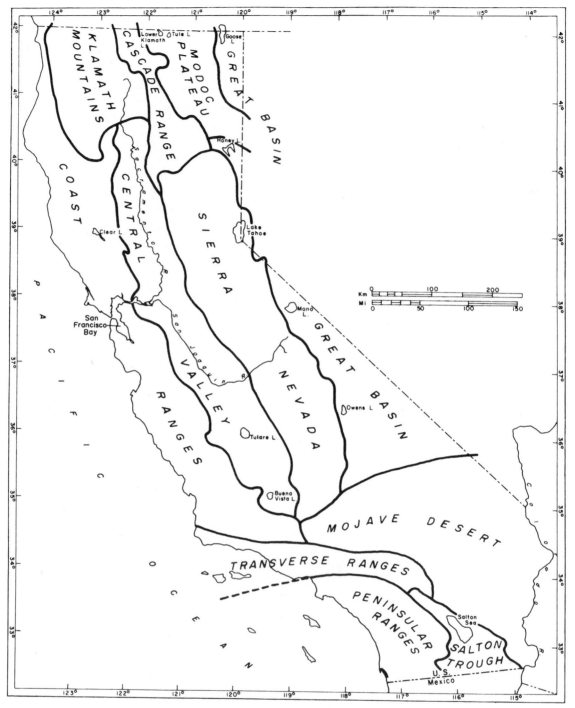

**Figure 1.2** Geomorphic provinces of California. Each province is characterized by particular geologic structures and lithologic units and their entailed landforms. (After Bailey 1966; Ernst 1979; Jenkins 1941.)

granitic, metamorphic, and sedimentary rocks—is an outlier of the northern Sierra Nevada, but the granitic bedrock linking the two ranges is covered by younger alluvium of the upper Sacramento Valley and volcanic extrusives of the Modoc Plateau and Cascade Range (Oakeshott 1971). Prominent peaks in the Klamaths are 2000–2500 m high, the tallest being Mt. Thompson (2723 m) in the once-glaciated Trinity Alps near the heart of the province. The extensively folded and faulted Klamath Ranges give rise to a dendritic pattern of streams, most of which empty into the great Klamath–Trinity River system (Figure 1.3). Bounteous riverine and upland resources sustained the archaeological populations in this region (see Chapter 10).

## Cascade Range

East of the Klamath Mountains rise the volcanic peaks and lava rims of the Cascade Range (Figure 1.2). These mountains extend southward from British Columbia through Washington and Oregon, reaching 240 km into California. Mt. Lassen (3187 m), an active volcano that last erupted from 1914 until 1917, is the most southerly peak (Loomis 1958). About 110 km north of Lassen, Mt. Shasta (4317 m) dominates the southern Cascades. Shasta is one of the few mountains in California still harboring alpine glaciers (Figure 1.4). The Cascades are drained mainly by the Pit and McCloud rivers, both of which flow into the Sacramento River (Figure 1.3). Of archaeological interest are ubiquitous basalt outcrops, along with deposits of obsidian in the Medicine Lake Highlands (an easterly projection of the Cascades). Both types of rock were prized by the Indians as raw material for chipped-stone tools.

## Modoc Plateau

The separation between the Modoc Plateau (Figure 1.2) and the eastern border of the Cascade Range is indefinite in northern California because the fault systems and rocks characteristic of the two regions are intermingled (Macdonald 1966). The Modoc volcanic platform is actually the southwestern tip of the great Columbia Plateau that covers much of eastern Oregon, Washington, and southern Idaho. Topographically, the Modoc Plateau is a jumble of lava flows and fissures, ridges, small cinder cones, and basalt plains averaging 1400 m above sea level (Figure 9.1). The southern part of this region is drained by Hat Creek, Fall River, and other tributaries of Pit River, whereas the Plateau country near the Oregon line has internal drainage. Sluggish streams empty into such large, shallow basins as Goose Lake, Tule Lake, and Lower Klamath Lake (Figure 1.3).

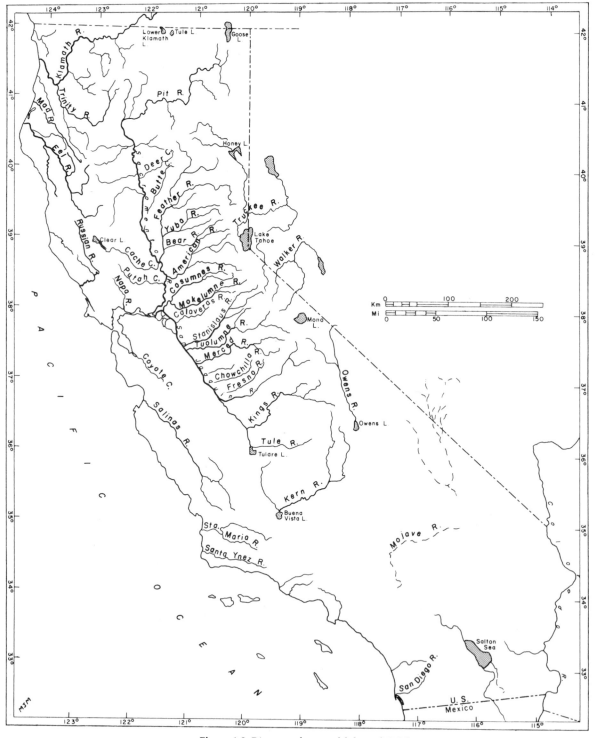

**Figure 1.3** Rivers and natural lakes of California, A.D. 1980. (Map by the author.)

**Figure 1.4** Looking north from an altitude of 5500 m, along the chain of Cascade volcanoes in California. Lassen Peak is near the center and Mount Shasta is in the background. (Photograph by Ernest S. Carter; courtesy of the U.S. Geological Survey, Menlo Park.)

The streams and lakes of the Modoc Plateau were the foci of prehistoric settlement and economic activity (see Chapter 9).

## Great Basin

The Great Basin (or Basin and Range) province covers an immense area south of the Columbia Plateau, between the Cascade–Sierra Nevada cordillera and the Rocky Mountains (Figure 1.2). Parallel north-trending fault-block ranges (horsts) and intervening basins (grabens) give the region its peculiar relief. Surprise Valley in northeastern California and Owens Valley east of the Sierra Nevada (Figure 1.5) are typical Great Basin valleys. Throughout the Basin, drainage is interior; streams flow into saline lakes or sinks without reaching the sea. The Mojave Desert, sometimes included in the southwestern Great Basin, is treated here as a separate province. Although folded and faulted sediments are the most common geologic features, important volcanic rocks (including obsidian) also occur, particularly in the zone of contact with the Sierra Nevada.

The Great Basin has long been an arid land sustaining only relatively small, dispersed, and often nomadic groups of hunter–gatherers. Before 7500 years ago, however, the Basin landscape featured lakes and grasslands richly endowed with game. Human use of the Great Basin was more intensive at that ancient time than during many subsequent periods (see Chapters 3 and 8).

*Sierra Nevada*

The magnificent Sierra Nevada extends 650 km along California's eastern border (Figure 1.2). This 130-km-wide range was created by the uplift of a granitic batholith (actually a group of plutons)—one of the largest on earth (Hill 1975). Subsequent tilting of this block resulted in a gentle western slope of about 2°, beginning with the band of foothills along the eastern margin of the Central Valley, and a dramatic eastern scarp where the Sierran wall rises abruptly from the floor of the Great Basin (Figure 1.5). U-shaped valleys and sharp alpine features record where former glaciers chiseled the high country (Figure 7.1).

**Figure 1.5** Eastern escarpment of the Sierra Nevada in the vicinity of Lone Pine and Mount Whitney, seen from above the north end of Owens Lake. Total relief in this picture, from Owens Lake (1085 m) to Mount Whitney (4418 m) is 3333 m. (Photograph by U.S. Air Force; courtesy of U.S. Geological Survey, Menlo Park.)

The Sierran backbone of California includes more than 500 peaks over 3000 m high. Of these, Mt. Whitney (4418 m) is the loftiest in the contiguous 48 states. Viewing the Sierra Nevada as a massive barrier to human movements is tempting but inaccurate. Numerous river valleys transect the western slope, connecting the foothills with high-altitude passes leading to the Great Basin. These natural corridors allowed native peoples to traverse the entire width of the Sierra in a few day's time. In fact, most transmontane trade occurred in the southern Sierra across the highest part of the range (Elsasser 1960).

The western Sierra is well supplied with moisture. Annual precipitation normally ranges from <50 cm in the low hills to >180 cm in the high country. The yearly discharge of Sierran rivers is more than 3.7 billion m³ (≈30 million acre-feet)—nearly half of California's total runoff. Snowfall is an important part of Sierran climate. Winter occupation by prehistoric Indians was largely restricted to elevations below the snowline (≈1000–1500 m) (see Chapter 7). East of the mountain crest, a rain shadow limits precipitation to ≈25 cm/year (Figure 1.10). As a result, the eastern face of the Sierra is an arid part of the Great Basin rim (Figure 1.5).

## Great Central Valley

A dominant feature of central California's landscape is its interior lowland. The Great Central Valley is 750 km long and from 30 to 80 km wide, covering approximately 50,000 km² (Figure 1.2). Enclosed by the Siskiyou, Sierra Nevada, Tehachapi, and Coast Ranges on the north, east, south, and west, respectively, this huge basin is underlain by sediments (derived mainly from Sierran streams) to a maximum depth of nearly 17 km. The Valley floor, which seems monotonously flat, rises gradually from sea level near Stockton (Figure 6.4) to elevations of about 100 m at its northern and southern limits. Westward from the Sierran piedmont, the gradient of the Valley's broad eastern plain declines gently, whereas the narrower western slope is beveled more sharply to the foot of the Coast Ranges (Oakeshott 1971). The only real break in the flatland topography is provided by the 600-m-high Sutter Buttes (volcanic remnants) near Marysville (Figure 1.6).

The Sacramento River, flowing southeast for 260 km, drains the northern 40% of the Valley. From the south, waters of the San Joaquin River system flow northwest for some 440 km. The combined discharge of these streams averages ≈5 billion m³/yr, nearly all of which is collected on the Sierra–Cascade watershed. Toward the center of the Valley, the two great rivers swing to the west and eventually merge in the labyrinth of channels and marshes comprising the Sacramento–San Joaquin Delta. The waters then flow into Suisun Bay, pass through a gap in the

**Figure 1.6** Looking northwest across the Sacramento Valley at Sutter Buttes. (Photograph by John S. Shelton.)

Coast Ranges at Carquinez Strait, and empty into San Pablo Bay (Figures 1.3, 6.1, and 6.4). The separation between the Sacramento and San Joaquin valleys is usually set at the Mokelumne River. At sea level, the Mokelumne channels are so confused that the river is variously thought of as the lowest tributary of the Sacramento or the most northerly effluent of the San Joaquin (Schenck and Dawson 1929). Large archaeological populations were concentrated near the courses of Valley streams and wetlands (see Chapter 5 and Figure 5.1).

*Coast Ranges*

The Coast Ranges—actually formed of many separate ranges, mountains, and valleys—extend north–northwesterly along the Pacific Ocean, west of the Central Valley and Klamath Mountains, into Oregon (Figure 1.2). In California, these ranges are roughly 640 km long and from 15 to 110 km wide (excluding the parts of the Coast Ranges that reach out into the continental shelf under the sea). San Francisco Bay marks the division of the North and South Coast Ranges (Figures 6.1 and 6.4). Hills and ridges tend to be rounded by erosion in the southern and central parts of the ranges (Figure 1.7), but more spectacular highland topography appears in the north. Peaks seldom rise above 1800 m; most ridge crests average between 600 and 1200 m. Where these mountains meet the sea, "the coast itself is extremely rugged and is marked by nearly vertical sea cliffs, sea stacks. . . and steep mountains at the shore line, in many places with gently sloping, narrow terraces a few feet to a few hundred feet above the sea" (Oakeshott 1971:4; Figures 6.3 and 10.2).

Geologically, the Coast Ranges include two distinct core assemblages: (1) a vast, disordered array of sandstone, shale, conglomerate, volcanics, chert, limestone, and serpentine, and (2) a complex group of granitic intrusives and metamorphic rocks. Much of the basement structure is covered by diverse younger sediments. To complicate matters further, the extreme folding and faulting that accompanied the uplift of the Coast Ranges have created in these mountains numerous independent ranges and valleys, few of which are more than 150 km in length. One of the longest is the Diablo Range, trending southward for 210 km from Mt. Diablo (Figure 1.7) along the western margin of the San Joaquin Valley (Oakeshott 1971; Page 1966).

**Figure 1.7** View east across part of the central Coast Ranges, climaxing at Mount Diablo (1173 m). (Photograph by Commercial Photo and View Company; courtesy of the California Division of Mines and Geology.)

Coastal streams are typically smaller than those of the Sierra, with a few important exceptions in the North Coast Ranges. The largest is the Eel River, which discharges about 2 billion m³ of runoff annually from the Mendocino Range. Other notable coastal streams are the Russian and Salinas rivers (Figure 1.3). Native peoples of the Coast Ranges lived not only near major streams, but also in the hill country, around lakes (e.g., Clear Lake), along the seashore, and especially near such large coastal estuaries as Humboldt, San Francisco, and Monterey bays (see Chapters 4, 6, and 10).

*Transverse Ranges*

Of California's mountain chains, the Transverse Ranges alone trend east–west as they cut across the state for a distance of 500 km, separating central and southern California. The Transverse Ranges meet the Coast Ranges and Sierra Nevada on the north, the Mojave Desert on the north and east, and the Salton Trough and Peninsular Ranges on the south (Figure 1.2). Like the Coast Ranges, the Transverse system embodies many ranges—the Santa Ynez, Santa Monica, San Gabriel, San Bernardino, Eagle, and Orocopia mountains, to name a few. Rising from the Mojave Desert on the east, only 100 km from the Colorado River, the Transverse Ranges extend westward in a band 25 to 95 km wide into the sea, where the nearly drowned mountains are seen as San Miguel, Santa Cruz, and Santa Rosa islands. Maritime adaptation to the island and the coastal (Santa Barbara Channel) zone of these ranges sustained the highest population densities known in California prehistory (see Chapter 4).

The intensely folded and faulted Cenozoic sediments of the Transverse Ranges are among the thickest on earth—up to 21.5 km! Massive erosion has cut deep valleys, leaving high, often narrow ridges and peaks. Crests in the western ranges tend to be 1000–2000 m high; more easterly ridgetops climb to 2500 m and above. San Antonio Peak in the San Gabriels is 3072 m in elevation, and the summit of San Gorgonio Mountain at 3500 m looms above the San Bernardino Range as the highest point in southern California (Oakeshott 1971). Streams in this region— the Santa Ynez, San Gabriel, and Los Angeles rivers—are of relatively little consequence, except during heavy rainstorms when they may be transformed into raging torrents for periods of a few days or weeks.

*Mojave Desert*

This sprawling, arid province covers ≈50,000 km² of southeastern California. It merges with the desolate Yuma and Colorado Deserts on the southeast and south, respectively; on the north, it confronts the Sierra Nevada and is separated from the Great Basin rather arbitrarily at the

Garlock Fault. West of the Mojave are the Transverse and Peninsular ranges (Figure 1.2). From Mojave (838 m), the desert plain slopes gently eastward to Barstow (642 m), now and then giving rise to small hills. Continuing eastward toward the Colorado River, the desert is increasingly mountainous. Prominent ranges are the Granite, Bristol, Providence, Bullion, Turtle, María, and Chocolate mountains.

Throughout the desert lowlands are broad *playas*, or dry lake beds, typically formed of sand and gravel basins sloping toward central salt flats—testimony to the many pluvial lakes that once covered much of the land (see Chapter 3). Because of interior drainage, these playas may become ephemeral lakes following occasional heavy downpours. Similarly, the Amargosa and Mojave rivers and other intermittent streams may carry flashfloods during storms. The archaeological record is closely linked to shifting water sources in this ever-changing desert province (Figure 1.8).

### Colorado Desert (Salton Trough)

The Colorado Desert, or Salton Trough, is a depressed block, 135 km long and 50 km wide, between forks of the San Andreas Fault. Elevations

**Figure 1.8** View across part of the ancient Manix Lake playa to the eroded foothills of the Calico Mountains, Mojave Desert; note the alluvial fans near the base of the hills. (Photograph by the author.)

in this forbidding land fall to 75 m below sea level. Much of the trough anciently was covered by Lake Cahuilla, of which only playa surfaces, weathered beach terraces, and the Salton Sea remain. North of this inland sea lies the Coachella Valley; stretching southward is the Imperial Valley. Bordered on the west by the Peninsular Ranges and on the east by the Mojave Desert (Figure 1.2), the Colorado Desert extends into Mexico, where its southern end is flooded by the upper Gulf of California.

The Colorado Desert has not always been a sere and desolate province. Several times in the geologically recent past the entire basin, from the lower Coachella Valley to the upper Gulf, brimmed with the fresh water of Lake Cahuilla. This immense lake (as much as 55 km wide and 98 m deep) formed whenever the Colorado River drained into the Salton Basin for extended intervals of time. Each lacustral period was followed by centuries when the river did not flow into the region but instead deposited sediments across its southern end. The waters of Lake Cahuilla then evaporated, leaving the desert and Salton Sea (Beck and Haase 1974; Wilke and Lawton 1975). As one might expect, the vicissitudes of ancient Lake Cahuilla strongly affected the course of prehistory in the Colorado Desert (see Chapters 3 and 8).

### Peninsular Ranges

So named because they run the full 1200-km length of the Baja California peninsula, the Peninsular Ranges reach about 225 km into southwestern Alta California (Figure 1.2). Like the Sierra Nevada, the Peninsular Ranges formed when granites were intruded into older metamorphics and sediments. At the northern end of the province are the Los Angeles Basin and adjacent highlands, along with a series of offshore

**Figure 1.9** Lake Hodges, near Escondido, San Diego County. This landscape is typical of the granitic–metamorphic terrain a few kilometers from the coast in the Peninsular Ranges. (Photograph by Mary Hill.)

ridges forming San Nicolas, Santa Catalina, San Clemente, and tiny Santa Barbara islands. Prominent mainland ranges, from north to south, are the Santa Ana, San Jacinto, Santa Rosa, Agua Tibia, and Laguna mountains. San Jacinto Peak at 3293 m is the highest point in the Peninsular Ranges, but most ridgetops lie below 2000 m (Figure 1.9). Streams in this province, such as the Santa Margarita, San Luis Rey, and San Diego rivers, drain westward and seldom carry large volumes of water (Oakeshott 1971).

Common Peninsular Range features are sheltered bays and lagoons, open coast, broad river terraces, and steep upland terrain. Ancient societies used these diverse settings for millennia, leaving a rich archaeological heritage in southwestern California (see Chapters 2–4).

## Climate

Unique in North America is California's dominant Mediterranean climate (Kesseli 1942), featuring but two seasons each year: mild, wet winters and warm, dry summers. The influence of the Pacific Ocean ameliorates air temperatures year-round, especially near the coast. Only the interior mountains and deserts exhibit harsh Continental climates (D. Johnson 1977b).

Precipitation generally increases with latitude and elevation. A mere 7–10 cm of rain falls annually in the Colorado Desert, whereas 10–35 cm/year is normal for the Mojave Desert. Less than 2 cm/year has been recorded in parts of Death and Imperial valleys. In contrast, rainfall along the coast between San Francisco Bay and the Oregon line averages 100–200 cm/year, and wet years may deliver more than 300 cm of rain to California's northwest corner. The greatest annual precipitation on record in the state was 468.5 cm on Ship Mountain, Del Norte County, during the 1977–1978 water year (Goodridge 1980:8).

Annual rainfall in the Central Valley increases gradually from about 16 cm at Bakersfield in the south to 98 cm at Redding in the north. Precipitation levels in the Sierra Nevada rise dramatically from <50 cm/year in the foothills to >180 cm/year in the high country (Figure 1.10). Snowfall accounts for a significant part of the moisture at elevations above 1000 m, and snowpacks 1500 cm or more in depth may accumulate in the northern Sierra. The winter of 1906–1907 brought to Tamarack, Alpine County, 2144 cm of snow—the largest amount ever recorded during a single season in the lower 48 states (Beck and Haase 1974).

Transmontane California, including the western Great Basin and the Mojave Desert, experiences a Continental climate: hot, dry summers and cold winters with little moisture. The aridity and isolation from Mediter-

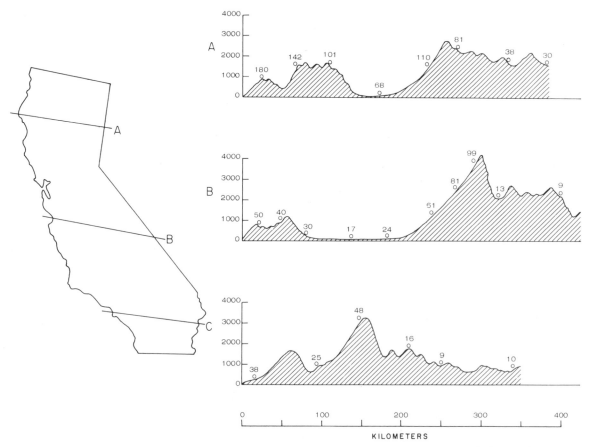

**Figure 1.10** Transects across California, showing variations in relief (m) and precipitation (cm). (Compiled by the author from various sources.)

ranean conditions are caused largely by the rain shadow of the Sierra Nevada and Cascade ranges, which capture on their windward slopes most of the moisture in the eastbound storms (Figure 1.10). To illustrate, precipitation of ≈30 cm/year is normal at Honey Lake in the western Great Basin, but, in the mountains only 75 km west of the lake, precipitation reaches ≈185 cm/year.

Temperatures in California are similarly varied except on the coast. Mean maximum temperatures in July range from 60° (F) along the north coast to 116° in the northern Mojave Desert. The highest temperature on record was a sizzling 134° on July 10, 1913, in Death Valley. Typical mean highs for July are 60–72° near the ocean, 92–102° in the Central Valley, 68–92° in the mountains, and 90–116° in the deserts.

Low temperatures also vary considerably. Mean minimum temperatures in July range from 8° (F) near Squaw Valley to 46° on the southern coast. The record low temperature if 56° below zero, suffered on Mt. Lassen during the winter of 1932–1933. Typical mean low temperatures for January are 38–46° on the coast, 32–38° in the Central Valley, 8–38° in the Sierra Nevada, 28–46° in the Coast Ranges, and 16–40° in the Great Basin and desert areas (Beck and Haase 1974).

In brief, California has not one but many climates. Mild Mediterranean conditions prevail in most regions, with harsh Continental climates affecting only the eastern mountains and deserts. Mean low winter temperatures are above freezing in most parts of the state, and even high summer temperatures are made tolerable by low humidity. Mild climates thus permitted aboriginal occupation of nearly all regions throughout the year. As Baumhoff (1978:18) has observed, California's climates are not so rigorous as to "impose of themselves certain modes of living" (as in the Arctic); rather, they are of most importance as a determinant of vegetation (Major 1977) and, less directly, of faunal assemblages. Biotic resources consequently affected, more directly than climate, the cultural ecology of prehistoric California.

## Life Zones and Vegetation Types

Reflecting the influence of climate, soil, elevation, aspect, and slope, California's vegetation is richly diverse. Included in California are more than 30 natural vegetation types, or about one-fourth of all types identified by Küchler (1964) in the entire coterminous United States. One convenient way to view California's biota is in terms of distribution bands or life zones. Each zone is distinguished by particular plants and animals, although boundaries between zones are not always sharp and some vegetation types or species occupy two or more zones. Generally, any given life zone will occur at lower elevations in the north than in the south.

The overview given below has been adapted and synthesized from Barbour and Major (1977), Küchler (1977), Storer and Usinger (1970), and Wieslander and Jensen (1946). Estimates of land areas for each vegetation type are from Barbour and Major (1977:4).

### Lower Sonoran Zone

The Lower Sonoran life zone is represented chiefly in the Mojave Desert, Colorado Desert, and Central Valley—areas of low elevation having minimal rainfall, high summer temperatures, and low humidity. Characteristic of the desert lowlands are the creosote bush (65,500 km$^2$) and creosote

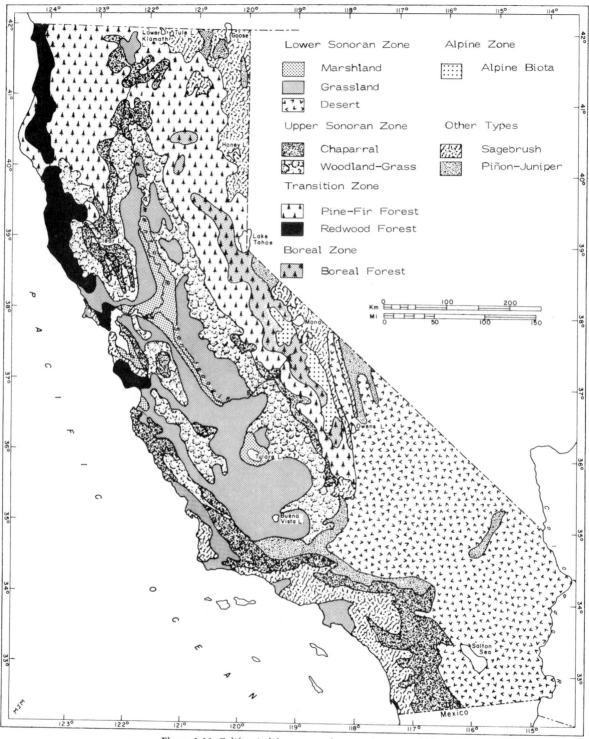

**Figure 1.11** California life zones and vegetation types. (Adapted from Durrenberger 1965 and Grinnell 1935; map by the author.)

bush–bur sage (21,500 km²) vegetation types, with local occurrences of saltbush–greasewood, paloverde–cactus shrub, and saltbush types. Animals found in such desert environments are jackrabbit, bobcat, coyote, and numerous small rodents, birds, and reptiles.

In the Central Valley, the Lower Sonoran zone finds expression mainly in the California steppe or prairie grassland (52,900 km²) and tule marsh (7400 km²), with areas of saltbush in the southern Valley and riparian woodland in the northern Valley (Küchler 1977). The latter vegetation type is marked by a few kinds of trees (valley oak, cottonwood, sycamore, and willows) that once grew in curtains along Valley streams. Animals peculiar to the marsh and grassland types are the tule elk,* pronghorn,* grizzly bear,* coyote, jackrabbit, reptiles, and waterfowl and other birds (Figure 1.11).

### Upper Sonoran Zone

Typical of semiarid foothills and desert country at elevations between ≈150 and 1220 m, the Upper Sonoran life zone is composed of two major vegetation types: savanna or oak woodland–grass (38,200 km²) and chaparral (34,000 km²). The former is a grassland type with scattered oak trees found in the foothills of the Sierra Nevada, Transverse Ranges, and coastal mountains. This was perhaps one of the most important vegetation types for the Indians because it produced abundant acorns and edible grass seeds, as well as forage for deer (Baumhoff 1978:18). In northern California, the black oak, canyon live oak, Oregon oak, and buckeye predominate in the northern oak woodland. Throughout the Sierran foothills and interior Coast Ranges, the foothill woodland is composed of blue, valley, and live oaks, accompanied by buckeye and digger pine. A southern oak woodland, extending from the Tehachapis to Mexico, sustains coast live oak, Englemann oak, and black walnut trees. Common woodland animals are deer, jackrabbit, brush rabbit, fox, coyote, grizzly bear,* valley quail, mourning dove, and various woodpeckers.

Chaparral is a formation of dense brush normally found on steep, rocky slopes between the oak woodland–grass and coniferous forest belts. The most widespread and characteristic chaparral plants are manzanita, chamise, mountain mahogany, scrub oak, and ceanothus. Chaparral is a "fire-type" formation, showing the effects of fire ravage for many thousands of years (Jepson 1925). Chaparral country is by and large unfit for human occupation. Nonetheless, it was valuable to the Indians as deer habitat and as a place to gather amole, brodiaea, soap plant, and manzanita berries.

* Locally or areally extinct.

*Transition Zone*

The Transition life zone is California's main forest belt, accounting for some 86,000 km² of timberland. Among its major types are cedar–hemlock–Douglas fir forest (8100 km²), mixed conifer forest (55,000 km²), California mixed evergreen forest (13,600 km²), redwood forest (9300 km²), and coastal sagebrush (9900 km²). The Transition zone contains a greater number of species of trees and shrubs than any other zone in the state. This zone lies between ≈600 and 1500 m in the Sierra Nevada and somewhat higher in the mountains of southern California. In the Coast Ranges, from Oregon to Monterey, the redwood forest type extends in a strip less than 55 km wide from sea level to altitudes of only 600–900 m. Similarly, the California mixed evergreen forest occurs in the Coast Ranges below ≈1000 m.

In the Sierra Nevada, the Transition zone is recognized by ponderosa and sugar pines, incense cedar, white fir, and black oak, with groves of sequoia in the central and southern parts of the range. In the much wetter northern Coast Ranges are pure stands of redwood or redwood mixed with tanbark oak, Douglas fir, coast hemlock, tideland spruce, and grand fir. On the inner side of the redwood belt is a distinct band of madrone, Douglas fir, and Oregon oak. Last, an arid Transition subzone or ponderosa–shrub forest type (6800 km²) occurs in the Great Basin below the Sierran forests. Typical of this drier and more exposed type are ponderosa pine, bear brush, manzanita, and Sierra plum (Jepson 1925).

The wildlife of the Transition overlaps with higher and lower zones and is accordingly varied. Canadian elk, beaver, rabbits and other rodents, foxes, black and grizzly* bears, coyote, mountain lion, and numerous birds belong to this zone. The Transition was generally, although not always, the upper limit for year-round settlement by precontact Indians.

*The Upper Zones*

In the Sierra Nevada entirely above snow line at elevations of ≈1500–2150 m is the Canadian life zone. Its principal vegetation type is the red fir forest (7600 km²), composed of red and white firs and silver and Jeffrey pines. Between the Canadian zone forests and the treeline (≈2750 m) lies the Hudsonian life zone, a timberline band of lodgepole pine subalpine forest (8600 km²), with scattered lodgepole and whitebark pines, western juniper, and a few types of bushes, such as currant and Lemmon's willow. Above 2700 m is the Boreal zone, a cold and windswept alpine landscape with scant soil (except in meadows), no large trees, and a few hardy plants

---

* Areally extinct.

of types common to the Arctic. Alpine meadows (3000 km$^2$) occur in all the upper zones. The high-elevation fauna consists mainly of summer visitors from lower zones, along with such residents as the Allen chipmunk, marmot, wolverine, and mountain sheep. The high country above 3250 m was usually visited only in the summer by Indians engaged in hunting, gathering, and trade with Great Basin peoples (Bennyhoff 1953).

*Great Basin Types*

The western Great Basin, from Modoc County to the northern Mojave Desert, exhibits two main vegetation types: sagebrush steppe (13,000 km$^2$) and piñon–juniper/juniper–steppe woodland (13,500 km$^2$). Sagebrush, bitterbrush, and rabbit brush predominate in the lower reaches of this zone (≈1200–1700 m), whereas piñon pine and Utah juniper form scattered woodlands at the higher elevations (≈1700–2200 m). Great Basin environments provided sparse archaeological populations with piñon nuts and other edible seeds along with pronghorn, mountain sheep, and small game.

# Historic Transformations

California's natural setting is very different today than it was in the geologically recent past. Climate, wildlife, and even coastal geography have changed significantly even during the span of human occupation (see Chapters 2, 3, and 6). Remarkable changes also have occurred during the historic era. For example, some of the richest biotic communities in the state have been eliminated as coastal estuaries from San Diego to Eureka have been polluted, filled with spoils and silt, and built upon. In A.D. 1800, San Francisco Bay and its marshlands covered nearly 1800 km$^2$; today the Bay system is only half that size as a result of landfill projects and extensive siltation. To the east, much of the Delta and nearly all the former marshlands in the Central Valley have been drained since about 1870 to create agricultural land. This "reclamation" was done at the cost of wetland habitat for millions of waterfowl and other animals.

Salmon were so numerous in early historic times that horses often were reluctant to ford streams during spawning runs. By the 1870s, however, the best salmon fisheries of coastal and interior rivers had been largely destroyed; overfishing, water diversion, pollution, and soil runoff due to farming, deforestation, and, above all, hydraulic mining took their toll. Of an estimated 8000 km of spawning grounds along the Sacramento

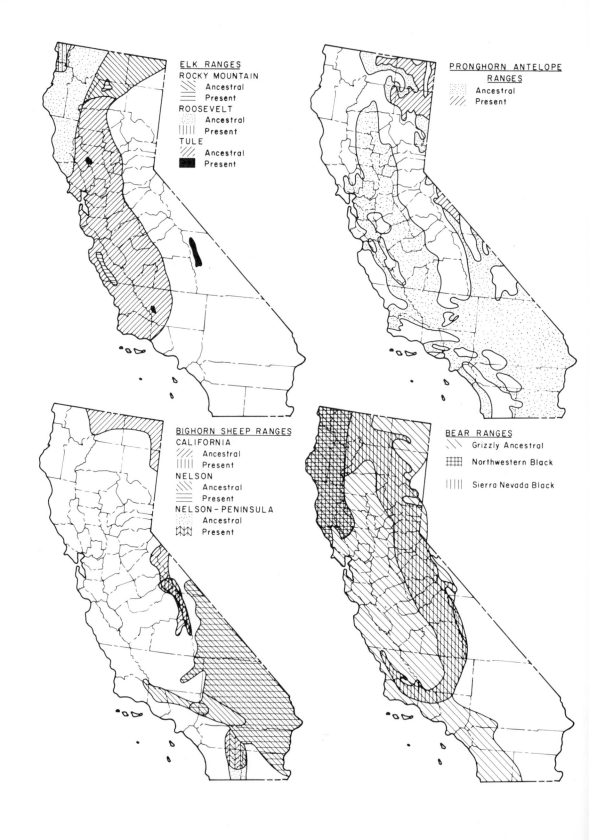

**ELK RANGES**
ROCKY MOUNTAIN
 ⧄ Ancestral
 ☰ Present
ROOSEVELT
 ⦙⦙ Ancestral
 ‖‖ Present
TULE
 ⧄ Ancestral
 ■ Present

PRONGHORN ANTELOPE
RANGES
 ⦙⦙ Ancestral
 ⧄ Present

BIGHORN SHEEP RANGES
CALIFORNIA
 ⧄ Ancestral
 ‖‖ Present
NELSON
 ⧄ Ancestral
 ☰ Present
NELSON-PENINSULA
 ⧄ Ancestral
 ⋀⋀ Present

BEAR RANGES
 ⧄ Grizzly Ancestral
 ▦ Northwestern Black
 ‖‖ Sierra Nevada Black

River system, only 480 km remained in 1929 (Clark 1929; Swezey and Heizer 1977).

Until the nineteenth century, dense redwood forests skirted the coast from Monterey to Oregon. Relentless logging has obliterated nearly all the virgin forest, leaving only remnants in parks and private groves. Less dramatic perhaps was the removal before 1900 of the Central Valley woodlands. Countless oaks were felled to provide firewood for local ranches and fuel for steamers plying Valley waterways. Plowing and the grazing of seedlings by cattle and sheep made reforestation almost impossible.

Tule elk, once abundant in marshy areas, were nearly extinguished by commercial hunters before 1900. They persist now only in a few small reserves. Likewise, the formerly widespread herds of pronghorn were hunted to extinction locally and are now limited in California to parts of the western Great Basin (Figure 1.12).

An estimated 10,000 grizzly bears once roamed throughout cismontane California. Following an early nineteenth-century explosion of the bear population in the South Coast Ranges, where great herds of Spanish cattle increased their food supply and the removal of Indians to the missions opened new bear habitat, grizzlies were exterminated rapidly. They were captured for bear-and-bull fights, shot, trapped, caged, and poisoned with *bear bait* (chunks of raw meat laced with massive doses of strychnine). The last known California grizzly bear was seen in eastern Tulare County in 1924 (Storer and Tevis 1955).

The histories of the sea otter and Guadalupe fur seal further exemplify the recent changes in California's environment. Before 1800, sea otters were incredibly numerous all along the coast; but by 1850, Russians and Americans had hunted the otters nearly to extinction. Similarly, the Guadalupe fur seal ranged from the Farallons to Baja California until 400,000 of them were killed for profit during the nineteenth century (Gordon 1974).

It is clear from the foregoing that the Indians and early colonists beheld a California very different from the one we know today. It is that unspoiled California that we must envision as we seek to understand how prehistoric cultures interacted with their environments.

## Synopsis of Natural History

Although the California landscape is enormously diverse, several key concepts may be summarized: (1) the dominant geomorphic features are

---

**Figure 1.12** Past and present distributions of big-game animals in California. (From *Historical Atlas of California*, by Warren A. Beck and Ynez D. Haase; copyright © University of Oklahoma Press.)

north–northwest-trending mountain ranges and valleys marked by varied local physiography; (2) relief is extreme, including the lowest and highest points in the contiguous 48 states—Death Valley (−85 m) and Mt. Whitney (4418 m); (3) all of California's large rivers, except the Colorado, belong to either the north coastal or the interior (Cascade–Sierra–Valley) watershed; (4) California embraces landforms and hydrographic features of every description—deserts, volcanic peaks and plateaus, rugged coastline, tidelands, marine channels, estuaries, islands, hill country, high mountain ranges, river valleys, broad alluvial plains, wetlands, streams, and both saline and freshwater lakes; (5) Mediterranean climates typify all regions but the deserts, high cordillera, and Great Basin, where Continental conditions prevail; and (6) the endless combinations of terrain, soil, climate, and biota result in microenvironments of immense variety and resource potential.

Because of this environmental diversity, prehistoric Indians of any given locality faced an abundance of certain resources and a dearth of others—a circumstance favoring trade, economic interdependence, and ultimately the evolution of complex redistribution networks. This is not to say that the environment determined how cultures would develop or interact, but rather that patterns of resource availability would have influenced local population size, settlement location, exploitative strategy, and the like.

The Indians found in California an ideal climate and material resources to meet their basic needs. Theirs was a "Goodly Ilande," and they found it provident through the millennia. Before this shore of the Pacific was maimed by Western Civilization, California was indeed "very near to the Terrestrial Paradise."

# 2. The First Californians

Out of Asia an unknown number of centuries ago came these
Wanderers, the first to set foot on the Western Hemisphere.
Omnivorous Pleistocene predators, they followed their prey as it
moved and sought new sources in a land that was to them only an
extension of the country with which they had long been familiar—a
land we now conveniently call a land bridge.

*Cressman (1977:57)*

[Drawing by Randall Engle.]

# Introduction

It is generally known that humans did not evolve in the Western Hemisphere and that the first Americans drifted into the New World from Siberia. They came by way of the Bering Land Bridge, exposed by low sea levels of the Ice Age. Theirs was the last great migration of the human species, yet only the first step toward settling and adapting to the vast continents unknown to their predecessors.

The timetable of man's entry into America and settlement of its various regions is the subject of ongoing research. Although a 12,000-year record of New World prehistory is firmly established, evidence of earlier cultural activity is more tenuous. One possible ancient site is at Tlapacoya, Mexico, where several flaked-stone tools reportedly were found with Pleistocene mammal bones on an old lakeshore, now buried under volcanic ash, dated by the radiocarbon ($^{14}$C) method at circa 18,000 to 22,000 B.C. (Lorenzo 1970). Radiocarbon dates on the order of 17,000 B.C. have been obtained for the lowest cultural stratum at the Meadowcroft Rockshelter in Pennsylvania (Adovasio *et al.* 1979:34), and the discovery of stone tools along with fossil sloth and horse bones in deposits ≈19,600 years old at Pikimachay Cave, Peru (MacNeish 1972, 1979a), would imply that North America was initially populated somewhat earlier. However, each of these finds has been questioned (particularly as regards dating), and on present evidence none can be accepted as definitive proof of New World human occupation 19,000 or 20,000 years ago.

Even greater antiquity is claimed for possible and certain bone artifacts—including a caribou-tibia fleshing tool—from the Old Crow River vicinity, Yukon Territory, which have yielded $^{14}$C ages of ≈25,750 to 29,100 years (Irving 1982; Irving and Harington 1973; Morlan 1980). Unfortunately, the Old Crow specimens have come from secondary deposits and do not make a strong case for human population of the American Arctic at such an early time (Dumond 1982:887, 890).

California, too, contains sites alleged to be older than 12,000 years, including some for which ages of 40,000 to several hundred thousand years have been proposed. Most of these claims are highly controversial, as we see in this chapter, which takes up the Ice Age archaeology of California. First, however, we examine glacial and other environmental conditions that would have influenced the origins, adaptations, and spread of the earliest North Americans.

## Glaciers and Seas

During the Pleistocene epoch, or Ice Age, enormous sheets of glacial ice up to 3 km thick repeatedly covered much of the Northern Hemisphere. In America the Pleistocene glacial sequence included at least four stages or major episodes of glaciation separated by interglacials (warmer intervals of ice retreat). The stages, in turn, were composed of stadials (smaller advances) and interstadials. For example, the Wisconsin Stage of ≈60,000 to 11,000 years ago featured a number of stadials and interstadials (Figure 2.1). The Holocene, or Recent, interval of circa 11,000 B.P. (before present) to the present is a post-Pleistocene epoch, or so it would seem; ultimately it too may prove to be an interglacial.

As ice shields expanded in the Northern Hemisphere, so much water was trapped in the glaciers that sea levels fell more than 85 m and continental shelves were exposed around the world (Hopkins 1979:19). Whenever the oceans receded, terrestrial plants and animals invaded the "offshore" realm and established themselves as viable communities. When the ice melted during interglacial and interstadial times, marine waters rose again and flooded coastal zones. Glacial fluctuations, related to alternate cooling and warming of climates, led to sea-level oscillations throughout the Pleistocene (Figure 2.1).

No less than six Wisconsin ice advances caused ocean levels to fall enough to expose the floor of the Bering Sea—actually a landmass, Beringia, up to 2000 km wide connecting Siberia and Alaska (Hopkins 1967). At such times humans and other creatures could have moved easily between the Old and New Worlds. The Bering Land Bridge was open during most of the time from ≈25,000 until 13,000 years ago. About 16,000 years ago, sea level began to rise gradually. Then an abrupt, global shift to warmer climates at circa 14,000 B.P. triggered rapid deglaciation and meltwater runoff. By circa 13,000 B.P., the Bering and Anadyr straits had been submerged (Hopkins 1979:17, 28–29).

## Peopling America

America likely was first settled by small bands of hunters and foragers who drifted gradually across Beringia, probably over a span of generations.

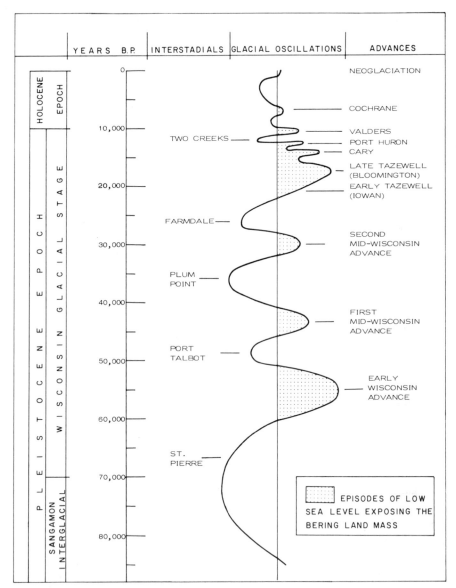

**Figure 2.1** Chronology of late Pleistocene and Holocene glaciation in North America. (Adapted from Ancient Native Americans edited by Jesse D. Jennings, W. H. Freeman and Company, copyright © 1978; drawing by the author.)

The number of migrants was doubtless small because Siberia was sparsely populated and moving farther north meant more cold and generally fewer resources in a land dominated by the wolves, bears, and tigers of the Soviet Far East (Laughlin and Wolf 1979:3). The earliest Americans probably lived in Arctic refugia, such as the nearly ice-free environments of Beringia and interior Alaska. But population growth inevitably hastened their spread into other parts of the New World, then a beckoning wilderness extending over an area of 40 million km$^2$.

When North American glaciers were most extensive, the Cordilleran (western) and Laurentide (eastern) ice sheets coalesced, at least briefly, to form a single glacial mass from the Pacific to the Atlantic and from the Arctic Ocean to the northern tier of the United States. Migrations into lands south of the glaciers would have taken place chiefly along a mid-continental, ice-free corridor between the Cordilleran and Laurentide fronts. This corridor may have existed during much of the interval from ≈20,000 to 14,000 years ago, during which time the joining of the eastern and western ice shields probably was never a barrier to human dispersal for periods longer than a millennium or two. Communications between eastern Beringia and central North America were possible after circa 14,000 B.P. through a steadily widening, ice-free inland zone (Hopkins 1979:15–17, 33–35).

Some researchers have questioned whether the interior corridor was open during and immediately after the glacial maxima. Fladmark (1979:64), for example, argues that the early Americans may have migrated southward from Beringia along "a chain of sea level refugia" on the North Pacific coast—a view supported by Borden's (1979) observation that many parts of the Pacific Northwest were already occupied between ≈14,500 and 11,500 years ago. Nonetheless, although both the coastal and interior routes probably were used at various times, it is doubtful that the first southerly migration was by way of the coastal zone. Coastal movements between Beringia and Puget Sound most likely were prevented until circa 12,000 years ago by the presence of ice caps and piedmont glaciers on the continental shelves during major glacial intervals (Hopkins 1979:35).

There is no scholarly consensus as to when subglacial America was initially settled. P. S. Martin (1973) has proposed that specialized big-game hunters first emerged south of the ice sheets circa 12,000 B.P. and that, through normal population growth and expansion, they spread as far south as Tierra del Fuego in less than a millennium. Many researchers cite the previously mentioned finds (in Peru, Mexico, Pennsylvania, etc.) as evidence for widespread human population of the New World 20,000–30,000 years ago. Other investigators assert that America was first occupied more than 40,000 years ago, and a few believe that human antiquity in the Western Hemisphere can be traced 200,000 years or more into the remote past. Some of the data upon which these differing views are based are examined in this chapter. For the moment, however, we shall say that America was settled by people of Asian origin at some time earlier than 12,000 years ago, that is, during late Pleistocene times.

# Pleistocene California

The environment of Ice Age California was very different than that of today. During stadial periods the climate was relatively cool and moist; montane and valley glaciers covered large areas of the high Sierra and Cascade Range; pine forests stood in the foothills where oak woodlands now grow; and hundreds of lakes occupied the lowlands where deserts and arid valleys now exist. Along the coast, ocean waves pounded beaches many kilometers west of the present shoreline—the result of lower sea levels (Figures 2.1 and 6.2). Before 10,000 years ago, regions that are now deserts provided verdant habitats for huge bison and mammoths together with such awesome predators as the short-faced bear and saber-toothed cat (Figure 2.2).

## Climate and Water

From late Pleistocene times onward, California's climate has been sub-humid or semiarid with cool–moist and warm–dry seasons like those of today. Both inland and on the coast, pollen analyses and paleobotanical studies show that summer drought conditions prevailed even during late Wisconsin stadials. The influence of this Mediterranean climate in much of California during the late Pleistocene contrasts with the marked climatic changes recorded in glacial North America (Adam 1974; D. Johnson 1977b).

Nonetheless, when viewed region by region, California changed significantly between 60,000 and 10,000 B.P. due to generally cooler temperatures and increased precipitation. The coastal region was more moist during the last glacial stage than it is now, "as reflected by the presence of more extensive coastal coniferous forest and by the occurrence of certain fossil tree species considerably south of their present limits" (D. Johnson 1977b:171). Similarly, in the Sierra Nevada, temperatures were cooler, the treeline and life zones shifted downslope, montane glaciers expanded, and the snowline fell as much as several hundred meters below that of today (Adam 1967, 1973; Birkeland *et al.* 1976; Birman 1964; Curry 1968; Wahrhaftig and Birman 1965).

Perhaps the most dramatic late Pleistocene changes occurred in the interior valley and desert regions where increased rainfall and lower temperatures, coupled with reduced evaporation, led to a downward shift of biotic zones (Wells and Berger 1967) and created numerous pluvial lakes (Figure 3.1). Between circa 22,500 and 12,000 B.P., during the Bonneville and Provo Pluvials, more than 100 lakes were formed in the Great Basin; others appeared in California's Central Valley and even in the Coast Ranges (Eardley *et al.* 1973; Morrison 1965; Snyder *et al.* 1964). During

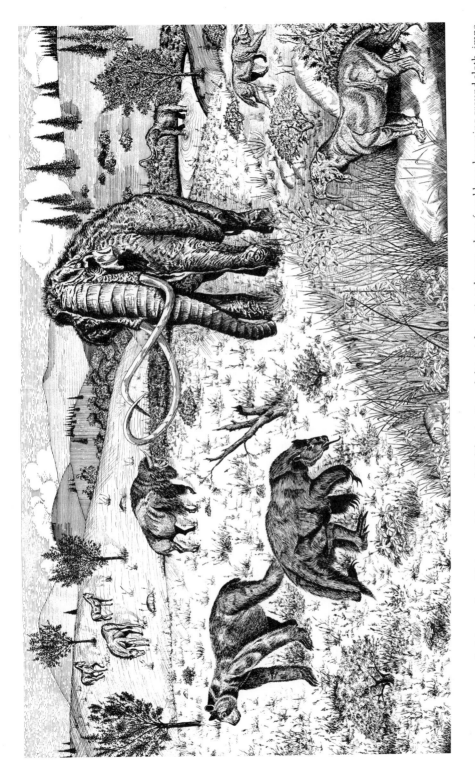

**Figure 2.2** Rancholabrean (late Pleistocene) fauna of California. From left to right, extinct horses, short-faced bear, browsing ground sloth, imperial mammoths, saber-toothed cat, and dire wolf. For scale, the short-faced bear stood about 130 cm at the shoulder when on all fours. (Drawing by Randall Engle.)

this period the Mojave Desert was a region of deep lakes and fertile marshes, surrounded by xeric woodland and cold steppe (Mehringer 1967, 1977).

The largest of the pluvial lakes was Lake Bonneville, covering more than 50,000 km² in Utah, Nevada, and Idaho to a maximum depth of ≈335 m. Remnant lakes of the ancient Bonneville system include Provo, Sevier, and Great Salt lakes. Lake Lahontan in the western Great Basin flooded an areas roughly half the size of Lake Bonneville and was about 170 m deep (Flint 1965). Modern vestiges of Lahontan include Pyramid, Winnemucca, and Walker lakes in Nevada and Honey Lake in northeastern California (Figure 3.1).

During the cool–moist pluvial episodes, the lakes were deep and water was generally available throughout the Great Basin. Then, around 11,000 B.P., temperatures began to rise, forests and grasslands gave way to more xeric plant communities, and deep lakes evolved into shallow lakes and marshes (Bedwell 1970; Weide 1968; Wells and Berger 1967). These transformations seem to have developed earlier in the south than in the north, but within a few centuries the entire Great Basin was affected.

The emergence of shallow lakes and marshes is of special archaeological interest because they produce far more biomass than do deep lakes of equal extent. Marshes offer not only the seeds, roots, and stems of waterplants, but also the opportunity to take waterfowl and their eggs, fish, frogs, turtles, shorebirds, and various small mammals adapted to wetland habitats (Weide 1968). Moreover, during times of desiccation large mammals would have congregated increasingly near the lakes and marshes as water sources elsewhere dried up. Clearly, the late Pleistocene lakeshores were ideal places for human occupation (see Chapter 3).

*Rancholabrean Fauna*

California's Pleistocene animals are best known from fossils preserved in the tar pits of Rancho La Brea in Los Angeles. This is the type site for the Rancholabrean faunal assemblage, defined by such creatures as the imperial mammoth, horses, bison, tapirs, sloths, camels, dire wolf, California lion, cheetah, and saber-toothed cat (Figure 2.2). From the human perspective, this fauna must have been an impressive part of the Pleistocene landscape.

Imagine the animals encountered by early people in the Far West. In this area ranged the California lion—the largest cat that ever lived (roughly 25% larger than an African lion). Smaller, but capable of pursuit speeds of ≈ 35 m/sec, was the North American cheetah. Another felid was the saber-toothed cat, about the size of a Bengal tiger and equipped with scimitar canines and slashing teeth. Numerous dire wolves evidently hunted in packs. Comparable to a good-sized timber wolf, the dire wolf had a powerful neck and jaws for dragging downed game. The most awesome predator was the giant short-faced bear. The largest carnivorous mammal ever to live in America, this bruin stood ≈130 cm high at the shoulder (compared with ≈100 cm for a grizzly bear) and was armed with a battery of shearing teeth unlike those of omnivorous true bears. Although it weighed more than a ton, the giant short-faced bear had long legs designed for great speed (Adams 1979; Downs and Miller 1971; Kurtén and Anderson 1980; Stock 1930).

Grazing and browsing animals were also important in the Rancholabrean fauna. The western horse was in most respects like its modern counterpart, a herd animal about 150 cm high. Some species of ancient bison, however, were considerably larger than the modern "buffalo." With a shoulder height of ≈200 cm and a weight of nearly 2000 kg, these ponderous beasts roamed widely in the California lowlands. Other common herbivores were the musk ox, shrub-ox, deer, tapir, camelids, several species of sloths, mastodons, and mammoths. Of these, the Columbian mammoth was one of the largest land mammals ever known. With great curved tusks up to 4.6 m long, this massive beast stood 3.5–4.0 m high at the shoulder and weighed as much as 11,000 kg (Downs and Miller; Kurtén and Anderson 1980; Stock 1930). Because such gigantism was common, the term *megafauna* is often applied to the larger of the Rancholabrean species.

### Summary

The impact of the Pleitocene epoch in California was seen most directly in sea-level fluctuations caused by glacial oscillations farther north. Important, too, were the fairly cool–moist climates that sustained glaciers in the high country, depressed life zones and the snowline in elevation and latitude, and led to the emergence of pluvial lakes. While these conditions prevailed, California supported diverse Rancholabrean animals. Together, these factors comprise the environmental background against which the pre-Holocene archaeological record is to be considered.

# Evaluating the Archaeological Evidence

This chapter examines certain remains alleged to be archaeological and of Pleistocene age. Interpreting such materials is difficult on several accounts. One problem is the scarcity of human bones and definite artifacts in reliably dated contexts, which limits any reconstruction of cultural patterns from the ancient past. At times, the data are so equivocal that one cannot distinguish between natural and cultural remains.

Even when finds are clearly archaeological, it is not always possible to determine their age by radiocarbon or other reliable methods. For instance, the degree of fossilization alone is not a good indicator of antiquity: highly permineralized human bones found embedded in the travertine rock of Calaveras County caves—once thought of to be of Pliocene age (Whitney 1867, 1872) and later estimated to be 12,000 years old (Orr 1952a)—are, on present evidence, no more than 3000 to 4000 years old (see Chapter 7). Neither does deep burial necessarily indicate great antiquity. In 1960 a human calvarium was found north of Seal Beach in marine deposits 5.3 m below sea level and 10.5 m below the surface. Associated shell yielded a $^{14}$C date of A.D. 970 ± 80 (UCLA-119); rapid deposition and vertical shifts of the local crust had contributed to deep burial (Brooks, *et al.* 1965).

Another difficulty is that geologic processes have obscured archaeological traces over the millennia. Consequently, most discoveries of ancient sites in California have been made in deserts and in the eroded south coastal zone where the remains may occur on or near the surface. This does not mean that early materials are absent elsewhere, but rather that we know less about nonarid lands where sediments and vegetation obscure old surfaces. As T. F. King put it, "seeking Pleistocene Man on the California desert is a little like looking on 10th Street for a dime lost on 4th because the light is better" (1975:33). Yet desert archaeology is a mixed blessing; the deflation and devegetation that expose artifacts also destroy stratified deposits that might otherwise provide a context and dating for the discoveries.

Unpublished and unreliable data are also troublesome. Many reports of finds have appeared only as newspaper articles or brief notes lacking key information, and even some accounts in scholarly journals are so vague as to be of scant value. The sad truth is that a large proportion of the archaeological discoveries in California has never been reported fully and professionally.

A final yet basic challenge is to confirm the archaeological evidence: What constitues valid proof of human activity? C. W. Meighan has noted that "skeletons and unquestionable tools may be regarded as definitive evidence, charcoal and burned bone as only 'possible,' with greater or lesser degree of probability depending on subsidiary lines of evidence" (1965:710). To be really acceptable to most archaeologists, an "Early Man" site ideally should have a clearly identifiable geologic context, definite artifacts or human skeletal material, faunal and floral remains, and substances amenable to dating by reliable methods; "insofar as finds that have been proposed fail to satisfy such criteria they are inevitably open to question, rejection, or suspended judgment" (Griffin 1979:44).

With this background, we now examine some of California's possibly ancient archaeological sites and remains.

## Possible Early Sites

### Lake Manix

Lake Manix in the Mojave Desert (Figures 1.8 and 2.3) consists of a central playa and the Coyote, Troy, and Afton basins. At various times in the past Lake Manix was a sink at the end of the Mojave River. Fossils from lakeshore strata indicate a Pleistocene age for the highest stand of the former lake, and $^{14}$C ages of 17,340 B.C. (UCLA-121) and 17,540 B.C. (UCLA-296) were derived from tufa samples found just below the highest shoreline.

In 1948 amateur archaeologist Ritner Sayles discovered crude flaked-stone artifacts in the desert pavement and lacustrine sediments throughout the hills above the ancient playa. Six years later, Ruth Simpson, then with the Southwest Museum, began a systematic survey of the Manix Basin and adjacent foothills east of the Calico Mountains. She encountered artifact scatters like those found by Sayles as much as 545 m above the highest shoreline of the Pleistocene lake (Leakey *et al.* 1969). The artifacts—mostly percussion-flaked choppers, scrapers, bifaces, cores, and waste flakes, with a few hammerstones and blade cores (Figure 2.4)—were described by Simpson (1958, 1960) as the *Manix Lake Lithic Complex*. Equating these artifacts with Lower Paleolithic materials of the Old World, she has applied such terms as *Clactonian, Chellean,* and *Acheulian* to the complex. Simpson (1958, 1964) avers that the Lake Manix specimens are approximately 20,000 years old.

Differing with Simpson, W. S. Glennan suggests that the Manix Lake Industry "reflects a workshop activity area and not the cultural remains of a pre-projectile point stage occupation of the Mojave Desert" (1976:43). Glennan argues, first, that late artifacts are commonly embedded in desert pavement and that finding Lake Manix specimens in desert pavement does not necessarily indicate great age; second, that the general similarities between Lake Manix and Old World artifacts prove neither formal relationships nor contemporaneity; and, third, that almost none of the Lake Manix pieces shows edgewear or other use marks, but they do resemble debris from known lithic-quarry sites elsewhere in the desert.

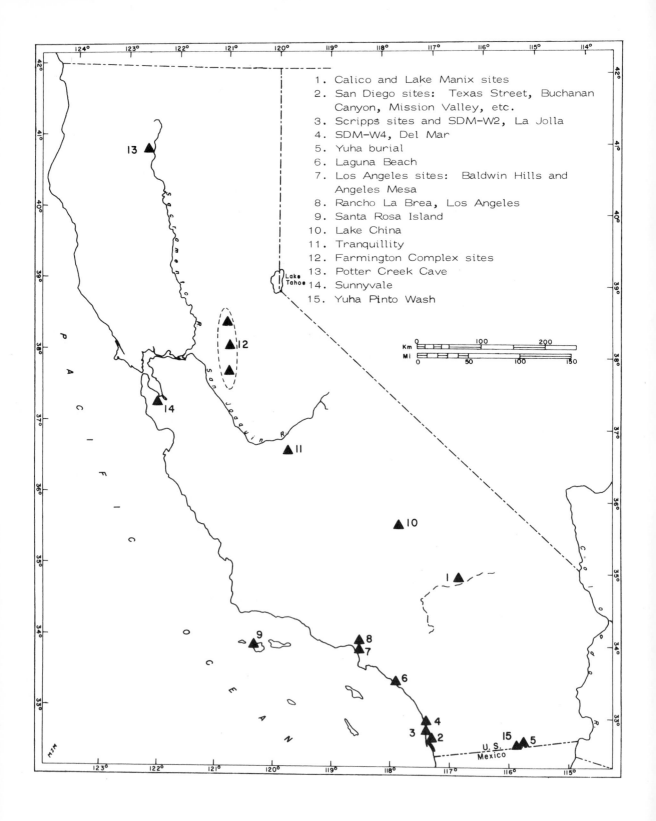

1. Calico and Lake Manix sites
2. San Diego sites: Texas Street, Buchanan Canyon, Mission Valley, etc.
3. Scripps sites and SDM-W2, La Jolla
4. SDM-W4, Del Mar
5. Yuha burial
6. Laguna Beach
7. Los Angeles sites: Baldwin Hills and Angeles Mesa
8. Rancho La Brea, Los Angeles
9. Santa Rosa Island
10. Lake China
11. Tranquillity
12. Farmington Complex sites
13. Potter Creek Cave
14. Sunnyvale
15. Yuha Pinto Wash

Glennan (1976:58) concludes that the Lake Manix assemblage includes only blanks, preforms, and workshop rejects scattered widely over alluvial fans wherever high-quality chalcedony is found, and that the claims of Pleistocene antiquity cannot be supported.

Simpson has replied that Glennan's study was "premature, weakly supported by background data, [and] inaccurate" (1976:65). She cites the ostensible diversity of archaeological sites in the Lake Manix vicinity to counter the view that the area was a single workshop or quarry. Simpson affirms that Glennan neglected important data and that the entire Lake Manix issue will come into better focus when her *Eastern Calico Mountains Archaeological Survey Report* is published.

The Lake Manix controversy may persist for some time. There is no doubt that the specimens are artifacts and that they occur in nonrandom densities and patterns at various places above ancient Lake Manix. Although some of the pieces *may* be quite old, efforts to link them to $^{14}$C dates from fossil lakeshores have been unsuccessful. Hence, the age of the complex remains unknown, and there is no good reason to view it as related to Old World industries. Most of the lithic inventory at Lake Manix probably reflects quarry–workshop activity over a long span of time. The hypothesis that some of the chipping stations were left by "pre-projectile point" cultures of circa 20,000 B.P. remains to be confirmed.

*The Calico Hills Site*

In an attempt to resolve the Lake Manix problem by finding artifacts in a datable context, excavations were begun in 1964 at the Calico Hills site under the guidance of L. S. B. Leakey and R. D. Simpson. Located above the Manix playa at an elevation of ≈670 m in foothills 7 km northeast of Yermo (Figure 2.3), Calico is one of the most controversial sites in America. The deposits in question rest on the eroded and faulted remnant of an old pediment or inactive alluvial fan reaching from the Calico Mountains eastward to Lake Manix. The excavated strata belong to the Pleistocene Yermo formation (Figure 2.5), unconformably overlying Miocene ash beds and mudstones of the Barstow formation (Haynes 1973).

Digging meticulously, field crews have opened two "master pits" (7.6 m square with depths of ≈6.4 and 8.8 m; Figure 2.6), 22 smaller "control pits," and five trenches in the cemented alluvium (Simpson 1980:9). By 1968, the researchers had identified several hundred chert and chal-

**Figure 2.3** Location of possible early (Pleistocene) archaeological sites in California. (Map by the author.)

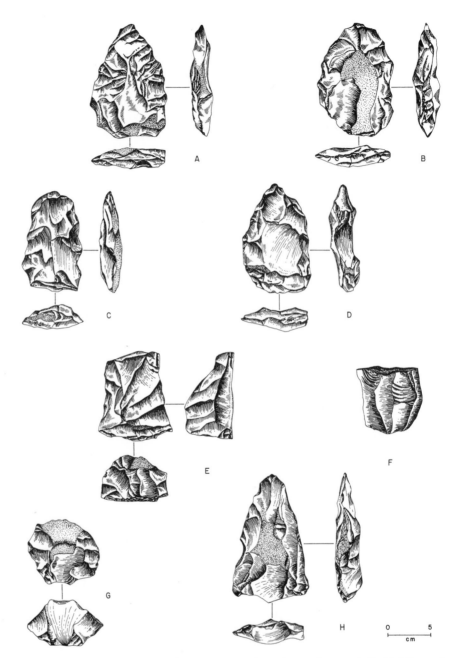

**Figure 2.4** Artifacts of the Lake Manix Complex, Mojave Desert. A–D, H, bifaces; E, scraper-plane; F, G, cores. (Modified from Glennan 1976: Figures 2, 5, 6, 8; drawing by Randall Engle.)

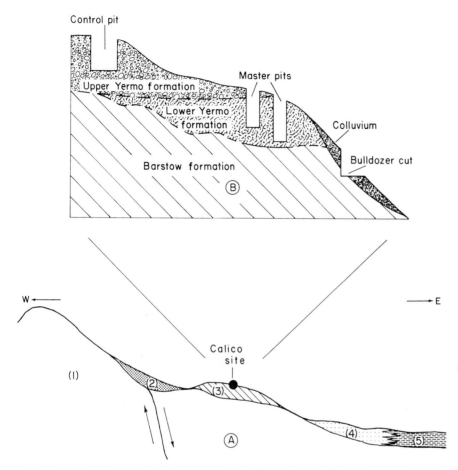

**Figure 2.5** Generalized geologic cross-section of (A) the Calico Foothills area and (B) the Calico site area; not to scale. (1) bedrock of pre-Pleistocene age; (2) alluvial fans of Wisconsin age; (3) alluvial-fan remnants of the pre-Wisconsin Yermo formation; (4) Wisconsin-age beach ridge on late Pleistocene alluvial-fan deposits; and (5) late Pleistocene lacustrine deposits of the Manix Lake Basin. (After Haynes 1973: Figures 1,2; drawn by the author.)

cedony "tools, some of which appear to have been primitive hand axes and scrapers" (Leakey *et al.* 1969:78). These were selected from many thousands of rocks judged to be natural. By 1977, more than 4000 specimens had been set apart as "artifacts" (Simpson 1977), and by 1981 the number of "significant lithic artifacts" had risen to 11,400 (Budinger 1981:2). This inventory is said to include more than 400 prismatic flakes and blades, unifacial tools, bifacial tools with patterned flaking, and prepared cores, to name a few of the types identified by Simpson (1980:2–8) (Figure 2.7).

**Figure 2.6** Calico Hills site: excavation units in Master Pit 1. The central column has been maintained for future studies. Excavation units measure 1.52 × 1.52 m (5 × 5 feet). Maximum depth below surface shown here is 6.40 m (21 feet). (Photograph by Fred E. Budinger, Jr.; courtesy of the San Bernardino County Museum.)

An analysis of lithic items from Master Pit II has revealed nearly 1000 pieces of débitage and "over 800 tools and other worked artifacts" with "distinctive use-wear patterns" on more than 40% of the material examined (Singer 1977:109). This assemblage also contained "flake and blade tools including burins, gravers, borers, perforators and knives, utilized burin spalls and microblades, seven retouched scraper forms, and a variety of cores, angular picks, choppers and anvils" (1977:109).

In 1970 Leakey and his co-workers announced the discovery of a "hearth" at a depth of ≈7 m in Master Pit II. This was an ovoid arrangement of 18 cobbles enclosing a shallow basin about 35 cm wide by 45 cm long (see Berger 1979:Figure 1). No radiocarbon was detectable in the basin. However, a chalcedony cobble from the feature was sent to the Czechoslovak Academy of Sciences in Prague where V. Bucha determined that the stone evidently had been heated appreciably more on the end into the "hearth" than on the other end. A control rock from the same deposit but away from the feature showed no effect of heat. From this it was concluded that fire once burned within the stone enclosure (Berger 1979:34). The alleged hearth and "tools" comprise the testimony for Early Man at Calico, a site to which project geologist T. Clements initially assigned a minimum age of 50,000 years and a probable age of 70,000 to 100,000 years (Clements 1979; K. Dixon 1970b; Leakey *et al.* 1968, 1969, 1972; Schuiling 1979; Simpson 1977, 1980; Simpson *et al.* 1981).

**Figure 2.7** Lithic specimens from the Calico Hills site, identified by personnel of the San Bernadino County Museum as follows: 1, 2, choppers; 3, cutting tool; 4, side-scraper; 5, handaxe-like tool; 6, multiple scraper; 7, chopper; 8, multiple scraper; 9, side-scraper; 10, blades and bladelets; 11, 12, flakes; 13, multiple scraper; 14, side-scraper; 15, blade cores; 16, graver; 17, blade; 18, beaked scraper–graver; 19, end- and side-scraper. Despite the similarity of certain of these specimens to artifacts, most archaeologists consider the Calico lithic items to be *geofacts*—products of natural forces within the alluvial fan environment. (Photograph by Daniel J. Griffin; photograph courtesy of Fred E. Budinger, Jr., and the San Bernardino County Museum.)

C. V. Haynes, Jr., of the University of Arizona, has cast doubt on the claims of Pleistocene human activity at the Calico site. Haynes (1969, 1973) mustered a series of observations to support his conclusion that the Calico flints are geofacts and not tools: (1) the stones are of local origin and occur in the alluvium naturally; (2) flaking of the rocks could have resulted from mass wasting, fluvial transport, and pressure caused by deep burial; (3) no item from Calico is an obvious artifact, and there seems to be a gradual transition between what are considered artifacts, probable artifacts, possible artifacts, and nonartifacts; (4) the vertical distribution of the collection is random throughout some 3 m of mudflow gravels, indicating that the pieces are all redeposited; and (5) the geological age of the Lower Yermo formation is thought to be at least 500,000 years. If the Calico "artifacts" are of such mid-Pleistocene age, they necessarily would have been made by pre-Neanderthal people; yet there are no known fossils of such hominids in America (Haynes 1973).

In partial reply to Haynes, it has been argued that (1) the "tools" in fact were found in distinct concentrations and were not randomly distributed, (2) some specimens exhibit unifacial or bifacial retouch that could not have been produced naturally, and (3) the collection includes bladelets and blades as much as 4 cm long, most without cortex, which must be cultural (Budinger 1981:2–4); moreover, (4) some of the "artifacts" are made of moss agate and other materials said not to occur naturally in the Calico fan, and others exhibit "indubitable" wear marks from tool use (Witthoft 1979:48); and, finally, (5) certain items from Calico simply cannot be explained as geofacts because they were produced by the sequential removal of dozens of flakes in a controlled and patterned way (Bryan 1979:78).

L. A. Payen at the University of California, Riverside, has studied Calico lithic specimens with the goal of distinguishing between geofacts and artifacts. Payen's analysis was based on more than 14,000 measurements of "angle platform scars" in 54 sample collections of controlled (artifactual) and uncontrolled (natural) fracturing. Comparisons of the artifactual and natural series indicate clearly that the two kinds of fracturing exhibit different flake-angle distributions, the weighted means being 72 and 88° for artifactual and natural fracturing, respectively. Nine lots of chalcedony items from Master Pit II, thought by Calico excavators to be "prime tools," registered a mean angle of 87°—almost identical to the mean for known geofacts. Two lots of chalcedony artifacts from the Lake Manix industry averaged 71°. These observations reinforce Haynes' view that the lithic specimens from the Calico excavations are the result of natural fracturing and are not artifacts (Payen 1982; Taylor and Payen 1979:265, 273).

The case for geofacts has been supported further by Duvall and Venner (1979), who measured dimensions and angles of lithic specimens from the

categories *Calico tools* and *nontools,* as segregated by Leakey *et al.*
(1972). Statistical analyses demonstrated that the Calico tools are much
more closely related to the Calico nontools than to known Paleoindian
artifacts studied. Duvall and Venner (1979:455, 461) concluded that the
Calico objects are not artifacts and that the excavators appear to have
selected naturally fractured lithics that resemble artifacts.

In brief, Leakey, Simpson, and their colleagues have argued that Calico is the oldest known archaeological site in the New World. Haynes and
other scholars have countered that natural processes can explain the discoveries. The issue boils down to two basic questions: (1) How old is the
Yermo formation? and (2) Is there solid evidence of human activity in the
Yermo levels?

The first question seems the easier to answer. Although Clements
initially estimated the age of the lower Yermo strata at 70,000 to 100,000
years and Haynes preferred 500,000 years, the best available data suggest
an intermediate age. Recently, Bischoff *et al.* (1981) have determined that
the soil on the surface of the Yermo fan deposit at Calico is a strongly
developed relict paleosol comparable to paleosols 80,000–125,000 years
old elsewhere in the greater Southwest. Calcium carbonate from near the
base of this soil unit has been dated by the uranium–thorium method at
≈200,000 years, indicating that the "artifact-bearing" strata are slightly
older than 200,000 years (Bischoff *et al.* 1981:576, 582).

The second question is more difficult. Technical studies have convinced Singer, Bryan, Witthoft, and of course Leakey and Simpson that
some of the Calico pieces are tools. Other analyses by Haynes, Payen,
Duvall, and Venner indicate that the items are not artifacts, or at least
that their attributes are quantitatively different than those of known
artifacts. And what of the "hearth"? Again there is no consensus. Although it is possible that a fire once burned among the stones, evidence of
its kindling by humans is lacking; it seems more likely that a natural fire
heated the cobbles.

In the final analysis, the archaeological status of the Calico site remains dubious at best. This is so partly because of the tenuous nature of
the collections, but also contributing to the problem is the fact that no
full, systematic report of findings has ever been published. Some archaeologists may wish to reserve final judgment until the expected final report on the Calico specimens and their provenience is available, but
others doubt that such a report will ever appear. Meanwhile, several
observations are worth pondering. If the site indeed were to contain tools
more than 200,000 years old, then California would have been occupied
by pre-Neanderthals, as Haynes (1973) has noted. Yet no hominid fossils
of middle or early Wisconsin age, much less older ones, have ever come
to light in the Americas. Remarkable, too, is the absolute lack of definite
cultural material from these early periods. Acceptance of the Calico finds

as artifacts would thus create a rather conspicuous gap of 2000 centuries in the New World archaeological record. All things considered, this seems highly implausible.

### Yuha Pinto Wash

In September 1976, torrential rains caused massive erosion in the Yuha Desert, exposing a nearly vertical cliff in Yuha Pinto Wash, just north, of the Mexican border (Figure 2.3). Subsequently, 80 "Paleolithic flaked stone tools and utilized flakes" were found on the cliff in a re-deposited stream conglomerate overlain by sediments 21 m thick (Childers and Minshall 1980:297). An age of more than 50,000 years has been proposed on the grounds that the "artifact concentrations" (Imp-905 and -906) in Yuha Pinto Wash occur in the same geomorphologic unit as an alluvial fan dated previously by the $^{14}C$ assay of freshwater tufa and mussel shell at 37,400 ± 2000 B.P. (LJ-959) and >50,000 B.P. (LJ-954).

Childers and Minshall (1980:303) have compared the "generally amorphous" Yuha Pinto Wash specimens to an assemblage of stone tools more than 300,000 years old from China and to lithics from Buchanan Canyon, San Diego County, the latter not being cultural in my opinion (discussed below in the section on La Jolla and San Diego). A full description of the putative tools and their context must be published before their possible archaeological status can be evaluated.

### The Yuha Burial

In 1972 W. W. Childers of Imperial Valley College found a remarkable human skeleton in the Yuha Desert about 20 km southwest of El Centro, near the Mexican border (Figure 2.3). While exploring a small ravine, Childers happened upon a stone cairn. Excavations by Childers and E. Burton revealed a nearly complete, semiflexed adult skeleton in a shallow grave within a matrix of indurated sand at a depth of 15–40 cm below the eroded surface. Associated were two crudely worked flake scrapers of metabasalt (Barker *et al.* 1973; Bischoff *et al.* 1976, 1978; Childers 1974).

Samples of caliche ($CaCO_3$) adhering to the bones yielded $^{14}C$ ages of 21,500 $^{+2000}_{-1000}$ and 22,125 ± 400 years, whereas caliche from an adjacent boulder was dated by the thorium ($^{230}Th$) method at 19,000 ± 3000 years (Bischoff *et al.* 1976). These dates should be viewed with caution. Because caliche is formed by the precipitation of groundwater carbonates (compounds that often include geologically old carbon), the dates on the Yuha calcareous material may be older than the true age of the bones (Weide 1976). Moreover, the degree of soil development and the landform associated with the burial suggest a Holocene age inconsistent with the reported dates (Payen *et al.* 1978). Last, interpreting this find is difficult because of "an apparent discrepancy between the original excavation account and later published discussions concerning the stratigraphic position of the skeleton" (Payen *et al.* 1979:598).

Wilke (1978a) has observed that cairn burials from the California deserts generally are dated from circa 3000 B.C. to historic times, and he suggests that the Yuha burial may also belong to this period. A small scatter of ceremic (Tizon Brown Ware) shards found 6 m north of the burial shows that the immediate vicinity was used during late prehistoric times (Payen *et al.* 1978). Given the general lateness of cairn burials in the desert, the inherent problems of soil carbonate dating, the discrepancy in reporting, recent artifacts nearby, and the possible Holocene soil association, there is good reason to doubt the pre-Holocene age assignment of the Yuha burial. Although Bischoff *et al.* (1979) reaffirm that the skeleton is approximately 20,000 years old, $^{14}$C dating of the bones directly would be the best way to establish the age of this find.

## La Jolla Shores and Del Mar

Two sites near La Jolla in coastal San Diego County are of special interest here. Between 1920 and 1935 Malcom J. Rogers of the San Diego Museum of Man collected a series of human skeletal fragments that he thought to be quite old. One of the sites investigated was SDM-W2 at La Jolla Shores, about 1.2 km south of the Scripps Institution of Oceanography (Figure 2.3), where in 1926 a steam shovel exposed a partial human skeleton beneath a midden in a bed of compacted red sand, 46 cm below the surface. Recently, an amino-acid date of ≈6000 years was calculated for these bones. Underlying the red sand, at the base of a white sand stratum 1.7–1.9 m below the surface, Rogers found a human frontal bone; this has yielded an amino-acid date of ≈44,000 years. Finally, several ribs and other human bone pieces were salvaged from a matrix of gray–white sand at SDM-W2; the amino-acid date for this sample was ≈28,000 years (Bada *et al.* 1974). At least one published account has referred to an "*Ollivella* bead" found with the ribs. In fact, there are three *Olivella* shells (two cemented to a rib and the third to a humeral shaft), all of which are so eroded that their identification as beads is simply not possible (Tyson 1976).

Roger's second locality was SDM-W4 on the northwest edge of the San Diego River Slough between Del Mar and Solana Beach (Figure 2.3). The site consists of upper and lower middens, the latter nearly destroyed by tidal action. In 1929 Rogers happened upon a relatively intact human skull (Figure 2.8) and ribs in the seacliff at the base of the lower midden.

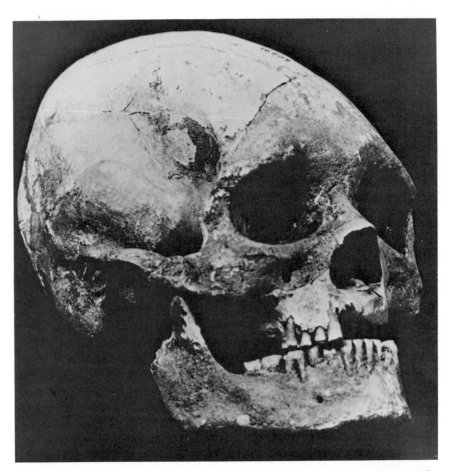

**Figure 2.8**  The Del Mar skull, discovered in 1929 at site SDM-W4 near Del Mar, California. An amino-acid racemization date of ≈48,000 years has been proposed for these human bones, but this estimate is probably incorrect. (Courtesy of the San Diego Museum of Man and Scripps Institution of Oceanography.)

An amino-acid age of ≈48,000 years has been calculated for these bones (Bada *et al.* 1974).

These amino-acid values include some of the oldest absolute dates ever derived from New World human remains. Whereas the determination of ≈6000 years is not surprising, the ≈44,000- and ≈48,000-year estimates, if correct, would require a thorough revision of present concepts about early American prehistory.

It is well to bear in mind that amino-acid dating is a relatively new method and that the factors affecting racemization rates are not yet fully understood or controlled. Also, as discussed later in this chapter, the

Laguna Beach skull, used to calibrate the formula for computing the dates, is a poor specimen upon which to base a chronometric method (see Hare 1974; von Endt *et al.* 1975). The skull had a "rather bizarre post-excavation history," and it is not certain that the [14]C-dated skull used in the calibration was in fact the one from Laguna Beach (Bada and Masters 1978:19). Knowing the precise archaeological provenience of the dated bones is important in this case because Laguna Beach reconstructed temperature averages were used along with the [14]C date to calculate the amino-acid racemization rate for the southern California coast.

Most important, amino-acid dates often differ greatly from those established by radiometric methods of proven reliability. For example, aspartic-acid ages of ≈40,000 years on human bones from Scripps Estate sites in La Jolla do not agree at all with four [14]C dates arrayed between 5460 ± 100 and 7370 ± 100 B.P. from the same sites (Protsch 1978:59–60). Likewise, the amino-acid age of ≈70,000 years applied to a human skeleton from Sunnyvale (Anonymous 1975; Bada and Helfman 1975) does not check with geologic and archaeological indications of burial less than 6000 years ago, confirmed by a [14]C date of 4460 ± 95 B.P. on charcoal from the same stratum (Bickel 1978a:20). Recent analyses of materials from numerous archaeological sites in California show that errors of −61 to 9080% exist between aspartic-acid ages on the one hand and radiocarbon, thorium, and protactinium ages on the other (Table 2.1). In this regard,

TABLE 2.1

**Comparison of [14]C, [230]Th, and [231]Pa Ages with Aspartic-Acid Ages of Archaeological Samples from California**[a]

| Site | Aspartic-acid age (yr) | Radiometric age (yr) | Percentage error of aspartic-acid age |
|---|---|---|---|
| Scripps Estate | ≈ 40,000 | 6,317 C ($\bar{X}$ of 4 ages) | 683 |
| Sunnyvale | ≈ 70,000 | 9,000 Pa | 778 |
| | | 8,300 Th | 843 |
| | ≈ 62,000 | 4,500 C | 1,280 |
| Stanford II | ≈ 5,600 | 4,375 C | 28 |
| Stanford III | ≈ 6,880 | 2,270 C | 200 |
| Castro | ≈ 11,700 | 2,710 C | 330 |
| Del Mar | ≈ 48,000 | 11,300 Pa | 425 |
| | | 11,000 Th | 436 |
| University Village | ≈ 10,900 | 3,170 C | 244 |
| BART | ≈ 1,900 | 4,900 C | −61 |
| Mountain View Dump[b] | ≈ 44,000- ≈413,000 | 22,350 C 19,900 Th 20,800 Pa | 9,080 |

[a]C: radiocarbon ([14]C); Pa: protactinium ([231]Pa); Th: thorium ([230]Th). (Data synthesized from Bischoff and Rosenbauer 1981; LaJoie *et al.*, 1980; and Protsch 1980.)
[b]Nonarchaeological bone.

LaJoie *et al.* (1980:488) have concluded that "Amino acid D/L values from 14 independently dated fossil samples in the south San Francisco Bay region show no consistent relationship to age, burial depth, mean annual temperature, soil pH, or residual nitrogen. Apparently, racemization is controlled by a complex, poorly understood combination of factors."

These findings indicate that amino-acid dates from coastal California cannot be trusted. Hence, the ages of the Del Mar and La Jolla Shores material remain to be determined precisely. It seems probable, however, that they will prove to be of mid-Holocene age (see Chapter 3).

### Laguna Beach

In 1933 teenagers M. H. Wilson and E. H. Marriner dug the upper portion of a human skull from a sandy loam matrix in a road cut in Laguna Beach (Figure 2.3). The context was that of late Wisconsin sediments redeposited during the Holocene. The calvarium and a few pieces of long bones, but no artifacts, reportedly came from a depth of ≈1.75 m. Over the years following its discovery, the skull was sent to Europe and Africa for examination by specialists, including L. S. B. Leakey. After viewing it in 1967, Leakey asked Rainer Berger of UCLA to date the skull by $^{14}$C. The age of its bone collagen was determined to by 17,150 ± 1470 B.P. (UCLA-1233A) (Berger *et al.* 1971; Borden 1969), whereas postcranial fragments yielded a $^{14}$C age of >14,800 B.P. (UCLA-1233B) (Protsch 1978).

The unexpected date of ≈17,150 B.P. prompted archaeologists to test the discovery site to see if additional material could be found. Excavations to a depth of 5 m by Sackett (in 1968) and Tomchak (in 1969) disclosed only alluvial sands and sandy loam with occasional layers of ocean mussel shells. Shells from the 0.6- and 2.0-m levels gave enigmatic $^{14}$C dates of 8950 ± 80 and 8300 ± 80 B.P., respectively. It is possible that either the shell or collagen age determinations, or both, are in error ($^{14}$C dates derived from bone and shell generally are not as reliable as those from charcoal), or the skull actually may have been found somewhat deeper than remembered. It is not even certain whether the skull that was dated was indeed the original specimen (Bada and Masters 1978:19). In any event, the Laguna Beach skull is of dubious scientific value and does not necessarily indicate early occupation of southern California. As Berger *et al.* have concluded, "the likelihood is great that the origin of the Laguna Beach remains and their subsequent depositional history . . . may never be known" (1971:45).

### "Los Angeles Man"

Fossilized human bone fragments were found in January 1936 by WPA workers digging a storm drain along the Los Angeles River north of the

Baldwin Hills in Los Angeles (Figure 2.3). Recovered were an occipital, two parietal fractions, and seven postcranial bones from gray sandy clay at a depth of ≈3.4 m in the bed of an ancient stream (Lopatin 1940). In March of the same year, the bones and two teeth of an imperial mammoth were exposed at the same depth in the Pleistocene deposits, 370 m distant from the human remains (Clements 1938). Later determinations of fluorine content indicated that the mammoth and human fossils were of approximately the same age (Heizer and Cook 1952).

Unfortunately, all but the human cranial fragments seem to have been lost. These, however, are of some interest. A $^{14}$C age of >23,600 B.P. (UCLA-1430) was obtained from collagen samples (too small for a finite date), making the Los Angeles skull the oldest radiocarbon-dated human remains in the Western Hemisphere (Berger *et al.* (1971). The skull also has been dated at ≈26,000 years by the aspartic-acid racemization method (Bada *et al.* 1974). Nonetheless, although the geologic context, possible stratigraphic association with mammoth fossils, and fluorine content of the bones are suggestive of antiquity, it must be remembered that the absolute date is based upon a very small—and therefore possibly unreliable—$^{14}$C sample. "Los Angeles Man" *may* have lived earlier than 22,000 B.C., but that postulate has not yet been confirmed.

### Angeles Mesa

Construction work by the Thomas Haverty Company in 1924 brought to light six human skeletons at depths of ≈6.2 to 7.5 m in loose sands and sandy clays in the Angeles Mesa vicinity between Los Angeles and Culver City (Figure 2.3). Associated were a quartzite boulder, a small awl-like object, and shells of recent mollusks (Stock 1924). The deep burial, lack of evident disturbance, and permineralization of the bones may imply respectable antiquity (Wallace 1955a). Without absolute dates, however, one may only speculate about the age of the Angeles Mesa skeletons.

### Rancho La Brea

The tar pits of Rancho La Brea in Hancock Park, Los Angeles (Figure 2.3), are internationally renowned as a rich paleontological site. More than a million superbly preserved fossils, representing some 200 plant and animal species 5000–40,000 years old, have been recovered from these asphalt pits.

In 1914 the partial skeleton of a gracile young woman (about 153 cm tall and 25 years old at the time of death) was discovered by L. E. Wyman in Pit 10 at Rancho La Brea. Nearby were western horse and *Teratornis* (a large condorlike vulture) fossils (J. Merriam 1914). The human bones are in excellent condition, even though *pit-worn* (i.e., ground and polished by the abrasive action of mineral grains suspended in the fluid asphalt). The dolichocephalic skull is similar to those of many historic southern California Indians. The cranium features a curious irregular hole, suggestive of a depressed fracture, just above the glabella; but it is virtually impossible to know whether this reflects the cause of death or postmortem damage. A mano, which might have caused such a fracture, was found only 10 cm above the skull (Berger *et al.* 1971; Kroeber 1962a). Manos, incidentally, first appeared in southern California approximately 9000–8500 years ago (see Chapter 4).

Another archaeological specimen from Rancho La Brea is an atlatl dart foreshaft from Pit 61–67, $^{14}$C-dated at 4450 ± 250 B.P. (LJ-121) (H. Howard 1960). This date does not apply to the human bones because Pit 61–67 lies nearly 100 m southeast of Pit 10. A greater age for the skeleton was proposed some time ago on the basis of the associated avifauna (H. Howard and Miller 1939; cf. Heizer 1962a). More recently, complex chemical methods were used to decontaminate the human bones of intrusive carbon (Ho *et al.* 1969), and a treated collagen sample was dated at 9000 ± 80 B.P. (UCLA-1292 BB) (Berger *et al.* 1971).

Apart from the "Brea Maid," as the skeleton was called by J. C. Merriam, no other human remains have been found in the tar pits. But Rancho La Brea has yielded bones of three species of extinct animals—saber-toothed cat (one tibia and three femora), California lion (one femur), and bison (one radius)—with what appear to be artificial cuts and grooves oblique to the axes of the bones (Figure 2.9). Three of these bones also exhibit round, possibly drilled, holes; one of the cut bones has been $^{14}$C-dated at 15,200 ± 800 B.P. (G. Miller 1979). Experiments and examination of the fossils by many archaeologists and paleontologists indicate that the cuts were made on fresh bone; they were not made by animal teeth; they are nonrandom; and that they are best explained as tool marks or butchering scars (Downs and Miller 1971; Miller 1969). Thus, the presence of humans at Rancho La Brea ≈15,000 years ago seems plausible, assuming that the $^{14}$C date is valid and does not reflect residual contamination by the asphalt.

*Santa Rosa and San Miguel Islands*

Several locations on Santa Rosa and San Miguel islands have been alleged to be late Pleistocene cultural sites. Santa Rosa Island (Figure 2.3), 75 km southwest of Santa Barbara, is the second largest of the northern Channel Islands—23 km long and 16 km wide, covering 220 km². Razorback ridges up to 475 m high, steep arroyos, and marginal seacliffs charac-

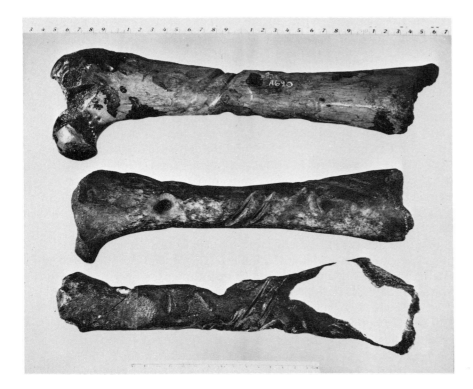

**Figure 2.9** Fossil bones of saber-toothed cat from Rancho La Brea with possible tool marks. Each bone has two oblique, parallel cuts medially. Top: left femur; center; left femur; bottom: right tibia with plaster filling in place where bone was taken for radiocarbon dating. The age of the tibia was determined to be 15,200 ± 200 [14]C years. (Photograph courtesy of George J. Miller, Imperial Valley College.)

terize the physiography. Nearby San Miguel Island is appreciably smaller (14 × 7 km) but equally rugged. During Pleistocene glacial episodes, lower sea levels exposed all the northern Channel Islands as a single island with an area as large as 2200 km². At such times cool, moist climates would have favored the growth of pine and fir forests on the ridges. Dwarf mammoths (1.2–2.4 m tall at the shoulder) then ranged over the island(s) and faced no predators except possibly humans.

As early as the 1870s, and repeatedly thereafter, discoveries of artifacts and mammoth fossils attracted scientific attention to the islands (Bowers 1878; Cessac 1951a; Eisen 1904; Heizer and Elsasser 1956; Heye 1921; Schumacher 1875b, 1877b; Stock and Furlong 1928). In 1946 Phil C. Orr of the Santa Barbara Museum of Natural History began geological, archaeological, and paleontological studies of Santa Rosa Island. Orr (1968) described several Quaternary formations, of which the Santa Rosa Island formation deserves mention because it contains mammoth bones reportedly associated with cultural remains. The Tecolote member of this formation has been $^{14}$C-dated between ≈37,000 and 10,400 B.P. (Berger and Orr 1966; Orr and Berger 1966).

Archaeological materials abound on Santa Rosa Island, where several hundred sites have been recorded (Glassow 1977). In 1959 Orr encountered human bones, 11.5 m deep and below a midden, projecting from Tecolote sediments at Arlington Springs on the island's northwest edge, about 400 m from the beach. Orr removed the bones following a 1960 field conference attended by 12 prominent earth scientists and archaeologists who expressed reservations about the association of "Arlington Man" with Pleistocene strata. Some observers noted that the bones seemed to rest in an intrusive channel cut into the formation, and most felt that additional work would be needed before any conclusion could be reached.

Abalone shells collected by James Griffin from a depth of 3.3 m (8.2 m above the bones) provided a $^{14}$C date of 7350 ± 350 B.P. (M-1133), and a small sample of organic earth and charcoal in apparent contact with the bones was dated at 10,400 ± 2000 B.P. (L-568A) (Orr 1960b). Because of the large standard deviation tied to this date, another carbon sample was collected and processed; the result was 10,000 ± 200 B.P. (L-650) (Olson and Broecker 1961). To address further the question of the age and possible intrusion of the Arlington bones, Orr noted that the 10,000 B.P. date was backed by three more age determinations arrayed between ≈11,300 and 7350 years. Also, "the entire hillside was cleared of vegetation and talus material, exposing the strata above, and on both sides of the bone, proving conclusively that there was no landslide or crevice fill" (Orr 1968:90). Thus, an age of ≈10,000 years seems reasonable for the Arlington bones. This is consonant with the series of $^{14}$C ages—9050, 7440, 7070, and 6800 years B.P.—determined from other, stratigraphically later deposits nearby (Orr 1962a, 1962b).

Considerably older remains have been found on Survey Point (Figure 2.10), just west of Arlington Canyon, on Santa Rosa Island. Many concentrations of hearths (saucer-shaped or U-shaped pits of brick-red earth with bands of dark soil and charcoal) and the split, darkened bones of dwarf mammoths occur on alluvial seacliffs and on the sides of arroyos leading to the beach. A $^{14}$C date of >37,000 B.P. was derived from landsnail shells taken from the lower part of the fossil beds in the same stratum as some of the "burned" features. Blackened mammoth bone found on the seacliff, 11.5 m below the surface, provided a $^{14}$C date of 29,650 ± 3000 B.P. (LJ-290R). These bones came from a pit or basin with "burned" sides (Orr 1956a, 1956b); unburned bone from the same feature yielded a $^{14}$C date of 30,400 ± 2500 B.P. (UCLA-1898) and an aspartic-acid age of ≈33,000 years (Bada *et al.* 1974). Although the age of the mammoth

**Figure 2.10** Survey Point, Santa Rosa Island, showing dated levels. (A) 7070 B.P., "Dune Dweller" cemetery deposit; (B) 29,650 B.P., blackened mammoth bones from Quarry 10; (C) third interglacial level with a $^{14}$C age older than 37,000 B.P. (Courtesy of Phil C. Orr, Santa Barbara Museum of Natural History.)

bones seems established at circa 30,000 B.P., the nature of the "hearths" remains equivocal.

Summarizing his case for "Pleistocene Man" on Santa Rosa Island, Orr notes that the numerous hearths often contain "tiny fragments of charred bird bones or mammoth bones . . . , and large pieces of mammoth bones occur in several" (1968:68). These hearths are, according to Orr, restricted to one part of the island, suggesting that natural fires were not the causal factor. A pattern is seen also with respect to the mammoth bones. Literally thousands of animals are said to be represented, yet no complete skeletons have been reported. The high frequency of burned rib and vertebra pieces appears to indicate selectivity; long bones generally are not charred. Moreover, the pit dated at circa 30,000 B.P. contained the unburned innominates of a mammoth, but the sacrum was entirely charred. In another case, Quarry 15 yielded both burned and unburned mammoth bones, including two dorsal vertebrae adjoining the sacrum and a femur "articulated" to a scapula.

Orr further calls attention to abalone shells found in terrestrial soils of Wisconsin age in cliffs and canyon walls as far as 4.5 km from the sea.

Similarly, numerous "intrusive" stones have come from Pleistocene strata on the island; some of the chert and chalcedony specimens have been declared to be artifacts, and all were found outside of natural geologic contexts (Orr 1968). Finally, Orr (1968:82–85) has described several "probable kill sites" where charcoal, mammoth bones, and chipped stones were found in close proximity. Two mammoth skulls from Tecolote Canyon had their vaults destroyed, exposing the brain cases, which Orr has interpreted as evidence of butchering. Burned cypress wood "a few feet below" the skulls provided a $^{14}$C date of 15,820 ± 280 B.P. (L-244) (Orr 1956b).

In 1976 Rainer Berger of UCLA investigated a hearth that had been discovered the previous year by John Wooley, a geologist representing the owners of Santa Rosa Island. Within the sediment fill of this circular feature, measuring 3 m in diameter, Berger found mammoth bones and "what are by Paleolithic standards rather advanced stone tools" (Anonymous 1977a:62). Three of the apparent tools—"pick, knife, and core tool"—have been illustrated but not described (Berger 1982:169–170). No traces of radiocarbon were detectable in four charcoal samples (UCLA-2100A–D), indicating to Berger that the fire in the hearth had burned more than 40,000 years ago (Anonymous 1977a,b, 1978; Berger 1982:168; Payen and Taylor 1976:275). Subsequent excavations of this feature sponsored by the Leakey Foundation yielded no artifacts or mammoth bone. Moreover, several reddened rootlike extensions were noted, suggesting that the hearth may have been a burned tree stump (Wendorf 1982).

One should approach the Santa Rosa Island discoveries with caution. As F. Riddell admonished in his report of noncultural carbon found with mammoth bones in Merced and Orange counties, "what may seem to be remains of ancient campfires, including burned, fragmented bones. . . , burned red or orange earth, and charcoal may be natural phenomena and readily explainable in those terms" (1969:180). At Santa Rosa Island, however, the reported pattern of basins or pits with red earth, charcoal, bird bones, intrusive flaked stones, and both burned and unburned mammoth bones may prove to be the result of cultural rather than natural processes *if* that pattern is confirmed by meticulous archaeological research in the future.

Similar "exposures of oxidized soil and oxidized shattered rock," many containing proboscidean bone, have been found on barren, deflated surfaces and in ancient soil profiles on San Miguel Island (Greenwood 1978a:91). One of these contained cypress charcoal, $^{14}$C-dated at 16,600 ± 350 B.P., directly associated with burned and calcined mammoth bone (Greenwood 1978a:85). Visiting scholars, who in 1969 examined a number of possible hearths on San Miguel Island, proposed that these features be investigated further.

One Santa Rosa Island mammoth bone has yielded a $^{14}$C date of circa 8000 B.P. If the older dates (i.e., 30,000–40,000 B.P.) were to be accepted in connection with bona fide hearths, one would confront the unlikely inference that the island's mammoth population survived for 20,000 to 30,000 years in the face of hunting pressure. Of course it is possible that early islanders subsisted chiefly on vegetal foods, sea mammals, birds, and shellfish, and did not consider the elephants as a major food resource; but this too seems unlikely. In any event, the diminishing area of the island(s) and the growing human populations probably hastened the extinction of the dwarf mammoths.

A Pleistocene habitation of the islands would imply use of watercraft and basic navigation skills at a very early time. The Channel Islands have been separated from the mainland for nearly a million years, and even during Wisconsin interstadials several kilometers of open water divided the islands from the Santa Barbara coast. It is doubtful, but not inconceivable, that ancient peoples moving southward along the Pacific shore arrived in California with a knowledge of boats and coastal navigation. The early use of boats and maritime skills farther north is attested by dolphin hunting off the British Columbia coast approximately 9000 years ago (Conover 1972) and by the presence of a large community of sea hunters on Anangula Island in the eastern Aleutians by 8700 years ago (Laughlin 1975). Still, these examples related to a time almost 30,000 years later than the putative first occupation of the Channel Islands, and they do little to support that chronology.

To sum up, allegations that humans lived on the Channel Islands as early as 30,000 to 40,000 years ago are based mainly on "hearths," dated both geologically and radiometrically, that are said to contain flaked stones together with burned/calcined bones of mammoths, small mammals, and birds. Also cited are "intrusive" stones and shells in Pleistocene strata. A careful, multidisciplinary investigation of some of the "hearths" would perhaps show conclusively whether they are natural or cultural. Until this sort of research is completed, the notion of Pleistocene archaeology on the islands must be viewed as unconfirmed.

## La Jolla and San Diego

For more than three decades, George F. Carter and his associates have sought to establish that "pre-projectile point," "Lower Paleolithic" cultures existed in southern California as long ago as 80,000 to 100,000 years. Carter's unorthodox views have not been generally accepted.

In the late 1940s, Carter explored the Scripps alluvial fan at the base of Linda Vista Mesa in La Jolla (Figure 2.3). There he observed a large midden capping the fan and eroding along its edges. In the gullies and weathering beach face of the 15-m-thick alluvium, Carter found mussel and abalone shells, and what he took to be hearths and stone flakes produced by man. Carl Hubbs of the Scripps Institution of Oceanography reportedly also discovered streaks of burned earth and a hearth containing broken and partly charred bones and charcoal in the seacliff exposure. A few fossils, among them a Pleistocene horse tooth, were collected nearby (Sellards 1960). Although admitting that "developed artifacts" were lacking, Carter (1949, 1950) claimed that La Jolla materials were about 40,000 years old. A $^{14}$C date of 21,500 ± 700 B.P. was later obtained by Hubbs from one of the Scripps fan samples, but two others were dated at 600 and 500 B.P.

Archaeologists have criticized Carter's work at La Jolla because his reports are imprecise at crucial points; the specimens—most of which seem not to be artifacts—were taken from weathered surfaces rather than from controlled excavations; his interpretations of geological processes and dating are questionable; and the stratum dated at 21,500 years is almost certainly natural instead of cultural (F. Johnson and Miller 1958; Treganza n.d.b; Wormington 1959:22).

In 1952 Carter described an array of stone "artifacts" from terrace gravels at the Old Mission, Sweetwater River Valley, Valley Road, and Emory School gravel-pit sites in and near San Diego. Using climatic, geomorphologic, and soils data, Carter (1952) assigned these deposits to a Third Interglacial (Sangamon) age. This dating is probably irrelevant, however, because the stones appear to be natural streamworn flakes and battered cobbles without the patterned scars one would expect on artifacts (see Carter 1952:Plates 4 and 5). Few, if any, archaeologists share Carter's interpretation of the gravel-pit sites.

More controversial were Carter's discoveries at the Texas Street site in San Diego. This location is a bench, formed of stratified gravels and finer sediments representing a fan on ancient valley fill, on the south side of the San Diego River. The Texas Street formation, more than 35 m thick, has produced hundreds of flakes and cobble cores believed by Carter to be artifacts. There are also a few bits of unprovenienced bone and areas of discolored earth and rocks identified as hearths (Carter 1954a, 1957). These "burned" surfaces range from less than 1 to 80 m long in the exposed cuts. Two of the Texas Street "hearths" shown to me by Dr. Carter in 1977 seemed to be only amorphous clusters of cobbles in an alluvial matrix. The "charcoal" in one of these clusters turned out to be a hard black mineral, possibly manganite. No dark matter was found in the other "hearth."

In his various writings, especially *Earlier than You Think* (1980) and *Pleistocene Man at San Diego* (1957), Carter has argued that Lower Paleolithic cultures existed in America as early as the Sangamon Interglacial (Figure 2.1). He has asserted further that "the presence of bipolar flaking

at Choukoutien [in western China] suggests that the Texas Street industry [which includes 'bipolar flaking'] may also belong to the Soan tradition of stonework" (Carter 1957:369). But even if one were to accept the
estimate of >80,000 years as the age of the Texas Street deposits, this
could not be reconciled with the middle Pleistocene age of the Soan
industries in Asia. Moreover, the Third Interglacial (Eem and Mikulino)
cultures of Eurasia include the Upper Acheulian and proto-Mousterian
industries that are anything but crude compared with the stones from
Texas Street. Excepting Sellards (1960), Simpson (1954), and a few others,
archaeologists familiar with the San Diego materials agree that they are
naturally fractured stones and not artifacts (Haury 1959; Heizer 1978a; F.
Johnson and Miller 1958; Krieger 1958; Meighan 1965; Treganza n.d.b).

Yet the search for Interglacial Man in San Diego continues. In 1972 J.
Moriarty and H. Minshall reported finding core and flake tools in
Buchanan Canyon about 1.5 km from the Texas Street site. The context
was that of gravels exposed in stream cuts by heavy runoff. Without
explicit basis, the Buchanan Canyon locale has been assigned an age "far
greater than any presently accepted radiocarbon dates on Early Man in
the New World" (Moriarty and Minshall 1972:12). Subsequently, Carter
and Minshall (1976) stated that the Texas Street and Buchanan Canyon
collections overlap extensively, representing a "bipolar complex" of interglacial age. The supporting evidence (stone-flaking experiments, amino
acid-dated bones from *other* nearby sites, etc.) seems dubious or im-
material. Also, Taylor (1975, 1982) has tentatively dated the Buchanan
Canyon specimens at ≈5000 years on the basis of the fluorine-diffusion
profile measurement method. Hence the case for Buchanan Canyon being
a Pleistocene cultural site is without merit.

One of the more lengthy discussions of Pleistocene man in southern
California is embodied in Herbert Minshall's popular book, *The Broken
Stones* (1976). To support the notion that southern California was inhabited more than 125,000 years ago, Minshall argues that the "tools" from
Buchanan Canyon and Texas Street are similar to those from Siberian and
Chinese sites ≈250,000 to 400,000 years old. Further comparisons are
drawn with materials from Calico and Yuha as well as Blacks Fork in
Wyoming and Manitoulin Island in Ontario. Needless to say, these unsystematic comparisons of artifacts and natural stones from several continents and sites spanning ≈400,000 years do nothing to advance Minshall's views about San Diego County prehistory. A professional critique
of his concepts and methods perhaps would be unfair, because *The Broken Stones* obviously was not written for a scholarly audience. The volume is best identified as an interesting foray into the realm of speculation.

By way of summation, Carter, Minshall, and their associates have
declared that early and even pre-Wisconsin peoples occupied California.

Yet they have found no certain artifacts, hearths, or human bones in the ancient deposits to which they allude. The Texas Street and other San Diego sites may be quite old, but their status as archaeological sites has not been demonstrated.

### The Farmington Complex

In 1952 Adán E. Treganza of San Francisco State College reported crude stone tools from the Farmington Reservoir locality, 35 km east of Stockton on the eastern edge of the San Joaquin Valley (Figure 2.3). Thousands of specimens were found eroding out of unsorted cobble and gravel terraces at 40 streambed stations. The assemblage, named the Farmington Complex, is typified by core tools and large reworked flakes. Tough, olive-green chert is the chief material, along with rare pieces of felsite and porphyry. Some of the artifacts are waterworn, but most have sharp (although heavily patinated) flake scars. Although types are difficult to define, one could single out hammerstones, choppers, crude plano-convex blades, and an array of heavy-flake scrapers (Figure 2.11); knives, projectile points, or other refined bifaces seem to be absent (Riddell 1949; Treganza 1952; Treganza and Heizer 1953).

The temporal and cultural placement of the Farmington Complex has vexed archaeologists since it was first identified. In the earliest studies, a terminal Pleistocene to early Holocene age was proposed on geologic evidence, with the period from circa 7000 to 5000 B.C. favored (Antevs 1953a; Treganza 1952; Treganza and Heizer 1953). Most later writers also advocated an age greater than 8000 years for the complex, but R. F. Heizer (1964:130–131) published [14]C dates of 1660 ± 220 and 1170 ± 70 B.P. (UCLA-133, -132) on the charcoal from the Farmington gravels at site Sta-44, "which seem effectively to dispose of this site as ancient." A third charcoal sample, secured from Sta-44 gravels by Eric Ritter in 1973, yielded a radiocarbon age of 1195± 75 years (GaK-4088). Excavations in the gravels by Ritter and others seem to indicate that the carbon resulted from riparian woodland fires long after the Farmington materials had been deposited. Because the charcoal apparently came from burned tree roots and stumps, the [14]C dates do not pertain to the sediments and may be disregarded (Ritter *et al.* 1976).

In the years since the initial discoveries, Farmington-type artifacts have turned up at several other locations between the Cosumnes and Stanislaus River drainages (J. Johnson 1967; Payen 1973). Geomorphologic studies along the Central Valley–Sierra Nevada interface currently offer the best means of dating these materials. Five major Quaternary alluvial units are identified in this zone, each represented by a stream terrace with a distinctive capping soil. The lowermost terrace (containing

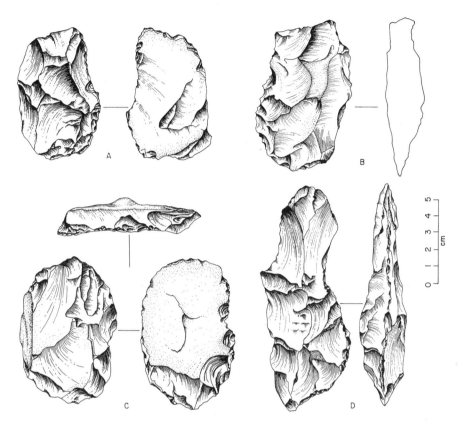

**Figure 2.11** Flake and core tools of the Farmington Complex. (A, C, D, after Treganza 1952; B, after Ritter *et al.* 1976. Drawing by Randall Engle.)

the artifacts) belongs to the Modesto Formation. Modesto terraces correlate with the late Pleistocene Tioga glaciation, a Sierran advance coeval with the Valders stadial. Excavations by Ritter and others have shown that the artifacts are contemporaneous with, or older than, the Modesto gravels. It seems likely, therefore, that the Farmington sediments and stone tools were deposited during late Tioga or early Holocene times, 12,000–7000 years ago (Ritter *et al.* 1976).

The apparent lack of refined bifaces or projectile points in the Farmington collections was seen by Alex Krieger (1964) as support for his hypothetical "Pre-projectile Point Stage." This interpretation is questionable. The probable age of the Farmington tools falls within a period when foliate and lanceolate points and other well-made bifaces were in use throughout California (see Chapter 3). Also, the complex may represent specialized nonhunting activities that did not require flaked-stone weapon points. In any event, the redeposited Farmington artifacts do not comprise the full lithic ensemble to be expected at primary habitation sites, so it is not possible to say for sure that refined bifaces were or were not made by the Farmington people.

Possibly related to the Farmington Complex is an industry of percussion-flaked quarry detritus and crude tools discovered in 1979 by A. S. Peak and Associates at Rancho Murieta in the Calero Basin, approximately 15 km east of Sacramento (Peak 1981b). Sites Sac-370 and -379 produced numerous preform and lanceolate bifaces, both informal and bifacially worked cores, chunks of tabular raw material, and other specimens thought to result from quarry operations (Crew 1981:135). These materials were recovered from gravel stratta estimated on the basis of geomorphologic observations to be 12,000–18,000 years old (Shlemon 1981:126). Unfortunately, no radiocarbon dates are yet available to confirm or refute this age estimate. Without more precise dating, the significance of the Rancho Murieta assemblage remains uncertain.

*Potter Creek Cave*

More than a century ago, Livingston Stone discovered a fossil bone deposit in Potter Creek Cave, Shasta County (Figure 2.3). Later digging by paleontologists E. L. Furlong in 1902 and W. Sinclair in 1903 produced the remains of 52 Quaternary faunal species, of which 21 are extinct. This assemblage included such creatures as the horse, mammoth, short-faced bear, shrub-ox, Shasta ground sloth, and camelids (J. Merriam 1906; Sinclair 1904). Among the specimens were broken, split, and polished bones that Putnam (1906) and Sinclair (1904) accepted as probable artifacts. Other scholars have expressed varying degrees of skepticism on the matter.

During nearly seven decades, specialists were unable to confirm or dismiss the evidence for Pleistocene man at Potter Creek Cave. As recently as 1964, Alex Krieger asserted that there are "one polished bone tube with square-cut ends; a large stone chip with sharp edges; and deposits of charcoal found deep in the cave in 1904, which can hardly be ignored" (1964:47–48). Writing in the same volume, Robert Heizer took the opposing view that "a few bone scraps that have features suggesting artifactual modification, found in the midst of thousands of bone fragments that are clearly not artifacts, make their fortuitous production the most probable explanation" (1964:119). The characteristics of the bones in question could have been caused by the teeth and digestive tracts of large carnivores and by the action of water in the cave (Heizer 1964; Payen and Taylor 1976).

In an effort to solve the problem, Louis Payen in 1965 conducted further investigations at Potter Creek Cave. Although the large lower chamber had been dug completely in 1904, Payen was able to excavate parts of the entrance chamber, upper room, and passage leading to the lower cavity. Three $^{14}$C age determinations on midden charcoal (UCR-150) and atlatl dart-shaft wood (UCR-148, -151) were 1910 ± 150, 1915 ± 150, and 2010 ± 150 years. Corrected for secular variation, the dates of these samples are identical at A.D. 50. In contrast, a value of 8250 ± 330 $^{14}$C years (UCR-381) was obtained on shrub-ox bone imbedded in breccia ≈1.7 m below the surface in the entrace chamber (Payen and Taylor 1976:53–55).

Taking into account stratigraphic observations and obsidian hydration measurements as well as the $^{14}$C dates, Payen and Taylor conclude that a 6000-year hiatus separates the archaeological and paleontological strata. They also point out that the bones of giant short-faced bear were abundant in all levels of the lower cave; it is doubtful that this immense carnivore would have shared its lair with (living) humans. Even though Indians were present in north-central California in early Holocene times, they evidently did not occupy Potter Creek Cave as contemporaries of the Rancholabrean animals (Payen and Taylor 1976).

## The Tranquillity Site (Fre-48)

Situated about 4 km north of Tranquillity in Fresno County, Fre-48 (Figure 2.3) was, until recently, considered a possible late Pleistocene archaeological site. During a 1939 survey, G. Hewes and W. Massey of the University of California discovered at Fre-48 several highly per-mineralized human skeletons, exposed by wind and water. Additional fieldwork between 1940 and 1942 showed a possible association of human burials and artifacts with the fossilized bones of extinct bison, camel, and horse, along with remains of recent fauna (Hewes 1943). Excavations in 1944 by L. Satterthwaite of the University of Pennsylvania Museum revealed two strata: a clay loam ≈90 cm deep with human bones and artifacts, and an underlying Fresno Hardpan (caliche). The remains of at least 25 adults, 8 children, and 2 infants were exhumed from the loam and from grave pits dug into the hardpan (Angel 1966; Hewes 1946).

Whereas Hewes (1946) had expressed doubts as to the association of the artifacts and fossils, Heizer and Cook (1952) determined similar fluorine levels in the faunal and human bones. From this, some researchers inferred that "the contemporaneity of the extinct mammal and human bones has been virtually proved" (Angel 1966:2). However, at least three lines of evidence refute such a claim: (1) the fossils and archaeological remains at Fre-48 are separable stratigraphically; (2) the artifacts (*Olivella* beads, stemmed and concave-base points, quartz crystals, pestles, etc.) are indistinguishable from specimens known to be less than 4500 years old elsewhere in central California; and (3) a $^{14}$C date of 2550 ± 60 B.P. on human bones from Burials 3 and 4 confirms that the proximity of humans and extinct fauna at Tranquillity is "more a matter of geographical coincidence than a true tight association in space and time" (Berger *et al.* 1971:48). Incidentally, the $^{14}$C date calls into question the fluorine dating method, at least insofar as it was applied at Fre-48.

## China Lake

The China Lake basin is the arid western lobe of the ancient Lake Searles–Lake China system in the northwestern Mojave Desert (Figure 2.3). It occupies the Indian Wells Valley, which is bordered by the Sierra Nevada on the west, the Coso and Argus mountains to the north and east, respectively, and by several smaller ranges to the south. The basin is rich in evidence of former environments as well as in fossils of Pleistocene fauna—notably mammoths, camels, bison, horses, wolves, saber-toothed cats, and various birds (E. Davis 1975, 1978; Fortsch 1972, 1978).

Beginning in 1969, Emma Lou Davis of the Great Basin Foundation directed a program of archaeological reconnaissance and surface collecting at China Lake. In the following decade, Davis expanded her work to include excavations, intensive surveys, and research by specialists in varied fields. Especially notable was the design of a meticulous survey system to locate and record on maps the exact provenience of each specimen. Davis and C. Panlaqui "set up a system of 23 'stakes,' each on the summit of a slight elevation. . . . Eventually each stake became the center or instrument station for a square 305 m on each side" (Davis and Panlaqui (1978:23). By 1978 the survey effort had produced about 5350 artifacts, 15,700 flakes, and 900 fossil bones from the desert surface. With the aid of instruments, each find was plotted on a map relative to the nearest stake (E. Davis 1978).

During an early phase of the research, fascinating insights were gained when the artifact distribution was mapped and analyzed. Davis found artifacts to be scarce on the upwind side of the lakebed; there were occasional scrapers and broken-point tips, but virtually no flakes. In contrast, the downwind side of the playa held artifacts in great variety and abundance: flakes, broken-point bases, and "pounding and grinding rocks." The inference drawn from this pattern was that birds and mammals were hunted in the upwind area, whereas in elevated places downwind hunters occupied shelters and blinds, foraged, made and repaired tools, and kept watch on the movements of game (E. Davis 1973a:8).

Davis has reported a number of China Lake sites with both artifacts and bones of extinct animals, among them Mammoth No. 1 in immediate association with a chert chopper and "less close association" with two very weathered jasper flakes; Stake 8, where a white chert flake was found near a mammoth pelvis, and other artifacts estimated to be 17,000–10,000 years old were scattered among fragments of horse, camel, bison, and mammoth bones; the Henry site, where horse and camel bones occurred with 47 flake implements and 2 ovoid features suggesting the outlines of shelters or huts; and the Basalt Ridge locality where smashed bones and teeth of mammoth and camel were scattered among hundreds of flake and core tools (E. Davis 1974a, 1978).

Davis and Panlaqui suggest a hypothetical outline of Lake China prehistory featuring a sequence of eight cultures. The criteria for temporal and cultural placement in this series are, in order of importance: (1) weathering, (2) technology, (3) inferred function, and (4) lithic material. Five of the cultures are assigned to the Pleistocene. These, with their tentative ages, are summarized as follows:

1. Early and Late Core Tool Traditions (ca. 45,000–25,000 B.P.): Chert and nonobsidian volcanics preferred; coarse, irregular precussion-flaking technology; extreme weathering of specimens with deep pitting and scouring of all flake scars; and such tools as large choppers and spoke-

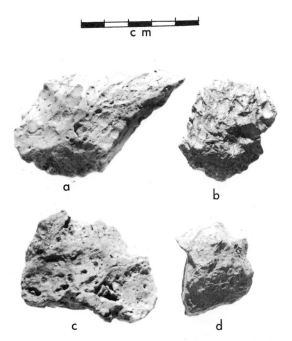

**Figure 2.12** Artifacts of a postulated Core-Tool Tradition from the basin of Pleistocene Lake China: "a, fragment of chopping tool with spokeshave at top, chalcedony; b, biscuit scraper with spur beak, jasper; c, chopper fragment, chalcedony; d, spur beak, jasper" (E. L. Davis (1978:10). (Photograph courtesy of E. L. Davis, Great Basin Foundation.)

shaves, long ovate knives–points, cordiform knives–points, and "pound-ing and grinding rocks" (Figure 2.12).

2. Late Wisconsin Cultures I (ca. 25,000–20,000 B.P.): Jasper and non-obsidian lithics worked by irregular precussion into smaller, more refined implements than before; fewer, smaller choppers and chopping tools, an array of spokeshaves, crescents, and scrapers, and long ovate knives–points (Figure 2.13). All artifacts are heavily weathered and sandblasted.

3. Late Wisconsin Cultures II (ca. 20,000–15,000 B.P.): The previous inventory is expanded to include smaller, more refined tools, and obsi-dian is used for the first time; pressure retouch augments the percussion technology; varied spokeshaves, borers, gravers, crescents, side-knives, and flake cutting implements are distinctive; weathering is moderate to heavy.

**Figure 2.13** Artifacts of "Late Wisconsin Cultures I," basin of Pleistocene Lake China: "a, large end-scraper with spur beak left side, chalcedony; b, long ovate knife/point, rhyolite; c, four-sided scraper, chalcedony; d, 'slug' scraper, chalcedony; e, biscuit scraper, chal-cedony; f, broad beak, long borer, chalcedony" (E. L. Davis 1978:10). (Photograph courtesy of E. L. Davis, Great Basin Foundation.)

**Figure 2.14** Artifacts of the "Proto-Clovis Phase" from the basin of Pleistocene Lake China; "a, Proto-Clovis [point] base with shallow flutes, chalcedony; b, knife/point base with 2 flutes, gray chert; c, large jasper knife with 3 flutes and one shoulder. . . ; d, base of knife/point, 1 shoulder right side. . . , chalcedony; e, knife/point base weathered, with shoulder and sub-shoulder recess (right), jasper; f, base of knife/point with 1 faint shoulder (left), pink chalcedony" (E. L. Davis 1978:10). (Photograph courtesy of E. L. Davis, Great Basin Foundation.)

4. Proto-Clovis Cultures (ca. 15,000–13,000 B.P.): New technologies entail heat treatment of silicates, basal fluting of knives/points, and the use of a punch to remove wide, thin spalls; notable in the great range of flake tools are lanceolate knives/points, beaks, crescents, stemmed knives/points with flutes, saws, and, rarely, blades (Figure 2.14); artifacts are moderately weathered.

5. Classic Clovis Phase (ca. 13,000–10,800 B.P.): Marked by exquisite workmanship of the finest available stone, heat treatment, fluting, and microtools; most Proto-Clovis artifact types survive, but are more refined; fluted knives/points are diagnostic; and the impact of sand blasting is moderate to light (Davis and Panlaqui 1978:38–39). (The Clovis material is discussed more fully in Chapter 3.)

In sum, Davis and her colleagues have used artifact weathering, form, function, material, and technology to define a series of late Pleistocene cultures in the China Lake basin. It is not yet possible to assess these cultures fully, especially the oldest ones, or their proposed ages. There is no doubt that, on typologic grounds, the fluted biface assemblage is evidence of human presence in southeastern California more than 10,000 years ago (see Chapter 3). Ten samples of carbonaceous earth from backhoe straticuts provided $^{14}$C dates of 11,330 ± 550 to 30,500 $^{+ 3000}_{- 2200}$ B.P., and 2.75 kg of ivory from Mammoth No. 4 was $^{14}$C-dated at 18,600 ± 4500 B.P., but none of these dates is linked directly to cultural material. Only two $^{14}$C age determinations—6775 ± 260 and 10,275 ± 165 years— are clearly associated with living surfaces (Davis and Panlaqui 1978:16–17). Thus, to develop a chronology for cultural remains older than 10 or 11 millennia, we are left with the necessarily imprecise and uncontrolled age estimates inferred from the degree of weathering and other artifact variables.

In spite of chronologic uncertainties, Davis and Panlaqui have drawn attention to a wealth of early archaeological remains in the Mojave Lakes country. Their meticulous fieldwork has brought to light possible associations of tools with bones of extinct animals at China Lake, and it has led to new information about terminal Pleistocene environments and cultural adaptations. Important, too, Davis and Panlaqui (1978:180) have advanced research objectives to guide future archaeological studies in the Mojave Lakes country.

## Summary and Conclusions

For some inexplicable reason, California has produced far more than its share of putative Early Man sites—most of which are easily disqualified. Typically these sites are kept in the limelight by small cadres of patron zealots who manage to issue an endless stream of brief, often sensational tracts witnessing the great antiquity of their finds, but who never seem to publish full descriptive reports. But archaeology is not a matter of faith or dogma; the burden of proof, after all, rests upon the data. For lack of adequate data, many of the sites discussed in this chapter cannot be accepted as Pleistocene archaeological remains.

It is conceivable, but highly improbable, that America was populated in the remote past more than 50,000 years ago. At the Calico Hills site, alluvial deposits thought to be older than 200,000 years have yielded flaked stones declared by certain investigators to be "tools." These claims have been undermined, first, by technical analyses that indicate that the recovered items probably are not artifacts; second, by the knowledge that acceptance of the Calico site as cultural would create a most unlikely gap of 2000 centuries in the New World archaeological record; and, last, by the absence of a comprehensive site report. Similarly, little can be said of the Yuha Pinto Wash site and materials until they are described systematically. Texas Street, Buchanan Canyon, and other sites of their genre in the San Diego vicinity almost certainly are not archaeological.

The case for humans in California between 50,000 and 30,000 B.P. is also far from compelling. Further examination of the "hearths" on San Miguel and Santa Rosa islands will be required to evaluate the notion of insular occupation 30,000–40,000 years ago. Severely weathered core tools from the China Lake Basin may be quite ancient but, due to their provenience on deflated surfaces, dating has proved to be a refractory problem. Not to be trusted are the amino-acid dates on human bones from La Jolla, Del Mar, and Sunnyvale; these remains surely are of Holocene age and do not fall within the published range of 40,000–70,000 years.

The testimony on behalf of California's settlement 30,000–15,000 years ago is more promising but still inconclusive. The northern Channel Islands possibly were inhabited during this period. Perhaps also assignable to this interval is the Laguna Beach skull, $^{14}$C-dated at circa 17,150 B.P., but uncertainties regarding provenience make this ascription tenuous. The Los Angeles skull, which has yielded the oldest radiocarbon age yet obtained from New World human bones (23,600 years), is possibly the earliest known trace of a California population; but again reservations must be expressed on account of the very small sample of material available for dating. Finally, at least one of the Rancho La Brea fossil bones with apparent tool marks has been $^{14}$C-dated circa 15,000 B.P. In the negative column, the 21,500-year age assigned to the Yuha burial is likely skewed by geologically old carbonates. Burial mode, stratigraphy, and nearby ceramic sherds suggest a late prehistoric age for this skeleton (Figure 2.15).

There can be little doubt that California was inhabited, albeit sparsely, between 15,000 and 10,000 years ago. "Arlington Man" and possibly the Angeles Mesa people lived near the end of this interval. The eastern flanks of the Central Valley were populated as well, judging from the Farmington Complex artifacts found in geologic contexts <12,000 years old. Geomorphologic observations suggest that the Rancho Murieta greenstone quarry sites also may be on the order of 12,000 years old, but no substantiating absolute dates have been reported. Perhaps the best indicators of widespread occupation in terminal Pleistocene times are the Clovis-like fluted points (Figures 3.2–3.4) and related artifacts from numerous sites throughout California (see Chapter 3).

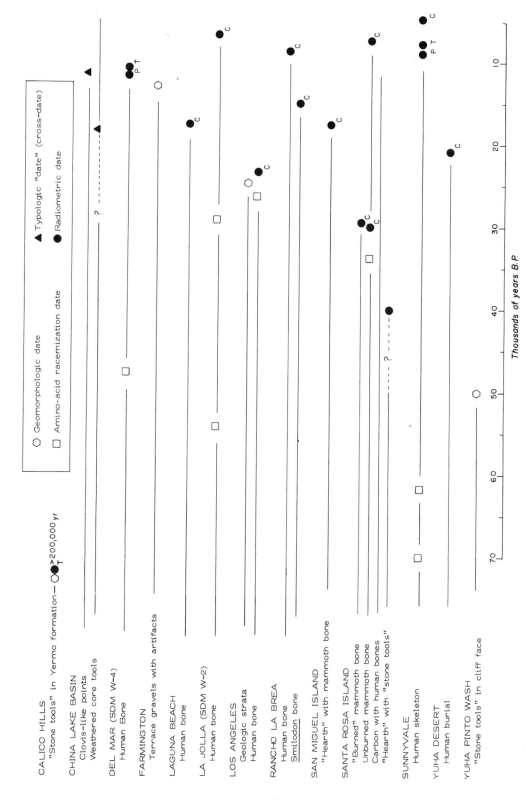

**Figure 2.15** Summary of age determinations for putative and confirmed archaeological material of claimed Pleistocene antiquity. C, radiocarbon ($^{14}$C); P, protactinium ($^{231}$Pa); T, thorium ($^{230}$Th). (Chart by the author.)

Very little can be said about the lifeways of California's Pleistocene pioneers. Although associations between tools and extinct faunal remains are rare and mostly tenuous, and direct evidence of plant use is lacking altogether, one may assume that these early people subsisted by gathering, collecting, and hunting. Lakes and seashores, marshlands, estuaries, and riparian zones would have been especially attractive to the first Californians. One may speculate that they might have used traps, nets, digging sticks, clubs, possibly slings or bolas, and spears in the food quest; the bow and arrow were unknown. No ground-stone artifacts have been discovered in the late Wisconsin sites, but toolkits were furnished with stone choppers, scrapers, perforators, and knives. Presumably other implements of stone, bone, wood, shell, skin, and fiber also were employed, but these remain to be identified archaeologically.

Initial populations would have been small, possibly being composed of nomadic bands with 15 to 30 persons each. Population densities would have varied from one locality to the next, but overall they must have been low as compared with those of the protohistoric Indians. Almost nothing is known of the physical features or linguistic traits of the earliest Californians. Fortunately, archaeologists can sketch a better picture of the early Holocene cultures. This is the task of Chapter 3.

# 3. Early Cultures

We have come to think of these PaleoIndians, in this part of the Americas, as Marsh/Grassland People. . . . The folk who subsisted in this varied countryside were wiley foragers, commanding a number of highly developed skills as beaters, trackers, botanists, hunters, herbalists, builders of snares, collectors, weavers, artisans and butchers, and last but not least, cooks. Primary marsh dependency seems to have persisted until the onset of . . . the Holocene, causing extinction of much of the marsh and grassland habitat.
*E. Davis and Panlaqui (1978:81)*

(Courtesy of the R. H. Lowie Museum of Anthropology, University of California, Berkeley.)

# Introduction

Research during the past few decades has shown that people lived in many parts of California between 12,000 and 8000 years ago. Archaeologists have begun to learn about terminal Pleistocene and early Holocene cultures—economic systems, technology, and settlement patterns—and how they adapted to California's diverse and changing environments. This is the topic of the present chapter.

Between circa 10,000 and 6000 B.C., cultures in widely separated regions of the Far West shared related yet distinctive cultural patterns. Although most archaeological remains assigned to this early period have been found in the Great Basin and in the southern California coastal and desert country, central and northern California are also represented (Figure 3.1). Certain general traits characterize the early western traditions, as they will be referred to collectively:

1. Interior sites often are located on shorelines of ancient lakes and marshes; those in coastal areas tend to occur along old stream channels and near estuaries. These distributions seem to reflect the attraction of early hunter–gatherers to the varied and abundant resources in lacustrine, marshland, and estuarine settings (Warren and Pavesic 1963; Weide 1968).

2. The lithic technology is sophisticated. It often features heat pretreatment of stone, along with advanced percussion- and pressure-flaking techniques; finished pieces reflect superior craftsmanship. Ground-stone artifacts are rare or absent early in the period but more common later. The bow and arrow are unknown, but the atlatl and dart are recorded by engaging spurs and heavy projectile points.

3. Stone tool assemblages include an array of specialized cobble, core, flake, and blade implements. Common artifacts are large foliate points or knives (Figure 3.5: A, D), trianguloid points with tapering or wide stems (Figure 3.5: B, C, G, I), lanceolate fluted points (Figures 3.2–3.4), "crescents" (Figure 3.5: E, F), an assortment of scrapers and scraper-planes (Figures 3.6 and 3.7), perforators, choppers, and hammerstones. Even though little is known of nonlithic artifacts, except on the coast where a few bone and shell items have survived, one may assume that devices of wood, skin, fiber, bone, and shell were utilized.

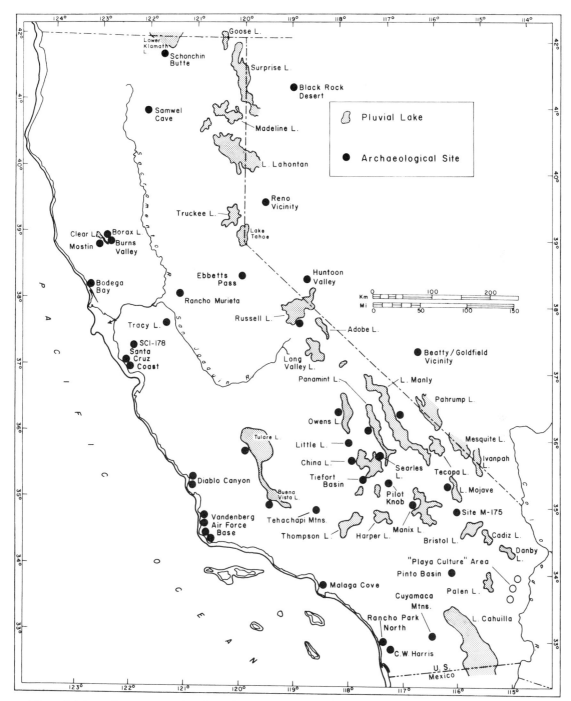

**Figure 3.1** Late Pleistocene and early Holocene archaeological sites in California and western Nevada. The reconstructed coastline represents the conditions of 10,000 B.P. when sea levels were ≈60 m lower than those of today. (Pluvial lakes after Snyder *et al.* 1964; coastal bathymetry after Welday and Williams 1975; map by the author.)

4. Inland groups presumably hunted large and small game, fished, took waterfowl, and collected eggs, mollusks, and other wetland products. Vegetal foods probably were harvested as well, but firm evidence is wanting. Coastal people collected shellfish, hunted marine and land mammals, took birds from the surf and shore, occasionally caught small fish, and probably gathered both littoral and inland plants.

5. Some early Holocene peoples may have wandered from place to place; others may have followed an annual round, moving systematically from one place to the next in order to take advantage of seasonal resources. However, one should not assume that before 6000 B.C. all Californians were nomadic. In some favored localities, such as near large marshes and estuaries, the natural bounty would have been adequate to sustain more or less permanent settlements and possibly did so.

## Environments

The Pleistocene to Holocene transition was a time of marked environmental changes in North America. Major, synchronous adjustments in temperature and precipitation affected the distribution of water, floras, faunas, and the human populations dependent on them (Aschmann 1958; Baumhoff and Heizer 1965; Mehringer 1977). As well, numerous local environmental shifts occurred during this interval. Adapting to these evolving conditions, early cultures became increasingly diverse and locally specialized through time.

Late Pleistocene cool–moist climates of circa 22,500 to 14,000 B.P. favored glaciation in the mountains and formation of deep pluvial lakes in the basinlands (see Chapter 2; Figure 3.1). The amelioration of Pleistocene conditions between circa 14,000 and 8000 B.P. brought warmer temperatures, glacial retreat (causing sea levels to rise from $\approx -85$ to $-40$ m), and the opening of "ice-free" routes from the north. San Francisco Bay and other coastal embayments began to emerge toward the end of this period (see Chapter 6).

Climates in the Greater Southwest before circa 11,000 B.P. were generally cool with mild, wet winters. Pluvial lakes achieved their maxima at this time and persisted, as increasingly shallow lakes and marshes, during the somewhat warmer Anathermal climatic interval of $\approx 11,000$ to 8000 years ago. After circa 8000 B.P. the lakes receded, leaving at first marshes and then only playas and fossil shorelines to mark their former extent.

The late Pleistocene vegetation of the Southwest and Great Basin was a mosaic of forest, woodland, grassland, and cold desert communities. Beginning circa 11,000 B.P., piñon–juniper woodlands were replaced by xeric juniper or juniper–oak woodlands in much of this area. In Arizona and southern California the juniper woodlands below ≈1600 m persisted into the early Holocene, whereas above ≈1800 m conifer forests gradually gave way to essentially modern vegetation types after circa 11,000 B.P. (Van Devender and Spaulding 1979). In central and northern California, postglacial conditions caused a general shift of life zones to higher latitudes and elevations.

In brief, the period between circa 12,000 and 8000 B.P. experienced warming temperatures, glacial retreat, rising seas (along with increased coastal erosion and flooding of continental-shelf lands), evaporation of pluvial lakes, major vegetative shifts, and the extinction of the Rancholabrean fauna—all of which profoundly influenced human societies in California.

## The Fluted-Point Tradition

*Introduction*

The 1926 discovery of fluted projectile points clearly associated with the bones of extinct bison near Folsom, New Mexico, established a much greater human antiquity in the New World than had been accepted previously. Since then, fluted points (Figure 3.2: C–E) have been found in virtually every state and province in North America (J. Hester 1972, 1975; Wormington 1959). In the central part of the Continent, fluted points have long served as markers of the Big-Game-Hunting Tradition (BGHT), manifested chiefly in the Great Plains and Southwest. The BGHT is usually defined to include three phases—Llano (or Clovis), ≈11,800– 11,000 B.P.; Folsom, ≈11,000–10,000 B.P.; and Plano, ≈10,000– 7000 B.P.—although "retention of a brief Folsom period is based more on sentiment than on logic, because on cultural grounds the Folsom and Plano lifeways are but variations on a single theme whereas the first or Llano stands to some degree distinctive" (Jennings 1978:23).

In the Rocky Mountains and Great Plains, Clovis points (Figure 3.2: D) occur at mammoth kill sites, often near ancient lakes or streams. Also found at such Llano sites are the remains of bison, horse, camelids, tapir, four-horned antelope, and sloth. (J. Hester 1972). Although Llano people surely killed large animals, it does not necessarily follow that they were exclusively or even preferentially big-game hunters, as were the later Folsom–Plano societies. In the Great Basin and Pacific coastal areas at least, the groups who left Clovis-like points seem to have been foragers who exploited a wide range of plants and animals (E. Davis 1978) and who

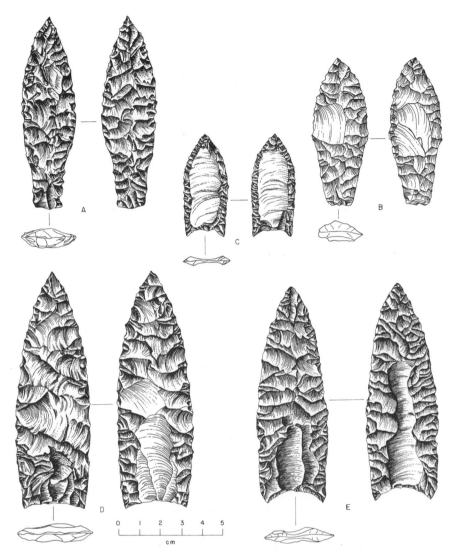

**Figure 3.2** Early projectile point types from the western United States. A, Hell Gap point (ca. 10,500–9000 B.P.), Casper, Wyoming; B, Parman point (ca. 9000–8000 B.P.), Calaveras County, California; C, Folsom point (ca. 11,000–9700 B.P.), Lindenmeier, Colorado; D, Clovis point (ca. 11,800–11,000 B.P.), Blackwater Draw, New Mexico; E, Clovis Point, Schonchin Butte, California. (A, C–D drawn from Denver Museum of Natural History casts; drawings by Randall Engle.)

were more diversified economically than the BGHT concept would imply. Neither Folsom–Plano artifacts* nor typical BGHT kill sites have

---

*A possible exception is a Scottsbluff-like projectile point from Secret Valley, near Honey Lake, reported in a private collection (Riddell 1958:44–45).

been found in California or the western Great Basin; hence the mere presence of fluted points does not necessarily signal BGHT activity in the Far West.

Until recently, fluted points were viewed as rare exotics in the area west of the Rockies, or as marginal vestiges of a technology properly endemic to lands east of the Continental Divide. Wallace (1978b:26) nicely summed up the majority opinion: "The close resemblance of the [western] specimens to Clovis–Folsom probably means that California formed a peripheral outpost of the Great Plains Fluted Point Tradition." However, the abundance and wide distribution of fluted points in California and the western Great Basin seem better explained as results of a viable, *in situ* cultural tradition and not one marginal to more easterly "centers" of fluting technology.

The Clovis-like fluted points in the Far West are found along ancient lakeshores, in piedmont zones of former grassland, and in mountain passes between fossil lakes. They occur with flaked-stone crescents, gravers, perforators, scrapers, and choppers (E. Davis 1968b, 1974b; E. Davis and Shutler 1969; T. Hester 1973). Recent discoveries in the Mojave Desert suggest that Fluted-Point Tradition hunters might have taken some large-game animals (E. Davis 1978), but there is no indication that big-game pursuit was central to their way of life. Other archaeological remains attest to a general hunting–foraging subsistence regimen. It is worthwhile here to examine some of the evidence for this tradition in California.

### Tulare Lake

The old shorelines of Tulare Lake (Figure 3.1) in the southern San Joaquin Valley have yielded numerous fluted points, of which 30 Clovis-like specimens in a private collection have been described in print. Most of these are fashioned of variously colored chert, and all exhibit well-controlled horizontal flaking (Figure 3.3). Twenty pieces are fluted, 8 bifacially and 12 unifacially, and 7 are basally thinned (Riddell and Olsen 1969). The lakeshore also has produced various scrapers, chipped crescents, Lake Mojave type points, and other stone artifacts ascribable to the Fluted-Point Tradition and/or the Western Pluvial Lakes Tradition (discussed below).

The fluted points and other artifacts had been collected by D. Witt over a span of three decades within an area roughly 2.4 km long and 0.8 km wide. The 59-m elevation of this locale was a major lake level until Holocene times, but this stand has not been dated precisely. The Witt site also yielded the bones of horse, bison, and mylodont ground sloth, as well as a bit of proboscidean tusk—all surface finds in possible but uncon-

**Figure 3.3** Flaked-stone artifacts from the Witt site on an old shoreline of Tulare Lake, Tulare County. On typologic grounds, these lanceolate, concave-base points are thought to be 12,000–11,000 years old. All specimens are surface finds. (Photograph courtesy of Francis Riddell, California Department of Parks and Recreation.)

firmed association with the artifacts. Although none of these materials has been dated directly, on typologic grounds the Clovis-like points argue for occupation of the ancient Lake Tulare vicinity earlier than 11,000 B.P. (Riddell and Olsen 1969).

*Borax Lake (Lak-36)*

Prior to 1938 amateur archaeologist Chester Post discovered several Clovis-like fluted points at the Borax Lake site (Lak-36) in the heart of the

North Coast Ranges (Figure 3.1). Located on the edge of a dry lakebed between the Lower and East Lake arms of Clear Lake, the Borax Lake site was first excavated by M. R. Harrington of the Southwest Museum in 1938, 1942, and 1945, and then by R. Sayles in 1946 (M. Harrington 1938a,b, 1945, 1948a). The artifacts—fluted lanceolate points, foliate bifaces, points resembling Lake Mojave and Silver Lake types, flaked-stone crescents, scrapers, and choppers—occurred from the surface to depths of ≈250 cm in rather confused alluvial deposits thought to be ancient. "Geological indications [are] that our deposit, with its contained implements, possesses a very respectable antiquity, dating apparently from the Great, or Provo, Pluvial period . . . 10,000 or 15,000 years ago" (M. Harrington 1948a:59).

Of 20 reported fluted points and fragments (Figure 3.4), 2 are unifacially fluted, 14 are channeled on both faces (the remaining 4 pieces being too small for analysis), 11 are basally ground, and 7 exhibit scratched channels (M. Harrington 1948a). "The fluting was accomplished by the removal of three or more flakes. In a few instances the removal of a final broad flake tended to obliterate the scars left by the first flutes. . . . All lacked the characteristic Folsom base" (Wormington 1959:61). Assuming (incorrectly) that these points marked a late expression of the Folsom Culture, Harrington assigned the "Borax Lake Folsoms" a tentative age of 10,000 years. He concluded (1948a) that nomadic groups of early hunter–gatherers had been attracted to the Borax Lake obsidian source (see Chapter 10) and that various groups had camped at Lak-36 over a long span of time. Subsequently C. W. Meighan (1955a) recognized the fluted points from Lak-36 and from site Nap-131 farther south (cf. Heizer 1953:316) as markers of the Borax Lake Complex (see Chapter 10).

Soil disturbance and artifact mixing at Borax Lake initially led to uncertainty about the nature and age of the site's components (Treganza n.d.a; Wormington 1959). To clarify the stratigraphy of the Borax Lake sediments, Meighan and Haynes (1970) dug 20 backhoe trenches to an average depth of 3 m at Lak-36. Resting on a bed of lacustrine clay was an alluvial fan composed of gravel and sand units with intrusive lenses of mud, silt, and sand. Artifacts occurred throughout the alluvium but not in the clay. Comparison of the Borax Lake geologic profiles with Quaternary deposits from Lake Lahontan in the western Great Basin suggested, albeit tenuously, a minimum age of ≈12,000 years for the basal cultural stratum at Lak-36. This estimate is bolstered by measurements of 77 hydration rims on obsidian artifacts from the site. Of these, 26 are 8.0–13.3 μm thick. The five measured fluted points had rims 7.5–9.8 μm thick ($\bar{X}$ = 8.7 μm) (Meighan and Haynes 1968, 1970; Meighan *et al.* 1974).

David Fredrickson (1973:28) recognizes three cultural components at Borax Lake. The first may be a variant of the "Clovis Culture" with an

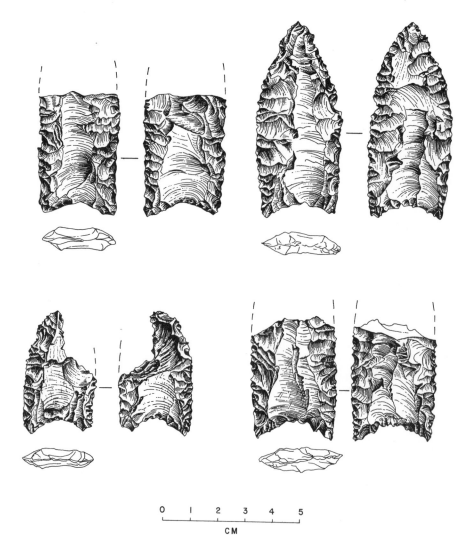

0   1   2   3   4   5
CM

**Figure 3.4** Fluted lanceolate points of obsidian from the Borax Lake site (Lak-36), Lake County. (Redrawn by Randall Engle from Harrington 1948a:62, 65, 66, 70; courtesy of the Southwest Museum.)

age of ≈11,000 to 12,000 years. The second, apparently ≈6000–8000 years old, represents the major part of the site's occupation and forms the type component for the "Borax Lake Pattern." The latest occupation, circa 3000 to 5000 B.P., is related to the "Middle Central California Complex." Fredrickson refers to the earliest cultural manifestation at Lak-36 as the Post Pattern (after Chester Post), with fluted points, single-shoulder points, and crescents as diagnostic. The crescents possibly served as transverse projectile points for hunting waterfowl (Clewlow 1968b). The Post Pattern economy may have been oriented toward lacustrine gathering, fowling, and hunting large and small animals (Fredrickson 1973).

## China Lake

Since 1969 E. L. Davis and her co-workers have found in the China Lake Basin (Figure 3.1) at least 10 sites and localities with fluted bifaces and other traces of an early occupation designated by them "Classic Clovis" (Davis 1978). Most of the artifacts are carefully documented surface finds, sometimes associated with old shorelines or paleosols and occasionally found near remains of Pleistocene animals. Unfortunately, none of the Clovis-like points from ancient Lake China has been dated absolutely.

Especially characteristic of the China Lake fluted-point industry are: (1) the selection of high-quality cryptocrystalline silicates and obsidian for stone tool production; (2) heat pretreatment of stone; (3) refined flaking; (4) fluted lanceolate points or knives; and (5) varied flake and core artifacts, among them crescents, flake knives, lanceolate knives or preforms with square bases, saws, scrapers, "beaks," and pounding/grinding stones (E. Davis and Panlaqui 1978:33, 47–51).

One of the most productive localities at China Lake was Basalt Ridge, where an outcrop of basalt rises above a once shallow marshy bay. Along the ancient shoreline was a mix of flakes, "Clovis" artifacts like those just noted, and carbonate crust along with both charred and unburned bones of extinct mammals. Altogether, more than 500 artifacts were documented at Basalt Ridge—some in direct contact with camel, horse, and mammoth bones; but whether this association is cultural or fortuitous remains unclear. Radiocarbon dates of 12,200 ± 200 and 13,300 ± 150 B.P. on separate tufa layers record the approximate times of high-water stands on Basalt Ridge and thus fix the maximum age of the overlying artifact scatter (E. Davis and Panlaqui 1978:89–95).

Basalt Ridge is said to differ from other China Lake "Clovis" sites more in quantity than in substance because other locales also feature artifact scatters with fluted points, old shorelines, paleosols, and Rancholabrean fossils. Davis has incorporated these findings (along with the evidence of artifact form, material, weathering, technology, and inferred function, as discussed in Chapter 2) into a hypothetical model to account for development of the Fluted-Point Tradition:

1. By 15,000 B.P. the Far West was culturally and linguistically complex, and many different groups of people had long since occupied Central and South America.

2. At Lake China (and presumably elsewhere in the Great Basin), a technology of broad pressure flaking replaced irregular percussion work between 14,000 and 11,000 years ago. "Thick, ovate bipoints and cordiforms were supplemented by a new tool—long, lanceolate knives with a single, weak shoulder and multiple, basal flutes" (E. Davis 1978:1). This marks a "Proto-Clovis Phase."

3. A cultural peak identified by a climax of population, hunting activity, distinctive artifacts, and a mastery of lithic technology—the "Classic Clovis Phase"—was reached prior to 11,500 B.P. (E. Davis 1978:1, 13).

4. The Proto-Clovis to Clovis development occurred in the lakes country of the Pleistocene Great Basin. The environment was one of cold steppe, mesic woodland, and grassland ideally suited for megafauna. After circa 11,500 B.P., however, the climate grew warmer and drier, reducing the savannas and grasslands in the Great Basin. Simultaneously, prairie grasslands were replacing boreal forests east of the Rockies (E. Davis 1978:1, 178; Van Devender 1977:198).

5. As the intermontane habitats of the megafauna receded (Guilday 1967), the savanna-adapted animals and Clovis people began to radiate eastward and then northward into the opening ranges of the Great Plains. This scenario accounts for the sudden emergence of Clovis technology east of the Great Divide as well as its "apparent long development" in the southeastern Great Basin (E. Davis 1978:1, 13, 178).

Certain aspects of this intriguing model may be confirmed by future research. Meanwhile, it would be well to remember that the suggested late Pleistocene cultural phases have not yet been demonstrated by stratigraphic occurrences that would establish their temporal order. Also, despite strong typologic similarities between the California fluted-point assemblages and the true Clovis industry farther east, any *sociocultural* linkage or equivalence between them is, for the present at least, conjectural. Finally, none of the Clovis-like points (or, for that matter, any of the markers of the putative earlier phases) at China Lake has been dated directly or found in definite cultural association with Pleistocene fossils. This is not to fault the researchers, however, for their fieldwork has been meticulous. Still, for the moment, one can say only that the Fluted-Point Tradition is well represented at China Lake, and that the combined evidence of geology, typologic cross-dating, and possible faunal associations is not incompatible with an age of 11,000 years or more.

*Other Fluted-Point Discoveries*

Fluted, lanceolate points have been found isolated or with other artifacts at many California localities in addition to those already mentioned (Figure 3.1). Clovis-like points have been collected on the shores of ancient Lake Mojave, at Ebbetts Pass south of Lake Tahoe, at passes in the Cuyamaca Mountains and Mojave Desert, in Owens Valley, and in the vicinities of Little Lake, Searles Lake, Panamint Lake, and the Tiefort Basin (E. Davis 1973b; Davis and Shutler 1969; Glennan 1971b; Simpson 1947; Warren and Ranere 1968). Amsden (1973) described surface finds of fluted points in Owens Valley, Pilot Knob Valley, and Pinto Basin. A lone Clovis-like point fragment, nicely fluted and basally ground, was discovered in the Tehachapi Mountains (Glennan n.d.); a particularly fine specimen of obsidian (Figure 3.2E) reportedly was found several decades ago by a collector near Schonchin Butte in Modoc County (Woodcock 1977); Tracy Lake has yielded a fluted point and a crescent (Beck 1971; Heizer 1938a); and a bifacially fluted point with basal grinding was collected at Samwel Cave in Shasta County (Beck 1970a; Treganza 1964c).

Fluted points are also known from many parts of Oregon and Nevada (Beck 1970a; Clewlow 1968b; E. Davis and Shutler 1969; Hester and Jameson 1977; Strong 1969; Warren and Ranere 1968). Few of these specimens have been studied adequately. Even so, their number and wide distribution indicate the pervasiveness of the fluting technology in the Far West, and their strong similarity to $^{14}$C-dated specimens farther east implies production during the millennium after 12,000 B.P.

## Summary

The western Fluted-Point Tradition shares the technology of the Llano Complex farther east. Distinctive are the fluted Clovis-like bifaces; no Folsom points are known from California. Techniques of manufacturing fluted points apparently were much the same throughout the West. Obsidian or fine cryptocrystalline stone was selected as the raw material, the latter often being heated before flaking. Refined percussion gave shape to the points and produced the channels, whereas pressure flaking was used to detail and contour the final product (E. Davis and Shutler 1969:159).

Although fluted points in California have not yet been $^{14}$C-dated, obsidian hydration measurements and geologic context of the Borax Lake specimens imply an age of 11,000–12,000 years. The discovery of fluted points on pluvial lakeshores and their tentative affiliation with Rancholabrean fossils at Tulare and China Lakes would also fit this chronology. Nonetheless, the ages of most fluted points in California have been estimated only by reference to similar specimens in the Llano Complex, and this assumes that the Llano and western points are coeval. But as E. L. Davis has postulated, the fluting technology might have evolved in the Far West from "Proto-Clovis" antecedents. Such a reconstruction would agree with archaeological data from the Arctic that Dumond (1980:991) has interpreted to mean that "Clovis culture developed in America south of the ice sheets from some ancestor already present. The first American immigrants, whoever they were, were then clearly pre-Clovis."

The fluting technology may have accompanied the rapid dispersion of groups sharing a common origin (Martin 1973), but that origin probably was not in the Arctic and could have been in the pluvial lakes country of the western United States. In that case, one would expect some fluted points in California to be older than their counterparts in the Southwest and on the High Plains. Testing this proposition will require absolute dating of California fluted-point assemblages.

Big-game hunting is one economic specialization linked to the fluting technology, but surely not the only one. Clovis-like points in the Far West occur in coastal, valley, pass, and lakeshore settings along with the remains of mollusks, birds, and both large and small mammals. No unequivocal big-game kill sites have been reported. These varied settings and faunal remains, coupled with a diversified toolkit, suggest a generalized hunting–gathering way of life. In California and the Great Basin the proximity of fluted points to old pluvial lakes is especially notable. It seems likely that in such areas the Fluted-Point Tradition peoples would have adapted increasingly to lake and marsh environments, gradually evolving into the Western Pluvial Lakes Tradition (discussed below) by circa 11,000 B.P.

In brief, the Fluted-Point Tradition cultures of North America possibly developed from a common origin, perhaps somewhere in the western United States, roughly 12,000 years ago. The subsequent appearance of specialized economic patterns may have been largely a response to the emergence of diverse regional environments in early Holocene times.

## Faunal Extinctions

Researchers have long sought to explain the massive faunal extinctions of late Pleistocene times. During the Wisconsin stage alone North America lost 77 species (26%) of the Rancholabrean fauna (Kurtén and Anderson 1980:357). Among these were the Columbian and woolly mammoths, ground sloths, five species of horses, all but one species of antelope, giant beaver, two genera of musk oxen, a large moose, several species of camelids, and such large carnivores as the dire wolf, giant short-faced bear, saber-toothed cat, and California lion (Chartkoff 1970:2; Kurtén and Anderson 1980: 364–365). Of 67 genera of North American mammals known to have become extinct during the Pleistocene, about 35 vanished between circa 13,000 and 8000 B.P. (Downs and Miller 1971; J. Hester 1960; Martin 1973).

Many possible causes of the extinctions have been suggested. Van Valen (1969), for example, lists 86 reasons proposed to account for the late Pleistocene extinctions. One school of thought favors rapid, adverse climatic shifts as a primary causal factor (Axelrod 1967). Another view is that new diseases were introduced into America's nonresistant animal populations (Corbett 1973). One of the most persistent hypotheses, however, is that "overkill" by humans was largely responsible for the late Pleistocene extinctions. P. S. Martin (1958, 1967, 1973) has advanced the thesis that big-game hunters spread explosively throughout America, briefly attaining sufficient numbers to "overkill" many of their prey species. Martin (1973:973) reasoned that the invading hunters could have swept from Canada to the southern tip of South America, decimating animal populations in their swath, between 11,500 and 10,500 B.P. Martin (1973, 1975) and Mosimann and Martin (1975) argued that the larger herbivores—horses, elephants, camels, and sloths—could not reproduce fast enough to offset their numbers lost to hunters, nor did they have enough time to evolve behavioral defenses in the face of mankind's sweeping conquest of the Americans.

D. L. Johnson (1977a:151) has noted that the impact of humans may have been especially deleterious to megafauna in California where the vegetation mosaic is patchy: "Thus, by necessity, during droughty summers the Rancholabrean grazing and browsing herbivores would have been 'ecologically concentrated' in the watered stream valleys, basins, and water holes where, for the same reasons, their human predators must also have dwelled." Because coastal California sustained a Mediterranean climate and served as a refugium for cold-sensitive floras and faunas throughout Quaternary times, "man, not climate, probably was the principal agent in the late Quaternary extinction of the Rancholabrean fauna in California" (D. Johnson 1977a:152). Similarly, Van Devender (1977) noted that because the shift to desert conditions in southeastern California occurred ≈3000 years after most of the megafaunal extinctions, changes in climate or vegetation probably did not cause them.

Coastal as well as terrestrial species have been reduced by human predation. As examples, Steller's sea cow, the walrus, and the flightless cormorant—all vulnerable to hunting—once ranged widely around the North Pacific. Steller's sea cow and the walrus previously occupied coastal waters as far south as central California, but by early historic times their territories had been greatly diminished as a result of hunting pressure (Hopkins 1979:33).

Notwithstanding these observations, many aspects of the extinction problem are not explained by reference to humans:

1. Grayson (1977) has pointed out that 10 genera of California birds vanished between circa 13,000 and 10,000 B.P. and that, with one possible exception, the avian extinctions cannot be related directly either to the

demise of the mammals or to human hunters. The late Pleistocene brought extinction to species ranging from blackbirds and pocket gophers to *Ternatornis* and mammoths—an array of creatures too diverse to be accounted for by the overkill hypothesis (Grayson 1977:692).

2. Although *possible* associations of Rancholabrean fossils and artifacts have been reported from Secret Valley (Riddell 1958), Santa Rosa Island (Berger 1982), China Lake (E. Davis and Panlaqui 1978), and Tulare Lake (Riddell and Olsen 1969), definite megafaunal kill sites as yet have not been discovered in California.

3. Although Paleoindians did kill members of some species that ultimately became extinct, they also intensively pursued others (e.g., *B. bison*) that survived (J. Hester 1967; Krantz 1970).

4. In large areas of western North America, the climate and flora changed dramatically during the Pleistocene to Holocene transition (Axelrod 1967). Many habitats previously suited to Rancholabrean animals vanished at that time. Also, $^{14}$C-dated early Holocene climate changes were often swift, not gradual or complacent (Bryson *et al.* 1970). The abrupt shifts would have been particularly devastating to faunas with limited ranges.

To sum up, it would appear that no single factor caused the late Pleistocene extinctions. Habitat replacement brought about by rapid climatic shifts probably struck with considerable impact. Hunters surely abetted the demise of some big-game species, especially those with populations already reduced by diminished habitats. Any congregation of animals in favored places, seasonal or otherwise, would have raised their vulnerability to predators, including humans, and this may have hastened local extinctions. As Kurtén and Anderson have concluded:

> Extinction did not occur uniformly across the continent. Local conditions affected local populations. No one cause can account for it; rather, a mosaic of adverse conditions prevailed. We believe that changes in vegetation, sudden storms, droughts, loss of habitat, interspecific competition, low reproduction rates, and overspecialization, to name a few factors, reduced or weakened populations, making them vulnerable to environmental pressures, including man, the hunter, who probably delivered the *coup de grâce* to some of the megafauna between 12,000 and 9,000 years ago. (1980:363)

## The Western Pluvial Lakes Tradition

### Introduction

As defined by Bedwell (1970), the Western Pluvial Lakes Tradition (WPLT) occurred in the western Great Basin from the vicinity of Fort Rock, Oregon, on the north, southward along the east side of the Cascade–Sierra Nevada uplift, and into the (now) arid lands of southern California. Because of numerous pluvial lakes (Figure 3.1), similar adaptations to lake, marsh, and grassland environments could be made throughout this area. The WPLT flourished for several millennia after 11,000 B.P., then gradually disappeared early in the Altithermal climatic period. By 8000–7000 B.P., the Pluvial Lakes way of life was replaced by traditions better adapted to arid lands (Bedwell 1970:230–233).

## Nomenclature

As a legacy from decades of Early Man studies, we have inherited myriad names for variants of the WPLT and related traditions. Elements of these traditions were first recognized in coastal San Diego County by Malcom Rogers, who initially (1929c) identified two ancient cultures: "Shell Midden People" and "Scraper-Maker Culture." The Shell Midden People (or "Proto–Scraper-Maker Culture") were at first thought to be the older, but Rogers (1939, 1945) later reversed the order and substituted the terms *San Dieguito* for *Scraper-Maker* and *La Jolla* for *Shell Midden* (Table 3.1) (Warren 1967a). In 1939 Rogers also defined a sequence of Malpais, Playa I, and Playa II Industries in the arid lower Colorado River country. Rogers apparently included the Lake Mojave Culture (Campbell *et al.* 1937) in his Playa Industries.

Seeing typologic relationships between his inland and coastal assemblages, Rogers (1958) converted Malpais, Playa I, and Playa II into San Dieguito I, II, and III, respectively. Later, William Wallace (1962a) lumped

**TABLE 3.1**

**Concordance of Terms Referable to the Western Pluvial Lakes Tradition and Paleo-Coastal Tradition**[a]

| A: Lower Colorado River and Interior Desert Areas | | | | | |
|---|---|---|---|---|---|
| *Rogers (1939)* | *Rogers (1958)* | *Campbell* et al. *(1937)* | *Wallace (1962)* | *Warren (1967a)* | *Bedwell (1970)* |
| Playa II | San Dieguito III | Lake Mojave Culture | Lake Mojave Culture | San Dieguito Complex | Western Pluvial Lakes Tradition |
| Playa I | San Dieguito II | | | | |
| Malpais | San Dieguito I | | | | |

| B: Southern California Coast | | | |
|---|---|---|---|
| *Rogers (1929)* | *Rogers (1939, 1945)* | *Warren (1967a)* | *Davis* et al. *(1969)* |
| Scraper-Maker Culture | La Jolla[b] | | |
| Shell Midden People | San Dieguito | San Dieguito Complex | Paleo-Coastal Tradition |

[a]Modified from Warren 1967a.

[b]La Jolla apparently developed and spread after ≈8000 B.P. and thus does not belong to the Paleo-Coastal Tradition. It is a unit of the Encinitas Tradition (see Chapter 4).

the Playa, Lake Mojave, and his Death Valley I materials into a single Lake Mojave Complex (Table 3.1) (Warren 1967a).

In a synthesis of exceptional clarity and value, Claude Warren (1967a) defined a San Dieguito Complex to incorporate the Lake Mojave, Death Valley I, and Playa I and II expressions as well as coastal units (to be discussed below). Warren proposed that the San Dieguito Complex reflects a generalized hunting tradition, 9000 to 10,000 years old, distinct from the coeval Desert Tradition (Jennings 1964). California units of the San Dieguito Complex include the C. W. Harris site (San Diego County), Playa I and II (San Bernardino County), Lake Mojave, Death Valley I, Panamint Basin, Mono Lake, and Owens Lake assemblages characterized by leaf-shaped knives and points, Lake Mojave and Silver Lake points, scrapers, engraving tools, and crescents (Warren 1967a).

Lastly, E. L. Davis, C. Brott, and D. Weide (1969) have defined a Western Lithic Co-Tradition—a series of lithic industries, as old as ≈10,000 years, identifed by percussion-flaked core tools, choppers, ovate bifaces, and large flakes (including distinctive side-struck flakes). The Western Lithic Co-Tradition entails the San Dieguito Pattern, Lake Mojave Pattern, Panamint Basalt Industry, and other manifestations distributed widely in the Far West, from Wyoming to the Pacific shore (Davis *et al.* 1969). As a synthetic device, the Western Lithic Co-Tradition allows for the classification of any number of discrete but technically related archeological units.

It is clear that much confusion about early California prehistory has been caused by a terminological jungle that has obscured basic archaeological patterns and relationships. The Western Pluvial Lakes Tradition seems a good concept to bring order to some of the taxonomic chaos without planting any new vines in the jungle. Following Bedwell (1970) and T. Hester (1973), the WPLT is taken to include the entities formerly called Playa, San Dieguito, Lake Mojave, and Death Valley I, and the nonfluted-point assemblages from the ancient shorelines of pluvial lakes (Figure 3.1). Wallace (1978b:27) anticipated this synthesis when he noted that the close correspondence between the Lake Mojave and San Dieguito materials betray their common ancestry: "In all probability they represent regional variants of an early hunting tradition that prevailed over a wide area."

*Characteristics and Origins*

Determining the age and cultural aspects of the Western Pluvial Lakes Tradition assemblages is difficult because they usually occur on exposed surfaces, lacking stratification, where artifact mixing is possible or likely. Nonetheless, the WPLT apparently is defined by:

1. A tendency for sites to be located on or near the shores of former pluvial lakes and marshes or along old stream channels;
2. Dependence on hunting various mammals, fowling, collecting, and gathering vegetal products;
3. An absence of ground-stone artifacts such as millingstones, hence a presumed lack of hard seeds in the diet;
4. A developed flaked-stone industry, marked especially by percussion-flaked foliate knives or points, Silver Lake and Lake Mojave points, lanceolate bifaces, and points similar to the long-stemmed variety from Lind Coulee (T. Hester 1973). (Tuohy [1969] found that nearly half of the Lake Mojave, Silver Lake, and long-stemmed points in large collections from three Nevada sites exhibited burin facets. The discovery of a burin technique for shaping and resharpening these points underscores the relationship among the types.);
5. Lastly, the WPLT toolkit, which commonly includes chipped-stone crescents, large flake and core scrapers, choppers, scraper-planes, hammerstones, several types of cores, drills, and gravers, and diverse flakes (Figures 3.5 and 3.6).

The origins of the WPLT are obscure. Wallace (1978b:27) postulated that the tradition may have originated in an old culture stratum distributed over large areas of western North America. One possibility is that the Fluted-Point and Pluvial Lakes Traditions form a historical continuum, the latter being a more highly specialized adaptation to the shallow lake and marsh habitats that prevailed after 11,000 B.P. Apart from the conspicuous fluted points, the former tradition is set apart only by its *presumed* greater age, local adaptation to cold steppe and savanna lands, and *perhaps*, a stronger emphasis on hunting. Still, the repeated discoveries of fluted points on fossil lakeshores along with ovate points, crescents, and other distinctive artifacts show clearly that the Fluted-Point and Western Pluvial Lakes Traditions were related both technically and economically.

If better data from stratified deposits are acquired in the future, the two traditions may be defined more precisely: the Fluted-Point Tradition may come to be viewed as the precursor of the WPLT; or the two may be merged into a single "Early Western Tradition" or something of the kind. Meanwhile, it seems best to treat them separately.

## Lake Mojave Complex

The Lake Mojave Complex is one of the best-known expressions of the Western Pluvial Lakes Tradition. Pleistocene Lake Mojave (Figure 1.4) in the northern Mojave Desert is today represented by the Silver Lake

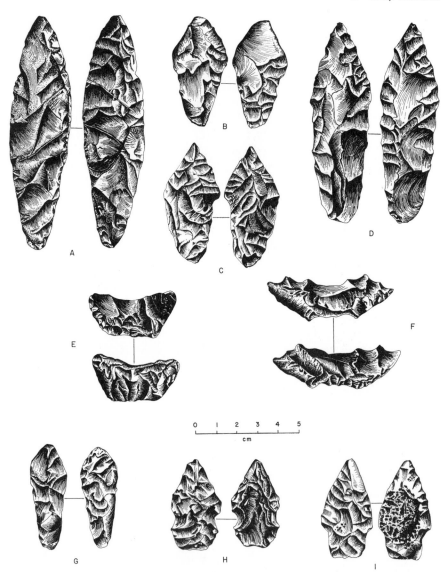

**Figure 3.5** Typical artifacts of the Western Pluvial Lakes Tradition from the shorelines of ancient Lake Mojave. A, D, Foliate points; B, C, G, Lake Mojave type points; E, F, stone crescents; H, I, Silver Lake type points. (Redrawn by Randall Engle from Amsden 1937: Plates 38, 40, 41, 42; courtesy of the Southwest Museum.)

and Soda Lake playas. Campbell *et al.* (1937) assigned to the Lake Mojave Culture a large artifact collection from two dozen sites located between the 286- and 288-m beaches of pluvial Lake Mojave. Subsequently, Lake Mojave artifacts were reported from the shorelines of many other pluvial

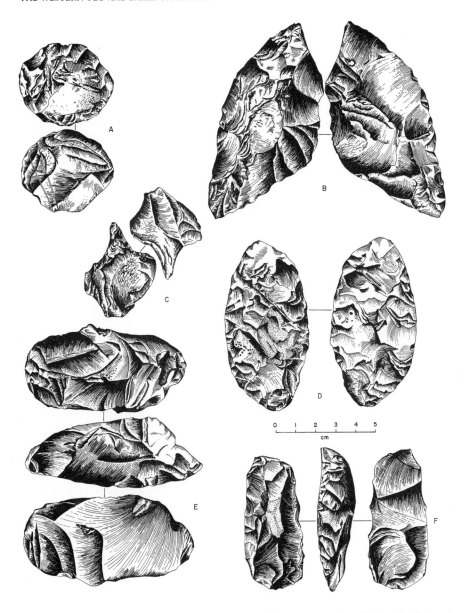

**Figure 3.6** "Lake Mojave Culture" specimens of the Western Pluvial Lakes Tradition. A, Round scraper; B, flake knife; C, perforator; D, oval knife; E, elongate keeled scraper; F, end and side scraper. (Redrawn by Randall Engle from Amsden 1937: Plates 28–30, 34, 37, 39; courtesy of the Southwest Museum.)

lakes in the southwestern Great Basin. Similarities between the Lake Mojave and San Dieguito materials (discussed below) are particularly evident in terms of percussion-flaked foliate knives and points, scrapers, and flaked-stone crescents (Warren and Ranere 1968) (Figure 3.6).

Whether the Lake Mojave channel outlet site was occupied when the lake was full has long been debated. M. Rogers (1939) thought that the site was below the lake's drainage channel level and would have been submerged at high water, but an instrument survey by G. Brainerd (1953) showed that the overflow channel crossed part of the site but did not cover it. Thus, there seems no reason to doubt the contemporaneity of human settlement with the full lake: "The fact that virtually every remnant of beach formed at the overflow level has some indication of human occupation, and that the only cultural remains not associated with these beaches are late, suggests that most of the occupation occurred when the lake was overflowing" (Warren and Ranere 1968:14).

Based upon paleoclimatic data, Ernst Antevs initially (1937:48) estimated that the Lake Mojave artifacts "may be at least 15,000 years old," but he later endorsed the more conservative age of 9000 years (1952:28). Subsequently, Warren and DeCosta (1964) obtained a $^{14}C$ date of 9640 ± 200 B.P. (LJ-200) on *Anodonta* shell from the shoreline of the lake's highest stand (≈283 m). This date evidently applies to the Lake Mojave Complex, including the specimens found at the Lake Mojave outlet channel site.

Although radiocarbon dates on freshwater mollusk shells may be unreliable because they contain unknown amounts of geologically old carbonates (Michels (1973), the Lake Mojave date of ≈9640 B.P. seems to be fairly accurate. A $^{14}C$ age of 9630 ± 300 years (LJ-528) on the high pluvial shoreline of nearby Lake LeConte is remarkably close to the Lake Mojave date (Meighan 1965), and such an age is compatible with dates on charcoal in the 8490-to-9030 B.P. range from the San Dieguito type site (which contained artifacts like those of the Lake Mojave Complex).

Warren and Ore (1978) report an effort to date cultural material at Lake Mojave by (1) reconstructing the geomorphic history of the lake, (2) developing a model to account for lake margin deposits, and (3) deducing the most probable deposits with which archaeological remains would be affiliated. Testing at one site, Bench Mark Bay, yielded buried artifacts (three gravers and a foliate-point base) in a lacustrine stratum with *Anodonta* shells $^{14}C$-dated at 10,270 ± 160 B.P. (Y-2406), and surface material representing a second early occupation apparently associated with the final recession of Lake Mojave about 8000 years ago (Warren and Ore 1978:179, 184–186).

To sum up, the Lake Mojave Complex is an expression of the Western Pluvial Lakes Tradition. Lake Mojave sites provide evidence of cultural activity coeval with several early Holocene lake stands dated by $^{14}C$

between circa 10,000 and 8000 B.P. Late artifacts such as pottery and arrow points are not found with Lake Mojave's pluvial features, but they do occur near springs and mesquite groves in sand dunes near Soda Lake and with ephemeral lakeshores at low elevations in Silver Lake Playa (Warren and Ranere 1968).

## San Dieguito: The C. W. Harris Site

The C. W. Harris site (SDi-149), located on the San Dieguito River 15 km from the sea, is the type site for Warren's (1967a) San Dieguito Complex. SDi-149 is important because its strata provided the initial cultural sequence for western San Deigo County. Malcom Rogers originally discovered this site in 1928 after flooding in 1926 had exposed a cultural stratum in the river channel. First investigated by Rogers in 1938, the archaeology of SDi-149 was further defined in later excavations by Warren and True (1961). Because the artifacts in the river gravels at several loci are not waterworn, and because a charcoal-stained lens (evidently a hearth remnant) was found in the San Dieguito gravels, it is thought that the deposits record a series of old camps on gravel bars in the wide riverbed (Warren 1966, 1967a).

The San Dieguito component is a gravel conglomerate more than 2 m below the river floodplain. Artifacts from this component in Locus I at SDi-149 include two forms of leaf-shaped knives, foliate to ovoid bifaces (knife blanks?), foliate and short-bladed shouldered points, a crescent, engraving tools, choppers, core hammers, pebble hammerstones, cores, and many types of scrapers (Figure 3.7). These materials are technically similar to the Lake Mojave collections (Figures 3.5 and 3.6).

Overlying the San Dieguito component is a stratum of sterile river silt about 1 m thick. Above this is a thicker deposit with La Jolla cultural remains; in the uppermost levels are recent tools, presumably left by late prehistoric Diegueño Indians. The La Jolla implements represent a seed-grinding, small-game-hunting, shellfish-collecting culture as contrasted with the earlier nonmillingstone San Dieguito component (Meighan 1965; Warren 1967a). Both stratigraphy and $^{14}C$ dates clearly evince the relative ages of the San Dieguito and La Jolla materials at the Harris site. Charcoal from a roasting platform in La Jolla levels yielded a date of 6300 ± 240 B.P. (LJ-202), whereas charcoal and carbonaceous earth samples from San Dieguito contexts gave $^{14}C$ ages of 8490 ± 400 (A-724), 8490 ± 400 (A-725), and 9030 ± 350 (A-722A) B.P. (Warren 1967a). These age determinations are important not only because they date key units of the southwestern California archaeological sequence but also, in the case of the San Dieguito component, because they suggest the approximate age of typologically similar WPLT materials on surface sites farther east. Also

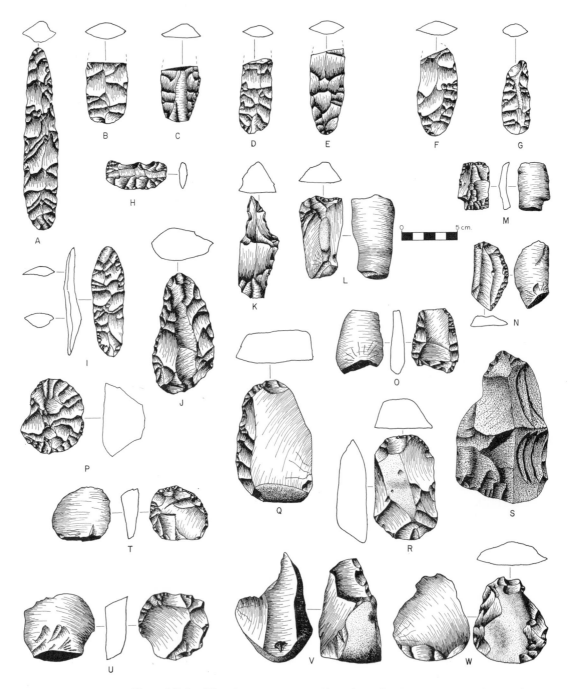

**Figure 3.7** San Dieguito component artifacts from the C. W. Harris site (SDi-149), San Diego County. A–G, Foliate knives or points; H, crescent; I, knife; J, knife blank; K, beaked scraper; L, M, end scrapers; N, O, side scrapers; P, scraper plane; Q, not identified; R, double-ended scraper; S, cleaver; T, U, ovoid scrapers; V, chopper; W, primary flake scraper. (After Warren 1967a:Plates 12, 14, 16.)

notable is the discovery of pine nuts in the La Jolla hearth—apparently the first known instance of their use in California.

### Buena Vista Lake (Ker-116)

In 1933 and 1934 E. F. Walker and W. R. Wedel directed Civil Works Administration crews in the excavation of five sites on the southwestern edge of Buena Vista Lake in the southern San Joaquin Valley (Figure 3.1). Sites 1 and 2 were middens (actually parts of a larger site now designated Ker-116), whereas Sites 3–5 were cemeteries. Wedel (1941) defined three cultural strata at Ker-116. The lowest—Stratum III, 160–200 cm deep—yielded manos, millingstones, heavy stemmed and foliate points, a mortar, red ochre, and extended burials, none of which seemed to be of great antiquity.

In 1964 and 1965, however, D. A. Fredrickson and his co-workers discovered below Stratum III at Ker-116 a component beneath 280–350 cm of more recent soils. This light-green, indurated, sandy loam deposit, speckled with bits of *Anodonta* shell, yielded 14 artifacts and a small piece of human parietal bone. Among the artifacts were two fragments of large points, three crescent fragments, a scraper, two knife fragments, and a stone atlatl engaging spur—an assemblage not unlike that of the C. W. Harris site (Fredrickson and Grossman 1977:Figure 4). Burned and unburned *Anodonta* shell from the cultural level gave $^{14}$C dates of 7600 ± 200 (I-1928), 8200 ± 400 (LJ-1356), and 8200 ± 400 (LJ-1357) B.P. (Fredrickson 1964b, 1965a, 1967; Fredrickson and Grossman 1977; Grossman 1968).

The deeply buried Buena Vista Lake component thus appears to represent the Western Pluvial Lakes Tradition in the southern San Joaquin Valley. The basal stratum registers human activity at a time when the lake stood about 87 m above sea level, approximately 8000 years ago as indicated by stratigraphy, artifact types, depth of overburden, and three $^{14}$C dates.

### The Mostin Site (Lak-380/381)

The Mostin site lies along a low terrace and in the bed of Kelsey Creek, a short distance south of Clear Lake (Figures 3.1 and 6.4). Landowner Julian Mostin first called archaeological attention to this site in 1973; prior to that time, an estimated 20 to 25 human burials had been exposed and washed away by the creek (R. King and Berg 1973; T. King 1973a).

The site consists of no fewer than nine cultural and natural levels.

The deepest archaeological stratum (5.3 m below the surrounding valley floor) consists of charcoal, obsidian flakes and tools, fish and bird bone, freshwater clam shells, fire hearths, pit-like features, ochre, and human burials in a matrix of dark organic mud. Charcoal from this deposit has been radiocarbon dated at 11,250 ± 240 B.P. (Kaufman 1980:111, 102).

The distribution of human skeletons in the creekbed suggests the presence of several deeply buried cemeteries. In 1973 and 1974 archaeologists from Sonoma State University and Cabrillo College removed nearly 25 human skeletons threatened by erosion. These burials had been interred in semiflexed or tightly-flexed positions without consistent orientation. *In situ* with the burials, or washing out of the cultural deposits, were large percussion-flaked lanceolate, lozenge-shaped, and shouldered bifaces of obsidian and chert, pointed-bone artifacts, and two ground-stone lenticular "tablets" (Figures 3.8, 10.16) (R. King and Berg 1973; T. King 1973a).

Additional fieldwork at Lak-381 in 1978 by a team of archaeologists and physical anthropologists from UCLA included the excavation of a

0  1  2  3  4  5
cm

**Figure 3.8** Imperforate and drilled ground-stone tablets from the Mostin site (Lak-380/381), Lake County. These specimens are probably of early Holocene age. Their function is unknown. (Photograph courtesy of David A. Fredrickson, Sonoma State University.)

burial directly associated with two modified stream cobbles and a well-made pestle. The burial yielded a bone collagen $^{14}$C date of 10,470 ± 490 years. This agrees with the previously cited age of 11,250 years for the deposit in which the burial was found (Kaufman 1980:181). If this $^{14}$C date is correct (questionable because of the material dated), the associated pestle would be the oldest such implement known in California and could be taken to indicate milling activity more than 10,000 years ago.

On present evidence, Lak-380/381 seems to reflect an early adaptation to the Clear Lake Basin by people who hunted, fished, took waterfowl, collected mollusks, and gathered food plants. This subsistence orientation at the Mostin site may have been derived from the presumably earlier Post Pattern, as represented at the Borax Lake site (Lak-36) only 15 km to the east. The Mostin site seems to hold great potential for future research. The multiple strata and abundant material suitable for dating at Lak-380/381 compensate in part for the disturbed strata and lack of $^{14}$C dates at Lak-36. Also, the deeply buried midden deposits at Lak-381 may yield information about late Pleistocene and early Holocene environments and cultural ecology in the Clear Lake Basin. In this regard, it is notable that pollen grains in deep sediment cores from the lake show a transition from pine to oak between 15,000 and 8200 years ago, bracketing the earlier dates of occupation at the Mostin site (Kaufman 1980).

The Lak-380/381 burials promise to shed light on both the physical anthropology and mortuary customs of ancient populations in the North Coast Ranges. In all, four burials have been $^{14}$C-dated, resulting in age determinations arrayed between 7750 ± 400 and 10,470 ± 490 B.P. (Ericson 1977b; Ericson and Berger 1974; Kaufman 1980:120). These dates, along with two others on charcoal from cultural deposits, indicate that the Mostin site was occupied over a span of about 3000 years, beginning circa 9000 B.C. If the $^{14}$C dates are correct, the Lak-380/381 skeletons would comprise one of the oldest known cemeteries in America. More significant than mere age, the very existence of large cemeteries and dense midden deposits may imply a degree of sedentism not usually credited to Paleoindians. All things considered, the lakeshore setting, economic focus, and apparent age argue that the Mostin site represents a northern California variant of the Western Pluvial Lakes Tradition.

## Burns Valley (Lak-741, -742)

Excavations in 1977 by Ann S. Peak and Associates at two Burns Valley sites, about 1.5 km east of the Borax Lake site, yielded evidence of ancient cultural activity. Situated ≈100 m apart, Lak-741 and Lak-742 contain deep, stratified soils, without discernible midden, under colluvial overburden (Weber 1978). Three soil units are recognized: Unit A (<5 m thick), of late Wisconsin age, unconformably overlying metamorphic bedrock of the Franciscan Formation; Unit B (<4 m thick), of early Holocene age, unconformably imposed on Unit A; and Unit C (<3 m thick), of late Holocene age, conformably resting on Unit B. Artifacts occur in the upper 2–3 m of Unit B, as well as in Unit A. The stratigraphic position, lithology, and pedogenic development of Soil Unit B at Lak-741 is distinctively similar to the Paleoindian deposit at Borax Lake (Haynes 1978).

The artifacts from the Burns Valley sites include obsidian bifaces, keeled and plano-convex scrapers, chopping tools, a few foliate and lanceolate points, and a possible (dubious) fluted-point fragment; no millingstones were found (Weber 1978). Hydration rims on 60 obsidian samples from Lak-741 measured from 2.7 to 10.2 ± 0.2 μm in thickness, whereas the rims on 47 pieces from Lak-742 were arrayed between 3.8 and 8.4 ± 0.2 μm. Rim thickness was highly variable and did not seem to correlate with depth of burial (Kaufman 1978a,b). To the extent that obsidian hydration measurements indicate age, the Burns Valley deposits would appear to be highly mixed.

Lacking $^{14}$C dates, the obsidian hydration method was used to build a chronology for these sites. Assuming a "conversion rate of 1000 years per micron," Weber (1978:82) proposed the following sequence:

circa 4000 B.P.: Abandonment
8400–4000 B.P.: Occupation of Lak-741 and Lak-742
9600–8400 B.P.: Occupational hiatus
pre-9600 B.P.: Occupation of Lak-741

Although some of the obsidian samples may be quite old—six have hydration rims thicker than any from the Mostin site—the specific chronology given above cannot be deduced from the available hydration measurements. As L. Johnson (1969a:1354–1355) has shown, obsidian hydrates at a diminishing rate; the regression line depicting the relationship between time and hydration rim thickness is curvilinear, not linear as would be produced by a simple, direct "conversion rate."

The Burns Valley sites remain enigmatic. Radiocarbon dates are lacking, and a thermoluminescence date of 525 ± 500 B.C. (Ericson 1978) on burned clay from Lak-741 (17–30 cm deep) does little to clarify the age of the deposits. Nonetheless, stratigraphy, pedology, artifact types, thick obsidian hydration rims, and absence of millingstones or other markers of mid-Holocene or later periods would suggest a terminal Pleistocene to early Holocene age for Soil Unit B. The older cultural levels in this unit may correspond to intervals of higher water when Burns Valley and the Borax Lake vicinity would have been connected by shallow arms of Clear Lake (M. Harrington 1948a:123–125; Weber 1978). If so, the Burns Valley sites may relate to the Western Pluvial Lakes Tradition or, alternatively, may reflect a different sort of lacustrine adaptation derived from the Post Pattern. Until the ages of Lak-741 and -742 and their relationships to former lakestands can be worked out, one can only speculate about their place in prehistory.

## WPLT Summary

Cultures adapted to wetland environments seem to have emerged wherever pluvial lakes existed in California. Distinctive lithic assemblages have been found, usually at surface sites, on fossil lakeshores in the Colorado Desert (M. Rogers 1939; Weide 1976), at Death Valley (Wallace and Wallace 1978), in the Mojave Desert (Campbell *et al.* 1937; E. Davis 1978), western Great Basin (T. Hester 1973), northeastern California (Riddell 1958), San Joaquin Valley (Arguelles with Moratto 1982; Fredrickson and Grossman 1977; Riddell and Olsen 1969), and in the North Coast Ranges (Fredrickson 1973). Other sites ascribable to the WPLT, including the San Dieguito type site, occur along the courses of ancient streams.

The exceptional carrying capacity of wetlands, coupled with the nearly ubiquitous association of artifacts with early Holocene streams and lakeshores, implies that WPLT populations could have been sizable. In the western Great Basin, WPLT populations may have been larger than those of later traditions. Also, one must not assume that these groups were invariably nomadic. Although most WPLT remains occur at surface sites that do not offer much information on this point, the Mostin site at least raises the prospect of some degree of sedentism among Paleoindians more than 10,000 years ago.

The WPLT may have evolved from Fluted-Point Tradition antecedents as woodlands and deep lakes gave way increasingly to grasslands and shallow lakes after 12,000 B.P. This view is supported by (1) the repeated co-occurrence of fluted points with crescents and other WPLT traits on pluvial lakeshores and (2) the virtual absence of fluted points in the eastern Great Basin, where early cultural developments around pluvial lakes differ significantly form those of the WPLT (Bedwell 1970). It seems probable, therefore, that the Fluted-Point Tradition and the WPLT form a culture-historical continuum. The WPLT flourished from circa 11,000 B.P. until Altithermal climates led to the evaporation of the lakes, beginning approximately 8000 years ago (Bedwell 1970). In places where remnants of the larger lakes persisted into mid-Holocene times, the WPLT endured somewhat longer, but both the pluvial lakes and the cultural tradition largely vanished by circa 7000 B.P.

# A Paleo-Coastal Tradition?

*Introduction*

Several early components on the southern California coast are distinctive yet apparently related to the Western Pluvial Lakes Tradition. The coastal sites tend to be located on estuary and bay shores—a parallel to the lakeshore and marshside settings of the interior sites. Coastal subsistence activities emphasized taking mollusks, waterfowl, sea mammals, and fish, as well as land animals and plants. Unlike most inland WPLT lithic scatters, the coastal sites are often stratified, multicomponent deposits from which cultural sequences can be defined and absolute dates obtained.

The provisional separation of a Paleo-Coastal Tradition (PCT) from the WPLT is based more on economic than technical differences. Comparable flaked-stone tool inventories, found throughout southern California between 11,000 and 8000 B.P., evince widespread technological relationships. The coastal manifestations are set apart mainly with respect to exploitative practices, settlement patterns, apparent degree of sedentism (although this has been defined only tenuously), and artifacts other than flaked stone.

The term *Paleo-Coastal Tradition*, first proposed by E. Davis *et al.* (1969) as an element of their Western Lithic Co-Tradition, here includes certain coastal components dated between circa 11,000 and 8000 B.P. Some of the PCT materials have been assigned by Wallace (1955a) to his Horizon I or Early Man Horizon and, more recently (1978b), to his Period I: Hunting. Other archaeologists (e.g., Kaldenberg 1976) have called attention to the lithic industries shared by early coastal and inland (WPLT) groups by relating both to a "San Dieguito Tradition." The term *Paleo-Coastal Tradition* is preferred here because it highlights a distinctive littoral focus while allowing more exploitative diversity than is implied by *Hunting Period*. Nonetheless, the PCT is not yet well defined and, as more is learned, it may prove to be only a coastal variant of the WPLT.

*Rancho Park North (SDM-W-49)*

The best-known PCT component occurs at Rancho Park North, Site A (also called Great Western Site A or SDM-W-49), ≈3.5 km southwest of Batiquitos Lagoon in north coastal San Diego County (Figure 3.1). Excavations there in 1974 by P. Ezell and R. Kaldenberg revealed cultural stratification paralleling the San Dieguito–La Jolla–Yuman sequence at the C. W. Harris site (Kaldenberg 1976) (Figure 3.9).

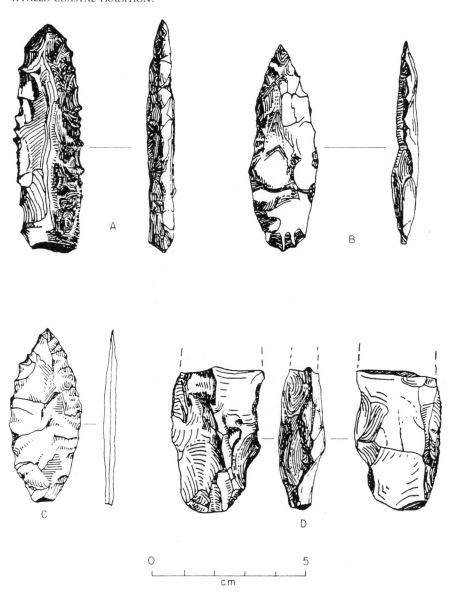

**Figure 3.9** Percussion-flaked stone bifaces from Rancho Park North, Site A, San Diego County. A, Elongate projectile point or knife of basalt; B, foliate knife or projectile point of basalt; C, ovate to foliate knife or projectile point of basalt; D, heavily patinated biface fragment of felsite. (Drawing courtesy of Russell Kaldenberg.)

The uppermost 30 cm of SDM-W-49 yielded pottery and other remains of fairly recent (circa 710 B.P.) Diegueño (Ipai–Tipai) occupation. Between 30 and 50 cm were millingstones and other traits of the La Jolla Complex (see Chapter 4). Below 50 cm, to a depth of 140 cm or more, was a "San Dieguito" component with distinctive scrapers, planes, cores, blades, and bifaces, but lacking millingstones (Kaldenberg 1976:232 ff.). Five radiocarbon dates, tightly clustered between 8010 ± 90 and 8280 ± 80 B.P., were obtained on *Chione* shell from separate levels between 50 and 120 cm. Dates of 8040 ± 80 and 6900 ± B.P. relate to the 40–50-cm level (Kaldenberg 1976:320).

The people of Rancho Park North relied heavily on marine and estuarine food resources, exploiting no less than 13 molluscan species from calm lagoons, sandy beaches, and rocky shores. Large pectens were the preferred shellfish in earlier times, giving way to a predominance of banded cockle after circa 8000 B.P. Oysters, mussels, and the speckled scallop were also important into the La Jollan period. Although a few bones show that waterfowl, deer, rabbits, hares, and small rodents were taken, a hunting emphasis is not indicated. Recent work by C. S. Bull and R. L. Carrico has produced large quantities of fish bone, indicating that both lagoon and coastal waters were being fished as early as 8000 years ago. Heavy exploitation of yucca for cordage is inferred from yucca pollen and abundant pushplanes in the lower strata (Kaldenberg 1976, 1980).

Rancho Park North seems to have been occupied most intensively from circa 8300 until 8000 B.P. by people who subsisted on shellfish, fish, and plant foods, augmented by small game. Technically and formally, their lithic toolkit is linked to that of San Dieguito, suggesting that the Paleo-Coastal Tradition was not far removed from its WPLT antecedents. Economically, however, the PCT is distinguished by an emphasis on coastal resources. The accumulation of roughly 1 m of midden deposits in a span of only ≈300 years, along with the discovery of a "structural pavement"—a possible housefloor of cobbles set into clay and associated with a series of hearths—may attest to seasonal, or maybe year-round, settlement at SDM-W-49 earlier than 8000 years ago.

The presence of pine, sea-blite, deer grass, and lace-pod pollen grains in the lower levels at Rancho Park North records a local environment moister and with more surface water than now exists in the area. Increasingly xeric conditions after 8000 B.P., as confirmed by pollen types above ≈50 cm, coincided with the advent of the La Jolla Complex. By 7000 B.P., the older technology, dominated by scraper-planes, blades, and knives, had been replaced by tools associated with seed processing (Kaldenberg 1976).

One problem yet to be resolved is whether the "San Dieguito" to La Jolla shift was an *in situ* economic and technical response to environmental change or the result of La Jollan immigration into the area. For nearby Agua Hedionda Lagoon, Moriarty (1967) has described a transitional, continuous occupation from San Dieguito (ca. 9070 B.P.) to La Jolla components. If confirmed, this would suggest that the shift to millingstone cultures from PCT antecedents in coastal San Diego County occurred without population replacement. However, the archaeological record—particularly in terms of the dramatic shift of technologic emphasis from flaked- to ground-stone implements and associated exploitative changes—may also be interpreted as a result of new social and cultural influences on the coast. Future studies of PCT and La Jollan human skeletal populations may help resolve this problem.

## Diablo Canyon Sites

At Diablo Canyon in coastal San Luis Obispo County (Figure 3.1), Greenwood (1972) has reported two multicomponent sites with basal dates of circa 9320 and 8410 B.P. The lower levels of these sites may represent the Paleo-Coastal Tradition.

Site SLO-2 at the mouth of Diablo Creek is a deep (340-cm) midden at which Millingstone, Hunting, and Chumash (see Chapter 4) components were recognized. Two $^{14}C$ dates were obtained: $8960 \pm 190$ B.P. (GaK-2044) on red abalone shell from 290 cm, adjacent to Burial 5, and $9320 \pm 140$ B.P. (UCLA-1688A) on human bone from Burial 20 at 320–330 cm (Greenwood 1972:86). Burial 5 was a flexed (?) interment with a "mano nearby." The shell date may apply to the 290-cm level, but not necessarily to the burial that would have been intruded after the midden at 290 cm had been deposited. Burial 20 (dated directly) was found with flakes, a core, a pitted stone, and a hammerstone, but no milling implements. In fact, the two provenienced millingstones from SLO-2 came from depths above 190 cm, and all 12 of the manos were found above 290 cm (Greenwood 1972:34). Because the associations between these milling tools and the $^{14}C$-dated samples are dubious, the data from SLO-2 do not substantiate a millingstone technology at circa 9000 B.P. They do indicate, however, that Diablo Canyon as occupied as early as circa 9320 B.P.

The case for a very early Millingstone component is better made at another Diablo Canyon site, SLO-585, a midden $\approx 220$ cm deep. Abalone shell from below a shell lens at 200 cm gave a $^{14}C$ age of $8410 \pm 190$ years (GaK-2040) (Greenwood 1972). Although the dated shell was not associated directly with grinding tools, 4 millingstones and 10 manos were found at or below the 200-cm level. Assuming that the date is correct, the basal stratum at SLO-585 would be essentially coeval with the oldest known millingstones in coastal San Diego County, dated $8360 \pm 75$ B.P. (see Chapter 4).

Various Diablo Canyon artifacts appear to be older than $\approx 8400$ years, that is, to occur below 200 cm at SLO-585 and below 290 cm at SLO-2. Included are blades, foliate knives, contracting-stem points similar to Lake Mojave points, scrapers and scraper-planes, a chopper, hammerstones, pitted stones (mollusk tenderizers?), a bone awl and bipoint, and *Olivella* spire-lopped shells (Greenwood 1972).

Several inferences may be drawn from the early Diablo Canyon materials. This part of the coast evidently was occupied long before millingstones first appeared; premillingstone strata seem to exist in lower SLO-2 and possibly at SLO-585. As at Agua Hedionda and Rancho Park North, the Diablo Canyon data do not shed much light on the question of population continuity, mixing, or replacement associated with the advent of millingstone technology.

Like their contemporaries farther south, the early Diablo Canyon people harvested abundant marine, littoral, and land resources. At SLO-2, for example, 71 molluscan genera have been identified. The proportions among major food remains persist with remarkable constancy from the base to the top of the midden. California mussel predominates with an overall average of about 85% of all shell. Other important species are the black turban snail, barnacles, and red and black abalones. Game animals and birds number 20 species, among them Steller's sea lion, California sea lion, harbor seal, northern sea elephant, bear, badger, mountain lion, sea otter, mule deer, rabbit, brown pelican, cormorant, and snow goose (Greenwood 1972:50–51). Of 41 fish species identified at SLO-2, 13 were known from the deepest part of the site (below 270 cm). Some of these fish may have been taken by predatory birds or mammals that were subsequently killed by hunters, but the lingcod, plain midshipman, rock prickleback, wolf eel, and pile perch could have been caught by hand or in traps (Fitch 1972). The faunal remains from SLO-2 are thus significant, for they show that nearly 100 species of animals were being used by Paleo-Coastal Tradition peoples at Diablo Canyon some 9300 to 8000 years ago.

*Summary*

The southern California coastal zone sustained a Paleo-Coastal Tradition earlier than 8000 years ago. Because dependence on marine and littoral resources was already well established by circa 9300 B.P., one should expect to find a series of yet older sites evincing progressively more specialized adaptations to the coastal environment. That such sites have not been found, or have not survived, may be a result of marine encroachment in early Holocene times (see Chapters 2 and 6). Even 10,000 years ago, the shoreline was as much as 10 km farther west than it is today along many stretches of the southern coast (Figure 3.1).

The PCT shared with the Western Pluvial Lakes Tradition a distinctive lithic technology and many types of flaked-stone tools, which argues for a common origin, or other close relationship, of these traditions. The coastal toolkit, however, is set apart by pitted stones, asphaltum, pointed-bone objects, and shell spoons and ornaments. This distinction may be more environmental than cultural, however, since bone and shell normally do not survive on the deflated inland sites, and other tools (e.g., pitted stones) may be linked functionally to processing of coastal materials.

Subsistence economy most clearly separates the PCT from the WPLT. The remains of more than 100 species of mollusks, birds, marine and land mammals, and fish have been identified in the middens at Diablo Canyon, Agua Hedionda, and Rancho Park North. Even so, it is conceivable that the PCT and more westerly of the WPLT expressions are no more than environmental and/or seasonal variants of one another; that is, the perceived differences between the PCT and the WPLT may be largely a result of different environments and subsistence foci. The lower C. W. Harris component, for example, may represent seasonal use of an inland environment by people who lived during another part of the year at a caostal site, such as Rancho Park North. However the PCT and WPLT ultimately prove to be related, they provided the cultural matrix into which millingstones were introduced some 8400 years ago. A growing reliance on hard seeds, evidenced by the rapid acceptance of milling technology between circa 8000 and 7500 B.P., signals the ebb of the Paleo-Coastal Tradition and the emergence of a different (Encinitas) tradition on the coast (see Chapter 4).

## Early Sites in West-Central California

Recent work in west-central California has revealed early Holocene components at several sites not far south of San Francisco Bay. In Scotts Valley, near Santa Cruz, excavations by R. R. Cartier in 1980 and 1981 at SCr-177 yielded "C-14 dates of 7,180 ± 290 (RL-1374) and 10,080 ± 460 B.P. (RL-1373) from two test units. The dates were [reported as] associated with chert dart points, a large chert biface, obsidian flakes, charcoal, fire-altered rock, and ground stone artifacts"; a similar collection was made at SCr-33, some 400 m from SCr-177 (Cartier 1982:229).

Regrettably, further studies of the ancient deposits at SCr-177 have been compromized by recent damage to the site. In 1981 the site was partly bulldozed, to make way for a parking lot, by the then-mayor of Scotts Valley who was later praised by the City Council for his cost-effective approach to construction schedules (Anonymous 1982:5–6). Yet even with the minimal information on hand, SCr-177 is known to have been a very important site. It contains what may be the oldest known [14]C-dated component in the region, with ground-stone artifacts (reported but not described) said to be more ancient than those elsewhere in California except possibly at the Mostin site. Also, the obsidian from lower SCr-177 would imply that trade networks in California were functioning ≈100 centuries ago; the nearest obsidian sources are approximately 200 km north and east of SCr-177. Large-scale rescue excavations at SCr-177 took place during the spring of 1983. It is hoped that the early Holocene prehistory of the Santa Cruz Mountains will be better understood when the results of this fieldwork are published.

East of Santa Cruz County, another Holocene component was discovered recently at SCl-178, a deeply stratified site near Coyote Creek in the southern part of the Santa Clara Valley (Figures 3.1 and 6.4). Covering more than 70,000 m³ are lithic scatters and cultural deposits on and within an alluvial fan. Limited testing of upper levels during the 1970s was followed by intensive sampling, between 1979 and 1981, directed by E. G. Stickel of Daniel, Mann, Johnson, and Mendenhall (DMJM), Inc. All work at the site has been sponsored by the California Department of Transportation. Excavation of 29 test units by DMJM revealed approximately 20 soil horizons, among them no less than six cultural layers, extending to a maximum depth of 6.5 m (Stickel *et al.* 1980:6).

The cultural and natural strata at SCl-178 apparently span the entire Holocene epoch. Upper components are said to be related to the "Late and Middle Horizons" of the Central California Taxonomic System (see Chapter 5). Descriptions of these and of the lower components were not available at the time of this writing. However, four [14]C dates have been published; these range from 8050 ± 300 B.P. (UCLA-2329B) at the 330-cm level to 9960 ± 500 B.P. (UCLA-2329D) at the 510-cm level (Breschini and Haversat 1982). Of note are a mano from the 460-cm level, a notched stone from 420 cm, and an *Olivella* shell bead from 500 cm (Stickel *et al.* 1980:6). SCl-178 is one of the oldest known sites in west-central California. Its deeply stratified deposits may serve as a key for seriating other ancient components and could provide a record of environmental changes to help interpret cultural adaptations during a 10,000-year span of prehistory.

## Conclusions

This chapter has reviewed the early Holocene archaeology of California and has discussed the Fluted-Point, Western Pluvial Lakes, and Paleo-Coastal Traditions. Although details regarding the ages, relationships, and origins of all of these traditions remain to be worked out, the dating of the Fluted-Point Tradition has proven especially difficult. Most of the FPT finds have been isolated pieces or surface scatters estimated, on the strength of typologic likeness to $^{14}$C-dated Clovis artifacts, to be 12,000 to 11,000 years old. Some of the California fluted points (e.g., those from Lakes China and Tulare) may be associated with Rancholabrean fossils, and geologic observations at Borax Lake suggest an age of ≈12,000 years for the oldest cultural deposits, but no firm conclusions can be drawn from these observations. Likewise, even the cultural distinctiveness of the tradition is open to scrutiny. It is at least possible that the Fluted-Point assemblages merely represent an early phase of the Western Pluvial Lakes Tradition; that is, the western fluted points may identify only a technical horizon within a larger cultural (and social?) continuity. More data, particularly information from stratified deposits, will be needed to resolve this problem.

The ages of the Western Pluvial Lakes and Paleo-Coastal Traditions are better known. Bedwell (1970:232) assigned the WPLT to the period between 11,000 and 8000 B.P., with dates clustering between circa 10,500 and 9400 B.P. The $^{14}$C dates on WPLT units in California range from circa 10,270 to 8200 B.P. (Table 3.2). The temporal placement of the PCT is suggested by remarkably consistent $^{14}$C dates—all within the span from circa 9320 to 8000 B.P.—from several components (Table 3.2). Older PCT sites almost certainly exist, or did exist, near the early Holocene coastline.

The origins of these early traditions are obscure. The Western Pluvial Lakes Tradition apparently evolved *in situ* throughout much of the western Great Basin and California when productive shallow lake and marsh environments emerged after circa 11,500 B.P. The WPLT may have developed from the Fluted-Point Tradition or, less likely, from other antecedents.

A common origin of the Western Pluvial Lakes Tradition and Paleo-Coastal Tradition seems indicated by their shared lithic technology and tool forms and by their similar adaptive strategies. Indeed, the WPLT and PCT may have been no more than environmental specializations within a broader cultural continuum. It is possible that interior (WPLT) peoples spread to the coast roughly 10,000 years ago as a result of population pressures in the pluvial lakes country. For such groups the transition from lakeshore to seashore adaptation, particularly in the vicinity of coastal lagoons and marshes, would have been relatively uncomplicated. Certainly by circa 9000 B.P. coastal dwellers were exploiting an array of littoral and intertidal zones.

An alternative, though improbable, model would have the PCT developing from older coastal predecessors. Rising seas after circa 14,000 B.P. would have obliterated coastal sites as the ocean inexorably pushed eastward; some parts of the the southern California coastline shifted landward as much as 10 to 20 km during terminal Pleistocene and early Holocene times. This model would view the PCT as a geographic displacement of more ancient shoreline cultures rather than as a coastal adaptation by interior peoples. Accordingly, the technical similarities between the PCT and the WPLT would be seen as the result of diffusion from the interior to the coast sometime before circa 9500 B.P. (Figure 3.10).

Much remains to be learned about these early traditions. Although a beginning has been made toward understanding their subsistence practices, technologies, and settlement arrangements, almost nothing is known about their linguistic affiliations, demography, or social organiza-

**TABLE 3.2**

**Radiocarbon Ages of Early Post-Pleistocene Components**

| Component | Radiocarbon date |
|---|---|
| Western Pluvial Lakes Tradition | |
| Lake Mojave, cultural stratum | |
|   *Anodonta* shell | 10,270 ± 160 (Y-2406) |
| Lake Mojave, shoreline | |
|   *Anodonta* shell | 9640 ± 200 (LJ-200) |
| Lake LeConte shoreline | |
|   Tufa | 9630 ± 300 (LJ-528) |
| Buena Vista Lake (Ker-116) | |
|   *Anodonta* shell | 7600 ± 200 (I-1928) |
|   *Anodonta* shell | 8200 ± 400 (LJ-1356) |
|   *Anodonta* shell | 8200 ± 400 (LJ-1357) |
| Mostin Site (Lak-380) | |
|   Human bone collagen | 10,260 ± 340 (UCLA-1795) |
|   Human bone collagen | 9040 ± 200 (UCLA-1795B) |
|   Human bone collagen | 7750 ± 400 (UCLA-1795C) |
|   Charcoal | 11,250 ± 240 (UCLA-2165) |
|   Human bone collagen | 10,470 ± 490 (UCLA-2171) |
| C. W. Harris Site (SDi-149) | |
|   Charcoal | 8490 ± 400 (A-724) |
|   Charcoal | 8490 ± 400 (A-725) |
|   Charcoal | 9030 ± 350 (A-722A) |
| Paleo-Coastal Tradition | |
| Rancho Park North (SDM-W-49) | 8030 ± 80 (LJ-3160) |
| | 8280 ± 80 (LJ-3161) |
| | 8110 ± 80 (LJ-3246) |
| | 8040 ± 80 (LJ-3243) |
| | 6900 ± 280 (UCR-432) |
| | 8010 ± 90 (LJ-3244) |
| | 8060 ± 90 (LJ-3245) |
| Diablo Canyon (SLO-2) | |
|   *Haliotis* shell | 8960 ± 190 (GaK-2044) |
|   Human bone collagen | 9320 ± 140 (UCLA-1668A) |
| Diablo Canyon (SLO-585) | |
|   *Haliotis* shell | 8410 ± 190 (GaK-2040) |

| Years B.P. | Northern California | Central California | Southern California Interior | Southern California Coast | | | | | |
|---|---|---|---|---|---|---|---|---|---|
| 7000 | *Borax Lake Pattern* | | (Depopulation) | ENCINITAS TRADITION | | | | | |
| 7500 | ? | | | | | | | | |
| 8000 | | Buena Vista Lake IV | | Malaga Cove 1 Rancho Park North | Intensification of Plant Resource Use | Increasing Sedentism | Increasing Population | Technological Diversification | Increasing Regional Specialization |
| 8500 | | | | Rancho La Brea | | | | | |
| 9000 | | | | Diablo Canyon | | | | | |
| 9500 | | SCI-178 | Owens Valley Death Valley I | | | | | | |
| 10,000 | | | Lake China | PALEO—COASTAL TRADITION | | | | | |
| 10,500 | Mostin Site Burns Valley ? | ? | Lake Panamint Lake Mojave | | | | | | |
| 11,000 | WESTERN | PLUVIAL | LAKES | TRADITION | | | | | |
| 11,500 | Borax Lake Site *Post Pattern* Samwel Cave | Tracy Lake ? Tulare Lake ? | Lake China Owens Valley | | | | | | |
| 12,000 | FLUTED | POINT | TRADITION | | | | | | |
| | ? | Farmington Complex ? Rancho Murieta ? | | Laguna Beach ? Angeles Mesa ? Baldwin Hills ? | | | | | |

**Figure 3.10** Concordance of early archaeological units.

tion. In broadest terms, one may say that California was inhabited before 8000 B.P. by people who, in appropriate environments, congregated near wetlands where they lived by gathering, hunting, fowling, fishing, and collecting. Most groups presumably were more or less nomadic, moving from one ephemeral or seasonal camp to the next. Other groups, particularly those in favorable coastal and lakeshore settings, might have lived year-round, or nearly so, at a single settlement. The economic success of the Fluted-Point Tradition and subsequent Western Pluvial Lakes Tradition and Paleo-Coastal Tradition seemingly permitted their rapid spread throughout lowland California and assimilation or replacement of older peoples and cultures in those areas. One would expect, therefore, that any survivals of older cultural patterns into mid-Holocene times would be found in mountainous regions where the WPLT–PCT way of life could not be followed.

# 4. Southern Coast Region

The natives are well appearing, of good disposition, affable, liberal,
and friendly toward the Spaniard. As to their government, it is by
captaincies over villages. . . . They have cemeteries set apart for the
burial of their dead. The god whom they adore, and to whom they
offer their seeds, fruits, and all that they possess, is the sun. . . . Their
houses, shaped like half-globes, are neatly built; each one is capable
of sheltering four or five families. In their manufactures, these Indians
know how to make very beautiful inlaid work of mother-of-pearl on
the rims and sides of stone mortars and various other utensils.

*Fages [1775] (1972:46–47, 51)*

(Courtesy of the Santa Barbara Museum of Natural History.)

# Introduction

Stretching along the magnificent shore of the Pacific from Morro Bay southward is the Southern Coast archaeological region (Figure 1). This chapter examines the singular archaeological record of this region, especially along the Santa Barbara coast, and traces prehistoric developments after circa 6000 B.C. A brief survey of southwestern California's environment and native cultures will provide a background for discussions of archaeology.

## Environment

Varied coastal and mountain zones between Morro Bay and Santa Monica typify the Santa Barbara subregion (Figures 4.1 and 4.4). Uplands, often separated from the shore by piedmont and terrace lands, are close enough to have been visited easily by coastal Indians. Although warmer and less foggy than the central California coast, Santa Barbara receives enough rainfall ($\approx$45 cm/year) to sustain a rich biota. Of the local resources:

> There is an abundance of all seeds needed for [the Indians'] use, and many acorns. There are birds and land animals. . . . The fishing is so good, and so great is the variety of fish, . . . that this industry alone would suffice to provide sustenance to all the settlers which this vast stretch of country could receive. In the mountains there are seen many pines like those of Spain, *mollares,* and oaks and live oaks. (Fages [1775] 1972:35)

Further assets are the islands—San Miguel, Santa Rosa, Santa Cruz, and Anacapa—that border the Santa Barbara Channel and shelter it from the full impact of the open sea (Figure 4.3). Notable too is the strategic location of this province, surrounded as it is by parts of the Coast and Transverse ranges, San Joaquin Valley, Mojave Desert, and Peninsular Ranges (Figure 1.2). This situation made Santa Barbara a natural center for early trade networks.

The San Diego subregion extends from Santa Monica to upper Baja California (Figures 1 and 4.13). In this part of California, low hills and terraces separate the mountains from the shore. Here, as near Santa Barbara, chaparral is the dominant vegetation type. Oak groves dot the foothills, interior valleys, and canyons, and sycamores grow along streams. Grasslands and shrubfields occur in lowlands, and forests of pine, fir, and cedar cover the higher ranges dividing the coast from the desert (Wallace 1955a). Low rainfall ($\approx$25 cm/year) in the south makes the hinterland east of San Diego an arid country; streams are typically small and intermittent.

The coastal landscape (Figure 4.1) features bays, lagoons, and long sandy beaches giving way now and then to rocky points. A profusion of mollusks, fish, and waterfowl thrives in this littoral zone. Mitigating the forces of sea and storm along the San Pedro Channel are the offshore islands: San Nicolas, Santa Barbara, Santa Catalina, and San Clemente (Figure 4.13). Given this distribution of natural resources, it is not surprising that archaeological populations were concentrated along the western edge of the San Diego subregion.

## Native Cultures

The Southern Coast in the eighteenth century was occupied by speakers of Chumashan, Serran, Cupan, and Dieguéño languages (Figure 11.1).

**Figure 4.1** Batequitos Lagoon, San Diego County, one of many lagoons along the southern California coast. Fed by San Marcos creek and other small watercourses, Batequitos Lagoon extends 5.6 km inland from the ocean beach (bottom). More than 40 archaeological sites in the immediate vicinity attest to the abundant natural resources of such lagoon environments (Crabtree *et al.* 1963) and to the exploitation of these resources over a span of 9000 years or more (Kaldenberg 1976; Kaldenberg and Ezell 1974). (Photograph by M. Jay Hatley; courtesy of M. Jay Hatley, Cornerstone Research.)

Spanish missions established in this region, beginning with San Diego de Alcalá in 1769, devastated Native populations and cultures (Castillo 1978; Cook 1940, 1943c, 1976). Consequently, many Indian lifeways vanished rapidly and without being documented historically.

Southern Coast peoples were distinguished from other Native Californians by their social complexity, art styles, economic practices, and technical skills. The best known of these Southerners were the Chumash, who held the Santa Barbara Channel Islands and mainland, from San Luis Obispo to Malibu Canyon on the coast, and inland to the western edge of the San Joaquin Valley (Grant 1978a).

Chumash culture was as elaborate as that of any hunter–gatherer society on earth. Theirs was a true maritime adaptation focused on sea mammal hunting and fishing, but not to the exclusion of collecting shellfish or taking various land animals and plant foods. Of the latter, acorns and chia (sage) seeds were notable. The seagoing plank canoes (Figure 4.2) of the Chumash and their Gabrielino neighbors were unique in North America (Heizer 1938b; Hudson *et al.* 1978), and their fishing tackle was remarkably specialized (Hoover 1973). The Chumash apparently followed a seasonal round to optimize their use of local resources. Spring and early summer found them in widely dispersed camps from which they hunted, fished, and harvested wild crops. Populations gathered in large coastal villages during the late summer and fall when fishing for pelagic species was at its peak. Then came a dispersal for the late fall pine nut and acorn harvests, followed by winter sedentism in the main villages where food supplies were stored (Landberg 1965:102–103).

Chumash society featured pronounced status differentiation, inher-

**Figure 4.2** The unique plank canoe (*tomol*) of the Chumash and Gabrielino served in fishing, sea-mammal hunting, and transportation. A reconstruction of this craft, named *Helek* (Sea Hawk), is shown here on a Santa Barbara beach being prepared for its voyage to the Channel Islands as part of the American Bicentennial. (Photograph by Dick Smith; courtesy of the Santa Barbara Museum of Natural History.)

ited chieftainship, and intervillage alliances. Economic activities were so successful that Chumash villages counted as many as 1000 residents—the most populous settlements in the aboriginal Far West. The total Chumash population in A.D. 1770 was on the order of 15,000 to 20,000 (Brown 1967; Cook and Heizer 1965).

The exceptional artistry of Chumash craft specialists is shown in basketry and in items of shell, bone, wood, and stone (Figures 4.7, 4.10, 4.11, and 4.18). Chumash rock art, including both petroglyphs and vari-colored pictographs, is the most spectacular of any north of Mexico (Grant 1965). Some of the best-known examples are from Painted Cave (SBa-506) near Santa Barbara (Figure 4.3). This rock art, thought to have been the work of shamans and other specialists, is usually found in caves and rockshelters in remote places inland from the coast (Grant 1978b:517– 518). The motifs are of two general kinds: abstract (zigzags, dots, grids, and other geometric designs) and representational (depicting the sun, stars, humans, birds, swordfish, rattlesnakes, etc.). Although the precise meaning of most Chumash rock art is unknown, much of it is thought to have had a religious purpose. Some of the motifs are probably related to astronomy and calendrical systems (Hudson and Underhay 1978), and at least five rock-art sites in Chumash territory evidently functioned as solstice observatories (Hudson *et al.* 1979:46).

South of the Chumash, the Gabrielino occupied the coast in what is today the Los Angeles and Orange County area. Second only to the Chumash, the Gabrielino were the wealthiest, most populous, and most powerful ethnic group in southern California (Bean and Smith 1978a). Their culture was similar to that of the Chumash, the main differences being that the Gabrielino spoke a Cupan language, cremated their dead, and made pottery. Santa Catalina Island provided the Gabrielino with valuable deposits of steatite, which they quarried and traded, often as finished vessels and ornaments, to other Indians (Heizer and Treganza 1944).

Farther down the coast were the Luiseño (including the people formerly called Juaneño) who moved seasonally between mountain and sea-shore camps to hunt both land and sea mammals, collect intertidal species, and harvest such vegetal foods as acorns and hard seeds (Bean and Shipek 1978; Sparkman 1908). The Luiseño are known for elaborate initiation rituals involving sand painting, ordeals, and the use of the hallucinogenic Jimsonweed. Luiseño religion is documented by Father Gerónimo Boscana's (1933) classic study *Chinigchinich*, written around 1822.

Between Luiseño territory and northern Baja California were semi-nomadic bands of Diegueño who, like the Luiseño, followed a seasonal round to exploit wild plants, fish, small game, and occasionally deer or mountain sheep. The Diegueño, along with other Indians of the San Diego subregion, made pottery and cremated their dead—reflections of

**Figure 4.3** Painted Cave (SBa-506) near Santa Barbara. Recent studies by the Santa Barbara Museum of Natural History indicate that some of the pictographs found in Chumash territory represent astronomical subjects. The black disc in this panel (far right center) may depict a total eclipse of the sun. (Photograph courtesy of the Santa Barbara Museum of Natural History.)

Yuman influence from desert cultures farther east (Luomala 1978; True 1966).

## Early Archaeology

### *Explorations*

When R. L. Olson of the University of California began excavations near Santa Barbara and on Santa Cruz island in 1927, he was dismayed to find that most of the sites had been "plundered by relic hunters" (1930:3). During the late 1800s, southern California's middens had been looted extensively to provide artifacts for private and museum collections in Europe and the United States (Nelson 1936:199).

Early antiquarians were drawn to San Miguel Island, for example, where winds had exposed cemeteries in sand dunes. W. G. Harford of the U.S. Coast Survey was the first known collector on San Miguel, in 1872 and 1873, followed in 1875 by Paul Schumacher of the Smithsonian Institution. The vagabond naturalist Jean Léon de Cessac dug on San Miguel in 1877, and Stephen Bowers further rifled the island's cemeteries in 1878 (Grant 1978d).

In the decade after 1877, Reverend Stephen Bowers was perhaps the most ardent collector of antiquities in southern California (S. Bowers (1878, 1883, 1884, 1885a,b, and 1887). In 1885 he described and then sold to the Peabody Museum a spectacular cache of more than 100 "relics" from a cave (now Bowers Cave) in the San Martín Mountains of Los Angeles County. This cache of baskets, feather bands, bone whistles, wooden bullroarers, stone "clubs" with wooden handles, and other items most likely had been left in the cave by the Chumash around A.D. 1800 (Elsasser and Heizer 1963). The location of Bowers Cave remained a mystery for 65 years until its rediscovery in 1951 by R. van Valkenburgh, who found in it some blue glass beads, basketry fragments, and sherds of thirteenth-century pottery traded from the Southwest (van Valkenburgh 1952). With regard to the cache, Bowers doubtless saved perishable specimens from the ravages of wood rats; elsewhere, his antiquarian pursuits were less justifiable.

Rampant digging before 1900 damaged countless sites on the Southern Coast (Figure 4.4). Paul Schumacher was one of the more ambitious collectors of this era. Under the aegis of the Smithsonian Institution, he dug into scores of sites on the Santa Barbara Channel Islands and mainland (Schumacher 1874, 1875a,b,c,d, 1877a,b, and 1878b). In 1875 Schumacher unearthed in a single month more than 700 burials at seven sites on Santa Cruz Island. Beyond amassing such collections, Schumacher made some substantive contributions to archaeology. His interest in material remains and technology led to valuable observations on the manufacture of pottery, baskets, steatite *ollas,* and other products (Schumacher 1878a,c, 1880).

Schumacher was also quite territorial. He saw as a principal competitor Jean Léon de Cessac, a member of the ill-fated French scientific expedition led and funded by Alphonse Pinart. Between 1877 and 1879, Cessac gathered prehistoric remains along the Santa Barbara Channel (Hamy 1951). Near Santa Barbara, he found that zealous "members of the Smithsonian Instituion [viz., Schumacher] had very nearly exhausted the coastal sites" (Cessac 1951a:8), adding:

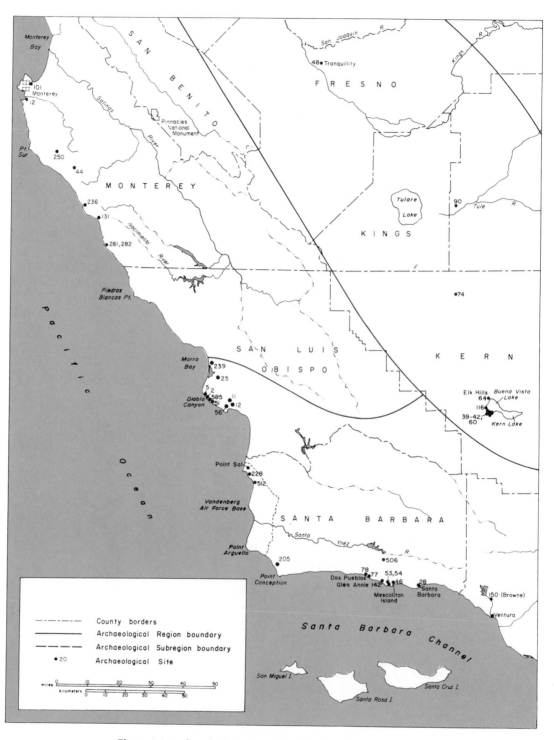

**Figure 4.4** Archaeological sites of the Southern Coast and Valley. (Map by Allan Childers and Thad Van Bueren.)

> Meanwhile my researches and their happy result, having awakened the "patriotic" or "interested" touchiness of . . . one of my archaeological competitors. I was forbidden to excavate a very important cemetery in the very town of Santa Barbara. I succeeded, however, thanks to the help of an Italian gardener who tilled this site in obtaining a number of skulls. (Cessac 1951a:9)

Schumacher did his best to stop the digging by Cessac, threatening him with a law that did not exist and even trying to persuade the Secretary of the Smithsonian Institution to ask the U.S. Senate to enact a law prohibiting the export of antiquities (Reichlen and Heizer 1964). Weathering these storms, Cessac dug on the mainland coast and on four of the islands and later exported most of his specimens to France.

Among Cessac's accomplishments were his discovery of steatite bird and sea mammal effigies on San Nicolas Island and his recognition that the San Nicolas (Nicoleño) materials were different from those of the northern Channel Islands (Chumash). Cessac (1951a,b) was also the first to report the archaeological caves and chert quarries on Santa Cruz Island and to identify on San Nicolas Island traces of Kodiak occupation related to early nineteenth-century Russian fur trapping. Moreover, Cessac elicited from local Indians detailed information about the production and use of artifacts collected. Regrettably, some of these data may have been lost due to his (and Pinart's) later misfortunes in France (Reichlen and Heizer 1964).

Collecting activities in California persisted on a grand scale well into the twentieth century. Witness a 6-month expedition to San Miguel Island in 1919, when crews representing the Museum of the American Indian, Heye Foundation, exhumed 343 burials from 23 sites (Heye 1921). At about the same time, J. P. Harrington was excavating the Burton mound (SBa-28; Figure 4.4). in Santa Barbara on behalf of the Smithsonian Institution. From that great mound, covering nearly 1 hectare, Harrington in 1923 recovered mortars, pestles, shell fishhooks, steatite vessels, and other items probably left by the late prehistoric Chumash. A component datable to the Spanish–Mexican period also was noted (Harrington 1928). Prior to Harrington's work, the Burton mound had been mined for artifacts by Schumacher, Cessac, Bowers, A. F. Hinchman, and a host of casual pot hunters. The Burton mound was, unfortunately, a typical victim of the era when harvesting relics took precedence over stratigraphic excavations or efforts to reconstruct culture histories. By about 1920 scores of archaeological sites along the Southern Coast had been excavated. Although no reliable age estimates or cultural sequences had been developed, the range of prehistoric materials (including local variations) to be found in this region was fairly well known.

## Culture Change

In their *History of American Archaeology,* Willey and Sabloff (1974) refer to 1914–1940 as the *Classificatory–Historical Period,* because during that interval chronology was the dominant interest and theme in American archaeology. In California, as elsewhere, this concern was shown by attention to stratigraphy and culture change through time. By 1930 such studies had produced archaeological sequences in the Santa Barbara and San Diego localities.

David B. Rogers, who had been Harrington's assistant at the Burton mound, went on after 1923 to excavate widely on the coast between Carpintería and Gaviota. In 1929 Rogers defined three prehistoric phases in the Santa Barbara vicinity: Oak Grove, Hunting, and Canaliño—a sequence based on stratification at key sites and inferred differences in economic patterns. At Oak Grove sites on high ground away from the sea were found semisubterranean pit houses, extended burials with red ochre, abundant millingstones, and a few rather crude projectile points. The later Hunting People left mortars and pestles, sandstone bowls (Figure 4.8), few millingstones, numerous projectile points (Figure 4.7), and flexed burials at their villages near the ocean. Lastly, domed pole and thatch houses (Figure 4.12), plank canoes (Figure 4.2), flexed burials, and elaborate shell and steatite industries typify the Canaliño; by the style and refinement of their products, the Canaliño were identified as the ancestors of the Chumash (D. Rogers 1929).

Rogers proposed separate migrations to account for each of the Santa Barbara cultures. He felt that the Oak Grove People may have succumbed to disease or moved away before the arrival of the Hunting People, who in turn were assimilated in place by the Canaliño. Although there is little to support this migration scheme, the basic outline of Roger's (1929) cultural succession still appears valid after 50 years.

R. L. Olson of the University of California, Berkeley, (UCB) generally confirmed Rogers's sequence. In 1928 and 1929 Olson excavated 4 sites near Santa Barbara and 10 on Santa Cruz Island. He explored each midden with a trench, then followed out features and cemeteries with smaller units. Approximately 725 burials were unearthed by this technique. Olson's (1930) report emphasized stratigraphy and variations among sites in their relative frequencies of artifact types. Observing that the millingstone–mano to mortar–pestle ratio increased with depth at some sites, Olson concluded that "while both the mortar–pestle and metate–muller modes of grinding were present almost throughout, there was a real change in the prevailing method" (1930:8–9). On the basis of cultural stratification and other evidence of relative age (e.g., induration of deposits, numbers of perishable items, and presence of historic artifacts), Olson seriated his sites and developed a sequence of five cultural periods on the mainland and three on Santa Cruz Island (Figure 4.5).

A hypothetical Archaic Period was followed by an Early Mainland Period, marked by plentiful millingstones but few mortars. "Local specialization" was present from the beginning of this period, as evidenced by shellfish and sea mammal remains, bone fishhooks, steatite work, and

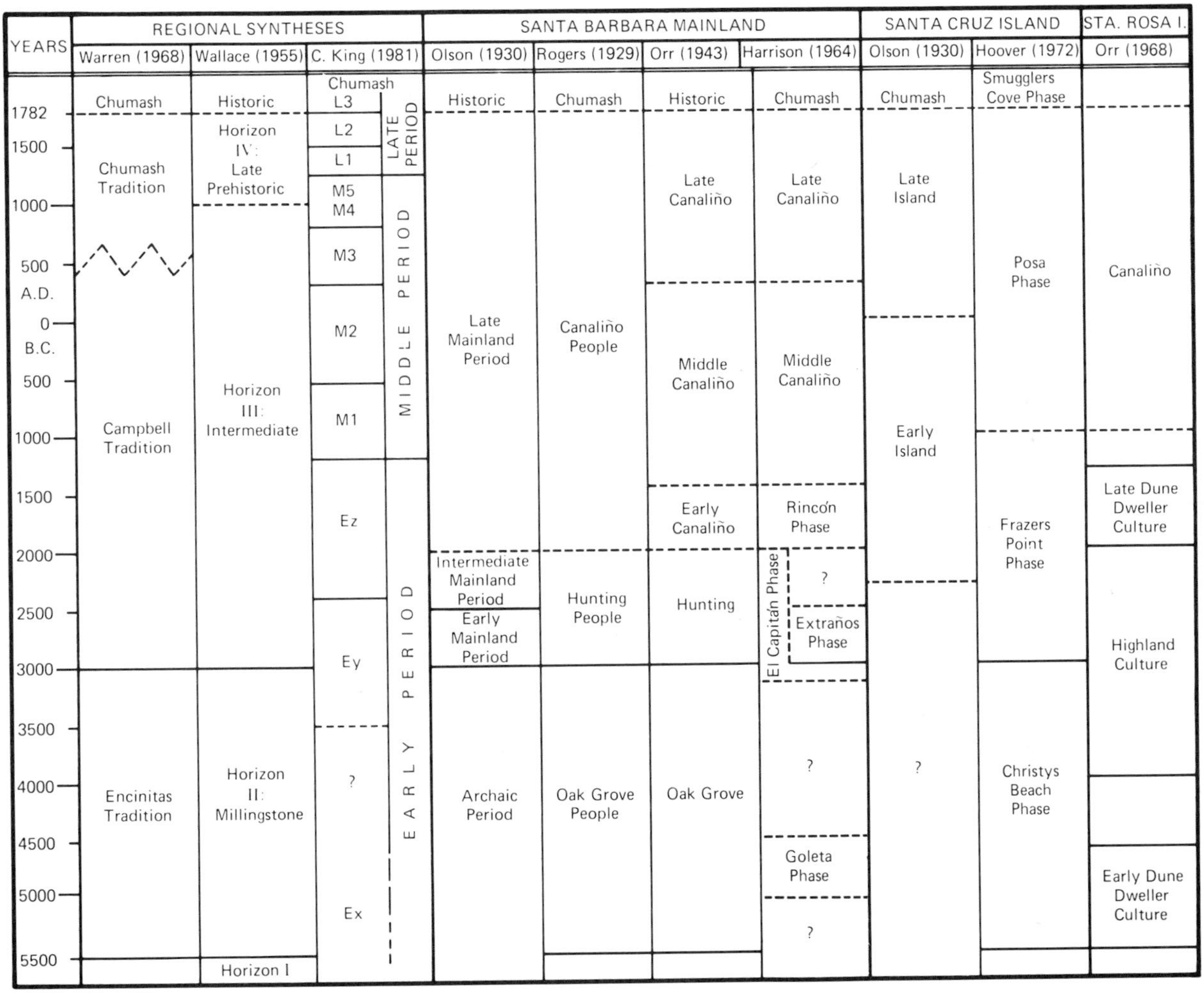

| YEARS | REGIONAL SYNTHESES | | | SANTA BARBARA MAINLAND | | | | SANTA CRUZ ISLAND | | STA. ROSA I. |
|---|---|---|---|---|---|---|---|---|---|---|
| | Warren (1968) | Wallace (1955) | C. King (1981) | Olson (1930) | Rogers (1929) | Orr (1943) | Harrison (1964) | Olson (1930) | Hoover (1972) | Orr (1968) |
| 1782 | Chumash | Historic | Chumash L3 — LATE PERIOD | Historic | Chumash | Historic | Chumash | Chumash | Smugglers Cove Phase | — — — |
| 1500 | | Horizon IV: Late Prehistoric | L2 / L1 | | | Late Canaliño | Late Canaliño | Late Island | | |
| 1000 | Chumash Tradition | | M5 / M4 — MIDDLE PERIOD | | | | | | | |
| 500 A.D. | | | M3 | | | | | | Posa Phase | Canaliño |
| 0 B.C. | | | M2 | Late Mainland Period | Canaliño People | | Middle Canaliño | | | |
| 500 | | Horizon III: Intermediate | | | | Middle Canaliño | | | | |
| 1000 | Campbell Tradition | | M1 | | | | | Early Island | | |
| 1500 | | | Ez | | | Early Canaliño | Rincón Phase | | Frazers Point Phase | Late Dune Dweller Culture |
| 2000 | | | | Intermediate Mainland Period | Hunting People | Hunting | ? — El Capitán Phase | | | |
| 2500 | | | Ey | Early Mainland Period | | | Extraños Phase | | | Highland Culture |
| 3000 | | | | | | | | | | |
| 3500 | | | ? | | | | | | | |
| 4000 | Encinitas Tradition | Horizon II: Millingstone | | Archaic Period | Oak Grove People | Oak Grove | ? | ? | Christys Beach Phase | |
| 4500 | | | | | | | Goleta Phase | | | Early Dune Dweller Culture |
| 5000 | | | Ex | | | | | | | |
| 5500 | | Horizon I | | | | | ? | | | |

**Figure 4.5** Concordance of archaeological units, Santa Barbara subregion.

the use of asphaltum. In the Intermediate Mainland Period, millingstones were lacking, whereas steatite *ollas*, inlay work of shell and beads, circular shell fishhooks, (Figure 4.7) and bone beads and tubes appeared for the first time. The Late Mainland Period included steatite *comales* and more *ollas* than before, but otherwise retained Intermediate traits (Olson 1930:16–17).

Olson deemed his Early Island Period to be coeval with the terminal Early Mainland and initial Intermediate Mainland periods (Figure 4.5). Early Island sites yielded few millingstones; bone pendants and charmstones were distinctive. European goods marked the recency of the Late Island Period, recognized by abalone shell ornaments in a "bewildering array of shapes and sizes," steatite *ollas* and *comales*, numerous fish-hooks, and occasional pottery (traded wares) (Olson 1930:18).

Unlike Rogers, Olson implied that the Santa Barbara cultures had developed in place, "even though the tribal or linguistic groups may have changed a number of times" (1930:20). He also allowed for the possibility of some Oceanian influence in the form of plank canoes, stone "club heads," circular shell fishhooks, and general maritime orientation (1930:21).

While R. L. Olson and D. B. Rogers investigated cultural change in Santa Barbara prehistory, Malcom J. Rogers of the San Diego Museum of Man defined a series of three complexes in western San Diego County. These he named the *Shell Midden, Scraper-Maker,* and *Historic Yuman Cultures* (Rogers 1929c). Initially, Rogers (1929c:466–467) guessed that a depletion of mollusks had caused Shell Midden groups to move inland and evolve into Scraper-Maker hunters. Rogers later (1939, 1945) reversed the order of the Scraper-Maker and Shell Midden Cultures and renamed them *San Dieguito* and *La Jolla,* respectively (Table 3.1 and Figure 4.17).

The sequences worked out by D. Rogers, R. Olson, and M. Rogers were pioneering efforts to identify and to order prehistoric complexes in southwestern California. These models of cultural succession differed from prevailing opinions that California cultures had not changed appreciably through the millennia. Although lacking absolute dates, the general outlines of Southern Coast prehistory sketched in 1929 and 1930 remain valid. Fifty years of additional research have confirmed that early Holocene complexes gave way to a series of related "millingstone cultures" (e.g., Oak Grove and La Jolla), which in turn were followed by increasingly specialized late prehistoric expressions (e.g., Canaliño and Yuman).

## Prehistoric Reconstructions: Santa Barbara Subregion

Much archaeological work was done in the Santa Barbara subregion during the first few decades (1930–1960) after the first local chronologies had been proposed. This period witnessed improved field methods, the advent in 1949 of radiocarbon dating, and a growing interest in prehistoric cultural ecology and social organization. Data gathered during this interval led to refined local sequences and provided the basis for regional syntheses. Some of the more important investigations are reviewed here.

*Topanga Canyon*

In 1946 R. F. Heizer and E. M. Lemert of UCB discovered and tested several sites on ridges and hilltops, about 6 km from the sea, in Topanga

Canyon, Los Angeles County (Figure 4.13). Compacted deposits with large, heavily patinated stone tools and a lack of obviously recent material suggested that these sites were fairly old (Heizer and Lemert 1947). Adán Treganza, assisted by C. Malamud in 1947 and A. Bierman in 1948, excavated two of the Topanga Canyon sites: LAn-1 (the Tank site) and LAn-2 nearby. The former proved to be a stratified habitation site exceptional for its yield of artifacts—nearly 80 per m³. In the lower of two components scraper-planes were the most common artifacts, with scrapers, choppers, core hammerstones, and a few projectile points rounding out the chipped-stone inventory (Figure 4.6). These tools were made of local fine-grained basalt, quartzite, porphyry, chalcedony, and chert. Several thousand millingstones and manos indicate that processing hard seeds was a major subsistence activity. A few mortar fragments and pestles in the upper component may attest to the use of acorns. Disposal of the dead was by secondary burial under millingstones (Treganza 1950; Treganza and Malamud 1950).

Treganza and Bierman (1958) identified two phases of the Topanga Complex: Phase I, described above, and Phase II as manifested at LAn-2 and in the upper 45 cm of LAn-1. Phase II is distinguished by small projectile points, incised and cogged stones, and fewer core tools than in Phase I; reburial continues along with the introduction of extended burials oriented to the south.

Further work at LAn-2 in 1957 allowed K. Johnson of UCLA to define a third Topanga phase, the hallmarks of which were large rock-lined ovens of circular plan, flexed burials (sometimes under stone cairns), mortars, pestles, pressure-flaked points, core tools, and plentiful millingstones (Greenwood 1959; K. Johnson 1966). Charcoal from Phase III levels at LAn-2 yielded five $^{14}$C dates ranging from 750 ± 150 to 490 ± 200 B.C. These $^{14}$C dates, along with artifact cross-dating, chronologically place Topanga Phase I earlier than 3000 B.C.; Phase II at circa 3000–1000 B.C.; and Phase III at circa 1000–0 B.C. (K. Johnson 1966:15, 20).

To sum up, the flake, core, and millingstone industries of the Topanga Complex seem to register an adaptation to, and perhaps seasonal occupation of, the Los Angeles County uplands by groups who hunted game and harvested seeds. As discussed in the following section, economic and technical similarities link the Topanga Complex with Oak Grove to the north and La Jolla to the south (Figures 4.5 and 4.17).

## Coastal Sites

Topanga-like components have been discovered at the Zuma Creek, Little Sycamore, Glen Annie, and many other coastal sites in the Santa Barbara subregion. From indurated deposits at the Zuma Creek site near Point Dume (Figure 4.13), S. L. Peck in 1947–1948 recovered mill-

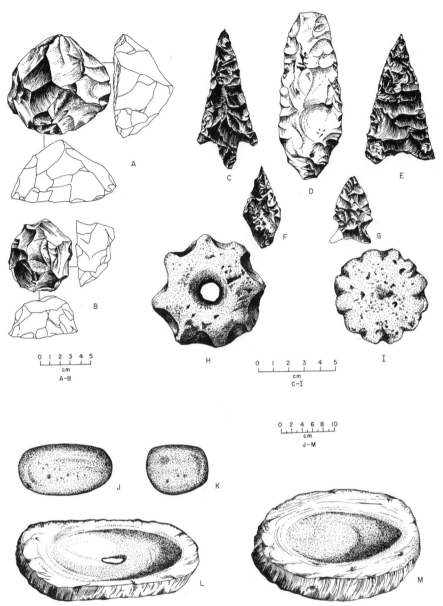

**Figure 4.6** Topanga Complex artifacts: A, B, scraper planes, Phase I; D, E, projectile points of Phase I types; C, F, G, projectile points of Phase II types; H, I, cogged stones; J, K, manos; L, M, millingstones. (After Treganza and Bierman 1958, Treganza and Malamud 1950; drawing by Randall Engle.)

ingstones, varied projectile points, core tools, and cogged stones—all similar to Topanga Phase II materials. This assemblage was duplicated at the nearby Zuma Mesa site (Ruby 1961). Of the small amount of shell present in the Zuma Creek site, California mussel accounted for the largest percentage of 16 identified species. The only other reported faunal remains were a few bits of artiodactyl, sea lion, and rabbit bones. Small pitted stones, not found inland, may have served to tenderize shellfish. Twelve graves were excavated at Zuma Creek, among them both reburials under millingstones and primary interments in various postures (Littlewood 1960; S. Peck 1955). The similarity of these burials and artifacts to those of Topanga II indicate a single component approximately 3000 to 5000 years old. In 1968 the Zuma Creek site was totally destroyed to make way for "terrace upon terrace of mobile homes" (T. King 1973d:13).

Located on the coast between Topanga Canyon and Santa Barbara, the Little Sycamore site (Ven-1) (Figure 4.13) was sampled in 1953 by W. J. Wallace of the University of Southern California. Two components were identified: an upper, friable black shell midden ≈60 cm thick with late prehistoric (Chumash) artifacts, and a lower stratum of compacted yellowish-red soil with caliche-encrusted artifacts and the remains of bay mussel, black abalone, deer, sea otter, and waterfowl (Wallace 1954). In the lower deposit Wallace found a large cairn of millingstones, many of which had been "killed" (ritually broken); human bones reposed below the cairn. Millingstones, manos, and hammers (including pitted stones) comprised about 70% of all artifacts. Completing the array were cores, choppers, scrapers, a few ovoid and foliate points, bone awls, shell ornaments, and two whelk shells with cut or gound ends—possibly bird calls or trumpets (Wallace 1954; Wallace *et al.* 1956).

The stratigraphic and cultural separation of the upper (Chumash) and lower (Millingstone) components at Ven-1 may imply either that Chumash culture did not evolve from Millingstone antecedents or that such evolution took place elsewhere during the period when the Little Sycamore site was unoccupied. Although Ven-1 has not been radiocarbon-dated, its earlier component is typologically like Topanga II and is probably 3000 to 5000 years old. Hence, the occupational hiatus and subsequent Chumash habitation must have occurred more recently than 3000 years ago.

Another coastal site related to the Topanga Complex is Glen Annie (SBa-142), excavated in 1960 by University of California, Santa Barbara, archaeologists under the direction of R. C. Owen. Resting on a small hill overlooking Goleta Slough (Figure 4.4), SBa-142 was an extensive, dark shell midden. Prominent among 27 identified species of marine mollusks in this deposit were the wavy chione, Washington clam, California mussel, speckled scallop, and banded chione. Recovered artifacts were like those of the Tank site (LAn-1). Eight burials were exhumed; all but one of

these were associated with large millingstone features (Owen *et al.*
(1964:454). Four radiocarbon dates place the occupation of Glen Annie
Canyon between 6380 ± 120 (UCLA-608) and 7270 ± 120 (UCLA-607)
B.P. Stratification and artifact analyses suggest possibly two components
representing "a temporarily inhabited, irregularly visited camp site utilized by a highly nomadic population" during the "Oak Grove Period"
(Owen *et al.* 1964:469, 435).

Briefly, then, the Glen Annie, Little Sycamore, and Zuma Creek/
Mesa sites shared a millingstone technology, a mortuary pattern of burial
under millingstone cairns, and indications of a diverse subsistence economy. Floral and faunal remains, along with subsistence-related artifacts,
indicate that seeds and other vegetal foods, fish, mollusks, waterfowl, and
both land and sea mammals were taken from diverse marine, seashore,
slough, and terrestrial environments. Apart from this subsistence and
littoral setting, however, the coastal Millingstone components shared
basic technologic and stylistic traits with those of the inland Topanga
Complex. It seems likely that the coastal and inland Millingstone assemblages were left by culturally, and perhaps socially, related peoples.
One possibility is that the Topanga and coastal Millingstone components
represent seasonal exploitation of different resource areas by a single,
mobile population.

Also important for reconstructing prehistory in the Santa Barbara subregion is the Malaga Cove site—a large, stratified midden near Santa
Monica Bay (Figure 4.12). In 1936–1937 Edwin Walker of the Southwest
Museum identified four cultural levels at Malaga Cove in deposits some
8.5 m deep. Levels 2–4 existed in a loose sand dune matrix, whereas the
basal stratum was a dense yellow detritus "almost as hard as stone" with
a thoroughly weathered upper surface (Walker 1951:38, 53). Millingstones first appeared in Level 2 ($\approx$7.0–7.7 m below the surface), as did
stone disks, pebble hammers, incised stones, and secondary burials under
rock cairns—all comparable to the Topanga II assemblage.

Later prehistory is documented by Canaliño materials in Level 3
($\approx$4.6–7.0 m deep): large mortars and long pestles (Figure 4.10), *Haliotis*
shell fishhooks (Figure 4.7), tarring pebbles, and steatite vessels. That the
Level 3 people were successful in hunting and fishing is shown by plentiful bones of seals, sea lions, sea otters, porpoises, deer, coyotes, and rabbits, along with those of albatross, ducks, gulls, loons, and many kinds of
fish. The Canaliño assemblage is retained throughout Level 4 (the upper
4.6 m), but with the addition of arrow points, basket-hopper mortars,
painted pebbles, glass beads, and flexed burials identifiable with the protohistoric and historic Gabrielino (Walker 1951).

Beneath the sand dune, within a "light, tan-colored, cliff-fed detritus,"
Level 1 yielded hundreds of chert flakes, flake knives and microliths, a
foliate-point fragment, asphaltum, hammerstones, red ochre and white

**Figure 4.7** Hunting and fishing implements of the Santa Barbara subregion. Example of (A) mounted harpoon point and (B) bone barb from Pitas Point (Ven-27) and Prisoners Harbor (SCrI-246), respectively; these are depicted as they would have been attached to a wooden shaft; (C–E) other harpoon barbs from SCrI-246; *Haliotis* shell fishhooks from *Kaxas*, Prisoners Harbor, SCrI-240 (F, H) and *Noqto*, SBa-210 (G); late period projectile points from *Soxtonokmú*, Alamo Pintado site, SBa-167 (I, J) and SBa-485 (K, L). (Courtesy of the Department of Anthropology, University of California, Santa Barbara.)

diatomaceous earth, shell spoons, scoops, beads, pendants and inlays, cut bone tubes, and pointed to spatulate objects of bone. The remains of no fewer than 12 mammalian and 14 avian species, along with numerous unidentified fish bones, were taken from Level 1. Of special interest were the bones of porpoises, sea otters, seals, and sea lions—probable evidence for the use of watercraft—and the permineralized remains of an extinct flightless scoter. Level 1 also contained thousands of mollusk shells accounting for 33 species, mostly cockles, scallops, and cove oysters (Walker 1951).

Walker's (1951) opinion that Level 1 may be quite old is supported by several observations: (1) the unconformity separating Levels 1 and 2 is thought to represent a long interval of weathering prior to the time of dune midden accumulation; (2) Level 1 lacks millingstones, and elsewhere in southern California millingstones first appear between circa 8500 and 7500 B.P.; (3) chipped-stone artifacts from Malaga Cove 1 resemble those from components at the C. W. Harris and Rancho Park North sites, $^{14}$C-dated circa 8000 to 9000 B.P.; (4) the Level 1 material occurs in a late Pleistocene terrace deposit, whereas the overlying dune is of Holocene age (Walker 1951); and (5) K. Johnson (1966:21) has reported a $^{14}$C date of 6510 ± 100 B.P. on shell "equitable with . . . level 1" at Malaga Cove. All things considered, Level 1 probably is older than 6500 years. That the first residents of the Malaga Cove site were well adapted to the seashore is confirmed by the abundant remains of mollusks, sea mammals, fish, and waterfowl in the subdune stratum; this implies that their origins were elsewhere on the coast. For reasons as yet unknown, Malaga Cove was abandoned and not reoccupied until sometimes after circa 5000 B.P. Subsequent intensive use of the site culminated in the Canaliño developments, which, at the protohistoric–historic level, are associated with the Gabrielino.

Further information about cultural succession, as well as unexpected insights into mortuary practices, in the Santa Barbara subregion resulted from George Carter's 1937 testing of a site near Point Sal (Figure 4.4). This 10-m-deep midden exhibited three strata with progressively darker soils, more shell and ash, and less clay from the bottom stratum (I) to the top (III). Strata I and II were ascribed to the Hunting Period, whereas Stratum III was identified as Canaliño (Carter 1941). The continuous development from Hunting to Canaliño at Point Sal, along with the hiatus between Millingstone and Chumash levels at Little Sycamore, seems to imply that Chumash culture evolved—at least in part—from Hunting antecedents.

In Stratum III at Point Sal, Carter exposed an unusual cemetery. Of 47 burials, fully half of the skeletons (most identified as female) lacked mandibles; 71% of all skulls were broken; the foramen magnum had been enlarged in 61% of the skulls (reportedly all male); and 69% of the skeletons were incomplete yet without signs of postinterment disturbance. Carter (1941:219) proposed that these observations might be explained by a complex burial ritual involving mutilation of the corpse, followed by delayed or secondary burial. It seems just as plausible, however, that Carter may have found the result of hostilities. In either event, grave goods indicate that the cemetery had been used by early Chumash people. Many of the graves were funished with distinctive beads, asphaltum-coated baskets, knives, and *Haliotis* shell ornaments.

## Summary

Building upon the earlier studies of D. Rogers (1929) and R. Olson (1930), research between 1930 and 1960 led to a more detailed understanding of mainland prehistory in the Santa Barbara subregion. Excavations in Topanga Canyon during the late 1940s and again in 1957 disclosed a record of three Millingstone phases, beginning as early as circa 6000–5000 B.C. and persisting until circa A.D. 1. At Zuma Creek a single component with mortuary traits and artifacts like those of Topanga II (ca. 3000–1000 B.C.) further verified the close relationship between coastal and inland (or pericoastal) Millingstone expressions.

At the stratified Little Sycamore site Canaliño materials rested unconformably upon a lower cultural unit resembling Topanga II and Zuma Creek. More complex stratigraphically was the Malaga Cove site, where an early (6500–4500 B.C.?) nonmidden level was separated unconformably from later Hunting and Canaliño midden deposits. The Hunting to Canaliño transition was also documented at Point Sal. As a result of these and other discoveries, by about 1960 the basic outlines of prehistory had been sketched for the Santa Barbara mainland, and local variations were being defined. This work provided a basis for subsequent regional syntheses and studies of cultural change.

## Channel Island Prehistory

As noted previously, much of the early (ca. 1870–1930) archaeological work on the Channel Islands was exploratory, unsystematic, and intended mainly to produce artifact collections for museums. With the stratigraphic excavations by R. Olson (1930) on Santa Cruz Island, however, attention began to shift toward chronology and the definition of cultural sequences. Notable progress in this direction was made by P. C. Orr of the Santa Barbara Museum of Natural History. Some 20 expeditions between 1947 and 1968, allowed Orr to identify and radiocarbon date four cultural phases of Holocene age on Santa Rosa Island (Figure 4.4). The first is the Early Dune Culture (ca. 5500–2000 B.C.), known from cemeteries and habitation sites in coastal sand dunes. From Early Dune middens, composed predominantly of *Haliotis* shell and the bones of large fish, have come crude chert projectile points, "digging stick weights" (perforated stones), and distinctive shell beads and ornaments. Burials in sitting positions are accompanied by red ochre.

The following Late Dune Dweller Culture (ca. 2000–1000 B.C.) is known from dune sites containing shells of mussels and more black than red abalone. Flexed burials occur with "Gypsum Cave" type points, mortars, certain kinds of *Olivella* beads, and more steatite and bone artifacts than before. Culminating the Santa Rosa Island sequence (Figure 4.5) is the Canaliño Culture (ca. 1000 B.C.–A.D. 1600), for which there is ample evidence of dense populations subsisting on abalones, mussels, cockles, fish, and sea mammals. Richly furnished burials and reburials with stone or wooden grave markers occur in crowded cemeteries (Orr 1951a, 1952b,c, 1956b, 1960b, 1968).

Orr has also described a Highland Culture (ca. 4000–2000 B.C.), so named because of sites on ridges away from the shore. Apart from its inland setting, the Highland culture is identified by abundant mortars and a dearth of mollusk shells; diagnostic types of artifacts are said to be lacking (Orr 1968:100). The Highland occupation seems not to have been a distinct culture, but rather a reflection of special (seasonal?) use of inland resources, such as acorns or pine nuts, by groups whose main settlements were closer to the sea.

During the 1950s and 1960s other investigators (e.g., McKusick 1959a; Roziare 1959b, 1962a, 1965, 1967) also conducted fieldwork on the northern Channel Islands. As summarized by Glassow (1980:80), two key objectives of this work were to "systematically inventory the archaeological resources [and] identify the major periods of prehistoric development." Since circa 1970 additional survey and evaluation studies, including some testing, have been carried out, mainly to satisfy cultural resources management data needs of the federal government (Glassow 1977; Greenwood 1978a; Rozaire 1978). The 1970s also witnessed a program of basic research, initiated by A. Spaulding and M. Glassow of the University of California, Santa Barbara (UCSB), to investigate the evolution of maritime adaptions (Glassow 1980:81).

Although progress is being made, the basic outlines of Channel Island prehistory have been sketched only tenously. Orr's Santa Rosa Island sequence, for example, is based upon so few [14]C-dated components that significant refinements may be expected as more data become available. The same can be said of R. Hoover's chronology for Santa Cruz Island, derived from his (1971) analysis of materials collected during the 1920s by R. Olson. A more detailed and recent study is C. D. King's (1981) analysis of diachronic changes in artifact types, and the social implications of these changes, throughout the Santa Barbara Channel region. King's reconstruction is discussed later in this chapter.

M. Glassow (1977, 1980) has summarized the major results of past archaeological investigations on the northern Channel Islands. Regarding populations and settlement patterns, he observes that site densities tend to be much higher on the islands than on the mainland. This is believed to be a result of higher population mobility, rather than higher population density, on the islands:

> That is, whereas mainland population aggregates may have seasonally occupied, perhaps, only five sites in the course of an annual cycle, the population aggregates on the islands may very well have occupied a far greater number, largely because of a much greater dependence by the islanders upon intertidal resources such as various species of shellfish. (Glassow 1981:84)

Based upon C. King's (1971) estimates of Chumash village sizes, the northern Channel Islands (excluding Anacapa) supported population densities on the order of 2.9 to 4.8 people per km², in contrast with densities of ≈8.1/km² on the mainland coast between Rincón Point on the east and Gaviota on the west. Glassow (1980:86) attributes this difference to the much lower terrestrial resource diversity on the islands than on the mainland coast and to the circumstance that "the relatively greater abundance of marine resources around the peripheries of the islands did not offset the mainland advantage of having bountiful supplies of different kinds of terrestrial food resources."

Although the islanders collected shellfish, took waterfowl, and gathered vegetal products, their principal subsistence activities were fishing and sea mammal hunting. The archaeological record shows that fishing technology became more elaborate and specialized with time, suggesting an evolution of fishing strategies and emphases. L. J. Tartaglia's (1976) functional analysis of fishhook forms representing various periods of island prehistory shows that bone gorge hooks were employed as early as circa 3000 B.C. to catch shallow-water fish; later, circa A.D. 1, circular or J-shaped fishhooks (Figure 4.7:F–H) of shell or bone came into use for catching near-shore bottom feeders. The taking of certain schooling fishes (e.g., herring) by net or seine seems to have been a late prehistoric development; other kinds of schooling fishes were taken by hook much earlier in time. Glassow (1980:89–90) has proposed that the diachronic increase in the importance of fishing, along with the elaboration of fishing technology to obtain a broader range of species, may have been a result of insular population pressures and the need to obtain ever larger amounts of food from marine sources.

Analyses of faunal remains from Channel Island sites have shown that sea mammals, too, figured prominently in the prehistoric diet. Abundant seal and sea lion bones may attest to hunting at rookeries with clubs and harpoons; dolphins and porpoises most likely were harpooned from boats.

The early economy of the Channel peoples also included both inter-island trade and commerce with the mainland. For instance, eth-nohistoric accounts indicate that the Chumash of the northern Channel Islands may have produced nearly all of the shell beads found at mainland sites in Southern California (C. King 1971), a conclusion supported by the archaeological evidence: "Nearly every late prehistoric site on Santa Cruz Island contains abundant olivella shell detritus resulting from bead manufacture, along with small chert bladelets with narrowed chipped tips that were used to drill holes in the beads" (Glassow 1980:94).

Thus, Channel Island groups appear to have survived and prospered in large measure because of their flexible and mixed economic strategy. Their subsistence was derived not only from the resources of island lit-toral and inland zones, but also from the marine realm. Necessary and desirable items not available on the islands could be obtained through trade with mainland peoples—a system that fostered technical specializa-tion (e.g., in bead manufacturing) on the islands.

Before leaving the Channel, mention should be made of underwater discoveries. During the past half century, numerous artifacts have been found in underwater locations along the southern California coast. At least 33 marine sites off the Santa Barbara mainland and Channel Islands have produced more than 90 artifacts, chiefly mortars, millingstones, and grooved stones. Mortars weighing as much as 165 kg have been recovered from waters 2–15 m deep off the islands, and more than 100 stone vessels have been found off La Jolla in waters deeper than 30 m (Hudson 1976:7, 8, 16).

The seabed location of these artifacts has given rise over the years to many speculations about their origins, ranging from the idea that some of the heavier stone items had anchored Indian boats to the notion that local archaeological materials had been included with ships' ballast jettisoned during the historic period. Having reviewed many such ideas in light of a careful analysis of the specimens and their discovery sites, Hudson (1976) concluded that there are five plausible explanations for the marine dis-coveries: (1) some artifacts may have fallen into the ocean as a result of seacliff erosion of archaeological sites; (2) some coastal sites probably were inundated by rising seas during early and mid-Holocene times; (3) occasional accidents may have involved the sinking of Indian boats and their cargo; (4) the grooved stones were evidently fishnet sinkers and would have been lost from time to time in the course of normal use; and (5) certain stone vessels may have been thrown into the sea intentionally for ceremonial reasons (Hudson 1976:29–49). These possibilities would seem to account for most if not all of the known Indian artifacts from seabed locations off the southern California coast.

# The Santa Barbara Sequence Revisited

*Coastal Phases*

In 1941 P. C. Orr excavated at the Mescalitan Island site (SBa-46) near the mouth of Goleta Slough (Figure 4.4). The results led him to redefine D. Rogers's Canaliño Period into Early, Middle, and Late units (Figure 4.5), each distinguished by mortuary patterns and by types and relative numbers of such artifacts as shell ornaments and steatite vessels (Orr 1943). As there was no hiatus from Early to Late, the entire Canaliño sequence was thought to chronicle Chumash prehistory.

Further adjustments to cultural chronology resulted from excavations during the 1950s by N. E. Gabel and W. M. Harrison of UCSB at six sites on the Santa Barbara coast. Five of these were single components; the sixth (*Mikiw*, SBa-78) contained four components (Figure 4.4). A series of 19 radiocarbon dates from three of the sites indicates that all, except a historic Chumash living area at SBa-78, were occupied between circa 5100 and 1500 B.C. These investigations led Harrison (1964) to modify greatly D. Rogers's (1929) local sequence.

Harrison's chronology (Figure 4.5) begins with the Goleta Phase (ca. 5100–4500 B.C.?), marking the arrival of Oak Grove (Millingstone) People on the Santa Barbara Coast. Following a gap in the archaeological record, the Oak Grove occupation resumes with the El Capitán Phase (ca. 3350–1950 B.C.). Both the Goleta and El Capitán phases reflect a land-oriented economy mainly focused on vegetal foods but with minor use of small mammals and littoral resources. These subsistence patterns, along with large numbers of millingstones, implied to Harrison (1964:365) that the Oak Grove People had come from the inland deserts.

The Extraños Phase (Figure 4.5) is said to record the intrusion of Hunting People at circa 2900 B.C. Thereafter, culturally and ethnically distinct Oak Grove and Hunting societies are thought by Harrison (1964) to have coexisted along the Santa Barbara Channel for nearly 1000 years. Phases of each, dated circa 3000–2500 B.C., occur in identical environments near Goleta Slough. Just as the Oak Grove economy was attuned to land resources, the Hunting People exploited the sea. The bones of seals, porpoises, dolphins, whales, swordfish, and sharks, coupled with large accumulations of mollusk shells, attest to this maritime orientation in Extraños Phase components at the Aerophysics (SBa-53) and Corona del Mar (SBa-54) sites (Harrison and Harrison 1966) (Figures 4.8–4.10).

Harrison (1964:368–369) discounts the possibility of Extraños origins in the mainland California area because it lacks maritime cultural expressions, at 2900 B.C. or earlier, with artifact inventories comparable to the SBa-53 assemblage. Instead, he offers this amazing scenario:

The Hunting People were originally a maritime people who immigrated southward along the Pacific coast from Alaska, possibly following the yearly southern migration of the Northern Fur Seal. . . . It is further suggested that the immigration occurred by way of coastal navigation in substantial boats, possibly the plank canoe or its predecessor. (Harrison and Harrison 1966:68)

**Figure 4.8** Hunting Period or Campbell Tradition projectile points. A, B, San Miguel Island; C–F, Vandenberg Air Force Base. (Courtesy of the Department of Anthropology, University of California, Santa Barbara.)

**Figure 4.9** Hunting Period or Campbell Tradition gound-stone artifacts: A, mortars; B, pestles. All from the Aerophysics site (SBa-53). (Courtesy of the Department of Anthropology, University of California, Santa Barbara.)

Calling attention to similarities between Extraños Phase artifacts and those of the Palisades II Phase from near Cape Krusenstern, Alaska, Harrison (1964:371) argues that the Hunting People may have originated with a landfall by Palisades II seafarers. An alternative view is presented later in this chapter.

Around 2000 B.C., the Hunting and Oak Grove Peoples are said to have merged into a single Rincón Phase (ca. 1950–1450 B.C.)—the beginning of the Canaliño culture (Table 4.1). Thereafter, until historic times, the Canaliño continued to evolve as a single ethnic group ancestral to the Chumash (Harrison 1964:376).

Harrison attempted to redefine the Santa Barbara sequence by positing the long coexistence and later merging of Oak Grove and Hunting Peoples. This differed from D. Rogers's (1929) sequence in which Hunting People followed, and were separate from, Oak Grove People. Now, with the benefit of hindsight and more data, the technical differences between coeval late "Oak Grove" and early "Hunting" assemblages seem better explained in terms of specialized site function than in terms of intrusive and autochthonous populations. That is, differences between sites with a predominance of millingstones and those with the products of marine exploitation may simply represent seasonal or other economic activities

**Figure 4.10** Late Period or Chumash ground-stone artifacts. The flat-rimmed, "flower pot" mortars are from SBa-734, Vandenberg Air Force Base, and the pestles are from (left to right) SBa-126 (El Capitán) and SBa-167 (*Soxtonokmú*, or Alamo Pintado, site). (Courtesy of the Department of Anthropology, University of California, Santa Barbara.)

by a single, mobile population rather than many centuries of sympatric ethnic and cultural parallelism.

The averred Alaskan origin of the Hunting People seems most improbable. Even the sudden appearance of a developed maritime economy, suggested at SBa-53, seems doubtful in light of considerable evidence for the gradual evolution of maritime adaptations elsewhere in the region (Glassow *et al.* 1975; Greenwood 1972; C. King 1981; Meighan 1959c; Tartaglia 1976).

The gradual intensification of marine resource exploitation is especially well documented for the Channel Islands. On Santa Rosa Island the Early Dune Dwellers (ca. 5500–2000 B.C.) took large fish and at least some sea mammals, presumably with the aid of boats; by circa 500 B.C. fishing had become a very important enterprise (Orr 1968). Likewise, on Santa Cruz Island fish were taken throughout the prehistoric sequence (Figure 4.5), and sea mammals were hunted intensively during the Frazers Point Phase, beginning circa 3000 B.C. (Hoover 1971). Schooling fish in the open channel probably were taken as early as circa 3000 B.C. (Glassow 1980:90). Such observations imply that the maritime orientation in Santa Barbara prehistory was a local development and not intrusive.

## Coastal–Inland Relationships

While highlighting maritime economic strategies of the Chumash, it is worth remembering that these people also occupied substantial inland areas. Archaeologists have investigated many of the interior village- and camp sites, among them Conejo Rockshelter or Ven-69 (Glassow 1965), Triunfo Rockshelter (Kowta and Hurst 1960), Rancho Cañada Larga or Ven-58 (Greenwood and Browne 1963), Ven-70 (Leonard 1966), and Mulholland or LAn-246 (Galdikas-Brindamour 1970). Interior areas appear to have been settled both seasonally by coastal groups and permanently by Inland Chumash populations who hunted deer, caught salmon, and gathered acorns, sage seeds, and other vegetal products.

Three sites—LAn-225, -227, and -229—on the Century Ranch in western Los Angeles County (Figure 4.13) have provided evidence of inland–coastal economic relationships over a long span of time. Excavations in 1961 and 1962 by UCLA showed LAn-225 to be a single-component "Millingstone Horizon" site. Sites LAn-227 and -229, dated to circa A.D. 500–1300 and 1550–1800, respectively, contained fewer millingstones and more projectile points, drills, beads, steatite vessel fragments, pipes, mortars, pestles, and bone tools (C. King et al. 1968). Despite their location nearly 7 km from the sea, these sites yielded the bones of 19 species of fish. Among these are albacore and skipjack—tuna-like pelagic species occurring in waters far from land in southern California. Also represented are large rockfish, which inhabit the sea bottom zone in relatively deep water (Follett 1968:137). Other faunal remains attest to the hunting of deer and smaller animals, especially rabbits and squirrels. From these and other data, C. King et al. (1968) concluded that LAn-227 and -229 probably were base settlements or villages from which parties ventured out to specialized activity sites, both farther inland and on the coast.

A few kilometers north of Century Ranch, the Oak Park vicinity in the upper Medea Creek drainage (Figure 4.12) has been investigated as part of the Inland Chumash Archaeological Project. Directed by C. W. Clewlow, Jr., the Project in 1977 and 1978 excavated four sites (Ven-123, -125, -294, and -375) and collected surface materials at 13 others (Clewlow et al. 1978; Clewlow and Whitley 1979). This work confirmed occupation of 3000 years or more at both permanent and seasonal sites. Earlier sites were identified with Millingstone cultures; later ones with the protohistoric Chumash. The researchers at Oak Park defined a series of *site complexes*—coeval, functionally linked settlements and diverse activity stations presumably used by a single population. The most significant shift discerned in the Oak Park archaeological record was "a sociological change in the spatial distribution of activities" at circa A.D. 500 (Clewlow and Whitley 1979:174); otherwise, the basic subsistence economy seems not to have changed appreciably over time.

Chumash adaptation to inland areas such as the Santa Monica Mountains was part of a complex socioeconomic system deeply rooted in prehistory (Leonard 1971). Social ranking and trade relationships among headmen may have permitted the exchange of goods between inland and coastal resource areas. Indeed, one view is that some of the Interior Chumash required coastal goods in order to maintain population levels (Galdikas-Brindamour 1970).

Several archaeologists have proposed models to account for social and economic interaction between coastal and inland Chumash groups (Spanne 1975; Tainter 1972, 1975). For example, Tainter has observed that the Ynez Valley Chumash may have experienced marked annual fluctuations in the availiabity of deer, salmon, and certain food plants. To ensure demographic stability, they reportedly "bought" coastal surplus foods and "sold" their own surplus when yields were high—a system of redistribution controlled by headmen. According to Tainter (1972:97–98), the economic preeminence of the coast would have led to a generally lower ranking of interior villages in the exchange network; at least some coastal villages held interior settlements under their jurisdiction.

Glassow (1979), however, has shown that acceptance of such models may be premature because several key assumptions (e.g., the idea that the Inezeño Chumash exploited salmon runs) have not been confirmed archaeologically. He argues cogently (1979:158–159) that more archaeological and environmental facts will be needed before patterns of Interior Chumash cultural ecology and their place in the larger Chumash interaction sphere can be worked out.

## Social Status and Mortuary Patterns

Archaeological mortuary patterns that may reflect social ranking have been reported at the Medea Creek cemetery (LAn-243) near Agoura in the

Santa Monica Mountains (Figure 4.13). Excavation of the entire cemetery by UCLA archaeologists revealed a western area with the remains of 259 to 300 individuals in relatively shallow graves, often associated with rock features, and an eastern area with 137 to 164 deeper burials and no rock features. Exact burial counts were not possible because of poor bone preservation, secondary interments, and disturbance of some burials by later grave digging. Shell beads (Figure 4.11) indicate a protohistoric to

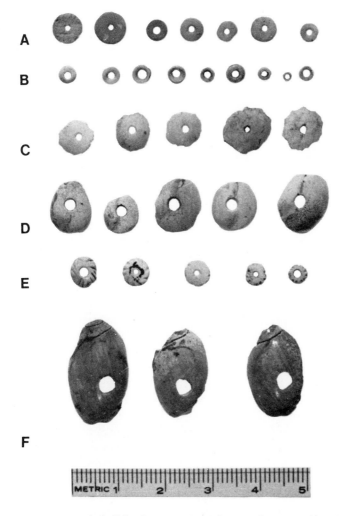

**Figure 4.11** Late Period shell-bead types: A, *Haliotis rufescens* epidermis discs; B, *Olivella* callus cupped beads; C, *Olivella* rough-chipped wall discs (Mission Period); D, *Olivella* callus full-lipped beads; E, *Olivella* incised-wall discs; F, *Olivella* split-punched beads. A–E from Ker-307, *Kashtiq*; F from SBa-72. Types after C. King (1974). (Courtesy of the Department of Anthropology, University of California, Santa Barbara.)

early historic age and approximate contemporaneity of the graves (L. King 1969).

Burials at Medea Creek displayed significant variablity of age, sex, depth of burial, position, orientation, and grave accompaniments between the eastern and western portions of the cemetery. Whereas eastern graves tended to be furnished with few items, western graves often included conspicuous wealth. Of 23 types of *Olivella* beads found in the Medea Creek cemetery, 21 were more frequent in the west and many of these were entirely lacking in the east. Caches of shell beads and ornaments, projectile points, shark teeth, ochre, fuchsite, and crystals of quartz, sulfur, and gypsum also were significantly more numerous in the western lobe of the cemetery. These differences have been interpreted as due to "the use of these areas by kinship groups of differing statuses" (L. King 1969:27).

The Medea Creek cemetery research is important because it shows that mortuary remains may reflect social behavior. This implies that, in regional perspective, analyses of mortuary patterns at other, earlier sites may illuminate aspects of social evolution in Chumash prehistory.

## Channel Prehistory: An Integrated Chronology

Over the years scholars have grappled with problems of cultural chronology in the Santa Barbara subregion. Diverse schemes featuring from three to eight phases (Figure 4.5) have been advanced to represent Channel Island or mainland prehistory after circa 6000 B.C. (Harrison and Harrison 1966; C. King *et al.* 1968; Meighan 1959b, 1965; Olson 1930; Orr 1943, 1968; D. Rogers 1929; Wallace 1955a, 1978b; Warren 1968). The most recent, comprehensive, and definitive research along these lines is embodied in C. King's *The Evolution of Chumash Society* (1981). To construct a detailed temporal sequence for the Channel area, King analyzed numerous grave lots (each lot being a group of artifacts found together in a single grave and thus thought to be more or less contemporaneous) from several major collections. Among the materials studied were those collected by R. Olson in 1927–1928 on the mainland coast and Santa Cruz Island, by P. M. Jones in 1901 on Santa Rosa Island, and by D. Rogers, P. Orr, and others at various mainland and island sites. Temporal control for King's study was provided by stratigraphy, radiocarbon and obsidian hydration dating, cross-dating (i.e., comparison of items in the grave lots with typologically identical items in dated contexts elsewhere), and of course by seriating the lots themselves.

King's study depends mainly on analyses of shell beads and ornaments, but it also encompasses myriad other types of bone, shell, and stone artifacts. His temporal sequence, like that of the mid-Central Valley (Lillard *et al.* 1939), consists of Early, Middle, and Late periods. King has divided each period into phases (Figure 4.5) and each phase into more refined subdivisions. Many of the characteristics used to differentiate the periods and some phases are the same in both southern and central California:

> The large temporal divisions of Early, Middle, and Late Periods are closely parallel, and subdivisions of the Late Period Phase 1, Phase 2a, Phase 2b and Phase 3 are also based on bead type change common to both areas. Finer time distinctions and the phases of the Middle and Early Periods recognized in this work have at present poorly defined correlations with subdivisions in Central California because many of the artifacts used to distinguish finer periods in Central California are not found in the Channel region. (C. King 1981:45–46)

The higher frequencies of southern California beads and ornaments in Late Period central California probably attest to the increasing economic integration of the two areas—a development previously recognized by B. Gerow's (1974b) model of "co-traditions and convergent trends in prehistoric California" (see Chapters 5 and 6).

King's *Early Period* (>5000–1000 B.C.) incorporates the cultural units previously identified as Oak Grove and Hunting (D. Rogers 1929), Archaic, Early Mainland, and Early Island (Olson 1930), the Millingstone Horizon and much of the Intermediate Horizon (Wallace 1955a), Dune Dweller (Orr 1968), and the Encinitas and early Campbell Traditions (Warren 1968). The Early Period entails no fewer than three phases. The *Middle Period* (ca. 1000 B.C.–A.D. 1100) exhibits more types of beads and ornaments than before, and is marked in part by a shift from rectangular to circular *Haliotis* and *Olivella* beads. Encompassed by the Middle Period are Middle Canaliño, early Late Mainland, late Intermediate Horizon, and late Campbell expressions (Figure 4.5). Five Middle phases (M1–M5) are recognized. The *Late Period* (A.D. 1100–1804), marked in southern California by the occurrence of *Olivella* callus beads and clam disk and cylinder beads, subsumes Late Canaliño. Late Mainland, Late Prehistoric, Late Island, and Chumash Tradition manifestations (C. King 1981:46–74) (Figures 4.5 and 4.12).

King's widely accepted chronology includes both Channel mainland and island prehistories in a single sequence. This reconstruction is more temporal than cultural in the sense that diachronic changes in artifact assemblages mark time and distinguish periods but do not necessarily imply cultural replacement. In Fact, King (1981:327) opines that Chumash society was developing in place for more than 7000 years. Through time, however, changing types and frequencies of beads, ornaments, and other valuables probably reflected economic and social evolution. In this regard, King has shown that the primary function of certain valuables shifted from ornamental in early times to economic in later times. Beads, for instance, came to be used less for display and more for exchange or as

**Figure 4.12** Reconstruction of Chumash coastal village. In protohistoric times, Chumash villages of 50 to 1000 or more residents were situated along the shores of the Santa Barbara Channel. (Drawing by Adán E. Treganza.)

"storable" wealth. Also, certain types of beads apparently were used only by "members of the families of hereditary leaders," whereas others were used by those "affiliated with families of political leaders" (C. King 1981:323–324). King's cultural sequence, therefore, provides a record of economic and social evolution as well as stylistic changes in Santa Barbara Channel prehistory.

## Prehistoric Reconstructions: San Diego Subregion

The prehistory of the San Diego subregion roughly parallels that of Santa Barbara insofar as early Millingstone cultures preceded locally distinctive cultures of later times. Also, both areas were exposed to some of the same external influences. Nonetheless, the particulars of cultural development differed in each subregion and became increasingly divergent by late prehistoric times.

## La Jolla Complex

Throughout much of southwestern California, San Dieguito and related premillingstone occupations were followed by various expressions of the La Jolla Complex (originally termed *Shell Midden Culture*). As described by M. Rogers (1939, 1945) and redefined by Harding (1951), the La Jolla Complex is recognized by millingstone assemblages in shell middens, often near sloughs and lagoons. Geographically, it extends from coastal Orange County to central Baja California (Kaldenberg 1976:46). Characteristic of La Jolla are basined millingstones, unshaped manos, a preponderance of flaked cobble tools, a few Pinto-like projectile points, and, occasionally, perforated stones. Burials tend to be flexed, heads to the north, under stone cairns (Rogers 1939, 1945; Warren *et al.* 1961).

The age of the La Jolla Complex has been well established by radiocarbon dating. Radiocarbon ages of 6300 ± 240 and 4720 ± 160 years have been determined for La Jolla levels at the C. W. Harris site (SDi-149) (Warren 1967a), and at the Scripps Estates site (SDi-525) in La Jolla, mussel shells from a La Jollan midden and cemetery yielded four $^{14}$C dates ranging from 7370 ± 100 to 5460 ± 100 B.P. (Hubbs *et al.* 1960). Corroborating dates have been obtained from La Jollan components at Rancho Park North (SDM-W-49), 6900 ± 280 B.P. (Kaldenberg 1976); Monument Mesa (SDi-222), 7260 ± 80, 6540 ± 70, and 3640 ± 60 B.P. (Bingham 1978); and at many other sites (M. Bright 1965). The oldest known La Jollan remains in southwestern California were found at SDi-4669, where bone collagen from a skeleton buried under a cairn of "killed" millingstones yielded a $^{14}$C age of 8360 ± 75 years (Ike *et al.* 1979:526). (Site locations are shown in Figure 4.13.) On the near end of the temporal scale, the La Jolla Complex seems to have persisted in the San Diego subregion until ≈3000–2000 years ago (Kaldenberg 1976:47).

Some writers divide the La Jolla Complex into phases to reflect developmental changes (Figure 4.17). Rogers (1945) distinguishes La Jolla I and II based on cemeteries, evidence of Channel Island trade, and improved lithic technology in the latter. Moriarty (1966) allows for three phases, as "suggested by typological change coordinated with stratigraphically controlled radiocarbon dating." These are La Jolla I (5500–3500 B.C.), identified by flexed burials, the first appearance of millingstones, and crude percussion-flaked scrapers; La Jolla II (3500–2000 B.C.), with true cemeteries, ground-stone discoidals, and several types of projectile points in addition to the Phase I inventory; and La Jolla III (2000–1000 B.C.), showing Yuman cultural influence from the east (Moriarty 1966:21–23).

It is notable that one of the oldest ceramic industries in America is preserved in a La Jollan site. C. E. Drover (1975) has described a series of vessel sherds and cylindrical to figurine-like forms from the Irvine site (Ora-64) near upper Newport Bay (Figure 4.12). Fifteen pieces have been

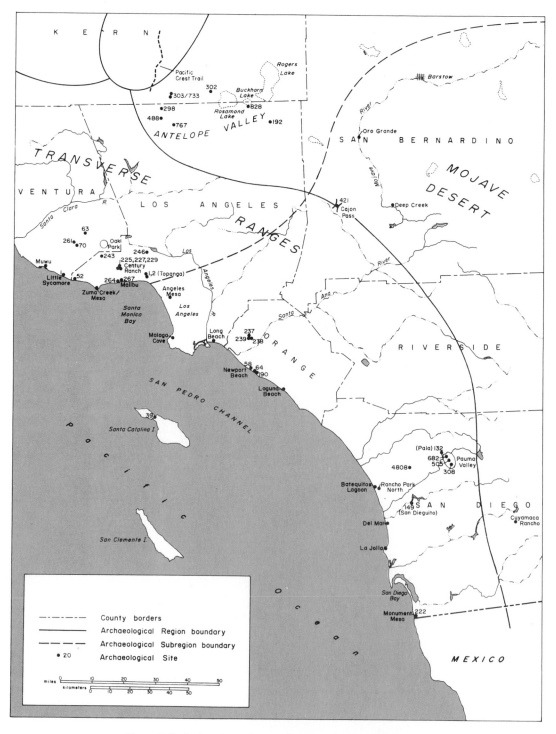

**Figure 4.13** Archaeological sites of southwestern California. (Map by Allan Childers and Thad Van Bueren.)

recovered from less than 0.1% of the deposit (which covers ≈70,000 m²!). Colors grade from yellowish brown to very dark brown. Some specimens have punctate or shell-incised decorations. These ceramics occur in a cultural context typified by large-stemmed and indented-based points, millingstones, and flexed, highly permineralized burials (Drover *et al.* 1979:287). In all, 23 $^{14}$C age determinations ranging from 8045 ± 270 to 4900 ± 80 years have been obtained on marine shell carbonate from the Irvine site. Shell samples apparently associated with the ceramics have yielded $^{14}$C dates of 7150 ± 150 to 6220 ± 130 B.P. Thermoluminescent dating of two artifacts gave *minimal* ages of 3200 and 3650 years (Drover *et al.* 1979:293). Two figurine-like fired clay objects also have been found at the Little Harbor site (SCaI-17) on Santa Catalina Island in a stratum $^{14}$C-dated at 3880 ± 250 B.P. (Drover 1978:81). These findings show that there was an early, indigenous ceramic industry in southern California quite separate from the later (ca. A.D. 900) introduction of pottery from the southern Great Basin and Colorado River. However, because the early ceramics are known from only two sites, any definition of their range in time and space would be premature until more data are available.

Among the more intriguing artifacts from La Jollan sites are discoidal and cogged stones. The former are usually round to ovoid ground stones with flat to slightly convex faces and edges (Figure 4.14). Specimens in two measured collections averaged ≈9.3 cm in diameter and ≈ 5.3 cm thick (Moriarty and Broms 1971; Warren *et al.* 1961), whereas Sutton (1978) reports discoidals averaging ≈14.5 cm in diameter and ≈6.2 cm thick from SDi-4575 near San Elijo Lagoon. Two of the largest examples (>20 cm in diameter) occurred in a collection of 39 discoidals from Ora-83 in Bolsa Chica (Herring 1968). Most stone discoidals are well made and, although a few have slight concavities pecked into one or both faces, none shows any obvious use-wear. Some broken stones were found glued together with asphaltum (Dixon 1975). Cogged stones are like the discoidals with respect to size and workmanship, but have grooves or indentations along their edges giving them a gearlike appearance (Figure 4.14). The number of grooves ranges from 1 to more than 20, with 10 to 15 common. Likewise, the size and form of the cogs are highly variable, and the stones may be either perforate or imperforate (Eberhart 1961; McKinney 1968). Cogged and discoidal stones are found from southern Ventura County to Baja California, mainly in the coastal drainage, but rare specimens have turned up as far from the coast as Cajon Pass and Fossil Falls (K. Dixon 1968; Herring 1968).

Most cogged and discoidal stones seem to have been made between circa 4000 and 1000 B.C. (K. Dixon 1968, 1975; Moriarty and Broms 1971). Interestingly, the two are often found together, but seldom with other kinds of artifacts. Frequently there is evidence of purposeful burial; for example, Winterbourne (1938, 1968) reported finding cogged and discoidal stones in clay below middens in Orange County sites. At one of these,

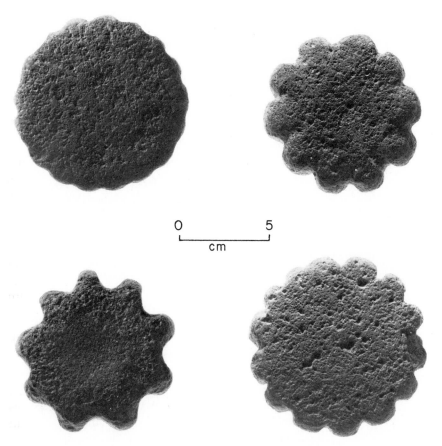

**Figure 4.14** Cogged stones from southwestern California. These were part of a cache of 11 cogged and discoidal stones, reportedly buried in a pile or stack, discovered in 1930 at Rancho Los Cerritos in Long Beach. (Photograph courtesy of Keith Dixon, Department of Anthropology, California State University, Long Beach.)

the Banning–Norris site (Ora-58) near Costa Mesa, cogged stones were buried intentionally in submidden pits, and there were many stones cached side by side or superimposed (K. Dixon 1968). Similarly, four discoidal and seven cogged stones (Figure 4.14) recorded in 1930 at Los Cerritos Ranch had been buried purposely in a "straight stack" (K. Dixon 1975:26). Such occurrences, along with the enigmatic form of the artifacts, have led variously to speculations that the stones were used as club heads, gaming pieces, oil lamps, rope-making tools, nut crackers, or, invariably, as "ceremonial objects" (Eberhart 1961; Moriarty and Broms 1971; G. Smith 1950). The fact is, however, that we do not know the function of the discoidal and cogged stones (although a purely utilitarian function is difficult to imagine). Even so, it is notable that these artifacts distinguished the La Jolla Complex before circa 1000 B.C., prior to the intrusion of desert traits from the east.

There are several hypotheses to account for the origins of the La Jolla Complex. Warren *et al.* (1961:28) proposed that it began sometime prior to 7500 years ago with the arrival on the coast of a simple gathering people from the interior desert. The reason for this westward movement may have been that the California deserts became increasingly unfavorable for human habitation as Altithermal climates set in (Warren and Pavesic 1963:420–421). Once on the coast, early La Jollan groups would have learned quickly to exploit shellfish and other littoral resources.

A related model was advanced by M. Kowta (1969), who showed that the preparation of agave and, later, yucca for food and/or fiber most likely was a primary function of the numerous scraper-planes found in Millingstone components. Kowta proposed that "agave exploitation entered southern California from the interior at the onset of the Altithermal when the agave itself diffused into the area as a result of shifting climatic conditions" (1969:68). Thereafter, the intensity of agave utilization would have been locally conditioned by competition with shellfish- and acorn-gathering activities.

A third proposition, favored by Moriarty (1966, 1967), Kaldenberg (1976), and others, views the La Jolla Complex as derived *in situ* from San Dieguito antecedents. This notion finds support in the apparent continuity between San Dieguito-like and La Jollan components at Agua Hedionda Lagoon and Rancho Park North (see Chapter 3). Finally, it is possible that all three models are partly correct. Climatic warming after circa 6000 B.C. may have stimulated movements to the coast of desert peoples who then borrowed littoral adaptations from older groups while sharing with them their millingstone and scraper-plane technologies and seed- and agave-processing skills. In this regard, the La Jollan economy and toolkit seem to indicate a fusion of coastal and desert traits and not outright cultural replacement.

## The Pauma Complex

In 1958 D. L. True identified a complex similar to both La Jolla and San Dieguito in an area east of Escondido in the Peninsular Ranges of northern San Diego County. An examination of nearly 25 sites revealed San Dieguito-like flaked-stone crescents and leaf-shaped points or knives associated with La Jollan millingstones, core scrapers, and stone discoidals. The name *Pauma Complex* was assigned to these materials, after the Pauma Valley (Figure 4.13) where some of the sites occur (True 1958). Geologic aspects of the sites and stone tool types suggested an age of some 8000 years for the Pauma Complex. Moreover, "a rather abrupt break and considerable separation in time between the Pauma Complex and San Luis Rey I [ca. A.D. 1400–1750] is indicated by obvious dissimilarities in artifact types and site locations" (True 1958:257).

As a result of additional surveys after 1958 and further analysis of artifacts, True recognized that the Pauma Complex as originally defined may have been a conglomerate of San Dieguito-like materials, Millingstone elements, and assemblages with Millingstone artifacts unlike those typical of the La Jolla Complex (True 1977:6).

Several of the sites provisionally related to the Pauma Complex have been sampled by excavation. Two of these, the Molpa (SDi-308) and Pankey (SDi-682) sites, seem to include San Luis Rey and Millingstone (La Jollan?) components, but no San Dieguito elements (True 1977, 1980:6–8). Another possible Pauma site is SDi-4558 in Moosa Canyon near Escondido (Figure 4.13), tested in 1977 by R. Cook of the California Department of Transportation. Apart from a few San Luis Rey pot sherds near the surface, excavations at SDi-4558 revealed 130 cm of Millingstone cultural deposits with several San Dieguito-like points in the upper levels (R. Cook 1977, 1978). Pending further work, the stratigraphy and identification of a Pauma component at SDi-4558 remain equivocal.

True has summed up what is known of the Pauma Complex:

> (1) The Pauma Complex inventory is very similar to that of the adjacent coastal La Jollan . . . and some undefined but close relationship is proposed between the two; (2) the Pauma Complex as defined here includes very little actual evidence of San Dieguito elements . . . ; and (3) there may be evidence in the area (sometimes associated with Pauma Complex sites) of the Campbell intrusion proposed by Warren. (True 1980:37)

All things considered, the Pauma Complex may be an inland variant of the La Jolla Complex associated in some way with the Campbell intrusion. Pauma site locations, paucity of stratified deposits, and large numbers of surface sites with millingstones may imply seasonal occupation by La Jollan groups whose main settlements were on the coast.


*Sayles Complex*

A long prehistory has been defined at the Sayles site in Cajon Pass—a narrow gap in the Transverse Ranges linking the San Gabriel Mountains on the west with the San Bernardino Mountains on the east, and the Mojave Desert on the north with the Los Angeles Basin on the south (Figure 4.13). Because of its geographic location, Cajon Pass lies in close proximity to the varied resources of desert, mountains, and coastal plain.

Archaeological research in the Cajon Pass vicinity began during the late 1940s when various sites were recorded by G. A. Smith, R. J. Sayles, A. Mohr, and A. Bierman. The first excavations in the area were conducted in Summit Valley at Las Flores Ranch, the location of a major village, *Guapiabit*, occupied by either the Vanyume (W. Strong 1929:7) or Serrano (Kroeber 1925:615). Pottery, mortars, arrow points, and circular house depressions at *Guapiabit* typify the protohistoric occupation of the area (Moseley and Smith 1962; Bowers 1976).

The prehistory of the Transverse Ranges is best known from M. Kowta's (1969) report of 1965 excavations at the Sayles site (SBr-421). Kowta's chronology, which relates the effects of environmental change on economic and social systems, begins before 6000 B.C. with the San Dieguito Complex during the Anathermal climatic period. The next period, 6000–3000 B.C., is interpreted as one of warming and drying—the Altithermal climatic phase (Antevs 1948, 1952, 1955)—when populations moved from the mountains toward the coast (Kowta 1969:36). The millingstones, manos, and scraper-planes in coastal Millingstone Horizon (Wallace 1955a) assemblages from this period are seen as evidence for growing reliance on seed collecting and processing brought about by climatic change.

Kowta (1969) interprets the period from 3000 until 1500 B.C. as a time of cooler, moister conditions—the Medithermal climatic episode (Antevs 1948, 1955)—when the Mojave Desert was more intensively used, as evidenced by the Pinto Basin Complex. Assemblages from this period in the Transverse Ranges document a blending of Millingstone and Pinto Basin expressions (Kowta 1969:39). Characteristic of the period between 1000 B.C. and A.D. 1000 is the Sayles Complex, consisting largely of percussion-flaked scraper-planes, cores, plano-convex scrapers, choppers, and hammerstones (Kowta 1969:1). The Sayles Complex and the late Topanga Complex are similar; both exhibit a "superabundance of scraper planes, milling stones, manos, hammerstones, other percussion flaked core and flaked tools, cogstones, quartz crystals, small incised stone objects, blades, and side-notched, contracting stemmed, lozenge-form and foliate points" (Kowta 1969:45). Differences between the two complexes, such as the absence of mortars and pestles at the Sayles site, are attributed to the effects of the Shoshonean intrusion forming a wedge across the Transverse Ranges. Kowta concludes that the Sayles Complex "represents a post-1000 B.C. remnant of a Milling Stone Horizon–Pinto Basin continuum that existed along the Transverse Ranges in early Medithermal times" (1969:1).

## Late Prehistory

The late prehistoric period in southwestern California was a time of cultural transformations brought about by trait diffusion, immigration, and *in situ* adaptation to environmental changes. Along the coast, subsistence practices in the later phases of the La Jolla Complex evolved in response to changes in the littoral environment after circa 2000–1000 B.C. (Warren 1964; Crabtree *et al.* 1963). These developments included (1) a shift toward land-based gathering in place of lagoon-based shellfish collecting (diminished because of lagoon silting) and (2) retention of marine-oriented subsistence patterns in certain favored locales and the ultimate emergence of a weak or quasi-maritime economy (True 1966:290).

At some time during or following these adjustments, acorn processing (as evidenced by mortars and pestles) was introduced, probably from the north. Because of this new subsistence focus, land-use patterns shifted to interior upland areas and away from the previously favored coastal zone (True 1966:290). At about the same time as, or soon after, the appearance of acorn-related traits, the practice of cremation appeared on the Southern Coast. It is possible that cremation was brought into some coastal areas as a result of the Shoshonean intrusion from the deserts (True 1966:291). In the southern part of the region, however, "relationships with the Colorado River region are more obvious, and it is almost certain that Diegueño ceramics and mortuary practices [cremation and urn burial] had a Colorado River origin with possible influences reaching as far as the Hohokam in southwestern Arizona" (True 1970:58). As for chronology, Moriarty (1966:23) reports that the "Yuman" practice of cremation had replaced La Jollan inhumation by circa 500 B.C. at the La Jolla Beach and Tennis Club site in coastal San Diego County.

For inland San Diego County there appears to be a hiatus in the cultural sequence between the time of occupation by Millingstone (La Jolla, Pauma?) groups and the late prehistoric period (Figure 4.17), but this may indicate reduced activity rather than abandonment of the inland tracts (True 1977:10). The late period is represented by several complexes that can be correlated with specific linguistic groups. One of these is the *San Luis Rey Complex*, first identified by Meighan (1954) and later refined by True *et al.* (1974). Excavations in 1953 by C. W. Meighan at SDi-132, near Pala ≈35 km from the ocean in San Diego County, revealed cremations, bedrock mortars, millingstones, triangular arrow points, bone awls, and stone and shell ornaments. This became the type component for the protohistoric San Luis Rey I Complex, tentatively dated by Meighan at circa A.D. 1400–1750. A San Luis Rey II Complex featured the earlier assemblage along with pottery vessels, cremation urns, red and black pictographs, and such nonaboriginal items as metal knives and glass beads (Meighan 1954:223) (Figure 4.15). Inferred San Luis Rey subsistence activities include hunting and gathering with an emphasis on acorn harvesting.

Many other San Luis Rey components have been reported since the time of Meighan's work (R. Cook 1978; McCown 1955a; True 1966). Data now indicate that pottery may have been introduced to the San Luis Rey

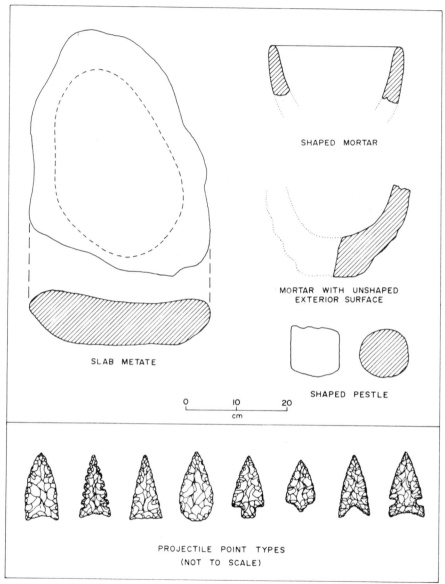

SHAPED MORTAR

MORTAR WITH UNSHAPED
EXTERIOR SURFACE

SLAB METATE

SHAPED PESTLE

0    10    20
cm

PROJECTILE POINT TYPES
(NOT TO SCALE)

**Figure 4.15** Artifacts typical of the San Luis Rey Complex from site SDi-132 near Pala, San Diego County. These materials are thought to represent activities of late prehistoric Luiseño Indians. (After Meighan 1954: Figure 2; redrawn by Thad Van Bueren.)

culture, probably from the south, as early as circa A.D. 1200–1600 (True *et al.* 1974). Also, the San Luis Rey materials initially were attributed to the ancestors of the Diegueño, but True (1966:204 ff.) has shown that this complex almost certainly represents the forebears of the Luiseño.

In coastal Orange County, Ross (1969) has defined the Irvine Complex (ca. A.D. 600–1800). Like San Luis Rey, the Irvine Complex represents late prehistoric to historic Luiseño occupation. The main difference between the Irvine and San Luis Rey Complexes seems to be economic: The former reflects littoral adaptation, whereas the latter is inland-oriented. Ora-190, an Irvine Complex shell midden near Newport Bay (Figure 4.13), yielded remains of 65 species of marine invertebrates, 3 marine mammals, and 11 species of fish (Ross 1970), whereas San Luis Rey sites contain virtually no traces of coastal products. Three $^{14}$C dates ranging from A.D. 405 ± 350 to A.D. 1100 ± 250, along with typological cross-dating, support Ross's (1970:110) view that Ora-190 was inhabited between circa A.D. 600 and 1450. The earlier date would imply as well that the predecessors of the Luiseño had settled near Newport Bay at least 1350 years ago.

D. T. Hudson has extended the known range of the San Luis Rey Complex to the interior mountains of Orange and southern Los Angeles Counties. Hudson (1969) analyzed data from Ora-237, -238, and -239 in Santiago Canyon, ≈20 km inland, excavated in 1935 and 1937 by the Federal Works Progress Administration (WPA) and the State Emergency Relief Administration (SERA). Artifacts from these and nearby sites are basically like those of San Luis Rey I and are included within that phase (Hudson 1969:58). A historic Intermontane Phase (ca. A.D. 1750–1850) also was tentatively defined for interior Orange County. Mortar styles, deer-tibia whistles, apparent lack of pottery, and the placement of cremated remains in stone vessels distinguish this phase from San Luis Rey II (Hudson 1969:58–59).

In the southern interior of San Diego County the protohistoric Diegueño are known archaeologically as the *Cuyamaca Complex*. Based upon investigations in Cuyamaca Rancho State Park, True (1970:53–54) identified the following as traits that set the Cuyamaca Complex apart from San Luis Rey, despite a number of shared items: cemeteries apart from living areas, use of grave markers, cremations placed in urns, use of specially made mortuary goods (miniature pots, elaborate projectile points, etc.), abundant ceramics in a wide range of forms, a steatite industry, and numerous millingstones (Figure 4.16). The Cuyamaca Complex is thought to be the end product of a continuous development from La Jollan antecedents, with influence from Colorado River peoples (True 1966, 1970).

As True (1966:294) has noted, the continuity between La Jolla and the historic Diegueño (speakers of a Hokan language) is significant. Because there is no break in the sequence, it is probable that speakers of Hokan languages were responsible for the Millingstone cultures, at least in the San Diego subregion. A comparable situation likely occurred in the Santa Barbara vicinity, where the Chumash seem to have developed from a

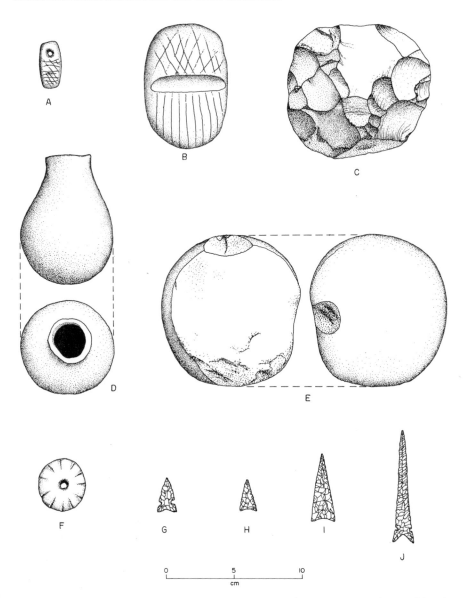

**Figure 4.16** Artifacts typical of the Cuyamaca Complex, representing late prehistoric Diegueño occupation, from Cuyamaca Rancho State Park, San Diego County. A, incised steatite pendant; B, incised steatite shaft-straightener; C, domed scraper plane; D, ceramic miniature olla; E, pebble hammerstone; F, molded, incised pottery disc; G–J, projectile points. (After True 1970: Plates 2, 4–6; redrawn by Thad Van Bueren.)

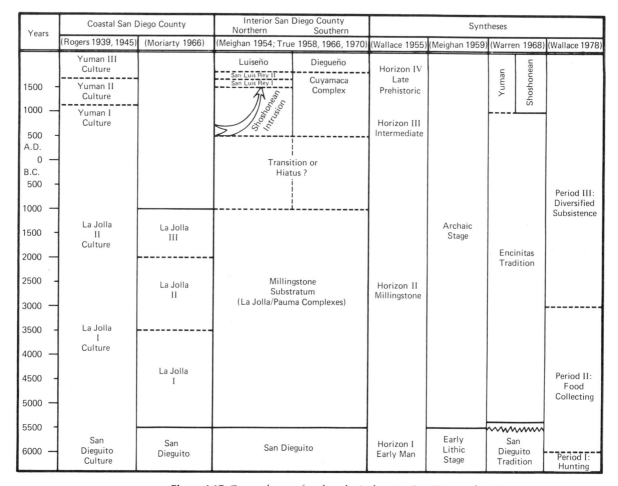

**Figure 4.17**  Concordance of archaeological units, San Diego subregion.

similar, related Millingstone culture (True 1966:294–295). The northern (Oak Grove) and southern (La Jolla) Millingstone cultural continuum would have been broken between 3500 and 2000 years ago by the spread of Shoshonean (Takic) groups in the coastal area between the Chumash and Diegueño (Figure 4.17).

## Regional Syntheses

In 1955 W. J. Wallace advanced a pioneering synthesis of Southern Coast prehistory. Four widespread cultural horizons were proposed, each with significant local variation: Horizon I, Early Man; Horizon II, Millingstone Assemblages; Horizon III, Intermediate Cultures; and Horizon IV, Late Prehistoric Cultures (Figure 4.17). To Horizon I Wallace (1955a: 215–218) tentatively assigned the San Dieguito, Angeles Mesa, Malaga Cove I, "Los Angeles Man," and the Rancho La Brea materials.

The better-known Horizon II was characterized by extensive use of millingstones and core tools, but a paucity of projectile points, bone, or shell artifacts. Rock cairns over primary or secondary burials with meager grave goods were typical. Within this horizon Wallace (1955a) placed Oak Grove, Little Sycamore, Topanga, Zuma Creek, Malaga Cove II, and La Jolla. Horizon II peoples relied heavily upon shellfish and vegetal resources; hunting and fishing, according to Wallace, were less important.

Abundant projectile points, along with faunal remains confirming dependence on both land and sea mammals, distinguished Horizon III. Shellfish also contributed materially to the diet, but fishing apparently did not. A shift from millingstone and mano to an emphasis on mortar and pestle may signify increased reliance on acorns. Mortuary customs included both cremation and diverse forms of burial. Assigned to this horizon were the Hunting Culture and La Jolla II (Figure 4.17). One Horizon III site, Big Tujunga Wash in Los Angeles County, yielded about 40 Hohokam pot sherds (ca. A.D. 600–800) from southern Arizona; these provided one index as to the age of Horizon III (Wallace 1955a:222).

Horizon IV was recognized by dense populations and cultural elaboration. Typical were skillfully made artifacts, increased use of the bow and arrow, pottery vessels (in the south), circular shell fishhooks, generous use of asphaltum, and numerous bone and shell artifacts. Intensive fishing and sea mammal hunting accompanied the continued interest in collecting. Flexed burials were common in the north, whereas cremation was the preferred disposal mode in the south. The Canaliño and San Luis Rey cultures were assigned to this horizon (Wallace 1955a).

Wallace's (1955a) synthesis was basically descriptive and classificatory, emphasizing the content of archaeological cultures and the relationships among them. As a normative model, it defined *horizons* on the basis of typical or "normal" elements rather than the range of traits and how or why they changed through time. With few absolute dates available, Wallace's sequence lacked chronological precision. Even so, it remains valid to this day as a broad outline of prehistory in southwestern California.

By 1965 enough radiocarbon dates were available for C. W. Meighan tentatively to order West Coast prehistory by periods and to identify certain cultural trends through time. Meighan (1965:712) posited that, before circa 2000 B.C., coastal peoples were land-oriented nomadic hunters who left "little evidence of utilization of marine resources even though many of [their] sites overlooked the Pacific." From circa 2000 B.C.

until historic times the coast was settled by more sedentary groups adapted to various environmental niches. Some coastal people depended primarily on ocean resources and became progressively more skilled at acquiring them. Through time, the archaeological record shows increasing populations and cultural diversification (Meighan 1965:712–713).

In a now-classic overview, C. N. Warren (1968) synthesized Southern Coast prehistory using the concepts of cultural tradition and cultural ecology. *Cultural tradition* was defined as "a generic unit comprising historically related phases," and *cultural ecology* was viewed as "the interrelationship between a cultural tradition and its environment(s)" (Warren 1968:1). The model built upon these concepts allows for more cultural variation at one time than does a model based upon horizons.

Warren proposed five traditions (Figure 4.5 and 4.17), the first being San Dieguito (see Chapter 3). The second tradition, Encinitas, incorporates La Jolla, Oak Grove, Topanga, and related Millingstone complexes. Hence, Wallace's Horizon II would be subsumed under this tradition. Encinitas assemblages share crude chopping, scraping, and cutting tools, numerous millingstones, discoidal and cogged stones, and infrequent projectile points; shell is present in variable quantity, but bone is rare. Weaving is known from a rush mat and basketry impressions on asphalt at a few sites (F. Curtis 1964; Moriarty 1966). Loosely flexed and extended burials predominate in the north, reburials are common in the Los Angeles County area, and flexed burials typify the San Diego subregion. Grave goods, other than cobble or millingstone cairns over burials, are unusual (Warren 1968:2).

Available $^{14}$C dates indicated to Warren that the Encinitas Tradition began at about the same time (ca. 5500 B.C.) in both San Diego and Santa Barbara Counties. In the south, this tradition evidently persisted until sometime after A.D. 1, but near Santa Barbara it ended between circa 3000 and 1500 B.C. (Warren 1968:2). The earlier part of this chronology is now open to revision. At Diablo Canyon, San Luis Obispo County, Greenwood (1972:86) has reported $^{14}$C dates of 6460 ± 190 and 5570 ± 170 B.C. for a millingstone component at site SLO-585 (see Chapter 3). Similarly, Glassow *et al.* (1975) reported testing at Vandenberg Air Force Base a number of sites, including four thought to contain millingstone components more than 7500 years old. Five $^{14}$C dates arrayed between 6040 ± 350 and 5630 ± 300 B.C. support this estimate (Martz 1976:34). Finally, Ike *et al.* (1979:526) reported a $^{14}$C date of 6410 ± 75 B.C. for a millingstone cairn burial from coastal San Diego County. It would thus appear that the Encinitas Tradition was established from Diablo Canyon to the San Diego vicinity, and probably beyond, by circa 6000 B.C.

Warren's next tradition, Campbell, incorporates the Hunting Culture (Harrison 1964, 1965) and related expressions along the Santa Barbara coast. Campbell sites contain mortars and pestles, flake scrapers, a variety of shell and bone ornaments, and numerous projectile points along with quantities of sea and land mammal bone and fish remains. Burials, often accompanied by red ochre or Haliotis shell dishes, are flexed with heads to the north or west. The Campbell Tradition is dated as early as 3030 B.C. at SBa-53 in Goleta (Figure 4.4). In this area the Campbell and Encinitas traditions apparently overlap in time because at SBa-78 the Encinitas burials are dated at 3350 and 2500 B.C., bracketing the dates for the Campbell component at SBa-53. Harrison (1964) sees this as evidence for two contemporary populations and traditions, of which Campbell was intrusive. Campbell Tradition influence is seen also in the Topanga II Complex, at Zuma Creek, and in the Little Harbor site on Santa Catalina Island. The Goffs Island site (Winterbourne 1967) near Laguna Beach may be an Orange County manifestation of the Campbell Tradition (Warren 1968:3).

The Campbell Tradition evidently gave rise to the Chumash Tradition, archaeologically recognized by a maritime economy, elaborate technology, and a profusion of beads, ornaments, and ceremonial and artistic items. Chumash assemblages feature stone bowls, mortars, "digging stick weights," animal effigies, and projectile points; bone awls, scepters, hairpins, fishhooks, whistles, and tubes, the latter often overlain by shell bead appliqué (Figure 4.18); and shell beads, ornaments, and fishhooks. Burials tend to be flexed, face down, with heads to the north or west, in cemeteries with marked graves and copious funerary offerings (Warren 1968:3–5).

Between Chumash territory and northern San Diego County there is evidence—as yet not well dated—of a "Shoshonean" movement from the interior to the coast. Inland sites seem to be related to those of the deserts farther east (Ruby 1970:116–117). Among the Shoshonean Tradition elements are cremation, pottery, and small triangular arrow points. This

**Figure 4.18** Bone tube with *Olivella*-shell bead overlay, late Middle Period or early Campbell Tradition, from SBa-46 on Mescalitan Island. (Courtesy of the Department of Anthropology, University of California, Santa Barbara.)

tradition is represented in inland San Diego County by the San Luis Rey I and II phases, assignable to the forebears of the Luiseño. Farther south, the Cuyamaca Phase is linked to the protohistoric Diegueño and represents the Yuman Tradition—a blending of Colordo River area traits with those of the older Encinitas Tradition in far southwestern California (Warren 1968:5).

Each of these traditions also is distinguished by certain economic patterns or ecological adaptations. According to Warren (1968), Encinitas Tradition peoples intensively harvested seeds and collected shellfish, but did little hunting. This reconstruction has been challenged by Koerper (1981), who shows that hunting, fowling, fishing, and shellfish collecting—as well as gathering vegetal foods—were important Encinitas Tradition activities. Campbell Tradition peoples added acorn processing to their subsistence repertoire, gathered mollusks, hunted terrestrial game, took waterfowl, and gradually developed a maritime economy (i.e., an emphasis on marine fishing and sea mammal hunting), culminating in the Chumash Tradition. It may be that the Campbell–Chumash lifeways never fully penetrated the San Diego subregion because the environment there was not as rich in fish and game as it was near Santa Barbara (Warren 1968:12). The intrusive Shoshonean Tradition borrowed heavily from the Chumash, adopting a maritime economy in the northern part of its coastal domain. In terms of adaptation, the Yuman Tradition was the most generalized. Yuman peoples hunted (mostly small game), collected shellfish, gathered acorns and other plant products, and did some fishing (Warren 1968).

## Summary and Conclusions

California's southern coast has experienced a long and rich prehistory. The earliest inhabitants are little known archaeologically, yet one may assume that they were hunter–gatherers who entered the region prior to 9000 B.C. (see Chapter 2). The early Holocene cultures are better known. At Diablo Canyon, Agua Hedionda Lagoon, Rancho Park North, and other sites, the material record attests to fishing, intensive shellfish collecting, and some hunting by nomadic or possibly semisedentary groups between 7370 and 6060 B.C. A $^{14}$C date of 7100 B.C. from SBa-210 (Martz 1976) shows that coastal Santa Barbara County also was occupied during this period.

The subsequent Encinitas Tradition may have developed *in situ* from coastal antecedents, with the addition of Millingstone elements from the east, or it may reflect the westward migration of desert peoples. The apparent continuities from San Dieguito to Encinitas components at Agua Hedionda Lagoon, Rancho Park North, and Diablo Canyon support the proposition that Millingstone traits diffused to coastal dwellers. The Topanga I Complex, on the other hand, may reflect migration because it has no known predecessors locally. Although more data will be needed to resolve this problem, it seems clear that a new subsistence emphasis appeared on the coast soon after 6500 B.C. The rapid spread of millingstone technology, with or without population movement, may have been triggered by the onset of Altithermal climatic conditions and resultant biotic changes.

While recognizing millingstones as a marker of the Encinitas Tradition and as evidence of new technoeconomic practices, one should not assume that hard-seed processing eclipsed other subsistence activities. As H. Koerper (1981) points out, the roles of hunting, fowling, and fishing in the Encinitas Tradition have been greatly underestimated in the past. Analyses of faunal remains from two sites in Orange County, for example, revealed "a tremendous diversity in vertebrate procurement with respect to kinds of animals taken, habitats exploited, and capture techniques utilized beginning in the Milling Stone Tradition. Even sea mammal hunting was an important factor" (Koerper 1981:481).

After circa 3000 B.C., coastal cultures became increasingly diversified and economically specialized (Wallace 1978b). In the San Diego subregion, the La Jolla Complex persisted as a distinctive expression of the Encinitas Tradition. On the Santa Barbara coast the Campbell Tradition emerged as a blend of new fishing and marine mammal hunting emphases with the older collecting, hunting, and gathering foci. Many Encinitas traits, among them millingstones and coarse flaked-stone tools, were retained by the Campbell Tradition even as it evolved into the Chumash Tradition (Leonard 1966:223; Warren 1968:8).

The origins of the Campbell Tradition have vexed archaeologists for many years. In 1929 D. Rogers (355–357) proposed a migration from the interior to explain the advent of the Hunting People (i.e., the Campbell Tradition). Like Rogers, Wallace (1978b:30) reasoned that "since the artifacts closely parallel those found farther east in the Pinto Basin and elsewhere, movement of an inland hunting–gathering population to the Pacific shore seems a logical conclusions." Earlier, Harrison (1964:368) had rejected such a mainland California origin because he thought that it would not account for the maritime orientation of the Hunting Culture. Instead he offered the amazing idea that maritime adaptation in the Santa Barbara Channel area began with a migration of seafarers from Alaska.

None of these proposals is especially satisfying, mostly because they attempt to explain a problem that may not exist, namely, the "sudden" appearance of a maritime tradition along the Santa Barbara Channel. Several lines of evidence demonstrate that the maritime economy evolved gradually, *in situ,* and was not implanted abruptly as a result of migration. For example, C. King's (1981) meticulous analysis of artifacts from numerous sites on the Channel mainland and islands shows only incremental formal and stylistic changes, implying fundamental cultural continuity from Encinitas to Campbell times (Ex to Ez Periods; Figure 4.5); no wholesale cultural replacement is indicated. In fact, King (1981) argues that the ancestors of the Chumash lived in the Santa Barbara subregion for more than 7000 years. Moreover, as Koerper (1981) has shown, the previously assumed sharp distinction between Encinitas and Campbell adaptive strategies is open to question. Both Encinitas and Campbell Tradition sites contain the remains of shellfish, fish, water-fowl, and sea and land mammals. Shellfish were taken on the southern California coast by 6000 B.C. or earlier, and direct evidence of both fishing and sea mammal hunting extends through all of the known Holocene prehistory of the Channel Islands and mainland coast; what changed through time were the intensity and emphases of marine resource exploitation (Glassow 1980; Tartaglia 1976).

All factors considered, the Encinitas to Campbell transition seems to reflect progressive economic changes rather than population replacement. In this regard the Pinto projectile points in Campbell Tradition sites probably found their way to the coast by trade and not by a westward migration of desert peoples. Many of the points are made of obsidian and other exotic materials, indicating that they were produced in the desert interior. The points may have been obtained from eastern groups in exchange for shell ornaments or other coastal products.

Over a span of millennia, the Campbell Tradition evolved into the Chumash Tradition—certainly one of the more elaborate cultural developments in California prehistory. Archaeologically, as well as ethnographically, the Chumash are recognized by large villages (Figure 4.12), dense populations, social ranking, intensive trade, craft specialization, and a distinctive art style. A specialized, partly maritime economy sustained Chumash society. Cyclical rounds of population dispersion and aggregation were followed to optimize the use of seasonally available resources, especially seed crops, pelagic fishes, and sea mammals. The appearance of these traits in prehistory signals the emergence of an increasingly complex and successful economic system attuned to the environments of the Santa Barbara subregion.

Turning to linguistic matters, the Encinitas Tradition probably represents occupation of the Southern Coast region by speakers of Hokan languages (see Chapter 11). Since the Campbell Tradition apparently gave rise to the Chumash Tradition, the Campbell people most likely spoke a Hokan language or languages ancestral to Chumashan. South of Chumash territory, old Hokan groups are thought to have lost ground when "Shoshoneans" (the Takic subfamily of Uto-Aztecan) from the interior moved westward and spread along the coast. Ultimately, these Takic peoples came to occupy the coast from southern Los Angeles County (Gabrielino) to northern San Diego County (Luiseño) (Figure 11.1).

Although the Takic expansion chronology has not been worked out precisely, it seems clear that population movements were not synchronous in all parts of the coastal zone. For example, the Irvine Complex, identified with the Luiseño, first appeared in Orange County circa A.D. 600 (Ross 1969), but comparable evidence of the Luiseño (the San Luis Rey Complex) is not found in San Diego County until circa A.D. 1400 (Meighan 1954; True 1958, 1966). Considering both linguistic and archaeological data, C. Bull (1977:56) sets the western movement of the "Luisenic language family" at circa 500 B.C. Finally, C. King has interpreted the discovery of Middle Period Phase 1 and terminal Early Period beads with cremations (ascribed to Takic peoples) in the Tataviam, Gabrielino, and Northern Serrano areas to mean that "Uto-Aztecan speakers [sic] probably moved into eastern and southern California at the end of the Early Period" (1981:327–328). This would imply that the Takic expansion into the Southern Coast region occurred as early as circa 1500 to 1200 B.C.

Once on the coast, the "Shoshoneans" adapted quickly to their new surroundings. In large measure this was accomplished by borrowing the technology and economic practices of their Hokan neighbors: Witness the maritime orientation of the (Takic) Nicoleño and Gabrielino. During later prehistory, the Southern Coast peoples were influenced by agriculturalists of the American Southwest. Among the items introduced to California's far southern coast were cotton blankets, grooved stone axes, pottery, cremation urns, sand painting, and certain pictograph styles (J. Davis 1961; Heizer 1941a, 1946). Although some cultigens also reached the coastal zone (Treganza 1947b), agriculture did not spread effectively into this area until the mission era.

# 5. The Central Valley Region

The banks of the Sacramento and San Joaquin, and the numerous tributaries of these rivers, and the Tule Lake (i.e., Tulare Lake), were at this time studded with Indian villages of from one to twelve hundred inhabitants each. The population of this extensive valley was so great that it caused surprise, and required a close investigation into the nature of a country that without cultivation, could afford the means of subsistence to so great a community, and who were such indifferent hunters.

*(Trapper 1832, in Cook 1955b:319)*

VIEW OF AN INDIAN RANCHERIA, YUBA CITY, CALIFORNIA.

(Courtesy of the R. H. Lowie Museum of Anthropology, University of California, Berkeley.)

# Introduction

Three natural and archaeological divisions are recognized within the vast Central Valley region: the Sacramento Valley, Delta, and San Joaquin Valley (Figure 1). Ethnographic peoples of this region spoke more than 30 dialects of the Wintu, Nomlaki, Patwin, Konkow, Nisenan, Plains Miwok, Saclan, and Yokuts languages—all of which traditionally have been assigned to the California Penutian linguistic stock (Figure 11.1). Such diversity of languages implies a complex prehistory, and indeed Valley archaeology reflects population shifts and cultural replacement as well as the evolution of regionally distinctive social and economic patterns. The Valley was both a crossroads, marked by lively trade, and a center of dense populations at the heart of the "California climax culture" area (Kroeber 1939:53–55).

## Environment

Valley cultures are best understood with reference to their natural environments. Indian residents of the Valley witnessed dramatic environmental changes over the centuries: a major episode of faunal extinctions and replacement at the end of the Pleistocene; the emergence of wetlands as sea levels rose and filled San Francisco Bay and its inland backwaters (see Chapter 6); flooding and massive siltation of bottomlands; cyclical appearance and evaporation of shallow lakes; and biogeographic shifts in response to climatic fluctuations. Such wholesale changes in the effective environment would have greatly influenced prehistoric Valley societies.

Because of its vast area and central location, the Central Valley shares common borders with more cultural and natural regions than does any other physiographic province in California. Topographically, the Valley is a low-elevation "flatland" composed of alluvial plains, river channels, old lakebeds, sloughs, marshes, and uplands of low relief. Before modern reclamation projects, tidal action in the Delta and seasonal flooding along streams produced extensive wetlands. Lakes, marshes, and sloughs once covered more than 5000 km$^2$ in the San Joaquin Valley alone. The largest

**Figure 5.1** Typical Central Valley landscape and archaeological site (beneath structures) near the confluence of Dry Creek and the Mokelumne River, San Joaquin County. (Courtesy of the R. H. Lowie Museum of Anthropology, University of California, Berkeley.)

of these was ancient Tulare Lake (Figure 4.4)—as much as 45 km across—which occupied a structural basin formed by downwarping (G. Davis *et al.* 1959).

Tulare Lake, along with Buena Vista Lake farther south (Figure 4.4), was also contained in part by geologic features peculiar to the southern end of the region. Alluvial fans reaching into the Valley from the Kings River on the east and Los Gatos Creek on the west coalesced long ago into a ridge; lands to the south were so arid that runoff was often not able to maintain a discharge through the alluvium. The natural dam thus contributed to the impoundment of Tulare Lake and its swampy basin (Gifford and Schenck 1926:7). A similar projection of the Kern River fan westward to the McKittrick Hills formed a second dam behind which lie Kern and Buena Vista Lakes. At times of flood, Buena Vista and Tulare Lakes formerly spilled into a single basin and, with the waters of the Kern, Kaweah, and Kings rivers (Figure 1.3), flowed into the San Joaquin River system (Oakeshott 1971; Wedel 1941). Both Kern and Tulare lakes fluctuated greatly in response to paleoclimatic changes, but both are now dry most of the time as a result of historic drainage projects (Arguelles 1982:13–19).

Valley bottomlands experiencing tidal or seasonal flooding produced lush swamp vegetation, especially coarse grasses, tules, and cattails, valued by Indians as sources of food, fiber, and building material. Along watercourses grew riparian woodlands of sycamore, cottonwood, Oregon ash, and box elder. These trees, often draped by curtains of California grape vines, formed a canopy over undergrowths of willow, blackberry, wild rose, button bush, and elderberry.

Except for stream corridors and the Delta, the prehistoric Central Valley was mostly a Lower Sonoran grassland—the California prairie. In its primitive condition the prairie blossomed with such annuals as tom-cat clover, gilia, fiddle neck, blow-wives, and mimetanthe. Early travelers described seas of tall grass and countless oak groves on the expanses of prairie and savanna above the floodplains. Spear grass was joined on the perennial grassland by grindelia and California poppy. The Valley grass-land extended upslope to the foothill chaparral and woodlands of the Coast Ranges and Sierra Nevada. Only upon the alkaline flats and arid southwestern flanks of the Valley was vegetation sparse, being limited to sagebrush, salt grass, yerba mansa, nitrophilia, alkalai heath, saltbush, and short grasses (Heady 1977; Jepson 1925; Munz 1959).

The marsh belt of the Central Valley sustained abundant wildlife. The tule elk* was common here, as were the mink, weasel, river otter, rac-coon, and beaver. Each winter the Pacific flyway brought flocks of migra-tory waterfowl—geese, brants, ducks, and swans—to Valley wetlands where they joined resident white pelicans, great blue and black-crowned herons, ibis, cranes, cormorants, and eagles.

On higher ground were badgers, coyotes, skunks, ground squirrels, jackrabbits, and cottontail rabbits, together with herds of pronghorn. Bighorn sheep* were limited to a horseshoe of rugged terrain around the southern end of the Valley, whereas such predators as mountain lions,* wolves,* kit foxes, bobcats, and grizzly bears* ranged widely (Beck and Haase 1974; Gifford and Schenck 1926; Storer and Tevis 1955).

Central Valley waterways provided habitats for river mussels and many fish species. Five fish zones, each with a particular mix of water chemistry, temperature, depth, and current, have been identified in the Sacramento–San Joaquin system: (1) the Rainbow Trout Zone (mostly in Sierran streams), with Pit sculpin, speckled dace, and rainbow trout; (2) the California Roach Zone, featuring California roach; (3) the Squawfish Zone, inhabited by Sacramento squawfish, tule perch, Sacramento sucker, and occasional rainbow trout and speckled dace; (4) the Deep-bodied Fishes Zone, with thicktail chub, hitch, tule perch, Sacramento sucker, and Sacramento squawfish; and (5) the Estuarine Zone, a habitat for Delta smelt, longfin smelt, and starry flounder. This aquatic fauna is supplemented by anadromous fishes such as Chinook salmon, steelhead rainbow trout, Pacific lamprey, and white sturgeon, which pass through or temporarily occupy all zones except the first (Moyle 1976).

The 1833 observations of George Yount suggest how the Valley's nat-ural resources may have appeared to the Indians. Deer, elk, and antelope

*Locally or areally extinct.

were numerous beyond parallel. In herds of many hundreds, they might be met so tame that they would hardly move to open the way for the traveler to pass. They were seen lying or grazing in great herds, on the sunny side of every hill and their young, like lambs, were frolicking in all directions. The wild geese and every species of water fowl darkened the surface of every bay and firth, and upon the land in flocks of millions, they wandered in quest of insects and cropping the wild oats which grew there in abundance. When disturbed, they arose to fly, the sound of their wings was like that of distant thunder. The rivers were literally crowded with salmon, which since the pestilence [i.e., the epidemic of 1833] had swept away the Indians, no one disturbed. (Yount 1923:52, *in* Bennyhoff 1977a:7)

The Valley climate is locally varied but generally pleasant. Mean temperatures in January fall between 40 and 50° F. In July temperatures average 70–80° in the Delta locality and 80–90° on the valley floor to the north and south. Summers are hot, particularly in the San Joaquin Valley, where temperatures of 90° may be surpassed 60 to 120 days each year and daytime highs well above 100° are common. The mean annual precipitation is ≈50 cm, rising to >75 cm in the upper Sacramento Valley and falling to <25 cm in the southern San Joaquin Valley. Snowfall is negligible (Durrenberger 1965; Goodridge 1980).

The Central Valley was immensely attractive to early Indians. Its plains and wetlands teemed with game and offered rich harvests of vegetal foods. Only in terms of rocks and minerals were parts of the Valley impoverished. The region lacked obsidian, and some localities (e.g., the Delta) were entirely devoid of stone. On the other hand, steatite and asphaltum occurred in the southern Valley, and valuable salt deposits existed in the north (Heizer 1940a). Local deficiencies were made good by the substitution of baked clay for stone and by trading for rocks and minerals from adjacent regions (Heizer and Treganza 1944).

One way to give perspective to the environmental potentials of the Central Valley is to note that its aboriginal (eighteenth-century) population was about 105,000, with roughly 53,500* people living in the Sacramento Valley and 52,000† in the San Joaquin (Cook 1955a, 1976). These figures amount to ≈93 persons/100 km²—a population density nearly 20 times the average for preconquest America north of Mexico (Kroeber 1939:143).

*Native Cultures*

In late prehistoric times, no fewer than five ethnic groups occupied parts of the Sacramento Valley (Figure 11.1). The Patwin held the southern end of the Valley, mostly west of the river, from the area of Princeton south to San Pablo and Suisun Bays (P. Johnson 1978). The eastern Valley

---

*Including Patwin, Valley Nisenan, River Nomlaki, Konkow, and River Wintu.
†Including Plains Miwok and Northern and Southern Valley Yokuts.

between modern Sacramento and Marysville was the domain of Valley Nisenan (Wilson and Towne 1978). North of the Nisenan on the eastern valley floor and in the foothills east of Chico and Oroville were the Konkow (Riddell 1978), and the River Nomlaki lived to the west between Cottonwood and Toomes Creeks (Goldschmidt 1978). The upper Sacramento River drainage north of Cottonwood Creek was Wintu country (LaPena 1978).

Throughout the Sacramento Valley, the basic political unit was the village community, or tribelet, consisting of one primary and a few satellite villages under the authority of a headman. Permanent or winter settlements of 15 or 20 to several hundred persons usually were situated on low knolls near streams and above marshy floodplains. Houses were of several types, including both conical and dome-shaped structures covered with earth (Figure 5.2), tule mats, grass thatch, or (among the Wintu) bark. Ceremonial lodges or chief's residences in the principal villages were large, circular or elliptical, semisubterranean houses finished with earth or bark (Figure 5.18).

Subsistence activities were essentially the same among the Wintu and Patwin. Deer, elk, and antelope were snared, driven over cliffs, shot with arrows, and even run down by relays of hunters. Black bears were killed occasionally, but grizzlies in the Valley were greatly feared and rarely hunted. Waterfowl and small game, such as rabbits and quail, were hunted or taken by a variety of ingenious nets, snares, and traps. All Valley groups fished, especially for Chinook salmon, which usually ran in the Sacramento River system from about May until December. Trout, perch, chub, sucker, hardhead, eels, and sturgeon were taken variously by hook, net, harpoon, trap, wier, and poison. Most Valley groups followed a yearly gathering cycle that led them away from the lowlands into the hill country each summer. In the course of this annual round the Indians harvested acorns, nutmeg and pine nuts, buckeyes, and sunflower seeds—all of which could be stored—in addition to greens, tule and cattail roots, brodiaea bulbs, manzanita berries, blackberries, and California grapes, which were consumed as they ripened (Dixon 1905a; Du Bois 1935; Goldschmidt 1951, 1978; Kroeber 1925, 1929, 1932).

The Plains Miwok occupied the southeastern end of the Sacramento Valley north of the confluence of the Sacramento and San Joaquin Rivers. Adjoining them on the southwest, the Saclan (Bay Miwok) extended mainly along the southern shore of Suisun Bay but also north of the Sacramento River near Rio Vista (Figure 11.1). Unfortunately, these mid-Valley–Delta groups were so devastated by missionization, disease, and the Gold Rush that only scant records of their former cultures have been preserved except archaeologically. It is known that the tribelet was the largest political unit among them, and that the Plains Miwok had about 28 such divisions (Bennyhoff 1977a:15). Large multiple-family villages

VIEW OF AN INDIAN RANCHERIA, YUBA CITY, CALIFORNIA.

**Figure 5.2** View of the Nisenan village of *Yupu* near Yuba City, first published in Gleason's (1882) *Pictorial Drawing Room Companion*. Depicted are acorn granaries and large dome-shaped, earth-covered dwellings. (Courtesy of the R. H. Lowie Museum of Anthropology, University of California, Berkeley.)

were situated on elevated landforms near streams. Most settlements were inhabited permanently, except for a period of several weeks each year during the fall acorn harvest. Acorns were a staple food, augmented by various seeds, nuts, roots, berries, and greens. Fishing and hunting were important also, but not developed to full potential. Tule balsas provided transportation across sloughs and streams. A major industry among the Plains Miwok was the production of baked-clay substitutes for items made of stone elsewhere: net weights, cooking "stones," pipes, and crude vessels (Bennyhoff 1977a; J. Johnson *et al.* 1976; Levy 1978b).

The late prehistoric Yokuts claimed nearly all of the San Joaquin Valley as well as the lower Sierra Nevada foothills south of the Fresno River (Figure 11.1). Eighteenth-century Valley Yokuts may have numbered ≈41,000 persons (Cook 1955a), making them the largest ethnic group in precontact California. Three divisions of Yokuts—Northern Valley, Southern Valley, and Foothill—were composed of about 60 tribelets, each with a few hundred to several thousand members. Like their Sacramento Valley congeners, the Yokuts lived in permanent villages on high ground

near watercourses and subsisted by fishing, hunting, fowling, and intensive collecting. Although large communal residences sheltering 10 or
more families (Powers 1877:Figure 39) were built in some places, most
Yokuts houses were circular or oval single-family dwellings of tule mats
over pole frames (see Latta 1977:345–382). Differences between the
Northern and Southern Valley Yokuts were mainly ecological: the Southern groups were adapted to a lake–marsh–prairie environment, whereas
their Northern kin had better access to salmon and acorns in riverine and
oak savanna environments (Gayton 1948a, b; Latta 1977; Wallace
1978a, c).

After A.D. 1770 Indian populations were reduced and settlement patterns were disrupted in the Delta and San Joaquin Valley areas as a result
of Spanish colonial expeditions and mission recruitment (Cook 1943a, b,
1960, 1962; Cutter 1950). However, even more traumatic impacts to Central Valley populations were caused by the epidemic of 1833 and subsequent years. The disease (probably malaria) struck with such enormous
virulence that about 75% of the Valley people were swept away before
1846 (Cook 1955b:322). The destruction of Valley cultures and societies
was completed soon after 1848 by the American invasion (Cook 1943c,
1968, 1970; Heizer, ed. 1974b, c; Heizer and Almquist 1971).

## Early Archaeological Work

Scientific archaeology in the southern San Joaquin Valley began with a
series of University of California expeditions to the San Joaquin Valley,
initiated by P. M. Jones' 1899 exploration of mounds in Kern County. In
1909 N. C. Nelson visited the Elk Hills near Buena Vista Lake to recover
a cache of baskets and other artifacts exposed in a dry arroyo. A few years
earlier, C. H. Merriam, working independently, had visited the same
general area to record a different group of perishable items discovered
around 1903 by a local resident, James Stockton, in a small rockshelter
some 15 km east of Bakersfield. This find included the mummified body
of a child in a large coiled basket, along with a smaller basket, milkweed
fiber net, hemp cordage, and fragments of rush mat and rabbit skin
blanket. "The position of the articles [suggested] that the larger basket
was placed upright, mummy in sitting posture, weeds packed about it,
mat over its head, and second basket used as a lid" (Merriam 1905, *in*
Heizer 1951a:30). Artifact types assign this unusual burial to the late
prehistoric Yokuts (Heizer 1951a).

During the 1920s and 1930s artifact collecting for the quasi-scientific
purpose of increasing museum acquisitions (e.g., Heye 1926) was a com-

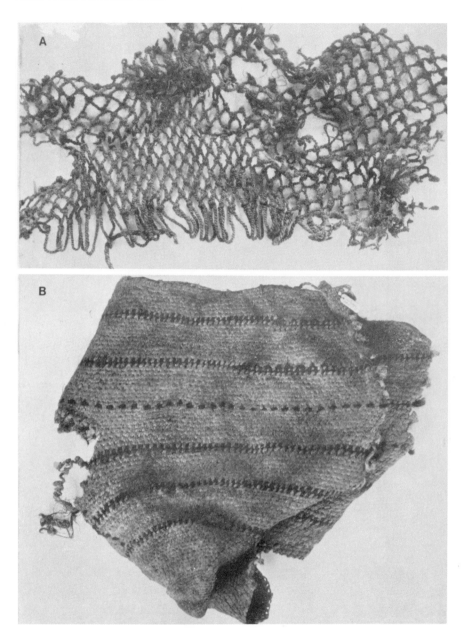

**Figure 5.3** Perishable late period (Yokuts) artifacts from the southern San Joaquin Valley: A, netting bag; B, bag of needle-stitched braid. (After Gifford and Schenck 1926, courtesy of the R. H. Lowie Museum of Anthropology, University of California, Berkeley.)

A     B     C     D     E     F     G     H     I     J     K     L     M     N     O

mon practice in the Central Valley. The first large project in the southern San Joaquin Valley involved the excavation of nine sites and recording of many others, along with the documentation of private collections, in the vicinities of Kern and Tulare Lakes (Figure 4.4). In the resultant *Archaeology of the Southern San Joaquin Valley*, Gifford and Schenck (1926) assigned to the ancestral Yokuts a late prehistoric complex of flexed burials, Brown Ware pottery, obsidian arrow points, both millingstones and mortars, and an elaborate steatite industry. Perishable cordage and textiles (Figure 5.3) were thought to have been left either by the Yokuts or by Indians from the coast who sought refuge in the Valley during the mission era.

In retrospect, it seems remarkable that Gifford and Schenck did not define a long archaeological sequence. They maintained that the "deposits examined were too shallow to yield much information as to culture change with the passage of time" (Gifford and Schenck 1926:114). Although they observed some evidence of time depth (stratification, caliche on certain artifacts, and varying degrees of bone preservation), Gifford and Schenck did not recognize the relative antiquity of atlatl weights and spurs, large projectile points, and chipped-stone crescents. They concluded that, even though the southern Valley might have been occupied in ancient times, "the material culture recovered would seem to be as readily assignable to the last century as to the last millennium" (Gifford and Schenck 1926:118).

In the northern San Joaquin Valley, between 1893 and 1901, avocational archaeologist J. A. Barr excavated and recorded nearly 2000 artifacts from a dozen mounds in the Stockton locality (Figure 6.4). H. C. Meredith also collected near Stockton, and on the basis of his and Barr's findings, published two early accounts of Delta archaeology (Meredith 1899, 1900). W. H. Holmes of the Smithsonian Institution further described the archaeology of the "Stockton District" and illustrated various artifacts donated by Barr and Meredith to the U.S. National Museum (Holmes 1902). Additional research near Stockton included P. M. Jones' 1900 excavation of several sites, most notably Sac-82, a mound from which Barr previously had exhumed more than 50 burials and where 7 strata had been exposed in a drainage ditch. Jones ultimately published his findings along with a description of Barr's collection from Sac-82 (P. Jones 1923).

---

**Figure 5.4** Artifacts from the Lodi vicinity, northern San Joaquin Valley. Scale variable. A, incised bird-bone tubes; B, fish spear of antler; C, *Haliotis* shell ornament; D, perforate charmstones; E. baked-clay objects with punctate decorations; F, bird effigy of fired clay; G, large bone needle; H, bone awl or thatching tool; I, steatite earspool; J, pair of bone whistles; K, L, Stockton Serrated projectile points of obsidian; M–O, side-notched projectile points of obsidian (O is 130 mm long). (After Schenck and Dawson 1929, courtesy of the R. H. Lowie Museum of Anthropology, University of California, Berkeley.)

As a high school student trained by Barr, Elmer J. Dawson in 1912 began the first systematic exploration of archaeological sites near Lodi (Figure 6.4). Dawson continued digging until around 1930, keeping careful notes of provenience and grave associations for nearly 8000 specimens. Based upon observations at stratified sites, Dawson recognized that significant cultural changes had occurred with time. When Dawson made his collections and data available to the University of California, W. E. Schenck used them as the foundation for an overview of northern San Joaquin Valley archaeology (Schenck and Dawson 1929). This publication was important as a systematic record of 92 sites and as a summary and comparison of all previous discoveries in the Delta area by Barr, Meredith, Jones, Dawson, and others. Schenck did not accept the cultural sequence recognized by Dawson, but proposed instead a tenuous archaeological succession with little room for culture change or time depth. As Sonia Ragir (1972:2) put it, "if Schenck had been less cautious about taking Dawson's suggested sequence, the 'early,' 'middle,' and 'late' traditions might have been recognized ten years earlier in 1929."

Schenck did divide the excavated mounds into three "age-groups" according to their artifact types and topographic location. Group I contained a single American Period site with many non-Indian artifacts; the midden base was on the same plane as the surrounding land. Late prehistoric to early historic Group II sites produced delicate serrated points and curves of obsidian, abundant clay artifacts, incised bird bone tubes, small mortars, and a few charmstones. Group II mounds usually were situated on high ground above marshy places along the banks of the Cosumnes and Mokelumne Rivers. Group III included the oldest prehistoric components, found below the adjacent terrain in marshlands as far as 2 km distant from modern river courses. The indurated deposits of Group III sites yielded quartz crystals, charmstones, distinctive *Haliotis* and mica ornaments, foliate bifaces, and slate pendants (Schenck and Dawson 1929:402–403) (Figure 5.4).

Despite obvious differences among site groups, Schenck concluded that 1500 years was the probable age of the oldest site near Lodi, and that in central California "little if any evidence has been produced to show that the culture revealed by archaeology was different from that of the eighteenth century, or that gave geological proof that the sites were very old" (Schenck and Dawson 1929:410).

## Origins of a Central Valley Sequence

*The Delta Sequence*

Archaeological research during the 1930s in the mid-Valley profoundly affected later interpretations of central California prehistory. The well-known three-horizon sequence was developed first in the Delta locality between 1936 and 1939 and later refined and expanded to include the San Francisco Bay area (see Chapter 6).

Beginning in 1931 Sacramento Junior College (SJC) teams excavated various sites near the Deer Creek–Cosumnes River confluence. This work was stimulated by the enthusiastic participation of the college president, J. B. Lillard, and several faculty members. Investigations focused on the Augustine (Sac-127), Booth (Sac-126), and Windmiller (Sac-107) mounds, all situated on clay knolls above the floodplain (Figure 6.4). One of the students who gained field experience at these sites was R. F. Heizer, who recalled 40 years later (1974b:179) that he had "learned something about scientific excavation from the president, J. B. Lillard, and a very good archaeologist, Richard van Valkenburgh, whose support was managed by a part time job in the college library." Such was central California archaeology during the 1930s.

In 1936 Lillard and W. K. Purves (a music teacher at SJC) announced that three "cultural levels"—Early, Intermediate, and Late—could be identified at the excavated sites. The Windmiller mound (Figure 5.15), which was to become the type site for the Early Culture, was a key deposit because it was physically stratified and showed the temporal separation of components. The cultures were distinguished by artifact types, burial patterns, and the condition of human bones (Lillard and Purves 1936). This study validated Dawson's initial discovery of culture change in Delta prehistory.

After 1934 University of California, Berkeley, and Sacramento Junior College investigators sampled numerous sites in the Delta and lower Sacramento Valley (Heizer 1936, 1937b; Heizer and Fenenga 1938; Heizer and Krieger 1935–1936; Heizer et al. 1934; Riddell and Riddell 1940; Wedel 1935a–c). This work ultimately contributed to important research dealing with the chemical analysis of human bones as a means of dating (Cook and Heizer 1949; Heizer and Cook 1949); physical analysis of midden constituents as an approach to reconstructing economic practices (Cook and Heizer 1951); the Sacramento Valley baked-clay industry and its possible relationship to ceramic traditions of the Southwest (Heizer 1937a; Heizer and Beardsley 1943); and the intentional burial of dogs, coyotes, bears, raptorial birds, and other creatures as evidence of animal ceremonialism in central California prehistory (Haag and Heizer 1953; Heizer and Hewes 1940). More significant, however, the investigations during the 1930s challenged prevailing views to the effect that central California's native cultures had been static or immutable through the ages; they supplanted this view with a model of cultural succession.

By 1939 a series of one historic and three prehistoric cultures, including manifestations unknown in 1936, could be identified (Figure 5.5). At Sac-107 (Figure 5.15) excavators observed four components: Postcontact, Late (protohistoric), and Transitional materials in midden deposits, and

| Lillard and Purves (1936) | Lillard et al. (1939) | Heizer and Fenenga (1939) | Heizer (1949) | Ragir (1972) |
|---|---|---|---|---|
| Recent Level | Historic Period | (Historic) | (Historic) Phase III | |
| Intermediate Level | Phase 2 | Phase 2 | Phase II | Hotchkiss Culture |
| | Phase 1 | Phase 1 | Phase I | |
| | Late Period | Late Horizon | Late Horizon | |
| | Transitional Period | Transitional Horizon | Middle Horizon | Cosumnes Culture |
| Early Level | Early Period | Early Horizon | Early Horizon | Windmiller Culture |

**Figure 5.5** Concordance of terms for the Delta cultural sequence. (See also Figure 5.11.)

an Early cemetery in hard-packed clay below the midden. Relating these cultural units at Sac-107 to components at other sites, Lillard, Heizer, and Fenenga (1939) defined three archaeological periods in terms of mortuary patterns and ornamental artifacts:

1. *Early Period:* This is represented at Sac-107 and SJo-56, -68, -142, and -168 (Figure 6.4) by fully extended burials oriented westerly and normally with funerary artifacts (Figure 5.13); large projectile points of slate and chert; distinctive *Haliotis* and *Olivella* shell ornaments and beads; perforate charmstones; quartz crystals; varied items of baked clay; and infrequent mortars, pestles, and millingstones (Figure 5.12).

2. *Transitional Period:* First recognized at the Morse mound (Sac-66), this period was investigated at 12 sites where components yielded a predominance of tightly flexed burials oriented variably, often with red ochre and sometimes accompanied by grave goods; large foliate and concave-base projectile points; imperforate charmstones; bone awls, spatulae, bipoints, and fish spear tips; varied baked-clay objects; millingstones, cobble mortars, and pestles; and an array of shell beads and ornaments (Figure 5.16).

3. *Late Period:* Diagnostic of the Late Period are flexed or (occasional) extended burials as well as cremations; preinterment burning of artifacts; serrated points and curves of obsidian; incised bird bone tubes; elaborate *Haliotis* shell ornaments; clamshell and magnesite disk beads as well as *Olivella* beads; and shaped, flat-bottomed mortars (Figure 5.17; Lillard *et al.* 1939).

Lillard *et al.* expressed the view that their series was a genetic progression, that is, that the Early Culture was the "parent" of the Transitional Culture, and so on. The Delta locality was seen as a "center of cultural specialization" from which influences spread with different intensities to most parts of central California. The assemblage from the Maltby site (CCo-250) at the western end of Suisun Bay (Figure 6.4) was taken as evidence that the Carquinez Strait–San Francisco Bay region did not receive cultural stimuli directly from the Valley, and that when influences did reach the Bay "they were few in number and met a conservative, established culture which was developing along its own individual lines" (Lillard *et al.* 1939:61). The Delta sequence and its place in central California archaeology are discussed more fully later in this chapter.

## The Central California Taxonomic System

In his landmark study, *Temporal and Areal Relationships in Central California Archaeology,* Richard Beardsley (1954) refined the Delta sequence and extended it to include the prehistory of the San Francisco Bay region. The result was the Central California Taxonomic System (CCTS), which inherently assumed that a basically uniform cultural succession had developed in central California from the coast to the interior. Beardsley's monograph introduced into the California literature several concepts that University of California archaeologists had adapted prior to 1946 from the Midwestern Taxonomic Method (McKern 1939). The term *component* was used to designate an archaeological record of occupation at a single site during a brief interval of time. A group of closely related components made up a *facies,* and related facies comprised a *province.* The province thus entailed both geographic and cultural significance. *Horizons* were seen as broad cultural units that could be arranged in a temporal sequence. Lastly, *zones* were set apart as geographic entities that separated coastal and Central Valley areas (Figure 5.6) (Beardsley 1954).

### Central California Horizons

Beginning in 1936, a series of papers defined with increasing precision the Delta sequence of cultural horizons (Lillard and Purves 1936; Heizer and Fenenga 1939; Lillard *et al.* 1939). Detailed studies of the Early Horizon appeared subsequently (Heizer 1949, 1974b; Ragir 1972), but comparable treatments of the Middle and Late Horizons never materialized. The cited works identified the central California horizons as follows:

1. *Early Horizon:* (1) known sites predominantly in the Delta locality; (2) ventral or occasional dorsal extension of burials (Figure 5.13) with westerly orientation (Figure 5.14), and very rare cremations; (3) high frequency ($\approx 85\%$) of graves with artifacts, often ($\approx 26\%$) with quartz crys-

| | | LITTORAL ZONE | | INTERIOR VALLEY ZONE | | | | |
|---|---|---|---|---|---|---|---|---|
| | | MARIN PROVINCE | ALAMEDA PROVINCE | COSUMNES PROVINCE | | COLUSA PROVINCE | | |
| LATE HORIZON | PHASE II | ESTERO FACIES: Estero A, McClure A, Cauley A, Toms Point | FERNANDEZ FAC: Fernandez A, Newark #1A | MOSHER FACIES: Mosher; Hicks A, Johnson, Goethe, Nicholas 4, Nicholas 5, Hotchkiss A | | MILLER FACIES: Miller A, Howells Point A | | |
| | PHASE I | MENDOZA FACIES: Mendoza, Cauley A | EMERYVILLE FACIES: Emeryville A, Greenbrae B, Bayshore A, Ponce A, Maltby, Glen Cove | HOLLISTER FACIES: Hollister, Brazil A, Hotchkiss B, Hicks B | | SANDHILL FACIES: Sandhill, Miller B | | |
| | | COSTAL PROVINCE | | INTERIOR PROVINCE | | | | |
| MIDDLE HORIZON | | McCLURE FACIES: McClure B, Estero B, Cauley B | ELLIS LANDING FACIES: Emeryville B, Greenbrae B, Bayshore, Ponce B, Ellis Landing, Stege, Potrero, W. Berkeley, San Rafael B, Newark #1B, Fernandez B?, Monument ?, Princeton | MORSE FACIES: Morse, Van Lobensels, McGillivray A, Calquhoun, Koontz, Hicks C | DETERDING FACIES: Deterding, Wamser | BRAZIL FACIES: Brazil B | NEED FACIES: Need Vail | ORWOOD FACIES: Orwood 2 |
| EARLY HORIZON | | (Unknown) | | PROVINCE UNNAMED | | | | |
| | | | | WINDMILLER FACIES: Windmiller C, Blossom, McGillivray B, Phelps | | | | |

**Figure 5.6** Cultural sequences in central California archaeology. (After Beardsley 1954.)

tals and sometimes ($\approx 11\%$) with red ochre; (4) *Olivella* beads of Types A1a and L; (5) rectangular *Haliotis* beads; (6) perforate, often edge-incised *Haliotis* ornaments in geometric shapes, some with asphaltum and bead appliqué; (7) perforate biotite, canid teeth, and turtle-carapace ornaments, and slate pendants; (8) well-made charmstones, typically perforate, of amphibolite schist, granite, and translucent alabaster in spindle, biconical, phallic, and other forms; (9) thick, conical smoking pipes of stone; (10) heavy stemmed and foliate projectile points, usually ($\approx 60\%$) of nonobsidian materials, and inferred use of the atlatl; (11) a paucity of bone artifacts, though cannon bone "daggers," flattened matting needles, spatulae, and beveled-base pins may be distinctive; (12) hand-molded baked-clay objects, especially net weights; (13) infrequent mortars, pestles, millingstones, and manos; and (14) inferred hunting and fishing, but apparently little dependence on acorns or hard seeds (Figure 5.12).

2. *Middle Horizon:* (1) sites found throughout the mid-Central Valley; (2) tightly flexed burials of variable orientation are normal, but ≈5% of the dead are cremated; (3) nearly all cremations, but only ≈40% of the primary inhumations have funerary artifacts, while red ochre stains and stone cairns are common in graves; (4) *Olivella* beads of Types C1, F, and G; (5) circular and subrectangular *Haliotis* beads; (6) abundant *Haliotis* ornaments of varied geometric shapes, frequently made of *H. cracherodii* rather than *H. rufescens* shell; (7) perforate canid teeth and bear claws; (8) distinctive "fishtail" and asymmetrical spindle-shaped imperforate charmstones, sometimes with asphaltum and cord impressions at the neck; (9) cobble mortars and evidence of wooden mortars in the form of chisel-ended pestles; (10) an extensive bone industry of flakers, bipoints, basketry awls, spatulae, fish spear tips, saws, etc.; (11) large, heavy projectile points, often of nonobsidian lithics, with foliate and lanceolate concave-base types predominating, and inferred use of the atlatl; (12) much evidence of violent death, such as disarticulated skeletons and weapon points imbedded in >5% of the skeletons; (13) baked-clay objects; and (14) a diversified subsistence with inferred hunting, fowling, fishing, and seed processing (Figure 5.16).

3. *Late Horizon:* (1) sites distributed throughout central California with influence extending into adjacent areas; (2) various types of primary burial, often in flexed positions, and cremations; also pre-interment burning of basketry and other artifacts; funerary red ochre less common than before and found in lumps rather than as powder in graves; (3) abundance of baked-clay artifacts; (4) *Olivella* beads of Types E and M; (5) elaboration and proliferation of *Haliotis* ornaments with "banjo" (dancer effigy?), trapezoidal, and triangular shapes; (6) magnesite disk beads and drilled cylinders; (7) clamshell disk beads; (8) flanged, tubular smoking pipes of schist and steatite; (9) small, side-notched obsidian points, locally with deep angular serrations; (10) bow and arrow inferred from small points and arrow-shaft smoothers and straighteners; (11) shaped, flat-bottomed mortars and cylindrical pestles; (12) bird bone tubes with incised geometric designs; (13) items of non-Indian origin late in the sequence; and (14) subsistence focus on gathering acorns and other plant foods, as well as hunting, fowling, and fishing (Figure 5.17).

*Chronology*

Efforts to date the central California sequence have been fraught with problems. Ten years before radiocarbon dating was available, Heizer and

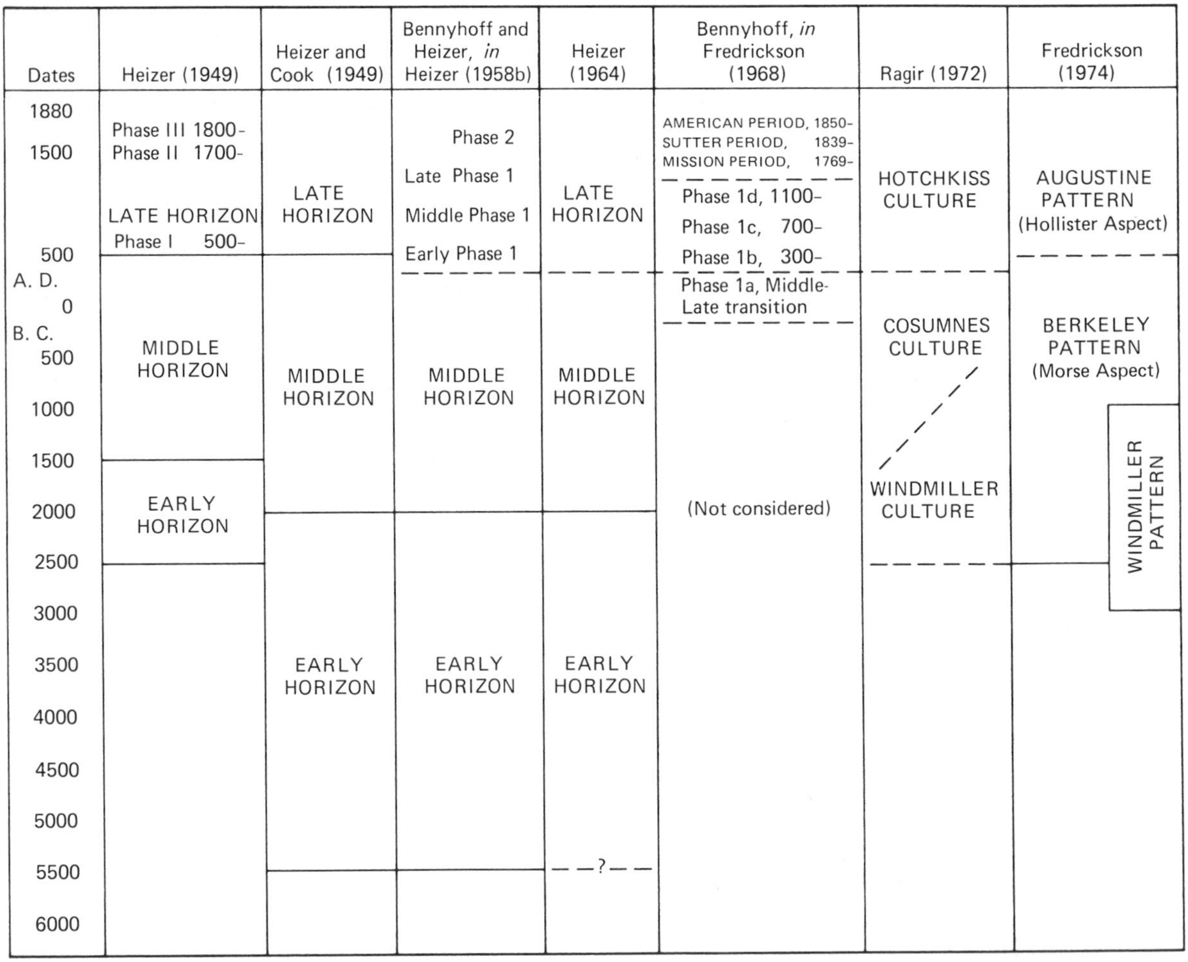

| Dates | Heizer (1949) | Heizer and Cook (1949) | Bennyhoff and Heizer, *in* Heizer (1958b) | Heizer (1964) | Bennyhoff, *in* Fredrickson (1968) | Ragir (1972) | Fredrickson (1974) |
|---|---|---|---|---|---|---|---|
| 1880 | Phase III 1800– | | Phase 2 | | AMERICAN PERIOD, 1850– | | |
| 1500 | Phase II 1700– | LATE HORIZON | Late Phase 1 | LATE HORIZON | SUTTER PERIOD,      1839– | HOTCHKISS CULTURE | AUGUSTINE PATTERN |
| | LATE HORIZON | | Middle Phase 1 | | MISSION PERIOD,     1769– | | (Hollister Aspect) |
| | Phase I      500– | | Early Phase 1 | | Phase 1d, 1100– Phase 1c,   700– Phase 1b,   300– | | |
| 500 A.D. | | | | | Phase 1a, Middle-Late transition | | |
| 0 | MIDDLE HORIZON | | | | | COSUMNES CULTURE | BERKELEY PATTERN |
| B.C. 500 | | MIDDLE HORIZON | MIDDLE HORIZON | MIDDLE HORIZON | | | (Morse Aspect) |
| 1000 | | | | | | | |
| 1500 | | | | | | | |
| 2000 | EARLY HORIZON | | | | (Not considered) | WINDMILLER CULTURE | WINDMILLER PATTERN |
| 2500 | | | | | | | |
| 3000 | | | | | | | |
| 3500 | | EARLY HORIZON | EARLY HORIZON | EARLY HORIZON | | | |
| 4000 | | | | | | | |
| 4500 | | | | | | | |
| 5000 | | | | | | | |
| 5500 | | | | — —?— — | | | |
| 6000 | | | | | | | |

**Figure 5.7** Concordance of central California archaeological sequences.

Fenenga (1939) prudently avoided the question of absolute age, but drew attention to the progressively greater degree of bone mineralization and induration of deposits going back in time from the Late to Early horizons. A decade later, Heizer (1949:39) suggested on the basis of stratigraphy, soils development, and artifactual cross-dating that the initial dates of the Early, Middle, and Late Horizons were, respectively, 2500 B.C., 1500 B.C., and A.D. 500 (Figure 5.7). Later in the same year Heizer and Cook's (1949) chemical analyses of human bone led to the estimate that the Early Horizon had flourished between 7500 and 4000 years ago. This contention seemed to be validated by $^{14}$C dates of $4052 \pm 160$, $4100 \pm 250$, and $4350 \pm 250$ B.P. on charcoal and cremated bone from the Blossom site

(SJo-68), which Heizer (1958b) placed toward the recent end of the Early Horizon (Figure 5.7). By 1958 Heizer could also cite 10 radiocarbon dates from Newark (Ala-328), West Berkeley (Ala-307), and University Village (SMa-77) as evidence that the San Francisco Bay shore was occupied by "Middle Horizon" shellfish gatherers around 1500 B.C.

In an overview of western North American prehistory, Heizer (1964:126–127) reaffirmed his acceptance of the three horizons and their ages as set forth in 1958, except that he did not give an initial date for the Early Horizon. A later refinement of the CCTS was Bennyhoff's definition of six Late Horizon phases (Figure 5.7), following a Middle–Late transition phase (ca. 100 B.C.–A.D. 300) and including three phases each in the late prehistoric (A.D. 300–1769) and early historic (A.D. 1769–1881) periods (Bennyhoff, *in* Fredrickson 1968:137).

One of the limitations of the horizon concept, as applied in central California, was that it did not permit much cultural variability at any point in time. To address this problem, S. R. Ragir (1972) proposed that *Windmiller Culture* be substituted for *Early Horizon*, *Cosumnes Culture* for *Middle Horizon*, and *Hotchkiss Culture* for *Late Horizon* (Figure 5.7). This nomenclature allowed for additional developments earlier than Windmiller and/or within any of the named cultures.

Ragir also corrected the CCTS chronology by demonstrating, with the aid of radiocarbon dates and seriations of charmstone and projectile-point types, that the Blossom site (SJo-68) was the oldest Windmiller site known and not the youngest as previously thought. The many radiocarbon dates now available from Windmiller components (Figure 5.11) are arrayed from 4350 ± 250 to 900 ± 250 B.P. Although the latter date may be anomalous, the others show that past age estimates of "Early Horizon" origins were too liberal and that the Windmiller Culture persisted until circa 500 B.C. or later (Heizer 1974b; Ragir 1972). This revised chronology and its effect upon the Central California Taxonomic System are discussed later in this chapter (see pp. 199–214).

## Further Investigations

### San Joaquin Valley

In 1939 G. Hewes of UCB explored parts of the mid–San Joaquin Valley in an effort to link the Delta and Tulare Lake areas, both "fairly well known" archaeologically. Hewes surveyed 14 tracts of land between the southern limits of Schenck and Dawson's work and the northern end of Gifford and Schenck's study area. In all, 107 sites were found. Most were near streams and marshes on the east side of the Valley. Some of the middens were quite large—up to 170 m across, with as many as 66 surface housepits. One of the discovered sites was Fre-48 (Figure 4.4), the putative Early Man site near Tranquillity (see pp. 65–66). Hewes noted the resemblance of mid-Valley artifacts to those of the Delta, but was careful not to advance a San Joaquin Valley chronology on the strength of limited survey data. Still, the high density of large sites, variable states of bone permineralization, and diversity of artifacts were cited as evidence of large populations and major cultural changes over a long interval of time (Hewes 1941:126–132).

In 1941 W. R. Wedel reported on excavations, done in 1933 and 1934, by the Civil Works Administration at five sites—two middens, two cemeteries, and a small grave site—on the southwestern edge of Buena Vista Lake (Figure 4.4). The middens (Ker-39 and -60) were actually parts of the much larger site Ker-116, where Fredrickson and Grossman (1977) later found a deeply buried component related to the Western Pluvial Lakes Tradition and dated to circa 6250 B.C. (see p. 99). Ker-39 and -60 were stratified, each with a lower, compact deposit containing a few hearths, millingstones, manos, and, at Ker-60, extended caliche-encrusted burials. Overlying these older components were middens with loose soils, flexed burials, circular patterns of post molds, and abundant bone, shell, asphaltum, clay, and stone artifacts (Figure 5.8) (Wedel 1941:136).

As for external relationships, Wedel noted the likeness of extended burials, millingstones, and stemmed and leaf-shaped points at Buena Vista Lake to Oak Grove materials (see Chapter 4) on the Santa Barbara coast, 80 km to the southwest, and to the Early Horizon of the Delta, 400 km to the north. The lack of charmstones, quartz crystals, shell ornaments, or other "Early" diagnostics with the burials convinced Wedel that "the Early Delta horizon [was] a later and considerably more developed phase than that suggested by the lower level remains at Buena Vista" (1941:147).

Although Wedel did not determine the ages of the two lower deposits, he showed clearly that the upper components at Ker-60 and -39 were of prehistoric and protohistoric–historic ages, respectively. The upper prehistoric component at Ker-60 is set apart by roasting pits secondarily used for flexed burials, charmstones, bone strigils and bipoints, limpet shell ornaments, *Olivella* half-shell and saucer beads, and other artifacts rare or absent at Ker-39. With respect to dating, Wedel (1941) cautiously repeated Kroeber's (1936b) opinion that this assemblage was contemporary with the Delta Middle Horizon and perhaps also with the Mainland Intermediate period on the Santa Barbara coast (see Chapter 4).

From the Buena Vista Lake hilltop cemeteries (Ker-40 and -41), 418 flexed burials were exhumed. Funerary artifacts were like items from the

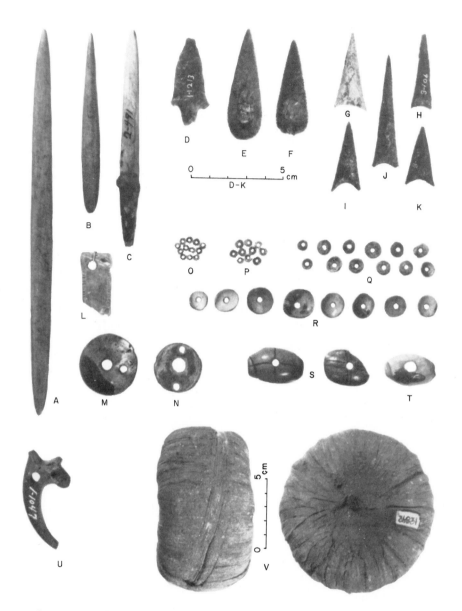

**Figure 5.8** Artifacts from Buena Vista Lake shore sites, Kern County (after Wedel 1941): A–C, pointed bone objects (spears or awls?), length of A is 147 mm; D–K, chert projectile points; L–N, *Haliotis* shell ornaments, diameter of M is 22 mm; O–T, *Olivella* shell beads, diameter of O is 2.5 mm; U, perforated raptor claw, length 39 mm; V, tule-wrapped asphaltum. (Courtesy of the Smithsonian Institution, National Anthropological Archives.)

upper midden levels, suggesting that Ker-40 and -41 may have served as the burial grounds of people from Ker-39 and -60, respectively (Wedel 1941:138–140). As known from Ker-40 and upper Ker-39, the proto-historic–historic phase is distinguished by triangular arrow points, wooden grave markers, preserved textiles, pottery, and an elaborate steatite industry. Although Wedel calls attention to similarities between the late Buena Vista Lake phase and the Delta Late Horizon, he concludes that Buena Vista Lake was influenced mainly by southern California cultures:

> Traits at Buena Vista which stand as a link with this general area include coiled basketry on bundle foundation, hopper mortars of flat and globular form, transversely grooved arrow straighteners, . . . and perhaps pottery. . . . More specific connections are implied in the soft twined milkweed string bags . . . and in a whole host of features whose appearance is unmistakenly Santa Barbaran [a well developed steatite industry, extensive use of bitumen, abalone shell receptacles, limpet shell ornaments, long heavy bone daggers, exquisitely made triangular "swallow tail" and lanceolate projectile points, and carefully made chert and jasper "blades" 150 to 260 mm long]. (Wedel 1941:149)

It thus appears that the Buena Vista Lake vicinity experienced at least four phases of prehistoric activity, beginning at Ker-116 more than 8000 years ago. At some later time (ca. 2500 B.C.?), roughly coeval with the Delta "Early Horizon", the Buena Vista Lake shore (lower Ker-39 and -60) was again occupied; little is known of this phase. Settlement during the third phase (ca. 1000 B.C.–A.D. 500?) was by people with strong cultural ties to the Delta, perhaps the ancestral Yokuts. The latest phase (ca. A.D. 1500–1850?) shows influence from both the Santa Barbara coast and the southern California interior (cf. Kroeber 1925:934). At least some of these episodes of human occupation and abandonment may be correlated with past climatic conditions and cycles of lake filling and drying (see Arguelles 1982; Moratto *et al.* 1978).

Even though completed nearly 50 years ago, the 1933–34 project at Buena Vista Lake stands as the most intensive scientific excavation work so far in the southern San Joaquin Valley. Another notable project in this area was E. F. Walker's 1935 excavation of a jeopardized Yokuts cemetery (Ker-64) at Elk Hills near Buena Vista Lake (Figure 4.4). From sandy deposits containing "hundreds, possibly thousands, of burials," Walker exhumed 46 historic and 53 pre-Spanish era interments (1947:5, 10, 13). Graves had been marked by Juniper posts, and the skeletons, all but one of which were flexed, were covered variously by juniper wood, tule mats, or milkweed fiber clothing. Grave goods indicated late prehistoric and early historic (17??–1860?) use of the Elk Hills cemetery by Yokuts, possibly from the village of *Tulamniu* (Walker 1947:7–14).

A similar Yokuts cemetery was reported by F. A. Riddell at Ker-74, 19 km west of Delano (Figure 4.4), where in 1949 a natural mound containing burials was being destroyed by a land-leveling project and local collectors were removing grave goods. Through interviews and examination of private collections, Riddell obtained information about nine burials. Most had been accompanied by items of non-Indian manufacture (glass beads, bottles, pocketknives, religious medallions, etc.) as well as traditional *Haliotis* ornaments, *Olivella* and clamshell disk beads, bone tubes, flaked-stone tools, and artifacts of steatite (Riddell 1951).

Many other protohistoric and early historic cemeteries in the southern San Joaquin Valley have been investigated (Anonymous 1938; Estep 1933; Latta 1977:109–119, 174; von Werlhof, see Schiffman and Garfinkel 1981:3.5). In 1958 UCLA archaeologists excavated a small group of prehistoric burials—mostly semiflexed and without definite associations other than red pigment on bones and mussel shells in graves—at Tul-90 (Figure 4.4) near the edge of former Tulare Lake, 85 km north of Bakersfield (Warren and McKusick 1959). Comparing their findings with those earlier reported by Gifford and Schenck (1926), Walker (1947), and Wedel (1941), Warren and McKusick (1959:20) proposed the following sequence of burial modes in the Buena Vista and Tulare lakes area:

*Late:* Preferred position is tightly flexed on side or supine; moderate amount of burial goods often with European items. (A.D. 500–ethnographic present.)

*Middle:* Preferred position is supine semiflexed; few burial goods. (1500 B.C.–A.D. 500.)

*Early:* Preferred position is extended, supine or prone; no burial goods? (? B.C.–2000 B.C.)

Viewing this succession as "related to, but considerably different from the Central Valley sequence," Warren and McKusick (1959:21) used cross-dating with the Delta sequence to infer the ages of their Early, Middle, and Late manifestations. This was the first, albeit tentative, attempt to seriate mortuary practices in the southern San Joaquin Valley.

In the northern San Joaquin Valley, prior to 1955, UCB archaeologists tested several middens to assess research prospects in the area (e.g., McGeein 1950; Mohr 1948). These studies were followed by occasional, mostly small-scale projects, including salvage excavations at Mer-66 in Dos Palos (Wildesen 1969) and at *Gewachiu*, Fre-398 (McAlexander and Upson 1969). More intensive fieldwork during the 1960s along the east side of the Diablo Range led to definition of an archaeological sequence in many respects distinctive but in others comparable to that of the Delta.

Between 1962 and 1968 various federal and state agencies collaborated to salvage archaeological remains jeopardized by the construction and filling of San Luis, Los Banos, and Little Panoche Reservoirs about 75 km east of Monterey Bay (Figure 6.4). Work began at San Luis Reservoir, where A. Treganza's (1960b) survey was followed by excavations of cemetery and midden deposits at Mer-14 directed by R. Crabtree in 1962 and F.

**Figure 5.9** Housepit 2, looking south, at the Menjoulet site (Mer-3) in the Los Banos Dam project area; Trench A in foreground. The hard earthen floor of this feature measured ≈23 m in diameter, making it one of the largest aboriginal structures known in California. On the floor were the remains of 30 secondary cremations. The structure represented by Housepit 2 is thought to have been used by a protohistoric Yokuts community (Pritchard 1970:32–35, Figures 4, 5, 14a). (Photograph by W. Pritchard, courtesy of F. A. Riddell and the California Department of Parks and Recreation.)

Riddell in 1963. Two saucer-shaped housefloors of puddled adobe mud, 7–9 m in diameter, and 92 flexed and extended burials were documented. Recovered projectile points, mortars and pestles, millingstones, bone whistles, steatite ornaments, and *Olivella* shell beads indicate that Mer-14 was a single-component site inhabited between circa A.D. 300 and 1000 (Olsen and Payen 1969; Riddell and Olsen 1965).

As part of the Los Banos Dam Detention project (Figure 6.4), excavations were conducted in 1964–1965 by W. Pritchard at the Menjoulet site (Mer-3). Among the remains of 12 structures at Mer-3 was a housepit more than 23 m in diameter—one of the largest known to California archaeology (Figure 5.9). Pritchard's (1967, 1970) research goals were to define a local temporal sequence, to examine architectural features for information about social, political, religious, and demographic patterns, and to discover culture markers that might identify the residents of the site as Yokuts, Costanoan, or possibly Miwok.

Two components were recognized at Mer-3, the earlier (A.D. 300–1000) characterized by extended or semiflexed burials, beveled-rim and slab mortars, and distinctive shell ornaments of types like those from Mer-14. A second, protohistoric to early historic component featured large semisubterranean structures, a developed bone industry, small side-notched projectile points, shell ornaments, and secondary cremations, 30 of which were found on the largest housefloor. A $^{14}C$ age of <185 years (I-3164) applies to this component. Although it had been generally thought, prior to work at Mer-3, that the west side of the San Joaquin Valley in ethnographic times was "unimportant" and "had few residents" (Kroeber 1925:476), Pritchard (1970:45) determined that the Menjoulet site was a major year-round village, possibly a Yokuts tribelet center, inhabited by an estimated 50–100 people.

In 1966 W. Olsen and L. A. Payen investigated three sites at Little Panoche Reservoir, approximately 35 km south of San Luis Dam (Figure 6.4). Excavations at Fre-128 revealed several structures, two burials, and artifacts signifying occupation between circa A.D. 1700 and 1800 by a small group whose cultural affiliations were with the south and west rather than with the Delta (Olsen and Payen 1968:39). At Fre-129 Olsen and Payen found evidence of a late prehistoric temporary camp or village site, along with a cemetery from which 16 tightly flexed burials were exhumed. Also discovered at Little Panoche Reservoir were "three distinct occupation zones" buried to a maximum depth of ≈4 m and exposed in the walls of an arroyo (Salt Canyon). Stratigraphic trenching, minimal archaeological testing, and preliminary geologic and soils studies indicate a probable age of 3000 years for the lower cultural stratum and 500–1000 years for the upper (Olsen and Payen 1968:63–69).

Continuing salvage work on the west side of the San Joaquin Valley, in 1966–1967 Olsen and Payen excavated the Grayson site (Mer-S-94) in the San Luis Reservoir area (Figure 6.4). Research here was designed to reconstruct exploitative practices at the juncture of valley and foothill biotic zones and to develop a local cultural chronology. Eight cultural and natural strata were recognized. Burials, features, artifacts, and midden constituents occurred above 220 cm in "Zones" (Strata) A–D, whereas "Zones" E–H were devoid of cultural material (Figure 5.10).

On the basis of distinctive artifact types and mortuary patterns at Mer-S-94 and other western Valley sites, Olsen and Payen (1969) defined a series of four cultural complexes:

1. *Positas Complex* (ca. 3300–2600 B.C.): Known from the basal cultural deposit at Mer-S-94, this complex is distinguished by small shaped mortars, short cylindrical pestles, millingstones, perforated flat cobbles, and spire-lopped *Olivella* beads. Two $^{14}C$ dates of A.D. 1305 ± 90 and 450 ± 100 B.C. are mutually inconsistent and contribute little toward the dating of the Positas Complex.

| Stratum | Depth (cm) | Characteristics | Cultural Complex |
|---|---|---|---|
| ZONE A | 0-30 | Dusty, dark-gray, loose, flourlike midden with a high proportion of fire-altered rock | Panoche |
| | 30-80 | As above, except lighter in color and with more evidence of rodent disturbance | |
| ZONE B | 80-175 | Darker in color than Zone A; uncompacted; with evidence of intensive cultural activity | Gonzaga |
| ZONE C | 175-195 | Basal midden deposit; extremely compacted or cemented light gray to yellow soil with numerous small, natural waterworn pebbles | Pacheco |
| ZONE D | 195-220 | Cemented, yellowish colored sand with high clay content; lowest cultural stratum | Positas |
| ZONE E | | Localized coarse yellow sand | None |
| ZONE F | | Localized rounded stream cobbles | None |
| ZONE G | | Red soil and cobbles | None |
| ZONE H | | Poorly consolidated shale or sandstone bedrock | |

**Figure 5.10** Stratigraphy at the Grayson site, Mer-S-94. (After Olsen and Payen 1969.)

2. *Pacheco Complex* (ca. 2600 B.C.–A.D. 300): Represented by Zone C at Mer-S-94, this complex is divided into two phases—Pacheco B (until ca. 1600 B.C.), marked by foliate bifaces, rectangular *Haliotis* ornaments, and thick rectangular *Olivella* beads, and Pacheco A (after ca. 1600 B.C.), with *Olivella* beads of spire-ground, modified saddle, saucer, and split-drilled types, *Haliotis* disk beads and ornaments, perforated canine teeth, bone awls, whistles and grass saws, large stemmed and side-notched points, and abundant millingstones, mortars, and pestles. The Pacheco shell and bone industries are most like those of the Delta "Middle Horizon," but other traits evince relationships to the west and south.

3. *Gonzaga Complex* (ca. A.D. 300–1000): With known manifestations at Mer-3, Mer-14, Mer-S-94, and other sites on the west side of the Valley, this complex is recognized by extended and flexed burials, bowl mortars and shaped pestles, squared and tapered-stem projectile points, a few bone awls and grass saws, distinctive *Haliotis* ornaments, and thin rectangular, split-punched, and oval *Olivella* beads—altogether an assemblage like that of the Delta "Late Horizon," Phase 1.

4. *Panoche Complex* (ca. A.D. 1500–1850): Evidenced at many western Valley sites, the Panoche Complex features large circular structures, flexed burials as well as primary and secondary cremations, a few millingstones, varied mortars and pestles, bone awls, saws, whistles and tubes, small side-notched arrow points, clamshell disk beads, *Haliotis*

epidermis disk beads, and *Olivella* lipped, side-ground, and rough disk beads. These traits are most comparable to those of the Delta "Late Horizon," Phase 2.

Olsen and Payen (1969) concluded that the western edge of the Valley was long occupied by groups basically oriented to an acorn-gathering and hunting economy. Although minimal evidence of the Panoche Complex was found at Mer-S-94, intensive late period activity is well represented at Mer-27 (Nissley 1975) and at Mer-S-119, where Pritchard (1968b) excavated three structures ascribed to the protohistoric Kawatchwa Yokuts, as well as at Mer-3, Fre-128, and Fre-129. "Middle" and "Late, Phase 1" occupations are recorded in Pacheco and Gonzaga components at Mer-3, -14, -27, -S-94, and possibly at Salt Canyon. Separating these from the later Panoche Complex is an apparent hiatus of ≈500 years between circa A.D. 1000 and 1500. This may reflect abandonment due to adverse environmental conditions.

Throughout the Pacheco to Panoche sequence, trade relationships were maintained with peoples of the Delta and more southerly coastal and inland areas. While the Panoche Complex, and perhaps Gonzaga, may register a Yokutsan presence, the earlier complexes are not easily linked to any particular ethnic or linguistic groups. Additional fieldwork will be needed to address such problems and, more important, to reconstruct paleoenvironmental conditions and examine prehistoric cultural adaptations to them on the western flanks of the San Joaquin Valley.

## Sacramento Valley

Scientific archaeology in the Sacramento Valley north of the Delta was minimal until the 1950s. Prior to that time UCB had sponsored a few reconnaissance projects, such as N. C. Nelson's (1907a) survey of mounds near Tehama and Red Bluff (Figure 9.5), and excavations during the 1930s at Sha-47 and Col-1, -2, and -3 (Heizer 1936; Heizer and Fenenga 1938; Heizer and Krieger 1935–1936; Wedel 1935a). Much of this work was done to test the geographic extent and cultural variability of the cultural "horizons" first identified in the Delta (Lillard *et al.* 1939; Smith and Weymouth 1952b).

In 1951 UCB archaeologists M. A. Baumhoff and R. F. Heizer, along with soils scientist F. Harradine, excavated a loosely flexed human skeleton that was eroding from a stream bank near Capay in Yolo County (Figure 6.4). The bones of "Capay Man," an adult male, lay at a depth of 1.94 m in a "fairly consolidated calcareous aluvium" (Heizer and Cook 1953:24). Soil conditions suggested that roughly 2000 years had elapsed since burial (Harradine 1953:27), whereas bone chemistry and degree of permineralization indicated an age of ≈4000 years (Heizer and Cook 1953:26). Because the Capay burial was not found with cultural material and has not been dated by radiocarbon, its significance and age are uncertain; it does illustrate, however, that Sacramento Valley archaeological remains are often buried under natural sediments of considerable depth.

Despite early surveys, testing, and investigations of such discoveries as the Capay burial, the archaeology of the greater Sacramento Valley remained poorly known until the 1950s and later when intensive fieldwork was done in connection with water projects. In 1952, for example, A. E. Treganza of San Francisco State College (now University; SFSU) directed surveys of seven proposed reservoir areas in and near the Sacramento Valley as part of the River Basin Survey program. In all, 181 sites were documented in the areas of Nimbus, Oroville, Lost Creek, Little Grass Valley, Redbank, Lewiston, and Trinity reservoirs (Treganza 1953).

Following this reconnaissance, Treganza undertook salvage excavations in 1953 at Nimbus and Redbank reservoirs. At Nimbus, in Sacramento County, the principal archaeological sites had been destroyed by construction before archaeological work could begin, and limited testing at Sac-169 yielded "near negative results as far as cultural remains were concerned" (Treganza 1954:4). At Teh-58 in Redbank Reservoir (Figure 9.5), Tehama County, Treganza excavated 77 burials in a cemetery apparently used by the Wintu between circa A.D. 1800 and 1850. Although stratified sites were not sampled at Redbank and little was learned about cultural succession, valuable information was gained about external cultural relationships with this northern border area of the Sacramento Valley:

> Artifacts such as magnesite cylinders, medium clam disc beads, abalone ornaments, and half shell olivella beads indicate a former contact with the central valley. Features such as arrow shaft smoothers, concretion "charm" stones, and arrow point types find parallels in the McCloud river areas to the north. These last items plus pine nut and glycymeris beads, ceremonial blades, fish knives, and projectile points with extended barbs are all traits of the northwest coast of California. Of local occurrence are large stone and shell disc beads, ground obsidian blades, and flaked obsidian pendants. (Treganza 1954:36)

These observations served not only to define protohistoric and early historic (Wintu) manifestations, but also to show that the northern Sacramento Valley, at least during the late period, was not an outlier of the Delta cultural province. Rather, northern Valley assemblages are more like those of the Shasta Lake area to the north where, in 1941 and 1942, UCB archaeologists R. K. Beardsley and W. D. Weymouth documented 37 river, terrace, and hill sites. Excavations in 1942 at three of these sites in the McCloud River canyon (Figure 9.5) yielded 37 burials accompanied by protohistoric and early historic materials nearly identical to those found later by Treganza at Teh-58 (Smith and Weymouth 1952a).

Based upon these and other findings, C. W. Meighan (1955a:32–33) proposed the *Shasta Complex* as characteristic of the northern Sacramento Valley and adjacent uplands, extending northward into Oregon, during the period after circa A.D. 1600. In addition to the traits mentioned above with regard to Teh-58 and the McCloud River sites, the Shasta Complex is recognized by settlements near streams, semisubterranean dwellings, a hunting–gathering subsistence base, acorn processing in hopper mortars, and paucity of charmstones and certain other "Californian" items. The Shasta Complex—now designated the Shasta Aspect of the Augustine Pattern (see Chapter 10)—is thought to signal "an intrusive group from the north" (Meighan 1955a:34) and most likely can be identified with the spread of Wintuan peoples and cultural influences (see Chapter 11).

In 1960 Treganza continued his northern Valley investigations by sampling Sha-169 and -170 on the Sacramento River north of Redding (Figure 9.5). Both midden and cemetery deposits were excavated, the latter yielding 40 flexed burials (Treganza and Heiksen 1960). *Glycymeris* and pine nut beads, *Haliotis* ornaments, arrow-shaft smoothers, Gunther Barbed arrow points, and other distinctive artifacts identify Sha-169 and -170 as expressions of the Shasta Complex. Calling attention to the numerous protohistoric sites nearby, Treganza and Heiksen (1960:43) proposed that the Redding vicinity had been a cultural center for this complex. One of these late sites near Redding was Sha-46 (Figure 9.5) where, during the late 1950s, D. Boyd of Shasta College exhumed 118 burials and associated grave lots of typical Shasta Complex materials (Woolfenden 1970).

In the Black Butte Reservoir area, along the Glenn–Tehama County border (Figure 9.5), A. E. Treganza in 1961 directed SFSU salvage excavations at the Brownell Indian Cemetery (Gle-10) and at two middens, Gle-11 and -15—all assignable to the Shasta Complex. Of special interest at Gle-15 were the saucer-shaped pits of a large (10-m-diameter) dance house and 23 smaller (4- to 6-m) structures. Considering both archaeological and ethnographic information, Treganza and Heiksen (1969) determined that Gle-11 and -15 had been protohistoric settlements of the Stony Creek Nomlaki.

At Gle-10 Treganza excavated a small portion of the jeopardized and disturbed cemetery after the Corps of Engineers had relocated marked historic graves. Two unusual buried features consisted of elongate river cobbles arranged in a rosette pattern, radiating outward from a circular center stone; the "petal" stones were inclined downward toward the center to form a shallow basin approximately 65 cm across and 18 cm deep (Woolfenden 1970:22). The function of these rock features was not determined. The interments at Gle-10 numbered 4 protohistoric and 13 historic burials, the latter furnished with abundant artifacts—Euro-American ceramics and tableware, metal containers, knives, watches, jewelry, and clothing along with traditional black bear robes, magnesite cylinders, *Olivella* and clamshell disk beads, *Haliotis* ornaments, Gunther Barbed points, and large "ceremonial" bifaces—indicating a late nineteenth-century period of acculturation (Woolfenden 1970:22–107). Comparing the Gle-10 assemblage with the remarkably similar inventory from Sha-46 (as just described), Woolfenden (1970) interpreted local variation in detail as a reflection of minor cultural differences between the Stony Creek Nomlaki and the Wintu, respectively. The patterns of acculturation seen archaeologically at Gle-10 and Sha-46 show that, "although the Wintun people were forced to orient themselves to the dominant Euro-American society, taking to them much of its material culture, they retained much of their traditional values and patterns of status" (Woolfenden 1970:198).

During the 1950s and 1960s archaeologists were also investigating sites in the southern Sacramento Valley (Gallup 1963; Jewell and Clemmer 1958; Various Authors 1958). One of these sites was Bamert Cave (Ama-3), a large rockshelter in weathered andesitic tuff, located near Ione at the eastern edge of the Valley (Figure 7.2). Dry deposits at Ama-3 were excavated in 1950 and 1951 by UCB (Heizer and Treganza n.d.), and in the 1960s by archaeologists from the University of California, Davis (UCD), and California State University, Sacramento (CSUS) (J. Johnson 1967; Mabry and Theodoratus 1961; Payen and Johnson 1965). Bamert Cave yielded remarkably well-preserved materials, among them complete and fragmentary digging sticks, arrow shafts and hardwood arrow points, cordage, a carrying net, twined and coiled basketry, and a tule mat. Projectile points and bead types, along with items of non-Indian manufacture, attest to the use of Bamert Cave in late prehistoric and early historic times (Heizer and Hester 1973:19).

That Bamert Cave was used for mortuary and ceremonial purposes is indicated by at least one burial and by pit-and-groove petroglyphs. Storage and food-processing functions are represented by artifact caches and bedrock mortars in the cave. Faunal remains as well as projectile points and bone gorge fishhooks attest to hunting, fishing, and foraging variously to acquire deer, squirrel, kangaroo rat, desert cottontail, white-tailed jackrabbit, king salmon, hardhead, Sacramento sucker, and freshwater mussels. Coprolites and abundant plant tissues preserved in the dry deposits provide evidence for dietary use of acorns, pine nuts, buckeye seeds, and various parts of tarweed, Mariposa lily, storksbill, and dogbane (Heizer and Hester 1973:19). Bamert Cave thus provided a unique record of occupation, most likely by the Northern Sierra Miwok, during a protohistoric to historic period of cultural transition and acculturation.

A much longer archaeological sequence in the Bamert Cave locality has been identified at Camanche Reservoir on the Mokelumne River (Figure 7.2). The Camanche Reservoir area was investigated by CSUS, archaeologists between 1962 and 1964, during which time 77 sites were recorded; of these, 12 caves and 5 open sites were excavated (J. Johnson 1967; Palumbo 1967). On the basis of this work, Johnson defined five prehistoric phases. The earliest, tentatively dated circa 8000–6000 B.C., is a "purely hypothesized Early Man component" suggested by 14 cores and a flake tool found in Pleistocene gravels at three separate sites (Johnson 1967:283–284). The second cultural phase at Camanche is known only from human skeletal remains, without surviving artifacts, found in a Post-Pleistocene yellow alluvium at the stratified Old Bridge site (Cal-237). The thorough permineralization of these bones implied to Johnson (1967:285) "an antiquity comparable to the oldest human remains found in the Central Valley of California," that is, an age of more than 4500 years.

Corresponding with the Delta cultural sequence, the three later phases at Camanche Reservoir are identified, respectively, by (1) ventrally extended and partly fossilized skeletons accompanied by Windmiller artifacts at the Old Bridge site; (2) flexed, moderately calcified skeletons with *Olivella* saucer beads and other "Middle Horizon" artifacts at two sites; and (3) loosely flexed burials and several cremations, along with both historic and "Late Horizon, Phases 2 and 3" artifacts, at several sites (Johnson 1967:285–286). Johnson's work at Camanche Reservoir not only showed that the cultural succession initially defined in the Delta was paralleled as far east as the edge of the Sierra Nevada foothills, but also shed light on archaeological remains intermediate in time between the Farmington Complex (see Chapter 3) and the "Early Horizon." That such remains have not been found also in the Delta locality is more likely a result of natural sedimentation and deep burial than of an absence of pre-"Early" cultures in the lower parts of the Valley.

The problem of buried archaeological deposits is further illustrated by Arcade Creek, north of Sacramento, where erosion revealed an archaeological stratum under 2.75 m of natural soil (Curtice 1961:20–25). Among 75 artifacts collected, excluding flakes and cores, are millingstones, manos, a mortar, pestles, large stemmed points, flake choppers, and hammerstones. Based upon the stratigraphic position and high frequency (35%) of milling tools, the Arcade Creek assemblage was assigned by Wallace (1978b:29) to his Period II: Food Collecting, dated circa 6000–3000 B.C. Although this assignment is not unreasonable, the depth of burial and proportion of milling tools do not necessarily indicate such antiquity. Alluviation has deeply buried archaeological remains of modest antiquity throughout the Valley. Examples would include a Windmiller type charmstone found at a depth of 9 m near Woodbridge; an occupational stratum beneath 5.5 m of alluvium just south of Sacramento; and a curious drilled artifact of granite found near Thornton at a depth of approximately 3 m (Heizer 1949:39).

Cultural developments akin to those of the Delta have been identified at the Applegate site (Ama-56) on Jackson Creek, 6.5 km north of Camanche Reservoir (Figure 7.2). UCD archaeologists excavated this site in 1965 when it was jeopardized by pipeline construction. Mortars, pestles, and a few manos attest to the processing of vegetal foods, whereas faunal remains showed that the residents of Ama-56 collected mussels and turtles from an adjacent slough and hunted or trapped deer, elk, black-tailed hare, small rodents, and numerous birds. Notable were the disarticulated bones of eight or more canids (coyotes?) found buried in two separate features (J. Johnson 1970a).

Human remains in an apparent cemetery at the Applegate site included a cremation, 1 extended and 17 flexed burials, and 11 fragmentary skeletons. Associated artifacts registered long occupation. Although bifaces from a lower component are like those of the "Early Horizon," most artifacts are of "Middle Horizon" types. Obsidian hydration measurements suggest an age of 2300 to 4600 years for this component (Johnson 1970a:118). Also present, although less frequent, are markers of the "Late Horizon," Phase 1 (ca. A.D. 300–1400). Ama-56 is important not only for its record of "the transitional period between Early and Middle Horizon," but also as "a link between the Sacramento Valley and the burial caves of the Sierra Nevada foothill region to the east" (Johnson 1970a:67).

W. G. Roop (1981) has reported an important yet little studied aspect of prehistoric subsistence and settlement patterns in the Valley and other lowlands of central California. In Placer, Merced, Solano, and Napa counties, Roop found millingstones, manos, pestles of a type designed for use in wooden mortars, and occasional flaked-stone tools on the margins of vernal pools. These pools are small, hardpan-floored depressions in the valley grassland that fill with water during the winter and gradually dry up during the spring, at which time they support a distinctive flora (Holland and Jain 1977:56). Vernal pools are especially common along the eastern edge of the Sacramento Valley. Roop (1981) has proposed that Indians camped near these pools for brief intervals each spring to harvest freshwater shrimp, take occasional waterfowl, and especially to gather the greens, bulbs, and seeds of clover, hairgrass, eryngium, navarretia, tarweed, brodiaea, and other plants associated with the pools.

Numerous other archaeological projects have been completed in the Sacramento Valley during recent years. Significant among these were excavations at Sut-34 and -44 at Sutter Buttes (Jensen 1970); the King Brown site, Sac-29 (Olsen 1963); the Jonson site, Sac-65 (Schulz *et al.* 1979); the Safflower site, SJo-145 (Schulz and Ritter 1977); the Blodgett site, Sac-267 (J. Johnson 1976); and the Deterding and Governor's Mansion sites (unpublished). This work has led to a better understanding of the nature, areal extent, age, external connections, and internal relationships among the archaeological cultures of the Sacramento Valley. However, as discussed below, it has led as well to a number of problems in cultural classification not easily resolved by reference to the traditional succession of three "horizons."

## Rethinking the Central California Sequence

Beginning in 1954 Bert Gerow of Stanford University has repeatedly questioned the model of widespread, parallel cultural succession in central California (Gerow 1954, 1968, 1974a, 1974b). Gerow's objections have been sustained by various data, including radiocarbon dates showing that the "Early" and "Middle" Horizons were at least partly contemporaneous. The oldest available date from an "Early" site (SJo-68) is 4350 ± 250 B.P., but a "Middle" component at CCo-308 has been dated at 4450 ± 400 years (Figure 5.11). Although the latter age was determined from a small sample of charcoal and may not be precisely correct, many other $^{14}$C dates show that "Early" and "Middle" expressions coexisted for a millennium or more (Figure 5.11). Hence the concepts of Early and Middle *Horizons* would appear to be misleading as broad, sequential developments. Moreover, as Gerow (1968) and J. Johnson (1971a) have noted, many of the traits supposedly typical of particular horizons are absent in various parts of the Central Valley and San Francisco Bay regions. Therefore, variability in the archaeological record is not easily accommodated by the horizon scheme.

Bickel (1974) has called attention to other problems with the Central California Taxonomic System (CCTS). First, since no minimum of characteristic traits was ever set for the definition of horizons, assemblages sharing few common elements often were classified together when the CCTS was applied in places distant from the Delta locality. Second, the dimensions of time and culture sometimes were confused:

> [the] presence of a shell bead diagnostic type in one context (such as a Nevada dry cave) might suggest temporal equivalence to other sites of a horizon, whereas in another context it would be invoked as evidence for cultural equivalence. In less than extreme cases the nature of identity (cultural or temporal) implied by horizon membership often remained unclear and unspecified. (Bickel 1974:2)

Because the CCTS was composed of discrete, sequential units, it obscured gradual changes through time. Consequently, the processes of cultural evolution could not be represented by the static taxonomy. This was reflected in a concern for "diagnostic" traits rather than broad patterns of behavior. That is, the CCTS led to the reconstruction of particulars in ever more detail without much attention to the development of settlement patterns, economic systems, or social organization. It now

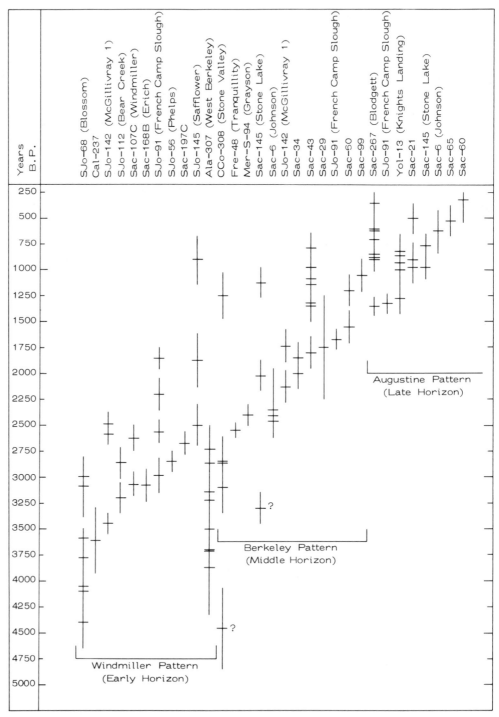

**Figure 5.11** Selected central California radiocarbon dates. Vertical lines indicate the range of 1 standard deviation. (After Fredrickson 1974; Schulz 1975.)

seems clear that central California prehistory was far too complex and dynamic to have been represented by a monolithic scheme such as the CCTS.

## Central California Patterns

Recent years have seen the emergence of archaeological sequences for many localities in central California. For example, J. Bennyhoff has divided this area into a number of geographic *districts* (Diablo, Colusa, Cosumnes, etc.) and defined for each a succession of cultural phases (Bennyhoff 1972, cited in Elsasser 1978b:38–44). However, the current emphasis on local developments does not mean that regional or areal models have been abandoned. One such model, formulated by D. Fredrickson in collaboration with J. Bennyhoff, advances the concept of *pattern* as an integrative cultural unit without temporal implications:

> A pattern is an adaptive mode extending across one or more regions, characterized by particular technological skills and devices, particular economic modes, including participation in trade networks and practices surrounding wealth, and by particular mortuary and ceremonial practices. (Fredrickson 1973:7–8)

As a general way of life shared by peoples within a defined geographic space, the pattern is the unit most readily perceived in the archaeological record. The smaller units of *aspect* and *phase* are detectable only through detailed analysis of the pattern. Thus, "a pattern is defined in terms of generalized forms and types, whereas aspects and phases are defined in terms of certain distinctive features which characterize these general forms and types" (Fredrickson 1973:124). Fredrickson has defined several patterns, of which Windmiller, Berkeley, and Augustine are especially relevant to Central Valley prehistory.

### Windmiller Pattern

To infer from the fairly common mortar fragments in at least some Windmiller sites, the grinding of acorns and/or other seeds was relatively important. Enormous numbers of baked-clay balls may have substituted for rocks in basket cooking of acorn mush and other foods by "stone" boiling. Large quantities of projectile points along with faunal remains indicate that deer, elk, pronghorn, rabbits, and waterfowl were hunted in quantity. Fishing is attested not only by the remains of sturgeon, salmon, and smaller fishes, but also by a unique trident fish spear, two types of angling hooks, and pecan-shaped objects of baked clay thought to have been fishline sinkers (Heizer 1949; Ragir 1972).

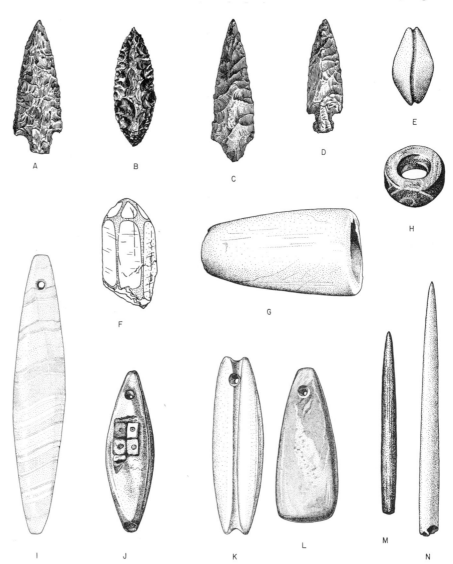

**Figure 5.12** Artifacts of the Windmiller Pattern from the Delta locality. A–D, large projectile points of chert and obsidian; E, pecan-shaped, grooved object of baked clay; F, battered quartz crystal; G, pipe of steatite; H, steatite bead; I–L, charmstones of alabaster or calcite (I, K) and blue amphibolite schist (J, L); M, N, ground-slate pins. (After Heizer 1949:Figures 8, 9, 11, 12, 14, 15, 16; courtesy of the R. H. Lowie Museum of Anthropology, University of California, Berkeley.)

As for Windmiller technical skills, flaked- and ground-stone industries are well represented. Especially notable are ground and polished charmstones of alabaster, marble, diorite, and other rocks (Figure 5.12). In the extensive inventory of baked-clay artifacts are vessels, disks, sinkers, and cooking "stones." Twined basketry is known from impressions on baked clay. Work in shell, including *Haliotis* ornaments, *Olivella* beads, and shell bead appliqué, is well developed. The minimal bone industry consists mainly of awls, needles, and flakers (Fredrickson 1973; Ragir 1972).

Trade seems to have been focused upon acquiring utility goods as well as ornamental and ceremonial objects, many of which apparently were obtained as finished items rather than as raw material. Windmiller groups in the Delta acquired (1) obsidian or finished obsidian artifacts from no fewer than two Coast Range quarries and three trans-Sierran sources; (2) *Haliotis* and *Olivella* shells and ornaments from the coast; (3) asphaltum from an undetermined source; (4) quartz crystals and alabaster from the Sierra foothills; and (5) many other exotic materials (Heizer 1949, 1974b; Ragir 1972). This implies that California was already settled extensively by 4000 years ago, and that the Windmiller Pattern was effectively integrated into the economic matrix of that time.

In the Delta locality, Windmiller burial of the dead occurred both in village grave plots and in cemeteries separate from the habitation sites. The ceremonial aspects of the mortuary complex are reflected by red ochre in graves and by funerary artifacts with ≈85% of all burials. Skeletons are most often extended ventrally and oriented toward the west, although westerly oriented dorsal extensions are also common. Flexed burials, nonwesterly orientation, and cremations occur infrequently (Fredrickson 1973; Ragir 1972).

It is significant that nearly all Windmiller burials were oriented toward the west (Figure 5.13). P. D. Schulz (1970) determined that in four Windmiller sites the predominance of orientations fell between 223° and 282° (magnetic), which are, respectively, the positions of the sun at the winter and summer solstices. Assuming that the burial orientation was toward the setting sun, the body positions would indicate that ≈80% of the deaths occurred in the winter. The highest frequency of burials at all sites is oriented toward 240°, which corresponds either to mid-February or to October–November (Figure 5.14).

Further assuming that the Windmiller economy was focused on hunting rather than gathering storable seeds (and particularly acorns), Schulz (1970) proposed that, in lean years, episodes of near-starvation may have combined with disease to decimate Valley populations. Supporting this hypothesis are human remains that seem to show evidence of recurrent starvation among Windmiller children (McHenry 1968). Skeletal analysis revealed that Harris lines—thought to result from disease or trauma—

**Figure 5.13** Windmiller Pattern (formerly "Early Horizon") burial at the type site, Sac-107 (see Figure 5.15). Extended skeletons, often oriented toward the west and furnished with charmstones and other artifacts, typify the Windmiller mortuary pattern. Photograph circa 1935. (Courtesy of the R. H. Lowie Museum of Anthropology, University of California, Berkeley.)

decreased in frequency from "Early" to "Late," and that dental hypoplasia was least common during "Middle" times, phenomena attributed to the adoption of acorns as a major food resource in the "Middle Horizon" (McHenry and Schulz 1978:43).

Although McHenry and Schulz have made a case for Windmiller people suffering more developmental trauma than the other populations studied, this does not necessarily mean that acorns were not being used by "Early" groups. Indeed, the number of mortar fragments in Windmiller sites would suggest that the pulverizing of acorns or other seeds was an important activity (Ragir 1972:98). Moreover, certain edible

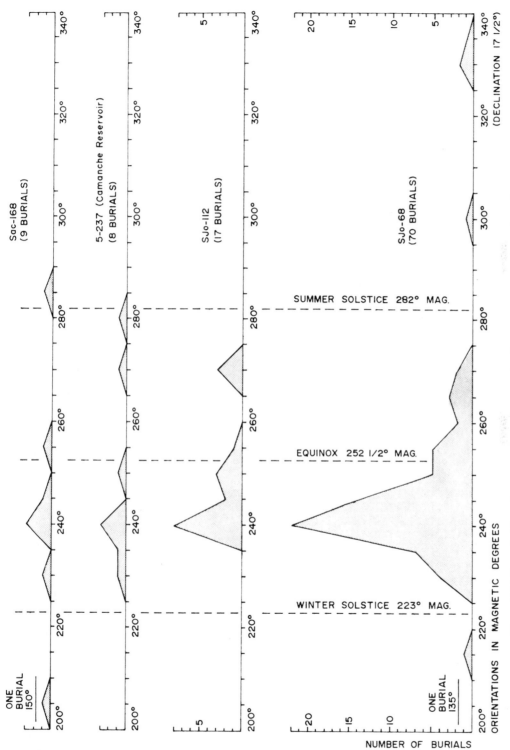

**Figure 5.14** Extended-burial orientations at four Windmiller Pattern sites. (After Schulz 1970; Figure 2.)

plants, such as cattail, tule-potato, amole, clover, and brodiaea, were so abundant in the Valley that it is difficult to imagine recurrent episodes of starvation unless the effective environment had been modified greatly by climatic changes.

It is suggested here that at least some Windmiller groups may have occupied the Sierra Nevada foothills during the summer and the Valley during the winter (Figure 5.15). Seasonal movements of this sort would explain why Windmiller types of artifacts occur in Sierran mortuary caverns along with human bones otherwise unidentified (see Chapter 7). This hypothesis also would account for the quartz crystals, calcite, alabaster, and schist artifacts—all of materials from foothill sources—found in Valley Windmiller sites. Finally, seasonal movements would explain why, according to solar orientation of skeletons, about 80% of the Valley Windmiller burials seem to have been interred during the winter. As early as ≈4000 years ago, Windmiller people may have established a pattern of summer movement to the Sierra Nevada from winter villages in the Valley. A comparison of Valley Windmiller skeletons with those from the Sierran ossuary caverns would be a good way to test this proposition.

Certain aspects of social behavior may be inferred from Windmiller mortuary practices as observed in Valley cemeteries. Ragir (1972:96–97) noted that the burial of males in separate areas, in deeper graves, and with more artifacts may indicate that men generally held higher status than women. However, the association of conspicuous grave goods with the remains of some women, children, and even infants suggests that status was at least partly inherited or ascribed rather than achieved. Although

**Figure 5.15** The Windmiller mound (beyond fenceline), Sac-107, near the Cosumnes River, Sacramento County (Figure 6.4). Excavations during the 1930s in stratified deposits at Sac-107 revealed four cultural components representing Early, Transitional, Late, and historic phases. Sac-107 is the type site for the "Early Horizon," now encompassed by the Windmiller Pattern. (Photograph by F. Fenenga, 1948; courtesy of the R. H. Lowie Museum of Anthropology, University of California, Berkeley.)

most Windmiller men and women were buried in an extended position, flexed burials seem to be exclusively those of old women. The significance of this is not readily apparent. Warfare or feuding is implied by depressed skull fractures, "nightstick" fractures of the forearm, weapon points embedded in bones, skull caches and isolated skulls, and the use of human bone artifacts (Heizer 1974b; Ragir 1972).

With respect to Windmiller origins, it is suggested that people well adapted to riverine and wetland environments, perhaps from the Columbia Plateau or western Great Basin, brought an early and generalized form of the Windmiller Pattern to the Delta locality at some time before 2500 B.C. (see Chapter 11). By circa 1800 B.C., strong Windmiller influence could be seen as far west as the San Francisco Bay shore in the lower component at West Berkeley (Elsasser 1978b) (see Chapter 6). At about the same time, and possibly as early as 2000 B.C., Windmiller populations came to occupy the central Sierra Nevada foothills, at least seasonally (see Chapter 7).

Gerow (1974a) has called attention to marked similarities between early Windmiller and Berkeley ("Middle Horizon") phases. For example, powdered red ochre in graves, nonventral position, nonwesterly orientation, flexed burial posture, and bone points appear more frequently in earlier Windmiller strata at the Blossom site (SJo-68) in the Delta (Gerow 1974a:241). The earliest Windmiller component at SJo-68 also produced cobble mortars, pestles, bone spatulae and ulna awls, lanceolate concave-base projectile points, and perforate "bipoint notched-end" charmstones like those of the early Berkeley Pattern to the west (Davis and Treganza 1959; Ragir 1972; Wallace and Lathrap 1975). These facts suggest that an earlier, generalized Windmiller culture may have been ancestral to the later, more specialized Berkeley and Windmiller Pattern expressions, and that these patterns evolved coevally, mostly in geographic separation, and with variable intensities of contact and diffusion through time.

It is possible that the appearance and spread of the early, generalized Windmiller culture in central California represents the arrival and initial diversification of Utian language groups (see Chapter 11). An early western or San Francisco Bay enclave of Utians, identified with the Windmiller-like component at West Berkeley (see Chapter 6), may have given rise to the Berkeley Pattern, which in turn relates to the emergence of Miwok and Costanoan. Heizer was probably correct in saying that Windmiller "is an early phase in what must be an unbroken cultural tradition" (1974b:190).

## Berkeley Pattern

The Berkeley Pattern includes those components previously assigned to the Middle Horizon, renamed by Ragir (1972) the Cosumnes Culture,

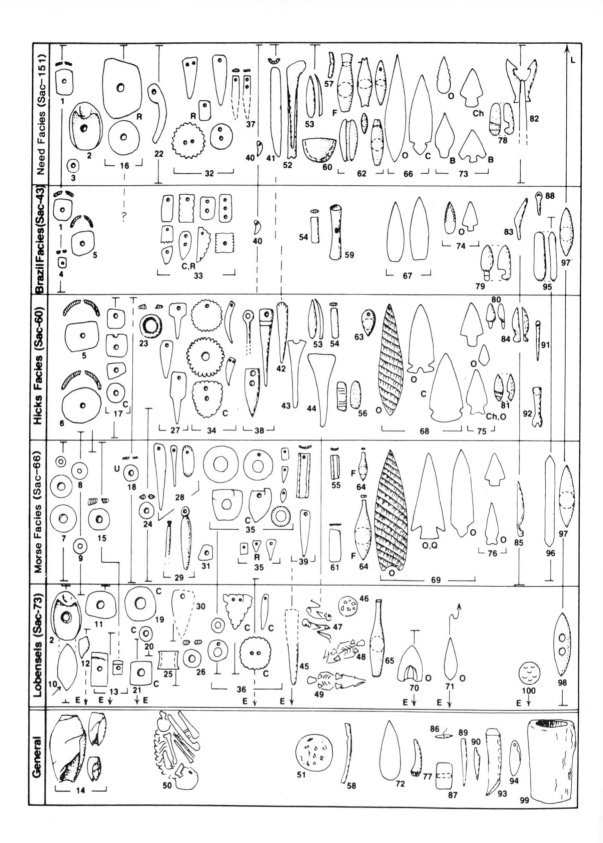

Need Facies (Sac–151)

BrazilFacies(Sac–43)

Hicks Facies (Sac–60)

Morse Facies (Sac–66)

Lobensels (Sac–73)

General

and referred to by Gaumer (1968) as the Emery Tradition (Fredrickson 1973:125a). Initially a San Francisco Bay region development, the Berkeley Pattern later spread to surrounding coastal and interior areas of central California. The shift to the Berkeley Pattern in many places was not an abrupt or total cultural replacement, but rather a gradual yet significant change in economic emphasis and particular material traits. Although the inception of the Berkeley Pattern does not seem to be the result of a separate migration into California, its appearance in some places may signal local population movements (see Chapter 11).

Because the Berkeley Pattern is discussed at length in Chapter 6, only a brief synopsis is given here. Berkeley Pattern subsistence activities focused upon acorns as a dietary staple. Technologically, the Berkeley Pattern is set apart from Windmiller by relatively more mortars and pes-

---

**Figure 5.16** Berkeley Pattern ("Middle Horizon"), Cosumnes District: Significant artifact types and temporal changes, from Lobensels ("Early–Middle Horizon transition facies") to Need (Late–Middle Horizon) facies. Drawings not to scale. Position of specimens shown within facies has no chronological significance. Bead typology from Lillard *et al.* (1939). B, basalt; C, *Haliotis cracherodii*; Ch, chert; E, trait persists from "Early Horizon"; F, "fishtail" charmstone; L, trait persists into "Late Horizon"; R, *Haliotis rufescens*; U, *Haliotis*, sp. unidentified. 1–14, *Olivella* beads: 1, modified "saddle," Type 3b2; 2, split-drilled, Type 3b1; 3, small "saucer," Type 3c; 4, small modified "saddle," Type 3b2; 5, full "saddle," Type 3b; 6, round "saddle," Type 3b; 7, ring, Type 3c2; 8, large "saucer," Type 3c; 9, small "saucer," Type 3c; 10, "beveled" bead (arrow points to bevel), Type 3b1; 11, oval "saddle," Type 3b; 12, diagonal spire-lopped, Type 1c; 13, thick-shelved rectangle, Type 2b; 14, spire-lopped, Types 1a, 1b. 15, *Macoma* disk bead. 16–21, *Haliotis* beads: 16, large, amorphous, Type H4; 17, small amorphous, Type H4; 18, nacreous disk, Type H3; 19, large disk, Type H3; 20, small disk, Type H3; 21, square, Type H1a. 22, Steatite "claw" pendant. 23, Steatite ring. 24, Steatite lenticular disk bead. 25. Steatite "hourglass" earspool. 26, Steatite flat disk bead. 27,28, Flat slate pendants. 29, Cylindrical slate pendants. 30, Flat slate pendant. 31, Biotite ornament. 32–36, *Haliotis* pendants. 37–39, Bone pendants. 40, Canid tooth pendants. 41–45, Deer tibia and antler spatulae. 46, Cremation. 47, Flexed burial, all orientations. 48, Burial, ventral, semiextended, all orientations. 49, Burial, ventral, extended, all orientations. 50, Burial, tight flexure (most distinctive of "Middle Horizon," though other positions, including rare extension, also occur), all orientations. 51, Cremation (rare, none for Brazil Facies). 52, Mammal tibia "wand." 53, Split rib strigil (Type 1). 54, Whole rib strigil (Type 2). 55, Flat bone strigil (Type 3). 56, Bone dice. 57, Bird-bone whistle, central stop. 58, Bird-bone whistle, end stop. 59, Mammal-bone whistle, central stop. 60, Steatite perforated cup ("cloud blower"?). 61, Flat stone bars. 62–65, Charmstones. 66–76, Chipped-stone artifacts: 66–69, probably spear points (note careful diagonal flaking, on 68, 69, to left); 70, knife designed for hafting; 71, bipointed knife (occurs in all facies but most common in Lobensels); 72, leaf-shaped knife; 73–76, dart points. 77, Antler-tine flaker. 78–81, Atlatl spurs (?) of bone. 82, Barbed-bone fish spear. 83–85, Unbarbed-bone fish spears (?). 86, Bone gorge hook. 87, Bone mesh gauge. 88, Cannon-bone awl, pointed distally. 89, Ground-bone awl. 90, Bone splinter awl. 91, Bone needle. 92, Socketed antler handle. 93, Antler wedge (rare). 94, *Margaritifera* spoon, perforated. 95,96, Flat slab pestle for use with wooden mortar. 97, Cylindrical bipointed pestle for use with wooden mortars. 98, Pitted bipointed pestle. 99, Wooden mortar. (After Elsasser 1978b: Figure 4; chart by J. A. Bennyhoff, 1972; courtesy of A. B. Elsasser, J. A. Bennyhoff, and the Smithsonian Institution.)

tles, a well-developed bone industry, distinctive diagonal flaking of large concave-base points, and certain forms of *Olivella* and *Haliotis* (especially *H. cracherodii*) beads and ornaments (Figure 5.16). Berkeley peoples normally interred their dead in flexed positions with variable orientations and fewer grave goods than are found with Windmiller burials. A small proportion of cremations with funerary artifacts may identify high-status individuals.

Berkeley Pattern assemblages appear in the lower Sacramento Valley soon after circa 500 B.C. It is proposed that the Berkeley components at such sites as Sac-6, Sac-142, Sac-34, and Sac-145 (Figure 6.4) may represent the arrival and spread of the ancestral Plains Miwok in the Cosumnes District (i.e., the area of the lower Cosumnes, Mokelumne, and Sacramento rivers) from a Proto-Miwok homeland in the Bay region. Radiocarbon dates bracket this spread between circa 500 and 0 B.C. (Figures 5.11 and 6.16). The ancient Plains or Bay Miwok probably also held the area north of Suisun Bay during this interval, later relinquishing this territory to the Patwin (Bennyhoff 1977b).

In the Stockton District farther south, the Berkeley Pattern is less evident. Instead, the Windmiller Pattern evidently continued much longer than in the Cosumnes District. One relatively late Windmiller settlement was at French Camp Slough (SJo-91) near Stockton, where J. Johnson in 1970 and 1971 rescued materials jeopardized by a construction project. Radiocarbon dates place the initial occupation of SJo-91 at circa 1000 B.C. The subsistence economy at this site was based upon the use of slough resources: Sacramento perch and squaw fish, freshwater clams, tules, and ducks and geese, along with deer, elk, and acorns from higher ground (J. Johnson 1971b:6).

At SJo-91 Johnson found two cemeteries in a dark midden deposit. One cemetery, with a $^{14}$C date of circa A.D. 630 ± 100, contained about 60 burials but only three artifacts. The other, dated between 984 ± 60 B.C. and A.D. 105 ± 190, yielded 115 extended burials in ventral positions with red ochre and abundant artifacts (large stemmed and concave-base points, bone pins and spatulae, *Haliotis* ornaments, pestles and other groundstone items) in the graves. Some skeletons were found to have been wrapped and buried in tule mats; others had remains of headdresses; and at the feet of one burial were bits of twined fabric, presumably remnants of sandals. Relative wealth or poverty of graves may indicate status differentiation. The survival of perishable items at SJo-91 was remarkable, "and in some cases the actual mold of the bodies was preserved. Had this been recognized early in the investigation some of them could have been filled with plaster, such as many of the body molds at Pompeii had been, and the actual physical appearance of the individuals might have been recovered" (J. Johnson 1971b:5).

SJo-91 might have been an early Yokuts settlement, or perhaps the residents of this community spoke a Utian language derived from the speech of earlier Windmiller populations. In any event, similarities between the French Camp Slough assemblage and components of the Chowchilla Phase (see Chapter 7) to the southeast argue for cultural unity from the Stockton District to the south-central Sierran foothills during some interval between circa 1000 B.C. and A.D. 500. James Bennyhoff, who first called attention to the *in situ* continuity of archaeological developments in the Cosumnes, Diablo, and Stockton districts over a span of 2000 years or more, relates these district sequences to the emergence of the Plains Miwok, Bay Miwok, and Northern Valley Yokuts, respectively (Bennyhoff and Fredrickson 1969, cited in Fredrickson 1973:66–68).

The cultural distinctiveness of the Stockton District (as well as that of the Colusa District and others) shows that the Berkeley Pattern did not spread uniformly throughout central California. Rather, the Berkeley Pattern seems best explicated as the archaeological record of Utian (Miwok–Costanoan) cultural developments in the San Francisco Bay Region after circa 1500 B.C. (see Chapter 6) and the subsequent spread of Miwok groups from the Bay northward to Clear Lake and eastward, across the mid–Central Valley, to the Sierra Nevada. Berkeley traits ultimately came to be distributed over a wide geographic area, but the pattern seems most closely linked to the "Utian radiation" (see Chapters 6 and 11).

## Augustine Pattern

As defined by Fredrickson (1973), this widespread central California pattern includes cultures previously assigned to the "Late Horizon" (or "Hotchkiss Culture"; see Ragir 1972). The Augustine Pattern is distinguished by intensive fishing, hunting, and gathering (especially of acorns); large, dense populations; highly developed exchange systems; social stratification, as indicated by considerable variability in grave furnishings; elaborate ceremonialism; and the mortuary practices of cremation (often reserved for high-status persons) and preinterment grave-pit burning of artifacts, coupled with flexed burial. Technologically, the Augustine Pattern exhibits shaped mortars and pestles, bone awls for making coiled baskets, and the bow and arrow (Fredrickson 1973:127–129). Pottery is also found in some parts of the Central Valley (Figure 5.17). The Augustine Pattern represents both local innovation and the blending of new traits with those of the older Berkeley Pattern.

An important stimulus to the Augustine Pattern was the southward expansion of Wintuan peoples in the Sacramento Valley, identified archaeologically by preinterment burning, harpoons, flanged tubular pipes, and arrows tipped with Gunther Barbed points. The later elaboration of

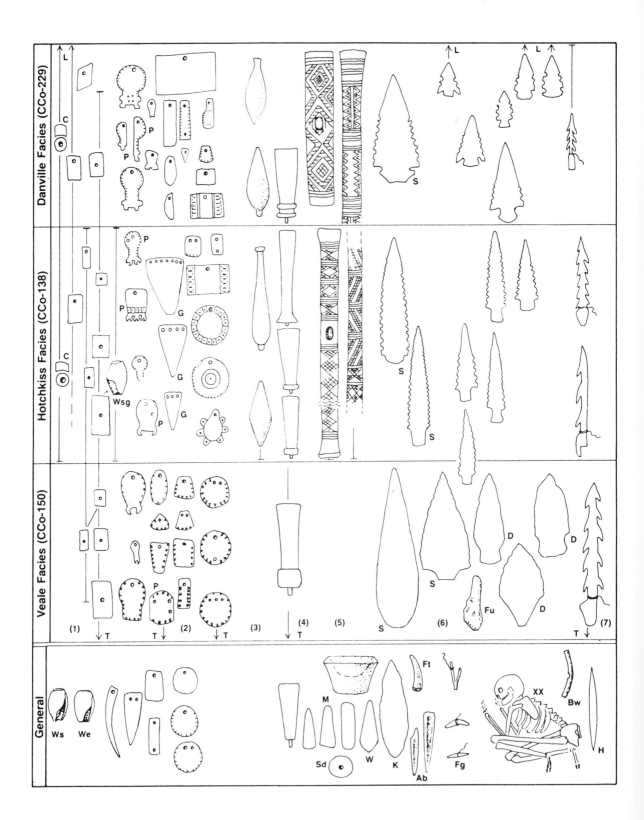

**Danville Facies (CCo-229)**

**Hotchkiss Facies (CCo-138)**

**Veale Facies (CCo-150)**

**General**

the Augustine Pattern—beginning circa A.D. 1400 and witnessed by a proliferation of settlements, intensification of trade, general use of clam-shell disk beads as money, and new levels of social and political complex-ity—is seen not as the result of additional immigration, but as a product of growth and increased contacts among resident populations, fostered by improved environmental conditions.

An important Augustine Pattern settlement in the Cosumnes District was located at the Blodgett site (Sac-267) near Sloughhouse (Figure 6.4). Excavations by J. Johnson revealed two prehistoric components, [14] C-dated at A.D. 580 ± 90 and A.D. 1605 ± 145. The earlier of these exhibits flexed burials with few accompaniments, rectangular *Olivella* beads, and Gunther Barbed arrow points (see Figures 10.5B and 10.7E). The later (Plains Miwok?) component is recognized by various triangular arrow points, clamshell and steatite disk beads, magnesite cylinders, *Olivella* disk beads, and pottery.

A surprising discovery at Sac-267 was a well-defined pottery-making technology. Large quantities of rolled, coiled, and pinched clay, along with finished rim and body sherds, allowed Johnson (ed. 1976) to define a Cosumnes Brown Ware. Similar pottery now has been identified at Sac-56, -67, -113, and -265, all within 25 km of Sac-267. The Brown Ware pottery is thought to be related to the extensive baked-clay industry (net sinkers, pipes, discoids, cooking "stones," etc.) already well known in the lower Sacramento Valley. Johnson concluded that "the Plains Miwok were making a Brown Ware type of pottery throughout the lower Cos-umnes area and that previous investigators may have missed the coiled clay fragments and sherds because they often did not use screens and they did not wetscreen the material before sorting" (1976:371).

Finally, Johnson (ed. 1976:336) sees the Gunther Barbed points at

---

**Figure 5.17** Augustine Pattern ("Late Horizon"), Diablo District: Significant artifact types and temporal changes. Drawings not to scale. Except for projectile points, position of specimens within subphases has no significance. Approximate order of artifacts repre-sented, from left to right: 1, *Olivella* beads; 2, *Haliotis* ornaments (note that first appearance of heavy incision on many ornaments is in "Middle–Late Horizon Transition"); 3, charm-stones; 4, stone pipes; 5, decorated-bone ear tubes and whistles; 6, stone projectile points; 7, bone harpoons. Legend: Ab, bone awls; Bw, bone whistles; C, "cupped" *Olivella* beads; D, dart point (undesignated points are presumed arrow points); Fg, fishhook or gorges of wood (top), shell, and bone (bottom); Ft, antler tine flaker; Fu, bone (ulna) flaker; G, ornaments worn as girdle; H, bone hairpin; K, stone knife; L, trait carries over to "Phase 2, Late Horizon;" M, stone mortar and pestles; P, ornaments usually found paired in mirror image; S, spear point; Sd, stone discoidal, perforated; T, trait appears for first time in "Transition Phase," between "Middle" and "Late Horizons;" W, stone pestle for use in wooden mortars; We, whole end-ground *Olivella* bead; Ws, whole spire-ground *Olivella* bead; Wsg, whole side-ground *Olivella* bead; XX, flexed burial position (27% grave pit burning; 32% have northwest orientation). (After Elsasser 1978b:Figure 6; chart by J. A. Bennyhoff, 1972; cour-tesy of A. B. Elsasser, J. A. Bennyhoff, and the Smithsonian Institution.)

Sac-267 (and at other sites farther north) as evidence that the Slough-house vicinity was near the southerly limit of immigration by a bow and arrow-using population (Patwin?, Nisenan?). That the incursion was not peaceful is shown by many cases of violent death at Sac-267 and other Valley sites, such as Yol-13 (ca. A.D. 650–1150) at Knights Landing on the Sacramento River (Figure 6.4) where mutilated skeletons and Gunther Barbed points embedded in human bones have been found (J. Johnson, ed. 1976, 1977). Nonetheless, one should not assume that all Gunther Barbed points in the Valley were left by invaders. This type is distributed widely in northern California (Dotta 1967), and technical analyses have shown that "the Gunther barbed projectile point is most commonly manufactured of obsidian derived from sources not included within the known spatial distribution of the type, and raw materials (blanks) are known from valley sites" (Jackson and Schulz 1975:4–7). It seems probable, therefore, that following an episode of contact, including violence, between Patwin (or Nisenan?) immigrants and established Valley populations, the latter adopted both the bow and arrow and the particular style of associated arrow points. Thereafter, Gunther Barbed points were manufactured by various central California groups not identifiable with the Wintuan incursion.

## Summary and Conclusions

During its long prehistory, the Great Central Valley witnessed many population movements, waves of cultural influence from neighboring areas, and a complex interplay between local and regional cultural forces—a drama always played against the backdrop of diverse and changing environments. Although the Valley possibly was first occupied in terminal Pleistocene times, as suggested by core and flake tools at Rancho Murieta, Camanche Reservoir, and the Farmington Complex sites, these assemblages remain to be dated precisely. Also undated, but probably 11,500 to 7500 years old, are Fluted-Point Tradition and Western Pluvial Lakes Tradition assemblages at Tracy, Tulare, and Buena Vista lakes (see Chapters 2 and 3). It is likely that most of the archaeological evidence of Central Valley habitation prior to circa 4000–5000 B.C. lies deeply buried under alluvium. This is especially true of the lower reaches of the San Joaquin and Sacramento River drainages where up to 10 m of sediments have accumulated during the past 5000 to 6000 years. Such rapid alluviation would account for the deep burial of the Capay skeleton, Arcade Creek artifacts, many Windmiller components, and other remains of modest antiquity in Valley lowlands.

Little can be said of early- to mid-Holocene archaeology in the Central Valley. Candidate pre-Windmiller finds include permineralized and badly eroded human bones in the lowest component at the Old Bridge site (Cal-237); the Positas Complex of perforated flat cobbles, small mortars, and millingstones in Zone D at Mer-S-94; and, conceivably, materials from the lowest levels of Ker-39 and -60 at Buena Vista Lake. It is expected that further discoveries of early Holocene archaeological materials will be made in the Valley during the next few decades.

Later manifestations, at least in the Delta and surrounding country, are better known. Long described in terms of widespread, synchronous cultural horizons, the late Holocene prehistory of the mid–Central Valley now seems better understood in terms of cultural "patterns," that is, archaeological units representing fundamental economic, technologic, and often social continuities over large areas and long intervals of time. Many distinctive attributes of Valley patterns are thought to have appeared or spread as a result of immigration—Windmiller being linked with the arrival of Utian peoples from outside California; Berkeley associated with the expansion of Miwok groups from the Bay Region eastward into the Valley and beyond; and Augustine being stimulated by southward Wintuan population movements in the Sacramento Valley.

External relationships between peoples of the Delta locality and those of the Bay Region and central Sierra Nevada generally were more important than relationships with Valley peoples to the north and south. This east–west emphasis was partly based upon social and linguistic ties, but also was a function of economic incentives to trade with peoples in different resource zones.

South of the Stockton District, the San Joaquin Valley remains one of the least-known archaeological areas in California. Other than the salvage of late-period Yokuts burial sites, large-scale excavations have been limited to Wedel's early work at Buena Vista Lake and a series of projects at San Luis, Los Banos, and Little Panoche reservoirs. Although Wedel's components have not been dated absolutely, cross-dating of artifacts would indicate periods of significant occupation between circa 2000 B.C. and A.D. 500 and from circa A.D. 1500 to 1850. Cultural affiliations with the Santa Barbara coast and the Mojave Desert are apparent at Buena Vista Lake, whereas Delta traits are few during late prehistoric times. In the Panoche–San Luis vicinity, a long series of phases is broken by a hiatus between circa A.D. 1000 and 1500; this may relate to a dry climatic interval. Otherwise, this sequence parallels that of the Delta but with notable elements from the South Coast Ranges. Findings at Buena Vista Lake and Panoche–San Luis indicate that populations expanded and settlements proliferated after circa A.D. 1500 in the southern and western portions of the San Joaquin Valley.

In the upper Sacramento Valley archaeological attention has focused

**Figure 5.18** Ceremonial roundhouse of the Hill Nomlaki at Grindstone Creek Rancheria, Glenn County, 1923. Such large, semisubterranean structures are common features at major Augustine Pattern sites and are presumed to have housed cult ceremonies, as they did in historic times. (Photograph by C. H. Merriam; courtesy of the R. H. Lowie Museum of Anthropology, University of California, Berkeley.)

mainly upon late cemeteries and middens. Consequently, older manifestations remain poorly known even though some 12,000 years of prehistory have been documented in the adjacent North Coast Ranges (see Chapter 10), and there is every reason to expect comparable time depth in the upper Valley. Much has been learned about the Shasta Aspect of the Augustine Pattern, thought to be associated with the spread of Wintuan peoples from the north. Farther south, the later appearance of an elaborated Augustine Pattern (Figures 5.17 and 5.18). may signal the expansion of Patwin groups into the lower Sacramento Valley and the emergence of central California as a distinctive "cultural climax" area.

# 6. San Francisco Bay and Central Coast Regions

This is certainly a fine harbour: It presents on sight a beautiful fitness, and it has no lack of good drinking water and plenty of firewood and ballast. Its climate, though cold, is altogether healthful and it is free from such troublesome daily fogs as there are at Monterey, since these scarcely come to its mouth and inside there are very clear days. To these many good things is added the best of all: The heathens all around this harbour are always so friendly and so docile that I had Indians aboard several times with great pleasure, and the crew as often visited them on land.

*Ayala (1775)*

(Photograph by John S. Shelton.)

# Introduction

When Juan Manuel de Ayala's brig *San Carlos* entered San Francisco Bay in 1775, the surrounding country was densely populated by Indians. At that time the Bay area was occupied by Coast and Saclan Miwok, Suisun Patwin, and speakers of several Costanoan languages (Figure 11.1). Although much has been written about these historic Indians (see Moratto 1974b), the prehistory of the Bay area is less well known—partly because urban sprawl has destroyed numerous archaeological sites and partly because many of the data from "salvaged" sites remain unpublished and generally unavailable. Also problematic is the complexity of the archaeological record. The Bay region was inhabited for more than 10,000 years by diverse peoples, and long ago it emerged as a distinctive cultural center with influences extending to and from the Central Valley and Coast Ranges.

South of San Francisco Bay, the Central Coast region encompasses that part of the South Coast Ranges between the latitudes of Año Nuevo and San Luis Obispo (Figure 1). This varied land features coastal terraces as well as mountains rising abruptly from the shore, forested uplands, fertile interior valleys, and rolling oak-studded hills. In early historic times, and probably through a long interval of prehistory, the Central Coast was held by the Esselen and Salinan Indians (Figure 11.1). Very little archaeological work has been done in this area; early cultural developments, particularly in the interior valleys and hills, remain poorly known. Even so, recent surveys and testing have identified some ancient occupation sites and have yielded important new information about prehistoric settlement and land-use patterns in the Central Coast region.

This chapter examines the archaeology and prehistory of the Central Coast and San Francisco Bay regions. It begins with an overview of natural history and a review of major environmental changes that may have affected local cultures over a span of 10,000 years or more.

# Natural History

*San Francisco Bay Region*

The San Francisco Bay region encompasses the bayshore and rolling hill and valley country on all sides for a distance of about 50 km (Figures 1 and 6.4). At the heart of this region is the largest estuarine system in California. Its principal features are San Pablo and San Francisco bays, Carquinez Strait, Suisun Bay, and a maze of peripheral channels and tidelands. Together these waterways are some 88 km long and from 5 to 20 km wide, covering roughly 1100 km². The Bay system previously was much larger, inundating ≈1800 km² before massive silting during the Gold Rush and recent landfill projects greatly reduced its area and altered the nature of its margins. Between 1850 and 1914, an estimated 875 million m³ of sediments from the Sierra Nevada were deposited in the San Francisco Bay system (Desgrandchamp 1976). Bay filling has continued, although at a slower rate, as a result of deforestation, poor farming practices, and other modern activities. Today the mud-choked Bay averages only 3–4 m deep (although its depth is 110 m at the Golden Gate due to tidal scouring), and much of its bordering marshland has been "reclaimed" for urban purposes.

San Francisco Bay occupies a late Pliocene trough that was flooded repeatedly during Pleistocene interglacials. The depression extends southward to form the Santa Clara and San Benito valleys, and northward across San Pablo Bay into the Petaluma, Sonoma, and Napa valleys. The Bay is bounded on the west by ridges of the San Francisco and Marin peninsulas, the latter dominated by Mt. Tamalpais (elevation, 794 m). Separating the Bay from the San Ramón and Livermore Valley system to the east are the Berkeley Hills, rising from the bayshore to an elevation of 581 m at Volmer Peak. The Diablo Ranges, stretching southward from Mt. Diablo (elevation, 1137 m), form the eastern border of the Bay region (Figures 6.1 and 6.4).

The most recent filling of San Francisco Bay occurred during the past 10,000 years. At circa 15,000 B.P., the coastal shoreline was more than 25 km west of San Francisco's present ocean beaches (Figure 6.2). Thereafter, rising seas (caused by the melting of continental glaciers) began to encroach upon California's coast. The waters rose quickly from approximately −128 m at 15,000 B.P., past −56 m at 10,000 B.P., to −18 m at 7000 B.P. (Milliman and Emery 1968). Before circa 10,000 B.P., the great Sacramento River surged through the rocky gorge of the Golden Gate and then flowed across what is today the submerged continental shelf, finally emptying into the ocean many kilometers west of the present shoreline.

**Figure 6.1** Aerial oblique view of the San Francisco Bay region, looking eastward across the Central Valley to the Sierra Nevada. Marin headlands and coast, lower left; San Francisco Bay and Peninsula, lower right and center. (Photograph by the United States Air Force.)

By 8000 years ago, marine waters had begun to invade San Francisco Bay. Since circa 6000 B.P. the rate of sea-level increment relative to land surfaces around the Bay has amounted to ≈1.5 ± 0.5 mm/year (Figure 6.2) (Atwater *et al.* 1977; Bickel *et al.* 1973; Fairbridge 1976; Henn *et al.* 1972; Pestrong 1972).

The Bay's recent geologic history is highly significant to archaeology. The geologic data imply, first, that local estuarine adaptations must have appeared less than 8000 years ago; second, that archaeological sites on old bayshores are probably buried deeply under sediments; and, third, that the microclimates and biotic communities along the edge of the Bay would have changed almost continuously during early and middle Holocene times. Many of the marshlands bordering the Bay were established no more than ≈3000 years ago (Atwater and Hedel 1976). Similarly, the lower reaches of streams that empty into this inland arm of the sea would have changed as the Bay expanded and caused marshlands to invade parts of the Delta and other lowlands. Rising Bay levels may account for such archaeological phenomena as submerged sites, paucity of early cultural remains, and shifts through time in the use of particular food resources (Bickel 1978a, b).

The primeval Bay area was rich in rocks and minerals that the Indians could fashion into tools or use as trade goods. Obsidian, the preferred material for projectile points and knives, was available from the Anadel and Napa Glass Mountain quarries immediately north of the Bay region (see Chapter 10). Franciscan chert was common in streambeds and outcrops of the north Bay area, whereas banded Monterey chert occurred in coastal deposits south of San Francisco. Hematite for pigment was obtained in Sonoma and Alameda counties. Cinnabar, a prized vermilion pigment, was mined at the New Almaden deposits in Santa Clara County; cinnabar was in such demand that Indians trekked to the New Almaden locality from as far away as the Columbia River (Heizer 1951d). Marin County groups exploited the asphaltum seep at Duxbury Point, using the natural adhesive for a variety of purposes. Also valued was a fine schist from Wildcat Canyon, Contra Costa County, which appears archaeologically as ornaments and charmstones. Other rocks and minerals that figured in the aboriginal economy were granite, basalt, sandstone, and steatite (Heizer 1951d; Heizer and Treganza 1944).

The Bay area's prehistoric landscape featured a mosaic of plant communities ranging from saltmarsh and redwood forest to grassland and mixed-evergreen woodland. Each community sustained a peculiar array of animals, and game was generally abundant. Early explorers reported vast numbers of deer, elk, and waterfowl in the area. Along the coast were seals, sea lions, and sea otters, as well as plenty of red abalone, mussels, oysters, and clams. In addition, sharks, bat ray, white seabass, sturgeons, Chinook and silver salmon, jacksmelt, surf perch, and many other fish

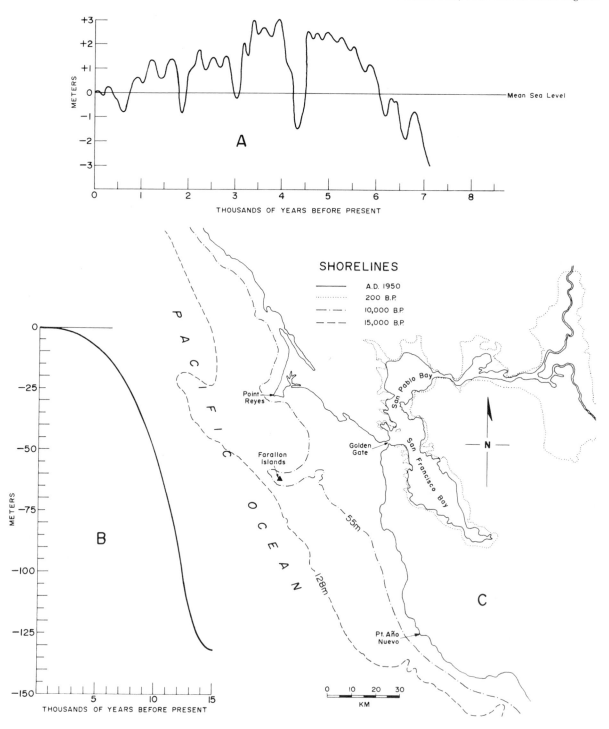

species were available to the Indians (Follett 1974, 1975b; Ingles 1965; Ricketts and Calvin 1962).

The local climate is salubrious, with few freezing days and almost no snowfall. January's mean temperatures are 45–55°F throughout the Bay region; in July the averages are 55–65° near the Bay and up to 15° higher inland. Precipitation normally varies from ≈50 to 100 cm per year, depending on the microenvironment (Durrenberger 1965).

In sum, the environment of the Bay region must have been nearly ideal from the Indian perspective. Local topography presented no barriers to overland travel and few places unsuited for habitation, and there was an abundance of game, fowl, fish, shellfish, vegetal foods, and lithic materials of value to the domestic economy and for trade.

## Central Coast Region

From Año Nuevo southward rugged mountains abut the sea to form the western edge of the Central Coast region. Because coastal terraces are infrequent and narrow (Figure 6.3), the western slope is drained by small streams of steep gradient. The surf-pounded, rocky shoreline supports a profusion of mussels and abalone, as well as fish, waterfowl, pinnipeds, and sea otters. The inland parts of this region feature north–south-trending mountains of the Diablo, Santa Cruz, Gabilan, and Santa Lucia ranges. Paralleling these uplands are valley systems, most notably the fertile Salinas River Valley, which extends nearly 250 km from its source in the Panza and Santa Lucia ranges to its mouth at Monterey Bay (Figure 4.4).

Seasons are weakly developed and temperatures are mild year-round in the Central Coast region, partly due to the effects of summer fog and sea breezes. Rainfall diminishes from north to south; precipitation averages ≈81 cm/year at Santa Cruz, 61 cm/year at Monterey, and 56 cm/year at San Luis Obispo (Beck and Haase 1974: Map 5). Inland, annual precipitation ranges from ≈25 cm/year in leeward valleys to >140 cm/year on the seaward aspects of the higher mountains. Diverse geology, landforms, soil types, and microclimatic conditions give rise to a rich mosaic of plant communities in this region. Among the major vegetation types are coastal strand, coastal saltmarsh, riparian, closed cone pine–cypress forest, redwood and mixed redwood–Douglas fir forest, broadleaf evergreen forest, coast live oak woodland, foothill woodland, chaparral, and grassland (Gordon 1974).

---

**Figure 6.2** Ancient shorelines and sea levels of the San Francisco Bay area. A, Holocene sea-level changes (after Fairbridge 1976: Figure 3); B, generalized late Pleistocene and Holocene sea-level curve (after Milliman and Emery 1968); and C, present and past shorelines of the San Francisco Bay area (after Atwater and Hedel 1976; Bickel 1978; Lajoie 1972).

**Figure 6.3** Marine terrace near Gorda, about 95 km south of Monterey, in the Central Coast region. Steep slopes rising abruptly from the rocky shoreline typify this part of the coast. (Photograph by John S. Shelton.)

The natural environment of the Central Coast region has changed significantly during the Holocene epoch and even during historic times. Coastal physiography is characterized by especially rapid natural change; studies of sea-cliff erosion indicate that in some places wave action is displacing the shoreline inland at an average rate of >15 cm/year (Gordon 1974:8). Some river valleys previously were occupied by extensive lakes. For example, the Sargent landslide at times blocked the Pájaro River to form a broad lake in the Bolsa de San Felipe or Hollister Valley (Jenkins 1973:158). In this same area, Don Pedro Fages in 1770 and 1772 recorded extensive marshlands, large flocks of geese, cranes, and ducks, herds of pronghorn, and "many reed patches crossed by numerous bear trails" (Bolton 1911:147–149; Treutlein 1972:344). These observations serve as a reminder that the archaeological cultures of the Central Coast region can be understood only with reference to their contemporary environments.

## Native Cultures

Before circa A.D. 1770, the San Francisco Bay region was occupied by speakers of Coast Miwok (Kelly 1978), Patwin (see Chapter 5), Bay

Miwok (Levy 1978b), and Costanoan (Figure 11.1). Typical of the Bay area groups were the Costanoans (from the Spanish *costaños*, "coast people") who held the South Coast Ranges between San Pablo Bay and Monterey. Although the Costanoans did not survive the impacts of the Spanish and American invasions, their culture was documented by early explorers, priests, and settlers and by later ethnographers. Useful overviews of Costanoan ethnography have been published by Breschini (1972b), Broadbent (1972), Harrington (1942), Heizer (ed. 1974), Kroeber (1925:462–473), Levy (1978a), and Margolin (1978). In addition, there exist at the Smithsonian Institution 117 boxes (nearly 80,000 pages) of Costanoan field notes, mostly linguistic data, recorded between 1929 and 1936 by J. P. Harrington (Walsh 1976:26).

Costanoan population in A.D. 1770 has been estimated at 7000 (Kroeber 1925:464) to 10,200 (Levy 1978a:485). The basic unit of Costanoan political organization was the tribelet, consisting of one or more socially linked villages and smaller settlements within a recognized territory. Tribelet leadership was vested in a chief and a council of elders who served mainly as advisers to the community (Harrington 1933:3). Principal villages were established at ecotones, that is, at the junctures of two or more biotic communities (e.g., oak woodland–bayshore marsh). Subsistence activities emphasized gathering berries, greens, and bulbs (especially soap root); harvesting seeds and nuts, of which the acorn was primary; hunting for elk, deer, pronghorn, and smaller animals; collecting shellfish; and taking varied fishes in stream, bay, lagoon, and open coastal waters.

South of the Costanoans were the Esselen, whose land encompassed the Big Sur and upper Carmel River drainages of the Santa Lucia Range, most of the Arroyo Seco drainage, and the ocean frontage south of the Little Sur River (Figure 11.1). Numbering approximately 1300 persons, the Esselen moved as small, seminomadic bands among favored camps to exploit both littoral and interior zones. Linguistic geography indicates that "the Esselen were a relict people driven into their mountain fortress by younger, perhaps Costanoan, invaders" (Cook 1974a:3). The San Carlos and Soledad missions (1770, 1771) brought an end to the Esselen, making them the first California Indians to become culturally extinct (Cook 1974a, 1974b; Hester 1978a).

South of Esselen country, Salinan peoples held the coast below Lucia and the mountainous upper Salinas River drainage as far north as Kings City (Figure 11.1). Like their neighbors, the Salinans hunted deer, bear, and rabbits; took waterfowl; fished; collected shellfish; and gathered acorns, sage seeds, and berries in their annual round (Hester 1978b). Although Mason (1912) and Harrington (1942) recorded aspects of Salinan culture, this group remains poorly known. It will be up to archaeology to shed light on the origins and development of Salinan lifeways.

# Exploratory Archaeology

*Introduction*

Although brief descriptions of Bay and Central Coast shellmounds and artifacts were published in various newspapers and journals during the second half of the nineteenth century (Hudson 1873; Yates 1875a), little scientific fieldwork was attempted in these regions until after 1900. Between the turn of the century and circa 1945, most investigations were exploratory: sites were excavated mainly to discover their depth, composition, and contents, rather than to seek answers to research questions. Archaeologists were concerned for the most part with learning the age of the deposits and whether any sort of cultural sequence might be inferred. About the time of World War II, interest began to shift toward comparative studies and the development of regional models of culture classification.

The attrition of archaeological sites around San Francisco Bay began as early as 1849 and gradually increased thereafter as a result of urban growth—especially on the Peninsula and east bayshore. Further damage was wrought by systematic collectors and casual antiquarians seeking charmstones and other "relics" (Yates 1875b, 1889). To the south, archaeological sites of the Central Coast also suffered at the hands of collectors and builders. Farming added to the toll: on the coast north of Santa Cruz was "a large shell mound about 270 feet [82 m] long and 90 feet [27 m] wide. How high it formerly was cannot be told as most of it has been removed by poultry men who used to haul it away by the wagon loads; at this time the mound was about 20 feet [6 m] high" (Dodge 1914:120). Such activities have damaged or destroyed more than 50% of the estimated 9675 archaeological sites formerly present in the nine Bay Area counties (Moratto 1970c, 1973b).

*Central Coast Region*

Excavations on the Central Coast began in 1875 when A. A. Saxe of the California Academy of Sciences tested the Sand Hill Bluff site (SCr-7; Figure 6.8) north of Santa Cruz (Saxe 1875). Subsequent archaeological studies in this region included P. M. Jones' reconnaissance of the U.S. Lighthouse Reservation at Pacific Grove in 1900; a cursory survey of 22 shell middens between Monterey and the Big Sur River (Gifford 1913); A. L. Kroeber's (1915) recording of nine sites near Monterey Bay; and three small-scale surveys of sites near Elkhorn Slough on the Monterey Peninsula (Golomshtok 1921–1922; Hill 1929; Wood 1930).

In 1935, E. M. Fisher—then a graduate student of zoology at the University of California, Berkeley (UCB)—carefully recorded 89 sites along the coastal strip between the Presidio of Monterey and the Carmel River. Fisher's (1935) report gave special attention to the identification and dietary significance of faunal remains observed at these sites. In the same year, W. R. Wedel (1935d) recorded a number of shellmounds in the Point Lobos State Reserve. During the decade following these surveys by Fisher and Wedel, archaeological work on the Central Coast was limited to a minor survey of the Monterey Peninsula in 1937 by the Works Progress Administration and the tracing of petroglyphs at Mnt-86 in 1938 by W. C. Massey. Despite these various surveys, controlled excavations were lacking and the Central Coast was to remain largely an archaeological *terra incognita* until after 1945.

## The San Francisco Bay Region

The first intensive survey of archaeological sites in the Bay region was conducted between 1906 and 1908 by N. C. Nelson, then working under the direction of J. C. Merriam at UCB. Nelson explored the San Francisco Bay shoreline and adjacent coast from the Russian River to Half Moon Bay, documenting 425 "earth mounds and shell heaps" (Nelson 1907b, 1909a, b). Nelson was the first to recognize the Bay area as a discrete archaeological entity, and to this day his fieldwork stands as the most comprehensive survey done in this region by a single person. Although he allowed for possible changes in culture through time, Nelson saw the intensive use of shellfish at both coastal and bayshore middens as evidence of a general economic unity throughout the region.

Along the bayshore of Alameda and Contra Costa counties, Nelson documented some of the more important archaeological sites in central California. This part of the bayshore, until recently bordered by salt-marshes 3 to 8 km wide, was especially rich in waterfowl, fish, and mollusks. More than 100 shellmounds were recorded in this littoral zone, and it was here that Bay region archaeology had its beginnings. Early findings at two of the northeast bayshore sites—Emeryville and Ellis Landing—and at the Fernandez site not far inland provided the basis for the first model of cultural succession in central California.

### Emeryville Shellmound (Ala-309)

Under the auspices of UCB, Max Uhle in 1902 excavated a large trench and tunnel at the Emeryville site (Ala-309), just south of Berkeley (Figure 6.4). The Emeryville shellmound was one of the largest in the Bay region, covering an area roughly 100 × 300 m to a maximum depth of

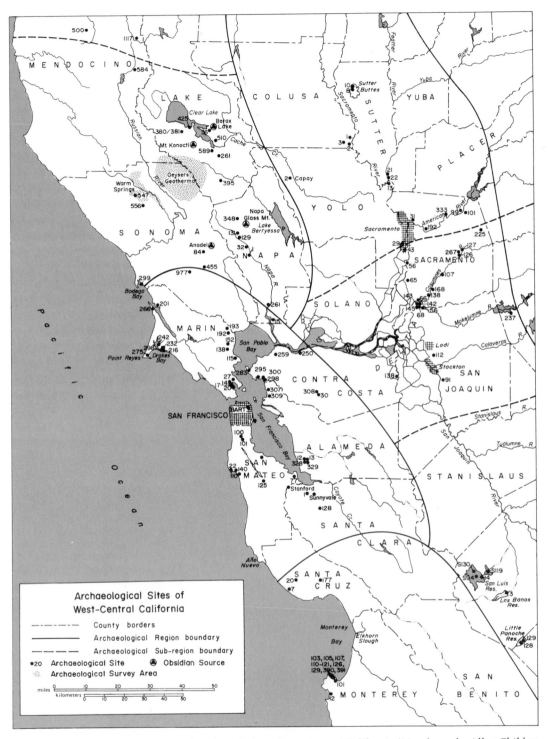

**Figure 6.4** Archaeological sites of west-central California. (Map drawn by Allan Childers and Thad Van Bueren.)

about 9.8 m. The volume has been estimated at ≈39,000 m³. Calling to mind the rising sea (and Bay) levels over time, the mound base at Ala-309 was 75 cm below the modern high-tide line.

Uhle segregated two components, each with five strata, at Emeryville. In the lower levels were flexed burials, red ochre, pointed-bone implements, perforate charmstones, chert bifaces, an emphasis on non-obsidian lithics for flaked-stone tools, and a predominance of bay oyster shells relative to those of bent-nose clams. The upper levels were marked by cremations, polished stone items, artifacts of flaked obsidian, and greater quantities of clam than oyster shells. Uhle's early recognition of diachronic change in Bay region prehistory was a significant innovation. Unfortunately, this idea was rejected by many of his peers, and even as late as the 1920s some Californianists were still highlighting the perceived "static" nature of local archaeological cultures (Kroeber 1925:930).

In 1924 W. E. Schenck of UCB rescued valuable data from the Emeryville mound when it was being leveled to accommodate a paint factory. A sizable quantity of material was salvaged from the upper 6.7 m of the midden, which was removed by steam shovel, and a smaller amount came from three manually dug trenches in the lower 2.4 m of the deposit. Schenck determined that about 60% of the midden was composed of shells—mostly of mussels, oysters, and small clams. Nearly 700 burials were noted; typically, these were flexed. One unusual feature was a mass of burned adult and infant bones, accounting for seven or more individuals, found 8.7 m below the surface. With respect to dating, Schenck (1926b) calculated an age of 1000 years for Ala-309, assuming an average population of 200 and a fixed rate of midden accumulation. This estimate is not supported by a ¹⁴C date of 2310 ± 220 years (LJ-199) later obtained on charcoal from the mound base (Hubbs *et al.* 1962).

Schenck's perceptions of Ala-309 were ultraconservative. While remarking on the "evenness of the culture" and the lack of evidence for stratification (1926b:270), he also reported that perforate charmstones occurred only below 6 m; stone pipes and Type M *Olivella* beads were found only above 5 m; and mica ornaments, imperforate charmstones, and "killed" (ritually broken) mortars appeared exclusively above 6 m. As Bert Gerow has observed, Schenck dismissed the evidence for the vertical separation of artifacts on the grounds on noncomparable sampling of the upper and lower portions of the deposit. However, if Schenck had analyzed his data more carefully,

> it seems that he could have made a plausible case for not only a change of charmstone types, but a decrease or absence in later times in the use of non-obsidian materials for flaked stone points, unelaborated barbs for composite fishhook or spear, unelaborated pestles, and circular forms of abalone and drilled mussel shell fractions with a single central perforation. (Gerow 1968:2)

Instead, Schenck criticized the idea of progressive development and the more liberal age estimates of his predecessors, concluding that artifactual differences within the mound could be attributed to its seasonal occupation by diverse groups from nearby localities who came to gather shellfish, take waterfowl, and hunt sea otter (Schenck 1926b). Later, however, H. Howard's (1929) analysis of bird bones showed conclusively that the Emeryville site had been occupied not seasonally but year-round.

### The Ellis Landing Site (CCo-295)

Located near Brooks Island on a saltmarsh in Richmond (Figure 6.4), the Ellis Landing mound (CCo-295; Figure 6.5) was a large and ancient bayshore site. Nelson's excavations revealed that the greatest midden depth was 8.5 m, of which 4.9 m were below the level of the surrounding marsh. In an effort to determine the age of CCo-295, Nelson computed its volume ($\approx$35,000 m$^3$) and estimated a probable rate of accumulation—a technique that yielded a time span of 3500 years (Nelson 1909a, 1910c).

The Ellis Landing mound was physically stratified. At a depth of about 2.5 m, Nelson observed that a lower compacted level with finely macerated shell was distinguishable from an upper level with larger shell fragments. This stratification appears in photographs and profile drawings, although Schenck later (1926b) denied its existence (Beardsley 1954).

Between 1906 and 1908, Nelson recovered 160 burials and 630 artifacts at Ellis Landing. These came chiefly from manual excavations

**Figure 6.5** Ellis Landing shellmound (CCo-295), facing west of south, showing N. C. Nelson's 1906–1908 excavations. (Courtesy of the R. H. Lowie Museum of Anthropology, University of California, Berkeley.)

(Figure 6.5), but some specimens were found on the beach and others were salvaged when the mound was graded. Nelson defined two components at Ellis Landing: the upper with perforate charmstones, incised bone tubes, *Olivella* saucer beads, stemmed projectile points, and mortars with flared sides; the lower marked by spatulate bone objects, triangular and rectangular *Haliotis* ornaments, red ochre, cobble mortars, an atlatl spur, grooved sinker stones, large nonstemmed points, and *Olivella* saucer and saddle beads (Figure 6.6). The lower cultural level was later selected by Beardsley (1954) as the type component for the Ellis Landing Facies (Figure 5.6). Beardsley placed the upper component in the Emeryville Facies, but cited the occurrence of clam disk beads in the upper 1 m of the deposit as a "weak hint" of a third, late prehistoric (Fernandez Facies) component at CCo-295.

### The Fernandez Site (CCo-259)

Remarkably, the Fernandez site (CCo-259) was a shellmound located fully 8 km from the Bay in Rodeo Valley (Figure 6.4). It was investigated sporadically by UCB archaeologists, beginning with excavations by Nelson in 1910. CCo-259 was sampled by L. Barker in 1935, R. Heizer in 1938, D. Perryman in 1958, and J. Davis in 1959 (Davis 1960b). When further research was contemplated during the 1960s, the landowner confessed that he had sold the site to a topsoil company for 25¢ per yard and that it was gone (Heizer 1973).

Even though CCo-259 was far from a source of mollusks, its midden was almost as rich in shell as any site along the bayshore. In the black, clayey lower part of the deposit, bay oyster and mussel shells predominated; most common in the upper, more friable soil levels were shells of bent-nose clams (Davis 1960b).

Three cultural strata were identified at Fernandez: Component A (0–137 cm), with clamshell disk beads, cylindrical beads of magnesite and steatite, *Olivella* punched and lipped beads, tubular stone pipes, imperforate charmstones, and baked clay balls—all associated with cremations; Component B (137–183 cm), characterized by thin rectangular *Olivella* beads, large *Haliotis* ornaments of diverse forms, and cremations; and Component C (mainly below 210 cm), set apart by *Olivella* saddle beads, perforate charmstones, large circular *Haliotis* ornaments, cobble mortars, and abundant red ochre with flexed burials (Davis 1960b). A charcoal sample from Component C provided a $^{14}$C date of 230 B.C. ± 250 (UCLA-297).

In 1954 R. K. Beardsley assigned Components B and C to the Emeryville and Ellis Landing facies, respectively, and selected the A level as the type component for the Fernandez Facies. The upper (Fernandez) component at CCo-259 is generally considered to be the best example of a Phase

**Figure 6.6** Artifacts from the Ellis Landing shellmound (CCo-295). A,B, pipes of polished steatite; C, incised bird bone; D,E, bone awls; F, polished bone "blade;" G, *Olivella* beads; H, I, obsidian arrow points; J,K, foliate bifaces of obsidian; L,M, imperforate charmstones; N,O, perforate charmstones; P,Q, part of a musical instrument made of bird bones and decorated with *Olivella* beads set in asphaltum. (After Nelson 1910: Plates 43–46; courtesy of the R. H. Lowie Museum of Anthropology, University of California, Berkeley.)

2, "Late Horizon" (i.e., late Augustine Pattern) settlement in the east bayshore locality. It would thus appear that CCo-259 represented a nearly continuous occupation from Ellis Landing Facies times (more than 2000 years ago) until the early historic period (Davis 1960b).

## The West Bay Area

Early archaeological fieldwork and discoveries west of San Francisco Bay largely paralleled those of the eastern bayshore. In 1910, for example, N. C. Nelson supervised major excavations at the Crocker mound or Bayshore site (SFr-7) near Hunters Point in San Francisco (Figure 6.4). Shell midden deposits as deep as 3 m yielded 23 burials and artifacts assignable to the Ellis Landing and Emeryville facies (Beardsley 1954:92). Similarly, Emeryville and Ellis Landing components were identified at the Ponce or Castro site (SCl-1) in northwestern Santa Clara County (Figure 6.4), where, in 1911, L. L. Loud singlehandedly excavated more than 350 m³ (12,000 ft³) of midden and found 50 burials (Beardsley 1954:92–94).

Early work in San Mateo County revealed materials comparable to those from the Bayshore and Ponce sites. At SMa-23, on the Mills Estate in San Bruno, three seasons of excavation by R. J. Drake in 1941 and 1942 produced both cremations and burials along with a cultural assemblage linked to the "late Middle Horizon" or "Phase 1 Late Horizon" (Drake 1948), that is, to the Ellis Landing or Emeryville Facies.

Even coastal sites evinced apparent close ties with bayshore cultures. At the Princeton mound (SMa-22), situated on the fringe of an old lagoon north of Half Moon Bay (Figure 6.4), L. L. Loud in 1915 unearthed one semiextended and seven flexed burials, the former with nine spatulate bone artifacts, a bone "knife," and *Olivella* saucer and rectangle beads. Found in the midden were whalebone wedges and numerous small pitted stones (Loud 1912, 1915). Beardsley (1954) fit SMa-22 into the Ellis Landing Facies (Figure 5.6), emphasizing the similarity of the Princeton burials and artifacts to those of the bayshore (20 km east) and Marin County (90 km north). Additional burials and artifacts found in 1962, coupled with three obsidian hydration measurements, further support the idea of an Ellis Landing affiliation for SMa-22 (Phebus 1973).

## The North Bay Area

In 1909 and 1910 N. C. Nelson sampled middens in Sausalito (Mrn-3), Greenbrae (Mrn-76), and San Rafael (Mrn-315) with the hope of finding evidence of cultural evolution. This work revealed two prehistoric complexes similar to those being investigated along the east bayshore: an older phase (later subsumed under the Ellis Landing Facies) with cobble mortars, large projectile points, *Olivella* saucer beads, mica ornaments, and elk bone whistles; and a younger phase (subsequently placed in the Emeryville Facies) distinguished by incised *Haliotis* ornaments, *Olivella* rectangle beads, imperforate charmstones, and shaped flat-bottom mortars (Nelson 1910a, b, 1911). These discoveries convinced Nelson that southeast Marin County was part of the San Francisco Bay cultural region and provided him with the basis for an archaeological sequence in the north Bay area.

In western Marin County, the Point Reyes Peninsula has witnessed over the years a great deal of archaeological work. Interest in this locality has been sustained largely by the conviction of many researchers that Francis Drake built his fort and careened the *Golden Hind* near Point Reyes in 1579. Drake's camp was the first English settlement in America, and not a few persons have spent decades searching for traces of it. The "Drake quest," a driving force in Marin County archaeology for some 40 years, was launched quite unintentionally by those seeking to unravel the area's prehistory.

Robert Heizer directed intermittent surveys of the Drakes Bay vicinity in 1938–1939 and the first scientific excavations there during 1940. At the Estero site (Mrn-232) Heizer discovered corroded iron ship's spikes and sherds of Ming Dynasty Chinese porcelain—the first sixteenth-century artifacts recognized in a Marin County archaeological site. In 1940 and 1941 UCB crews supervised by R. K. Beardsley resumed work at Mrn-232 and excavated three other Point Reyes sites: Mendoza (Mrn-275), Cauley (Mrn-242), and McClure (Mrn-266) (Figure 6.4); limited testing was done at nine others. More Chinese ceramics and bent iron spikes of "archaic character" came to light at six of these sites (Beardsley 1954). Heizer (1947) proposed that these materials most likely originated with Sebastian Cermeño's galleon *San Agustín*, which ran aground at Drakes Bay in 1595, but this interpretation is strongly contested by those who show that some of the artifacts almost certainly were left by Drake 16 years before Cermeño's mishap (Aker 1978; Aker and Von der Porten 1979; Moratto 1974a; Von der Porten 1963, 1965, 1970, 1972).

Beardsley and Heizer not only discovered sixteenth-century exotic artifacts in shellmounds at Point Reyes, but also established an aboriginal cultural sequence for the area. Based on work done through 1941, Beardsley (1954) defined three facies in western Marin County: (1) McClure, representing the "Middle Horizon" in the Coastal Province and linked to the Ellis Landing Facies on the Bay, (2) Mendoza, and (3) Estero, respectively the counterparts of Phase 1 and Phase 2, "Late Horizon", in the Marin Province (Figure 5.6). The characteristics of these facies are summarized in Table 6.1.

*Summary and Discussion*

Archaeological exploration in the Bay region increased rapidly after Uhle's early work at Emeryville and Nelson's far-flung survey and testing efforts in the first dozen years of the twentieth century. By 1916 UCB

**TABLE 6.1**

**Diagnostic Traits of Coastal Marin County Facies**[a]

| | McClure Facies | Mendoza Facies | Estero Facies |
|---|---|---|---|
| Central California concordance | Middle Horizon | Late Horizon: Phase I | Late Horizon: Phase II |
| Disposal pattern | Primary interment; high frequency of funerary offerings; beds of red ochre | Primary inhumation and cremation; numerous "killed" show mortars | Mostly cremations; associations are frequent |
| Artifacts | 1. Infrequent round-bottom mortars | Flat-based show mortars | Flat-based show mortars |
| | 2. Shaped pestles | Shaped pestles | Rare flanged pestles |
| | 3. Numerous crude stone sinkers | | |
| | 4. Net mesh gauges | | |
| | 5. Long, heavy projectile points; use of atlatl? | Small projectile points of obsidian; triangular body | Small obsidian projectile points often with square serrations |
| | 6. Some points with slight shoulder | | Points often triangular with corner notches |
| | 7. Finely chipped stone drills | | |
| | 8. Quartz crystals with pitch | | |
| | 9. Abundant bone artifacts: tubes head scratchers, needles, awls, chisels, daggers, etc. | Relatively few bone artifacts; hair-pins, awls, needles | Tubular bird bone artifacts are common: pyro-incised tubes, bird-bone whistles, bone beads |
| | 10. *Olivella* A1, F3a, G1, G2a | *Olivella* A1, G2a, E1 | *Olivella* E2 |
| | 11. — | — | *Tivela* tubular beads; great numbers of clam disk beads; steatite and magnesite beads. |
| | 12. Rectangular *Haliotis* ornaments | | Banjo shaped and triangular *Haliotis* pendants. |
| | 13. Baked-earth steaming ovens | | Historic spikes, porcelain, trade beads, glass. |

[a] After Beardsley (1954).

archaeologists had excavated 11 of Nelson's sites: Ellis Landing, Emeryville, West Berkeley, Stege, Fernandez, Castro, Bayshore, Princeton, Greenbrae, Sausalito, and San Rafael. Digging continued at a number of these mounds in later years, and work was initiated at Newark, Potrero, Filoli Estates, and at many of the Point Reyes sites. These investigations supported Nelson's concept of a distinctive San Francisco Bay archaeological region and showed that broadly parallel and synchronous changes in artifacts, mortuary practices, and shellfish remains were present throughout the area. Local differences were also apparent, but these seemed less important than the regional commonalities. The aggregate impression was that a series of closely related cultures, perhaps of common ancestry, had occupied the entire margin of the San Francisco Bay system for a long interval of prehistory.

The shellmounds also provided evidence of intensive adaptation to the littoral zone. Although the economic repertoire generally included fishing, shellfish collecting, fowling, hunting estuarine and land mammals, and gathering vegetal products, particulars of the food quest varied through time and from site to site. For example, the emphasis on mussels and oysters in earlier periods gave way to a predominance of clams in later times throughout the bayshore zone. Certain sites may have been specialized fishing villages; at one of the Stege mounds (CCo-300), for instance, heavy stone net-sinkers comprised 61% of all artifacts found (Loud 1924).

Another feature of many bayshore shellmounds is their great volume, which implies either recurrent settlement over long spans of time or sedentism by large populations. This is a matter of no small consequence when it is remembered that the central California Indians lacked agricultural crops to sustain their populations. At the same time, it is possible to overemphasize the shell content of the bayshore mounds. The great masses of shell have been interpreted traditionally to mean that mollusks were the dietary mainstay in the Bay area. One may argue, however, that the perceived importance of mollusks has been skewed by their high shell-to-meat ratio (often >1:1). An estimated 9390 whole shells (18,780 valves) would represent only 10 kg of edible meat from bay mussels; 1190 shells would register the same weight of meat from bent-nose clams (Cook 1946). In comparison, large and edible fish such as the bat ray (<95 kg), leopard shark (<32 kg), white seabass (<38 kg), and white sturgeon (<630 kg) are often known archaeologically by a few grams of bone. Here the preserved bone-to-meat ratio might be <1:1000! In other words, the remains of a single 10-kg fish might stand for as much edible meat as thousands of shells of mussels or clams. Hence, the sheer quantity of shell in the middens does not fairly reflect the importance of shellfish relative to other local foods.

Finally, exploratory studies revealed that many of the bayshore sites contained two or more components. By the 1940s enough information was on hand to permit a synthesis of these components into a tentative regional prehistory. As discussed in Chapter 5, R. K. Beardsley in 1948 expanded the Central California Taxonomic System so as to correlate Bay region sequences with those of the Delta. From studies of artifacts, mortuary patterns, and stratigraphy, Beardsley concluded that (1) the "Middle Horizon" was the oldest expression in the Bay region, and its components could be grouped into the Ellis Landing Facies; (2) the initial and greater part (Phase 1) of the "Late Horizon" was represented by components of the Emeryville Facies; (3) Fernandez followed Emeryville as the protohistoric phase (Phase 2) of the "Late Horizon"; and (4) the Ellis Landing to Fernandez progression appears to have been a developmental continuum (Figure 5.6). In the main, Beardsley's (1948, 1954) publication of new data and general synthesis were important contributions to central California archaeology.

## Regional and Local Prehistories

### Introduction

For more than two decades after 1948 the Central California Taxonomic System (CCTS) was the standard device for ordering prehistory in the Bay and Central Coast regions. The preoccupation with this model was a natural but tenacious reaction to earlier views of cultural stasis. Nonetheless, from about 1950 onward, archaeologists in central California typically found that their data did not fit neatly into the CCTS pigeonholes. To the extent that the CCTS was based upon time-sensitive mortuary practices and artifacts, it obscured more fundamental social and economic continuities over long periods of time. Also, the forcing of data into the CCTS often caused distinctive local manifestations to be overlooked. Another result of this typologic emphasis was that attention was focused more on subtle diachronic shifts in artifact forms than on broader patterns of cultural development or the reasons for changes seen in the archaeological record. Ultimately it became necessary to limit the particularism of the CCTS to local sequences and to seek new integrative models for regional and areal syntheses.

Archaeology in west-central California has advanced since 1950 in several important respects. Radiocarbon and obsidian dating have led to precise absolute chronologies that permit synchronic comparisons as well as refined diachronic studies. Fieldwork has continued around San Francisco Bay, and more than 30 sites have been excavated in the Central Coast region where preliminary cultural sequences have been worked out. In both the Bay and Central Coast regions archaeological manifestations different and older than the Ellis Landing Facies have been reported. Researches into prehistoric social organization, settlement patterns, and economic systems have been initiated with promising results, and investigations of prehistoric cultural ecology have been stimulated by geological and biological studies of Holocene environments in the Monterey Bay and San Francisco Bay areas. Some of these recent advances are discussed in the following sections.

## The Central Coast Region

Between 1946 and 1955, anthropology students at UCB gathered and organized a great deal of information about the archaeology of the Central Coast region. R. E. Greengo in 1950 sampled shellmounds near Elkhorn Slough (Figure 6.4) to examine relative quantities of molluscan remains (Greengo 1951); S. Broadbent surveyed the Carmel–Pacific Grove vicinity in 1950 and 1951 and tested the Berwick Park (Mnt-107) site (Broadbent 1951a, b); R. K. Beardsley (1946b) reported two aboriginal burials accompanied by *Olivella* shell beads at the Customs House site (Mnt-108) in Monterey; and UCB field classes tested several other sites in the area, among them Mnt-290, -300, and -351 (G. Breschini, personal communication, 1983). The most intensive and systematic work, however, was done by A. R. Pilling, who conducted extensive field surveys (1948a) and entered the first 350 Monterey County sites—mostly on the coast north of Big Sur—into the records of the University of California Archaeological Survey. Pilling (1948b) also described a series of petroglyphs and red, black, and white pictographs associated with caves in Vaqueros Formation sandstone of the Santa Lucia Mountains. Pilling and others further recorded archaeological sites and collections in the counties of Monterey (Pilling and Beardsley 1948) and San Benito (Pilling *et al.* n.d.). In many respects, Pilling's methods and observations prefigured the research to be conducted by others in the Central Coast region more than 20 years later.

As a graduate student at UCB, C. W. Meighan in 1952 directed the first excavations in Esselen territory at Isabella Meadows Cave (Mnt-250), roughly 60 km south of Monterey (Figure 4.4). Discovered by Pilling in 1949, Mnt-250 was a fissure containing soot-stained walls, six bedrock mortars, geometric pictographs rendered in charcoal, and both dry and wet midden deposits no less than 260 cm deep (Meighan 1955b). Excavations revealed basketry, cordage, arrow-shaft parts, and shell beads; a cache of deer and sheep skins; and the partially mummified body of a small child buried with a leather headband, pubic apron decorated with *Olivella* shell beads, and a necklace of shell, glass, and beetle leg beads. From these materials, Meighan inferred that Isabella Meadows Cave had been occupied by the Esselen from before A.D. 500 until historic times.

The cache and child burial were thought to have been left circa 1825 by people in contact with the missions.

Further UCB excavations were conducted in 1951 by R. F. Heizer and in 1952 by R. K. Beardsley at the Willow Creek site (Mnt-281 and -282) on the rocky coast of southern Monterey County (Figure 4.4). This work was later described by Z. S. Pohorecky (1964, 1976). First reported by O. P. Jenkins, Chief of the California Division of Mines, the Willow Creek site consisted of two extensive, vertically and horizontally stratified midden deposits, the upper (Mnt-281) separated from the lower (Mnt-282) by sterile gravels as much as 3 m thick (Figure 6.7).

Willow Creek midden features and stratification were highly variable, with discrete sand and shell deposits at Mnt-281 and concentrations of gravel, mussel shell, and abalone shell at Mnt-282. Food refuse and artifacts indicate both littoral and upland subsistence activities: fishing by hook and net, hunting of sea and land mammals, fowling, collecting shellfish, and gathering vegetal products. Cultural materials of Mnt-282

**Figure 6.7** Exposure of buried midden at Mnt-282 near Willow Creek, Monterey County, 1952; C. Meighan at left. (Courtesy of the R. H. Lowie Museum of Anthropology, University of California, Berkeley.)

**TABLE 6.2**

**Cultural Materials at the Willow Creek Site(s), Monterey County**[a]

| Trait | Mnt-281 | Mnt-282 | Stylistic differences |
|---|---|---|---|
| Flaked-stone bifaces (points) | 4 | 21 | yes |
| Stone sinkers | 2 | 6 | yes |
| Pitted stones | 12 | 1 | yes |
| Hammerstones | 129 | 8 | materials |
| Fire-cracked rocks | 79 | 8 | yes |
| Abrading stones | 1 | 1 | yes |
| Red ochre lumps | 1 | 1 | associations |
| Chert objects | 40 | 22 | no |
| Asphaltum-covered stones | 9 | 2 | — |
| Hopper mortars | 4 | 0 | NA[b] |
| Pestles | 15 | 0 | NA |
| Stone disks | 4 | 0 | NA |
| Incised ground slate | 21 | 0 | NA |
| Asphaltum masses | 5 | 0 | NA |
| Bone splinter awls | 0 | 4 | — |
| Cannon-bone awls | 3 | 1 | — |
| Deer-ulna awls | 2 | 1 | — |
| Bird-bone whistles | 1 | 1 | — |
| Worked antlers | 10 | 3 | — |
| Fishbone awl | 0 | 1 | NA |
| Broken base cannon-bone awls | 6 | 0 | NA |
| Worked head cannon-bone awls | 5 | 0 | NA |
| Haliotis ornaments | 10 | 4 | — |
| Worked Haliotis shell | 54 | 25 | — |
| Haliotis shell spoons or scrapers | 69 | 4 | — |
| Haliotis shell fishhooks and blanks | 7 | 6 | — |
| Other modified Haliotis shell | 58 | 4 | — |
| Olivella ground-spire beads | 2 | 2 | — |
| Olivella ground-spire, side-perforated beads | 4 | 0 | NA |
| Chipped Mytilus shell disks | 13 | 0 | NA |
| Mytilus shell fishhooks | 2 | 1 | — |

[a]After Pohorecky (1976:54–94).
[b]NA, not applicable.

differ from those of Mnt-281 variously in terms of style, type, and relative frequency (Table 6.2). Especially notable are the pitted stones, hammerstones, pestles, mortars, incised ground slate, cannon-bone awls, and *Mytilus* shell fishhooks common in the Mnt-281 deposits but rare or absent in deeper levels; in turn, Mnt-282 emphasizes projectile points, stone sinkers, and bone splinter awls. Flexed burials are reported from both components.

The occupation of Mnt-281 until historic times is confirmed by an asphaltum-coated pebble with cloth textile impressions; the lower boundary of this component has not been dated. Charcoal from the base of Mnt-282, however, has yielded $^{14}$C dates of circa A.D. 72 ± 250 (C-628) and A.D. 112 ± 400 (C-695) (Pohorecky 1976:97). The Willow Creek site thus appears to have been inhabited for 16 or 17 centuries after circa A.D. 50–100.

Pohorecky (1976:37–39, 124) interpreted the complex stratification at Mnt-281/282 as evidence of nine "alternate proto-Costanoan and proto-Salinan occupations at the Willow Creek site." This proposal has not been accepted widely, in part because of the small sample of artifacts and the difficulty in linking them to one ethnic group or the other; also, at least some of the strata may signify activity areas rather than distinct occupations.

The mix of "northern" and "southern" traits at Willow Creek has suggested to some writers that the site was near the Salinan–Costanoan boundary (Elsasser 1978b; Pohorecky 1976). Even this is equivocal, however, because "heavy influence from the Santa Barbara area" extended as far up the coast as northern Monterey County; southern influences throughout the Central Coast region are attested by basin millingstones, cairn burials, ceremonial bowls, hopper mortars, extensive use of asphaltum, abalone dishes, shell fishhooks, punctate bone decoration, specific types of projectile points, and certain pictograph motifs (Pilling 1955:71, 77). The absence or paucity of these traits in the San Francisco Bay region implies that "a major transition area between the Santa Barbara and San Francisco culture types should be found between Monterey and the southern end of the San Francisco Bay; this zone probably lies in the lower and middle Santa Clara Valley" (Pilling 1955:84).

A similar attempt to define the boundaries of cultural provinces was undertaken later at the southern end of the Central Coast region. M. A. Baldwin (1971a, 1971b) analyzed evidence of prehistoric cultural continuity between the Salinan and Chumash areas. Archaeological comparisons were necessarily limited because, apart from Willow Creek, only three sites had been excavated in Salinan territory: Pico Creek (Leonard 1968), Little Pico Creek (Abrams 1968), and a rockshelter (Mnt-483) near Bryson (Howard 1973a). Baldwin confirmed that many "southern" traits extended well into the Central Coast region, but argued that topographic factors had effectively limited the northern spread of the Chumashan maritime economy and attendant social elaboration. For the Salinans, "geography and climate militate against easy access to the offshore fish, and a coastal and land oriented subsistence is dictated" (Baldwin 1971:52).

Fieldwork in the Central Coast region during the 1960s included occasional surveys and excavations by both amateur and professional archaeologists. Reconnaissance work continued along the Monterey County coast, and the first survey of Pinnacles National Monument in San Benito County was undertaken (Olsen *et al.* 1966). In 1962 mineral prospectors in Willow Creek Canyon reportedly found a "mortuary fissure" (Mnt-609) containing the skeletons of 10 or more persons along with a grizzly bear humerus and teeth; this site was tested a decade later by the Monterey

County Archaeological Society (Howard 1974a). Another avocational effort was the salvage of eight burials after a bulldozer had disturbed graves at Mnt-619 near Dolan Creek (Howard 1969).

In 1965 R. K. Evans and N. N. Nakamura of UCLA recovered data from three Monterey Peninsula College sites (Mnt-371, -372, and -373) as part of a highway salvage project. A total of 73 small (5 × 5 ft) units was excavated. "Uniform middens without visible stratigraphy" yielded some 1300 artifacts—most comparable to specimens from Mnt-281 at Willow Creek (Evans 1968). Mnt-371 and -373 also produced Mexican pottery, a porcelain arrow point, brass buttons, and other traces of historic activities. Evans (1968) concluded that Mnt-371, -372, and -373 had served as protohistoric–historic Costanoan campsites rather than as permanent villages.

The Spanish fort of El Castillo in Monterey rests upon Mnt-101, one of the larger shellmounds near Monterey Bay (Figure 4.4). Excavations in 1967 by W. E. Pritchard of the California Department of Parks and Recreation revealed stratified midden deposits to a maximum depth of 280 cm. Housefloors were found as deep as 220 cm, and seven burials were recorded. Types of projectile points, shell beads and ornaments, and an atlatl spur in the lower levels are like items from dated sites, including Mnt-281, suggesting that aboriginal use of the El Castillo site may have begun 2000 to 3000 years ago (Pritchard 1968a).

Mussel and abalone shells accounted for most of the molluscan remains identified at Mnt-101, whereas seal and sea lion bones greatly outnumbered those of land animals. Midden stratigraphy and artifact distributions indicated that economic practices changed through time: "The majority of the milling stones were located below the 140 cm level, which is the approximate level that the heavy concentrations of shell begin and continue upward to the surface" (Pritchard 1968a:69). Mnt-101 thus exhibits two prehistoric components—the lower representing a hunting–gathering–seed-grinding economy with relatively little use of mollusks, and the upper characterized by a shellfish-collecting and marine mammal-hunting subsistence. As discussed later in this chapter, the economic shift recorded at the 140-cm level in Mnt-101 may relate to Costanoan replacement of older Esselen populations in the Monterey Bay area.

Since about 1970 hundreds of surveys and numerous testing and excavation projects have been conducted in the Central Coast region. This work has been encouraged by several factors: the establishment locally of new colleges and universities, such as Cabrillo College and the University of California, Santa Cruz; population growth (which has also brought about increased destruction of archaeological sites); and increasing interest in local prehistory (Fritz and Smith 1978:54). The most powerful stimulus to archaeological work, however, has been the passage of legislation—particularly the National Environmental Policy Act of 1969 and the California Environmental Quality Act of 1970—requiring the assessment of, and providing for the mitigation of certain impacts on, "cultural resources."

As in years past, most recent fieldwork has focused upon areas of development along the coast of Monterey and Santa Cruz counties. R. L. Edwards of Cabrillo College has been a leading figure in these investigations. In 1972 a joint Hartnell–Cabrillo College field class directed by Edwards recorded 77 new sites in the Nacimiento River watershed (Edwards 1973, 1975). Later surveys documented 5 sites in the lower Pájaro River Valley (Edwards and Farley 1974) and 34 sites along the upper Carmel River between San Clemente and Los Padres dams (Edwards *et al.* 1974). These and other surveys have led to the discovery and recording of more than 1000 sites along the western edge of the Central Coast region. Relatively little reconnaissance activity has taken place in the Salinas Valley and other inland localities. Fritz and Smith (1978) prepared an overview of Pinnacles National Monument, but otherwise very little archaeological work has been done in San Benito County.

Like the surveys, most recent excavations in this region have occurred in the coastal zone and have been designed to comply with environmental law. For example, Gibson *et al.* (1976) have described the results of a highway salvage project at the Kirk Creek site (Mnt-238) on the south coast of Monterey County. Farther north, important data were gained by testing the Serra Landing, or Doud, site (Mnt-298) in Monterey. Located adjacent to El Castillo, Mnt-298 was first tested in 1971 by D. Howard, who reported only a stratum of abalone shells and a few artifacts (Howard 1974c). Further testing in 1977 by W. Roop and K. Flynn revealed both prehistoric and historic components in the badly disturbed midden. In the absence of radiocarbon dates, "time-sensitive" artifacts suggested that Mnt-298 was first occupied sometime after 2000 B.C., and that the site was still inhabited as late as A.D. 500 (Roop 1978).

Of 35 molluscan species identified at Mnt-298, the more common were red abalone (76%), California mussel (17%), and acorn barnacle (4%). Fish remains show that Pacific herring, Pacific sardine, rockfish, pile and surf perches, white seabass, California barracuda, Pacific mackerel, and eight other species were taken in four zones ranging from the surf to open ocean (Craig and Roeder 1978). Marine mammal bones attest to the hunting of northern and Guadalupe fur seals, California sea lion, sea otter, and dolphin. Mule deer and tule elk also were taken, although the hunters seem to have emphasized sea and shore animals (Roop 1978).

More extensively sampled than Mnt-298 was the Brown site (SCr-20) in the mountains of western Santa Cruz County (Figure 6.4). SCr-20 was first tested in 1958 by A. B. Elsasser, then excavated in 1972–1973 variously by R. Edwards, J. Fritz, and M. J. Moratto. This work has been reported by W. Roop (1976). SCr-20 is a large earth midden with abundant shells of California mussels (≈95%) and 16 other mollusks (≈5%). Mammal bones at SCr-20 record the hunting of deer, rabbit, gray squirrel, and sea lion (Roop 1976; Stafford 1973). Based upon an analysis of faunal remains and more than 2100 artifacts, Roop (1976) concluded that SCr-20 was a year-round village of the Costanoans and their forebears between circa A.D. 200 and 1500.

Not far from SCr-20 is the Sandhill Bluff site (SCr-7), located near a small lagoon north of Santa Cruz (Figure 6.4). Although never excavated by archaeologists, SCr-7 is known to be one of the more ancient sites in the region. Two separate deposits are visible in the eroding seaward face of the site. Exposed at the edge of the bluff is a stratum of dark, compacted soil with clasts of fire-altered rock and occasional bits of shell and chert; the upper part of this soil unit has been eroded and is strongly weathered (Moratto 1974c). Resting unconformably on this deposit is a sand dune capped by a dark, shell-rich midden (Figure 6.8) approximately 1 m thick (Gordon 1974:15–17). Stratigraphically, SCr-7 resembles the lower levels at Malaga Cove (see Chapter 4).

Nearly a century elapsed between the initial testing of SCr-7 by Saxe

**Figure 6.8** Ancient sand dune midden at SCr-7, Santa Cruz County. Cultural materials here are associated with the remains of an extinct flightless scoter. Radiocarbon dates indicate that the midden was occupied earlier than 3000 B.C. (Courtesy of the R. H. Lowie Museum of Anthropology, University of California, Berkeley.)

(1875) and the next scientific investigations. In 1973 and 1974, V. More-john, Professor of Biology at San José State University, made surface collections and excavated several test pits to acquire faunal remains from the dune midden. Unexpectedly, this work produced the largest extant collection of bones of an extinct flightless scoter. This was a rather odd bird about the size of a Canada goose but with vestigial wings (the size of a teal's). Big drumsticks apparently made this bird attractive to hunters. Prior to the discoveries at SCr-7, the scoter was thought—based upon the age of fossils found on Santa Rosa Island—to have vanished some 33,000 years ago (Morejohn 1974).

Apart from the scoter bones, constituents of the SCr-7 dune midden include various bird and mammal bones and shells of mussels, barnacles, and, rarely, abalone and rock oyster. Local collectors have found hammerstones, large side-notched and foliate points of chert, and abundant débitage of Monterey chert. Samples of mussel shell from the upper and lower parts of the dune midden have yielded $^{14}$C dates of 3790 ± 110 B.P. (I-7828) and 5390 ± 100 B.P. (I-7827), respectively (LaJoie 1974). These dates would indicate that the dune was first occupied at circa 3500 B.C. Consequently, the subdune soil unit must be appreciably older than the dune midden and may be of early Holocene age.

To recapitulate, limited work at SCr-7 has shown that the Central Coast was inhabited 5400 years ago and probably much earlier; that the flightless scoter survived until after 3500 years ago—more recently than previously thought; and that hunting pressure may have hastened the extinction of the scoter.

No treatment of Central Coast archaeological remains would be complete without mention of the Monterey County Archaeological Society (MCAS) and its many field projects. Since about 1967 D. Howard and his associates have excavated in Monterey County no fewer than 40 aboriginal midden and cemetery sites, among them archaeological deposits at the Soledad, San Carlos, and San Antonio de Padua missions and at the Royal Presidio in Monterey. Surface collections have been made at an even larger number of sites. To date, this work has been reported only in cursory, often sensationalized accounts (Howard 1969, 1972, 1973b, 1974a–d, 1975, 1976). A few of the more notable MCAS activities and findings are reviewed below.

In 1973 and 1974 the MCAS dug extensively near Big Sur at the Post Ranch site (Mnt-88), described as "the oldest known archaeological site in Monterey County" and the largest of all known Esselen sites (Howard 1974b:31). The Mnt-88 midden was composed of dark soil with macerated shells of mussels, limpets, chitons, and gastropods; lithic débitage; and splintered bone. Twelve burials were exhumed. Howard says that "all burials at Mnt-88 were interred in flexed position" (1974b:32), but then reports several pages later that "careful excavations" revealed "older disarticulated burials and apparent newer secondary burials" (1974b:37).

Although projectile points, manos, mortars, pestles, "charms," and a "ceremonial bowl" are noted (Howard 1974a,b, 1976), the Post Ranch assemblage has never been described and access to the collection has been denied to professionals (Breschini and Haversat 1978:32, 1979:54). Two radiocarbon dates have been announced—one derived from mixed shell found within an overturned mortar associated with an adult female burial: 1240 ± 100 B.C. (GAK-4710); and the other (on shell?) from below the same burial: 1660 ± 105 B.C. (GAK-535) (Howard 1974b,d). Apart from the obvious inference that the Big Sur vicinity was inhabited as early as 3600 years ago, interpretations of Mnt-88 prehistory must await more complete publication of the findings.

Nearly as old as lower Mnt-88 was another site in Esselen territory, the Church Creek Rockshelter (Mnt-44) near Tassajara (Figure 4.4). Mnt-44 was first reported by J. Steward, who described pictographs "made up of vertical white dashes placed on the wall in groups which resemble human hands (1929:107–109). Excavations in 1972 by the MCAS revealed a "two-component" midden as much as 2.15 m deep. Mixed bone and shell from the bottom of this deposit produced a $^{14}C$ date of 1440 ± 95 B.C. (GAK-4947). Mnt-44, not yet reported fully, is thought to have been a permanent and long-used living area of the Esselen and their ancestors (Breschini 1973; Breschini and Haversat 1979:54).

The final MCAS project to be reviewed here involved digging in 1967 at the Hudson mound (Mnt-12) (Figure 4.4)—possibly the site of the Rumsen (Costanoan) village of ʔičxenta (Levy 1978a:485). Mnt-12 encompasses three shellmounds that together form the largest known archaeological site in Monterey County. A 3 × 3-m shaft into Mound I exposed cultural strata as deep as 6.19 m. Charcoal from this depth was assayed at 470 ± 165 B.C. (I-5736). A second date, A.D. 55 ± 95 (GX-1871A), applies to mussel shell from the 1.70 m level of Mound III. Eighteen burials recorded by the MCAS have not been analyzed. Some artifacts from the Hudson mound have been noted or illustrated (Howard 1974a, 1975; Howard and Cook 1971), but again this assemblage has not been described. Even so, the context of the earlier radiocarbon date would imply that a littoral settlement and economic focus, and particularly intensive use of shellfish, began as early as 470 B.C. in the southern Monterey Bay vicinity (Breschini and Haversat 1979).

Breschini and Haversat (1980) have proposed the terms *Sur Pattern* and *Monterey Pattern* to designate archaeological manifestations in the Monterey–Carmel area. The Sur Pattern, present by 3000 B.C. or earlier, relates to a generalized economy, with little in the way of specialization, and could possibly represent foragers as discussed by Binford (1980:4–19). Sites along the ocean are not characterized by "shell middens" as much as by "middens with shell." For the most part, these sites are probably village sites, even along the coast, and should reflect a wide variety of activities. On the coast this pattern includes the early component at MNT-170, and possibly portions of MNT-116 and MNT-16. Inland sites should be generally similar in most respects, with only slightly varying emphasis on local resources. Inland sites probably include the lower portions of MNT-44, MNT-88, and MNT-33a. (Breschini and Haversat 1980:14)

The Monterey Pattern, which became widely established in the "Monterey District" after circa 500 B.C., is characterized by

specialization of economic modes, probably along the lines of collectors as discussed by Binford (1980:4–19). The coastal sites are [typically] "shell middens" in which extremely large amounts of shell have accumulated. . . . These sites are often not village sites—in many cases they are marine collecting/processing stations or limited duration campsites. . . . The village sites are often located slightly inland of the more exposed coastal gathering/processing sites, and should contain evidence of more diverse activities. Examples of these living sites . . . may include MNT-12, MNT-101 and MNT-298. Included within the Monterey Pattern should be somewhat specialized exploitation/living sites used during other seasons of the year, and which should be characterized by somewhat different activities. Examples of these sites may include MNT-28 and other sites in the mid/lower Carmel Valley, MNT-14 at the mouth of the Carmel River, MNT-842 and MNT-728, east-southeast of Monterey, etc. (Breschini and Haversat 1980:14–15)

Breschini and Haversat also propose that the Monterey Pattern "almost certainly associates with the . . . Costanoans," whereas the Sur Pattern is probably identifiable with the "ancestors of the Esselen" (1980:14–15). These connections seem plausible in light of (1) the apparently unbroken cultural progression from early Monterey Pattern components to ethnographic Costanoan settlements near Monterey Bay, (2) the archaeological continuity from Sur Pattern expressions to Esselen culture in areas farther south, and (3) the evident replacement of the Sur Pattern by the Monterey Pattern throughout Costanoan territory. This replacement, first noted at Mnt-101 by Pritchard (1968a), has been documented at many other sites in the Monterey Bay area (Table 6.3). If the Sur Pattern–Esselen and Monterey Pattern–Costanoan associations are confirmed, as seems likely, then the Costanoan spread into former Esselen territory throughout the northern Central Coast region must have occurred rapidly, soon after circa 500 B.C.

Much valuable information about Central Coast prehistory has resulted from the largest project to date in this region, completed recently by S. A. Dietz and T. L. Jackson of Archaeological Consulting and Research Services (ACRS). A 1976 survey by ACRS along the northern shore of the Monterey Peninsula (Figure 6.4) established that 18 aboriginal middens and a non-Indian historic site would be affected by construction of

**TABLE 6.3**

**Central Coast Archaeological Patterns and Radiocarbon Dates**[a]

| Site | $^{14}C$ age | Date | | Laboratory number | Pattern | Reference |
|------|-----------|------|---|-------------------|---------|-----------|
| Mnt-12 | 1895 ± 95 | A.D. | 55 | GX-1871a | Monterey | Howard and Cook (1971) |
| | 2420 ± 165 | 470 | B.C. | I-5736 | Monterey | Howard and Cook (1971) |
| "Mnt-16" | 700 ± 75 | A.D. | 1250 | WSU-2389 | Monterey | Breschini and Haversat (1980) |
| (Mnt-170) | 4040 ± 100 | 2090 | B.C. | WSU-2390 | Sur | Breschini and Haversat (1980) |
| Mnt-33a | 2285 ± 100 | 335 | B.C. | WSU-2388 | Monterey | Breschini and Haversat (1982) |
| Mnt-44 | 3390 ± 95 | 1440 | B.C. | GAK-4947 | Sur | Breschini (1973) |
| Mnt-88 | 3190 ± 100 | 1240 | B.C. | GAK-4710 | Sur | Howard (1974b, d) |
| | 3610 ± 105 | 1660 | B.C. | GAK-5335 | Sur | Howard (1974b, d) |
| Mnt-111 | 1000 ± 100 | A.D. | 950 | RL-835 | Monterey | Dietz and Jackson (1981) |
| Mnt-112 | 340 ± 100 | A.D. | 1610 | RL-836 | Monterey | Dietz and Jackson (1981) |
| | 580 ± 100 | A.D. | 1370 | RL-837 | | Dietz and Jackson (1981) |
| | 720 ± 110 | A.D. | 1230 | RL-1359 | | Dietz and Jackson (1981) |
| | 4050 ± 130 | 2100 | B.C. | RL-1360 | Sur? | Dietz and Jackson (1981) |
| Mnt-113 | 260 ± 100 | A.D. | 1690 | RL-839 | Monterey | Dietz and Jackson (1981) |
| | 550 ± 100 | A.D. | 1400 | RL-838 | Monterey | Dietz and Jackson (1981) |
| | 660 ± 100 | A.D. | 1290 | RL-840 | Monterey | Dietz and Jackson (1981) |
| Mnt-114 | not dated | | | | Monterey | Dietz and Jackson (1981) |
| | 1890 ± 110 | A.D. | 60 | RL-844 | late Sur? | Dietz and Jackson (1981) |
| | 1970 ± 110 | 20 | B.C. | RL-842 | | Dietz and Jackson (1981) |
| | 2190 ± 120 | 240 | B.C. | RL-841 | | Dietz and Jackson (1981) |
| Mnt-115 | not dated | | | | Monterey | Dietz and Jackson (1981) |
| | 1780 ± 110 | A.D. | 170 | RL-846 | late Sur? | Dietz and Jackson (1981) |
| | 2140 ± 110 | 190 | B.C. | RL-845 | | Dietz and Jackson (1981) |
| Mnt-116 | 630 ± 100 | A.D. | 1320 | RL-1362 | Monterey | Dietz and Jackson (1981) |

(continued)

**TABLE 6.3** *Continued*

| Site | $^{14}C$ age | Date | Laboratory number | Pattern | Reference |
|------|-----------|------|-------------------|---------|-----------|
| | 710 ± 100 | A.D. 1240 | RL-1361 | Monterey | Dietz and Jackson (1981) |
| | 3550 ± 120 | 1600 B.C. | RL-848 | Sur | Dietz and Jackson (1981) |
| | 3640 ± 130 | 1690 B.C. | RL-849 | | Dietz and Jackson (1981) |
| | 3650 ± 130 | 1700 B.C. | RL-847 | | Dietz and Jackson (1981) |
| Mnt-117 | 650 ± 100 | A.D. 1300 | RL-1364 | Monterey | Dietz and Jackson (1981) |
| | 1040 ± 110 | A.D. 910 | RL-1363 | Monterey | Dietz and Jackson (1981) |
| Mnt-118 | 460 ± 90 | A.D. 1490 | RL-1365 | Monterey | Dietz and Jackson (1981) |
| | 590 ± 90 | A.D. 1360 | RL-1366 | Monterey | Dietz and Jackson (1981) |
| Mnt-170 | 700 ± 75 | A.D. 1250 | WSU-2389 | Monterey | Breschini and Haversat (1980) |
| | 4040 ± 100 | 2090 B.C. | WSU-2390 | Sur | Breschini and Haversat (1980) |
| Mnt-185 | 920 ± 100 | A.D. 1030 | RL-1154 | Monterey | Cartier (1979) |
| | 1040 ± 110 | A.D. 910 | RL-1155 | Monterey | Cartier (1979) |
| | 2030 ± 120 | 80 B.C. | RL-1156 | Monterey | Cartier (1979) |
| Mnt-228 | 6880 ± 135 | 4930 B.C. | UCR-1308 | | Breschini and Haversat (1982) |
| Mnt-254 | 4630 ± 110 | 2680 B.C. | WSU-2523 | ? | Breschini and Haversat (1982) |
| Mnt-282 | 1840 ± 400 | A.D. 110 | C-695 | (? Willow | Pohorecky (1964) |
| | 1879 ± 250 | A.D. 71 | C-628 | Creek) | Pohorecky (1964) |
| Mnt-391 | 3660 ± 100 | 1710 B.C. | WSU-2578 | Sur | Breschini and Haversat (1981) |
| | 3470 ± 70 | 1520 B.C. | WSU-2579 | Sur | Breschini and Haversat (1982) |
| | 3290 ± 95 | | WSU-2580 | Sur | Breschini and Haversat (1981) |
| Mnt-414 | 5540 ± 160 | 3590 B.C. | UCR-797 | Sur? | Breschini and Haversat (1982) |
| | 5200 ± 100 | 3250 B.C. | UCR-1075 | Sur? | Breschini and Haversat (1982) |
| Mnt-438 | 1020 ± 75 | A.D. 930 | WSU-2245 | Monterey | Breschini and Haversat (1982) |
| Mnt-445 | 110 ± 100 | A.D. 1840 | WSU-2155 | Monterey | Breschini and Haversat (1982) |
| Mnt-480 | 650 ± 90 | A.D. 1300 | I-6616 | (Esselen?) | Howard (1973) |
| Mnt-619 | 1010 ± 85 | A.D. 940 | WSU-2569 | (Esselen) | Breschini and Haversat (1982) |

*(continued)*

**TABLE 6.3** *Continued*

| Site | $^{14}C$ age | Date | Laboratory number | Pattern | Reference |
|---|---|---|---|---|---|
| Mnt-690 | 240 ± 85 | A.D. 1710 | WSU-2576 | Monterey | Breschini and Haversat (1982) |
|  | 330 ± 75 | A.D. 1620 | WSU-2577 | Monterey | Breschini and Haversat (1982) |
| Mnt-698 | 1760 ± 110 | A.D. 190 | UCR-796 | Monterey | Breschini and Haversat (1982) |
| Mnt-834 | 1230 ± 80 | A.D. 720 |  | Monterey | Breschini and Haversat (1982) |
|  | 1370 ± 80 | A.D. 580 |  |  | Breschini and Haversat (1982) |
|  | 4740 ± 100 | 2790 B.C. |  | Sur | Breschini and Haversat (1982) |
| Mnt-838 | 4310 ± 225 | 2360 B.C. |  | ? | Breschini and Haversat (1982) |
| SCr-7 | 3790 ± 100 | 1840 B.C. | I-7828 | Sur? | LaJoie (1974) |
|  | 5390 ± 100 | 3440 B.C. | I-7827 |  | LaJoie (1974) |
|  | not dated |  |  | pre-Sur? | Moratto (1974c) |
| SCr-33 | 3580 ± 260 | 1630 B.C. | RL-? |  | Cartier (1980) |
| SCr-93 | 2720 ± 90 | 770 B.C. | WSU-2552 | Monterey? | Breschini and Haversat (1981) |
|  | 3210 ± 100 | 1260 B.C. | WSU-2551 |  | Breschini and Haversat (1981) |
| SCr-177 | 7180 ± 290 | 5230 B.C. | I-3774 | ? | Cartier (1982) |
|  | 10080 ± 460 | 8130 B.C. | I-1373 |  | Cartier (1982) |

[a]Boxed items represent multicomponent sites.

sewer system improvements. The testing of all 19 sites in 1976 was followed by excavations in 1976 and 1977; in all, 200 1 × 2-m units were investigated (Dietz and Jackson 1981:4–7).

The ACRS effort was by no means a typical salvage project. Research objectives and methods were clearly defined at the outset with the goal of examining a large corpus of data in order to address archaeological questions in regional perspective. A key objective was to test several models regarding "subsistence strategies, settlement patterns, temporal sequences, and cultural affiliations of aboriginal populations" in the Monterey Bay area (Dietz and Jackson 1981:700). Temporal control was provided by artifact cross-dating, stratigraphy, seriation of assemblages and features, and by 20 radiocarbon dates (Table 6.3). The latter not only showed that the Monterey Peninsula had been occupied since circa 2000 B.C. or earlier, but also permitted refined dating of economic and technological shifts observed in the archaeological record.

The investigations by ACRS confirmed the existence of two archaeological "populations," identifiable with the Sur and Monterey Patterns

(Breschini and Haversat 1980), in the area of the ethnographic Rumsen Costanoans (Figure 11.1):

> These include foragers, probably of the *Hokan* language family [most likely ancestral Esselen], who apparently utilized a number of . . . sites as residential bases and locations at least 4000 years ago. . . . [Their subsistence] strategy included seasonal residential moves among a series of resource patches, gathering of foods daily on an "encounter" basis with return to a residential base near the end of each day, no use of storage, a limited foraging radius around residential bases, considerable variability in the size of foraging groups and the number of residential moves made in a year, considerable variability in the redundancy of land use from year to year, and the possible occasional occurrence of extended resource procurement trips from residential bases (Binford 1980). Project sites CA-Mnt-114, CA-Mnt-115, CA-Mnt-116 and possibly CA-Mnt-112 appear to contain forager components. (Dietz and Jackson 1981:700–701)

The second of the archaeological populations identified by ACRS on the Monterey Peninsula were "collectors"—presumably early Costanoans—who entered the Carmel Valley and eventually displaced or absorbed the foragers (Esselen) in what would become Rumsen territory. Characteristic of the collectors were

> storage of food during part of the year, logistically organized . . . labor groups, and the use of residential bases (permanent and seasonal), camps, locations, stations, and caches (Binford 1980). All of the sites excavated . . . appear to be the result of collector activities or have collector components. . . . From these sites, the collectors exploited various marine and littoral resources, as well as resources found on the area's marine terraces (grass seeds, game, etc.) and in the nearby pine forests (pine nuts). (Dietz and Jackson 1981:701)

Zooarchaeological studies registered specific differences between forager and collector adaptation on the Monterey Peninsula. Analyses of shellfish remains, for example, showed that older strata contained absolutely less shell but relatively more mussel shell than younger strata. Abalone shell dominates the late midden deposits, often accounting for more than 90% by weight of all shell, whereas abalone shell and mussel shell tend to occur in more nearly equal proportions in middle levels; mussel greatly outweighs abalone shell in lower levels—mostly older than 2000 years (Table 6.3). This pattern suggests that, although shellfish gathering was not emphasized by foragers, the Esselens (and perhaps initial Costanoans) still may have depleted the populations of easily obtained mussels, prompting later collectors (Costanoans) to specialize in abalone procurement (Dietz and Jackson 1981:698–699).

A comparable pattern was observed with respect to fish remains. Fish bones were found in deposits of all ages, but the frequency of fish remains diminished with depth. Fish were significantly better represented in later than in earlier strata, indicating that the Costanoans devoted more attention to fishing than did their predecessors. On the other hand, the local fishery seems to have been less important than in the Santa Barbara vicinity. In all, the bones of 46 species of fish were identified, among them jacksmelt, plainfin midshipman, California halibut, yellowtail, soupfin shark, cabezon, Pacific herring, eight species of surfperch, lingcod, bat ray, 16 species of rockfish, and California barracuda. These remains attest to the exploitation of varied marine environments by fishing from watercraft with hooks and long lines, net fishing, and inshore fishing with lines, traps, and possibly other devices (Dietz and Jackson 1981:700; Gobalet 1981:E5–E7).

Further knowledge of economic patterns has come from Simons' (1981) identification and analysis of bones representing 6 avian and 19 mammalian taxa. A comparison of bird and mammal bones from 10 Monterey County sites showed an inland–coastal dichotomy: coastal sites tend to contain abundant remains of sea mammals, moderate to large numbers of bird bones, and generally small "inventories of terrestrial furbearers"; inland sites tend to have no sea mammal remains, few bird bones, and "larger inventories of terrestrial furbearers, especially carnivores" (Dietz and Jackson 1981:649). Simons's (1981) faunal data also indicate that the coastal part of this dichotomy can be subdivided into Monterey Peninsula and Santa Lucia Range elements, with exploitative differences probably reflecting cultural (i.e., Costanoan and Esselen) preferences.

In sum, the ACRS project has contributed to Central Coast archaeology in several important respects. The findings confirmed the existence of two distinct prehistoric cultures—*foragers* (ancestral Esselen?) and *collectors* (early Costanoan?)—thus lending support to the concept of Sur and Monterey Patterns. A local cultural chronology was established on the strength of 20 radiocarbon dates, and faunal analyses provided detailed information about prehistoric settlement and subsistence patterns and their distributions in space and time. Through this and other studies, the outlines of Central Coast prehistory have begun to take form.

## San Francisco Bay Region

Since about 1950 archaeological work in the Bay area has encompassed numerous survey and excavation projects, including the first significant excavations in such places as the Santa Clara Valley and parts of interior Alameda and Contra Costa counties. Early Holocene sites have been discovered, and distinctive local and regional expressions, unlike those of the Central California Taxonomic System (CCTS), have been identified. Advances in dating methods have led to absolute chronologies and a better understanding of prehistoric cultural relationships. At the same time, much has been learned about paleoenvironmental changes associated with San Francisco Bay and their implications for archaeology.

Current perceptions of regional prehistory recognize more time depth and greater cultural variability than was evident at mid-century. In this section we examine some of these newer perceptions and the research that led to them.

East Bayshore

*Newark Vicinity:* Limited testing by W. Wedel in 1935 at the Patterson or Newark site (Ala-328)—a large shellmound on the southeastern edge of San Francisco Bay (Figure 6.4)—preceded 18 seasons of excavation (1949–1968) by Adán Treganza and his San Francisco State University (SFSU) field classes. On the basis of materials recovered through 1953, Treganza and J. T. Davis in 1959 summarized their findings and compared the Ala-328 collections with those from 68 other central California sites. Three components were defined: Component A, assigned to the Fernandez Facies of the "Late Horizon"; Component B, linked to the Ellis Landing Facies and for which a $^{14}$C date of 389 ± 150 B.C. (C-690) was available; and Component C, stratigraphically below the Ellis Landing level and tentatively described as the type component of the "Patterson Facies" (J. Davis and Treganza 1959). This basal component featured tightly flexed burials oriented north or west, red ochre in graves, perforate charmstones like those of the Windmiller Pattern, green abalone ornaments, shell bead appliqué on bird bone tubes, and an elaborate industry of such bone and antler tools as fiber strippers, needles, awls, wedges, and serrate pelves and scapulae (Figures 6.9 and 6.10).

Davis and Treganza (1959) proposed that Ala-328C and the lower levels of West Berkeley (Ala-307, discussed below), Ellis Landing (CCo-295), and Bodega Bay (Son-299) were approximately coeval as the oldest known archaeological strata in the Bay area. Ala-328B and other Ellis Landing Facies components apparently were later in time (J. Davis and Treganza 1959:69–70).

C. E. Smith of California State University, Hayward, supervised additional excavations at Ala-328 during the summers of 1966, 1967, and 1968. The only subsequent fieldwork at Ala-328 was the SFSU excavation of a single deep unit for a study of midden constituents (Ringer 1971). However, three nearby sites—Ala-12, Ala-13, and Ala-329 (Figure 6.4)—have been excavated. In 1965 F. Rackerby of SFSU directed salvage operations at Ala-12 and Ala-13; additional data were recovered from Ala-12 in 1968 by R. Oliphant, also of SFSU (Oliphant 1968; Rackerby 1967). Ala-329, the Ryan mound, was investigated by field classes from UCB (1949), Stanford University (1959, 1960, 1962), and San José State University (1960s). A report on the Stanford work, directed by B. Gerow, was published by Coberly (1973).

The data from Ala-12, Ala-13, and Ala-328 have been described, com-

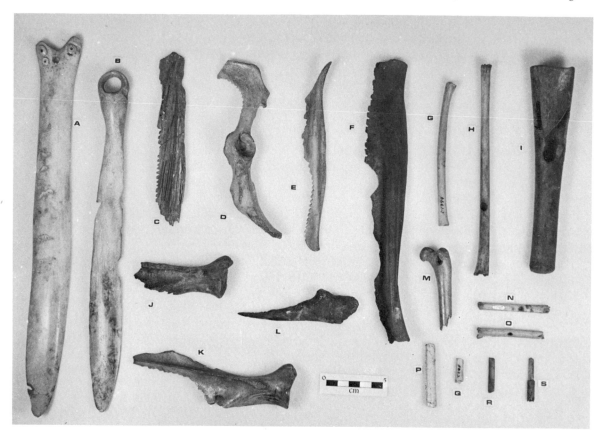

**Figure 6.9** Serrate, tubular, and spatulate bone artifacts from Ala-328 and nearby sites in the Newark vicinity. A,B, pointed thick spatulate bone objects found with Burial 226 at Ala-328; serrate (C) fish parasphenoid, (D) sea otter pelvis, (E) deer scapula, and (F) elk scapula; G, bird-bone tube; H, bird-bone whistle; I, mammal-bone whistle; J,K, modified deer scapulae; L, serrate deer or antelope ulna; M, drilled rodent femur; N, O, bird-bone whistles; P, bird-bone tube; Q,R, bird-bone beads; S, shimmed bird-bone bead. (Photograph courtesy of Polly Bickel and the A. E. Treganza Anthropology Museum, San Francisco State University.)

pared, and interpreted by P. Bickel (1976, 1981). Bickel notes that all three sites share mortars and pestles, shell beads, and burials predominantly in flexed positions as well as such typical Bay region traits as serrate bone implements, antler wedges, and distinctive hammerstones. Artifact types (Figure 6.11) indicate the relative ages of these sites: Ala-12 was coeval with much of the Patterson Facies occupation at Ala-328, and Ala-13 was settled later. Ala-328 lacks artifacts that cross-date to Valley types of the "Late Horizon, Phase 1," but a few thin rectangular and punched *Olivella* beads from Ala-13 might reflect a limited Phase 1 occupation in the

Newark vicinity. Clamshell disk beads, markers of the period after circa
A.D. 1400 were found at Ala-328 but not at Ala-13 (Bickel 1976:359–364).
Considering ¹⁴C dates and artifacts together, Ala-12 and Ala-328 evi-
dently were first occupied more than 2300 years ago, probably between
3000 and 4000 years ago, whereas Ala-13 evidently was settled by circa
A.D. 300 and saw intermittent use for at least a millennium thereafter.
Ala-328 seems to have been abandoned during much of the interval be-

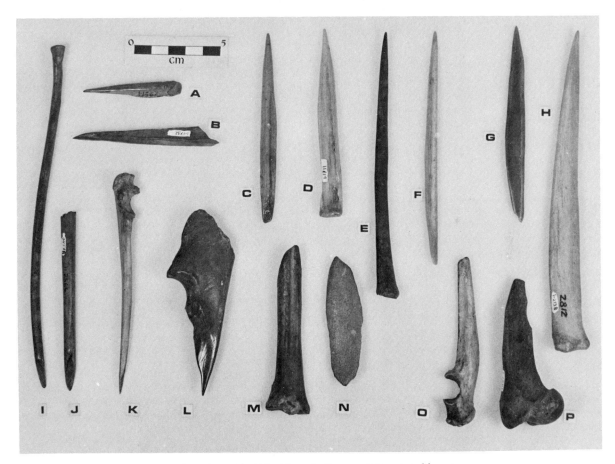

**Figure 6.10** Pointed bone artifacts from Ala-328, Alameda County. A,B, pointed bones
with angular tips; C,D, pointed bones with broad, smooth conical tips; E,F, pointed bones
with narrow, smooth conical tips; G,H, pointed bones with flat tips; I,J, pointed bird bones
with hollowbacked tips; K, pointed, non-cervid ulna with sharp tip; L, pointed cervid ulna
with sharp tip; M,N, pointed bones with nippled tips; O,P, pointed bones with dull, rounded
tips. (Photograph courtesy of Polly Bickel and the A. E. Treganza Anthropology Museum,
San Francisco State University.)

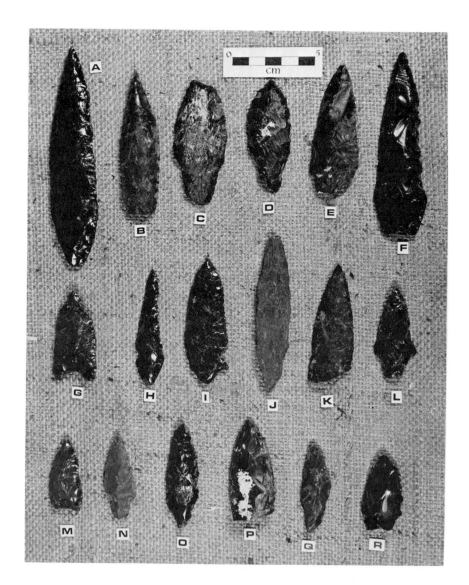

**Figure 6.11** Projectile points and other bifaces from sites Ala-12, -13, and -328, Newark vicinity. C–E, K, N, and P are of chert or flint; J is of phyllite; all others are of obsidian. (Photograph courtesy of Polly Bickel and the A. E. Treganza Anthropology Museum, San Francisco State University.)

tween circa A.D. 300 and 1500, but was reoccupied during the last few centuries of the prehistoric era.

With the large corpus of data available to her, Bickel was better able to define the components at Ala-328 originally sketched by Davis and Treganza. Component I (above ≈45 cm) is marked by clamshell disk and *Olivella* lipped beads, tubular steatite pipes, and imperforate sandstone charmstones (Figure 6.12). In Component II (mostly above 210 cm), the vertical distribution of three artifact groups is recognized: fishspear prongs, perforated mammal teeth, grooved stones, tabular *Haliotis* ornaments, and thick spatulate bones (Figure 6.9A,B) tend to occur in upper levels; cobble mortars and *Olivella* saddle and saucer beads cluster in middle levels; and abraded stones and pointed bones with flat tips appear in the lower part of the component. Component III (≈230–270 cm) has two artifact groups: an upper unit with perforated schist charmstones (Figure 6.12), pointed-bone objects with nippled tips, bird talons, and bone tubes and flutes with bead overlay; and a deep assemblage of

**Figure 6.12** Charmstones and other artifacts from Ala-328 and neighboring sites in the Newark vicinity. H, pecked-stone sphere; I, quartz pebble; all others are perforate (D–F, J) or imperforate (A–C,G) charmstones of steatite, schist, sandstone, or granite. (Photograph courtesy of Polly Bickel and the A. E. Treganza Anthropology Museum, San Francisco State University.)

*Haliotis* ring and shield ornaments and *Olivella* saucer and spire-lopped beads. Cremations, which account for 7% of all disposals, are limited to the upper and lower strata. Primary burials in flexed postures comprise the dominant disposal type throughout the midden (Bickel 1976:364–372).

Bickel has delineated changes in artifact types and mortuary practices at three sites. Paralleling these shifts are changes from schist to sandstone for charmstone manufacture and from obsidian of trans-Sierran origin to North Coast Ranges obsidian, suggesting adjustments in trade relationships over time. The fundamental economic practices seem to have changed very little, however, and, although individual sites were abandoned for brief or long periods, there is no indication of social and cultural replacement at any time in the sequence. Thus, like the shellmounds of Monterey Bay, the Newark sites may reflect continuous occupation by Costanoan peoples over a span of more than 2000 years.

*West Berkeley:* The West Berkeley site, Ala-307 (Figure 6.4), was excavated by UCB archaeologists first in 1902 and intermittently thereafter over a number of years. Before its destruction in the mid–twentieth century, Ala-307 was an enormous shellmound about 200 m long, 100 m wide, and 6 m deep. During 1950 and 1954 the University's Archaeological Survey excavated some of the last remaining deposits at Ala-307 (Wallace and Lathrap 1975).

Faunal analyses have shed light on prehistoric subsistence activities at West Berkeley. W. I. Follett has determined that the Indians of Ala-307 caught no fewer than 11 species of fish, mainly white and green sturgeons. Of secondary importance were king and possibly silver salmon; bat rays also were taken in some quantity. The diversity of the native fishery is further illustrated by the remains of leopard and thresher sharks, jacksmelt, plainfin midshipman, and surfperches in the Ala-307 collections. One may infer that fishing was done chiefly with gill nets and seines worked from watercraft (Follett 1975b).

The dominant identified mammal species is deer (36% of the bone by count), followed by coyote (20%), sea otter (14%), harbor seal (6%), and sea lion (5%). Pronghorn, elk, cottontail, jackrabbit, raccoon, common dolphin, and bay porpoise are also present in small quantities (Busby 1975). Intensive use of avifauna is clearly shown by the remains of 14 families of birds. Most of the West Berkeley bird bone represents visitant ducks, geese, and swans. Cormorants and murres also accounted for high numbers of specimens, and loons, grebes, gulls, owls, and many other kinds of birds were also in evidence—including one ceremonial burial of a California condor (Brooks 1975).

Mollusks were a staple in the diet at West Berkeley. Their remains averaged about 23% of the midden mass, although the proportion of shell

declined somewhat toward the bottom of the mound. Of 10 species identified by Greengo (1975), only the bay mussel, bay oyster, and bent-nose
clam were present in significant quantities. A notable species shift occurred from the bottom to the top of Ala-307. In the lower part of the
midden nearly one-half of the shells were those of oysters, to the virtual
exclusion of clams. At the top, however, bent-nose clams exceeded oysters by more than 26%. The clam is a mudflat dweller, whereas the oyster
favors a gravel bottom or a bed of its own shells. Since the habitats of
these two invertebrates are all but mutually exclusive, their distribution
at Ala-307 is taken to mean that environmental conditions of the nearby
Bay bottom changed significantly during the time that Ala-307 was occupied: "While the first 11 feet [3.35 m] of the midden was accumulating,
gravelly bottom conditions are indicated. . . . On the other hand, from
the top to a depth of six feet [1.83 m] the preponderance of *Macoma* over
the oyster points to mud flats" (Greengo 1975:68).

Corresponding changes in mollusks through time, reflecting a shift
from rocky or gravelly bottom to mudflat, also have been documented at
Ellis Landing, Emeryville, and numerous other bayshore sites (Bickel
1978a,b; Riley 1979). Parallel conditions exist in coastal middens (e.g., at
Mrn-266 and Son-299) where Washington clams tend to become relatively more abundant than California mussels through time. These data
may attest to the siltation of bays along the California coast during the
past several millennia.

In addition to the stratification of faunal remains noted above, two
cultural strata were recognized at Ala-307. Wallace and Lathrap (1975)
ascribe the upper 1.8 m of the deposit to the Ellis Landing Facies of the
"Middle Horizon," as proposed earlier by Beardsley (1954) (Figure 5.6),
but they attribute the lower 3.6 m to a coastal version of the "Early
Horizon" (i.e., Windmiller Pattern). Although the Ellis Landing component at Ala-307 has not been dated absolutely, charcoal from the "Early"
component provided eight $^{14}$C dates ranging from 1910 ± 450 B.C.
(M-125) at 396–427 cm to 750 ± 300 B.C. (M-121) at 244–281 cm (Figure
6.13).

Similarities between the lower two-thirds of Ala-307 and "Early"
components in the Valley are expressed by such traits as perforated
charmstones of diagnostic forms, heavy flaked-stone points of non-obsidian lithics, notched and grooved net sinkers, stone bars or "pencils,"
*Olivella* spire-lopped and thick rectangular beads, and distinctive abalone
beads and ornaments. The 95 skeletons recovered from West Berkeley
had been buried in various flexed postures without patterned orientation,
and most (71%) lacked mortuary artifacts. Wallace and Lathrap suggest
that Ala-307 provides the "first clear-cut evidence of Early Horizon occupation" in the San Francisco Bay area; they conclude that the mound

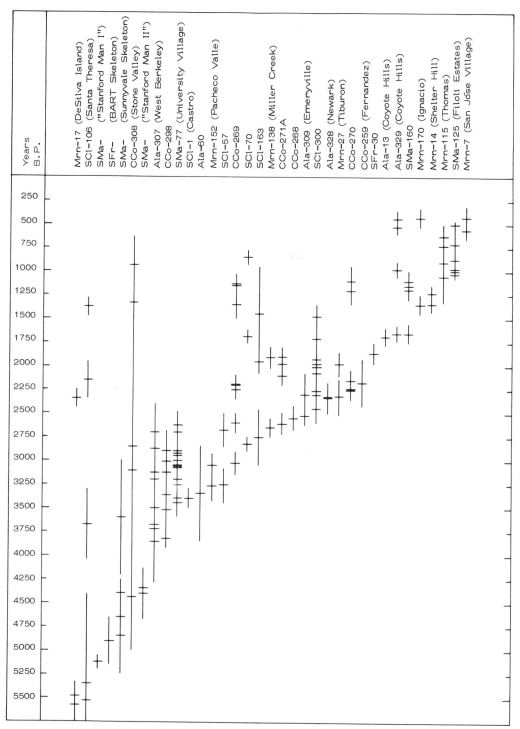

**Figure 6.13** Selected radiocarbon dates from the San Francisco Bay region. Vertical lines indicate the range of 1 standard deviation. (Compiled by the author from various sources.)

was settled as early as 3500 to 4000 years ago, abandoned in "early Middle times," and never again experienced aboriginal occupation (Wallace and Lathrap 1975:57–59).

Elsasser (1978b:37–40), in substantial agreement with Wallace and Lathrap, proposes an "Early Horizon, Berkeley Facies" to include lower Ala-307 and the University Village site, SMa-77 (discussed under "San Francisco Penninsula"). Fredrickson (1973:125a–126), however, has selected West Berkeley as the type site for his Berkeley Pattern (Figure 6.14) and apparently sees lower Ala-307 as the earliest known evidence of this pattern on the bayshore. As detailed later in this chapter, the Berkeley Pattern incorporates those components previously assigned to the "Middle Horizon," without the temporal restrictions of the horizon concept. Regardless of nomenclature, two important observations can be made: (1) lower Ala-307 represents a bayshore settlement of either Windmiller people or people strongly influenced by the Windmiller Pattern, and (2) continuities between lower and upper Ala-307 mark the evolution of the Berkeley Pattern from Windmiller or Windmiller-like antecedents. If the development of the Berkeley Pattern is related to the emergence of the Utian (Miwok and Costanoan) languages, as seems probable on the evidence of cultural geography and archaeological developments culminating with known ethnohistoric settlements, then the case can be made that the initial Utian presence in California associates with the early Windmiller Pattern before 2000 B.C. (see Chapter 11).

Interior Contra Costa County

Salvage excavations in interior Contra Costa County have led to the identification of seven different components at four sites: La Serena, CCo-30; Stone Valley, CCo-308; Rossmoor, CCo-309; and Alamo, CCo-311 (Fredrickson 1964a, 1965b, 1966, 1968, 1969; Mead and Moss 1967). These components range in time and cultural affiliation from early "Middle Horizon" (CCo-308C) to "Late Horizon, Phase 2," the latter [14]C-dated at A.D. 1665 ± 95 (I-1193). Other components represent "Late Horizon, Phase 1" (CCo-30A); a transition phase between "Middle" and "Late" Horizons (CCo-308A); late "Middle Horizon" (CCo-311); and middle "Middle Horizon" (CCo-30B, CCo-308B) (Fredrickson 1974b:58).

Of special interest is lower Stone Valley (CCo-308C), wherein 21 flexed burials and 93 artifacts were stratigraphically associated with the unexpectedly early [14]C date of 2500 ± 400 B.C. (UCLA-259) (Figure 6.13). Although burial posture, boulder mortars, and cobble pestles are compatible with "Middle Horizon" identification, heavy stemmed projectile points, a tabular schist object, and a very low frequency of bone artifacts suggest cultural affiliation with the "Early Horizon" of the Central Valley (Fredrickson 1965b). Any taxonomic confusion here is more a result of

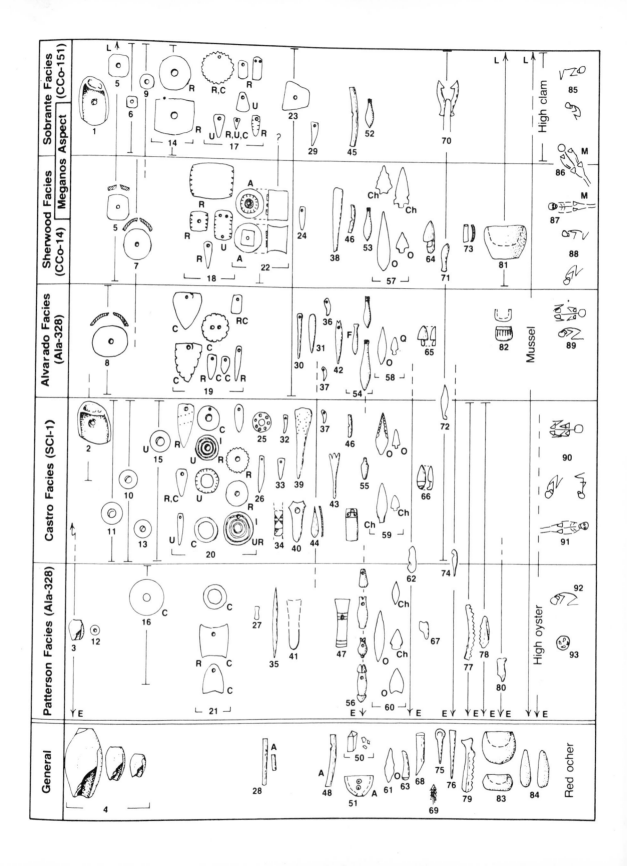

the CCTS than of the archaeological remains at CCo-308C. What seems clear is that a very early Berkeley Pattern component at Stone Valley also exhibits Windmiller traits. This blending, as at West Berkeley, may indicate either developments from Windmiller antecedents or strong influence from coeval Windmiller expressions. Again like West Berkeley, CCo-308C may relate to Utian peoples.

In any event, the large area of CCo-308B and -308C ($\approx$18,580 m²) may register sedentary village occupation between circa 2500 B.C. and A.D. 1. Mortars and pestles in the lower levels suggest that acorns may have been

---

**Figure 6.14** Berkeley Pattern ("Middle Horizon"), Alameda District: Significant artifact types and temporal changes from Patterson ("Early–Middle Horizon Transition") Facies to Sobrante Facies ("Late Middle Horizon"), taken from representative sites. Drawings not to scale. Position of specimens shown within facies has no chronological significance. Bead typology from Lillard, Heizer, and Fenenga (1939). A, appliqué in asphalt decoration; C, *Haliotis cracherodii*; Ch, chert; E, trait persists from "Early Horizon;" F, "fishtail" charmstone; I, double-line facial incision; L, trait persists into "Late Horizon;" MA, Meganos Aspect (hybrid expression of "Early" and "Middle Horizon" cultures) trait; O, obsidian; Q, quartzite; R, *Haliotis rufescens*; U, *Haliotis* unidentified. References to oyster, mussel, and clam indicate frequency of these mollusks in midden deposits through time. 1–12, *Olivella* beads: 1,2, Split-drilled, Type 3bl; 3, Small spire-lopped, Type 1a; 4, Spire-lopped, Types 1a, 1b; 5, Modified "saddle," Type 3b2; 6, Small "saddle," Type 3b2; 7, Round "saddle," Type 3b; 8, Full "saddle," Type 3b; 9,10, "saucer," Type 3c; 11, Ring, Type 3c; 12, Tiny disk, Type 3d. 13, *Mytilus* disk bead. 14–16, *Haliotis* beads: 14, Large amorphous beads, Type H4b; 15, Nacreous disk, Type H3a; 16, Large disk, Type H3b2. 17–21, *Haliotis* ornaments. 22, Earspool with *Haliotis* appliqué at one end. 23, Mica ornament. 24, Slate pendant. 25, Slate ring with *Olivella* appliqué. 26, Slate pendant. 27, Steatite "constricted" beads. 28, Bone tubes, beads (often with *Olivella* appliqué). 29, Antler pendant. 30, Perforated bone hairpin. 31, Flat bone pin. 32,33, Bone pendants. 34, Incised bone (pendant). 35, Long bi-pointed pin. 36, Bear tooth pendant. 37, Canid tooth pendant. 38–41, Bone, antler spatulae. 42, Perforated head scratcher (bone). 43, Forked head scratcher (bone). 44, Split-rib strigil. 45, Long bird-bone whistle, central stop. 46, Short bird-bone whistle, central stop. 47, Human (?) tibia whistle. 48, Bird-bone whistle, end stop. 49, Slate bar with *Olivella* appliqué. 50, Whole, fractured, quartz crystals. 51, Steatite or marble "cloud blower" (?), often with *Olivella* appliqué. 52–56, Charmstones (52–54 with asphalted ends). 57–60, Chipped-stone spear, dart points. 61, Obsidian knife. 62, Bone (ulna) flaker. 63, Antler tine flaker. 64–67, Bone atlatl spurs. 68, Antler wedge. 69, Stingray spine. 70, Barbed-bone fish spears. 71,72, Unbarbed-bone fish spears (?). 73, Ground beaver incisor. 74, Bone (ulna) awl. 75, Cannon-bone awl or punch. 76, Ground-bone awl. 77, Serrated rib. 78, Serrated fish bone. 79, Serrated mammal scapula. 80, Bone fiber-stripper. 81, Shaped stone mortar. 82, Incised (decorated) stone mortar. 83, Boulder mortar. 84, Cobble pestle. 85–93, Mortuary complex (available data not precise—emphasis is on variable flexed and semiflexed positions, with presumed local or no fixed orientation): 85, Flexed, with orientation to NW and NE quadrants; 86, Ventral extension, a marker for Meganos Aspect, significant at site CCo-151, orientation to SW, NW, and NE quadrants; 87, Dorsal extension, of rare and scattered occurrence; 88, Orientation to SW and NW quadrants; 89, Orientation to all points except NE quadrant; 90, Orientation to all quadrants, varying site to site within facies; 91, Dorsal extension, rare; 92, Orientation to NW quadrant; 93, Cremation, confined to Patterson ("Early–Middle Horizon Transition") Facies. (After Elsasser 1978b:Figure 3; chart by J. A. Bennyhoff, 1972; courtesy of A. B. Elsasser, J. A. Bennyhoff, and the Smithsonian Institution.)

utilized in the east Bay interior as early as 2000 B.C. However, products other than acorns may have been ground in the mortars and, even if acorns were processed, there is presently no good way to assess their importance in the diet. Finally, the sequence of mortuary patterning at Stone Valley implies an evolution from an egalitarian society (CCo-308C and B) to a system of social ranking based upon ascribed status (CCo-308A) (Fredrickson 1974b). This is discussed more fully in a later section.

### San Francisco Peninsula

The east bayshore sites were not the first to yield evidence of an "Early" presence in the Bay region. This distinction belongs to the University Village site (SMa-77) at the southwestern edge of San Francisco Bay (Figure 6.4). Buried under alluvium from San Francisquito Creek, SMa-77 came to light in 1951 when burials and artifacts were exposed by heavy equipment. In 1951 and 1952 B. A. Gerow of Stanford University excavated 43 burials, a cremation, and other features at University Village. The cultural deposits, ranging from 2.3 to 4.0 m above sea level, were not those of a shell midden, but rather a compact brownish-yellow loam with scattered lenses of shell, ash, and charcoal. The shell that did occur was mainly of bay oyster (94.2%), followed by bay mussel (3.6%), horn shell (1.9%), and several other mollusks in minute quantities. Charcoal associated with two burials provided $^{14}$C dates of 3150 ± 200 (L-187B) and 2700 ± 400 (L-187A) B.P. (Gerow 1968).

The skeletons found at SMa-77 were buried in various flexed postures without consistent orientation. Of approximately 3000 artifacts recovered from 35 graves, the most common were *Olivella* spire-lopped and thick rectangular beads, *Haliotis* square beads and geometric ornaments, large foliate and lozenge-shaped projectile points of Monterey chert (59.1%), obsidian (33.3%) and other rocks, and notched stone net weights. Also discovered were mortars and pestles, a sandstone bowl, chrysotile rods, perforated charmstones of Windmiller types, distinctive lunate or crescentic ground stones, and an array of bone tools including worked deer scapulae, polished mammal ribs, and pointed implements.

Considering the large number of graves relative to the amount of dietary refuse, together with soils stratigraphy, Gerow (1968:34) inferred that the University Village site was settled only briefly and then abandoned because of abrupt changes in the immediate environment: "A shift in the stream course of San Francisquito Creek might well have discouraged continued settlement, and the abandoned channel is evidence that such a change did take place."

Gerow's analysis of grave-lot data indicated that the University Village Complex antedated the "Middle Horizon" of the Delta but was dissimilar to the "Early Horizon" in many respects. Mortuary practices at SMa-77 contrasted with both "Early" and "Middle" graves in the Delta with regard to an absence of extended burials or westerly orientation, a high incidence of red ochre relative to ornamental artifacts as funerary accompaniments, a preponderance of whole *Olivella* shells over drilled shell fractions, and the small number of flaked-stone points, both absolutely and relative to crude flake and core tools. At SMa-77 quartz crystals, plummet charmstones, and artifacts of mica and slate were rare, whereas flat-ended pestles, cobblestone mortars, bone awls, polished ribs, and antler wedges were abundant. Moreover, the University Village Complex seems further removed typologically from the "Early Horizon" than is the Delta "Middle Horizon," and the SMa-77 skeletons contrast with the "Early" and "Middle" physical types in the Delta locality (Gerow 1968:12, 109–110).

Interpreting data from SMa-77 and lower Ala-307, Gerow postulated the existence of an Early Bay Culture. In rejecting Heizer's (1949) suggestion that the "Middle Horizon" was present in the east Bay area by 2000 to 1000 B.C. and that the bayshore was a marginal part of the Delta cultural province, Gerow concluded that two distinct cultures or traditions existed in central California between 1500 and 1000 B.C. and that subsequently these Bay and Valley cultures and populations gradually converged.

Gerow developed this idea more fully in his *Co-Traditions and Convergent Trends in Prehistoric California* (1974b). He observed in this monograph that the mid–Central Valley and southern California coast had been viewed traditionally as distinctive climax areas. The prevailing models of culture change in these areas had been essentially unilineal, accounting for local and regional differences as adjustments to varying environmental conditions. Gerow challenged the idea of parallelism or divergence between Valley and southern coast prehistories, arguing that (1) biological and cultural contrasts between the two areas were present at an early date, and cultural climaxes had already occurred in both areas as early as 1500 to 1000 B.C.; (2) skeletal data indicate greater rather than less populational differences between the two regions in early times; and (3) in terms of technology, style, mortuary patterns, and economic orientation the Valley and southern California coastal cultures, respectively, exhibit regional differences and subsequent converging trends.

Gerow's skeletal analyses resulted in the definition of two somatic types of population:

> earlier, metrically smaller lower vaulted group(s) and later, metrically larger higher vaulted group(s). The former are represented by the living Yuki and their neighbors along the north-central coast and prehistoric populations of the north-central and southern coast. The latter are represented by living Penutians, Shoshoneans, interior Hokans (Mojave, Yuma, Washo) and most prehistoric populations of the Central Valley. San Francisco Bay is both geographically and somatically intermediate. (Gerow 1974b:17)

The skeletal data show that there was a basic continuity of mid–Central Valley populations for some 4000 years; these Valley societies may be linked to Penutian languages. Similarly, the skeletons from Santa Cruz Island and the Santa Barbara–Los Angeles coast may derive from populations that spoke Hokan languages (Figure 11.1). Biologically and culturally, the University Village Complex is seen not as a marginal expression of Delta patterns, but as representing an Early Bay Culture in part intermediate between Valley and South Coast developments and in part uniquely characteristic of the San Francisco Bay region. In this light, the University Village site may have been inhabited by Esselen peoples whose biologic, linguistic, and cultural affiliations were mainly with the Central Coast region, but who also were being influenced by early Costanoan groups, together with their "Valley" traits, that were spreading throughout the east Bay area (Figure 6.16).

If this reconstruction is correct, one may assume that Costanoans did not settle the west Bay area until sometime after circa 1000 B.C., and that older archaeological remains on the Peninsula may relate to Esselen occupation. Four discoveries—the BART, Sunnyvale, and two Stanford skeletons—deserve mention in this regard.

In 1970 W. G. Henn and R. E. Schenk of SFSU recorded the partial skeleton of a 24–26-year-old male (described incorrectly as a female in some accounts) in situ in a stratum of gray clayey silt about 22.9 m below the present surface of San Francisco's Civic Center. The bones reposed ≈4.3 m above the base of the silt layer and ≈7.9 m below mean sea level. The skeleton had been discovered in the course of excavations for the Bay Area Rapid Transit (BART) tunnel, and it is believed that some of the remains, including the skull, were taken by workmen before the archaeologists arrived. No artifacts were found in the matrix embedding the bones.

Microscopic examination of silt adhering to the pelvis revealed both freshwater and marine diatoms and radiolaria. This mixture of organisms, along with a mineralogical analysis of the silt, indicated that the skeleton had come to rest in a brackish marsh near or within a freshwater channel that was covered intermittently by tidal water. Fragments of horsetail rush, bits of wood and bark, and other organic debris clinging to the bones gave a $^{14}C$ age of 4900 ± 250 years (W-185) (Henn and Schenk 1970; Henn et al. 1972); corrected for secular variation, the date would be circa 3710 B.C. The BART skeleton not only confirms that the northern Peninsula was inhabited more than 5500 years ago, it also shows that the rate of sea level rise during this period has averaged well over 1 m per millennium. Hence, any bayshore habitation sites on the order of 5000 years old probably lie buried under more than 5 m of sediments.

At Sunnyvale (Figure 6.4) a human skeleton, without directly associated artifacts, may be nearly as old as the BART remains. Although Bada and Helfman (1975) have published an amino-acid "date" of 70,000 years for the Sunnyvale skeleton (see Chapter 2), geologic, archaeological, and anthropometric relationships establish the age as mid-Holocene (LaJoie *et al.* 1980:483–486). Charcoal from a hearth less than 200 m distant and within the same stratum as the burial yielded a $^{14}$C age of 4460 ± 95 B.P. (I-6977) (Bickel 1978a,b).

Two skeletons from Stanford offer further information about early prehistory in the west Bay area. In 1922 Stanford University student B. Seymour discovered a human skull 6.1 m below surface in the bank of San Francisquito Creek on the Stanford campus (Figure 6.4). This calvarium of "Stanford Man 1" was found in a gravel stratum presumed on geologic grounds to be roughly 3000–4000 years old (Heizer 1950e), an estimate consistent with the physical characteristics of the skull (T. Mc-Cown 1950). Later, "Stanford Man 2"—a flexed skeleton associated with three large side-notched or expanding stem points of Monterey chert—was found nearby in the same gravel bed at a depth of 5.2 m below the modern surface. Bone collagen from the second burial provided $^{14}$C dates of 2450 ± 270 (UCLA-1425A) and 2400 ± 125 (UCLA-1425B) B.C. (Gerow 1974a:241).

Together, the Stanford, Sunnyvale, and BART materials show that the west Bay area was inhabited between circa 3500 and 2500 B.C. Although almost nothing is known of cultural manifestations on the Peninsula during this interval, it seems reasonable to suggest that a pre-Costanoan (Esselen?) population, likely with cultural ties to the Sur Pattern, may be represented.

A number of later (Costanoan?) archaeological sites on the Peninsula have been tested or salvaged, but large-scale investigations have been minimal and few of the resultant collections have been analyzed or published. In San Francisco County, for example, after more than 70 years, no one has excavated more than did Nelson in 1910 at Hunters Point (SFr-7) or Loud in 1912 at SFr-6 near the Palace of Fine Arts; even so, these sites have never been reported fully. More recent work in this area has included the salvage in 1972 of a partial human skeleton dated to A.D. 740 ± 85 (I-6939) and found, along with a cut-and-polished bird bone fragment, 250 cm below the modern surface at SFr-26 in the U.S. Army Presidio (Moratto and Heglar 1973); limited testing on Point Lobos at three shell middens—SFr-5, -21, and -24—apparently used as mollusk-gathering stations rather than as habitation sites (Holman *et al.* 1977); and testing in 1978 at three sites (SFr-29, -30, and -31) within Fort Mason, which yielded artifacts and features apparently representing "permanent or semi-permanent habitation sites rather than seasonal collecting stations" (Baker 1978:133).

Farther south, several excavations have been completed within the coastal, upland, and bayshore zones of San Mateo County (Figure 6.4). On the coast near Half Moon Bay, Asturias (1971) and Moratto (1971g), respectively, reported limited sampling of late prehistoric habitation (SMa-110) and shellfish-processing (SMa-140) sites. A few kilometers inland, in San Bruno, excavations during 1968 and 1969 at sites SMa-100 and -101 brought to light a housefloor, four burials, and a small inventory of "Late Horizon" artifacts from shell midden deposits $^{14}$C dated at A.D. 890 ± 95 (I-4798) (Oliphant 1971; Van Dyke 1971). Investigations elsewhere in the county at SMa-111 (J. Dotta, personal communication, 1971), SMa-112 (Lee 1970), and SMa-6 (Hansen 1974) also have yielded abundant dietary refuse but remarkably few artifacts.

An exceptional site is SMa-125, a large shell midden located on the Filoli Estates in the hills of Redwood City, about 10 km from the bayshore and 13 km from the ocean coast (Figure 6.4). First sampled in 1935 by H. Squires of San Mateo Junior College, the Filoli site was excavated annually between 1970 and 1976 by field classes from Cañada College. A master's thesis by J. Galloway (1976) describes mortuary and cultural remains from SMa-125. Forty-six burials, including the bones of 29 infants and children, are reported. Grave offerings totaling 4559 specimens were found with 19 burials, 2 of which were associated with more than 1000 items each. The inventory included 3528 *Olivella* spire-lopped and thin rectangle beads, 392 bat ray spines, 338 *Haliotis* ornaments, 164 bird-bone whistles, and smaller numbers of mortars, pestles, imperforate charmstones, and a few flaked-stone tools (Galloway 1976). Six $^{14}$C dates on charcoal and bone collagen from burials are arrayed between A.D. 895 ± 90 (I-6688) and A.D. 1450 ± 110 (I-7192) (Figure 6.13).

Significant variation in grave wealth at SMa-125 may signify status differentiation, although Galloway's (1976) assignment of a shaman's role to one individual is less certain. In general, the SMa-125 assemblage is comparable to that of Emeryville Facies components in the east Bay area. All things considered, it would appear that SMa-125 was a major village, presumably occupied by Costanoans during 6 or more centuries before A.D. 1500. The concentration of material goods at the Filoli site, unusual by west Bay standards, perhaps reflects its favorable geographic location between coast and bay resource zones and its status as an important social center.

### South Bay Area

Few parts of California experienced such rapid population growth since World War II as did the Santa Clara Valley. Inexorable urban sprawl in this sector of the Bay area has resulted in the damage or total loss of many archaeological sites. Lamentably, most salvage excavations in this area have been last-ditch efforts, often without the time or resources needed for adequate data recovery and reporting.

A case in point is the Holiday Inn site (SCl-128) in downtown San José (Figure 6.4). Minimal salvage work was permitted at this extensive site in 1973 and again in 1977 when construction activities destroyed large portions of the site. In 1977, for example, archaeologists were allowed to screen a small volume of the estimated 900 m³ of midden that had been piled by bulldozers. Nearly all the finds were out of context. Human bones representing no fewer than 29 individuals were recovered, but as many as 65 skeletons may have been obliterated by construction. Limited analyses of the salvaged bones indicated that the SCl-128 population was biologically intermediate between populations related to Hokan and Penutian languages (Breschini 1978).

Especially since 1970, when the California Environmental Quality Act became law (requiring the assessment of project impacts on the natural and cultural environment), the south Bay area has witnessed numerous archaeological survey and testing projects. These have documented hundreds of sites, some of which manifest considerable research potential (e.g., see Roop *et al.* 1981). The survey and testing work has also led to the discovery of inland sites older and of different character than the bayshore shell middens farther north. In the New Almaden Valley and foothills west of Morgan Hill two such early sites have been reported. In 1977 and 1978 J. Winter of San José State University tested SCl-64, the lower component of which yielded a ¹⁴C date of 6590 ± 200 B.P. In 1979 R. Cartier of Archaeological Resource Management sampled a nearby habitation site (SCl-106), which contained stratified cultural deposits to a depth of 265 cm; a series of five ¹⁴C dates indicates that SCl-106 was occupied as early as 4399 ± 570 B.C. (RL-1056) (Breschini and Haversat 1982; Cartier 1977b:5). Cartier tentatively assigns these components at SCl-64 and -106 to a Santa Theresa Complex.

At this juncture, any summation of south Bay prehistory would be premature. Although archaeological sampling in this area has shown that a long archaeological record exists, no large-scale, systematic excavations of deeply stratified deposits have been undertaken except at SCl-178 (see p. 110). It is anticipated that much will be learned about the prehistoric environments and cultures of the Santa Clara Valley area when such research is conducted.

## North Bay Area

Nearly 100 archaeological sites have been investigated since the late 1940s in the northern San Francisco Bay region. Details of this work have been summarized by T. King (1970a), Moratto (1974d), and Van Dyke (1972). The present treatment emphasizes general trends and discusses some of the more important research and findings.

As in earlier years, the principal motivation for fieldwork in the north Bay area was the "Drake quest." Of nearly 75 Marin County sites investigated since World War II, 32 middens on the Point Reyes Peninsula and 7 in southeastern Marin were excavated by those searching for evidence of Francis Drake's 1579 landfall (T. King 1970a; Moratto 1970a, 1974a). In the area east of the San Andreas rift, especially within the urbanized corridor along Highway 101, fieldwork was undertaken mainly to salvage jeopardized data and, since about 1970, to assess sites likely to be affected by various construction projects.

In 1949 and 1950 C. W. Meighan of UCB continued excavations on Point Reyes at the Estero site (Mrn-232) and at a smaller midden (Mrn-307) nearby, with the hope of finding some definite trace of Drake's activities. In this regard, Mrn-307 yielded Ming Dynasty porcelain—tentatively linked to the 1595 shipwreck of Cermeño's *San Agustín*—and Indochinese stoneware sherds stratigraphically below the porcelain, suggesting the possibility of a "pre-Cermeño stratum" (Meighan 1950a,b).

At about the same time (1949), the Drake Navigators Guild was established to study all aspects of Drake's voyage. The Guild conducted field surveys at Point Reyes as early as 1951 and thereafter excavated a number of historic Indian sites in the same area (Aker 1978; Von der Porten 1963, n.d.). Although this work has resulted in some first-rate analyses of sixteenth-century Asian and European materials (e.g., Shangraw and Von der Porten 1981; Von der Porten 1965, 1970, 1972), a full accounting of the Indian sites data remains to be published.

The Drake quest was also being pursued on another front during the 1950s. Nova Albion Explorations was organized to search for Drake's landing site on the Marin shore of San Francisco Bay. In 1955 Nova Albion Explorations commissioned A. E. Treganza of SFSU to look for sixteenth-century items in Indian shellmounds near Point San Quentin—a location chosen because it was there that the famous "plate of brasse," possibly linked to Drake, had been discovered, or rediscovered, many years earlier (see Heizer 1974a:34–36). Treganza's excavations at Mrn-78, -80, and -255 revealed porcelain sherds only at Mrn-255, but these were attributed to nineteenth-century Chinese laborers who had worked at brick kilns on the site of the older aboriginal midden (Treganza 1957). In 1957 and 1958 Treganza sought explorer-era remains in other bayshore Indian sites, again without success; sampling at Mrn-281, Dominican College (Mrn-254), and at the village site of *Olompali* (Mrn-193) failed to produce any pre-nineteenth-century non-Indian artifacts (Treganza 1958d). At Mrn-193, where a trench 1.5 m wide and 30 m long was opened, Treganza (1958d) reported two burials, cooking stones, and projectile points, beads, and mortars of types ascribable to the protohistoric Coast Miwok.

Meanwhile, back at Point Reyes, A. Neasham of the California Department of Parks and Recreation in 1957 found sixteenth-century items in the Murphy site (Mrn-308). Two years later, Treganza excavated about

80% of this site and recovered an iron spike, wax, and seven sherds of Ming porcelain (Treganza 1959c). Also in 1959, 31 porcelain sherds and a stoneware fragment came to light when Treganza excavated the Adams site (Mrn-298W) near the Estero de Limantour (Figure 6.15) (Treganza and King 1968).

The search for evidence of Drake was carried into the 1960s and 1970s at Point Reyes, where more than 20 sites were tested or excavated by archaeologists representing the Drake Navigators Guild, San Francisco State University, and Santa Rosa Junior College (Moratto 1974a; Treganza and King 1968; Upson 1967, 1968, 1969; Von der Porten and Péron n.d.a, n.d.b). Reflecting the primarily historical focus of these studies, the reports tend to be cursory with respect to aboriginal components. Indeed, some investigators seem to have viewed the Indian middens as little more than a matrix from which to extract iron spikes and porcelains. Consequently, many important data regarding Indian lifeways went unnoticed in the field or, if collected, were not analyzed or reported.

Exceptional in this regard were the nearly total excavation and full reporting by SFSU archaeologists of sites Mrn-216 and Mrn-298 on Lim-

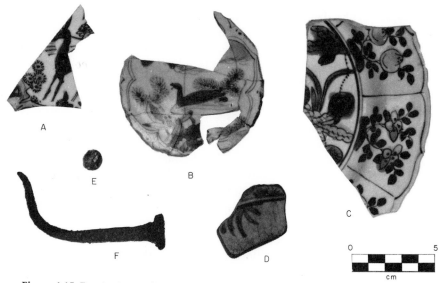

**Figure 6.15** Exotic sixteenth-century artifacts found in Indian occupation sites at Point Reyes National Seashore. A–D, sherds of Ming Dynasty blue-on-white Chinese porcelain; E, lead ball (musket ball?); F, clenched iron spike. Sherd B was chipped by an Indian into a discoidal shape. Sherd D is one of many surf-worn porcelain fragments found at Point Reyes; such pieces probably resulted from the shipwreck of the *San Agustín* in 1595, whereas most of the unworn porcelain is thought to have been left by Francis Drake in 1579 (see Shangraw and Von der Porten 1981). (Photograph courtesy of the A. E. Treganza Anthropology Museum, San Francisco State University.)

antour Sandspit at Point Reyes (Figure 6.4). Faunal remains here attest to winter occupation, and possibly occasional use during other seasons, by protohistoric Miwok groups who exploited varied resources of the Estero de Limantour, ocean shore, and nearby hills. They hunted deer, elk, and harbor seal; took brant, pelicans, snow geese, and ducks; caught perch and sculpin; collected crabs and 13 species of shellfish, predominantly Washington clams and rock cockles; and presumably gathered local vegetal foods to supplement acorns carried to the treeless spit from inland areas (Henn 1970; T. King and Upson 1970; Treganza and King 1968; Wilson 1970). Also notable at Mrn-216 and -298 was the manufacture of clamshell disk beads. As judged by the quantities of broken *Saxidomus* shells, rough bead blanks, ground disks, and finished beads, along with numerous chert drills, Point Reyes must have been a major source of the beads, which served both as ornamental items and as currency during protohistoric times.

Not all archaeological work in the north Bay area has been related to the Drake problem. Many sites have been investigated for salvage, student training, or "pure research" purposes. One such research project was C. W. Meighan's 1949 excavation of the Thomas site (Mrn-115), a large shell midden north of San Rafael (Figure 6.4). This was the first Marin County site to be dated by the radiocarbon method. Charcoal bits from the 274- to 335-cm levels produced an "average" date of A.D. 1230 ± 130 (C-186) (Meighan 1953d).

Together with 12 circular housepits (1.5–4.3 m in diameter), undisturbed since their initial discovery by Nelson in 1907, Mrn-115 contained the remains of a burned house and pieces of charred baskets from which M. A. Baumhoff (1953) was able to identify coiled, stiff-twined, and Catlow-twined weaving. Because only 75 artifacts and no burials were found, Meighan was hesitant to assign Mrn-115 to a particular facies of the CCTS. Even so, the $^{14}$C date and artifact inventory confirm thirteenth- to nineteenth-century occupation by Indians adapted mainly to the bayshore zone (Meighan 1953d).

Not long after Meighan's work at Mrn-115, D. J. McGeein and W. C. Mueller of UCB in 1950 and 1951 excavated Mrn-20 on Strawberry Point (Figure 6.4). Analyses of midden constituents indicate diverse subsistence activities on the shores of Richardson Bay. The shellfish most often collected were bent-nose clams and bay mussels, supplemented by bay oysters, heart and rock cockles, and rock scallops. Deer, sea otter, bay porpoise, and common dolphin were hunted. Of 23 avian species identified at Mrn-20, more than 50% are migratory waterfowl that populate the area only during fall and winter (McGeein and Mueller 1955:59). Fish remains showed that the Strawberry Point people took leopard shark, bat ray, green sturgeon, starry flounder, white seabass, and four species of perch (Follett 1957). Since the bat ray and white seabass do not occur locally during the winter (Follett 1957, 1974), the collective evidence of the fish and bird bones implies year-round habitation at Mrn-20.

Six of 19 flexed burials at Mrn-20 were of infants, one of whom wore in death a necklace of 277 *Olivella* thin rectangle (M1) beads and 4 *Haliotis* pendants. Four other graves contained such goods as red ochre, a nose ornament of bone, an obsidian point, and lots of 17 to 557 *Olivella* M1 beads. The remaining burials lacked visible associations (McGeein and Mueller 1955). "Middle Horizon" artifacts—imperforate fishtail and pyriform charmstones, stone net-sinkers, and cylindrical steatite labrets—along with small arrowpoints, *Olivella* M1 beads, and other "Late Horizon" markers were recorded. Basketry awls, foliate bifaces of obsidian, and gorge fishhooks were viewed as belonging to either horizon. In light of this assemblage, McGeein and Mueller (1955:62) concluded that "the site falls most easily into a transition period between the Middle Horizon and Late Horizon, with very little occupation in the Late, Phase I, Horizon." This "transition period" not only indicates that Strawberry Point was inhabited as early as A.D. 300–500, it also implies cultural continuity between "Middle" (Berkeley Pattern) and later manifestations linked to the ancestral Coast Miwok.

Much additional information about Marin County prehistory has been gained through more recent investigations. During the early 1970s, for example, C. M. Slaymaker of SFSU coordinated excavations at Mrn-138, -139, and -140 on Miller Creek in Las Gallinas Valley (Figure 6.4). Mrn-139 and -140 appear to have been late period camps, whereas Mrn-138 was a major settlement—possibly the Coast Miwok village of *Shotomoko-cha*. Cultural components at this deeply stratified shell-mound include a "Middle Horizon" unit, "Late Horizon, Phase 2" materials, and evidence of mission era or postmission occupation by Indians. The basal stratum at Mrn-138 has been $^{14}$C dated to 700 ± 95 B.C. (I-5797) and A.D. 40 ± 90 (I-5798) (Slaymaker 1974).

Slaymaker also expanded upon Treganza's earlier work at *Olompali* (Mrn-193), north of Novato (Figure 6.4). Archaeological deposits at *Olompali* may cover some 320,000 m², making it the largest known Coast Miwok village site. Excavations between 1971 and 1977 revealed several housefloors, both cremations and burials, and shaped mortars, *Saxidomus* disk beads, and small arrow points of obsidian—mostly of protohistoric age. A $^{14}$C date of A.D. 1420 ± 85 (I-6726) has been reported (Slaymaker 1972:10–19). The possibility of earlier components is suggested by cupule petroglyphs, cobble mortars, and certain types of beads and projectile points. The historic period (sixteenth to nineteenth centuries) also is represented by glass trade beads, square nails, bottle glass, and three items perhaps linked to Drake or Cermeño: two Oriental porcelain sherds (Von der Porten 1976) and an English sixpence struck in 1567 (Slaymaker, personal communication, 1978).

Several other Marin County archaeological sites were excavated during the 1970s. A "Late Horizon, Phase 1" site (Mrn-406) on Corte Madera Creek was sampled by J. McBeath (Van Dyke 1972:84); a series of excavations in stratified midden deposits at Mrn-170 near Hamilton Field showed apparently continuous occupation between circa A.D. 1 and A.D. 1600 or later (Chavez 1976); and at Echa-tamal (Mrn-402), near Nicasio, Dietz (1976) documented a protohistoric–historic Coast Miwok settlement. Also notable are T. L. Jackson's findings at the San José Village site (Mrn-7) in Novato. Radiocarbon dates of A.D. 1350 ± 80 (I-7625) and A.D. 1550 ± 80 (I-7626) at Mrn-7 apply to a "Late Horizon, Phase 2" assemblage marked by clamshell disk beads, *Olivella* lipped and rectangle beads, bone awls, saws and tubes, triangular side-notched and corner-notched arrow points of obsidian, and steatite beads and pipes (Jackson 1974b:1–22). The earlier [14]C date is of special interest because it "weakens the hypothesis that clam disc beads were an innovation prompted by historic contacts between aboriginal peoples and early explorers from Europe" (Jackson 1974:85). In this regard, clamshell disk beads at Mrn-170 also have been dated to the precontact period (Chavez 1976:219).

Not far south of Mrn-7, the multicomponent Pacheco Valle site (Mrn-152) has yielded two [14]C dates that, at the time of their reporting, were the earliest in Marin County. Both were derived from bone collagen obtained from submidden burials. Burial 4, associated with a tubular steatite bead and a nondiagnostic point fragment, yielded a date of 3270 ± 150 B.P. (UCLA-1891A), and Burial 5, found with red ochre and a point fragment, was dated to 3050 ± 130 B.P. (UCLA-1891B) (Clewlow and Wells 1981).

The Pacheco Valle site seems to have been occupied for a relatively long time before and after these dates. Most artifacts are of "Middle Horizon" types, but the "Late" period is also well represented and some specimens attest to "Early" activity. The "Middle" assemblages at Mrn-152 are most comparable to those of Mrn-266 (McClure site), Mrn-170 (Ignacio), and, to a lesser extent, Ala-307 at West Berkeley (Goerke and Cowan 1983:63). Lower Mrn-152 thus represents an early Berkeley Pattern settlement, possibly associated with the initial movement of Utian peoples (discussed below) into Marin County.

Considerably older than Mrn-152 are portions of Mrn-17 on De Silva Island near the shore of Richardson Bay (Figure 6.4). Recent excavations by G. Pahl of San Francisco State University have revealed both midden and submidden cultural deposits as much as 6 m deep at Mrn-17. Stratigraphically, an upper midden—approximately 4 m deep and dominated by shells of bent-nosed clam (75% of all shell)—is underlain by a thin sterile layer, and then 1.5 m of midden in which 75–80% of all shells are those of bay oyster. Basal, submidden deposits contained an "Early Archaic" hearth that has provided a [14]C date of 5480 ± 125 B.P. (Thieler

1983:n.p.). Although the full report of findings at De Silva Island is still in preparation, preliminary indications are that Mrn-17 includes the longest known archaeological record of cultural and environmental changes on the shore of the San Francisco Bay estuarine system. One would expect Mrn-17 to yield evidence of both Utian (ancestral Miwok) and pre-Utian occupation, as well as information about adaptive responses to the emergence and evolution of Richardson Bay.

Although Mrn-17 and -152 are the oldest sites known in Marin, their records of cultural development are paralleled, over shorter periods of time, at many other stratified sites in the county—Mrn-14, -27, -138, -170, -192, and -266, to name a few. Findings at these sites imply occupation by the Coast Miwok and their ancestors over a span of 3000 years or more. This is not to say that cultural patterns did not change, only that such change was mainly stylistic and technical, without evidence of population replacement. At the Shelter Hill site (Mrn-14) in Mill Valley, for example, three prehistoric components parallel the Ellis Landing–Emeryville–Fernandez progression on the east shore of San Francisco Bay. The transition between components at Mrn-14 was gradual and, through some 1800 years of occupation, the basic economic focus remained on Richardson Bay and its marshes. Essential patterns of collecting mussels and clams, fishing, and taking waterfowl persisted through time (Moratto *et al.*, eds., 1974; Riley 1979). Only particulars changed, such as the steady diachronic increase in the use of clams relative to mussels, but these can be explained in terms of natural factors rather than fundamental cultural adjustments:

> The combined effect of (1) intense human predation of the mussel beds during the early period of occupation at Mrn-14, and (2) increased silting and salinity (detrimental to the mussel beds) ultimately related to the world-wide rise in sea level led to an early decrease in mussels and concomitant increase in clams in the midden. (Riley 1979:88)

In addition to such studies of economic change, archaeologists recently have begun to learn something of prehistoric social organization in the San Francisco Bay region. In this regard, one of the more remarkable Marin County sites was Mrn-27, an earth and shell midden on the Tiburon Peninsula (Figure 6.4). In 1967 volunteers supervised by D. A. Fredrickson salvaged the cremations and burials of no fewer than 49 individuals within a small ($\approx$24 m$^2$) cemetery at Mrn-27. Clustered in certain graves were elk bone whistles, *Haliotis* shell ornaments, obsidian bifaces, imperforate charmstones, carved bone pendants, and numerous *Olivella* saucer beads—all "sociotechnic–ideotechnic" items thought to reflect social status (T. King 1974c). A "Middle Horizon" ascription based on artifacts from Mrn-27 agrees with $^{14}$C dates of 370 $\pm$ 190 B.C. (I-3149) and 30 $\pm$ 95 B.C. (I-3148) (T. King 1970b).

T. F. King (1970b, 1973e) has proposed that the grave wealth and mortuary spatial patterns at Mrn-27 attest to a ranked social structure. King observed that the central part of the cemetery consisted of the single and multiple cremations and fragmentary burials of 18 or more individuals (7 men, 5 women, and 6 children); 62% of all grave goods accompanied these remains, with by far the greatest number and variety of items being found with the cremations. Partly encircling the northern edge of the cremation area was a series of mostly male inhumations with few or no associated items. Indeed, outside of the central cluster only the burials of two adult females and an infant possessed large numbers of grave goods; these were in the southeastern quadrant of the cemetery. Single, often disarticulated adult burials without orientation lay farthest from the center (King 1970b, 1973e).

King believes that the Mrn-27 cemetery reflects in its structure a form of social organization characterized by ascribed ranking. He infers that

> the central cremation zone represents the interment of high-ranking individuals, while persons of lower rank are interred farther and farther from the center. The presence of children and infants in the central area, the slight evidence of sex-based role distinctions, the evidence of social distinctions cross-cutting age/sex divisions, and the "ideotechnic–sociotechnic" weighting of the artifact assemblage all suggest that rank . . . was not achieved on the basis of personal attributes but ascribed on the basis of kin-group membership. Such rank ascription is typical of a "Rank" society in Morton Fried's (1967) terms, or "Chiefdom" in the words of Elman Service (1962). (King 1974c:38)

One may question whether some of King's (1970b, 1973e) particular inferences about kinship structure can be validated by the archaeological data (Kautz 1972). Nonetheless, King has shown clearly that the Mrn-27 cemetery included two disposal modes (burial and cremation); that these modes were patterned spatially; that the distribution of "sociotechnic" artifacts was nonrandom; and that some children as well as certain adults merited grave wealth. These facts do seem to imply social ranking and status ascription in bayshore Marin more than 2000 years ago.

## Summary and Conclusions

Perceptions of Central Coast and San Francisco Bay region prehistory have changed rapidly during the past few years, partly as a result of intensive fieldwork performed to comply with environmental law. This mandated fieldwork has forced archaeologists to break away from their traditional bias toward coastal and bayshore middens and to investigate localities and types of sites not previously studied. One benefit of this change is seen with respect to studies of ancient cultures. As recently as

1970, midden sites dated to circa 1000–2000 B.C. comprised the oldest recognized evidence of occupation in the Bay region, and almost nothing was known of early prehistory on the Central Coast. Now it is known that these parts of west-central California were inhabited in early Holocene times. Even older archaeological traces may exist on the submerged continental shelf or below the waters and sediments of San Francisco Bay (Figure 6.2).

Radiocarbon-dated components at SCl-178 near San José and SCr-177 in Scotts Valley attest to cultural activity at circa 8000 B.C. in the area between San Francisco and Monterey bays (Table 6.3 and Figure 6.13). The lower, subdune deposit at SCr-7 may be of comparable antiquity. At present, little else can be said about these early components: SCr-177, although partly destroyed, is still being investigated; the materials from SCl-178 have not yet been published; and SCr-7 has never been excavated by archaeologists.

Bay and Coast prehistory between circa 5000 and 2000 B.C. is better documented. A dozen or more $^{14}$C-dated archaeological discoveries confirm occupation during this period in areas of the north Bay (lower Mrn-17), east Bay (CCo-308C), Santa Clara Valley (SCl-64, -106), west Bay (BART, Stanford, and Sunnyvale sites), Santa Cruz coast (SCr-7 dune), and Monterey Bay (Mnt-228, -254, -414, -834, and -838). Data from these sites indicate that widespread but relatively sparse populations of hunter–gatherers lived in the Bay and Coast regions before 2000 B.C. The locations of their settlements, in hill country as well as on bay and ocean shores, are marked by earth or sand deposits with significantly less shell than is found in later middens. Shellfish were collected, but this was not a major subsistence activity. Large projectile points and millingstones show that both hunting and vegetal food processing were important. Semisedentism, a foraging subsistence strategy, and technologic traits assign these early peoples to the Archaic Stage (Fredrickson 1974a; Willey and Phillips 1958). On the Central Coast, the origins of the Sur Pattern (Breschini and Haversat 1980) are seen in these early Archaic manifestations. This pattern apparently extended as well into the San Francisco Bay region. In both regions, the Sur Pattern probably was associated with speakers of Hokan languages.

Soon after 2000 B.C., bayshore- and marsh-adapted people representing a new and distinctive pattern settled at Ala-307 (West Berkeley). During the following millennium, similar bayshore settlements appeared at Bodega Bay (Son-299), De Silva Island (Mrn-17), and Pacheco Valle (Mrn-152) in the north Bay area, at Ellis Landing (CCo-295) and Newark (Ala-328) on the east bayshore, and at University Village (SMa-77) on the Bay's southwestern edge (Figure 6.4). By A.D. 1, numerous villages had been established throughout the San Francisco Bay region and along the Central Coast as far south as the Monterey Peninsula. Fredrickson (1973,

1974a) includes these developments in his Berkeley Pattern, the more southerly expressions of which apparently correspond to the Monterey Pattern (Breschini and Haversat 1980), discussed earlier. The Berkeley Pattern, including those components previously assigned to the "Middle Horizon," is characterized as follows:

> a. Technological skills and devices. The minimally-shaped cobble mortar and cobble pestle are employed as the virtually exclusive milling implements. Manos and metates [millingstones] . . . are rare. The dart and atlatl are present. . . . Chipped stone projectile points are less frequent than in the Windmiller Pattern, and nonstemmed forms predominate. There is a growing emphasis (through time) upon the bone industry. . . . The polished stone industry does not appear to be as highly developed as it is with the Windmiller Pattern.
>
> b. Economic modes. As indicated by a high proportion of grinding implements in relation to projectile points and by the regional accumulation of large shell heaps, the Berkeley Pattern has a collecting emphasis. The acorn is probably the dominant staple. The larger number of sites and great depths of deposit suggest a larger population than that supported by the Windmiller Pattern. . . . The use of local material predominates. Trade goods, when they appear, are finished specimens, rather than raw material.
>
> c. Burial and ceremonial practices. The mortuary complex is rarely elaborated. Flexed burials with variable orientation occur in village sites. Burial goods are restricted to a few utilitarian items or ornamental objects. . . . Ceremonialism is indicated predominantly by shamanism, that is, by the presence of single graves with objects compatible with known ethnographic "shaman's kits," e.g., quartz crystals, charmstones, bone whistles. Graves are sometimes accompanied by bird and animal bones, occasionally by articulated portions of skeletons. Birds and animals sometime[s] are found as ceremonial burials. (Fredrickson 1973:125a–126)

Fredrickson adds that the Berkeley Pattern is marked by considerable inter- and intraregional variation, but that its essential characteristics serve to distinguish it from more or less coeval manifestations, such as the Windmiller Pattern to the east and the late Borax Lake Pattern (see Chapter 10) to the north (1973:116–133). As evidenced by the lower Stone Valley (CCo-308) and West Berkeley (Ala-307) components, the Berkeley Pattern was emerging in the east Bay area by circa 2000 B.C. Stone Valley may have been near the boundary between the Berkeley and Windmiller patterns; similarly, University Village (SMa-77) possibly reflects a boundary zone between the Berkeley and Sur patterns.

Gerow (1968) included SMa-77, along with lower West Berkeley (Ala-307B), in his Early Bay Culture. However, several other bayshore components (e.g., at Ellis Landing, De Silva Island, Pacheco Valle, Newark, and Castro) evidently are as old as, or older than, the Early Bay type site. Excepting SMa-77, these are true shell middens reflecting intensive use of bayshore resources. Moreover, the distinctive foliate and lozenge-shaped projectile points of Monterey chert and large crescentic stones found at SMa-77 do not typify the other assemblages. As judged by its artifacts as well as human skeletal traits, the University Village material shows important affinities with archaeological manifestations of the Central Coast in addition to those of the Bay and Central Valley regions. In this light, one may question whether SMa-77 (i.e., the University Village Complex) is really typical of any widespread archaeological culture in the San Francisco Bay region per se.

All the bayshore sites named above, including SMa-77, share perforate charmstones of specific types, certain *Haliotis* shell bead and ornament forms, and *Olivella* spire-lopped and thick rectangle beads; but these also appear in coeval Delta sites and seem to be better markers of time than of culture. It is mainly in terms of a preference for flexed burials, a greater diversity and number of bone and antler implements, abundant stone mortars, and relatively more ground- than chipped-stone items that the older Bay region assemblages are separated from those of the Valley. However, these same traits persist in the Bay region long after the time of the University Village Complex and therefore must be viewed as indicators of San Francisco Bay area cultures in general rather than as diagnostic elements of an Early Bay Culture in particular.

The position taken here is that the University Village Complex is an expression of the Sur Pattern strongly influenced by the Berkeley Pattern. Thus, SMa-77 is seen as a relict Hokan settlement in contact with early Costanoan populations. The Berkeley Pattern then represents Utian (Miwok–Costanoan) cultural developments and geographic spread throughout the Bay and northern Central Coast regions (Figure 6.16 and Table 6.4). Old Berkeley Pattern components (e.g., Ala-307B, CCo-308C, and lower Mrn-152) share many traits with those of the Windmiller Pattern (see Chapter 5), suggesting a common origin.

Based on geographic distribution of [14]C-dated Berkeley Pattern components (Figure 6.16 and Table 6.4), it would appear that Utian populations first occupied eastern Contra Costa County at circa 2500–2000 B.C., then expanded westward to San Francisco Bay. By circa 1900 B.C., at least one Utian group had settled on the east bayshore (at Ala-307).Thereafter, Utian populations identifiable as ancestral Costanoans spread southward. By circa 1500 B.C., they occupied lands around the southern end of San Francisco Bay, whence they expanded northward onto the Peninsula, westward to the coast, and southward into the Santa Clara Valley. Costanoan dominions at circa 500 B.C. extended as far south as Mnt-12 on the Monterey Peninsula and included essentially all of the territory that they would hold until historic times (Figure 11.7).

Coeval with these events, ancestral Western Miwok populations were expanding into the north Bay area (Figure 6.16). Miwokan groups evidently first occupied the Napa Valley at circa 1500–1000 B.C., then reached northward as far as Clear Lake where they are recognized archaeologically as the Houx Aspect of the Berkeley Pattern, dated to circa 500 B.C. (see Chapter 10). Other groups of early Western Miwok settled in

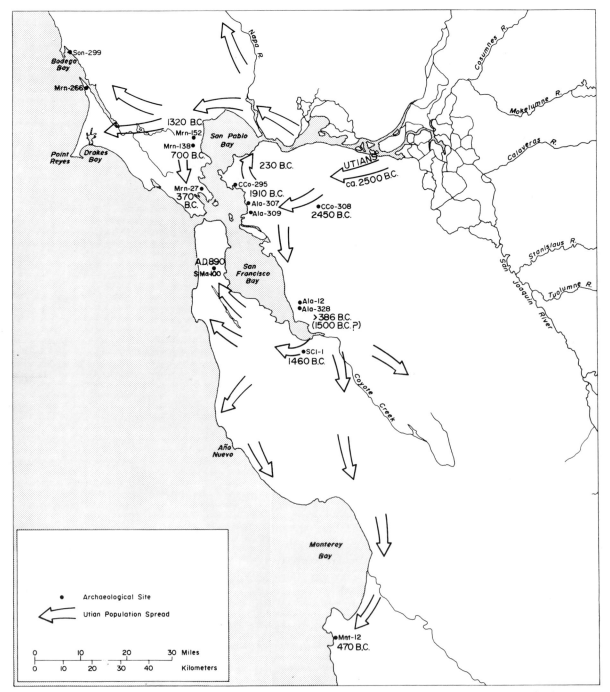

**Figure 6.16** The Utian radiation in west-central California. Arrows show the directions of Utian spread from the lower Sacramento Valley into the San Francisco Bay and Monterey Bay areas. (Map drawn by Thad van Bueren.)

**TABLE 6.4**

The Utian Radiation: Radiocarbon-Dated Components of the Berkeley Pattern in Central California[a]

| Date (B.C.) | Component | Reference |
|---|---|---|
| Berkeley Facies (early Utian or Utian-influenced) | | |
| 1910 ± 450 | West Berkeley (Ala-307) | Wallace and Lathrap (1975) |
| Patterson Facies (Proto-Costanoan) | | |
| 750 ± 300 | West Berkeley (Ala-307) | Wallace and Lathrap (1975) |
| 360 ± 120 | Emeryville (Ala-309) | Hubbs et al. (1962) |
| 389 ± 150 | Newark (Ala-328) | Bickel (1976) |
| 380 ± 90 | Newark (Ala-328) | Bickel (1976) |
| Monterey County shell middens (initial Costanoan) | | |
| 470 ± 165 | Mnt-12 | Breschini and Haversat (1979) |
| 330 ± 130 | Mnt-114 | Dietz and Jackson (1981) |
| 210 ± 200 | Mnt-115 | Dietz and Jackson (1981) |
| Marin County components (initial Coast Miwok) | | |
| 1320 ± 150 | Pacheco (Mrn-152) | Clewlow and Wells (1981) |
| 1120 ± 130 | Pacheco (Mrn-192) | Clewlow and Wells (1981) |
| 700 ± 95 | Miller Creek (Mrn-138) | Slaymaker (1974) |
| 410 ± 190 | Tiburon (Mrn-27) | T. King (1970b) |
| Houx Aspect of the Berkeley Pattern (Lake Miwok) | | |
| 150 ± 150 | Houx (Lak-261) | Fredrickson (1974a) |
| Delta locality (Plains Miwok) | | |
| 1350 ± 150[b] | Stone Lake (Sac-145) | Schulz (1975) |
| 230 ± 150 | McGillivray 1 (SJo-142) | Fredrickson (1974a) |
| Interior Contra Costa County (Bay Miwok) | | |
| 910 ± 120 | Stone Valley (CCo-308B) | Fredrickson (1974a) |

[a]See also Figure 6.16.
[b]Questionable date.

Marin County (Mrn-17 and -152) between circa 2000 and 1000 B.C. The nearby coast (e.g., at Mrn-266 and Son-299) probably came into Miwok possession between circa 1000 and 500 B.C. This north Bay radiation of Utians presumably involved Miwok replacement of Yukian (and Hokan?) populations, just as the Costanoans had supplanted Hokan peoples farther south.

T. F. King (1971a, b, 1974c) has proposed a model to account for this Utian radiation and spread of the Berkeley Pattern, although he did not identify them as such. King's model relies on positive feedback between population growth and natural environmental conditions to explain the development of sedentism, status ascription, and social ranking among early hunter–gatherers in the San Francisco Bay region. Coincidentally, the model defines a process by which the Berkeley Pattern and Utian peoples might have spread into previously occupied areas.

According to King, the prehistoric Bay region featured seven major resource zones: oak woodland, rocky shore and gravel bottom, marshland, mudflat, chaparral, open bay, and grassland (1971b, 1974c). The "typical" bayshore village of 4000 to 2000 years ago was in a marshside setting near a freshwater stream. This sort of ecotonal location permitted ready exploitation of the bay, mudflat, marsh, rocky shore, and inland zones. It is notable that the oldest sites in each vicinity were situated in catchments with the optimum mix of resource variety and abundance and that, later, usually smaller settlements were dispersed in the surrounding countryside.

King suggests that settlements would have been established first "where catchments contained a wide variety of biotic resources exploitable according to an annual schedule with few 'gaps'" (1974c:40). When rising populations in time began to exceed the carrying capacity of the catchment, the society might adapt by population-control measures, by development of new subsistence practices, or by fissioning, that is, "budding off" smaller groups to settle in nearby areas. This would have permitted further population growth in marginal areas until a point was reached at which the parent community was socially circumscribed by peripheral settlements. Considerable pressure toward readaptation would have built as the population approached the carrying limits of the environment. The needs of both parent and daughter communities could have been met through increased interaction in the form of warfare or resource sharing via exchange systems. Either kind of interaction would have required organization of the population, which amounts to the development of formalized, nonegalitarian political systems (King 1971a:11–14, 1974b:37–42).

Although King's model has not been tested systematically, it seems generally compatible with available data. Specifically, the older Berkeley Pattern settlements occur in locations with optimal resource diversity; there is clear evidence of population growth in the San Francisco and Monterey Bay areas between circa 2000 B.C. and A.D. 1; and settlement differentiation, trade, social ranking, and status ascription are indicated during the same period. The model also would explain how dense population fronts associated with fissioning parent settlements might have allowed Utian communities to expand into areas already occupied by groups with different land-use and settlement patterns and lower population densities.

Also with regard to the adaptive success of Utian peoples, it bears emphasis that virtually all the early Berkeley Pattern settlements were located near coastal or bayshore marshlands. These remarkably productive ecosystems offered fish, shellfish, waterfowl, shore birds, mammals, and marsh plants (Desgrandchamp 1976) and thus were able to sustain large aboriginal populations. It seems probable that the great expansion of marshlands in west-central California, associated with rising sea levels (Bickel 1978a), may have been a powerful stimulus to the spread of the Berkeley Pattern and a determinant of its early geographic extent.

Beginning circa A.D. 300 to 500, the Berkeley Pattern gradually developed into the Augustine Pattern (see Chapter 5). As defined by Fredrickson (1973:127–129), the Augustine Pattern incorporates those phases previously assigned to the "Late Horizon," namely, the Mendoza and Estero facies in western Marin County, the Emeryville and Fernandez facies in the east Bay area, and other facies (phases) elsewhere in central California (see Chapters 5 and 10). Unlike the Berkeley Pattern, Augustine does not mark general population replacement in the San Francisco Bay region; rather, it is identified by new traits such as the bow and arrow, harpoon, tubular tobacco pipe, and preinterment grave burning, that accompanied the southward movement of Wintuan (ancestral Patwin) peoples into the lower Sacramento Valley. Patwin expansion and concomitant displacement of Bay Miwok surely affected populations in the northeast Bay area; otherwise, Augustine traits seem to have diffused into the Bay region without social replacement.

Through time, the Augustine Pattern came to embody much more than a veneer of northern influences on a core of Berkeley cultural features. As compared with Berkeley, the Augustine Pattern manifested larger populations; a greater number of settlements and more evidence of status differentiation among them; a greater emphasis on gathering vegetal foods, especially acorns; more intensive trade and highly developed exchange systems; the spread of secret societies and cults together with their associated architectural features and ceremonial traits; and, in late prehistory, the appearance of clamshell disk beads as a currency for exchange. This was the emerging cultural pattern encountered and destroyed by the Spanish mission system and later historic developments.

# 7. The Sierra Nevada

When we reflect that the mountain valleys were thickly populated as
far east as Yosemite (in summer, still further up), and consider the
great extent and fertility of the San Joaquin plains. . . ; then add to
this the long and fish-full streams, the Mokelumne, the Stanislaus,
the Tuolumne, the Merced, the Chowchilla, and the San Joaquin
encircling all, along whose banks the Indians anciently dwelt in
multitudes, we shall see what a capacity there was to support a dense
population.
*Powers (1877:346)*

(Photograph by the author.)

# Natural History

One of the highest and longest mountain ranges in North America, the Sierra Nevada partitions the Great Basin on the east from California's coast and valley provinces on the west (Figure 1.2). Sierran landforms vary from low, rolling foothills, through ridge and canyon systems at midslope elevations, to meadows and rugged peaks in the high country (Figures 1.5 and 7.1). These topographic features, along with aspects of Sierran climate and hydrology, are discussed in Chapter 1.

Sierran flora and fauna are distributed in a series of lengthwise (north–south) belts or life zones roughly tied to elevation (see Chapter 1; Figure 1.11). The foothills lie mainly within the Upper Sonoran life zone ($\approx$150–1220 m elevation), marked by blue oak–interior live oak–digger pine woodland, woodland–grass savanna, and manzanita–chamise–ceanothus chaparral. Common animals are the mule deer, gray fox, ground squirrel, brush rabbit, valley quail, and mourning dove.

On the Sierran midslope the Transition life zone ($\approx$730–1950 m) or yellow pine belt is typified by ponderosa pine–incense cedar–black oak forest, with sugar pine, big tree, and golden oak as important adjunct species. Other notable Transition types are white fir–mixed conifer forest and manzanita–chinquapin–ceanothus–scrub oak chaparral. Inhabiting this zone are the black bear, mule deer, mountain lion, mountain coyote, and band-tailed pigeon.

At higher altitudes, where the winter snowpack is deepest, are red fir and Jeffrey pine forests of the Canadian life zone ($\approx$1500–2150 m); adjunct species include sugar pine, white fir, black oak, and lodgepole pine. Higher still are the sparse lodgepole pine and subalpine conifer (mountain hemlock–whitebark pine–foxtail pine) forests of the Hudsonian life zone ($\approx$2000–2800 m). Above treeline the windswept Alpine zone ($\approx$2440–4300 m) sustains only grasses, sedges, creeping plants, and occasional dwarf trees. Animals peculiar to the high country are the wolverine, varying hare, mountain sheep, marmot, and Allen chipmunk. East of the Sierran crest the sagebrush belt ($\approx$1280–2130 m) supports piñon pine, Utah juniper, mountain mahogany, and sagebrush, along with such creatures as the sagehen, desert jackrabbit, and Nuttal cottontail. In the

**Figure 7.1** Looking south toward the Kings–Kern Divide over glaciated peaks of the Sierra Nevada crest. Mount Gardiner is near the lower right corner; the high peak at the far left is Mount Whitney (4418 m). (U.S. Geological Survey photograph.)

southern Sierra, piñon–juniper woodland occurs at elevations of about 1700–2600 m (Barbour and Major 1977; Ingles 1965; Storer and Usinger 1970; Whitney 1979).

Among Sierran Indians the life zones often were of greater cultural importance than linguistic differences. While life zones run north–south, cutting across dialect boundaries, ethnic territories tended to reach east–west from the foothills to the high Sierra, providing access for each group to all life zones (Barrett and Gifford 1933:129–136). The territory of each language group thus afforded the widest possible array of biotic resources.

Prehistoric societies found the Sierra Nevada richly endowed with useful rocks and minerals. Although the mountain range is mostly granitic, many other kinds of lithologic units exist as a result of local vulcanism, metamorphism of foothill sediments, and glaciation, or as remnants of very old pre-Nevadan formations. Among the Sierran mineral resources of archaeological interest are alabaster, steatite, quartz crystals, basalt, rhyolite, slate, clay, hematite, chert, and chalcedony, as well as the nearly ubiquitous granitic rocks that were used in prehistory for varied artifacts (Bowen and Crippen 1948; Heizer and Treganza 1944; Wallace 1971). Along the east side of the range, at the geomorphic contact between the Sierra and Great Basin, is a series of obsidian sources. Eight quarries—at Bodie Hills, Mono Craters, Mono Glass Mountain, Casa Diablo, Mt. Hicks, Queen (Truman Meadows), Fish Springs, and Coso Hot Springs (Figure 7.2)—supplied nearly all the obsidian used by Sierran Indians (Ericson 1977a,b; Jackson 1974a).

In brief, the Sierra is not merely a rampart separating the California and Great Basin provinces, but an area of immense resource potential in its own right. It contains ample water, varied terrain, and abundant rocks and minerals. Because of its location, orientation, and relief, the Sierra features countless microenvironments, each with a distinctive mix of landforms, lithology, soils, microclimate, vegetation, and wildlife. Most impressive is the natural diversity along relatively short transects up and down slope. During the snow-free season, a person may trek from the edge of the Central Valley up through foothill oak woodlands and higher forests of pine and fir, across the Alpine crestal zone, and then down into the juniper and sagebrush of the western Great Basin—all within a span of 3 or 4 days. Few regions in America offer so much natural variety in so little distance.

In this book the Sierra Nevada is divided arbitrarily into three archaeological subregions (Figure 1). The northern Sierra encompasses the upper Feather, Yuba, Bear, and American River drainages; the central Sierra includes the watersheds of the Cosumnes, Mokelumne, Calaveras, Stanislaus, Tuolumne, Merced, Chowchilla, and Fresno rivers; and the southern Sierra takes in the upper San Joaquin, Kings, Kaweah, Tule, and Kern River systems (Figures 1, 1.4, 7.2).

## Native Cultures

The principal occupants of the Sierra Nevada in late prehistory were the Maidu, Washo, Miwok, Western Mono, Foothill Yokuts, and Tübatulabal (Figure 11.1). In addition, the Yana, Northern Paiute-Bannock, and Kawaiisu held peripheral tracts in the Sierra or used parts of the range seasonally. Together these groups represent nine language families assignable to three stocks and superfamilies (see Chapter 11). Such linguistic diversity attests to considerable population movement in Sierran prehistory.

The ethnographic homeland of Maiduan peoples—including Nisenan,

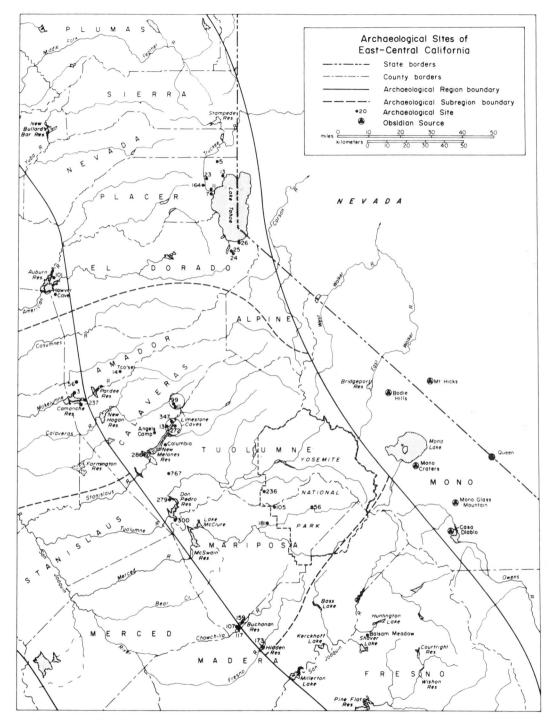

**Figure 7.2** Archaeological sites of east-central California. (Map by Allan Childers and Thad Van Bueren.)

Konkow, and (Northern) Maidu—was in the northern Sierra. Maidu country ranged from Lassen Peak eastward to the Honey Lake vicinity and southward to Sierra Buttes, while the Konkow held the lower reaches of the Feather River and adjacent parts of the upper Sacramento River watershed (Riddell 1978:370–371). West of Lake Tahoe, the Nisenan inhabited the Yuba, Bear, and American River uplands as well as lands along the lower Feather River (Beals 1933; Wilson and Towne 1978). South of the Nisenan, the Sierra Miwok domain fell between the Mokelumne and Fresno rivers. Maiduan and Miwokan peoples claimed the full width of the west slope, from the edge of the Central Valley to the Sierran crest, except for an area south of Lake Tahoe shared by the Central Sierra Miwok and the Washo (Figure 11.1).

A different arrangement of territories existed in the southern Sierra, where 15 separate tribelets of Yokuts occupied the foothills but not the higher mountains. Above them, at elevations from ≈ 900 to 2200 m, six tribal groups of Western Mono (Monache) formed a "second tier" with discontinuous holdings between the upper San Joaquin and Middle Fork of the Kaweah River (Spier 1978a,b). Similar to the Western Mono in their geographic position above the Yokuts, the Tübatulabal lived above ≈750 m in the mountains drained by the Kern and South Fork Kern rivers (C. Smith 1978).

Indians of the Sierran west slope lived in relatively permanent settlements in the Upper Sonoran and lower Transition zones. Some winter occupation did occur at favored places above snow line (Bunnell 1911; D'Azevedo 1963; Powers 1877). Otherwise, the higher zones were visited mainly during the warm season by parties engaged in hunting, gathering (e.g., piñon nuts), and trans-Sierran trade (Elsasser 1958).

Except in the far southern Sierra, permanent settlements of 10 or 15 to several hundred people were situated near water, typically along streams or on ridges or knolls with a southern exposure. A main village would consist of family dwellings, acorn granaries, bedrock mortars, one or more sweat houses, a headman's house, and a large communal dance house or ceremonial structure (Figure 7.3). In the surrounding countryside were smaller settlements of a few households related by kinship and economic ties to the principal village. Together the central and outlying settlements functioned as a "village community," under the leadership of a headman (Kroeber 1925:381; Merriam 1967:340). Among the Yokuts these communities were sufficiently large and well organized to be identified as tribes (Gayton 1948b; Spier 1978a).

Peoples of the western Sierra Nevada made their livelihood by harvesting plant foods, hunting, and fishing. A remarkable assortment of berries and other fruits, nuts, roots, bulbs, greens, and grass seeds was gathered. Of special importance as storable and nutritious foods were acorns of black and golden oaks, buckeye nuts, and pine nuts. Ingenious

**Figure 7.3** Murphys Rancheria, Calaveras County, 1906. This Miwok settlement features a large circular dance house (left) and smaller residential structures (right). (Photograph by S. A. Barrett; courtesy of the R. H. Lowie Museum of Anthropology, University of California, Berkeley.)

snares, traps, nets, and other devices were used, along with the bow and arrow, to take mule deer, pronghorn, black bear, rabbits, squirrels, quail, and pigeons. Fish—particularly salmon, trout, suckers, whitefish and sturgeon—were hooked, netted, trapped, poisoned, or captured by hand after being driven into shallows (Dixon 1905a; Faye 1923; Gifford 1932; Levy 1978b).

Subsistence and settlement patterns were quite different on the east side of the Sierran crest. Along this arid rim of the western Great Basin nomadic Paiute bands followed an annual cycle, moving among seasonal camps, in order to hunt mountain sheep, rabbits, and pronghorn; to harvest piñon nuts, seeds, and other vegetal products; and to acquire obsidian, salt, and other commodities for local use and for trans-Sierran trade (E. Davis 1965; Steward 1938).

Unusual among the peoples of the eastern Sierra were the Washo, who claimed the mountains between Honey Lake and the Walker River. The Washo were adapted both to the Great Basin and to the high Sierra. Like other Great Basin societies, they followed an annual round of hunting deer, rabbits, and pronghorn, and gathering pine nuts, chokecherries, and seeds; but they also fished extensively for trout and suckers in the streams around Lake Tahoe. Moreover, the Washo occasionally made gathering expeditions into the foothills nearly as far west as Sacramento (Downs 1966; Lowie 1939; Price 1962). The Washo used to good advantage every life zone in the Sierra Nevada. In this they resembled some of the more easterly Tübatulabal and Northern Maidu who sometimes ventured into the Great Basin to exploit particular resources (Dixon 1905a; Voegelin 1938).

The ancient harmony between Sierran cultural and natural systems ended abruptly in the mid-nineteenth century. During the Spanish and Mexican periods, contacts with Indians of the Sierra Nevada took the form of infrequent exploratory and punitive expeditions (Cook 1960, 1962). The Gold Rush, however, brought devastation to the central and northern Sierran societies whose country was invaded. By 1860 the impacts of disease, violence, forced relocation, environmental damage, and starvation had largely destroyed the native lifeways of the Sierra Nevada (Castillo 1978; Cook 1943c, 1968, 1970; Hall 1978).

## Early Archaeology

Widespread interest in California prehistory was kindled during the Gold Rush, when extensive mining operations in the Sierra led to numerous discoveries of artifacts and human bones allegedly in deposits of Tertiary age. In the 1850s and 1860s, for example, mortars, charmstones, a pestle, and a human skull reportedly were found in auriferous gravels beneath the latite cliffs of Table Mountain (Figure 7.4) in Tuolomne County (Becker 1891; Blake 1899). At nearby Gold Springs, miners claimed to have found mortars and millingstones associated with mastodon bones at a depth of 5 m in gold-bearing gravels (Sinclair 1908b). Similarly, at Clay Hill in the vicinity of Placerville, Dr. H. H. Boyce vouched for the discov-

**Figure 7.4** Tuolumne Table Mountain near Jamestown, Tuolumne County. This is a latite lava flow of Pliocene age that occupied an ancient river channel. During the nineteenth century, human bones and artifacts reportedly were found in auriferous quartz gravels of Eocene age underlying Table Mountain. These early claims have proven to be without merit. (Photograph by the author.)

ery of a human skeleton in dense clay at a depth of 11.6 m in sediments capped by basaltic lava 2.5 m thick (Whitney 1980).

Also publicized were a human skull supposedly taken from diggings 76 m deep near Columbia (Blake 1868), a collection of some 300 mortars exposed by hydraulic mining in Butte County's Pliocene gravels (Skertchley 1888), and a buried stone arrastra that was touted as "proof" of gold mining by Indians in the remote past (A. Taylor 1862). These reports stimulated careful research as well as speculations concerning the antiquity of man in the Sierra Nevada (Hanks 1901; Heizer 1948a; Winslow 1857; G. Wright 1891).

The most controversial discovery was the "Calaveras skull," a partial cranium found in 1866 at a depth of 40 m in a mine shaft penetrating Eocene gravels and lava beds on Bald Hill near Angels Camp (Figure 7.2), Calaveras County (Ayres 1882; Whitney 1867). The bones were fossilized and heavily encrusted with calcareous material, supporting the notion of great antiquity (J. Merriam 1910). The appelation of "Auriferous Gravel Man" persisted through 4 decades, until Ales Hrdlička (1907) showed conclusively that the Calaveras skull was that of a recent Indian, and Sinclair (1908b) discredited the story of its discovery.

In 1880 the respected geologist J. D. Whitney published a report culminating a long study of Sierran gold-bearing strata as related to Early Man. Whitney admitted the Calaveras skull, oral testimony from miners, and affidavits from "expert witnesses" as evidence that the remains of humans and extinct fauna were coeval with Tertiary gravels. Artifacts often identical to those made by historic Indians, reportedly found in auriferous deposits, were taken to support Whitney's belief that little or no cultural change had occurred in California since Pliocene times (Whitney 1867, 1872, 1880).

Reaction to Whitney's case for "Eocene Man" tended to be negative. Critical reviews by Holmes (1899, 1901) and Sinclair (1908a, 1908b) exposed the problems of using testimony and the like as scientific evidence; they offered no support for the idea of Tertiary archaeology. Nonetheless, Whitney's contentions and the reactions to them were important milestones. As Warren (1973) has observed, they mark the emergence of California archaeology.

Apart from the "Tertiary Man" studies, Sierran archaeology progressed slowly in the century after 1848. Although old village sites were recorded in several places, such as Yosemite National Park (Beatty 1933; R. Johnson 1937; Merriam 1917; Presnall 1930b), much of the Sierra Nevada remained *terra incognita*. Systematic field surveys were rare, and most published accounts from the period simply described artifacts and sites that fortuitously had come to the attention of the authors. Typical are Avery's (1873) observation of high-altitude lithic scatters north of Lake Tahoe, Powers' (1877) mention of a burial site on the Stanislaus

River, and early reports of rock art in Yosemite by Harden (1908) and Presnall (1930a). Holmes' (1902) monograph is notable for its comments on archaeological sites and specimens in diverse locations between Sonora and Nevada City.

Exceptional among the early twentieth-century works was Julian Steward's (1929) *Petroglyphs of California and Adjoining States.* Steward described, compared, and interpreted data from 121 California rock-art sites, about half being in the Sierra Nevada. Two rock-art style areas were identified in the Sierra: Area A, east of the crest, featuring geometric (curvilinear and rectilinear) petroglyph motifs, and Area B, in the southern Sierra foothills, characterized by painted (often polychrome) representations of humans and other animals. Steward's research was perhaps the most systematic work in Sierran archaeology before about 1950.

Further progress was made between 1947 and the early 1950s when Smithsonian Institution, River Basin Surveys archaeologists examined proposed reservoir areas throughout the Far West, including the Sierra Nevada. Preliminary field surveys were done in the areas of Folsom, Sly Park, New Melones, Mariposa, Pine Flat, Isabella, and Success reservoirs (Drucker 1947, 1948c,d,f,g; Fenenga 1947b, 1948a; Fredrickson 1949; Osborne 1948). In the main these were cursory studies with reports only two or three pages long, but they were of value because they brought archaeologists to many Sierran localities for the first time. Most of the River Basin fieldworkers—F. Fenenga, P. Drucker, A. Mohr, D. Fredrickson, F. Riddell, and C. Smith—also were affiliated with the University of California, Berkeley (UCB), where a new Archaeological Survey was being established in 1948 (Heizer 1948b). Knowledge and field experience gained during the River Basin surveys were important stimuli for later archaeological research by the University in the Sierra Nevada.

## The Northern Sierra

### Lake Tahoe Vicinity

In 1952 UCB archaeologists T. Bolt, A. B. Elsasser, and R. F. Heizer tested and made surface collections at 26 sites east of the Sierran crest near Lake Tahoe. The high elevation (≈1675 m), above snowline, indicated that these sites probably had functioned as warm-season camps only. Interpreting available data, Heizer and Elsasser (1953) defined two archaeological cultures separated in time and space. The more recent of these was the Kings Beach Complex, named after a site on the north shore of Lake Tahoe and distinguished by flaked obsidian and silicate implements, small projectile points, the bow and arrow, occasional scrapers, bedrock mortars, and a subsistence emphasis on fishing, piñon nut harvesting, seed gathering, and some hunting. This complex was ascribed to the ethnographic Washo and their ancestors after circa A.D. 1000 (Heizer and Elsasser 1953).

The earlier Martis Complex, first identified at site Pla-5 in Martis Valley, was marked by intensive use of basalt rather than obsidian for flaked-stone tools (Figure 7.5), large roughly shaped projectile points, "boatstones" (atlatl weights) and inferred use of the atlatl and dart, the mano and millingstone for seed grinding, bowl mortar and cylindrical pestle, abundant flake scrapers of basalt, and an economic focus on hunting and gathering. Comparison of Martis artifacts with dated assemblages in nearby areas suggested an age of 4000 to 2000 years B.P. for the compex (Heizer and Elsasser 1953).

Subsequent archaeological work in the Lake Tahoe vicinity included excavations in Martis Valley (Arnold 1957), at Chilcoot Rockshelter in Plumas County (Payen and Boloyan 1961), at Loyalton Rockshelter in Sierra County (Wilson 1963), and at two Martis sites in California, Nev-15 and Sie-20, and one in Nevada, Do-12 (Elsasser 1960). At Prosser Creek Reservoir, north of Truckee in Nevada County, J. T. Davis (1958) found evidence at Nev-11 and Nev-67 of seasonal occupation by Martis groups engaged in quarrying basalt, hunting pronghorn and smaller game, and perhaps taking cutthroat trout. A third site tested by Davis, Alp-22 in the Carson River–Watasheamu Reservoir area, represented seasonal fishing and harvesting of piñon nuts and grass seeds by Kings Beach peoples.

Also of interest are Payen and Olsen's 1967 excavations at two sites in the Stampede Reservoir area on the Little Truckee River, southeastern Sierra County (Figure 7.2). While Sie-44 was found to be a seasonal base camp used by Martis hunter–gatherers, Sie-28 was a large (23 m in diameter), circular stone enclosure that may have served as an impound for hunting pronghorn (Payen and Olsen 1969). Other investigations into the culture history of the Lake Tahoe vicinity have been reported by Elston (1970, 1972), Elston and Davis (1972), and Elston et al. (1976).

The archaeological sequence of the Lake Tahoe vicinity was revised and expanded considerably as a result of work by W. A. Davis and R. Elston, who excavated four sites just east of Lake Tahoe in order to explore relationships between Martis and Kings Beach and to test further the proposition that the latter corresponds to the ancestral Washo. Stratified deposits and radiocarbon dates indicated cultural manifestations both earlier than Martis and transitional between Martis and Kings Beach (Elston 1971). Based upon 10 $^{14}$C dates from the Jacks Valley (Do-37) and Spooner Lake Summit (Do-38) sites in Douglas County, Nevada, Davis (1967) proposed a chronology spanning about 7000 years.

Spooner I (5150–2970 B.C.) relates to a "possible buried archaeological

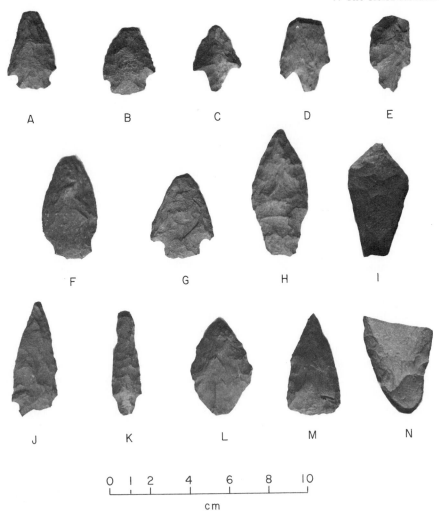

**Figure 7.5** Martis Phase bifaces of flaked basalt from Nev-15, North San Juan vicinity, Nevada County. All are projectile points except K, a possible drill, and N, a biface fragment unidentified as to type. A, B, G, Martis Corner-notched; C, E?, Elko Contracting Stem; D, Sierra Contracting Stem; F, H, Martis Stemmed Leaf; I, reworked Stemmed Leaf, or Lake Mojave?; J, Elko Eared; L, Martis Contracting Stem; and M, Martis Leaf-shaped. Type designations after Elston *et al.* (1977: 56–69), Hester and Heizer (1978), and Moratto (1972b). (Photograph by A. B. Elsasser; courtesy of the R. H. Lowie Museum of Anthropology, University of California, Berkeley.)

component which perhaps marks initial occupation of the high Sierra at the beginning of the Altithermal climatic period" (W. Davis 1967:282). Spooner II (1100 B.C.–A.D. 60) is characterized by millingstones, bifacial manos, unshaped pestles, and projectile points of Elko, Rose Spring, and

Martis types. This assemblage persists into Spooner III (A.D. 60–1385), but with the addition of cobble manos, several kinds of drills, and East-gate, Cottonwood, and Desert Side-notched points. Jacks Lake, *Spooner IV* (A.D. 1385 to historic times), is defined by materials from a winter village of the protohistoric Washo (W. Davis 1967; Elston 1971).

Recent surface collecting at seven sites and excavations at four others along the Tahoe Reach of the Truckee River (Figure 7.2) by Elston and others produced 3000 artifacts and enough new chronological data to permit a reassessment of the Lake Tahoe cultural sequence. Elston *et al.* (1977) defined seven phases that together span most of the Holocene epoch (Table 7.1). Martis and Kings Beach account for five phases, where-as Spooner is identified with a limited pre-Martis (Altithermal) occupa-tion. Significant differences between Spooner and Martis, however, re-main to be demonstrated, and it may be that the former is but an early, local expression of the latter (Elston *et al.* 1977:20). Earlier than Spooner is the Tahoe Reach Phase, evidenced by Parman points (Layton 1979) at Pla-23 and nondiagnostic artifacts in a component [14]C-dated to 8130 ± 130 B.P. (Tx-2548) at Pla-164 (Elston *et al.* 1977).

Several of these upper Truckee River phases are also represented at Nev-199 near Truckee, investigated in 1977 by archaeologists from Cal-ifornia State University, Sacramento. Testing revealed cultural remains assignable mostly to the Martis phases, but a veneer of Kings Beach materials was also noted and a basal component may relate to the Spoon-er Phase. Radiocarbon dates of <200 B.P. (GX-5226) and 6065 ± 175 B.P. (GX-5225) bracket the occupation of Nev-199 (Keesling and Johnson 1978:35). The Truckee River sites thus provide one of the longest cultural records known in the Sierra Nevada and one of the most valuable because of its correlation of Holocene environmental and cultural changes (Table 7.1).

## The West Slope

Dam building has led to "salvage archaelogy" in many parts of the Sierra. A case in point would be the investigations by Jewell (1964), Olsen and Riddell (1963), and Ritter (1968) at Lake Oroville along the Feather River in the foothills of Butte County (Figure 9.5). Summarizing the find-ings, Ritter (1970a) traced the development of the Mesilla, Bidwell, Sweetwater, Oroville, and Historic complexes through a period of approx-imately 3000 years (Figure 7.6). Certain artifacts, such as choppers, scrapers, hammerstones, and Spire-lopped *Olivella* beads, seem not to have changed through time, but others did vary, and those distinguish the complexes.

The Mesilla Complex known from sites But-84, -98, and -157, may

**TABLE 7.1**

**Cultural Phases of the Tahoe Reach of the Truckee River**[a]

| Phase | Time markers | Deposits | Age | Climate |
|---|---|---|---|---|
| Washo–Late Kings Beach | Desert Side-notched and Cottonwood series points, chert cores, utilized flakes, and other small chert tools | Surface and upper portion of sandy pebbly loam | Historic Contact– A.D. 1200 | Neoglacial; wet and cool, but with little summer precipitation |
| Early Kings Beach | Eastgate and Rose Spring series points, chert cores, utilized flakes, and other small chert tools | Surface and upper portion of sandy pebbly loam | A.D. 1200–500 | Nonglacial; dry, trees growing in former bogs; Tahoe may often not overflow |
| Late Martis | Corner-notched and eared points of the Martis and Elko series? Large side-notched points? Large basalt bifaces and other basalt tools | Within the pebbly sandy loam | A.D. 500–500 B.C.? | Neoglacial; wet but not necessarily cooler, increased summer precipitation |
| Middle Martis | Steamboat points, other types in Elko–Martis series? Large basalt bifaces and other basalt tools | Within the pebbly sandy loam and sandy cobbly loam | 500 B.C.?–1500 B.C. | Possible warm, dry interval centered on 1500 B.C. |
| Early Martis | Contracting stem points of the Elko–Martis series? Large basalt bifaces and other tools. Light-colored basalt artifacts? | Lower portions of pebbly sandy loam; on contact with orange sand at Pla-164 | 1500–2000 B.C. | Beginning of Medithermal; Neoglacial, wet but not necessarily cooler, increased summer precipitation; Tahoe begins to overflow |
| Spooner | Points in the Pinto and Humboldt series, light-colored basalt artifacts | Orange sand at Pla-164 | 2000–5000 B.C. | Altithermal; generally hot and dry; Tahoe does not overflow for long periods of time |
| Tahoe Reach | Parman points | Mottled silt at Pla-164 | 6000 B.C. | Anathermal; warming trend, climate similar to later Neoglacial intervals |

[a]After Elston et al. 1977:171.

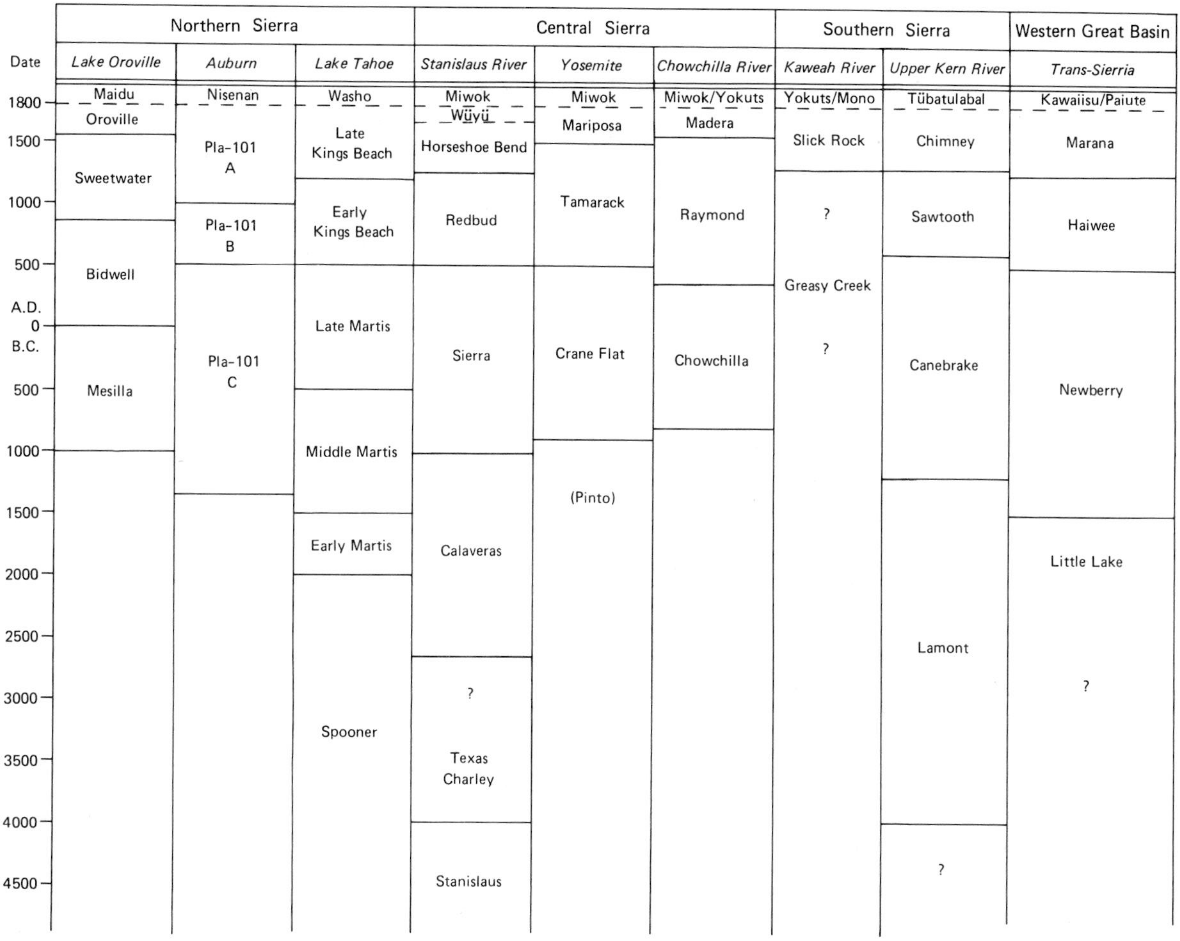

| Date | Northern Sierra | | | Central Sierra | | | Southern Sierra | | Western Great Basin |
|---|---|---|---|---|---|---|---|---|---|
| | Lake Oroville | Auburn | Lake Tahoe | Stanislaus River | Yosemite | Chowchilla River | Kaweah River | Upper Kern River | Trans-Sierra |
| 1800 | Maidu / Oroville | Nisenan | Washo | Miwok / Wüyü | Miwok / Mariposa | Miwok/Yokuts / Madera | Yokuts/Mono | Tübatulabal | Kawaiisu/Paiute |
| 1500 | Sweetwater | Pla-101 A | Late Kings Beach | Horseshoe Bend | Tamarack | Raymond | Slick Rock | Chimney | Marana |
| 1000 | | Pla-101 B | Early Kings Beach | Redbud | | | ? | Sawtooth | Haiwee |
| 500 | Bidwell | | | | | | Greasy Creek | | |
| A.D. 0 | | | Late Martis | Sierra | Crane Flat | Chowchilla | ? | Canebrake | Newberry |
| B.C. 500 | Mesilla | Pla-101 C | | | | | | | |
| 1000 | | | Middle Martis | | (Pinto) | | | | |
| 1500 | | | Early Martis | Calaveras | | | | | Little Lake |
| 2000 | | | | | | | | | |
| 2500 | | | | | | | | Lamont | |
| 3000 | | | Spooner | ? | | | | | ? |
| 3500 | | | | Texas Charley | | | | | |
| 4000 | | | | | | | | | |
| 4500 | | | | Stanislaus | | | | ? | |

**Figure 7.6** Concordance of archaeological phases in the Sierra Nevada.

reflect sporadic (seasonal?) occupation of the foothills between circa 1000 B.C. and A.D. 1 by people who hunted with the atlatl and dart and processed foods in bowl mortars and on millingstones. *Haliotis* and *Olivella* beads, along with charmstones, bone pins, and spatulae, show contacts with Sacramento Valley cultures, whereas Martis influence seems indicated by heavy basalt, slate, and chert projectile points. A $^{14}C$ date of 870 ± 100 B.C. from But-157 is assignable to the Mesilla Complex (Olsen and Riddell 1963; Ritter 1970a).

Between A.D. 1 and 800 Bidwell Complex people lived in relatively permanent villages from which smaller task groups moved out to hunt deer and smaller game, fish with the aid of nets (known from grooved and notched sinker stones), process hard seeds and acorns on millingstones and in wooden mortars (inferred), and collect freshwater mussels. The use of large slate and basalt projectile points continued, and steatite vessels for cooking were added to the inventory. At principal settlements, dead were buried in flexed, dorsal or lateral positions. Radiocarbon dates of A.D. 65 ± 100 (I-3169) and A.D. 730 ± 100 (I-3165) apply to the Bidwell component at But-157 (Ritter 1970a).

The Sweetwater Complex, A.D. 800–1500, was identified at But-90 and -131 by certain *Olivella* bead and *Haliotis* ornament forms, along with an industry of steatite cups, platters, bowls, and tubular smoking pipes. Small, lightweight projectile points of the Eastgate, Rose Spring, and Gunther Barbed types show that the bow and arrow were in use by A.D. 800. Around A.D. 1000, mortuary preferences evolved from flexed to extended or semiextended interments (Olsen and Riddell 1963; Ritter 1970a).

The Oroville Complex represents the protohistoric Maidu from A.D. 1500 until the epidemic of 1833 (Cook 1955b). Oroville components at But-131 and -182, respectively, have yielded ${}^{14}$C dates of A.D. 1580 ± 150 (I-1221) and 1615 ± 85 (I-3168). Bedrock mortars, probably initially used before Oroville times, were central to acorn processing; other seed-grinding implements continued unchanged. Oroville hallmarks are incised bird bone tubes, gorge hooks, gaming bones, and clamshell disk beads. Several kinds of structures, including large circular dance houses, were erected. Burials lay tightly flexed on their sides, occasionally under stone cairns; cremation was not in evidence. The Lake Oroville sequence ends with the Historic Complex. Witness to nineteenth-century abandonment of traditional settlements, this complex provides a sparse material record of Maidu acculturation and attrition (Olsen and Riddell 1963; Ritter 1970a).

Possibly related to the Bidwell Complex was the Rainbow Point site (Plu-S-94) at Bucks Lake (Figure 9.5), 40 km northeast of Lake Oroville, where lakeshore erosion in the 1960s exposed artifacts and features. Five stone circles, each about 3 m in diameter, have been interpreted as being places where summer shelters were built 2000 to 1500 years ago by families who camped near the edge of Bucks Meadow and harvested Indian potato, brodiaea, camas, tules, berries, and sugar pine nuts (Riddell 1969a; Riddell and Pritchard 1970).

The archaeology of other investigated localities in the northern Sierra is largely comparable to that of Lake Oroville. At New Bullards Bar Reservoir on the North Yuba River (Figure 7.2), about 30 km southeast of Lake Oroville, Humphreys (1969) defined three cultural phases, Bullards Bar I–III, on the basis of excavations at three sites. In content, particularly with regard to a transition from earlier use of large projectile points of basalt to a later inventory of small silicate points, the Bullards Bar sequence closely resembles the Mesilla to Sweetwater progression at Lake

Oroville as well as the Martis to Kings Beach phases at Lake Tahoe. Fifteen kilometers upstream from Bullards Bar, at Goodyears Bar, Elston (1974a, 1974b) excavated a seasonal "big game hunting base camp" site with heavy stemmed and side-notched points like those of Bullards Bar I and II. Southwest of Bullards Bar, J. Johnson and Theodoratus (1978) of California State University, Sacramento, documented more than 250 aboriginal sites—chiefly bedrock milling sites (219) and middens with numerous housepits—in the Marysville Lake project area along the Yuba River and Dry Creek. Future investigations at Marysville may shed light on Nisenan origins as well as the nature of prehistoric relationships among foothill peoples and their neighbors in the Valley and high Sierra.

Important archaeological work also has been done in the American River drainage. In 1964 F. Rackerby of San Francisco State University recorded nearly 50 sites in the areas of Auburn and French Meadow reservoirs along the Middle Fork of the American (Figure 7.2) at elevations of between 180 and 1525 m. Testing of the Craig site near Auburn showed that Martis traits had spread across the western slope of the Sierra to foothills as low as 245 m (Rackerby 1965b). Additional surveys on the Middle Fork of the American River in the Auburn and Sugar Pine Reservoir areas led to the discovery of more than 100 sites, mostly bedrock milling stations along with lithic scatters, rockshelters, quarry sites, and, at Auburn, middens (Childress and Ritter 1967; Ritter [ed.] 1970).

Research at Auburn Reservoir has included investigation of a chert quarry (Crew 1970) and excavation of five sites (Ritter [ed.] 1970). The stratified Spring Garden Ravine site (Pla-101), 7.2 km west of Foresthill at an elevation of 820 m, contained a record of occupation spanning 3 millennia. The lower (C) stratum yielded a Martis-like assemblage of large projectile points of basalt and slate, atlatl weights, bowl mortars, and many core tools and millingstones [14]C-dated at 1400 ± 110 B.C. (GaK-2246). The upper (A) stratum contained arrow points and numerous retouched flakes of silicates, hopper mortars (as well as bedrock mortars), a few core tools, and millingstones thought to represent the ancestral Nisenan and probably less than 1000 years old. Stratigraphically and culturally intermediate, the B stratum has been dated at A.D. 1039 ± 80 (GaK-2244) and A.D. 976 ± 90 (GaK-2245) (Ritter 1970a,b).

To reconstruct environmental conditions that may have affected prehistoric cultures in the Spring Garden Ravine vicinity, Matson (1972) analyzed fossil pollen from Pla-101. The pollen data indicate basic stability of vegetation patterns for some 3000 years, followed by a change within the past 500 years from oak grassland (savanna) with patches of chaparral to pine–oak woodland. This shift has been attributed to the cessation of selective burning by the Indians in historic times (Matson 1972), although climatic changes favoring the spread of pine also might have been a factor.

The Auburn and Oroville assemblages reflect prehistoric influences not only from the higher Sierra and Great Basin, but also from the Sacramento Valley. The latter is seen in the foothill occurrence of shell beads, certain bone artifacts, fishing tackle, architecture, and mortuary patterns typical of the Valley. Indeed, some Sierran assemblages appear to have come exclusively from the Valley and may relate to incursions of Valley people into the mountains. This is illustrated by materials found in limestone caves of the northern and central Sierra.

One such cavern—long ago destroyed by quarrying—was Hawver Cave, located at an elevation of 550 m, south of the Middle Fork of the American River near Cool, El Dorado County (Figure 7.2). Early in the twentieth century this vertical cave in fissured limestone was known to paleontologists as a storehouse of Pleistocene fossils (Furlong 1907; Stock 1918). Between 1908 and 1910 J. C. Hawver exhumed a quantity of human bones at the lower end of the main shaft, about 6 m below the entrance, from a loose mass of earth and rock. Some of the bones were mineralized and cemented into a dripstone breccia. Their position directly below the aperture suggests that they had been thrown into the mouth of the cave—an interpretation supported by the broken and disarticulated nature of the bones; no complete skeleton was found even though the remains of perhaps 30 or 40 individuals were present (Wallace and Lathrap 1952).

Artifacts from Hawver Cave, first reported by E. Hamilton (1910), consist of split and pointed deer cannon bones (awls?), stone pestles, a globular flat-bottomed mortar, and large projectile points (Wallace and Lathrap 1952). Although made of local chert, basalt, and slate, these points closely match types from Windmiller components in the Central Valley (see Figure 5.12). It is suggested that people of Windmiller affiliation may have used Hawver Cave as a natural tomb more than 2500 years ago. Discoveries at ossuary caves in the central Sierra (discussed below) support this proposition (Figure 7.7).

## Summary

Major advances have been made since 1950 toward understanding the prehistory of the northern Sierra Nevada. Early to mid-Holocene occupation of the high country by Great Basin people is evidenced by the Tahoe Reach (ca. 6000 B.C.) and Spooner (ca. 5000–2000 B.C.) phases. Martis, initially viewed as a high-altitude, seasonal hunting–gathering complex in the Lake Tahoe vicinity, is now recognized as a developmental series of phases, possibly of Great Basin origin but with a distribution from the western Great Basin to the Sacramento Valley. In spatial range Martis coincides generally with the combined ethnographic areas of Washo and

Maiduan groups. Martis is probably not ancestral to Washo (Kings Beach), but may represent Maiduan prehistory as indicated by the archaeological records at Oroville, Bullards Bar, and Auburn reservoirs (Elsasser 1978b; Ritter 1970a,b; Ritter [ed.] 1970; Ritter and Matson 1972). In this regard, J. Johnson has observed that "Martis like artifacts occur in the Central Sacramento Valley at the Patrick Site [But-1]; Finch Site [But-12]; and the Llano Seco Site. . . . The feeling expressed by Johnson is that Martis materials are present in the central valley on a much wider perspective than previously thought" (Keesling and Johnson 1978:12).

The Kings Beach Phase (ca. A.D. 500–1870) typically is recognized by sparse artifact scatters overlying deeper Martis components (Elston *et al.* 1977). The relatively higher artifact density and greater depth of Martis cultural deposits suggest that Martis population densities were higher than those of Kings Beach, and may indicate that permanent base camps and winter villages were used regularly in the Tahoe locality by Martis, but not Kings Beach, peoples. It is possible that the dry climatic episode between circa A.D. 500 and 1200 (Table 7.1) lowered the regional carrying capacity and dependability of certain key resources used by the Kings Beach populations (Elston *et al.* 1976).

The western slope of the northern Sierra was settled long ago by groups who, by 1000 B.C., exhibited both Martis and Central Valley traits. Whether initial populations came from the east or west, or both, is unknown. It is clear, however, that through time their cultures were increasingly molded into the California pattern. By A.D. 1500, central California architecture, ceremonies, economic patterns, tools, ornaments, and mortuary practices were to be found throughout the Sierran foothills.

Permanent villages were established in the northwestern Sierra Nevada by A.D. 1 or earlier, as seen in the Bidwell and related phases. Increasing sedentism accompanied population growth and settlement differentiation, that is, the emergence of settlement systems composed of principal and secondary villages, seasonal camps, and special activity stations. By A.D. 1500 principal villages functioned as social, political, and ceremonial centers for extended communities, and it was at the larger centers that dance houses (see Figures 5.18 and 7.3) were constructed. Small hunting, gathering, and trading camps in the mountains were visited intermittently or seasonally.

Key technologic shifts in northern Sierran prehistory were the replacement of the atlatl by the bow and arrow around A.D. 600–800 and the intensive use of mortars and pestles, including bedrock milling features, after A.D. 1400–1600. The latter presumably reflects a growing reliance on acorns as a staple food. One sees also a marked decline in the use of basalt and slate and a concomitant increase in obsidian as a raw material for chipped-stone artifacts. Obsidian was a superior material for many kinds of tools, but it was obtained only from non-Sierran sources. Thus, the popularity of obsidian in later prehistory is evidence of expanding trade relationships between the northern Sierra and adjacent regions (Jackson 1974a; Jackson and Schulz 1975). Quantities of marine shell artifacts in late components further show the range of trade contacts and the degree of Sierran integration into the central California economic system.

# The Central Sierra

## Mortuary Caves

Central Sierran archaeological caves have held great interest since the time of the Gold Rush. These include both rockshelters (exogene caves) and endogene caverns (which extend deeper into the earth than the entrance width). Endogene caverns occur at elevations of 250–650 m in limestone formations of the foothill cave belt (Figure 7.2). Rockshelters are distributed more widely, from the edge of the Central Valley to altitudes above 3500 m. Whereas rockshelters functioned as dwelling, milling, storage, and rock-art sites, endogene caves served mainly as burial chambers. Human bones, often in great numbers, have been found in limestone solution chambers such as Moaning Cave, Mercers Caverns, Winslow Cave, and Pinnacle Point Cave in Calaveras and Tuolumne counties (Heizer 1952b; Moratto 1976c; Payen and Johnson 1965). A few endogene caves also were used as quarries for calcite, which, after circa 2000 B.C., was fashioned into charmstones, ornaments, and pipes (Heizer and Treganza 1944; Payen 1964).

One of the best-known mortuary caverns is Moaning Cave (Cal-13), formerly called Solomon's Hole or Cave of the Sepulchre. This is a complex vertical solution cavity deeper than 140 m in a band of permeable limestone west of the Stanislaus River (Figure 7.2) near Vallecito in Calaveras County (Orr 1952a; Short 1970). The cave was first explored in 1851 by J. B. Trask, who noted human bones. Two years later, on October 31, 1853, the *Daily Alta California* carried an incredible account of explorers who, "at the depth of about 300 feet, . . . came upon a collection of over 300 human bodies perfectly petrified; that the hall contained an immense number of stalactytes [sic], some of which were incorporated with the bodies."

Nearly a century later, R. F. Heizer and A. E. Treganza of UCB investigated Moaning Cave and found a jumble of dissociated human bones in red clay below the mouth of the cave (Figure 7.8). Long bones and cranial parts of nine adults and two children were found along with hundreds of complete and fragmentary bones scattered about by earlier visitors. With the skeletons were *Haliotis* ornaments, *Olivella* beads, a cup-shaped pipe bowl, and an obsidian point (Wallace 1951a) of types that would date the ossuary deposits between circa 1000 B.C. and A.D. 500 (Figure 7.7).

Fossil deposits, including both human bones and those of the extinct Sierran ground sloth, occur at Mercers Caverns (Cal-11) in weathered limestone about 1.8 km north of Murphys (Figure 7.2). Mercers Caverns were visited by W. H. Holmes before 1900 and by J. C. Merriam and F. W. Putnam in 1901, and were excavated in 1902 by W. J. Sinclair. The position of the human bones indicated that bodies had been thrown into the upper chamber of the cave through the small entrance; no artifacts were reported.

Cave of Skulls and O'Neal Cave also have been investigated. Long ago, Whitney (1867) removed a number of crania from the Cave of Skulls (Cal-29), west of the Stanislaus River near Abbotts Ferry. Like the bones from Mercers and Moaning caves, these calcium carbonate-encrusted skulls reposed on the cave floor and had not been buried deliberately. Nearby, the limestone grotto of O'Neal Cave (Cal-6)—a vertical shaft more than 15 m deep—is described as "choked" with human and animal bones along with some unspecified artifacts and pieces of charcoal (Wallace 1951a).

One of the most important mortuary chambers is Winslow Cave (Cal-99), located about 2 km northwest of Murphys (Figure 7.2). A small pit dug by University of California archaeologists into sticky black clay 15 m below the cave entrance produced 1735 dissociated and mineralized human bones and fragments representing 12 adults, 3 children, and an infant. It is estimated that no fewer than 100 individuals had been dropped into Winslow Cave. Charcoal found on the deposit surface may be attributed to torches tossed from above by Indians, early gold seekers, or curious passersby. Testing yielded more than 4300 *Olivella* shell beads and 75 other artifacts, among them *Haliotis* shell ornaments, quartz crystals, a bone atlatl spur, a human-femur implement (atlatl?), fish-vertebra beads, and large projectile points (Gonsalves 1955). These items attest to the use of Winslow Cave chiefly during the millennium before circa A.D. 300.

Pinnacle Point Cave (Tuo-272) is a multichambered solution cavity at the base of a limestone pinnacle high above the Stanislaus River in Tuolumne County (Figure 7.2). Inside and below the cave opening was an archaeological deposit nearly 10 m deep consisting of angular limestone fragments, dark earth, human bones, and artifacts (McEachern 1968:56). Excavations in 1965 by archaeologists from California State University, Sacramento (CSUS), brought to light the skeletal remains of some 30 adults, adolescents, and children, along with more than 400 *Haliotis* shell ornaments and 10,500 *Olivella* shell beads; such bone artifacts as fish-

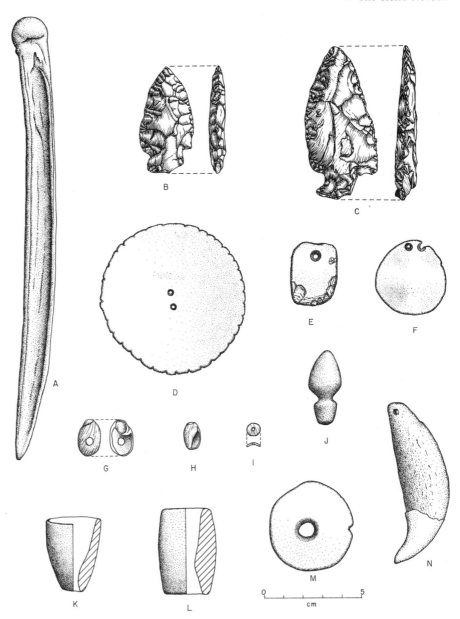

**Figure 7.7** Artifacts from mortuary caves in the central Sierra Nevada. A, bone dagger; B, C, projectile points of black chert; D–F, *Haliotis* shell ornaments; G, *Olivella* split-drilled bead; H, *Olivella* spire-ground bead; I, *Olivella* saucer bead; J, atlatl spur of bone; K, L, travertine pipes; M, steatite discoidal; N, perforated bear canine. Items A, D, and J–M are from Pinnacle Point Cave; B, C, and E–I are from Moaning Cave; N is from Winslow Cave. (After Gonsalves 1955; Payen 1964; Payen and Johnson 1965; and Columbia State Historic Park collections; drawn by Thad Van Bueren.)

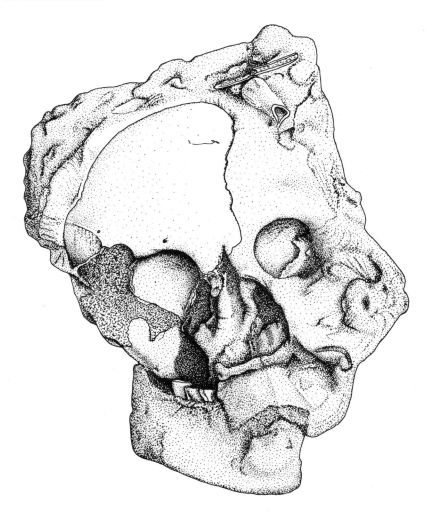

**Figure 7.8** Human bones embedded in speleothem (dripstone), from Moaning Cave, Calaveras County. Such fossils, evidently 1500–3000 years old, represent the use of central Sierran caves as mortuary chambers. (Drawn by Thad Van Bueren.)

vertebra beads, an atlatl spur, an incised rectangle, a bird-bone whistle, and perforated limb bones of the Pacific freshwater turtle; large projectile points of chert and obsidian; and limestone pipes, steatite beads, stone disks, and quartz crystals (Beck 1970b; Payen 1965; Payen and Johnson 1965) (Figure 7.7). Some perishable items also were recovered from the cave, including 80 fragments of cordage, 3 basketry pieces, and a problematical wooden object (McEachern and Grady 1977:25).

One of the more interesting questions about these ossuary caves relates to mortuary customs: Were bodies placed or thrown into the caves, or were loose bones deposited in the chambers? Although bodies may have been carried rather than thrown into the Cave of Skulls and Cave of Catacombs (Danehy 1951), clues elsewhere point to less delicate means of disposal. At Mercers and Moaning caverns, for example, broken bones were cemented in dripstone breccia; and Winslow Cave's black clay was crammed with dissociated skeletal parts. This suggests that bones and perhaps some bodies, along with artifacts, were cast into the void.

The case for secondary burial, at least in certain caves, is supported by Payen and Johnson's (1965) discovery of cremated bone, as well as un-burned but fragmented bone, throughout the matrix at Pinnacle Point Cave; only two instances of articulation were observed. Human remains apparently had been dropped into the cave and then covered by rocks thrown into the shaft. Payen (1965) opined that the fragmentary and scattered skeletal material may have resulted from secondary bundle burials being dropped into the cave. In any event, the dissociated and burned bone, charcoal, burned artifacts, and clast piles would seem to refute the notion that accidental death by falling was how the ossuaries came to be (cf. Orr 1952a:16).

The cavern burials evidently are of late Holocene age, despite a visitors' leaflet proclaiming that "more than 13,000 years ago, the bodies of prehistoric men fell or were thrown into the blackness of this huge cavern" (Anonymous 1981b:3). Other age estimates range from more than 12,000 years, based upon assumed dripstone accumulation rates (Orr 1952a), to historic times (Sinclair 1908a,b). C. H. Merriam (1909, 1910) noted that the Miwok Indians of the Sierran limestone belt normally cremated their dead and believed that a cannibal rock giant named *Che'-ha-lum'che* lived in the caves and caught people to eat. Merriam saw this belief as confirmation that the caves had been used in pre-Miwok times, several thousand years ago.

Although the mortuary cave specimens have not been dated directly, artifacts from Moaning, Winslow, and Pinnacle Point caves duplicate specimens from radiocarbon-dated Central Valley sites. Analysis and cross-dating of beads, pipes, and projectile points (Figure 7.7) from the caves suggest that the natural tombs were used mainly between circa 1000 B.C. and A.D. 500, with occasional burials in certain caves more recently (McEachern and Grady 1977; Payen 1964; Payen and Johnson 1965; Pritchard n.d.). The data suggest further that at least some of the cave disposals were left by people of Windmiller cultural affiliation (see Chapter 5). The practice of cave burial largely ceased about 1700–1300 years ago, possibly because Windmiller access to the caves and foothill resources was disrupted by environmental changes and settlement of the mountains by other populations (see Chapter 11).

## Yosemite National Park

Numerous surveys and testing projects, as well as some major excavations, have been completed in the south-central Sierra Nevada. Some of the more important studies have been done in Yosemite National Park (Figure 7.2), where there was early recognition of a cultural sequence that has become a milepost in Sierran archaeology. Since 1930 many archaeological surveys of variable scope and intensity have been conducted in Yosemite. Following several avocational surveys, UCB archaeologists documented 401 sites in the course of "intuitive" surveys in Yosemite during the summers of 1952, 1953, and 1954 (Bennyhoff 1953b, 1956; Grosscup 1954). The recorded sites ranged in altitude from 485 to 3250 m, with 83% of the village-size habitation sites (identified by large middens and numerous bedrock mortars) being in the Transition zone below about 2000 m (Bennyhoff 1953a, 1956).

During the 1970s, systematic inventory work by teams from California State College, Stanislaus (CSCS) brought to more than 560 the total of recorded sites in Yosemite (Napton 1974a,b; Napton et al. 1974b,c; Napton and Greathouse 1976). To date, an estimated 5% of the Park—mostly in areas of heavy use—has been surveyed by professional archaeologists (Napton 1978). This work has led to the recording of many types of sites, among them middens, lithic scatters, rockshelters, bedrock milling stations, cemeteries, pictographs, and stone alignments; nearly all of these types are correlated in their distribution with particular sets of environmental variables (Moratto 1981a).

Scientific excavations in Yosemite have consisted of minimal testing at 13 sites, "salvage" excavations at 4 sites, and the removal of several isolated interments. Based upon flaked- and ground-stone artifacts recovered from test excavations at four sites and from widespread surface collecting, Bennyhoff (1956) defined a local cultural sequence of three complexes: Crane Flat, Tamarack, and Mariposa, from oldest to youngest. The Crane Flat Complex is marked by heavy projectile points, inferred use of the atlatl and dart, and the mano–millingstone for grinding seeds, whereas the Mariposa Complex is distinguished by lightweight projectile points, inferred use of the bow and arrow, bedrock mortars (Figure 7.9) and cobble pestles (presumably used chiefly to process acorns), steatite vessels, and clamshell disk beads. Characterizing the intermediate Tamarack Complex are projectile points weighing between 1 and 3 g, inferred use of the bow and arrow, and use of the bedrock mortar and cobble pestle (Bennyhoff 1956).

Representing the protohistoric Sierra Miwok, the Mariposa Complex is dated between circa A.D. 1200 and 1800 on the basis of resemblances between Mariposa projectile-point types and those from dated contexts in

**Figure 7.9** Bedrock mortars on large outcrop of limestone at *Tco'se* (Ama-14), Indian Grinding Rocks State Park, Amador County. Scattered on this outcrop are 1185 bedrock mortars and 363 petroglyph designs. (Photograph by the author.)

the Central Valley and Great Basin (Bennyhoff 1956:53–54). The Tamarack Complex (A.D. 500–1200?) is defined only tentatively and not linked clearly to the predecessors of any historic group. The Crane Flat Complex (? B.C.–A.D. 500?) shares manos, slab millingstones, and several types of large projectile points with the Martis Phase farther north, but the emphasis on obsidian in Yosemite (most likely a function of proximity to obsidian sources) contrasts with the relatively greater use of basalt and other nonsilicate lithics in the northern Sierra. In sum, although the status of the Tamarack Complex was unclear in 1956, Bennyhoff showed that Yosemite had been occupied for 2000 years or more; that significant cultural changes, and perhaps population replacement, had occurred during this interval; and that Yosemite's prehistoric cultures had been influenced by those of the Great Basin, Central Valley, and other parts of the Sierra Nevada (Bennyhoff 1956).

Excavations in Yosemite at El Portal (Mrp-181), Crane Flat (Mrp-105), and Hodgdon Ranch (Tuo-236) (Figure 7.2) during the early 1960s led R. J. Fitzwater to replace Bennyhoff's sequence with a two-phase chronology, lacking Tamarack. Fitzwater (1962) subsumed Tamarack under the Mariposa Phase because to him they seemed virtually identical except for the weight of projectile points. The Crane Flat Phase, little changed in content from Bennyhoff's complex of the same name, was first evidenced in the Yosemite locality about A.D. 1. It was supplanted circa A.D. 1000 by the Mariposa Phase, which in turn persisted until the mid-nineteenth century. The earlier part of Fitzwater's chronology is supported by three ¹⁴C dates from Crane Flat: A.D. 1000 ± 70 (UCLA-276), A.D. 370 ± 80 (UCLA-277), and 90 ± 100 B.C. (UCLA-278) (Fitzwater 1962, 1968a,b).

Further work in Yosemite has included salvage excavations in 1966 at Ahwahnee (Mrp-56) to make way for a new visitors' center (Rasson 1966); surface collecting and testing in 1980 at five sites in the Wawona Valley (Whittaker 1981); and minimal testing in 1981 of several sites in areas of proposed development at El Portal (Baumler and Carpenter 1982). The Ahwahnee and Wawona sites were chiefly Mariposa Phase settlements, but they also yielded large projectile points and other traces of Crane Flat occupation. The El Portal sample was too small to permit reliable inferences about prehistory.

The development of an archaeological chronology for Yosemite in the 1950s and early 1960s was tenuous and based upon limited data. Nonetheless, in light of strong parallels between the Yosemite sequence and that of the nearby Chowchilla River area, where intensive excavations and 35 radiocarbon dates have been reported (T. King 1976; Moratto 1972b), Bennyhoff's original sequence would appear to be valid.

### North-Central Sierra Nevada

Dam and reservoir projects in the central Sierra have destroyed hundreds of cultural properties, but they have also led to archaeological investigations along every river in the area. For example, during 1970–1971 archaeologists from San Francisco State University (SFSU) and Merced Junior College (MJC) conducted a field survey and salvage excavations in the New Don Pedro Reservoir basin (elevation, 85–270 m) along the Tuolumne River (Figure 7.2). Remnants of 41 aboriginal sites were recorded, and 7 of these were sampled (Moratto, 1971f).

Excavations at the stratified Roger Creek site (Tuo-300) revealed two components. The lower levels yielded millingstones and manos, cobble mortars, atlatl weights, quartz crystals, and large quantities of percussion-flaked bifaces, preforms, and debitage. Tuo-300 appears to have been both a habitation site and a workshop for processing metachert, which outcrops nearby. Other remains in the lower midden included bone awls and a fish spear tip, *Haliotis* and *Olivella* beads, and large projectile points. A saucer-shaped earthen floor (≈9 m in diameter) represents a house constructed circa A.D. 915. Twelve fragmentary skeletons at and below the floor level indicate a mortuary pattern of flexed burial, without surviving artifacts, under stone cairns. On typologic grounds, this component is dated between circa A.D. 300 and 1500. Radiocarbon age determinations include A.D. 1200 ± 95 (I-5372), A.D. 915 ± 90 (I-5602), and A.D. 905 ± 90 (I-5601) (Moratto 1971d).

The late prehistoric culture (ca. A.D. 1500–1800) at New Don Pedro Reservoir is manifested in the upper levels of Tuo-300 and at Tuo-279 by steatite disk beads and cooking vessels, bedrock mortars with cobble pestles, small flake tools and arrow points of chert and obsidian, and circular dwellings averaging about 4 m in diameter. At Tuo-279 this component is $^{14}$C-dated at A.D. 1655 ± 90 (I-5603) (Henn 1971; Moratto 1971f).

Two cultural phases thus are well documented at New Don Pedro Reservoir: an expression of the Mariposa Phase, thought to represent Miwok prehistory, and an earlier phase comparable to Crane Flat. Evidence of yet other phases has been reported from two sites: a few points and beads of early (pre-Crane Flat) types were found in 1970 at the Moccasin site (Tuo-314) after it had been bulldozed and vandalized (Slaymaker 1971); and at Tuo-910, excavated during the 1970s by C. Ostrander of MJC, projectile points reflect several phases of occupation over a span of perhaps 3 to 4 millennia (M. Arguelles, personal communication, 1981). Tuo-910 yielded Pinto, Elko, and Windmiller stemmed points, probably 2500 to 5000 years old, as well as points datable to various intervals between circa 500 B.C. and A.D. 1800.

About 20 km north of New Don Pedro Reservoir, archaeologists from CSUS, in 1977 surveyed a proposed route of Highway 108 near Sonora. Among the sites recorded (and later tested) was the Sanguinetti quarry (Tuo-767)—a metachert quarry, lithic workshop, and habitation site covering nearly 45,000 m² (Rondeau 1978). Three other chert quarry–workshop sites have been reported in the general vicinity of Sonora (Moratto 1981b; Moratto et al., 1983; Motz 1978). The predominance of nonobsidian lithics at these sites and at Tuo-300 (just discussed) reflects both the local availability of chert and the relatively high cost of obsidian from distant sources.

Northwest of Sonora, the foothill country along the Stanislaus River has been the focus of extensive archaeological work in connection with the New Melones Dam and Reservoir project (Figure 7.2). Between 1968 and 1981 the federal government funded 10 phases of survey and excavation work at New Melones. Within the project area of ≈12,000 hectares (≈30,000 acres), nearly 700 archaeological sites have been documented (Gage 1969; Greenwood 1976, 1977; Moratto 1976b,c; Oman 1982; Orlins 1977; Payen et al. 1969). Approximately 90 of these sites have been sampled, a few intensively (Fitting et al. n.d.; Gage 1970; P. Johnson 1973; Moratto 1976a–d; Moratto et al. 1983; Peak 1973).

During the 1981 field season at New Melones, Holocene environmental and cultural changes were investigated at two deeply stratified sites: Redbud, Cal-S-347 (O'Brien 1983), and Texas Charley Gulch, Cal-S-286 (Moratto and Arguelles 1983). Multiple components were identified at Cal-S-286, the lower two being within a compacted yellow clay deposit of variable depth. The upper levels of this clay (Stratum D) yielded a $^{14}$C date of 5120 ± 170 B.P. (UCR-1439A). The lower levels (Stratum E)—as yet not dated directly but thought to be of early to middle Holocene age—contained cores, distinctive scrapers, and large percussion-flaked bifaces exhibiting remarkable craftsmanship (Singleton 1983). Above the clay strata at Cal-S-286 were midden deposits, the base of which has provided $^{14}$C dates of >3550 ± 160 B.P. (UCR-1488A–D) just below a structural floor with an associated large mortar (Goldberg 1983). Several prehistoric and protohistoric components have been defined in the midden deposits, among them one ascribable to the late prehistoric Miwok and another representing late nineteenth-century Indian mourning practices and habitation.

At the Redbud site, Cal-S-347, several prehistoric components were recognized in cultural deposits as much as 270 cm deep. One stratum, 110 cm deep, containing Elko series projectile points, has been $^{14}$C dated at 3200 ± 110 B.P. (UCR-1450A). A large, stemmed projectile point (Figure 3.2B) from Cal-S-347 is typologically like Hell Gap points on the Great Plains (see Frison 1974: Figure 1.37C) and Parman points in the western Great Basin; the latter have been $^{14}$C-dated at circa 8500 B.P. in northwestern Nevada (Layton 1979) and circa 8130 B.P. near Lake Tahoe (Elston et al. 1977).

Although some of the New Melones data remain to be analyzed and reported, a few preliminary observations can be made:

1. The archaeological sequence along this part of the Stanislaus River spans an estimated 8000 to 9000 years and included multiple prehistoric cultural phases (Table 7.2).

2. Stratified and seriated components reflect both cultural and environmental changes through time.

3. Some cultural changes (e.g., advent of the bow and arrow at ca. A.D. 500) may represent trait diffusion; others are linked to *in situ* adaptive shifts or to population replacement.

4. Nearly all the tested Indian sites include components less than 500 years old, and most of these are single-component sites. This recent proliferation of settlements probably reflects Miwok expansion after circa A.D. 1400.

5. After the Gold Rush, Indian use of traditional foods, milling equipment, houses, mortuary practices, and ceremonial structures persisted until the 1880s and later (Van Bueren 1982). Indeed, there is evidence that

parts of the New Melones project area may have been a refugium for displaced Indians from the surrounding country.

In the mountains east of the New Melones Reservoir a great deal of archaeological survey work and some testing have been sponsored by the U.S. Forest Service in its effort to inventory and assess cultural properties (ACRS 1975, 1977; Chartkoff and Chartkoff 1981; Goldberg 1983; Moratto 1981b; Napton 1974b–g; Napton and Greathouse 1982). For example, by 1981 nearly half the area of the Stanislaus National Forest had been examined in the course of 165 survey projects, and approximately 1100 sites had been recorded within ≈180,000 hectares (≈440,000 acres) of land (W. Woolfenden, personal communication, 1981). This work has documented two modes of late prehistoric settlement: High Sierran seasonal camps marked by lithic scatters but few bedrock mortars, and Transition zone settlements recognized by middens, numerous bedrock mortars, and structural remains (Moratto 1981b). Archaeological sites in the central Sierran forest belt occur near annual streams, on ridgelines, and in certain midslope (non–stream/ridge) settings. In this regard, T. Jackson (1979b:2) discovered "a near perfect correlation between mid-slope site locations and the contact between two major lithologic units of the area—the Mesozoic granitic basement complex of the Sierra Nevada batholith and overlying Pliocene pyroclastic rocks." These midslope site locations attracted Indian settlement because the lithologic contact zone featured relatively level terraces, springs, granite outcrops suitable for mortars, both intrusive and volcanic rocks, and biotic ecotones with diverse flora and abundant game.

Other notable research in the north-central Sierra has focused upon rock art and bedrock mortars. At *Tco'se* (Ama-14), northeast of Jackson (Figure 7.2), Payen and Boloyan (1963) documented 1185 mortars and 363 petroglyphs in a single limestone outcrop (Figure 7.9). *Tco'se* is of special interest not only as the largest known aggregation of bedrock mortars at any California site, but also because of the unusual association of mortars and petroglyphs, including the incorporation of mortars into rock-art motifs.

Central Sierran rock art has been described and variously interpreted by Steward (1929), Fenenga (1949), and Payen (1959, 1966, 1968). It occurs chiefly as angular and curvilinear motifs, some of which are representational, on rock panels at scattered sites—mostly in the foothills (Figure 7.10). Heizer and Clewlow (1973:25–29) designated this as the Central Sierra Petroglyph Style and, based upon its similarity to dated styles in the western Great Basin, estimated its age at 3000–500 years B.P. As the central Sierran petroglyphs seem not to have been made by the Miwok, they may represent pre-Miwok peoples of Great Basin origin or affiliation, or visits by Great Basin groups, or both.

**Figure 7.10** Petroglyphs on exfoliating red granite at site Cal-5 near Horseshoe Bend on the Stanislaus River, Calaveras County. Although found within the ethnographic territory of the Central Sierra Miwok, these petroglyphs stylistically resemble those of the western Great Basin. It is believed that the rock art at Cal-5 was left by pre-Miwok people of Great Basin cultural affiliation. (Photograph by the author.)

## South-Central Foothills

### Buchanan Reservoir

One of the more intensively studied areas in the Sierran province is the Buchanan Reservoir (Eastman Lake) vicinity in the Madera County foothills (elevation, 120–275 m), along the Chowchilla River, about 45 km east of Merced (Figure 7.2). Even before excations had begun, the discovery of 66 small to very large habitation sites and more than 3375 bedrock mortars within an area of only 9.75 km² seemed to indicate long and/or intensive occupation by a sizable population (Moratto 1968; Rackerby 1964).

In four seasons of fieldwork at Buchanan between 1967 and 1970, T. F. King and M. Moratto excavated several sites—notably Schwabacher (Mad-117), Dancing Cow (Mad-106), Jones (Mad-159), and Moby Rattlesnake (Mad-107)—and tested 23 others (King 1968, 1969; Moratto 1968, 1969b, 1970b,d). In all, some 20,000 artifacts, 140 burials, and 92 structural features were documented. Temporal control was provided by stratigraphy, cross-dating, seriation of grave and house lots, and 13 radiocarbon dates. By 1972 Moratto (1972b) was able to synthesize these data and define three phases of Chowchilla River prehistory (Table 7.2).

*The Chowchilla Phase* (ca. 300 B.C.–A.D. 300) marks an interval of prosperity. Three Chowchilla Phase settlements were found at Buchanan Reservoir in prime settings on the banks of the river. Fish spears, large projectile points, millingstones, and cobble mortars attest to the importance of fishing, hunting, and gathering vegetal foods, perhaps including acorns. Also characteristic are the atlatl and dart, and profesion of small obsidian flake tools, varied bone artifacts, and abundant ornaments and beads of *Haliotis* and *Olivella* shell (Table 7.2 and Figure 7.11). This inventory is generally comparable to that of the Crane Flat Phase in the Yosemite locality, 80 km to the northeast. Artifact types and materials reflect extensive trade with Indians east and west of the Sierra. Chowchilla people customarily buried their dead in extended or semiextended positions, furnishing their graves with red ochre and "killed" (ritually broken) artifacts (Table 7.2 and Figure 7.11). The nonrandom distribution of mortuary goods and quantity of artifacts with some buried children imply both nonegalitarian social status and status ascription (T. King 1976; Moratto 1972b).

**TABLE 7.2**

**Cultural Phase Markers at Buchanan Reservoir, South-Central Sierra Nevada**[a]

| | Chowchilla Phase (300 B.C.–A.D. 300) | Raymond Phase (A.D. 300–1500) | Madera Phase (A.D. 1500–1850) |
|---|---|---|---|
| Settlements | Few, large villages next to Chowchilla River; relatively large populations | Sporadic occupation of old sites near river; relatively small populations | Village community pattern; large, main villages near river; smaller settlements proliferate in the hinterlands; large populations |
| Architecture | No data | No data | Oval to circular plan, semi-subterranean ceremonial structures of wattle and daub, 8–17 |

**TABLE 7.2** (*Continued*)

| | Chowchilla Phase (300 B.C.–A.D. 300) | Raymond Phase (A.D. 300–1500) | Madera Phase (A.D. 1500–1850) |
|---|---|---|---|
| | | | m in diameter; smaller, circular plan houses |
| Subsistence | Hunting, fishing, gathering hard seeds; possibly some use of acorns | Acorns and hard seeds emphasized; hunting continues; no evidence of fishing | Acorns exploited intensively, along with other seeds; bulbs, greens, and berries gathered; hunting of elk, deer, and small game |
| Technology | Atlatl/dart; large projectile points of Types CLB, ECB, EE, ESN, SCB, SCS, PSS, SSN, TCS[b]; cobble mortar, cylindrical pestle; millingstones; bone fish spear tips | Bow and arrow replace atlatl/dart; medium projectile points of Types EES, ESS, RSCN, RSSN[b]; bedrock mortar and cobble pestle introduced; millingstones | Bow and arrow; small arrow points of Types DSN, CT, and a few EES, RSCN[b]; bedrock mortar, cobble pestle; millingstones |
| Ornaments | Abundant *Olivella* shell beads, Types A1a, B5b, C1b, C7, C8, F2, F3a, G1, G2a, G2b, G3b; *Haliotis* beads, H3a1, H3a2, H3b, H4[c]; *Acmaea* rings; numerous *Haliotis* ornaments | Few *Olivella* shell beads, Types B1, B2, B3a, C3, D1, M1a[c] | Abundant steatite disk beads; rare *Saxidomus* disks; some *Olivella* beads, Types B5, E1, E2, H1[c]; bird bone tubular beads; steatite pendants and ear/nose ornaments |
| Mortuary | Extended and semi-extended primary burials with copious grave goods; ochre in graves | Mostly tightly or loosely flexed primary interments; few mortuary artifacts; stone, daub, or millingstone cairns over burials | Flexed primary interments common; some cremations in houses; cremations are furnished with abundant artifacts |
| Miscellaneous | Evidence of trade with Great Basin and southwestern California groups; developed bone industry; artifacts reflect Windmiller affiliation | Little evidence of trade with coastal groups; violent death common; andalusite cylinders, spindles, earplugs | Brown Ware pottery (acquired in trade); elaborate steatite industry; ancestral Miwok |

[a]After Moratto (1972b).
[b]Projectile point type codes after Moratto (1972b).
[c]Shell artifact type codes after Bennyhoff and Fredrickson (1967).

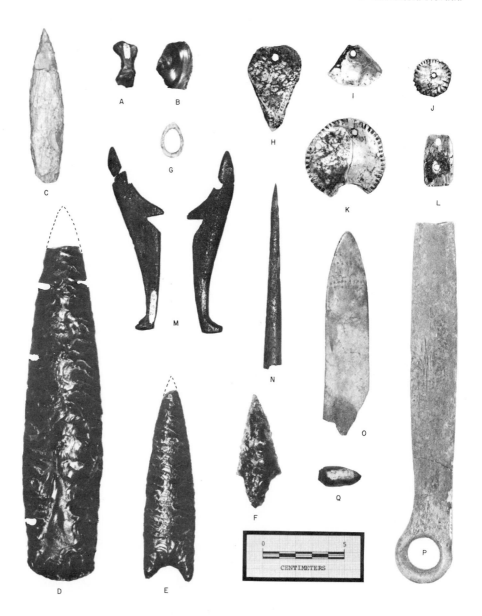

**Figure 7.11** Chowchilla Phase artifacts from sites Mad-117 and Mad-159, Buchanan Reservoir, Madera County. A, B, retouched obsidian flake tools ("scrapers"); C, phyllite foliate projectile point; D, obsidian large biface; E, obsidian Sierra Concave Base projectile point; F, obsidian Triangular Contracting Stem projectile point; G, *Acmaea* shell ornament; H–L, *Haliotis* shell ornaments; M, antler fish-spear guides; N, bone awl-tip; O, bone spatulate object (fragment) with punctate decorations; P, bone ringed-wand or dagger; Q, antler atlatl spur. (After Moratto 1972b.)

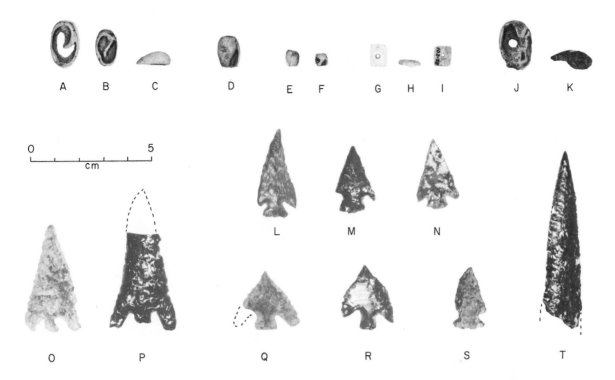

**Figure 7.12** Raymond Phase artifacts from Buchanan Reservoir, Madera County. A, B, Type B1 Side-Ground/End-Ground *Olivella* beads; C, Type B1 *Olivella* bead, lateral view; D, Type B2b End-Ground *Olivella* bead; E, F, Type B3a Small Barrell *Olivella* beads; G–I, Type M1a Thin Rectangular *Olivella* beads; J, K, Type D1 Split-Punched *Olivella* beads, ventral and lateral views; L–S, chert and obsidian projectile points of the Rose Spring or Eastgate ("Rosegate") series; T, well-made obsidian projectile point tip of uncertain type. (After Moratto 1972b.)

*The Raymond Phase* (ca. A.D. 300–1500) seems to reflect an episode of cultural instability and change. Although millingstones, core tools, and small retouched flakes continued to be important, *Olivella* beads were scarce and *Haliotis* ornaments were virtually unknown—presumably because the Chowchilla River people no longer had access to sources of marine shell or ornaments. Typical of the Raymond Phase are small-to-medium projectile (arrow?) points (Figure 7.12) and general use of the bedrock mortar and unshaped pestle (Figures 7.9 and 7.13). Populations were small and dispersed; old villages appear to have experienced chronic cycles of occupation and abandonment after circa A.D. 500. Violence was common. Primary interment of the dead in flexed positions was the normal mortuary practice, although some extended burials were interred

**Figure 7.13** Ground-stone artifacts from Buchanan Reservoir, Madera County. A, un-shaped cobble pestle of a type used extensively in bedrock mortars during late prehistoric times, length 245 mm; B, rectanguloid mano, length 73 mm; C, ovoid mano, length 118 mm. Manos and millingstones appear to have been in use throughout the known prehistory of the Chowchilla River vicinity. (After Moratto 1972b.)

during the early part of the phase. By contrast to Chowchilla Phase displays of funerary wealth, however, Raymond burials seldom were furnished with anything but cairns of boulders and millingstones (Moratto 1972b).

*The Madera Phase* (ca. A.D. 1500–1850) represents the spread and cultural florescence of ancestral Southern Sierra Miwok. Among the hallmarks of this phase are steatite disk beads, lightweight arrow points, bedrock mortars and cobble pestles, several types of *Olivella* beads, and occasional pieces of exotic Brown Ware pottery. Also diagnostic is a steatite industry featuring bowls, cooking vessels, pipes, arrow-shaft straighteners, and ornaments (Table 7.2 and Figures 7.13 and 7.14). This assemblage finds close parallels in the Mariposa Phase of Yosemite.

In Madera times the village community settlement pattern emerged, with main villages along the Chowchilla River and subsidiary hamlets on tributary streams. Dramatic population growth after circa A.D. 1550 coincided with the appearance of large (8–17 m in diameter) oval to circular, semisubterranean structures that probably functioned as ceremonial houses. Smaller (3–5 m in diameter) circular houses with slightly excavated floors and central hearths served as dwellings. Cremation, introduced around A.D. 1600, apparently was reserved for high-status individuals; primary interment in flexed positions was the more common disposal mode throughout the Madera Phase (Moratto 1972b).

A fifth season of excavations at Buchanan Reservoir in 1972, including the exhumation of 159 burials in three cemeteries jeopardized by construction, provided data for T. F. King's (1976) study of *Political Differentiation among Hunter–Gatherers* . . . King proposed that Chowchilla River society of 2000 to 1000 years ago was stratified and that social ranking was reflected in burial attributes (1976:89). He argued that mortuary variability at Buchanan Reservoir was better explained as a function of political differentiation than as a result of diachronic change in interment customs: "Flexed interment is a stable practice associated generally with low status *personae*, while disposal of high status dead is accomplished in several ways during the sequence including extended interment during perhaps the earliest period and cremation during the latest" (King 1976:86).

Analyses of the Buchanan data, including 10 additional burials (309 total) and 7 radiocarbon dates (35 total) obtained during some 1975 salvage work by A. S. Peak (1976), permit the following conclusions, some of which modify those of King (1976), about mortuary practices and their implications for Chowchilla River prehistory:

1. Chowchilla Phase social ranking and status ascription are indicated by cemetery patterning, nonrandom allocation of "expensive" grave goods, and burial of wealth items with certain infants and children (King 1976).

2. Both flexed and extended burials co-occur during the Chowchilla and Raymond phases, but extensions decline in frequency after circa A.D. 550 and are not found after circa A.D. 950 (Table 7.3).

3. To the degree that grave lots of valuable items (e.g., *Olivella* and *Haliotis* beads and ornaments) may reflect the status of the deceased, high-status individuals were buried in both flexed (36%) and extended (64%) positions ($n = 53$). Of 74 extended burials in the sample ($n = 309$), 38, or 51%, had no significant funerary associations. Extended burial, therefore, was not reserved exclusively for high-status persons. Rather, through time, flexure gradually came to replace extension as the normal burial position. A greater proportion of extended burials is associated

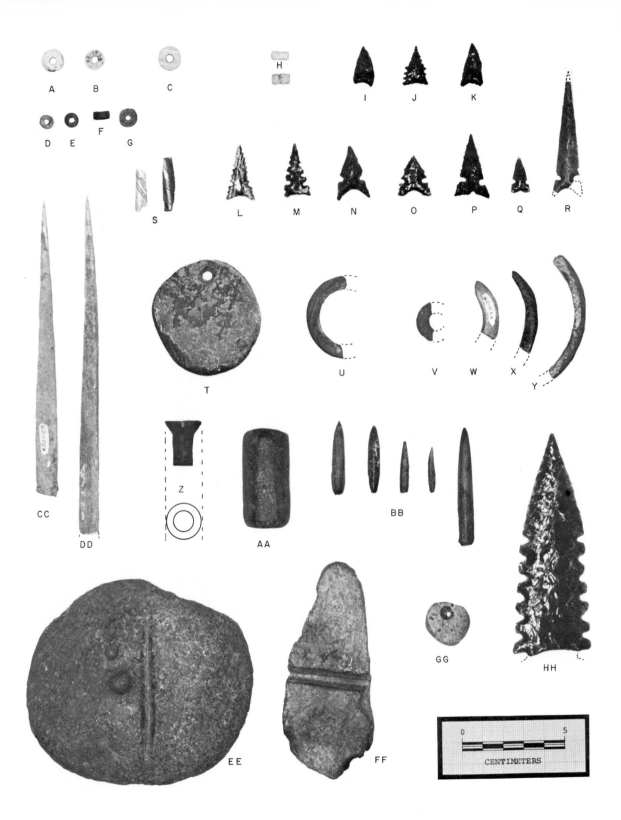

A    B      C       H        I     J     K

D   E   F   G

S      L    M    N    O    P    Q    R

T       U      V   W   X    Y

CC      Z       AA      BB      HH

DD

EE        FF     GG

0           5

CENTIMETERS

with wealth because the Chowchilla Phase, wherein extension was the dominant burial mode, was generally prosperous and burials tended to be well furnished. The millennium after circa A.D. 550, however, was evidently a time when luxury goods—particularly those from the coast—were in short supply, and the burial of expensive artifacts virtually ceased.

To summarize, Chowchilla Phase occupation (now dated circa 800 B.C.–A.D. 550) of the Buchanan Reservoir locality was centered at a few main villages along the Chowchilla River. Large, socially complex populations exploited local resources and actively traded with their neighbors. After circa A.D. 550, however, both population size and social complexity diminished; local Raymond Phase settlement was sporadic, violence was common, and trade was disrupted. Then, after circa A.D. 1500, scores of small settlements were established, and these maintained sociopolitical ties with the revitalized older centers. The Madera Phase, with its village community organization and distinctive economic patterns, represents the late prehistory of the Southern Sierra Miwok (T. King 1976; Moratto 1972b–d).

There is limited archaeological evidence of direct historic contacts between Indians and Euro-Americans at Buchanan Reservoir: an isolated glass bead at Mad-159, iron nails associated with native artifacts at Mad-111, and horse bones [14]C-dated at 185 B.P. (later than A.D. 1765) in a hearth at Mad-153 (King 1969; Moratto 1972b). The latter discovery may attest to the raiding of mission era corrals by Indians who took refuge along the Chowchilla River (cf. Cook 1960, 1962). In this regard, J. C. Frémont in the 1840s spoke of "Horse-thief tribes" of apostacized Indians who "took to the mountains" with stolen horses, "partly to use as saddle-horses but principally to eat. . . . The streams and springs hereabout were the waters of the Chauchilles and Mariposas River and the Indians of this village belonged to the Chauchilla tribe" (Frémont 1966:n.p.).

It is probable that the Buchanan area was largely depopulated by the malaria epidemic of 1833, which killed thousands of Indians as it swept

---

**Figure 7.14** Madera Phase artifacts from Buchanan Reservoir, Madera County. A–C, clamshell disc beads; D–G, steatite disc beads; H, bird-bone tubular beads; I–K, obsidian Cottonwood Triangular arrow points; L–Q, obsidian Desert Side-notched arrowpoints; R, chert Desert Side-notched arrow point; S, fragmentary, incised bird-bone artifacts; T, discoidal pendant of slate; U, V, fragmentary polished stone rings; W–Y, fragmentary polished stone arcs (nose or ear ornaments?); Z, polished steatite object (earspool?); AA, ground andalusite crystal; BB, pointed, ground, and polished andalusite crystals; CC, DD, bone awls; EE, arrow-shaft straightener on steatite pebble; FF, steatite vessel sherd, modified to function as arrow shaft straightener; GG, steatite pendant; HH, large serrated point of obsidian. (After Moratto 1972b.)

**TABLE 7.3**

Radiocarbon Ages of Interments at Buchanan Reservoir[a]

| Site/Burial | Position[b] | ¹⁴C date | Status[c] | Associations[a] |
|---|---|---|---|---|
| 133/76-03 | F (tight) | 1495 ± 150 (GX-4291) | L | Cobbles, point fragments, quartz flake, steatite bowl fragments |
| 159/72-05 | F | 1540 ± 110 (UCLA-1860J) | H | Large lot of *Olivella* G beads, *Haliotis* ornaments, cache of flakes |
| 159/72-06 | F | 1630 ± 80 (UCLA-1860P) | H | Large lot of *Olivella* G beads, *Haliotis* disks, bone wands, whistles |
| 106/72-24 | D | 1650 ± 80 (UCLA-1860D) | L | None |
| 159/72-32 | E | 1690 ± 100 (UCLA-1860A) | H | Steatite bowl, large lot of *Olivella* G beads |
| 106/72-11 | F | 1740 ± 100 (UCLA-1860E) | L | Atlatl weight |
| 117/69-08 | E | 1740 ± 110 (I-5361) | H | Millingstone, 3 *Olivella* G beads, 2 cannon bones, 4 cut antler bases, 1 bone awl, 1 mano |
| 117/72-16 | F | 1745 ± 100 (UCLA-1860G) | L | None (two projectile points in bones) |
| 159/68-03 | E | 1800 ± 95 (I-5363) | L? | Stone–daub cairn, 12 *Olivella* G beads, 1 *Haliotis* ornament |
| 106/72-01 | E | 2000 ± 80 (UCLA-1860O) | H | Large lot of *Olivella* G beads and *Haliotis* disks, 2 *Haliotis* ornaments |
| 117/72-44 | F | 2750 ± 90 (UCLA-1860B) | L? | Dubious association; 4 *Haliotis* disks, 2 *Olivella* G beads |
| 159/76-01 | F (loose) | 105 ± 120 | L | Dubious association; 1 *Haliotis* disk, 2 *Olivella* F beads |

*(continued)*

through marshlands and riverine tracts of the Central Valley and lower foothills (Cook 1955b). In the words of a contemporary witness:

> From the extreme northern part of the Sacramento valley to the Tulare lake, . . . the numerous villages which we had left filled with life were converted to Golgothas. The first struck down were buried. But the increasing dead gave not time to the living to thus dispose of their fellows. Huge piles of bodies were consumed with fire, and the ashes deposited in tombs near the village. ("Trapper" n.d., in Cook 1955b:319)

Cook (1955b:322) estimated the mortality rate at 75%. Assuming that the Chowchilla River populations were thus devastated by the epidemic, their numbers probably were small when the Fresno River Reservation was established in 1850 and Indians were removed to it from an area between the Merced and Kaweah rivers (Muñoz 1974, 1975a,b). Thus, the dearth of historic components at Buchanan may be the result of disease and the forced relocation of the Chowchilla River people.

**TABLE 7.3** (*Continued*)

| Site/Burial | Position[b] | ¹⁴C date | Status[c] | Associations[a] |
|---|---|---|---|---|
| 159/76-03 | F (tight) | 760 ± 125 (GX-4290) | L | Cobbles, dog burial |
| 133/76-01 | F (loose) | 830 ± 125 (GX-4285) | L | Two cobbles, 1 *Olivella* M1 bead |
| 133/76-02 | F | 960 ± 120 (GX-4286) | L | Cobble scatter, 1 *Olivella* M1 bead, 2 manos, 1 "polishing stone" |
| 117/72-21 | F | 970 ± 80 (UCLA-1860F) | L? | Two EES and ECN points, millingstone cairn |
| 106/72-33 | E | 1010 ± 80 (UCLA-1860I) | L | None |
| 133/76-05 | F (tight) | 1055 ± 130 (GX-4287) | L | None |
| 117/72-08 | E | 1305 ± 80 (UCLA-1860L) | L | Projectile points in bones, small lot of *Olivella* G beads in dubious association |
| 117/72-20 | E? | 1310 ± 80 (UCLA-1860K) | ? | Badly disturbed, small lot of *Olivella* C and G beads, millingstone |
| 159/72-13 | E | 1400 ± 90 (UCLA-1860H) | H | Bone pin, large bone wand, bone tool, large obsidian biface |
| 117/72-36 | F | 1425 ± 80 (UCLA-1860N) | L | Core tool |
| 117/72-59 | E | 1470 ± 100 (UCLA-1860C) | H | Millingstone and mortar cairn, large lot of *Haliotis* disk beads |

[a]Data compiled from King 1976, Moratto 1972b, and Peak 1976; artifact type codes after Moratto 1972b.
[b]D, disarticulated; E, extended; F, flexed.
[c]H, evident high status; L, evident low status.

## Hidden Reservoir

The foothill environment of the Hidden Reservoir area on the Fresno River is similar to that of Buchanan Reservoir, which lies only 15 km to the north (Figure 7.2). Initial archaeological work by W. Wallace in 1967 and 1968 included testing 9 of 18 documented sites (Wallace 1968, 1969, 1970a). Subsequently, F. Fenenga recorded 13 additional sites and excavated several large middens in the course of five field seasons between 1969 and 1975 (Fenenga 1973, 1975).

Investigations at China Diggings (Mad-173) and other stratified middens revealed cultural developments almost identical to the prehistoric sequence at Buchanan Reservoir as well as historic assemblages not found at Buchanan. The upper components of Mad-171 and -173, as examples, contained bottle-glass scrapers and projectile points, buttons, ceramics, and numerous glass trade beads, along with native artifacts reminiscent of the Madera Phase (Fenenga 1973; Kelly 1974). The glass beads were obtained by the Indians after 1850 from Americans rather than from earlier contacts with the Mexicans or Spanish (Martz 1974).

The Fresno River at Hidden Reservoir formed the ethnographic boundary between Miwok and Yokuts (Figure 11.1). However, relating archaeological material to one or the other of these groups has proved difficult for several reasons: first, the Fresno River vicinity apparently was a refuge for Indian neophytes fleeing from coastal missions during the half century after 1770; next, James Savage's 1851 trading post on the Fresno River attracted Indians from the surrounding country; and finally, the Fresno River Reservation, with its geographic center near Savage's trading post, accommodated no fewer than 16 "tribes" of Mono, Sierra Miwok, Foothill and Valley Yokuts, and "Capoos" (repatriated mission Indians?) between 1851 and 1860 (Heizer 1972b; Muñoz 1974, 1975b).

This intermingling of diverse cultures is reflected in historic components at Hidden Reservoir. Mad-179, where more than 50 saucer-shaped housepits were found on the surface, was littered with horseshoes, Staffordshire ceramics, and glass beads—evidence that this large site was occupied between 1850 and 1860. Mad-179 probably was a principal village of refugees from the southern mines who congregated near Savage's trading post (Fenenga 1973).

### Summary

Considerable archaeological work has been done since 1950 in the central Sierra Nevada. In the northern part of this subregion, a 12-year program of field investigations has been completed at New Melones Reservoir. A major study of the New Melones findings, now under way, promises to interpret a long record of archaeological and paleoenvironmental developments. In the Yosemite locality, Bennyhoff's (1956) pioneering chronology has served as a reference for archaeological work in the mid-Sierra. Paralleling the Yosemite sequence, the Buchanan and Hidden cultural phases are well substantiated by radiocarbon dates and large samples of excavated material. Together, the Buchanan, Hidden, and Yosemite researches have led to a fair understanding of the last 2000–3000 years of prehistory in the south-central Sierra. Earlier periods and the more northerly parts of the central Sierra remain poorly known.

# The Southern Sierra

### Kings and San Joaquin Uplands

The southern Sierra Nevada has witnessed many surveys, but comparatively few excavations. An important study of high Sierran archaeology was a survey of the Huntington Lake–Shaver Lake vicinity (Figure 7.2) conducted between 1953 and 1976 by Margaret Hindes (Molarsky). Trade trails, trading centers, camp sites, and large seasonal villages were identified among nearly 150 recorded sites—all of which were above an elevation of 1375 m. Common surface artifacts were Brown Ware sherds and projectile points like those reported by Bennyhoff in Yosemite (Hindes 1959, 1962, personal communications, 1976, 1980). The artifacts described by Hindes reflect no less than 3000 years of cultural activity in the upper San Joaquin watershed.

Northeast of Huntington Lake, W. and E. Wallace recorded five sites in Vermilion Valley (now Lake Thomas Edison) on the Mono Creek drainage about 16 km west of the Sierran crest. Subsequently, D. Lathrap and J. Nicoll dug at Vermilion Valley 1, a protohistoric–historic Mono campsite (elevation, 2300 m) that contained steatite disk beads, a profusion of small obsidian tools, arrow points, Owens Valley Brown Ware, and glass beads (Lathrap and Shutler 1955). The remarkable likeness of the Vermilion Valley assemblage to that from Iny-2, a historic Owens Valley Paiute settlement 100 km southeast of Lake Edison, shows the strong relationship between Great Basin and high Sierran cultures.

The Sierra National Forest has been the focus of considerable archaeological work, particularly as related to Forest Service activities, such as recreational developments and timber sales, and to commercial hydroelectric projects (K. Moffitt, personal communication, 1980). Examples would include Varner's sampling of the Recreation Point site (F. S. No. 57-20) at Bass Lake, where charcoal found near the base of a 120-cm-deep midden provided a $^{14}$C date of circa 200 B.C. (Varner 1976); minimal testing of an obsidian chipping site (53-674) endangered by road construction (Mundy 1980); and A. Peak's excavation of Mad-448, a culturally stratified midden in the Cattle Timber Sale area. The latter work is of interest because an age of 4840 ± 650 years (UCLA-2348B) was determined on carbon from near the bottom of the 110-cm-deep deposit (Peak 1981a). Although this date is not definitely archaeological, it seems compatible with the Humboldt, Elko, Pinto, and "Martis" projectile points found at the site.

Another study performed on behalf of the Sierra National Forest was T. L. Jackson's reconnaissance of about 600 ha (1500 ac) on Chawanakee Flats (elevation, 762–1463 m) near the Big Creek–San Joaquin River confluence. This area was first investigated in 1957 by M. Hindes, who documented several sites and reported that the Flats had been a major winter village area linked to the old Mono Trail. Jackson discovered 22 previously unknown sites, most of which are thought to have been related to one or two ethnohistoric Mono communities (Jackson 1979).

In the nearby Whiskey Ridge vicinity, north of Chawanakee Flats and west of Mammoth Pool (Figure 7.2), J. Kipps recorded a pictograph and 43 occupation and/or economic activity sites in a surveyed area of about 5600 ha (14,000 ac). Kipps (1981a) used artifact styles, obsidian hydration measurements, and documentary sources to show that the Whiskey Ridge sites had been occupied at various times over a span of 2000 years or more.

In the Wishon and Courtright Reservoir areas, about 25 km southeast of Huntington Lake (Figure 7.2), archaeological surveys by Payen (1974), Riddell, Olsen, and Hastings (1972), and Wren (1976) resulted in 66 sites being documented. Near Wishon Reservoir, on the North Fork of the Kings River, excavations by Sheets (1974) at the Mountain Rest site (elevation, 1250 m) revealed two prehistoric components, one estimated to date earlier than A.D. 1000 and the other later. Also near Wishon Reservoir, Wren sampled 14 sites jeopardized by the Helms Hydroelectric Project. The tested sites—typically middens with bedrock milling features, at elevations between 195 and 2535 m—most often yielded a protohistoric inventory of arrow points, obsidian flake tools, steatite beads and vessel sherds, and Owens Valley Brown Ware; glass beads and bottle-glass scrapers indicate the occupation of some sites during the historic period. Unexpectedly early materials, however, came to light at Fre-534/535, a large, high-elevation (2165 m) site located roughly 24 km west of the Sierran divide. The 100-cm-deep midden produced steatite vessels and numerous millingstones, along with Humboldt and Pinto series points in lower strata and Elko specimens above (Wren 1976). Radiocarbon ages of 5085 ± 100, 5220 ± 105, and 2080 ± 85 years have been determined on charcoal from Fre-534/535 (Wren, personal communication, 1976). These findings show that parts of the southern Sierra were occupied, at least seasonally, more than 5000 years ago by peoples of Great Basin cultural affiliation.

Under the auspices of the Kings River Conservation District, P-III Associates of Fresno in 1981 tested 18 potentially jeopardized sites in the Dinkey Creek Hydroelectric Project area southeast of Shaver Lake (Figure 7.2). Using stratigraphy, artifact types, and obsidian hydration measurements, Kipps (1981b) estimated that one of these sites (Fre-1023) had been occupied as early as 4000 B.C.; the others were assigned to various intervals between circa 1500 B.C. and A.D. 1900. Notable among these is Fre-1361, a large, high-elevation (1860 m) village site featuring some 150 bedrock mortars, diverse artifacts including exotic or trade items, and remains of permanent structures. Kipps (1981:*ix*) has proposed that this was "a large mountain population center occupied for much of the year during a time [ca. A.D. 500–1300] when the climate was warmer and dryer than today."

Recent archaeological work in the Huntington Lake–Shaver Lake vicinity has included recording 29 sites along power transmission corridors (Holman 1970; Van Dyke 1970), limited testing of a site at the

China Peak ski resort (Wren 1974), and Varner and Beatty's 1978–1979 intensive survey and documentation of 41 lithic scatters, milling stations, and midden sites in the 5900-ha (14,400-ac) Balsam Meadow Hydroelectric Project area (Varner and Beatty 1980).

Minimal testing at nine of the Balsam Meadow sites by Moratto and Riley (1980) and O'Brien (1981) yielded surprising results. "Lithic scatters" often continued to depths of a meter or more, and one such site (Fre-811) was [14]C-dated at 5380 ± 260 B.C. (UCR-1245). However, in 1983 additional fieldwork by S. Goldberg and Moratto—including both manual and backhoe excavations, geomorphologic and soils studies, and paleobotanical research—established (1) that the soils of Fre-811 had been disturbed greatly by historic logging, earthslides, and colluviation along the edge of Balsam Meadow, and (2) that the spatial association of obsidian artifacts with the dated carbon at this site was probably fortuitous. Also during the 1983 season, excavations at Fre-812 revealed extensive midden and non-midden cultural deposits with evidence of several occupations beginning as early as circa 5000 B.P. and culminating with late prehistoric use of the Balsam Meadow vicinity by the Western Mono.

Along the San Joaquin River at Kerckhoff Reservoir, 22 km west of Balsam Meadow, extensive sampling has produced evidence of settlement as early as A.D. 500. Later components with Owens Valley Brown Ware and Great Basin styles of arrow points probably reflect Mono occupation or affiliation (Beatty *et al.* 1978; Varner and Bernal 1976; Varner and McCormick 1977). Farther downriver, a 1961 survey of the Millerton Lake shoreline revealed some artifacts as much as 2000 years old, but most of the 33 documented bedrock mortar and midden sites were relatively late (Theodoratus and Crain 1962). Additional surveys and testing of Fre-444 near Millerton Lake in 1970 confirmed that local foothill populations had been largest during protohistoric times, and that Great Basin influences had extended as far west as the edge of the Central Valley (Moratto n.d.).

*Sequoia–Kings Canyon Locality*

Initial scientific work in Sequoia–Kings Canyon National Park (Figure 8.7) included reconnaissance projects by A. Elsasser (1959, 1962) and J. Davis' (1960a) excavation of the protohistoric Granite Creek midden (Fre-259) near Cedar Grove. Elsewhere in the Park, J. von Werlhof in 1960 excavated at Hospital Rock (Tul-24), a village site associated with the Potwisha group of Mono and well known for its pictographs. Stratified deposits in the open midden and in a rockshelter at Tul-24 were assigned by von Werlhof (1960, 1961d) to three intervals of occupation between circa A.D. 1300–1400 and historic times. One interesting aspect of von

Werlhof's research is his (1961a) documentation of aboriginal trails in the Kaweah Basin. Sequoia–Kings Canyon National Park also has been subject to many recent surveys, such as those in the areas of Mineral King (Jennings and Kisling 1971; Morehead 1975) and Giant Forest–Lodgepole (Napton *et al.* 1974a). This and other work in the Park has been summarized in an overview by Fee (1980).

For many years, an archaeological benchmark in the southern Sierra has been the cultural sequence defined in the Terminus Reservoir (Lake Kaweah) area (elevation, 150–225 m) along the Kaweah River, below Sequoia National Park (Figure 8.7). This part of the Kaweah drainage crosses the ethnographic boundary between the Wukchumni Yokuts and Potwisha Mono. Initial surveys revealed 19 habitation sites with midden, 14 bedrock milling stations, and 4 rock-art sites (Fenenga 1947a, 1948a). Among the more striking features were pictographs covering the faces of a rocky bluff with motifs in red, gray, violet, and white pigments. This rock art most likely was produced by the Wukchumni (Berryman and Elsasser 1966). Similar polychrome pictographs have been found in the Yokohl Valley, south of Terminus Reservoir, along with 37 habitation sites—all badly damaged by agricultural activity (Varner and Stuart 1975).

Slick Rock Village (Tul-10) was the first Terminus Reservoir site to be excavated, followed by Greasy Creek (Tul-1) and Cobble Lodge (Tul-145). Slick Rock Village featured 14 housepits (3.9–4.3 m in diameter) and 3 bedrock outcrops with 21 to 48 mortars each. Sampling by F. Fenenga in 1950 brought to light a few glass beads, obsidian arrow points, bone awls, tubular clay pipes, and steatite industry composed of disk beads, pendants and vessels, and more than 1000 sherds of Tulare Plain Ware (like Owens Valley Brown Ware)—a dark-brown to reddish-brown, fine-textured, coiled (or rarely modeled) pottery with flat-bottomed, vertically walled bowls and flat-bottomed "flowerpot" vessels predominating (Fenenga 1952). Also of interest at Tul-10 are numerous fist-sized choppers and scraper-planes, possibly woodworking tools used in house construction work. Considering architecture, burials, and artifacts, Fenenga concluded that Slick Rock Village had been a protohistoric Wukchumni settlement with minimal evidence of historic era occupation.

The Greasy Creek site was the only clearly stratified midden ($\approx 2$ m deep) sampled at Terminus Reservoir. Seven circular housepits were appreciably larger (8.2–14.6 m in diameter) than those at Slick Rock Village. The upper 40 cm at Tul-1 yielded arrow points, steatite disk beads, *Olivella* Full-lipped beads, pottery, and other materials comparable to the Slick Rock assemblage. A lower component at Greasy Creek is suggested by large projectile points, core choppers, and cobble mortars; millingstones, manos, and cobble pestles occurred in all levels. This site has not been dated except for the estimated appearance at circa A.D. 1300 of the pottery in levels above 30 cm (Pendergast and Meighan 1959).

According to local residents, numerous Indians lived at the Cobble Lodge site (Tul-145) until the 1860s, when they were annihilated by smallpox. The remains of their houses survived until destroyed by plowing in the 1930s. Excavations during 1960 revealed a large cemetery. In a pit near the edge of the site more than 50 individuals had been buried at one time, probably during the smallpox epidemic; in all, 130 burials were found. Funerary red ochre, traces of wooden grave markers, the use of fired clay as grave fill, and remains of flexed secondary interments in baskets were documented at Cobble Lodge. Although the stratification had been disturbed by aboriginal grave digging, two components could be inferred from the "late" pottery, arrow points, and steatite beads, and "early" cobble mortars and large projectile points (Berryman and Elsasser 1966; von Werlhof 1961b).

## Far Southern Sierra

The far southern Sierra Nevada encompasses that part of the range drained by the Tule and Kern rivers (Figures 1.3 and 8.7). Although intensive surveys and testing in this area have been undertaken only recently, sporadic archaeological work has been done since the 1920s. Early research included rock-art studies (Fenenga 1949; Steward 1929), documentation of Tübatulabal village sites (E. Voegelin 1938), surveys and surface collecting at the Lake Isabella project (Fenenga 1947b, 1948b), and the report of a dry cave near Walker Pass, where a prospector had found rush matting, a piece of twined juniper bark textile, and part of a conical burden basket (M. Harrington 1950:89–90). Also recorded were three other Kern County archaeological caves—Ker-185, -29, and -93—respectively containing the basket burial of a child, Owens Valley Brown Ware, and bedrock mortars and pictographs (Heizer 1951a, 1952b).

In 1957 G. Guthrie briefly summarized prior archaeological work in the southern Sierra. In a later, expanded overview, D. Griffin reviewed Kawaiisu and Tübatulabal site locations, synthesized available archaeological data, and noted her field observations at three rock-art and habitation sites on Erskine, Canebrake, and Kelso creeks, the first of which had been tested in 1962 (Griffin 1963).

Considerable fieldwork has been done in the vicinity of Lake Isabella at the confluence of the Kern and South Fork Kern rivers (Figure 8.7), beginning with the 1947–1948 seasons of survey and collecting by University of California, Berkeley, crews at sites Ker-1 to -26 (Fenenga 1947b, 1948b). Additional sites near Lake Isabella have been recorded by Wallace (1970b), Hanks (1973), and Schiffman (1974, 1976). Notable among these is Long Canyon Village (Ker-311) at an elevation of 915 m (3000 ft) on the South Fork Kern. This "permanent winter village" site, last occupied by the Tübatulabal between A.D. 1780 and 1830, covers about 20 ha (50 ac); its midden deposits, bedrock mortars, lithic scatters, rock alignments, and rock rings marking former dwellings and granaries were recorded and partly mapped in 1976 (Salzman 1977).

More recently, Glassow and Moore (1978) mapped and evaluated 50 sites around Lake Isabella. Habitation sites occurred mainly in the wooded, western part of the study area near sources of acorns and pine nuts. Although nearly all of the recorded sites were prehistoric, most evidently had been occupied only after circa A.D. 1000. Five historic aboriginal sites may be related to ethnographic Tübatulabal hamlets (Glassow and Moore 1978).

Excavations near Lake Isabella have been few, and findings remain largely unpublished. In 1971 archaeologists from California State University, Fresno, investigated several sites near Delonegha Springs in the Kern River canyon. Excavations also took place near the Erskine Creek–Kern River confluence and at the jeopardized Tübatulabal fishing village site of *Palakuc* (E. Voegelin 1938) near Bodfish, below the Isabella Dam, where a historic aboriginal structure was exposed (Salzman 1977:27). Other work in the Kern River locality has included studies of Tübatulabal pictographs (Andrews 1977a,b), among them what is alleged to be a calendar relating lunar cycles to the North Star (Schiffman 1977).

North of Lake Isabella a fair number of surveys, but few excavations, have been completed in the Tule River country (Jones 1969; Jones and King 1970). Typical are Varner and Davis' (1977) discovery of 53 sites in the South Fork Tule River Valley and Professional Analysts' 1979 survey of 10,800 ha (27,000 ac) on the Tule River Indian Reservation, where 29 sites were distributed geographically in two groups: (1) those at elevations below 1460 m on the valley floor near permanent streams and (2) those above 1660 m on ridgetops (Gehr 1979). It is likely that the former were base settlements, whereas the latter may have been hunting and/or gathering camps.

The most intensive archaeological work in the southern Sierra Nevada has been the systematic survey and testing of sites along the Pacific Crest Trail, most of which have been funded by the U.S. Bureau of Land Management (Clough 1976; Garfinkel *et al.* 1980; Sanborn 1964). Exemplary are K. McGuire and A. Garfinkel's investigations along the 29-km Bear Mountain segment of the trail in eastern Kern and Tulare counties (Figure 8.7). Situated between Lamont Meadow and Rockhouse Basin (elevation, 1980–2430 m) and about 4 km west of the Sierran crest, this is an area of rugged terrain characterized by meadow, piñon woodland, and sagebrush scrub vegetation types. Surface collecting and testing at 15 jeopardized sites revealed a settlement pattern featuring large "piñon-gathering base camps" and smaller, temporary piñon stations and hunting camps dated on the basis of projectile point types and obsidian hydration measurements. Synthesizing available data, McGuire and Garfinkel (1980:49–53) defined for the southern high Sierra the following prehistoric phases.

*Lamont Phase* (4000–1200 B.C.): Recognized by Pinto points and basalt as a material for flaked-stone tools, this phase is thought to represent sporadic forays into upland areas by hunting parties from base camps farther east (perhaps in the Owens or Indian Wells valleys). Occasional, limited gathering of piñon nuts is also suggested. McGuire and Garfinkel (1980:53–60) suggest that, due to warm, dry climatic conditions, piñon–juniper zones shifted downslope between circa 3000 and 1500 B.C. Because of steeper angles on the higher slopes, the downward shift would have caused piñon–juniper woodlands to occupy considerably more surface area than before. This postulated expansion of piñon during Lamont Phase times may have led to the settlement and subsistence strategy of the later Canebrake Phase.

*Canebrake Phase* (1200 B.C.–A.D. 600): Millingstones, along with Sierra Concave-Base, Elko, and Humboldt Concave-Base projectile points, are characteristic. "Piñon base camps" and temporary stations in upland areas are seen as evidence of settlement, exploitation of piñon nuts, hunting, and harvesting bulbs and seeds. As noted above, it is possible that substantial occupation of high-elevation areas during this phase was stimulated by environmental changes favoring the spread of piñon.

*Sawtooth Phase* (A.D. 600–1300): Intensified use of the uplands is recorded by more "piñon camps" and greater quantities of obsidian and artifacts than previously. The Sawtooth Phase is identified by Rose Spring and Eastgate series points, manos and millingstones, bedrock mortars and cobble pestles, steatite or serpentine disk beads, and (rare) *Olivella* Spire-lopped beads.

*Chimney Phase* (A.D. 1300–historic period): Subsistence and settlement patterns remain unchanged except that increased numbers of sites and artifacts imply more intensive occupation. Typical traits are Desert Side-notched and Cottonwood Triangular arrow points, Owens Valley Brown Ware, and stone disk beads; glass beads and *Olivella* rough disk beads appear in historic times.

In the Bear Mountain vicinity, the Sierran crest formed a boundary between the ethnographic Tübatulabal on the west slope and the Numic Kawaiisu and Panamint of the Great Basin (Figure 11.1). Synthesizing data from the Bear Mountain, Lamont Meadow, and Morris Peak segments of the Pacific Crest Trail, McGuire and Garfinkel propose that the Tübatulabalic and Numic groups have been differentiated since circa 1200 B.C. Archaeologically, this is shown by:

1. Rock art: Tübatulabal pictographs are mostly abstract with few representational forms. Rock art (assumed but not proven to be) of Numic

origin is distinctive and often depicts anthropomorphs, zoomorphs such as stylized bighorn sheep, and other realistic motifs. Petroglyphs are rare on the Kern Plateau, but pictographs are common. Rock-art sites more than 0.5 km west of the Sierran crest conform to the Tübatulabal pattern, whereas those to the east are similar in style and subject matter to the Coso Range petroglyphs (cf. Grant *et al.* 1968).

2. Settlement patterns: The location of Tübatulabal winter villages near the river in the South Fork Kern Valley may be contrasted with the desert location of Numic villages at the eastern base of the Sierran escarpment. Assuming that the seasonal piñon camps of a particular group were closer to its winter village than to that of another group, McGuire and Garfinkel ascribe the clusters of winter villages and piñon camps east and west of the divide to Numic and Tübatulabalic peoples, respectively.

3. Flaked-stone material: Chalcedony accounts for 5–75% (by weight) of the flaked-stone material found at archaeological sites along the Sierran crest, whereas the chalcedony–obsidian ratio seldom exceeds 1:20 at sites west of the crestal zone. Chalcedony was obtained from sources to the east and is thought to represent Numic activity.

4. Ground-stone artifacts: Sites along the Sierran crest produced millingstones made of desert volcanic rocks; by contrast, sites to the west yielded ground-stone artifacts manufactured only of local granitic rocks.

All things considered, McGuire and Garfinkel conclude that the Tübatulabalic and Numic occupations may be differentiated archaeologically; that Numic peoples inhabited and exploited the Sierran escarpment and crestal zones; and that the Pacific Crest Trail study area was part of the Tübatulabal homeland for at least 3000 years.

In many respects, the cultural sequence advanced by McGuire and Garfinkel is similar to Bettinger's (1974, 1977a, 1980) Owens Valley sequence. One notable difference, however, is that piñon nut procurement evidently did not begin until circa A.D. 600–800 in areas east of the Sierra (Bettinger 1976; Garfinkel and Cook 1980)—some 2300 to 2500 years later than suggested by McGuire and Garfinkel (1980) for the Sierran crest. Lacking piñon nut remains or other solid evidence of piñon exploitation in firmly dated Canebrake Phase deposits, it would seem best to reserve judgment about piñon use at such an early time.

## Discussion

The scope and focus of archaeological research in the Sierra Nevada have evolved over many decades. If one may characterize nineteenth-century studies as exploratory and often speculative, early twentieth-century work tended to be descriptive and analytic—a notable exception being Steward's classic synthesis (1929) of rock-art data. Research in the 1950s and 1960s emphasized chronology, typology, and comparison.

During the past few decades the Sierra has witnessed hundreds of archaeological projects ranging from the recording of individual sites to large, multi-year investigations involving hundreds of sites. This recent work has been concerned with prehistoric settlement patterns, social organization, exchange systems, paleoenvironmental reconstruction, cultural ecology, and various aspects of historical archaeology. Unfortunately, much of the recent effort also has assumed the guise of eleventh-hour rescue work in the context of dam and reservoir construction projects that have destroyed or inundated hundreds of archaeological sites.

Since about 1970 field surveys sponsored by the U.S. Forest Service and Bureau of Land Management have greatly expanded the inventory of known cultural properties in the Sierra Nevada. These surveys typically have been larger, better designed, and more intensive than their predecessors, and they have identified backcountry sites as well as those along major streams. Since the surveyed lands often transect several topographic and life zones, information has been gained about the distribution of sites in diverse elevation bands and biotic settings. Consequently, much has been learned about past settlement systems, not merely the whereabouts of large village sites. Current records of approximately 7000 sites in the Sierra will provide a basis for future computer-assisted studies of settlement patterns and their relationships to both environmental and cultural variables.

Survey and excavation data permit the definition of three cultural subregions within the Sierra Nevada. The northern part of the range is distinguished by extensive use of basalt, chert, and other nonobsidian lithics; projectile points of Martis, Hawver, and Gunther Barbed types; geometric and representational petroglyphs; subsistence based upon gathering (especially acorns), hunting, and fishing; and stylistic traits suggesting approximately equal influences from the Central Valley and Great Basin.

The southern Sierra features obsidian as the predominant material for flaked-stone tools; Pinto and Sierra Concave-Base points; polychrome, often abstract pictographs, steatite vessels and disk beads; Brown Ware pottery; subsistence emphasis on gathering (piñon nuts as well as acorns) and hunting, but relatively little fishing; and strong connections with desert and San Joaquin Valley cultures.

As one might expect, the central Sierra shared both northern and southern elements: petroglyphs and pictographs, significant use of obsidian and local lithics, steatite artifacts, and some Brown Ware pottery. Distinctive traits include certain forms of projectile points and stone pipes, cave burials (before ca. A.D. 500), a calcite–alabaster industry, and stronger cultural relationships with the Central Valley than with the Great Basin.

This subregional analysis must not obscure the basic unity of archaeological manifestations in the Sierra Nevada. Thoughout the entire range one finds evidence of similar land-use and settlement patterns, architecture, technology (witness the ubiquitous bedrock mortars), subsistence activities, seasonal population shifts to high-elevation camps, and enterprising east–west trade. Also, within any subregion, differences occur between (1) low-elevation base camp and village sites with numerous bedrock mortars, middens, cemeteries, and architectural remains—including community houses at larger sites—and (2) high-elevation seasonal camps and workshop sites with lithic reduction debris, few bedrock mortars, traces of small dwellings, and relatively little midden. Hence, archaeological manifestations in the Sierra vary not only according to age and culture, but as well by subregion, function, elevation, and season of use.

Turning now to chronology, it is not surprising that the preshistoric record is best known in the places where excavations have been most numerous: Lake Oroville, the Tahoe Reach of the Truckee River, New Melones Reservoir, Yosemite National Park, Buchanan Reservoir, and the upper Kern River watershed (Table 7.2). Still, much remains to be learned, especially with regard to explaining major cultural developments and reconstructing the early to mid-Holocene prehistory of the Sierra. This region probably was visited as early as 8000 to 9000 B.C. by peoples affiliated with the Farmington Complex and the Western Pluvial Lakes Tradition (see Chapters 2 and 3). Intensive settlement, however, seems to have occurred later. Occupation of the mountains is evidenced at circa 6000 B.C. near Lake Tahoe, 3000 B.C. at Balsam Meadow, 3200 B.C. near Wishon Reservoir, and 4000 B.C. (Lamont Phase) in the far southern high Sierra. Further confirmation of early high-elevation encampments and traffic across the Sierran Divide is shown by *Olivella* shell beads at Leonard Rockshelter, Nevada, in levels dated at circa 6600 B.C. (Heizer 1978:691).

At lower elevations on the Sierran west slope, land-use or settlement before 4000 B.C. is indicated by a Parman type projectile point at Cal-S-347, a flaked-stone crescent and ancient tools of basalt at Cal-S-276, and a distinctive biface and scraper industry in middle Holocene clay deposits at Cal-S-286—all within the foothills along the Stanislaus River. More widespread and intensive settlement of the west slope, recognized by old midden deposits, began at circa 1400 B.C. at Pla-101 on the Feather River, at 1500 B.C. at Cal-S-286 in the Stanislaus River drainage, and at circa 800 B.C. at Mad-117 on the Chowchilla River. The apparent recency of intensive occupation in the foothills is remarkable in light of the many older sites in adjacent regions.

Widespread settlement of the western Sierra may have been delayed because of low population pressures in surrounding areas and the relatively low resource potential of the foothills before acorns were used extensively. Unlike the rich marshlands, plains, and riparian woodlands of the Central Valley with their abundant vegetal foods and myriad waterfowl, salmon, elk, and pronghorn, the Sierra offered less exploitable biomass. Before the specialized acorn-related technology was available to utilize fully the oak savanna belt, early Indians probably viewed the inducements of the Valley as far more attractive than those of the Sierra. Nonetheless, certain ideal Sierran localities were occupied long before 1500 B.C., and people traversing the range or visiting it to quarry lithic materials surely camped in the mountains.

The eastern scarp and high country possibly were the first Sierran zones to be inhabited, albeit seasonably, 11,000–8000 years ago. From earliest times, the eastern Sierra witnessed a succession of Great Basin cultures whose influence throughout the range is marked by the use of obsidian, projectile points of the Pinto, Elko, Humboldt, Rose Spring–Eastgate, Desert Side-notched, and Cottonwood types, and, in late prehistory, distinctive rock art and Brown Ware pottery.

The initial widespread settlement of the Sierran west slope apparently coincided with the end of a long interval of prevailing warm–dry climate and the onset of more favorable cool–moist conditions about 3500 to 3000 years ago. Subsequently, the emergence of similar economic and settlement patterns can be traced in the west slope valleys for which data are available. These developments may be summarized as follows:

1. The first, and ultimately the largest, villages were situated near the rivers and their main tributaries at low elevations (usually below ≈1250 m). The intensive occupation of the Sierra after circa 1500–1000 B.C. is seen archaeologically in the Mesilla, Late Martis, Sierra, Crane Flat, Chowchilla, and Canebrake phases (see Table 7.2).

2. The highest population densities were found near ecotones (i.e., at the juncture of biotic communities) and in other settings permitting optimal access to diverse resource areas. Aggregations of people along foothill river courses were larger than those along higher reaches of the same streams. Few sites above snow line were inhabited year-round, and only warm-season camps and activity stations were to be found in the high Sierra.

3. Cultural innovation and social change between circa 1000 B.C. and A.D. 500 included expansion of trade, increasing use of acorns, and, as populations grew, the establishment of major villages in the Upper Sonoran and Transition zones. Mortuary patterns reflect the evolution of complex, nonegalitarian societies, at least in the central Sierra, by 500 B.C. or earlier.

4. Between circa A.D. 500 and 1400 many lower foothill villages were occupied only sparsely or intermittently; new settlements were located higher in the mountains. Trade with peoples to the west was disrupted; the bow and arrow were introduced; exotic artifacts (e.g., shell beads and ornaments) and other status markers seldom were buried with the dead; and violence was commonplace. These developments may reflect economic stress and social instability resulting from a deterioration of the effective enviornment brought about by climatic shifts (see Moratto *et al.* 1978). Archaeologically, this disquieting episode is recorded as the Sweetwater, Early Kings Beach, Redbud, Tamarack, Raymond, and Sawtooth phases (Table 7.2).

5. New levels of population growth and social integration were achieved after circa A.D. 1400–1500. This resulted in part from movements into the Sierra of new populations, notably the Miwok (Horseshoe Bend, Mariposa, and Madera phases) and Mono (Slick Rock, Vermilion). By circa A.D. 1600–1700, these and the older Sierran groups—the Washo (Kings Beach Phase), Maidu (Oroville), Nisenan (Pla-101A), Yokuts (Greasy Creek, Hidden), and Tübatulabal (Chimney Phase)—claimed the territories that would be identified with them ethnographically (Table 7.2 and Figure 11.1). By historic times all habitable localities were densely occupied, with large villages of perhaps 30 to 150 residents situated near the main streams and smaller hamlets in the backcountry. Principal villages functioned as the political, economic, and ceremonial centers of extended communities, and western Sierran cultures were reintegrated into the social and exchange networks of central California—factors that surely enhanced both demographic and economic stability. Late prehistoric population growth and cultural elaboration coincided with the onset of "improved" environmental conditions (see Moratto *et al.* 1978).

6. Rapid changes swept the protohistoric cultures. First, as a result of Ibero-American incursions and pressures, Indians from western California sought refuge in the Sierra during the half century after A.D. 1770. During this interval of unrest, the epidemic of 1833 devastated foothill Indians and left many of their villages deserted forever. Then, as coastal missions were being secularized in the 1830s, former neophytes of various ethnic origins and degrees of acculturation were repatriated in the Sierra Nevada. Next, the Gold Rush of circa 1848–1860 severely disrupted settlements in the Mother Lode country and often triggered the relocation of entire villages, either to aid or to avoid the miners. Finally, the establishment of foothill reservations during the 1850s further coalesced Indian groups, reduced their numbers, and accelerated cultural and social changes. All of this has resulted in an archaeological record of singular complexity in the Sierra Nevada.

# 8. The Desert Region

Claude N. Warren

The Indians who live in the little oases where fresh water is found
have a well-defined tradition of a great flood which once covered all
of this territory from the far south well up the slopes of the San
Jacinto and San Bernardino Mountains. They have no idea as to the
exact time of this flood, and the gray-haired old patriarchs relate that
their fathers told them of a time when they used to go into the valley
that is now a dry, sandy waste and catch an abundance of fish. But
there came a time when the waters receded and left millions of fish
on the beach, whereupon the wild animals came down from the
mountains to feast themselves, and were in such numbers that the
Indians were forced to flee for their lives.

*Anonymous (1891:2)*

Red Rock Canyon, Kern County. (Photograph by Mary Hill; courtesy of Mary Hill.)

## Environment

The deserts of southeastern California lie to the east of the Sierra Nevada, Transverse, and Peninsular ranges (Figure 1.2). These ranges block the eastward movement of the moist Pacific air mass, creating the characteristic arid conditions of the deserts. The Mojave Desert lies at the heart of this region, between the Great Basin deserts on the north and the Colorado Desert on the south. The desert area in general is characterized by north–south-trending mountain ranges, several of which reach over 2135 m and a few exceed an elevation of 3000 m. Wide, arid expanses extend across the low enclosed valleys, interrupted by an occasional spring, intermittent stream, or dry lakebed (playa) that marks the internal drainage pattern of these basins. Four major rivers are found in the deserts of California. The Colorado River, forming the southeast border of the California deserts, is the largest and the only one that flows into the ocean. It has deposited vast amounts of silt along its banks, which form rich soils that have been attractive to agricultural peoples. The river valley itself is an elongate oasis along the eastern border of the region, rich in plant and animal resources.

The Mojave and Amargosa rivers (Figures 8.1 and 8.7) are examples of "upside-down rivers" in which the water flows beneath the loose sand and gravel of the riverbed with water forced to the surface, at a few locations, by shallow bedrock. At times of heavy runoff, the Mojave and Amargosa rivers may flood, carrying respectable quantities of water and debris into desert playas. The Amargosa flows south, from higher elevations in Nevada, to the south end of Death Valley where it turns north to dump its water on the playas of that valley. The Mojave River originates in the San Bernardino Mountains and sinks at East Cronise Playa and/or Soda and Silver playas where a shallow lake may form after heavy rains. Neither the Amargosa nor the Mojave River flows in its lower elevations except at times of heavy runoff. Like many smaller streams flowing from the higher mountains, they disappear beneath the desert. However, at various times in the past, these rivers, especially the Mojave, have formed lakes at the present dry sinks.

**Figure 8.1** Archaeological sites of southeastern California. (Map by Allan Childers and Thad Van Bueren).

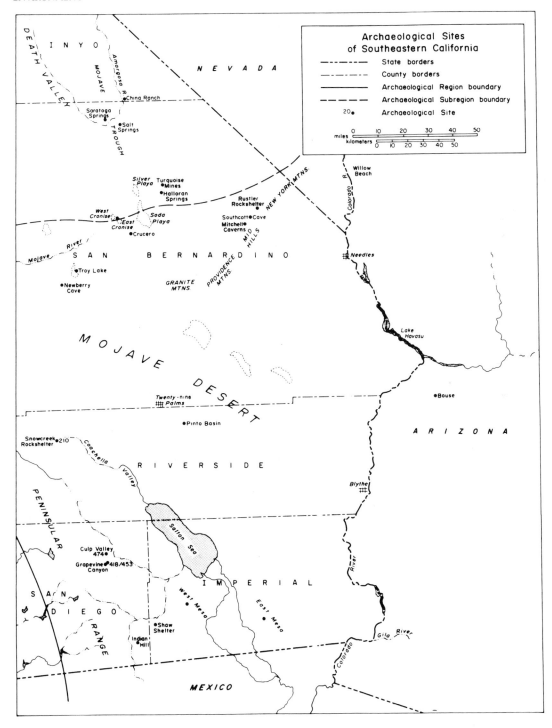

Archaeological Sites
of Southeastern California

| | |
|---|---|
| – – – – – – – – | State borders |
| – · – · – · – | County borders |
| ——————— | Archaeological Region boundary |
| – – – – – – – | Archaeological Subregion boundary |
| 20● | Archaeological Site |

The Owens River (Figures 7.2 and 8.1), which derives its water from the Sierra Nevada snowpack, flows year-round, but sinks into the desert at the south end of Owens Valley, where it formed Owens Lake. The Owens Valley is considerably more moist than the valleys of the Amargosa or Mojave rivers and supports more abundant plant and animal resources, which have influenced human demography.

The low central basin of the Colorado Desert, much of which lies below sea level, holds the Salton Sea. This basin has filled periodically in the past when the Colorado River shifted its course near its mouth and flowed north into the basin instead of south into the Gulf of California. When this occurred, a large freshwater lake was formed that supports rich plant and animal resources, which attracted man to its margins. When the Colorado again changed its course and flowed into the Gulf of California, the lake evaporated forming a salt sea and then a barren playa.

The California deserts are arid, with the average annual rainfall varying with elevation and other factors. Throughout much of the area rainfall is as sparse as 5 cm/year and only at few locations does it exceed 20 or 25 cm. However, some locations receive less than 2.5 cm of rain annually and others, at high elevations, receive more than 25 cm of precipitation a year.

The marked changes in elevation between the valley floors and the mountains also reflect changes in temperature. Through most of the low valleys and the Colorado Desert, summer temperatures hover between about 100 and 118°F in the shade. The highest recorded shade temperature is 134° from Death Valley. In the mountains above 1500 m, summer temperatures are closer to 90° F and even lower at the more northern latitudes. The winters are more variable and windier than the summers. Freezing temperatures (18–22° F) are recorded yearly in the higher Mojave Desert, whereas in the Colorado Desert freezing temperatures are far less frequent. At the northern latitudes, in the Great Basin desert, the winters are more like those of the central Great Basin, with freezing weather and moderate snowfall.

The vegetation of the California deserts reflects the arid environment, and the variations in rainfall and temperature result in regional differences in vegetation and rather distinctive plant communities. The creosote bush is the dominant plant type throughout the Colorado and Mojave deserts and forms uniformly monotonous cover over vast areas of mountain slopes and valleys. In desert valleys the creosote bush community surrounds riparian plant communities located where water is locally abundant. The riparian community includes a number of plants that were economically important to the Indians, especially mesquite, which sometimes occurs as large groves. Also found at low elevations, but more widely spread, was the saltbush community, which includes many edible seed plants.

At higher elevations the creosote bush community gives way to the black bush community, which includes yuccas and agaves, both important food plants. The black bush community is in turn replaced at still higher elevations by the piñon–juniper community. Piñon pine was an important aboriginal food source, but is found only in the higher mountain ranges of the eastern and northern Mojave and in the Sierra Nevada, Transverse, and Peninsular ranges on the western margin of the desert.

Plant communities localized around springs, marshes, and streambeds produce tules, cattail, and various grasses. In the washes of the Colorado Desert are found desert ironwood and palo verde—not found in the Mojave Desert—along with several other varieties of small trees and shrubs common to both deserts. In the Great Basin to the north, the plant communities change: yucca and mesquite are no longer found, sagebrush replaces black bush and to a large extent creosote bush, grasses increase, and piñon becomes more common on the mountain slopes.

Throughout the California deserts, large game animals are not plentiful and in most places are quite rare. The major large game animals hunted by Indians were most often mountain sheep, deer, and pronghorn. Jackrabbits and desert cottontail were commonly taken, as were wood rat and various small rodents, lizards, and desert tortoise.

Variations in elevation, combined with corresponding variations in temperature and rainfall, not only produce a varied distribution of plants, but also cause plants at higher elevations to mature later in the summer than plants at low elevations. Most aboriginal groups of the California deserts adapted to the harsh environment by developing a complex and detailed knowledge of the nature of the desert plants and animals and moved seasonally to take advantage of the plant resources as they ripened. This knowledge of desert resources made it possible for aboriginal peoples to live successfully over a span of millennia in some of California's harshest environments.

## Native Peoples of the California Deserts

Within the area of the California deserts were no fewer than 12 distinct Indian cultural groups. These represented two major linguistic divisions: the Yuman language family of the Hokan stock and the Numic and Takic subfamilies of the Uto–Aztecan family (see Chapter 11). To the north the Mono Lake and Owens Valley Paiute, Panamint (Koso), Kawaiisu, Kitanemuk, Serrano, Cahuilla, and Chemehuevi all spoke Uto–Aztecan languages; to the south and along the Colorado River the Mojave, Maricopa or Halchidoma, Quechan or Yuma, and Kamia spoke Yuman languages (Figure 11.1).

The Mojave, Halchidoma, and Quechan were river agriculturalists who were later joined by the Kamia from the Colorado Desert during historic times. The Chemehuevi also moved into the Colorado River Valley and took up agricultural practices, displacing the Halchidoma during the early historic period. Nonagricultural hunter–gatherers included all the remaining groups and some Chemehuevi. The southernmost of the hunter–gatherers—Cahuilla, Serrano, and Kitanemuk—developed sociopolitical and socioeconomic systems that set them apart from the other speakers of Uto–Aztecan languages in the Mojave Desert and apparently linked them with the coastal peoples of California as well as the Colorado River groups.

The Mono Lake Paiute, Owens Valley Paiute, Panamint, Kawaiisu, and Chemehuevi, throughout most of their history, were aligned more closely with Great Basin groups, both linguistically and culturally, than with the Kitanemuk, Serrano, or Cahuilla. They also spoke Numic languages, a subdivision of Uto–Aztecan found throughout the Great Basin, and shared the Great Basin pattern of nonsedentary small bands, with a generalized exploitive economy involving seasonal movement to take advantage of plant resources as they ripened. This movement over relatively great distances and the paucity of abundant reliable resources at a given location seem to have dictated a flexible social organization based on the nuclear family. Kinship ties often united several families into a small band for the annual round. Several such bands might come together for a particular harvest of wild seeds or a rabbit drive. Nuclear groups might also come together in winter, building shelters to form a small village. After such congregations, however, the nuclear groups again went their own ways resuming the hunting and gathering pattern.

> The outstanding sociopolitical units, consequently, were the biological family and the small winter village, consisting of a loose aggregate of families. . . .The headman. . .was little more than family leader or village advisor. Interfamily and intervillage alliances for cooperative enterprises were of limited scope and brief duration, occurring only at communal hunts or festivals, each of which has a special director. Because, however, of the erratic occurrence of wild seeds and the frequent variation in terrain covered, alliance did not always bring together the same families or village members. (Steward 1938:257)

An exception to this pattern are the Owens Valley Paiute, who were subdivided into true composite land-owning bands.

> Each village or cluster of villages was a band whose unity and independence was expressed in the habitual cooperation of all members in its own communal antelope, rabbit, and deer drives, in local festivals and mourning ceremonies, in the ownership of more or less exactly defined seed territories (and from Big Pine to Bishop, at least, of hunting territories), including irrigated areas, and in the possession of a chief, a common name, and a community sweat house . . .

> The functional basis of band organization, then, was the habitual cooperation of its members in joint enterprises and its objective expression was the common name, chieftainship, and ownership of territory. (Steward 1938:50–51)

Owens Valley is itself an exception in the California deserts. Over 160 km long, but less than 30 km wide, it lies at about 1200 m with high mountains rising to over 3000 m on both the east and west. Streams flow into the valley from the Sierra Nevada at narrow intervals and provide ample water. Deer and mountain sheep could be taken in the mountains, various seeds in the foothills, and seeds, roots, antelope, and rabbits in the valley. This varied environment provided the villages located in the valley with all essential food resources within 30 km of the village. Consequently, the villages were permanent and the populations were sedentary.

The Cahuilla, Serrano, and Kitanemuk are culturally more similar to southern coastal groups than are other desert peoples. They, like some of their neighbors on the southern California coast, spoke Takic languages. These three cultural groups appear to have had similar settlement patterns, although ethnographic data on this point are lacking for the Kitanemuk. The territories of all three groups extend from low or moderately low desert to mountains of the Peninsular and/or Transverse ranges. Among the Cahuilla and the Serrano, villages at higher elevation were situated in well-watered canyons or on fans near streams and springs. The lower elevation villages were located near springs or, in the case of the Cahuilla, at the lower end of alluvial fans near large clumps of mesquite where the high-water table enabled the Cahuilla to dig shallow wells. These villages were apparently permanent and, among the Cahuilla, the occupants had rights to land that included several life zones. In describing these villages, Bean states:

> Specific camp sites in gathering areas were claimed by lineages and were visited periodically by the same families, so the settlement situation of an acorn grove or pinyon forest tended to parallel that of the village, with each family being separated from other families to a greater or lesser extent. (1972:74)
>
> Collecting food plants required small groups of people to move throughout the area periodically on overnight trips, whereas game hunting required groups of men to go on trips which often lasted several days. The gathering of plant foods, such as pinyon, acorn, and mesquite, required as many as half the village population moving to the area to camp for weeks at a time. (1972:75)

The resources of the Cahuilla territory were unevenly distributed (e.g. piñon at high elevation and mesquite at low elevation). The Cahuilla compensated for this uneven distribution by a well-developed system of exchange. Bean and Saubel (1963:65) describe these conditions:

> The balance of food sources was further maintained by the Cahuilla through regular trade patterns with other Cahuilla and the neighboring Serrano, Luiseño and

Diegueño groups. This apparently developed from the differing food potentialities within each area. The desert Cahuilla, for instance, had less acorn than the mountain oriented groups; these other groups had less mesquite, and so it was customary for different groups to trade their surplus foods for other foods or for materials needed for tools, containers, or building.

This redistribution of resources provided a more reliable economy and undoubtedly contributed to the conditions that made permanent villages possible.

Although details are lacking for the Serrano subsistence patterns, they appear to have been similar to those of the Cahuilla; "Desert groups annually traveled into the foothills to collect nuts of various kinds and to trade with their kindred desert fruits and seeds for products not available in the desert" (Bean and Smith 1978:571).

The permanent villages and the subsistence patterns of the Cahuilla, Serrano, and presumably the Kitanemuk were supported by, or resulted in, a form of sociopolitical organization different from that of the Numic groups to the north. The Serrano were organized into exogamous clans, which in turn were affiliated with one of two exogamous moieties. "Each clan was the largest autonomous political and landholding unit with the core being the patrilineage and that included. . .all males recognizing descent from a common male ancestor plus descendants and wives of these males" (Bean and Smith 1978:572). All bonds among clans were "strictly ceremonial in nature with clans aligning themselves with one another along lines of economic, marital, or ceremonial reciprocity" (1978:572).

The Cahuilla were also organized into clans and exogamous moieties, with the clans being the largest autonomous political unit. Clans were composed of 3 to 10 lineages, which were dialectally different from those of other clans, shared a common name, claimed a common genitor, and recognized one lineage as original. Each lineage within the clan cooperated in defense, communal subsistence activities, and rituals. Each lineage owned a village site and specific resource areas, but most of the clan territory was open to all Cahuilla (Bean 1978:580).

There are no comparable data available for the Kitanemuk, although, as Blackburn and Bean (1978:567) note, "the close similarities between Kitanemuk and Cahuilla kinship terminologies suggest the presence of some form of the patrilineage system found elsewhere in southern California." Moieties are reported as absent among the Kitanemuk, and no mention is made of clans; however, social ranking and prestige systems were well developed and each village had an administrative elite including a chief and ceremonial manager similar to those reported for the Cahuilla and Serrano (Blackburn and Bean 1978).

The Mojave, Halchidoma, and Quechan of the Colorado River were Yuman groups who practiced agriculture as well as hunting and collecting. The typical Colorado River settlement was a scattering of houses up and down the riverbank rather than a centralized village. Houses were of two kinds: semi-subterranean winter houses made of cottonwood log frames and arrow-weed wattling covered with earth, and flat-topped ramadas that provided shade in the summer. Agricultural fields were near these permanent villages.

Colorado River peoples relied on agriculture for more than 50% of their subsistence. They supplemented their diet by collecting wild plants, fishing, and hunting. When crops failed, they gathered desert food plants as far as 5–10 km inland, in addition to wild crops along the river. Fishing was less important than collecting wild plants; hunting was relegated to a minor role in the economy (Knack 1981).

The Mojave had patrilineal clans; residence was patrilocal. The only office approaching political authority was the *Kohota*. A single *Kohota* lived in each district and acquired his position through skills, wisdom, ability, character, and validation of power dreams. In addition to the *Kohota*, in each community there were men recognized as leaders because of their wisdom and abilities. These offices do not describe the Mojave sociopolitical condition, however; as Kroeber (1925:727) states:

> They think in terms of themselves as a national entity. . . .They think also of their land as a country, and of its numberless places. . . .The man stands in relation to the group as a whole, and this group owns a certain tract rich in associations; but the village does not enter into the scheme. In fact, the Mojave were the opposite of clannish in their inclinations. Their settlements were small, scattering, and perhaps often occupied only for short times; the people all mixed freely with one another.

The Quechan, like the Mojave, had clans and a strong tribal identity. The Quechan identity was represented in the *Kwoxot*, or chief. There was normally only one *Kwoxot* in the tribe at a given time, and he served as economic, political, and religious leader. The Quechan and Mojave also shared many religious beliefs regarding the power of dreams, and they shared propensities toward a military spirit and military action in which they often united against the Halchidoma and western Arizona tribes (Knack 1981). "Tribes hundreds of miles away were attacked and raided. Visits carried parties of Mojave as far as the Chumash and Yokuts. Sheer curiosity was their main motive; for the Mojave were little interested in trade" (Kroeber 1925:727).

The Colorado River tribes were agricultural, with a material culture more complex than that of neighboring desert peoples. They were organized militarily and traveled great distances to do battle, to visit, and to trade. These peoples, no doubt, influenced their neighbors in the California deserts by introducing new items and ideas. Much of the late prehistory of the California deserts can be interpreted in light of these influences.

## Early Archaeology of the California Deserts

The prehistoric remains of the California deserts were brought to the attention of the general public in March 1898 when Gustav Eisen published a series of articles in the *San Francisco Call* describing the aboriginal turquoise mines and petroglyphs near Halloran Springs in the central Mojave Desert (Figure 8.1). For the next 20 years, only casual observations of prehistoric remains, most often petroglyphs, were described by explorers, military men, and travelers (C. King 1976; Wallace 1977a). It was not until 1926 that M. J. Rogers, after reading Eisen's reports and the early mining documents dealing with the history of the turquoise mines, made his first field trip to the Mojave Sink. He returned again in 1928 with four assistants for a more thorough survey. Archaeology in the California deserts was initiated with Rogers' *Report of an archaeological reconnaissance in the Mohave Sink region* (1929b).

In this report, Rogers was concerned primarily with the turquoise mines, which he attributed to Puebloan peoples. He also reported the presence of sites in the Cronise Basin and at the south end of Soda Playa that he identified as Puebloan, concluding that "there is no doubt that the Mohave Sink region had a scattered but permanent Puebloan population" (Rogers 1929b:12).

In addition to "Puebloan" sites, Rogers identified "Mohave" (Lower Colorado River) pottery and cremations at other sites. On these "Mohave" sites, a variety of shell beads (indicating contact with the California coast) was recovered, as was a piece of "filigree work ground from a *Glycymeris multicostata* shell (and). . .other carved fragments of this kind of work. . .in limited numbers, e.g., such as bracelets" (1929b:12). Rogers's first work in the Mojave Desert posed problems that were to form major research questions in years ahead.

Rogers' interest in Pueblo connections was influenced by M. R. Harrington's research in the Mojave Desert of southern Nevada less than 240 km to the east (Harrington 1933; Harrington and Simpson 1961; Shutler 1961). Between 1924 and 1933, Harrington not only had excavated the Puebloan site at Lost City, but also had extended his research to other sites on the Muddy River, the Tule Springs site, and Gypsum Cave. Harrington's identification of Basketmaker II through Pueblo II remains in the Muddy River Valley enabled Rogers to argue that Puebloan influence extended as far west as the Cronise Basin as well.

Elizabeth and William Campbell also began fieldwork in the 1920s, first in the area around Twenty-Nine Palms (Figure 8.1) but later throughout much of the Mojave and Colorado deserts. Elizabeth Campbell published *An archaeological survey of the Twenty-Nine Palms region* (1931), in which she described whole pottery vessels and other artifacts that were

**TABLE 8.1**

Elizabeth Campbell's Cultural Sequence for the California Desert (1936)

| Cultural remains | Environment of site locations |
|---|---|
| Sites with pottery and arrow points | Near present-day water sources |
| Sites with arrow points but no pottery | Near present-day water sources |
| Big Blade camps | Near present-day water holes and shores of sinks where water may still be found for short periods of time |
| Pinto and Silver Lake cultures | High terraces back from shore of present-day sinks or along the extinct rivers |

<sup>a</sup>From E. Campbell (1936).

to show affinities to the Lower Colorado River area and much of the Colorado Desert.

In 1936 Elizabeth Campbell published an article detailing a sophisticated environmental approach to the archaeological problems that was not to be appreciated for several decades (Campbell 1936; Warren 1970). In this paper she also presented the barest outline of a cultural sequence (Table 8.1). The terminology for her cultural sequence was never used again, except for the term *Pinto*, and it is difficult to correlate her cultural units with the sequences developed later by other archaeologists. The Pinto Basin report (Campbell and Campbell 1935) and the Lake Mojave Symposium (Campbell *et al.* 1937) clarified the earliest unit of her sequence. Campbell and others (1935, 1937) claimed a late Pleistocene–early Holocene date for the Lake Mojave and Pinto Basin material and identified the characteristic artifacts of each. Problems relating to the latter part of the sequence remained unexamined, as the Campbells turned their attention to Early Man studies.

The Pinto Basin Culture described by Campbell and Campbell (1935) was based on a series of sites associated with an ancient dry stream channel in the Pinto Basin (Figure 8.1) at the eastern end of Joshua Tree National Monument. Pinto points of several varieties (Figure 8.2 and 8.3), leaf-shaped points, drills, leaf-shaped knives, numerous heavy keeled scrapers, retouched flakes, choppers, hammerstones, manos, millingstones, and two pestles were collected from the surface of sites scattered along both sides of the channel for a little over 8 km. Since all artifacts were recovered from the surface, there is a possibility that later occupants of the area also left artifacts on these sites. Campbell and Campbell (1935) identified three oval millingstones, the two pestles, and one projectile point as identical to types found on sites of late occupation, and they eliminated them from the Pinto Basin Complex of tools. With the exception of the oval millingstones and pestles, the only remaining seed-processing tools were small, flat millingstones and manos. The asso-

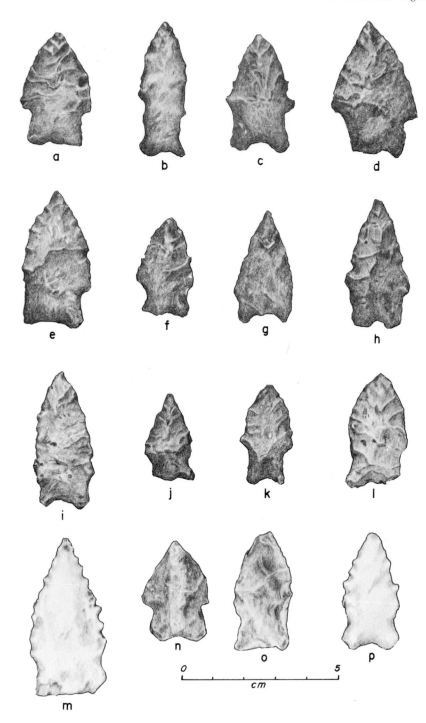

ciation of the Pinto Basin sites with an extinct river suggested to the authors of the Pinto report that they were occupied during a period of greater moisture than is now present. This interpretation has not been seriously questioned, but the date suggested for this moist period has stirred controversy.

While the Campbells were working at Pinto Basin and the Twenty-Nine Palms area, Rogers conducted wide-ranging surveys and limited excavations in the California deserts, publishing the results in 1939. Rogers' *Early lithic industries . . .* (1939) served as the basic cultural sequence for the California deserts for the next several decades, and is still of major importance today. Rogers disagreed with the Campbells' dates for both the Lake Mojave sites and the Pinto Basin Culture. He placed his Playa Industry (the equivalent of the Lake Mojave Complex) between 1200 and 800 B.C. and the Pinto material immediately after 800 B.C. in his Pinto–Gypsum Complex, at least 7000 years later than the Campbells' estimate. This ultraconservative chronology proved to be erroneous, but Rogers' basic sequence of cultural units, often under the guise of different terminologies provided with new dates, still forms the basic sequence of the California deserts.

Severe confusion over terminology makes the discussion of Rogers' sequence difficult. In 1939 Rogers defined three major cultural units that followed the Playa Industry. These were, in chronological order: Pinto–Gypsum, Amargosa I, and Amargosa II. He later subdivided Pinto and Gypsum into two units of the new sequence. In chronological order, they were Amargosa I, Amargosa II, Amargosa III, and Basketmaker III. This new arrangement meant that the new Amargosa III was the equivalent of the old Amargosa I, and the old Amargosa II was the equivalent of the new Basketmaker III (Table 8.2). Unfortunately, Rogers did not provide the rationale for these changes in terminology and failed to define the difference between Pinto and Gypsum. Some archaeologists continue to use his 1939 terminology, whereas others have adopted his later version. In the following discussion the 1939 terminology will be followed.

Rogers (1939:49–55) described his Pinto–Gypsum Complex based on material from 28 sites "within a long narrow strip of country extending north and south throughout the central part of the Mohave Desert" (1939:47). The complex contains a small range of tools including five types of Pinto points and the Gypsum Cave point, leaf-shaped and ovate knives that tend toward plano-convex cross-sections, large horse-hoof shaped pulping planes, drills, choppers, hammerstones, and smooth flat slabs. These slabs are made of "schist or some stone that splits into thin

---

**Figure 8.2** Pinto points from the Pinto Basin site. (After Campbell and Campbell 1935:Plate 13.)

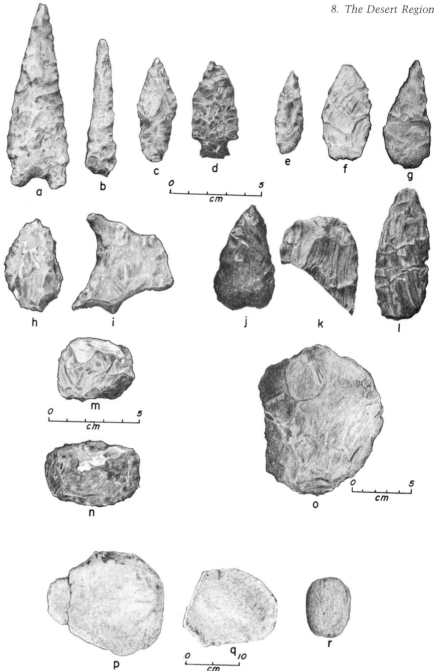

**Figure 8.3** Artifacts from the Pinto Basin site. a–d, miscellaneous point forms; e,f, leaf-shaped points; h,i, retouched flakes; j–l, knives; m,n, keeled scrapers; o, chopper; p,q, millingstones; r, mano. (After Campbell and Campbell 1935:Plates 7–12, 14.)

**TABLE 8.2**

**Concordance of Rogers' 1939 and 1950 Terminologies**

| Rogers 1939 | Rogers 1950 (Haury 1950:193) |
|---|---|
| Amargosa II | Basketmaker III |
| Amargosa I | Amargosa III |
| Gypsum | Amargosa II |
| Pinto | Amargosa I |

slabs" with "one rubbed surface, too smooth to have possessed milling power" (1939:52–53). Flake scrapers and retouched flakes are scarce and bone awls occur rarely (Figure 8.4).

Rogers' inclusion of the Gypsum Cave point in the Pinto–Gypsum Complex was at variance with Harrington's discovery of Gypsum Cave points in association with sloth dung at Gypsum Cave. Rogers' chrono-logical placement proved to be correct in this instance. Heizer and Berger (1970) have dated wooden sticks and a dart shaft that were in apparent association with sloth dung in two separate proveniences in Gypsum Cave. The sticks assayed at 450± 60 B.C. and the dart was dated at 950± 120 B.C.., several thousands of years younger than the sloth dung. The association of the sloth dung and the artifacts was secondary, the dung having been disturbed from its original position and moved into apparent association with the cultural remains.

That Pinto and Gypsum points have different temporal distributions is suggested by a few of the data that Rogers presents (1939:48). He notes that, of his 28 Pinto–Gypsum sites, 11 yielded both Pinto and Gypsum Cave points, whereas 5 yielded only Gypsum Cave points. Presumably, the remaining sites contained only Pinto points. This seriation of sites suggests temporal differences for the occurrence of Pinto and Gypsum Cave points, but with a period in which both types occur together.

The Amargosa Industry is dated by Rogers at A.D. 200–900, immediate-ly following the Pinto–Gypsum Complex, and may be derived from it (Rogers 1939:72–73). This industry, which consists of two phases, has its greatest concentration in the vicinity of the Amargosa River (Figure 8.1) in the north-central Mojave Desert. Phase I sites are often large enough to be considered permanent, though seasonally occupied. The artifact as-semblage is limited to only six categories: large projectile points with straight-based expanding stems and straight shoulders, drills with ex-panded bases for hafting, broad thin triangular knives, a few flake scrapers, incised and circular slate pendants, and fragmentary slate tubes that may be pipe fragments (Figure 8.5).

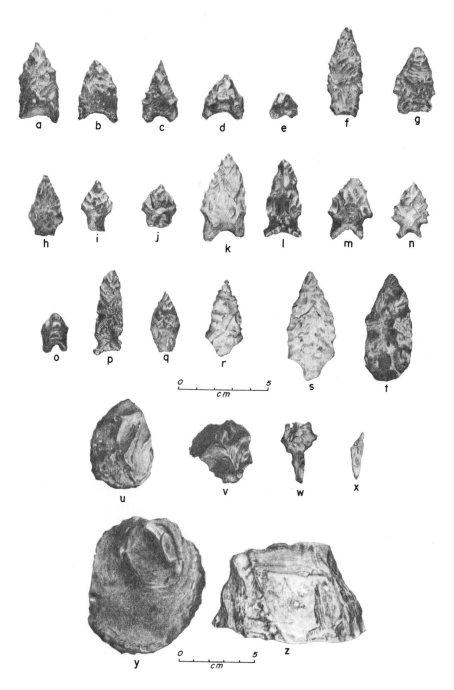

**Figure 8.4** Pinto–Gypsum artifacts. a–e, Pinto points, Type 1; f–j, Pinto points, Type 2; k–o, Pinto points, Type 3; p, Pinto point, Type 4; q, Pinto point, Type 5; r,s, Gypsum Cave points; t, leaf-shaped planoconvex knife; u, ovate scraper; v, biface disk; w, borer; x, bone awl-tip; y, cleaver; z, pulping plane. (After M. J. Rogers 1939: Plates 11–14.)

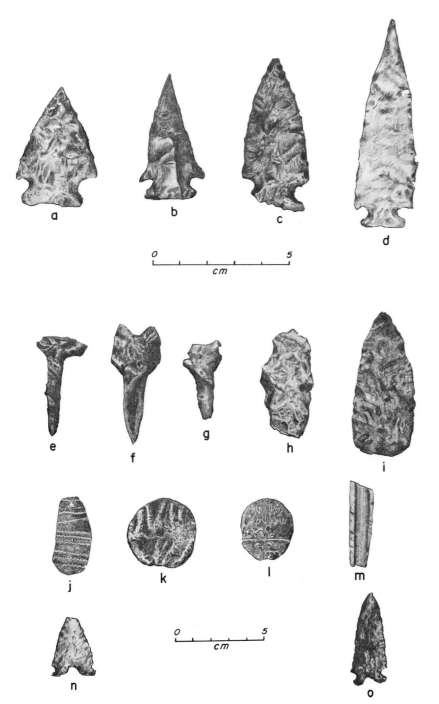

**Figure 8.5** Amargosa artifacts. a,b, Amargosa I dart points; c,d, Amargosa II dart points; e–g, drills; h, side scraper; i, knife; j–l, slate pendants; m, drilled slate tube; n,o, atypical Amargosa points (Elko Eared). (After M. J. Rogers 1939: Plates 16, 17, 20.)

Phase II sites are small and scattered and appear to represent temporary camps left by small, highly mobile bands. There are five categories of artifacts recovered from Phase II sites: dart points similar to those of Phase I but generally longer, arrow points that are stylistically very similar to the dart points but much reduced in size, millingstones and manos, plain Gray Ware pottery, and mauls and picks in sites associated with turquoise mining. The artifact assemblage of the Phase II sites shows close similarities to the Basketmaker III material of southern Nevada (Rogers 1939:61) and clearly represents Anasazi influence in the eastern Mojave.

Although the Amargosa phases are the latest cultural units described by Rogers in his 1939 monograph, he includes a plate illustrating points from the Mojave Desert in which he distinguishes between early and late "Desert Mohave" and between "Desert Mohave" and "Paiute and Shoshoni" (Rogers 1939:Plate 18). In a later paper concerning the cultural sequence of the Lower Colorado, Rogers (1945:173–174) writes: "Extending from the western boundary of San Bernardino County across the desert to the Colorado River and into Mohave County, Arizona, the Amargosa Complex is replaced with a pattern which needs only the addition of native pottery to make it Yuman; an element which it eventually acquired." During the initial stages, this "pattern" is characterized by "the shallow-basined metate, unshaped mano, small round mortar, triangular knife, triangular arrowpoint, and bone awl" (Rogers 1945:174). Pacific Coast shell jewelery and pelican-bone whistles reflect trade with the coast. Houses appear to be circular or oval brush-covered structures with a basal retaining ring of rock.

In time, this nonceramic "pattern" in the central Mojave became modified and enriched "until the aspect it presented eventually and throughout the latter half of its duration was more typically that of the Colorado River" (Rogers 1945:174). Corncobs had been found associated with pottery in house sites, which led Rogers (1945:174) to note that agriculture was apparently introduced along with pottery making and may have been practiced in favorable places. With this discussion, Rogers provides a brief outline of the final cultural units in his sequence. The triangular points of his early Desert Mohave (Figure 8.6) are correlated with the nonceramic Yuman, and the Desert Side-notched points of his late Desert Mohave (Figure 8.6) tally with the ceramic-using Yuman. Rogers' (1939:18, 1945:173–174) discussions of these assemblages never completely clarify the problems of the relationships between the nonceramic and ceramic Yuman or between the Yuman and the Paiute and Shoshone. His work does imply, however, that there is a cultural boundary between the "Yuman" assemblages to the south and the "Paiute and Shoshone" assemblages to the north.

The prehistory of the southern Mojave and Colorado deserts not only

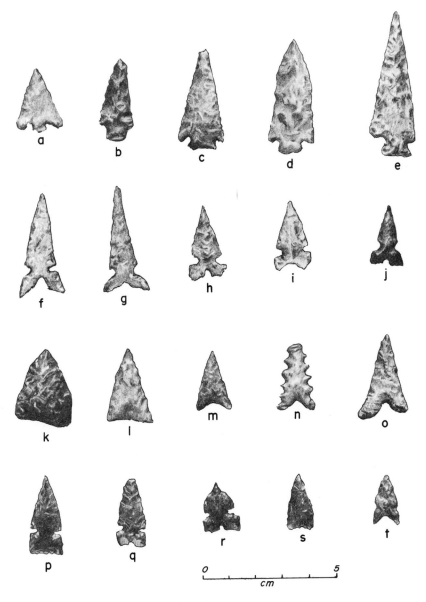

**Figure 8.6** Late projectile points from the Mojave Desert. a–e, "Amargosa II" points; f–j, "Desert Mohave (late)" points; k–o, "Desert Mohave (early)" points; p–t, "Paiute and Shoshonean" points. (After M. J. Rogers 1939: Plate 18.)

apparently exhibits a somewhat different cultural sequence from that of the northern Mojave, but has also been influenced by concepts introduced from the Southwest. Gladwin and Gladwin (1934) proposed a taxonomic system for major cultural divisions in the Southwest that was instrumental in the interpretation of the prehistory of the lower Colorado River Valley and the adjacent California deserts. In this taxonomic system (Table 8.3), the major divisions, on the order of Anasazi, Mogollon, and Hohokam, were termed *roots*, subdivisions of roots were called *stems*, and subdivisions of stems were called *branches*. The Gladwins included a *Yuman Root* to designate the prehistoric culture of western Arizona occupied by Yuman peoples. In 1939 Colton proposed that the term *Patayan* be used in place of *Yuman* to avoid the inference that these prehistoric peoples spoke Yuman languages and were necessarily ancestral to the historic Yuman groups. Later, Colton (1945) defined the Laquish, Cerbat, Coconino, and Prescott branches of the Patayan Root. The Laquish branch was centered near the delta of the Colorado River and the Cerbat branch near Needles, California. Both the Prescott and Coconino branches were located in western Arizona. All these brances were defined loosely, primarily on the basis of similarities in pottery and a few other characteristics (Colton 1945).

In 1945 Rogers entered this discussion, publishing a paper in which he reintroduced the term *Yuman*, apparently as defined by the Gladwins, but he subdivided this cultural unit into three chronologically distinct stages (Table 8.3) rather than into the branches and stems of the Gladwins' taxonomy. Yuman I (A.D. 800–900 to 1050) began with a drift of Yumans across the California deserts to occupy the Colorado River Valley below Black Canyon. The earliest use of ceramics and the development of agriculture took place at this time, but were confined to the area

**TABLE 8.3**

Concordance of Archaeological Sequences in the Lower Colorado River–Colorado Desert Area

|  | *Gladwin and Gladwin (1934)* | *Colton (1945)* | *Rogers (1945)* | *Schroeder (various)* | | *Harner (1958)* | |
| --- | --- | --- | --- | --- | --- | --- | --- |
| Root | Yuman | Patayan | Yuman | Hakataya | | Hakataya? | |
| Stem | None named | None named | None named | Patayan | Laquish | Upland Patayan | Lowland Patayan |
| Branch | None named | Laquish, Cerbat, Coconino, Prescott | None named | Cerbat, Coconino, Prescott | Amacava, La Paz, Palo Verde | None named | None named |

below Blythe, California. Anasazi and Hohokam ceramics are intrusive during this period. Local ceramics included Red and Red-on-Buff pottery types, shouldered jars, use of a red slip or wash, polishing, rim notching, incised decorations, and use of the paddle and anvil technique of manufacture.

The Yuman II (A.D. 1050–1450) development occurred during the time that Lake Cahuilla (Blake Sea) occupied the Salton Sink (Figure 8.1). Lake Cahuilla was a freshwater lake, created when the Colorado River shifted its course near the delta and flowed into the Salton Sink. It converted harsh desert into a large oasis with lush natural resources in the heart of the Colorado Desert. Yuman II occupation included the Salton Basin as well as the Colorado River and spread west along the Mojave River to near Barstow and northward to include the extreme southern portion of Nevada. During Yuman II times, the shouldered jar, rim-notching, and incised decoration disappeared. Stucco finish on pottery, recurved jar rims, and tab handles on scoops were introduced to ceramic manufacture. Cremation of the dead and circular, domed, brush-walled houses appeared for the first time. Pacific Coast shell beads and ornaments appeared along with Gulf Coast shell ornaments, which were present in Yuman I times. Yuman II terminated with the desiccation of Lake Cahuilla (Rogers 1945:190–192).

The area occupied during Yuman III times (A.D. 1450 to the nineteenth century) became more restricted as most of the Colorado Desert was abandoned owing to the desiccation of Lake Cahuilla. Along the Colorado River, the material culture continued with little change: the wattle and daub winter house as well as ramadas were used and semipermanent settlements of houses were scattered through the brush adjacent to the floodplain (Rogers 1945:192–194).

Schroeder (1952, 1957, 1961) conducted a survey of the Lower Colorado River and excavations at Willow Beach and used the resulting data as a basis for reexamining earlier interpretations and presenting his own modifications. Schroeder found that Rogers' diagnostic traits for Yuman I (Red and Red-on-Buff pottery, shouldered jars, use of red slip, and polished surfaces) were more numerous in western Arizona than in California and therefore rejected Yuman I as defined by Rogers. He also dated the beginnings of indigenous pottery at about A.D. 900 on the basis of the association of Pyramid Gray (an early plain, Lower Colorado Buff Ware) with dated Anasazi pottery at Willow Beach. This date was also supported by intrusive Hohokam sherds, dated prior to A.D. 1150, found associated with local pottery on surface sites both downriver from Willow Beach and in western Arizona.

Schroeder also modified Colton's early interpretation by demonstrating that the pottery in the Needles area was Lower Colorado Buff Ware rather than Cerbat Brown, as Colton had claimed, and that the Needles area should be grouped with the river valley farther south. Schroeder (1952) thus divided the region into two major groups, or stems, within a single root. He proposed *Hakataya* as the root name; relegated *Patayan* to the status of a stem, subdivided into the Cerbat, Coconino, and Prescott branches, all located in the uplands of western Arizona; and placed the Lower Colorado River and the Colorado Desert in the Laquish stem, subdivided into the Amacava branch at Needles, the LaPaz branch in the vicinity of Blythe, and the Palo Verde branch occupying the area from south of the Gila River to the Colorado delta (Table 8.3).

Harner (1958) presented another variation in terminology (Table 8.3) and a chronological sequence based on excavations at the Bouse site in western Arizona (Figure 8.1). Harner appears to have accepted the Hakataya as Schroeder defined it, but replaced the *Patayan* and *Laquish* stems with *Upland Patayan* and *Lowland Patayan*, respectively. He then defined three chronological phases of this *Lowland Patayan* in the Lower Colorado River Valley. The main features of this sequence were dated by intrusive Hohokam sherds.

During the Bouse Phase I, dated at A.D. 800–1000, horticulture was supplemented by considerable gathering and fishing, with hunting of minor importance. Settlements were located on bottomland adjacent to the river and near water sources in the desert. Ceramic traits include polished red-slipped pottery; unpolished, thin, white-slipped pottery; red slip over white slip; unslipped buff; and deep globular bowls and jars with slight or no necks. Stonework includes a variety of scrapers and choppers; slab to oval basin millingstones; one- and two-hand manos; rare polished ground-stone ornaments; three-quarter grooved axes possibly of Hohokam origin, rare projectile points; and whole *Olivella* shell beads.

Settlements were similar to those of Bouse I during Bouse Phase II (A.D. 1100–1300), but with a higher frequency in the Colorado Desert, Lake Cahuilla possibly being in existence at this time. Ceramics exhibit a continuation of previous styles with the addition of designs painted in red on unslipped buff or thin white-slipped surfaces. Some designs resemble those of the Gila Butte Red-on-Buff of Hohokam. New vessel forms include jars with vertical or recurved necks, shallow and deep bowls with slightly flaring lips, and trays.

The third phase, Moon Mountain (A.D. 1300–1700), is based largely on surface collections and is considered tentative. Bouse II traits continue, except for neckless globular jars; slipping declines and red painted designs increase; and stucco surface treatment and scoops are introduced. Vessel shapes gradually differentiate into those of historic times. Settlements are the same as in earlier phases but with large-scale occupation of the Lake Cahuilla shores.

The terminology applied to the prehistoric remains of the Lower Colorado River and the Colorado Desert appears complex and confusing; however, a brief summary of the points of agreement will clarify the situation somewhat. Most archaeologists agree that there is a single major cultural unit that extended along the Lower Colorado River and into the adjacent deserts. This major division, or root, has been termed *Yuman, Patayan,* and *Hakataya.* It is also agreed by most archaeologists that the Hakataya (the root name used hereafter in this chapter) was divided into lowland and upland divisions or stems. The upland stem has been called *Patayan* by Schroeder and *Upland Patayan* by Harner, whereas the lowland stem was referred to as *Laquish* by Schroeder and *Lowland Patayan* by Harner. Again, Schroeder's terminology is follwed in this chapter.

Finally, there is considerable agreement in the branches of each stem, although there is a confusion of names (Table 8.3). The Gladwins' taxonomic system was extensively modified by Rogers (1945) and Harner (1958) with the introduction of chronological phases. Each researcher identified three phases, but there is little agreement among them (Table 8.4).

The early archaeology of the California deserts was marked from the beginning by attempts to order the data chronologically. By the late 1950s, chronological sequences had been developed and some regional variation was beginning to emerge. It was becoming increasingly clear that the Colorado Desert was yielding data from only the earliest and latest periods of occupation and virtually nothing from the intervening period. Furthermore, the distribution of Lower Colorado River pottery across the Colorado Desert and into the southern Mojave Desert marked the influence of the Lower Colorado tribes, and it sets the area apart from the northern Mojave during the closing phases of prehistory.

The combination of Rogers' (1939, 1945) two papers was as much of a synthesis of the prehistory of the California deserts as was known in 1950, but the articles contain confusing inconsistencies in terminology and major errors in dates for the earlier cultural units. However, the accomplishments of Rogers and the Campbells are impressive when put in perspective. Rogers and the Campbells conducted virtually no excavations, directing their efforts toward surveying vast areas of the deserts and accumulating data of varying quality and quantity by collecting surface data. The harsh environment and isolation of the California deserts in the

TABLE 8.4

**Concordance of Rogers' (1945) and Harner's (1958) Sequences for Southeastern California and Western Arizona**

| *Rogers (1945)* | *Harner (1958)* |
| --- | --- |
| Yuman III (A.D. 1450–nineteenth century) | Moon Mountain (A.D. 1300–1700) |
| Yuman II (A.D. 1050–1450) | Bouse II (A.D. 1000–1300) |
| Yuman I (A.D. 800–1050) | Bouse I (A.D. 800–1000) |

early decades of the twentieth century placed stringent restriction on their approach, and the archaeological data were more amenable to accumulation through survey and surface collection than in other areas. Sites in the deserts of California often lack depth, but have large quantities of artifacts and other debris scattered across their surfaces. Large, deeply stratified sites are rare, and in the Mojave Desert during the 1920s and 1930s the manpower necessary for excavation was hard to find. Rogers and the Campbells essentially worked alone, although the Campbells did collaborate with Amsden, Antevs, and other geologists and archaeologists.

The wide-ranging surveys gave Rogers and the Campbells a broad perspective of the variation in sites, assemblages, and environmental conditions of the deserts, and they painted the prehistoric picture of past cultures in broad strokes. At the time that Kroeber (1936b) was carefully examining the chronological and typological characteristics of charmstones in the central California area, Elizabeth Campbell (1936) was arranging sites chronologically on the basis of environmental factors associated with the sites. Shortly thereafter, Rogers (1939) published a cultural chronology of the California deserts based on data accumulated without excavation, except for a few scattered test pits.

These early archaeologists' published reports of the California deserts included elements based on speculation and unstated hypothesis, which led later researchers to question their interpretations. Rogers' 1939 chronology was not wholly accepted by later archaeologists, but it became a theoretical model against which later archaeologists tested their own ideas. The numerous taxonomic and chronological schemes that have been proposed by later researchers reflect their doubts about Rogers' work. Nonetheless, Rogers' 1939 sequence has become the baseline from which progress in California desert archaeology is measured.

## Later Archaeology of the California Deserts

### Northeastern Mojave Desert

In 1952 William J. Wallace initiated research in Death Valley (Figure 8.7) that would extend over the next 25 years (Wallace 1955b, 1958, 1977b; Wallace *et al.* 1959; Wallace and Taylor 1955, 1959). Within 6 years he presented a cultural sequence of four complexes and four periods that formed the basic Death Valley sequence (Wallace 1958) and was used by Hunt in *Archaeology of the Death Valley salt pan* (1960). Later, Wallace (1962a) wrote "Prehistoric Cultural Development in the Southern

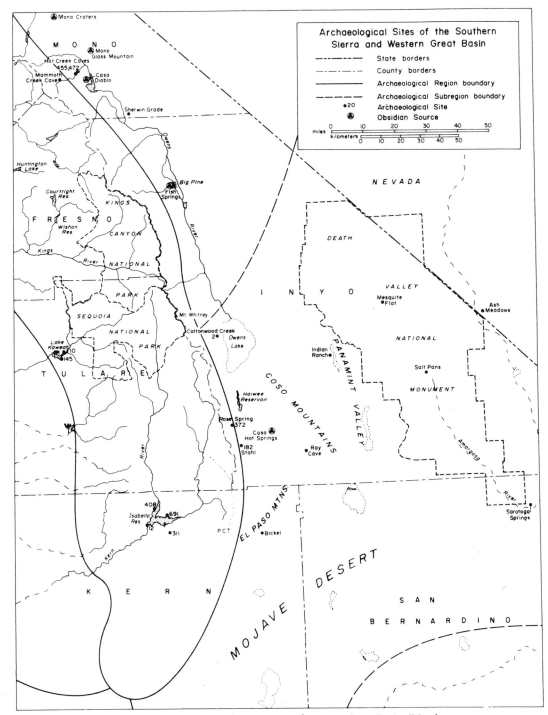

**Figure 8.7** Archaeological sites of the southern Sierra and western Great Basin. (Map by Allan Childers and Thad Van Bueren.)

California Desert," a more general paper that integrated Rogers' 1939 cultural sequence and his Death Valley sequence (Table 8.5). In 1977 Wallace (1977b) modified the earlier sequence as additional data required.

The first period, Death Valley I, began at circa 6000 B.C. and terminated at some unknown date. This period, a time of greater effective moisture, is correlated with the terminal glaciation. Death Valley was occupied during Death Valley I by people using the Lake Mojave Complex, which is now considered an expression of the Western Pluvial Lakes Tradition (see Chapter 3).

Period II and the Mesquite Flat Complex follow the Lake Mojave Complex, but according to Wallace they are separated from it by a long hiatus, for which no cultural remains have been discovered. This hiatus is thought to have corresponded to a long period of diminished rainfall, when the desert is presumed to have been even drier than it is today.

The Mesquite Flat Complex is assigned an initial date of 3000 B.C., the beginning of a time of increased effective moisture, during which a 10-m-deep body of water covered a large area of the valley floor. In 1958 Wallace identified only one phase of occupation during this period, and he (1958:12) noted that "the typical [projectile point] form has both side and basal notching, giving a characteristic 'footed' or 'eared' appearance" and "the typical Mesquite Flat point is like the Pinto form though differing in details."

Rogers (1939:68), however, made note of the same "eared" point type

**TABLE 8.5**

**Concordance of Terminologies for Sequences Proposed by Rogers (1939, 1945), Wallace (1958, 1962a), and Hunt (1960)**

| *California deserts (Rogers 1939, 1945)* | *Death Valley (Wallace 1958; Hunt 1960)* | *California deserts (Wallace 1962a)* |
|---|---|---|
| Late Desert Mohave | Death Valley IV (Desert Shoshone) | Period IV (Prehistoric Yuman and Shoshonean) |
| ------------------------------- | | |
| Early Desert Mohave | | |
| Amargosa II | Death Valley III (Stone mound or Saratoga Springs) | Period III (Amargosa II) |
| ------------------------------- | | ------------------------------- |
| Amargosa I | Late Death Valley II (Mesquite Flats) | (Amargosa I) |
| | ------------------------------- | |
| Pinto–Gypsum | Early Death Valley II | Period II (Pinto Basin) |
| Playa | Death Valley I (Lake Mohave) | Period I (Lake Mohave) |

but reported that these points are "undoubtedly variants of the Amargosa I dart point in which the side-notched point has been augmented with a basal notch. The type has never been encountered off an Amargosa site, and is not a rare type." Today, these eared points would be classed as Elko Eared points.

Hunt (1960:63) recognized early and late phases of the Death Valley II Period. She noted that early and late Death Valley II differ in projectile-point types, with the "Pinto type" typical of early phase and large corner-notched Amargosa types typical of the late phase. However, Hunt illustrated what appear to be Elko Eared types in her Pinto series.

Wallace (1977b:116–122) also recognized the two phases in his later work and placed Pinto points and Gypsum Cave points in the early phase and Elko Eared and Elko Corner-notched in the late phase. Although Wallace corrects the confusion in point identification, he continues to date both the Pinto series and Elko series at 3000 B.C. to A.D. 1. Wallace incorporated Hunt's data in his (1977b) later report on Death Valley and provided a much more complete statement than in the earlier papers. The early phase of Death Valley II, identified by the presence of Pinto and Gypsum Cave points, is known from only four open encampments, a shallow rockshelter, and a rock mound, all located in a restricted area in the central valley. The occupation sites are small and appear to have been temporary camps. There are no remains of structures, and even hearths are absent. In addition to the diagnostic points, large triangular knives with square bases are present, along with a few flake scrapers and an occasional chopper, scraper-planes, and a drill. One site also yielded a fragmentary crescent, an artifact type generally limited to sites of the Western Pluvial Lakes Tradition.

The rock mound was constructed of about 200 boulders and cobbles, over a shallow pit. A series of 11 projectile points, 8 knives, and 3 scrapers was found at the bottom of the pit and in the fill near the surface (Figure 8.8). The structure and placement of artifacts suggest a grave, but no human skeletal parts were recovered.

Hunt reported 24 sites that she identified as late Death Valley II. Nineteen of these are open campsites of varying sizes located in dunes (sometimes adjacent to mesquite), flat gravel-covered benches, and ridgetops. The sites have cleared circles rarely, but no other structural remains were reported. In addition to the campsites, there are two rock-shelters, one rock mound (possible burial), a quarry with hunting blinds nearby located on top of a ridge, and a site containing several hunting blinds, one of which produced late Death Valley II material.

Wallace (1977b:118) claims that late Death Valley II is best represented at five large settlements located along the margins of a dry arm of the lake at Mesquite Flat (Figure 8.7). These sites are on silty ground,

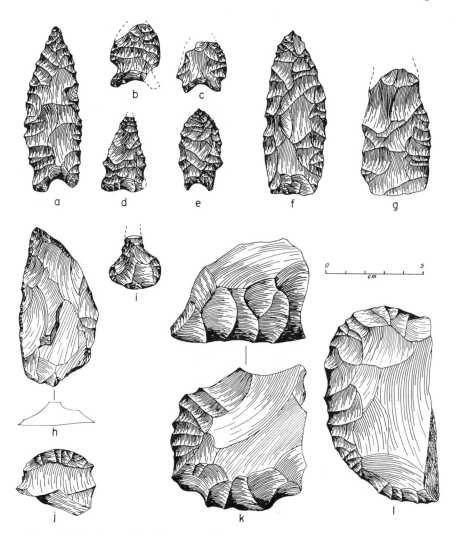

**Figure 8.8** Early Death Valley II artifacts. a–e, Pinto points; f,g, rectangular-based knives; h, flake scraper; i, drill base; j, flake scraper; k,l, scraper planes. (After Hunt 1960:Figures 22–25, 27, and 28.)

away from the sandy dunes, and are windswept and barren. The dimensions of the sites suggest occupation of some duration on a seasonal basis. Wallace interprets these as seasonal gathering sites of the early population where food and water were sufficient, and from which smaller groups split off, seasonally moving to other localities to hunt and forage.

The sites are littered with finished and unfinished stone artifacts, flakes, and chunks of raw materials. Projectile points are numerous and are more finely flaked than earlier points. The most distinctive of the dart points are the Elko Eared and Elko Corner-notched, but leaf-shaped points with rounded or concave bases also occur. There are a surprisingly large number of knives that are triangular in form with a squared base. Hammerstones, choppers, and scraper-planes are well represented, but flake scrapers are relatively rare. Large drills with expanded bases are another distinctive artifact.

The artifact assemblage is much like that of the early phase except for the changes in projectile points and the relative frequency of the various types. However, the late phase also has mortars and pestles. The mortars, made from coarse basalt, are bowl-shaped with rounded or nearly flat bottoms. Pestles are nothing more than elongated cobbles that have been used. The only sign of households are hearths composed of cobbles set in rough circles reported from three sites. Late Mesquite Flat (Death Valley II) sites (Figure 8.9) are found throughout the valley, but are rare in the central valley region. They also occur along the Amargosa River and in the surrounding mountains.

In 1958 Wallace defined Period III on the basis of data from two stone mound burials and distinguished it primarily by the presence of small corner-notched arrow points and shell beads. Even with such limited data he properly saw relationships with the Anasazi sites of southern Nevada. With the later work of Hunt (1960), Hunt and Hunt (1964), and Wallace and Taylor (1959), this period became better defined. Wallace (1977b) eventually designated these cultural remains as the Saratoga Springs Culture, and he identified the small projectile points as Eastgate and Rose Spring types. These were found with small triangular knives, scrapers, drills, hammerstones, choppers, millingstones and manos, pendants of green shist, Pacific Coast shell ornaments including *Olivella* Saucer beads, a single *Olivella* Barrel bead, and a limpet ring with squared ends. Plain, corrugated, and painted Gray Ware sherds of Puebloan origin were recovered on occasion. The only bone artifacts of the Saratoga Springs Culture were recovered from burials and included several spatualate objects made from long bones of large mammals, two bird bone tubes, a piece of mammal bone decorated with incised lines, and a large L-shaped bone tool that perhaps served as a sickle. The dead were placed in graves dug directly into the debris of the open campsites or rockshelters, or in shallow pits covered with boulders away from the camping places. The bodies were buried in a flexed position, usually with a few personal belongings.

The Saratoga Springs Culture (Period III) is dated between A.D. 1 and 1000 (Figure 8.10), which was a time when desiccation had once more set in and the climate had produced an arid environment much like that of today. Despite its aridity, the country appears to have been rather densely occupied. Small groups camped on low rises close to springs or on low terraces of the Amargosa River (Figure 8.7), often in rockfree areas be-

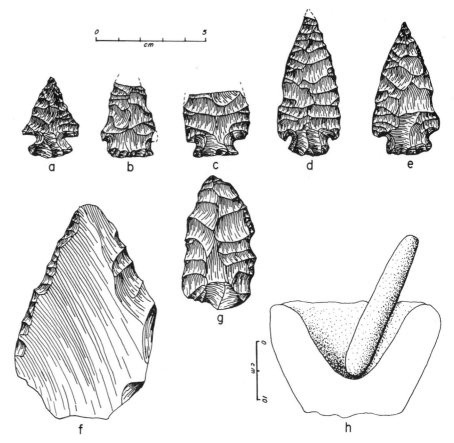

**Figure 8.9** Late Death Valley II artifacts. a–e, large stemmed points (Amargosa or Elko Corner-notched); f, ovate flaked knife; g, rectangular-based knife; h, mortar and pestle. (After Hunt 1960:Figures 26, 30, and 31.)

tween mesquite dunes. At higher elevations they occupied caves and rock overhangs, sometimes partially closing off the entrance or dividing the areas into smaller units with dry masonry walls. Remains of structures in the form of cleared circles and rock rings are found on some sites and the curious rock alignments of small and medium-sized rocks outlining large rectilinear or curvilinear designs may be attributed to the Saratoga Springs people.

Period IV is dated between A.D. 1000 and 1870 (Wallace 1977b:129). The cultural material from this period is attributed to the historic Panamint Shoshone and their ancestors. The artifact assemblage consists of millingstones and manos, mortars (sometimes of mesquite logs) and pestles, knives, small drills with expanding bases, quartzite hammerstones, Cottonwood Triangular, and Desert Side-notched points (Figure 8.11).

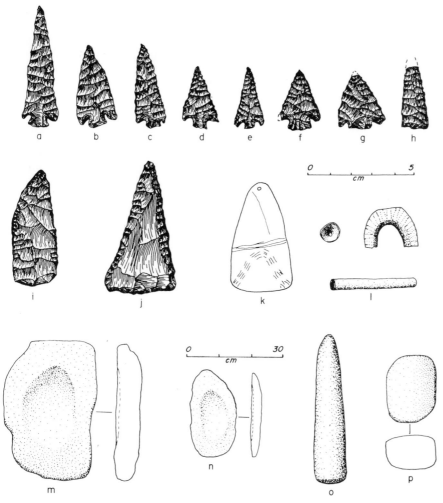

**Figure 8.10** Death Valley III artifacts. a–g, Rose Spring Corner-notched points; h, Cottonwood Triangular point; i, rectangular based knife; j, triangular knife; k, schist pendant; l, shell artifacts; m,n, millingstones; o, pestle; p, mano. (After Hunt 1960:Figures 41–43, 66, 68, and 70.)

Wallace reported only Owens Valley Brown Ware pottery, but Hunt (1960:193) identified Lower Colorado Buff Ware, Tizon Brown Ware, and Southern Paiute Utility Ware, made by the paddle and anvil technique, and Southern Paiute Utility Ware, Shoshoni Ware, and Owens Valley Brown Ware, made by coil and scraping, from the dunes along the edge of the central valley. Wallace (1977b:132) also reported oval and disk-shaped *Olivella* shell beads, whole shells with spires removed, and glass beads. Also present are perforated stone pendants and pieces of schist decorated

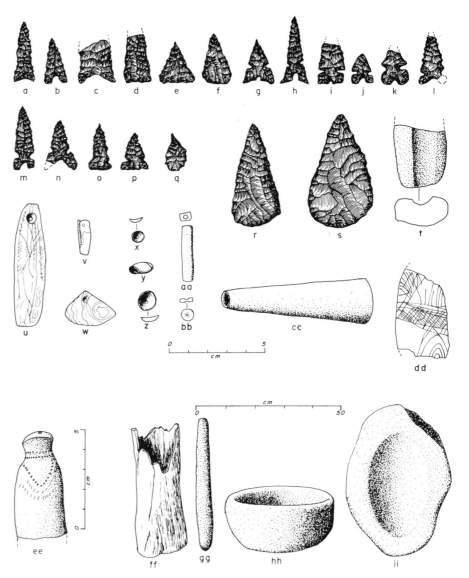

**Figure 8.11** Death Valley IV artifacts. a–f, Cottonwood Triangular points; g–p, Desert Side-notched points; q, drill; r,s, knives; t, shaft straightener; u, incised green-schist pendant; v,w, *Haliotis* shell pendants; x–z, *Olivella* shell beads; aa, shell bead; bb, steatite disk bead; cc, conical ceramic pipe; dd, incised blue schist; ee, unfired clay figurine; ff, wooden (mesquite) mortar; gg, long pestle; hh, stone mortar; ii, millingstone. (After Hunt 1960: Figures 60–65, and 69–73.)

with thin, incised lines forming a cross-hatched pattern. An unusual artifact is the unbaked clay figurine, most often of legless and armless females which resembles those made in the Southwest. Perishable remains from the dry sand dunes include twined and coiled baskets, the remains of circular houses made of mesquite framing, and semicircular windbreaks of upright poles. Cremations were practiced regularly, whereas interment in rock-covered graves occurred less frequently.

There are literally hundreds of sites dating from this period dotting the valley floor and adjacent mountains. On the valley floor camps were established among the mesquite-covered dunes, whereas in the higher country sites were located near springs or in rockshelters. It appears that the ethnographic pattern of seasonal movement from valley floor to mountain slopes was the continuation of a way of life established many centuries earlier.

In his "Prehistoric cultural developments in the southern California deserts," Wallace (1962a) presents a general cultural sequence of four periods for the California deserts, which is an integration of the Death Valley sequence and Rogers' (1939, 1945) general desert sequence. The changes made by Wallace (1962a) in terminology and arrangement of complexes appear to represent a workable compromise of the two sequences. The relative placement of cultural units in these three chronological sequences (Table 8.5) illustrates the changes made and the correlation of the Death Valley sequence with Rogers' 1939 sequence.

In his 1962 article, Wallace separated late Death Valley II from early Death Valley II and combined it with Death Valley III to form the two phases of the Amargosa Complex recognized by Rogers (Table 8.5). Early Death Valley II stands alone as an expression of the Pinto Basin Complex and is equated with Rogers' Pinto–Gypsum Complex. The only significant difference between Rogers' (1939) and Wallace's (1962a) general sequences for the California Desert is in the late period(s). Rogers (1945) identified both preceramic and ceramic units as having small triangular points. Wallace did not make this distinction.

Wallace's (1962a) chronological placement of the cultural periods differs significantly from that of Rogers. Wallace dates the Period I Lake Mojave to the early Holocene followed by a long hiatus that corresponds to the Altithermal, for which he could find no evidence of occupation in the California deserts. Following this lapse, the beginning of the Pinto Basin Period coincides with the beginning of the Little Pluvial. Rogers (1939) dates his entire sequence as beginning during the Little Pluvial.

The aboriginal turquoise mines are also important in the prehistory of the eastern Mojave Desert. Rogers (1929b) noted that these mines were used by Anasazi peoples probably dating to Basketmaker III and Pueblo I times, and at a later date by the Chemehuevi. Identifying the actual workers in the mines is not a simple task, however, because a number of different pottery types derived from widely separated points were found in the mines. Tools are generally nondistinctive crude hammers and picks, some of which are grooved for hafting (Figure 8.12). There are, however, a few three-quarter grooved axes and picks that are distinctive.

The turquoise mined at Halloran Springs was apparently traded to the south and east, because some of it has been found at Snaketown and dated to the Gila Butte Phase at A.D. 500–700 (Sigleo 1975). Turquoise occurs very rarely to the west of Halloran Springs and then usually as isolated flakes, not ornaments.

Leonard and Drover (1980:251–252) identified the pottery types recovered by Rogers and others from these mines and, on a basis of established Southwest pottery sequences, dated the mining activities and identified several changes in the cultural affiliations of the miners. This pottery sequence suggests that the Anasazi utilized or worked the mines between circa A.D. 700 and 900, followed by Hakataya peoples, who withdrew about A.D. 1200–1300, and finally by the Paiute in late prehistoric times. This sequence is partially supported by radiocarbon dates of A.D. 510–530 and 1090–1120 obtained by Leonard and Drover (1980:252).

The mining of turquoise by Anasazi groups indicates a use of the eastern Mojave that resulted in considerable influence in the region. Wallace (1977b) noted Anasazi sherds in components of the Saratoga Springs Culture, as did Hunt and Hunt (1964). Rogers (1929b) reported a concentration of Anasazi sherds on sites in the Mojave Sink and suggested that small Anasazi villages were present. This Anasazi pottery in south-

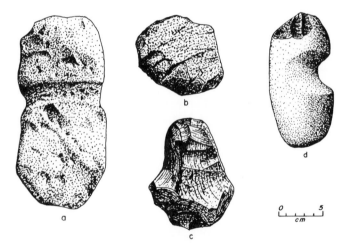

**Figure 8.12** Artifacts from Halloran Springs turquoise mines. a, unshaped grooved hammer; b,c, crude hammer–choppers; d, three-quarter grooved hammer. (a–c, after Leonard and Drover 1980: Figure 2; d, drawing of artifact collected by Rogers and housed in the San Diego Museum of Man.)

ern Nevada and adjacent California is associated with Rose Spring and Eastgate points and must be placed in the same chronological period as the Saratoga Springs Culture. The Anasazi influence, as seen by the distribution of sherds, extends westward from the lower Virgin River across southern Nevada and into California as far west as the Cronise Basin. This influence sets the northeastern Mojave apart from the rest of the California desert during the time of the Saratoga Springs Culture and creates an identifiable regional variation.

Following the decline of the southern Nevada Anasazi, the area apparently came under the influence of the Hakataya peoples, with the turquoise mines controlled by lower Colorado River peoples. During this period, a strong Hakataya influence can be seen in the southern Mojave Desert. The mines apparently were abandoned late in the sequence by the Hakataya, and the area was used occasionally by the Paiute.

## Owens Valley and Northwest Mojave Desert

During the 1950s, while Wallace was working in Death Valley, fieldwork was also being conducted in the lower Owens Valley (Harrington 1957; Lanning 1963; H. Riddell 1951; H. Riddell and F. Riddell 1956). This fieldwork resulted in the development of a cultural sequence for Owens Valley and the northwest Mojave Desert.

Harry Riddell (1951) excavated the Cottonwood Creek site (Figure 8.7), which was dated to the late prehistoric period. The site was an open campsite, located about 1.6 km west of Owens Lake on Cottonwood Creek, and contained Cottonwood Triangular, Cottonwood Leaf-shaped, Desert Side-notched, and Rose Spring series points. The Cottonwood Triangular and Desert Side-notched specimens together made up over two-thirds of the total number of points. Owens Valley Brown Ware pottery was found in the upper half of the midden, and small conically drilled steatite beads were found throughout the deposit. Other artifacts include cobble pestles and bedrock mortars, manos and millingstones, a pumice pipe, elongate slate pendants, thick leaf-shaped knives, drills, and *Olivella* beads of the Thin-lipped type characteristic of the central California "Late Horizon," Phase 2 (see Chapter 5).

On the basis of the Cottonwood Creek excavation, Cottonwood Triangular and Cottonwood Leaf-shaped points and Owens Valley Brown Ware were first defined. The site is also clearly a component of the late prehistoric occupation of the area and became the type site for the description of the Cottonwood Phase in Owens Valley.

Six years later M. R. Harrington (1957) published his final report on the excavations at the Stahl site (Figure 8.7). Like the Cottonwood site, the Stahl site played an important role in the interpretations of Mojave

Desert archaeology. Stahl is an occupation site located on a fan, adjacent to a dry stream channel, about 1 km north of Little Lake. It is ≈150 m in diameter and as much as 1.37 m deep. Patterns of post molds found during excavation are interpreted as house remains, and artifacts typical of several prehistoric cultures are present. The vertical distribution of artifacts suggests that the midden is at least partially disturbed (Harrington 1957:85–91). Harrington, however, argued that Stahl was a Pinto site with a few Shoshone artifacts near the surface. Although the bulk of the data seem to support this interpretation, the common occurrence of Lake Mojave and Silver Lake points suggests that other interpretations may be more accurate.

The artifacts include millingstones and manos, grinders of scoria, sharpening stones, hammerstones and anvils, a wide variety of scrapers, scraper-planes, elongate triangular drills, leaf-shaped knives, gravers, chipped disks, and some eccentric chipped forms. Several "charmstones" (one of which appears to be an atlatl hook), incised slate fragments, fragmentary bone awls, a cylindrical bone bead, and a few whole *Olivella* shell beads also were recovered. The projectile points recovered include 497 Pinto points classed into five subtypes—shoulderless, sloping shoulders, square shoulders, barbed shoulders, and one shoulder; 36 leaf-shaped points classed as "broad" and "willow-leaf" subtypes; 90 Lake Mojave and Silver Lake points; 13 wide-stem points similar to Silver Lake type; several miscellaneous large points; and 4 small arrow points.

Harrington (1957:70–72) argued that the Stahl site represented a single cultural unit, which he dated at 1000–2000 B.C. He based his argument on what he considered to be evidence that the site was occupied during a period of more effective moisture that does not correlate with the terminal Pleistocene. The evidence that Harrington presented for a moister period is questionable, but a "Little Pluvial age" has been generally accepted for the Stahl site.

The Rose Spring site (Figure 8.7) provided the sequence to which both the Cottonwood Creek site and the Stahl site could be linked. Rose Spring is a deep stratified site that was excavated by F. A. Riddell in 1956 and tested by J. T. Davis in 1961. The results of these excavations were analyzed and published by Lanning in 1963. The Rose Spring site is up to 3.7 m deep in some portions, but below 2.1 m the artifact yield was very small: only four nondiagnostic artifacts were recovered there. Lanning recognized four cultural units that he named, from earliest to latest, Early Rose Spring, Middle Rose Spring, Late Rose Spring, and Early Cottonwood (Table 8.6); they are distinguished primarily by changes in projectile-point types.

Early Rose Spring (Figure 8.14) is characterized by Humboldt Concave Base and Pinto-like points (called Little Lake series by Lanning). Found with these points were Gypsum Cave points and Elko series points, some

**TABLE 8.6**

**Concordance of Northwest Mojave Desert (Lanning 1963) and Death Valley (Wallace 1977) Sequences**

| Period | Death Valley (Wallace 1977b) | | Northwest Mojave (Lanning 1963) | |
|---|---|---|---|---|
| | | A.D. 1870 | | A.D. 1900 |
| V | Shoshone | | Late Cottonwood | |
| | | | | A.D. 1840 |
| | | | Early Cottonwood | |
| | | A.D. 1000 | | A.D. 1300 |
| III | Saratoga Springs | | Late Rose Spring | |
| | | A.D. 1 | | A.D. 500 |
| IIb | Late Death Valley | | Middle Rose Spring | |
| | | | | 500 B.C. |
| | | | Early Rose Spring | |
| | | | | 1500 B.C. |
| IIa | Early Death Valley | | Little Lake | |
| | | 3000 B.C. | | 3000 B.C. |
| | Hiatus | | | |
| I | Lake Mojave | | | |
| | | 6000 B.C. | Lake Mohave | |
| | | | Lanceolate | |

of which resemble Amargosa I dart points. Middle Rose Spring (Figure 8.15) also contains Elko series and Gypsum Cave points, but the small Rose Spring Side-notched and Rose Spring Corner-notched points are additions. Late Rose Spring (Figure 8.16) is marked by Rose Spring points and Cottonwood Triangular, whereas Early Cottonwood is distinguished by Desert Side-notched and Cottonwood Triangular points.

Lanning (1963:267–276) correlated the sequence from Rose Spring with other local sites and produced a cultural sequence for the northwest Mojave and Owens Valley that has served as a basic sequence for both the Mojave Desert and much of the western Great Basin (Table 8.6). Lanning's (1963:277–281) chronological placement of the phases within this sequence was based on cross-dating of diagnostic artifacts to areas for which an absolute chronology was established. He suggested two early phases: the Lanceolate Points Phase, which has not been confirmed by later work, and the Lake Mohave Phase, which is identified with the Western Pluvial Lakes Tradition. Both of these phases were based on data from a wide area and were not well represented in the local sequence.

Phase III, which Lanning termed *Little Lake,* is dated at circa 3000–1500 B.C. and is represented by the "whole of the Pinto assemblage at the Little Lake site" (Lanning 1963:268). Pinto points, chipped stone disks, and stone saws (Harrington's eccentrics) are listed as diagnostic. Also present are limited numbers of Lake Mojave and Silver Lake points, as well as large choppers, core scrapers, scraper-planes, leaf-shaped knives, broad-leaf and willow-leaf points, narrow round-base drills, millingstones, and shaped and unshaped manos (Figure 8.13).

Phase IV, Early Rose Spring (ca. 1500–500 B.C.), exhibits a "marked continuity" of types from Little Lake, including leaf-shaped knives, willow-leaf points, rare Pinto points, and narrow round-base drills. Shaped manos are present, but core tools and shaped scrapers are very rare. Humboldt Concave Base points are apparently limited to this phase, and the Elko series points, Gypsum Cave points, and large triangular points are all present (Figure 8.14).

Phase V, Middle Rose Spring (500 B.C.–A.D. 500), shows a continuity with Early Rose Spring by containing Elko series, Gypsum Cave, and large triangular points, as well as flat, shaped manos and, rarely, core tools and shaped scrapers. Middle Rose Spring is distinguished by the occurrence of Central California "Middle Horizon" shell bead types, pumice shaft smoothers, and slate tablets, and by the introduction of small projectile points of the Rose Spring series, asymmetrical and notched-base (Humboldt Basal-notched points?) knives, expanding base drills, and chipped ovals (Figure 8.15).

Phase VI, Late Rose Spring (A.D. 500–1300), is distinguished by the absence of the larger dart points. The projectile points are nearly all of the Rose Spring series, but a few Cottonwood Triangular and Eastgate Expanding-stem points occur. Artifacts that continue from Middle Rose Spring are asymmetrical and notched-base knives, expanding base drills, and flat-shaped manos. Split, punched *Olivella* beads occur, as do cobble pestles and steatite beads. Rose Spring Contracting-stem points appear for the first time, but core tools and shaped scrapers are no longer found (Figure 8.16).

Phase VII, Early Cottonwood (A.D. 1300–1840), is distinguished from earlier phases by Owens Valley Brown Ware pottery, ceramic and pumice pipes, thin-lipped *Olivella* beads, Desert Side-notched points, and small triangular drills. Rose Spring series points and flat-shaped manos continue from earlier phases, whereas broad triangular and leaf-shaped knives and expanded-base drills with long bits appear to be unique to this phase (Figure 8.17).

Phase VIII, Late Cottonwood (A.D. 1840–1900), is represented by part of the collection from the Cottonwood Creek site; it includes Owens Valley Brown Ware pottery, Desert Side-notched and Cottonwood Triangular points, notched-base knives, cobble pestles, steatite disk beads, and millingstones, all continuing from the previous phase. Cottonwood Leaf-shaped points appear for the first time, as do unshaped manos, slate pendants, and a drill with an unretouched, expanded base and a short bit. Shell beads of the central California "Late Horizon" (Augustine Tradition), Phase 2 occur, as do glass trade beads (Figure 8.18).

Lanning's chronological placement of these phases has been substan-

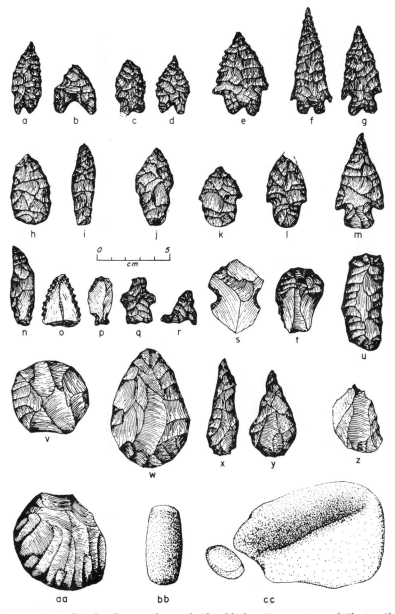

**Figure 8.13** Little Lake Phase artifacts. a,b, Shoulderless Pinto points; c,d, Sloping Shoulder Pinto points; c, Square Shoulder Pinto point; f,g, Barbed Shoulder Pinto points; h,i, leaf-shaped points; j, Lake Mojave point; k,l, Sliver Lake points; m, corner-notched stemmed point; n–r, eccentrics; s, concave scrapers; t,u, scrapers; v, chipped-stone disk; w, large knife; x,y, drills; z, spiked graver; aa large scraper-plane (13 cm long); bb, pestle (not to scale); cc, mano and millingstone (not to scale). (After Harrington 1957: Figures 34, 36, 39, 41–48.)

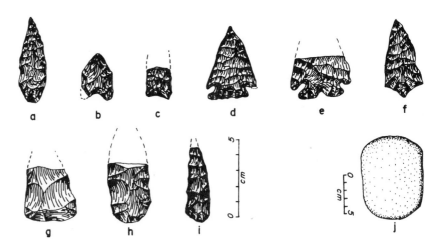

**Figure 8.14** Early Rose Spring artifacts. a, willow-leaf point; b, Pinto Shoulderless point; c, Humboldt Concave-base point; d, Elko Corner-notched point; e, Elko Eared point; f, Gypsum Cave point; g, large triangular point; h, knife, Type 1; i, drill, Type 1; j, shaped mano. (After Lanning 1963: Plates 6, 7, 9, 11.)

tiated in part by more recent radiocarbon dates (Clewlow *et al.* 1970). Of the five radiocarbon dates available for the Rose Spring site, three are derived from the deepest portion of the midden, in which so few artifacts were found that cultural affiliation is questionable. These dates are 1950 ± 180 B.C., 1630 ± 80 B.C., and 1570 ± 80 B.C. and refer to deposits that may be Early Rose Spring or Little Lake Phase, or they may be a phase not represented in Lanning's sequence. A radiocarbon assay of 950 ± 80 B.C. applies to Early Rose Spring, and another, 290 ± 145 B.C., dates to Middle Rose Spring; both substantiate Lanning's dates for those two phases.

Lanning (1963:292), like Wallace and Harrington, argued for a Little Pluvial date for the Pinto material (Little Lake Phase), but placed it at circa 3000–1500 B.C. and did not separate it from the Lake Mojave Phase by a hiatus of several thousands of years. The date for the Little Lake Phase, however, is based on cross-dating of the Stahl site with radiocarbon-dated sites in the western Great Basin by means of Pinto points and shell beads. The problem remains, however, of explaining the association of Pinto points with Lake Mojave and Silver Lake points at the Stahl site.

Shortly after Lanning's (1963) Rose Spring publication became available, the chronological placement of the Pinto point became the topic of an extended debate. Susia, in writing of the Pinto assemblage from the surface site at Tule Springs in southern Nevada, states that "The Pinto phase can be seen as probably the final time period in a tradition in western prehistory that can be traced back about 10,000 years to the Lake Mohave and Death Valley I surface finds. Documentation for the entirety

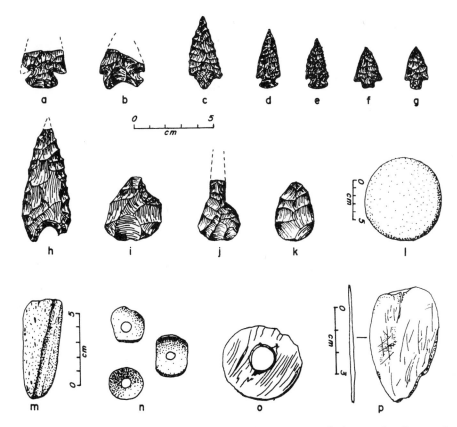

**Figure 8.15** Middle Rose Spring artifacts. a, Elko Corner-notched point; b, Elko Eared point; c, Gypsum Cave point; d,e, Rose Spring Side-notched point; f,g, Rose Spring Corner-notched point; h, knife, Type 4; i, knife, Type 3; j, drill, Type 3; k, chipped-obsidian oval; l, shaped mano; m, pumice shaft-smoother; n,o, shell beads and ring (not to scale); p, slate tablet. (After Lanning 1963: Plates 5–9, 11, 12, and J. T. Davis 1963: Figure I.)

of the period does not exist, so it remains a hypothesis, to be tested in the southern California desert" (1964:31).

Layton (1970) suggested that it was naïve for archaeologists to continue using the "Pinto type," because of the stylistic variation included within the "type." O'Connell (1971a) and Bettinger and Taylor (1974) proposed a separation of the Little Lake series from the Pinto type as a solution. Others have argued for the validity of the Pinto or Little Lake series of types (e.g., Hester 1973). There can be no doubt, however, that there is a great deal of confusion surrounding the Pinto point types, which makes their use in cross-dating suspect (Warren 1980a,b).

Wallace's Death Valley sequence and Lanning's sequence for the Owens Valley share many similarities (Table 8.6). They have essentially

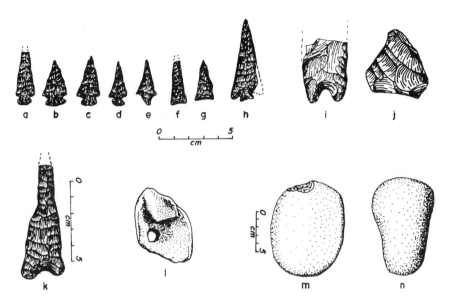

**Figure 8.16** Late Rose Spring artifacts. a,b, Rose Spring Side-notched points; c,d, Rose Spring Corner-notched points; e, Rose Spring Contracting-stem point; f,g, Cottonwood Triangular points; h, Eastgate Expanding-stem point; i, Type 4 knife; j, Type 3 knife; k, drill, Type 3; l, *Olivella* shell bead (3a2); m, shaped mano; n, pestle. (After Lanning 1963: Plates 6–9, 11.)

identical sequences of projectile points, and the addition of millingstones and manos and of California shell beads occurs about the same time in both sequences, as does Brown Ware pottery. There are some differences, however, which reflect regional variations: the presence of Anasazi pottery in the Saratoga Springs Culture of the Death Valley sequence, for example. When examining the cultural assemblages excavated elsewhere in the northern Mojave, these regional variations become better defined.

E. L. Davis and D. L. True conducted surveys and limited excavations in the Panamint Basin (Figure 8.11) during the early 1960s. True *et al.,* (1967) published the results of investigations of late occupation, and E. L. Davis (1970) presented a final report with a generalized description of the cultural sequence (Table 8.7).

Davis followed Wallace in assigning an earliest date of circa 4000 B.C. for the Pinto pattern, following a cultural hiatus. However, her Early Milling Archaic, which includes Pinto, Gypsum, and Silver Lake Patterns, is apparently poorly represented in Panamint Basin, and she relies primarily on the Campbells (1935) and M. R. Harrington (1933) for a description of this stage. The Milling Archaic stage apparently can be equated with Wallace's (1977b) Saratoga Springs Culture and Rogers' (1939, 1945) earlier description of the nonceramic Yuman.

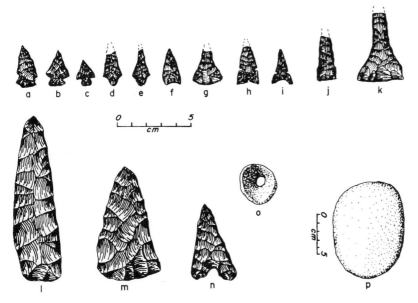

**Figure 8.17** Early Cottonwood artifacts. a,b, Rose Spring Side-notched points; c, Rose Spring Corner-notched point; d,e, Rose Spring Contracting-stem point; f,g, Cottonwood Triangular point; h,i, Desert Side-notched points; j, drill, Type 2; k, drill, Type 3; l,m, Type 2 knives; n, Type 4 knife; o, *Olivella* shell bead; p, shaped mano. (After Lanning 1963: Plates 7–9, 11, 12.)

The late Pottery Archaic stage is better represented in the Panamint Basin at the Indian Ranch site, where True *et al.* (1967) conducted a survey and collected artifacts from the surface of a series of dunes. Thirty-five more or less distinct occupation areas were mapped. The sites are associated with sand dunes, the majority exhibiting artifacts exposed by erosion. The artifacts include Cottonwood Triangular and Desert Side-notched points; a few small stemmed points of the Rose Spring series and larger Elko Eared varieties; drills of several types; bifacially flaked, triangular, and leaf-shaped knives; irregular flake knives and scrapers; a few fragmentary domed scrapers; scraper-planes; bifacially flaked heavy-duty chopping tools; hammerstones; slab and basin millingstones; shaped and unshaped manos; abraders of scoria; pestles but no mortars; incised and plain pendants of talc, slate, shist, mica, and possibly gypsum; shell beads; stone beads; and several types of glass beads. No burials were encountered, but cremation is suggested by fused glass beads and ashes. Pottery was also recovered but not identified in this report.

True *et al.* (1967) believe that the potential for subsistence within the locale and the larger area indicate that these sites represent winter occupation areas of a group of Panamint Shoshoneans, and that mesquite was probably a prime source of subsistence, along with the hunting of small game. This late occupation in Panamint Valley is clearly very similar to that described for Period IV in the adjacent Death Valley.

Excavations conducted by Hillebrand (1972) established for the Coso Mountains (Figure 8.7) a cultural sequence that exhibits similarities to the Rose Spring and Death Valley sequences. The Ray Phase (Hillebrand 1972), dated at about 2500 B.C., is characterized by Pinto points, Elko Eared and Elko Corner-notched points found with manos and millingstones, shell beads, slate pendants, twined basketry, and flexed burials. This cultural assemblage is shared in part with the following Chapman Phase, with manos and millingstones, slate pendants, shell beads, twined basketry, and the liberal use of obsidian for chipped-stone tools all continuing into the later phase.

The Chapman Phase is marked by an increase in the quantity and quality of obsidian tools, the disappearance of Elko points and the introduction of Rose Spring series points, as well as the later appearance of Desert Side-notched and Cottonwood Triangular points, and pottery. During the Chapman Phase, cremation is introduced, although flexed burials continue to be the preferred disposal method. Hillebrand (1972:108) dates

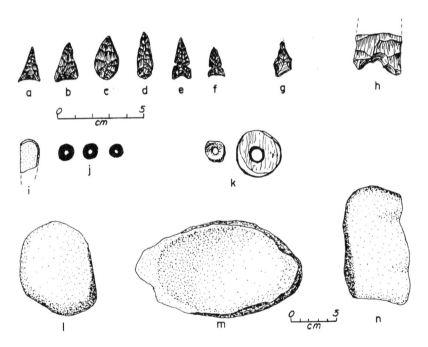

**Figure 8.18** Late Cottonwood artifacts. a,b, Cottonwood Triangular points; c,d, Cottonwood Leaf-shaped points; e,f, Desert Side-notched points; g, drill, Type 5; h, knife, Type 4; i, stone pendant fragment; j, steatite disk beads; k, shell beads; l, unshaped mano; m, millingstone; n, pestle. (After Lanning 1963:Plates 5–8, 11, 12.)

**TABLE 8.7**

**A Tentative Cultural Sequence for Panamint Valley**[a]

| Stage | Cultural tradition | Estimated dates |
|---|---|---|
| Postcontact Archaic | Paiute–Shoshone | A.D. 1550–1900 |
| Pottery Archaic | Shoshonean | 1000 B.C.–A.D. 1550 |
| Milling Archaic | Shoshonean–Yuman | 2000 B.C.–A.D. 1000 |
| Early Milling Archaic | Pinto, Gypsum, and Silver Lake patterns | 4000 B.C.–A.D. 1 |
| Paleoindian | Unknown pattern | 6000–4000 B.C. |

[a]After E. Davis (1970:117).

the Chapman Phase at circa 300 B.C. on the basis of the Rose Spring points. He would also subdivide the Chapman Phase into early and late subphases. Hillebrand (1972:108) notes that

> significant new traits that might be used as criteria for sub-phases are the bow and arrow, houserings, pottery, and cache pit. Although the date for the appearance of any of these traits is far from certain at this time, they all seem to be present by A.D. 1000 and perhaps even as early as A.D. 500. So then an early and late division of the Chapman Phase seems appropriate. The Early Chapman Phase begins in 300 B.C. and terminates sometime between A.D. 500 and A.D. 1000. Accordingly the Late Chapman Phase begins between A.D. 500 and 1000, and it closes in the middle of the 19th century.

Hillebrand's relative sequence fits well with data developed elsewhere, but his dates do not. The 300 B.C. date for the termination of the Ray Phase and the beginning of the Early Chapman Phase corresponds to the date for the beginning of the Middle Rose Spring phase, where the earliest Rose Spring points, dated at 290 B.C., occur in assocation with earlier point types. However, Hillebrand's A.D. 500–1000 date for the first occurrence of Brown Ware pottery is certainly too early by several hundred years.

Panlaqui (1974) described material from the two components of Ray Cave (Figure 8.7). The earlier of the two, consisting of all the buried material except a portion of the uppermost level, contains Elko Eared and Elko Corner-notched points and large concave-base points resembling the Humboldt Basal-notched type. This component is dated by radiocarbon at 1440 B.C. for the 106 to 122 cm level and at A.D. 450 for an ash lens at the 81 cm depth. This material was the basis for Hillebrand's (1972) Ray Phase description, but the date of A.D. 450 indicates that the Rose Spring points date after circa A.D. 500.

The second component at Ray Cave is a historic cache found on the surface of the shelter consisting of two twined conical burden baskets with round bottoms, a pitched water jug, a "seed beater," a number of Euro-American items, and a Desert Side-notched point from the 0 to 15 cm level. Although lacking pottery, this component is clearly a historic manifestation of the Late Chapman Phase.

Although only limited investigation has been conducted in the Coso Mountains, it is clear that a sequence has been demonstrated, that begins about 2500 B.C. and continues up to the historic period. Grant *et al.* (1968) have reported over 14,000 petroglyphs from the Coso Mountains (Figure 8.7) that depict mountain sheep, anthropomorphic figures, dogs, a few other animals, "medicine bags," "shield patterns," projectile foreshafts, atlatls, miscellaneous curvilinear and rectilinear patterns, and pit-and-groove patterns. These elements are arranged in scenes depicting mountain sheep being hunted by men or men and dogs, some with projectiles projecting from the sheep. Mountain sheep are depicted dead, alive, pregnant (a small sheep inside a large one), and, apparently, in the process of giving birth. There are hunting scenes with men using only atlatls (see cover of this book), others with men using only bows and arrows, and still other scenes depicting hunters with both bows and arrows and atlatls.

The Coso petroglyphs reflect a change in style through time that also illustrate the change from the atlatl to the bow and arrow. If the small Rose Spring points are interpreted as representing the introduction of the bow and arrow, then it is possible to date the petroglyphs as probably beginning during the Ray Phase and terminating in the following Chapman Phase. Grant *et al.* (1968:114) interpret the Coso Mountains as the heartland of a hunting ritual that diffused over a wide area of the western United States. However, perhaps more significant for interpretation of the cultural history of the Mojave Desert is the fact that the Coso petroglyphs represent a cultural tradition that persists through several archaeological phases, suggesting that there is considerably more cultural continuity than recognized in the archaeological assemblages. The artistic tradition and the presumed ceremonial tradition represented by the Coso petroglyphs suggest that the historic Shoshonean peoples of the Coso Mountain area have cultural origins that extend far back into the local prehistoric sequences.

Farther to the west in the Last Chance Canyon of the El Paso Mountains, McGuire *et al.* (1981) excavated the Bickel site (Figure 8.7), which is clearly related to Lanning's (1963) Late Rose Spring component. Cultural deposits are as much as 160 cm deep and produce lithic and faunal remains and charcoal as well as a number of artifacts. Four radiocarbon determinations place the occupation between circa A.D. 700 and 1300. The artifact assemblage includes 14 classifiable points, 11 of which were categorized as Rose Spring points; the other 3 were classified as Elko Corner-notched, Cottonwood Triangular, and Desert Side-notched points. Other tools included flake scrapers, biface fragments, cores, millingstones, manos and mano–pestle combination tools, hammerstones, and saucer- and disk-shaped *Olivella* beads.

The lithic débitage and the floral and faunal remains at the Bickel site were also analyzed. The faunal remains included an overwhelming abundance of jackrabbit bones (of the 978 identified bones, 708 were from jackrabbits) as well as smaller numbers of cottontail, wood rat, kangaroo rat, pocket gopher, ground squirrel, and artiodactyl remains. Because of the large number of jackrabbit bones, the Bickel site is interpreted as a base for communal rabbit drives (McGuire *et al.* 1981:97).

The floral remains were limited to digger pine nut fragments. Digger pine is not found locally in the El Paso Mountains, but is present about 12–18 km to the west in the lower elevations of the southern Sierra Nevada. This appearance of nonlocal pine nuts suggests that the inhabitants of the Bickel site followed a seasonal round that included some subsistence activities in the southern Sierra, and that the Bickel site was occupied in the fall shortly after the pine nut harvest (McGuire *et al.* 1981:94).

The lithic material at the Bickel site consisted largely of locally available chalcedony. However, the assemblage of chalcedony items "contained a paucity of specimens exhibiting bifacial, unifacial, or use wear" (McGuire *et al.* 1981:98). The few tools observed at this site were primarily large, percussion-flaked implements. Large, thinning, chalcedony flakes representing the primary stages of lithic reduction tended to be common in the débitage, whereas small pressure flakes, representing tool finishing and maintenance, were relatively scarce. The scarcity of chalcedony preforms and roughly made bifaces, characteristic of the primary stages of reduction, suggests that they were transported and used elsewhere (McGuire *et al.* 1981:99).

The Rose Spring projectile-point types and the radiocarbon dates indicate that the Bickel component is the chronological equivalent of Wallace's (1977b) Saratoga Springs Culture and Lanning's (1963) Late Rose Spring Phase. The Bickel site is perhaps best interpreted as a specialized, seasonally occupied site from which communal rabbit drives were conducted and as a place where local chalcedony was reduced to preforms and rough bifaces that were carried elsewhere.

Nearly all of the long oasis-like Owens Valley (Figure 8.7) lies to the north of the Rose Spring and Stahl sites and is known to have had a relatively dense population in early historic times. The many small tributaries that deliver water to the valley floor from high in the Sierra also made the Owens Valley an attractive place for habitation during the drier periods of prehistory.

Relatively little archaeological study has been done in Owens Valley, with Bettinger's (1975, 1976, 1977b) survey work being the most notable. Bettinger outlined a sequence of four phases for Owens Valley, based on a regional surface survey centered near Big Pine. Each phase is characterized by a series of diagnostic projectile points (Table 8.8). However,

**TABLE 8.8**

**Cultural Sequences for the Owens Valley**[a]

| Phase | Time span | Time marker projectile points |
|-------|-----------|-------------------------------|
| Klondike | A.D. 1300–1850 | Cottonwood series–Desert Side-notched series |
| Baker | A.D. 600–1300 | Rose Spring–Eastgate series |
| Cowhorn | 1500 B.C.–A.D. 600 | Elko series |
| Clyde | 3500–1500 B.C. | Little Lake series (Pinto) |

[a]From Bettinger (1976).

Bettinger's objective was not to set up a cultural chronology. Instead, he was concerned with testing models of cultural–ecological relationships. The data obtained from a survey of 95 tracts measuring 500 × 500 m, which were selected from an area 42 × 27 km, were analyzed in two ways. First, a statistical comparison was made of the actual distribution of certain functional artifact categories against a hypothetical set of artifact distributions based on ethnographic accounts. Second, an analysis was conducted to establish a functional taxonomy of archaeological site categories located in the survey. Inferences about the use of each category were based on the features, tools, and debris found at these sites, as well as on their settings with respect to potential food resources. Bettinger attempted to duplicate, where possible, the settlement types recognized from ethnographic accounts so that archaeological inferences could be augmented by direct historical analogy. Five categories of sites were identified: lowland occupation sites, piñon camps, riverine temporary camps, desert scrub temporary camps, and upland temporary camps.

Bettinger dated each site by means of time-sensitive projectile points and was able to identify elements of both change and continuity through time. In particular, Bettinger claimed: (1) that lowland occupation sites served as base camps and were the center of most activities in the spring, summer, early fall, and most winters throughout the period of prehistoric occupation; (2) that subsistence patterns in every phase revolved around the exploitation of lowland root and seed resources; and (3) that evidence points to the consistently small contribution of animal foods in the annual diet.

In contrast to these stable patterns, a site analysis indicated three important changes in the prehistoric settlement-subsistence system: (1) a shift in the emphasis of plant exploitation from riverine to desert scrub species between 1500 B.C. and A.D. 600, effected by a change in the location of lowland occupation sites from predominantly riverine settings to desert scrub localities; (2) the inception of regular piñon exploitation for food between A.D. 600 and 1000, shown by the appearance of piñon camps at this time; and (3) a decrease in large-game hunting after about A.D. 1000, reflected in the disuse of upland and desert scrub temporary camps as hunting stations after this date. Bettinger (1977:15) concluded, after reviewing changing climatic conditions, that, in Owens Valley, the prehistoric adaptation was "highly variable during the interval of aboriginal occupation" and that climatic shifts may be causally related to at least two of the three adaptive shifts reconstructed from archaeological data: (1) only after A.D. 600 were pine nuts an important staple food and (2) prior to A.D. 600 the subsistence system was specialized in intensive use of lowland, as opposed to upland, resources. The temporal variations in local subsistence adaptations, the climatically induced changes in human ecology, and the development of specialized subsistence strategies are all viewed by Bettinger as playing important roles in the changing settlement–subsistence systems of Owens Valley. In addition, Bettinger (1977:15–16) cites "population growth due to intrinsic increases, population movements, and the development of food production" (irrigation of native plants) as important in explaining adaptive shifts in the subsistence systems of Owens Valley.

Bettinger's interpretations are generally supported by surveys and excavations on the Southern California Edison No. 2 Control–Casa Diablo Transmission Line (Cowan and Wallof 1974). However, Munday and Lincoln (1979) questioned Bettinger's interpretations, claiming that the data were inadequate in some instances and that other potential determinants of archaeological variability were ignored. Hall (1981) also criticized Bettinger's conclusions on the basis of error in Bettinger's quantitative and statistical operations. Madsen (1981) criticized him on the basis of interpretation and inadequate data, and McGuire and Garfinkel (1976) and Garfinkel and Cook (1980) have taken issue with Bettinger's late date for the development of piñon exploitation. Bettinger (1976, 1979a,b, 1980, 1981a,b) responded to each of these criticisms and his work stands as a pioneering attempt to address questions dealing with the processes of cultural change. Bettinger's work, no doubt, contains weaknesses and errors, but it was innovative in approach and has stimulated research on new problems and the reevaluation of data, and it will at the very least be of historical importance in the development of California desert archaeology.

North of Owens Valley at higher elevations, where the arid conditions are lessened, the archaeological sequence still exhibits considerable similarities to that of the northern Mojave. The Casa Diablo project (Cowan and Wallof 1974), excavations on the Sherwin Grade (Garfinkel and Cook 1979) and in Mammoth Creek Cave (Enfield and Enfield 1964), and excavations and surveys in the Mono Lake region (E. L. Davis 1963, 1964) have yielded data that conform to the general sequence for the northern Mojave Desert (Figure 8.7).

E. L. Davis (1964) illustrated a sequence of projectile points from Elko through Desert Side-notched from two rockshelters at Hot Creek. Projectile points from a survey of the Mono area also suggest a sequence similar to that of Owens Valley, but Davis' excavations were too limited to demonstrate the sequence.

Enfield and Enfield (1964) reported a late occupation from Mammoth Creek Cave in Mono County. The Enfields argue, convincingly, that the site shows some cultural stratigraphy. The latest occupation is dated between A.D. 1200 and 1850 on the basis of Desert Side-notched points, Owens Valley Brown Ware pottery, and glass trade beads. Other items in this assemblage include steatite vessels, flake scrapers, manos, *Olivella* Disk beads, and a few other artifacts. The earlier strata are characterized by larger projectile points, including Gypsum Cave and Elko varieties; manos and millingstones; a square *Haliotis* bead; *Olivella* Disk beads; flake scrapers; and a few other items. The similarity of the projectile-point and pottery types to those of the northern Mojave are apparent. However, the Enfields (1964:418) view Mammoth Creek Cave as having relationships with the Yosemite area as well as with the Great Basin sites. There are some data to support their interpretation, such as the shell beads, but the data are so limited that the nature of these contacts cannot be determined.

The locations of Mammoth Creek Cave and other sites north of Owens Valley clearly indicate that they are all ecologically as well as culturally marginal to the California deserts, even though the projectile-point sequence appears to be similar. It seems likely that, in this area where streams flow year-round, the natural resources would have allowed, if not dictated, a somewhat different adaptation and seasonal scheduling from that of the lower, more arid deserts.

### Western Mojave Desert

In the western Mojave Desert south of Owens Valley, no local cultural sequence has been established. Most archaeological data accumulated through limited test excavations and surface surveys have been brought together by Sutton (1980, 1981) in two interesting papers.

A "Pinto age" assemblage was proposed for the western Mojave by W. S. Glennan (1971; Sutton 1981). On the basis of a rather extensive surface collection at the Sweetser site (Ker-302) in the Antelope Valley, Glennan (1971) defined the Rhyolite Tradition as consisting primarily of knives, choppers, scrapers, cores, and some millingstones. This assemblage is dated at circa 2000–4000 B.C. on the basis of an obsidian Pinto point with a hydration rind of 10.5 μm, and by cross-dating of artifact types with the Stahl site.

Rhyolite dominated the assemblage of the Sweetser site, as well as several other sites that Glennan investigated. One of these sites, LAn-298 at Fairmont Buttes (Figure 4.12), has been the object of investigations since Glennan's work there. Small test excavations have revealed cultural deposits 2 m in depth with late occupation in the upper 40–50 cm, marked by small triangular points of rhyolite and obsidian and late shell bead types. A nearly 100% rhyolite assemblage is present in the lower levels, however. Obsidian hydration readings from these deposits, although not in stratigraphic order, were up to 10.8 μm thick. The conclusion drawn from these test units is that the rhyolite sources at Fairmont Buttes were used for a long time, beginning perhaps during the Pinto Period (Sutton 1981).

The late prehistoric period, dated between circa 250 B.C. and A.D. 1650, is described by Sutton (1980:217) as having

> large permanent (or semi-permanent) villages with a variety of smaller special purpose sites occupied on a seasonal basis (Robinson 1977). The presence of large villages (which include cemeteries) and the number and complexity of other sites would suggest that the Antelope Valley supported a large population during the late prehistoric period, and was not a "fringe" area as suggested by the ethnographic data.

Sutton (1980, 1981) summarized data from three major prehistoric sites, all of which contained cemeteries. Site LAn-488, located in the southwest fringe of Antelope Valley, and Ker-303, in the western valley (Figure 4.12), are both large villages with deep middens. A number of smaller satellite sites including rock rings, lithic scatters, and milling stations are apparently associated with Ker-303. Artifacts found at these sites included many shell beads, ornaments, and steatite from the southern California coast as well as Rose Spring and Cottonwood projectile points. The third village, actually consisting of several sites, is located along the south shore of Buckhorn Lake on the eastern edge of Antelope Valley. Here, site LAn-828 (Figure 4.12) produced *Olivella* shell beads dated by Chester King at circa 200 B.C. to A.D. 600, and LAn-771 yielded a clay figurine very similar to one recovered from Ker-303.

Four radiocarbon assays available for Ker-303, one from Ker-733, and one from LAn-488 provide some indication of the age of these deposits (Table 8.9). Ker-733 is a small lithic scatter believed to be a satellite of Ker-303 (Sutton 1981:unpaginated). The 250 B.C. date for Ker-303 appears to be too early and presumably may date charcoal from a period earlier than the village occupation. No evaluation of this date is provided by Sutton (1981).

**TABLE 8.9**

**Radiocarbon Dates from Village Sites in Antelope Valley**[a]

| Site | Sample numbers | Material | Radiocarbon date |
|------|----------------|----------|------------------|
| Ker-303 | UCLA-1884a | Bone | A.D. 1650 ± ? |
| | UCLA-1699 | Surface bone | A.D. 755 ± 220 |
| | UCLA-1884b | Bone | A.D. 590 ± 40 |
| | UCLA-1927 | Charcoal from base of cemetery | 250 ± 40 B.C. |
| Ker-733 | UCR-970 | Charcoal from hearth at 60 cm | A.D. 1490 |
| LAn-488 | GAK-3010 | Charcoal from hearth | A.D. 1180 |

[a]After Sutton (1981:unpaginated).

Several cemeteries, without associated villages, also date from this period. They are LAn-192, near Lake Los Angeles; LAn-487, in the Sierra Pelona Mountains just south of Antelope Valley; and LAn-767, located in the foothills on the southwestern edge of Antelope Valley. Sutton (1980:220) attributed the large village sites with cemeteries to the Kitanemuk and the cemeteries without associated villages, located in the foothills to the south of the valley, to the Tataviam. Sutton also interpreted the differential distribution of wealth in the grave goods as evidence of systems of prestige and status and a more complex sociopolitical organization than that described for most peoples of the Mojave Desert. The economic basis for such social complexity is in part attributed to a heavy involvement in a trade network, in which the Antelope Valley population functioned as middlemen between the coastal and interior populations (Sutton 1980:221).

Such a trade system would presumably bring in ceramics from the eastern deserts. However, Sutton (1981:unpaginated) stated that ceramics of any type are uncommon in the Antelope Valley sites, but they appear more frequently toward the eastern end of the valley. Most ceramics recovered during formal archaeological investigations are a locally made undecorated brown ware. Sutton (1981) also noted that other pottery types do occur, citing Croasdale (1973:3, in Sutton 1981:unpaginated), who identified "Cerbat Brown, Sandy Brown, Panamint Brown, Coachella Brown, Parker Buff, Black-on-White Pueblo Ware, possible Red-on-Buff Hohokam, various types of stucco ware, and several other unidentified types of Buff Ware. All the pottery mentioned above except for the Black-on-White Pueblo type were found at one site location."

Sutton (1981:unpaginated) cautioned against accepting these identifications because the Black-on-White pottery probably did not come from the Antelope Valley, and there are no qualitative data or analytical reports available for these "types." It would appear, however, that Colorado

River influence can be seen in the Red-on-Buff and stucco wares found at the eastern edge of Antelope Valley.

The major occupation of Antelope Valley appears to have ended by A.D. 1650, after which the valley became a marginal area as reflected in the ethnographic record. The reason for the collapse of this cultural system remains unknown, but Sutton (1980:221) suggested that a disruption in the trade network must be considered as one possible explanation.

The late prehistoric period in Antelope Valley, as described by Sutton, appears to have few similarities to the late period in other areas of the Mojave Desert, but the Rose Spring and Cottonwood points serve as reliable time markers. Sutton's interpretations indicate that, in the late prehistoric period, large villages and systems of status and prestige may represent strong regional developments that set Antelope Valley apart from the rest of the Mojave Desert.

## Southeastern Mojave Desert

Schroeder's (1961) publication of the Willow Beach excavations provides the only long sequence available for the lower Colorado River. Willow Beach (Figure 8.1) is located on a river terrace 24 km south of Hoover Dam. It is a stratified site that was occupied sporadically for a period of more than 1000 years. It was, however, always a relatively small campsite, and some cultural units contain only a few tools.

Price Butte Phase, the earliest occupation, is dated by radiocarbon at circa 250 B.C. and contains large expanding stem points, square-based and leaf-shaped knives, wide-based drills, slab millingstone and unshaped mano, a series of flake scrapers, knife and point blanks, tubular stone pipes, stone disks, and hammerstones. Schroeder (1961:82, 89–90) noted similarities between the Price Butte Phase assemblage and that of a housepit at the confluence of the Virgin and Muddy rivers, and the material from the Shivwits Plateau. The large expanding stem points are virtually identical to Rogers' (1939) Amargosa dart points.

The next three phases have scanty assemblages but appear to represent a continuation of the basic assemblage of the Price Butte Phase, with a few additions. The Nelson Phase, dated at about A.D. 250, is distinguished by the first appearance of the shaped mano and oval basin millingstone, a new knife type and paint pigment. During the following Eldorado Phase, dated by radiocarbon at A.D. 450, a broad-stemmed dart point with narrow square shoulders appears. Material similar to both the Nelson and Eldorado phases is noted by Schroeder as occurring in housepits in the Muddy and Virgin river valleys. Schroeder, however, sees the broad-stemmed, narrow-shouldered points of the Eldorado Phase as being derived from the California deserts. The following Roaring Rapids Phase is dated at pre-A.D. 750 on the basis of intrusive Basketmaker III pottery from the Virgin Branch Anasazi. Verde Gray and Cerbat Brown from the Prescott Branch and Cerbat Branch of the Hakataya are also present. In this phase, small-stemmed projectile points that resemble the Rose Spring and Eastgate types are present.

The final phase, Willow Beach, dated at A.D. 900–1150, is characterized by an abundance of Pyramid Gray pottery, a lower Colorado River ware. Intrusive sherds (Moapa Gray, Prescott Gray, and Cerbat Brown wares) indicate continued contact with the Virgin Branch Anasazi, Prescott Branch, and Cerbat Branch. The Willow Beach Phase represents a continuation of the assemblage of the preceding phase with the addition of indigenous pottery, Pueblo II ceramics, Rose Spring points, worked turquoise and shell, bone beads, and a loaf-shaped mano. In the uppermost part of the stratum, Paiute Ware and Desert Side-notched and Cottonwood Triangular points appear, along with Tusayan Black-on-Red pottery, which give the last occupation a post-A.D. 1100 date. Because the Paiute pottery and small triangular points could not be separated stratigraphically at Willow Beach, Schroeder (1961:87) considers them intrusive.

The Willow Beach sequence illustrates the existence of a series of preceramic assemblages on the Colorado River that may be considered a regional variant of Rogers' Amargosa Complex. The parallels in projectile-point types and the sequence from large dart points to small Rose Spring points and Basketmaker III pottery are striking. The parallels stop there, however. The introduction of the lower Colorado River pottery represents a divergence that can be observed in a number of other sites in the southern Mojave Desert.

Southwest of Willow Beach, the New York, Mid Hills, Providence, and Granite mountains form a continuous range (Figure 8.1) in a northeast–southwest orientation with the southern end south and east of the Mojave Sink. Donnan (1964) published a suggested chronology for these mountains based on his excavations at Southcott Cave, J. T. Davis' (1962) report on the sequence at Rustler Rockshelter, and the limited material available on Mitchell Caverns (Farmer 1936; J. Smith 1958). Donnan's description of the earlier cultural units is based on published data from regions adjacent to the Providence Mountains (Hunt 1960; Rogers 1939; Wallace 1958), but following the "Amargosa Horizon," his sequence varies from that described by Wallace (1958, 1962a) and Hunt (1960).

Donnan (1964:11–12) argues that the lowest levels of both Southcott Cave and Rustler Rockshelter (Figure 8.1) are components of Rogers' (1945) "nonceramic Yuman Horizon" followed by the "Yuman Horizon." He does not provide the data from Southcott Cave, and Davis' (1962) data from Rustler Rockshelter does not provide clear evidence of a "nonceramic Yuman" occupation. The lowest levels of Rustler Rockshelter (76–152 cm) contain only four potsherds, and one may argue that they are intrusive due to disturbance. In these same levels there are only 1 small triangular point and 10 large dart points, including Elko Eared, large corner-notched points very similar to Rogers' Amargosa points, possible Eastgate points, and large leaf-shaped, triangular, and triangular side-notched points. Nearly all these point types are placed by Rogers (1939) in his Amargosa Complex. Found in levels between 46 and 76 cm were four Cottonwood Triangular points, one small triangular point with a convex base and side notches, two large triangular points, and a possible Eastgate point. The Cottonwood Triangular points in the 46- to 76- cm levels suggest the beginning of the "Yuman" occupation, but there are 10 sherds. The "nonceramic Yuman" occupation cannot be demonstrated at Rustler Rockshelter. It appears that the lowest levels at Rustler Rockshelter are better considered a component of the Amargosa Complex, followed by "Yuman" occupation.

J. T. Davis (1962:43–46) views the pottery-bearing later levels of Rustler Rockshelter as the Providence Complex of the "Western Upland Patayan," because of close ties with western Arizona and the lower Colorado River reflected in the pottery. Davis divides the Providence Complex into three phases based primarily on changes in pottery types. The estimated age of each phase was determined by cross-dating of pottery types with western Arizona and the lower Colorado River (Figure 8.19).

Phase I (ca. A.D. 800–1000) is characterized by plain brown pottery predominantly if not exclusively Tizon Brown Ware. Phase II (ca. A.D. 1000–1300) is marked by the addition of plain buff pottery from the lower Colorado River Valley. Phase III (A.D. 1300–1700) is characterized by stucco finish on plain buff pottery, painted red designs on plain buff pottery, and the introduction of numerous pottery types from the Colorado River Valley and upland Arizona.

Donnan (1964:11–13) incorporates the whole of the Providence Complex within his Yuman Horizon, which he dates between A.D. 800 and 1400. The Yuman Horizon is followed by the Shoshonean Horizon (A.D. 1400–1850) according to Donnan, but he fails to provide an artifact assemblage by which it can be identified archaeologically.

An archaeological survey of the Providence and New York mountains (Figure 8.1), conducted by True et al. (1966), identified 28 sites from which surface collections were made and analyzed. Only 10 rockshelters and small sites adjacent to springs yielded ceramics. Analysis of the ceramics indicated relationships with plain wares of northwestern Arizona, the Colorado River, and portions of southern California. On the basis of this surface collection, these late sites "appear to have been occupied by Yuman rather than Shoshonean peoples, although it is not always possible to separate the pottery of these two groups in the southern California

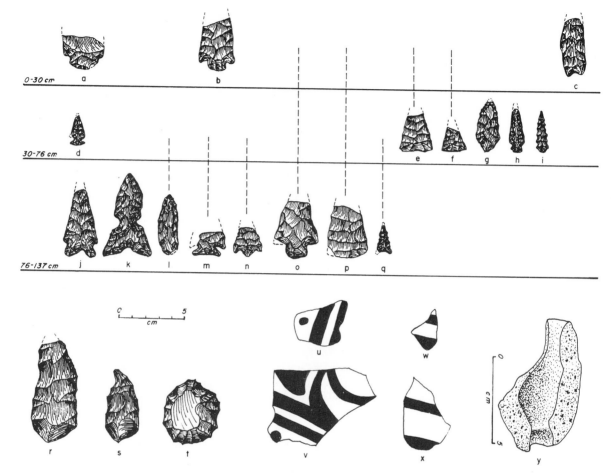

0-30 cm    a    b    c

30-76 cm    d    e  f  g  h  i

76-137 cm    j  k  l  m  n  o  p  q

0 ___ 5
cm

r    s    t    u    v    w    x    y

**Figure 8.19** Artifacts from Rustler Rockshelter. a, Type 4b point; b, Type 5b point (Elko Corner-notched); c, Type 7a point (Humboldt Concave Base); d, Type 4a point; e,f, Type 2a points (Cottonwood Triangular); g, Type 3a point; h, Type 3d point; i, Type M point; j, Type 4c point (Elko Eared); k, Type 4d point; l, Type 1 point; m, Type 5a point (Elko Side-notched); n, Type 6 point (Gypsum Cave?); o, Type 3c point (Elko Corner-notched?); p, Type 2b point; q, Type 2c point (Cottonwood Triangular); r, projectile point blank; s, crude "blank" (biface); t, "plano-convex 'turtle back' core scraper" (scraper plane); u,v, Parker Red-on-Buff pottery; w,x, La Paz Red-on-Buff pottery; y, stone pipe. (After J. T. Davis 1962: Plate 1 and Figure 4.)

area" (True *et al.* 1966:269). No significant aggregate of artifacts similar to the Shoshonean occupation of Death Valley, Panamint Valley, and Owens Valley was recovered from the survey of New York and Providence mountains (True *et al.* 1966:270). Assemblages from 11 nonceramic sites in the southern margin of the Mid Hills are said to

essentially duplicate the collections from the Kingman, Arizona area (True n.d., ms. in preparation). Likewise, they contain many elements suggestive of relationships with portions of the Willow Beach sequence (Schroeder 1961), and with artifacts recovered from surface surveys in the general area of Boulder Dam and the Shivwits Plateau (Harrington 1937, Schroeder 1961). Portions of the sequence from the Stuart Rockshelter in southern Nevada (Shutler [et al.] 1960) are also similar to the artifacts from these. . .sites (True et al. 1966:270).

The known cultural sequence from the Providence Mountains diverges from that of the northeastern Mojave Desert at the end of Amargosa I. Both Rose Spring points and Anasazi pottery are virtually absent from the assemblages described for the Providence Mountains. The Providence Complex, possibly preceded by a "nonceramic Yuman" assemblage, appears to represent the Hakataya influence in the southeast Mojave Desert.

## Mojave River Valley

During the 1940s and 1950s Gerald Smith (1963a) and Ruth Simpson (1965), in cooperation with the San Bernardino Museum Associates and the Archaeological Survey Assocation of Southern California, recorded large numbers of sites along the Mojave River (Figures 4.13 and 8.1). The data accumulated by these surveys have never been completely analyzed, and the reports vary from single-site sheets to reports on excavations and surveys. The quality of these reports is uneven, but a considerable quantity of data is presented.

Simpson's (1965) survey of Troy Lake Basin, 40 km east of Barstow (Figure 8.1), resulted in a large collection of artifacts from more than 20 sites. The data from these sites are presented in such a way that it is impossible to determine which artifacts were found on which sites. The projectile points, however, show a wide range of types, including Lake Mojave, various Pinto types, Elko Eared and Elko Corner-notched (Amargosa dart points), Gypsum Cave, Humboldt Concave Base, large leaf-shaped, Desert Side-notched, small triangular, and small leaf-shaped (probably Cottonwood Triangular and Cottonwood Leaf-shaped). Simpson also reports (1965:22) "Pueblo-like light projectile points" that strongly resemble Rose Spring points but are larger.

This range of projectile points suggests that the entire sequence outlined for the northern Mojave is represented at the Troy Lake Basin. Simpson (1965:45) states:

> Many of the Troy Lake weapon points are similar to those of late Death Valley II and early Death Valley III horizons (Hunt, 1960), and to those from Newberry Cave (Smith [et al.] 1957, 1963b). Such similarities strengthen the concept of Amargosa affinities for much of the Troy Lake material. The slab metates and slate pendants also suggest those of Death Valley III times.
>
> Lake Mojave and Pinto Basin appear to be the oldest phases represented. The Amargosa Complex would probably account for the major occupation of moderate age with an element, perhaps intrusive, of central Great Basin traits. Late Shosho-

nean and southern Nevada Pueblo elements are characteristic of the final period, at least around the fringes of the Troy Lake area.

Gerald Smith (Smith 1963b; Smith *et al.* 1957) excavated Newberry Cave (Figure 8.1), near the south end of Troy Lake Basin, a site that he believes is a single component with Amargosa affinities. The cave contained numerous perishable and nonperishable artifacts and pictographs painted on the walls near the opening. The occupational debris within the cave contained Gypsum Cave, Elko Eared, and Elko Corner-notched dart points, scrapers, choppers, a mano, a hearth for a fire drill, cordage, sandals, a bed of grass and grass-lined storage pits, an atlatl hook, dart shafts, foreshafts and butts, and a tortoise-shell bowl. A large number of items are interpreted as ceremonial in nature. These include a sheep dung pendant (sheep dung wrapped in sinew); a feathered plume; split twig figurines; quartz crystals painted green (one of which had pitch adhering to one end, suggesting that it was hafted to form a wand); painted stones; red, green, white, and black pigments; and pictographs.

C. A. Davis (1981)* recently analyzed the Newberry Cave material and obtained radiocarbon dates (Table 8.10) that generally substantiate the interpretations of Smith and co-workers (1957). Davis' analysis does, however, clarify some problems of the earlier work. Davis (1981:93–104) defines three components: Elko, Eastgate, and Historic, although vertical control during the excavation was lacking. Nearly all of the cave deposits are interpreted as falling within the Elko component. The basis for this interpretation appears to be the large number of Elko series points and a suite of 10 radiocarbon dates (Tables 8.10, 8.13).

Elko series points have been radiocarbon-dated elsewhere (Hester and Heizer 1973:5–6; Bettinger and Taylor 1974:10; O'Connell 1967:134–135) and cluster between circa 2000 B.C. and A.D. 600. Davis argues that, on the basis of the dates for the Elko point series elsewhere and the suite of radiocarbon dates from the Newberry Cave, it is reasonable to assign similar dates to the 28 Elko points at Newberry Cave. A similar argument is made for Gypsum Cave points that have been radiocarbon dated between 1500 and 450 B.C. elsewhere (Bettinger and Taylor 1974:10; Heizer and Berger 1970:17; Hester and Heizer 1973:13). Therefore, the five Gypsum points from Newberry Cave are thought also to date to the period represented by the Newberry radiocarbon dates.

One Eastgate point was also found at Newberry Cave. This point type is radiocarbon dated elsewhere between A.D. 600 and 1300 (Bettinger and Taylor 1974:10; Hester and Heizer 1973:7–8) and is therefore interpreted as representing a later occupation sometime after A.D. 600. Davis places nearly all the aboriginal items in the Elko component. He states (Davis 1981:103):

---

*Note added in proof: Davis' (1981) analysis of the Newberry Cave material has been published since this writing (see Davis and Smith 1981).

**TABLE 8.10**

**Radiocarbon Age Determinations from Newberry Cave**[a]

| Sample no. | Radiocarbon age | Calendar date | Material analyzed |
|---|---|---|---|
| LJ-993 | 2970 ± 250 B.P. | 880–1620 B.C. | Split twig figurine fragment |
| UCR-1095 | 3015 ± 90 B.P. | 1215–1470 B.C. | Elderberry dart shaft fragment |
| UCR-1093 | 3015 ± 200 B.P. | 1110–1600 B.C. | Cane dart shaft fragment |
| UCR-1092 | 3070 ± 185 B.P. | 1125–1615 B.C. | Cane dart shaft fragment |
| UCR-1097 | 3205 ± 170 B.P. | 1340–1690 B.C. | Split twig figurine fragment |
| UCR-1103 | 3300 ± 180 B.P. | 1470–2040 B.C. | Cane dart shaft fragment |
| UCR-1096 | 3320 ± 180 B.P. | 1485–2060 B.C. | Split twig figurine fragment |
| UCR-1094 | 3765 ± 100 B.P. | 2120–2480 B.C. | Willow dart shaft fragment |
| UCLA-759 | 7400 ± 100 B.P. | Uncalibrated | Woodrat midden |
| UCR-1143 | 11,600 ± 500 B.P. | Uncalibrated | Ground sloth ribs |

[a]From C. A. Davis (1981:94).

> Aboriginal use of Newberry Cave after Elko times seems to have been minimal. The only artifact that can definitely be attributed to the later Eastgate component is a single Eastgate projectile point. Some undated artifacts such as the mano–hammerstone, firedrill sets, sandals, cordage, leather thongs, and the sharpened bone pieces, may also be assigned to this component, but this possibility seems unlikely.

Artifacts from the historic component include machine-woven fabric, sisal cordage, glass fragments, and cartridge cases and apparently represent sporadic Caucasian visits from the nineteenth and twentieth centuries.

Like Smith and others (1957), Davis (1981:99) noted the specialized nature of the artifact inventory of the Elko component. He also commented that there is no evidence of extended occupation of the cave, that no food remains were identified in the deposits, and that the single mano–hammerstone could have been used to grind pigment as well as to process food. Davis agrees with Smith and others that the Elko component of Newberry Cave is best interpreted as parts of a magico-religious hunting assemblage. This interpretation is perhaps best supported by the 11 nearly whole figurines and 1049 fragments of split twig figurines (Figures 8.20 and 8.21).

Smith (1955) also reported data from test excavations conducted at the Deep Creek site near the headwaters of the Mojave River. This site, located on the western edge of the Mojave Desert (Figure 4.12), contains pottery that tentatively may be identified as Colorado Red-on-Buff, with decorations that "ranged from brick red to a dull reddish brown, and designs were made in circles, dots and wavey lines" (Smith 1955:33). Also recovered from the Deep Creek site were sherds of plain ware, Cottonwood Triangular and Desert Side-notched points, a few large stemmed points, a drill, a few scrapers, choppers, hammerstones, mortars and pestles, manos and millingstones, green slate pendants, shaft straighteners,

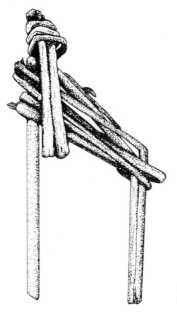

**Figure 8.20** Split-twig figurine from Newberry Cave. (After C. A. Davis and G. A. Smith 1981:Figure 21.)

actinolite crystals, awls and flakers of bone, pottery disks with central perforations, *Olivella* beads of three types, tubular clamshell beads, two small beads of calcite, and stones painted black (Figure 8.22). Also present are a number of what appear to be circular housepits.

Smith and his associates (Smith 1963a) also located sites along the Mojave River that yielded artifacts similar to those described for the Deep Creek site. This assemblage is characterized by Cottonwood Triangular and Desert Side-notched points, Buff and Brown Ware pottery, green slate pendants, manos and millingstones, mortars and pestles, Pacific Coast shell beads, arrow-shaft straighteners, ceramic pipes and pottery disks with central perforations, and occasional painting of utensils or unmodified rocks with a black, red, white, or green pigment.

No "nonceramic Yuman" sites are identified by Smith in this series of sites; however, more recent excavations at the Oro Grande site (Figure 4.12), on the Mojave River near Victorville, have yielded important data relating to a late nonceramic occupation (Rector *et al.* 1979). The Oro Grande site has two components of considerable interest. The earliest, dated by radiocarbon at 3120 B.C., contains no diagnostic artifacts, but is unusual because it is a human trackway where several people of different sizes left their footprints in the mud beside the Mojave River.

The second component is a midden bracketed by radiocarbon dates between A.D. 840 and 1300. Shell beads of southern California coastal origin suggest dates ranging from A.D. 500 to 1500. Rector (1979:137), however, notes that

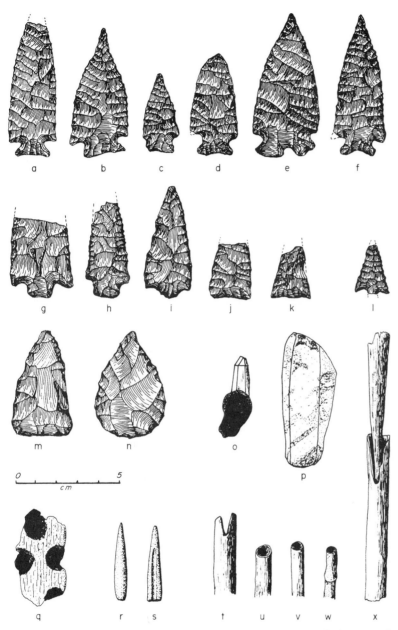

**Figure 8.21** Artifacts from Newberry Cave. a–c, Elko Corner-notched points; d, Elko Side-notched point; e,f, Elko Eared points; g,h, straight-stemmed points; i, Gypsum Cave point; j,k, large triangular points; l, Eastgate point; m,n, point blanks; o, quartz crystal with black adhesive; p, large quartz crystal; q, fire-drill hearth; r,s, bone points; t, notched end of dart foreshaft; u–w, cupped depressions in end of dart mainshafts for atlatl engagement; x, fragmentary socketed mainshaft. (After C. A. Davis and G. A. Smith 1981: Figures 5–8, 10, 12, 17, 19, 29.)

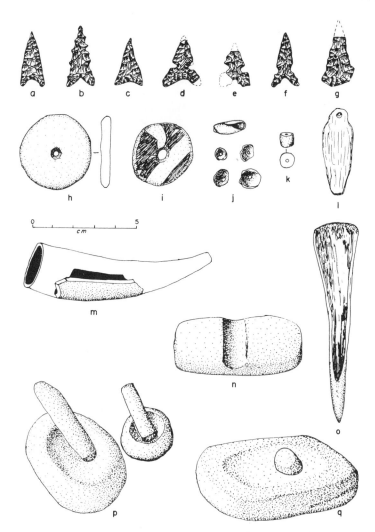

**Figure 8.22** Artifacts from protohistoric sites on the upper Mojave River. a–c, Cotton-wood Triangular points; d–f, Desert Side-notched points; g, leaf-shaped point; h,i, pottery disks; j, shell beads; k, stone bead; l, slate pendant; m, ceramic pipe; n, steatite shaft-straightener; o, bone awl; p, mortars and pestles (not to scale); q, mano and millingstone (not to scale). After G. Smith 1963.)

Time-sensitive stone artifacts recovered from the major component of the Oro Grande site are almost exclusively projectile points of the Cottonwood series. No pottery or Desert Side-notched points were found. Of projectile point styles dating prior to the Cottonwood series, only three specimens were recovered. Together the radiocarbon age determinations and projectile points suggest that most of the oc-cupation occurred within about a century of A.D. 1000.

The facts that 67 of the 74 classifiable points are Cottonwood Triangular, that none is of Desert Side-notched type, and that there is no pottery are important. The knives, drills and perforators, manos and millingstones, mortars and pestles, bone awls, stone pipes, and shell and stone ornaments (including incised slate items) all show close similarities to their counterparts in the pottery-bearing sites along the Mojave River. The Oro Grande site appears to fit Rogers' (1945:173–174) description of the nonceramic "pattern which needs only the addition of native pottery to make it Yuman" (Figure 8.23).

In Rogers' discussion of the Yuman development in the Mojave Desert, he placed the "seat of the culture climax" in the Mojave Sink region "where in the Mohave River during a rather prolonged moist period, maintained at least two permanent lakes for several centuries" (1945:174). Rogers proposed an initial date for the "nonceramic Yuman horizon" on the basis of intrusive sherds. His comments are of interest here (Rogers 1945:175):

> Although Lino Gray and Lino Black-on-Gray are the earliest type to occur, it is thought that they preceded the first Yuman incursion in that they and a few other Basketmaker III artifacts are associated chiefly with local turquoise-mining industry. The most widespread and common intrusive types occurring with the nonceramic Yuman horizon are Deadman's Gray, Fugitive Red, and Black-on-Gray. Judging from this and some other substantiating evidence, the inception date would fall sometime during the ninth century.

Rogers (1945:175) also maintained that because of their "advantageous intermediary position," the local group at the Mojave Sink served as middlemen in trade with Pacific coastal and inland areas. This trade brought intrusive pottery from both the Anasazi and Hakataya regions. However, Rogers also recognized temporary occupation of the area by small Puebloan groups. Lower Colorado pottery was the most common ware, probably indicating "intimate" relations between the Mojave Sink and the lower Colorado River. The latest "trade type" at the Mojave Sink was Jeddito Black-on-Yellow, found with local cremations, which Rogers (1945:176) used to date the abandonment of the sink at A.D. 1400.

Drover (1979) conducted a reevalation of the data from the Cronise Basin in the Mojave Sink, in terms of paleoecological data and radiocarbon dates. He found no archaeological data to document occupation earlier than "traces of 'Pinto' and 'Amargosa' artifacts which may correspond to lakestands of 5000 and 3500 B.C. respectively" (1979:172). According to Drover, intrusive ceramics suggest occupation between A.D. 800 and 1100, which may correspond to the moist periods of A.D. 100–1000 (Mehringer *et al.* 1971) or A.D. 450–1250 (Harper and Alder 1972). However, also according to Drover, 90% of the sites in Cronise Basin correspond to a series of lakestands dated at A.D. 1370–1390, 1550–1560, and 1740–1790 (Drover 1979:172).

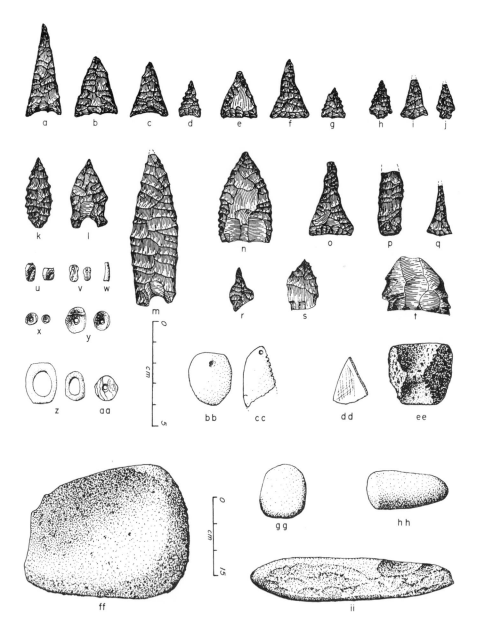

**Figure 8.23** Oro Grande artifacts. a–g, Cottonwood Triangular points; h,i, "small triangular points"; j, Rose Spring Corner-notched point; k, Cottonwood Leaf-shaped point; l,
Elko Eared point; m, Humboldt Basal-notched point; n, triangular knife; o,p, drills; q,r,
"perforating tools"; s, graver; t, scraper plane; u, Spire-ground and Barrel *Olivella* shell
beads; v, *Glycymeris* bilobates; w, *Dentalium* shell bead; x,y, *Olivella* disk beads; z, *Mega-
thura* rings; aa, *Haliotis* disk; bb,cc, shell pendants; dd, incised slate tablet; ee, vesicular
basalt pipe fragment; ff, millingstone; gg, mano; hh, pestle; ii, long pestle. (After Rector *et
al.* 1979: Figures 6–8, 11, 13, 14, 16, 17.)

Elsewhere Drover also noted (1979:221–222):

In an area whose prehistoric land tenure is thought to have been Shoshonean in recent periods, the finding of ceramics, mortuary patterns, architecture and trade items characteristic of Upland Arizona associated with late C14 dates is unexpected. A variety of intrusive ceramics originating from Upland Arizona and the Virgin River associated with several sites are indicative of Puebloid or Patayan site unit intrusions into the Cronise Basin ca. A.D. 1100. Lexico-statistical studies show a long duration of Yuman languages in both the Colorado River area and southeastern California deserts. The weight of ethnohistorical data when coupled with oral tradition strongly suggest a desert Patayan occupation in the vicinity of the Mohave Sinks with sporadic . . . "Shoshonean archaeology," such as described for Death Valley . . . *not* present in the Cronise Basin.

The Mojave River cultural sequence appears to parallel that of the Providence Mountains except for the period immediately following Amargosa I, when Anasazi pottery and Rose Spring points occur at the Mojave Sink and the nonceramic Oro Grande Complex occurs at Victorville. If the occupants of the Mojave Sink were middlemen, as Rogers proposed, then the presence of Anasazi pottery and Rose Spring points may be interpreted as intrusive items resulting from short-term occupation by neighboring groups and/or trade items. An alternative interpretation is that Anasazi peoples occupied the Mojave Sink during the time they controlled the turquoise mines, and that only after circa A.D. 900 did the Hakataya influence and trade network result in a local cultural climax.

The Oro Grande Complex, with Cottonwood Triangular points and the absence of pottery and Desert Side-notched points, is probably an expression of Rogers' "nonceramic Yuman." It appears to be coeval with the Saratoga Springs Culture of the northeastern Mojave, but outside the sphere of Anasazi influence. The Oro Grande Complex probably is the initial phase of Hakataya influence along the upper Mojave River and may not be present at the Mojave Sink where full-blown Hakataya may have replaced the Anasazi-influenced Saratoga Springs Culture.

Following the Oro Grande Complex, the Hakataya are clearly evident on the upper Mojave River at Deep Creek and other late village sites. The Hakataya appear to have persisted until historic times throughout the length of the Mojave River.

### Colorado Desert and Peninsular Ranges

The Mojave Desert south of the Mojave River, the Colorado Desert, and the adjacent eastern slope of the Peninsular Ranges (Figure 4.13) comprise an area where archaeological research has been conducted infrequently. The low-lying Colorado Desert has yielded few data relevant to the intermediate chronological periods. M. Weide (1976:85) reported that, in surveys of the Colorado Desert, Rogers found no sites away from the Colorado River dating from the period between San Dieguito I and Yuman II, suggesting a gap of some 6500 years by current dating. M. Weide (1976) also reported a few tantalizing scraps of information that suggest that man was present during that time, including a radiocarbon date of 3030 ± 100 B.C. for a quartz point of unspecified type from valley fill in San Felipe Creek Valley (Ferguson and Libby 1962); the Truckhaven cairn burial with a bone apatite date of 3840 ± 250 B.C. (Barker *et al.* 1973); and a date of A.D. 370 for a preceramic occupation on the shoreline of Lake Cahuilla, overlain by a ceramic-bearing deposit dated at A.D. 510 (Moriarty 1966:27).

Wallace *et al.* (1962) report a series of large dart points from beneath a pottery-bearing deposit of the Indian Hill Rockshelter in the Anza-Borrego State Park (Figure 8.1). The Indian Hill sequence is of major importance because, at the present time, it is the only sequence in the Colorado Desert that spans the transition from nonceramic to ceramic. The Indian Hill Rockshelter and a series of late sites (Michels 1964; Reinman *et al.* 1960; Townsend 1960; Wallace 1962b–d) on the eastern slopes of the Peninsular Ranges provide data for the local sequence.

The Indian Hill Rockshelter contains midden deposits up to 152 cm deep and is divided into ceramic and pre-ceramic components. Only 18 of 438 potsherds were recovered from below 61 cm deep, and Wallace *et al.* (1962:4) thought that they "could easily have been carried downward by human or rodent activity, or have been wind-eroded from a higher level during the course of the digging." They see similarities between the preceramic Indian Hill component and the Pinto Basin Complex on the basis of projectile points and other unspecified artifacts. It is apparent, however, from the line drawings of the projectile points in Wallace's report (Wallace *et al.* 1962:Figure 5) that these early points could also be interpreted as Elko Eared points. These large-notched points are associated with large scraper-planes (also limited to the lower levels of the rockshelter), leaf-shaped knives, flake scrapers, cobble and core hammers, choppers, millingstones and manos, *Olivella* shell beads, and bone awls.

In the ceramic component, the large points are replaced by Cottonwood Triangular and Desert Side-notched points. A single-stemmed point may be of a Rose Spring type. Pottery is relatively plentiful with Tizon Brown Ware accounting for almost 93% of the sample and Colorado Buff Ware comprising the remaining 7%. Tizon Brown Ware is plentiful above 60 cm, but the Lower Colorado Buff Wares are numerically significant only above the 30 cm level, suggesting a later date for the introduction of Lower Colorado Buff Ware. Tizon Brown is the dominant ware through the late deposits, however. Other artifacts from the late component include knives in reduced numbers, flake scrapers in increased numbers, millingstones and manos, choppers, and cobble and core hammers (Figure 8.24).

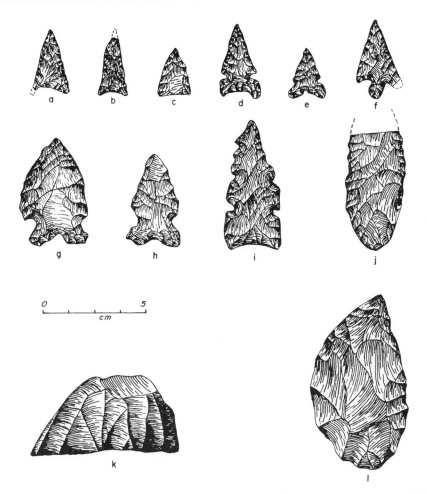

**Figure 8.24** Flaked-stone artifacts from Indian Hill Rockshelter. a–c, Cottonwood Triangular points; d,e, Desert Side-notched points; f, possible Rose Spring point; g,h, "eared" corner-notched point; i, large side-notched point; j, large leaf-shaped point; k, scraper plane; l, knife. (After Wallace *et al.* 1962: Figures 4–6.)

The later cultural component at Indian Hill Rockshelter appears to be essentially identical to the material excavated at Bow Willow 9 (Wallace 1962c) where Lower Colorado Buff and Tizon Brown pottery were present, with Tizon Brown making up about 87% of the sample; Cottonwood Triangular and Desert Side-notched were the most common projectile points, and manos and millingstones, leaf-shaped knives, flake scrapers, core and cobble hammers, choppers, and a few shell ornaments were present.

Townsend (1960) reported a similar assemblage from the Culp Valley and Grapevine Canyon area in Anza–Borrego State Park. Both Tizon

Brown Ware and Lower Colorado Buff Ware were present, and Tizon Brown again accounted for more than 80% of the sample. Points were limited to Cottonwood Triangular and Desert Side-notched types. A single mano and cylindrical stone smoking pipe were recovered and bedrock milling surfaces and mortars were recorded.

Snow Creek Rockshelter (Michels 1964) on San Gorgonio Pass yielded another similar assemblage from the mountain slopes. However, only 55% of the pottery is Tizon Brown; the remaining 45% is Lower Colorado Buff Ware. The projectile points from Snow Creek Rockshelter are Desert Side-notched and Cottonwood Triangular types. Other items from Snow Creek Rockshelter include a ceramic pipe fragment, few knives, a drill, a mortar, manos, hammerstones and a possible pestle, a bone awl fragment, a Barrel *Olivella* bead, and two fragments of unidentified wooden stem.

The Shaw Shelter (Reinman *et al.* 1960), near Carrizo Peak, was apparently a stopping place on a trail between the Colorado Desert and Carrizo Springs. It contained the bottom portion of a large ceramic vessel, a bundle of four wooden foreshafts, a hearth for a fire drill, a hooked stick tied with loose yucca fiber, a wooden paddle, two steatite shaft straighteners, a cut reed, a core, seven flakes of quartz, and a chopper. The single pot is identified as a "typical desert ware of a red brown color."

Surveys in the Anza-Borrego State Park (Meighan 1959a; Wallace 1962b, 1962d; Wallace and Taylor 1958, 1960b) produced the same range of artifacts as did the excavation. Tizon Brown and Lower Colorado Buff wares, Cottonwood Triangular and Desert Side-notched points, manos and millingstones, mortars and pestles, arrow-shaft straighteners of steatite, knives, choppers, hammerstones, and a few shell beads were reported.

Similar assemblages have been reported from lower elevations in the Colorado Desert and the southern Mojave Desert. The survey of Twenty-Nine Palms (Figure 8.1) (Campbell 1931) produced both Cottonwood Triangular and Desert Side-notched points. The large quantity of pottery was not typed by modern methods, but appears to include Lower Colorado Buff and Tizon Brown with some Red-on-Buff. Ceramic smoking pipes of two types (long conical and elbowed stem with upright bowl), steatite and granitic shaft straightener similar in form to those in the Anza-Borrego area, manos and millingstones, mortars and pestles, knives, hammerstones, small stone pendants, shell beads, and pendants are also reported. Numerous perishable items recovered from dry rockshelters include basketry, cordage, rare bits of textile and netting, wooden paddles, cane and wooden arrow shafts and foreshafts, hooked sticks, and fire drill hearths.

At lower elevations in the Colorado Desert, archaeological materials appear to be concentrated along the shoreline of Lake Cahuilla. Here, numerous sites yielding primarily Buff Ware have been reported on East Mesa and West Mesa (Brooks *et al.* 1977; Ellis and Crabtree 1974; Gallegos 1980) associated with high beach lines, bayous, and sloughs.

Wilke (1978b) investigated a number of sites at the north end of Lake Cahuilla where sites are also associated with lakeshore features. Wilke's analyses have provided information on ecological adaptation at four shoreline sites. Buff Ware is characteristic of these sites and Desert Side-notched and Cottonwood points make up the vast majority of projectile points (Wilke 1978b:56–57). Also present are large quantities of shell beads, which derive from the Gulf of California as well as the southern California coast. The beads were analyzed by Chester King and dated at circa A.D. 800–1500 (Wilke 1978b:56).

Wilke also undertook analyses of coprolites and floral and faunal remains, which resulted in a surprisingly detailed picture of the prehistoric resources at Lake Cahuilla during the recent high lakestand. The inventory of faunal and floral remains includes a heavy representation of shellfish, fish, aquatic birds, and freshwater marsh plants, as well as animals and plants from nearby lowlands, creosote bush scrub community, and adjacent uplands. Cattail pollen in some coprolites indicates occupation in spring, whereas *Dicoria* seeds in others indicate occupation in winter. A variety of other plant and animal remains indicate occupation in summer and fall. From these analyses Wilke postulated a permanent year-round occupation of certain lakeside sites and seasonal occupation of others, including small hunting and fishing stations at lakeside and temporary hunting and gathering sites in the uplands.

Wilke proposed a large population for the period of high lakestand, dated by him at between A.D. 900 and 1500, which was supported along the shoreline by an economic system that focused on lacustrine resources with secondary use of other nearby ecological zones. This was an effective subsistence pattern until the desiccation of Lake Cahuilla occurred. The adjustments to the changing lake can best be seen along the receding shorelines, where fish weirs appear in 15 construction eipsodes corresponding to the lake recession. The desiccation of Lake Cahuilla must have caused major outmigration to other areas of interior California, with a profound effect on the prehistoric developments of the area. This is seen as the explanation for the apparent increase in occupation density in other inland areas of California during the late period (O'Connell 1971b; Wilke 1978b:118).

M. Weide (1976:90–92) offered another interpretation, in which she suggests that, when Lake Cahuilla filled, it generally remained full for short periods of time, more on the order of 50 years rather than several hundred years as suggested by Wilke. She also noted that agriculture was not practiced at the site described by Wilke, although it was practiced along the Colorado River during the same period. Weide then argues that the middens associated with the final high lakestand were the remains of small nonsedentary populations that exploited the lake margins and underwent limited population increase. With the final desiccation, they added agricultural pursuits learned from the Colorado River peoples. C. White (1980:181) summarized these two alternative models in a table that is reproduced here (Table 8.11).

A third interpretation of Lake Cahuilla sites is presented by von Werlhof and von Werlhof (1979:30) for the East Mesa site. The von Werlhofs advance the hypothesis that numerous small bands exploited the East Mesa lakeshore resources for short periods between the middle of May and mid-summer. This schedule is postulated on the basis of floodwater-farming practices along the Lower Colorado River. C. White (1980:186–187) noted that the von Werlhof hypothesis appears to assume that the Lower Colorado River flow was relatively stable from year to year, but in fact the fluctuation in flow is great from year to year and had important consequences for crop cultivation and scheduling. Crabtree (1981:46) also noted that a preliminary analysis of ceramic types from East Mesa sites suggests the possibility of a more complex ethnic situation than Wilke found in Coachella Valley "with use of the southern part of the old lake by peoples from several parts of the Lower Colorado River."

The prehistoric data from lower elevations of the Colorado Desert are limited almost entirely to the late period of occupation. This is an occupation that exhibits marked influence from the lower Colorado River Valley. This late occupation is coeval if not contemporaneous with the late occupation along the Mojave River and the eastern flanks of the Peninsular Ranges where Buff Ware is found with the more common Brown Ware. Throughout the whole of the Colorado Desert and the southern Mojave Desert, Desert Side-notched and Cottonwood Triangular points are the dominant types, found in association with the Buff and Brown wares of the Lower Colorado and adjacent uplands.

The majority of known archaeological remains of the Colorado Desert and the eastern slopes of the Peninsular Ranges are very early sites or late sites containing ceramics. The nonceramic levels of Indian Hill Rockshelter represent the only component of the intermediate period. The nonceramic component of Indian Hill Rockshelter appears most closely related to the Amargosa I assemblage described by Rogers (1939) for the

TABLE 8.11

Alternative Models for Lake Cahuilla Prehistory

| Researcher | Lake level | Population | Occupation | Cultural consequences |
|---|---|---|---|---|
| Wilke | Stable | Large | Sedentary | Significant outmigration |
| Weide | Unstable | Small | Seasonal | Minor readjustment |

[a]From C. White (1980:184).

Mojave Desert. Following this occupation, Brown Ware, followed by Buff Ware, is introduced along with Cottonwood Triangular and Desert Side-notched points. This cultural sequence is very similar to those of the Mojave River and the Providence Mountains, the major differences being the relative frequency of the Brown and Buff Wares, and the possible absence of a nonceramic component comparable to the Oro Grande Complex. Although there are almost certainly some regional variations within the southern Mojave and Colorado deserts, the cultural similarities lead us to concur with Schroeder's (1979) placement of the whole area within the Hakataya stem.

# Synthesis

## Introduction

During the past two decades several attempts have been made to develop a cultural chronology applicable to the whole of the California deserts. Wallace (1962a) presented a four-period sequence in which he integrated the Death Valley chronology with Rogers' (1939, 1945) cultural sequence, but with a new set of absolute dates. Lanning's (1963) chronology based on the Rose Spring site received widespread use in the northern Mojave Desert and the western Great Basin. Archaeological data continued to accumulate from the California deserts, however, and in 1974 Bettinger and Taylor published a new chronology because they found the earlier sequences inadequate "for distinguishing and temporally ordering extinct socio-cultural groups" (Bettinger and Taylor 1974:4). In their chronology, the units were clearly stated to be temporal units, not prehistoric sociocultural groups. Each period was marked by a distinctive projectile-point type with wide distribution throughout the California deserts, and dated by radiocarbon. As prehistoric sociocultural groups were identified, they could be placed chronologically by identifying their characteristic projectile-point types.

At about the same time, Warren and Crabtree (1972) constructed a chronology of the Mojave Desert, which is to be published in the Great Basin volume of the *Handbook of North American Indians*. This chronology was also based on the temporal period concept and used projectile points as period markers and radiocarbon assays for absolute dates. Consequently, these two chronologies have a great many similarities. However, there were differences between the two, the chronological placement of the Pinto period being the most obvious (Table 8.12).

**TABLE 8.12**

**Concordance of Chronologies by Bettinger and Taylor (1974) and Warren and Crabtree (1972)**

| Bettinger and Taylor (1974) | Warren and Crabtree (1972) | |
|---|---|---|
| Marana | Period V: Shoshonean | |
| A.D. 1300 | | A.D. 1000 |
| Haiwee | Period IV: Saratoga Springs | |
| A.D. 600 | | A.D. 500 |
| Newberry | Period III: Gypsum | |
| 1200 B.C. | | 2000 B.C. |
| Little Lake | Period II: Pinto | |
| 4000 B.C. | | 5000 B.C. |
| Mojave | Period I: Lake Mojave | |
| ? B.C. | | 8000 B.C. |

More recently, a series of cultural chronologies for the California deserts has been published as part of the various cultural resource overviews by the Bureau of Land Management (e.g., Crabtree 1981; Garfinkel 1980; Hall and Barker 1975; C. King 1976; Norwood *et al.* 1980; Stickel *et al.* 1980; Warren *et al.* 1980; M. Weide 1976). The cultural sequences presented in these reports are in large part repetitive, most being restatements of one of the existing proposed sequences. They are confusing, however, because some authors simply apply new names to an existing chronological scheme, whereas a few attempt to develop new bases for a chronology. It is clear that the relative cultural sequence of the Mojave Desert is fairly well established, but the absolute dates of the intermediate and early periods are points of contention.

In his overview of the Amargosa–Mojave Basin Planning Units, Warren (1980a) presented a slightly modified version of the earlier Warren–Crabtree chronology. Warren (1980a) retained the temporal period as the basic unit, but made some changes in absolute dates. This chronology for the Mojave Desert forms the basis for the following discussion (see Figure 8.27).

The first two periods (Pleistocene and Lake Mojave) fall outside the discussion presented here. We begin with the Pinto Period, the most controversial of all periods.

*Pinto Period (5000–2000 B.C.)*

The transition from pluvial to arid conditions at the end of the Pleistocene was the most severe and dramatic environmental change in the California deserts during post-Pleistocene times. Rivers and lakes dried up, plant and animal life changed, and a new arid environment was created to which human populations adapted, or from which they withdrew to more desirable areas. It is this question of how people adjusted to this major environmental change that is central to the Pinto Period controversy.

Sites attributed to the Pinto Period are few in number, those of the Pinto Basin (Campbell and Campbell 1935), Salt Springs (Rogers 1939), and Death Valley (Hunt 1960; Wallace 1977b), as well as the Stahl site (Harrington 1957), being the best known. The time markers for the Pinto Period are the points of the Pinto series as described by Amsden (1935), Rogers (1939), and Harrington (1957). These descriptions of Pinto points generally stress the coarseness of their manufacture as well as their form, although Harrington notes some finely worked points at the Stahl site. None of these sites has been dated by radiocarbon, but absolute dates have been applied to Mojave Desert Pinto points by cross-dating with Pinto points in the Great Basin, where radiocarbon places them post-3000 B.C. (Hester 1973:38). Several scholars, however, have questioned the validity of the Pinto point type as currently used (Bettinger and Taylor 1974; Layton 1970; O'Connell 1971a; Warren 1980a,b) and suggest that the more crudely made Pinto point from the Mojave Desert may be typologically distinct.

At the present time there are two interpretations of the chronological placement of Pinto points, referred to here as the *short chronology* and the *long chronology*. Sites containing Pinto points are often associated with ephemeral lakes and now-dry streams and springs, suggesting wetter conditions that now prevail in the deserts. The proponents of the short chronology argue that this wet period, the Little Pluvial, occurred between 3000–2500 B.C. and the beginning of the Christian Era (Wallace 1962a:175). It is argued or implied that much of the California deserts went unoccupied during the warm–dry period preceding the Little Pluvial (Donnan 1964; Kowta 1969; Wallace 1962a; Wallace and Wallace 1978).

If this interpretation is correct, a cultural hiatus in much of the central Mojave occurred between circa 5000 and 4000–3000 B.C. If the desert was essentially devoid of people for 1000 years or so, a disjuncture in the cultural sequence would result. Those archaeologists who subscribe to the long chronology do so because they see no disjuncture in the archaeological record. Susia (1964:31), Tuohy (1974:100–101), and Warren (1980a) argue for a long cultural tradition that includes both the Lake Mojave and Pinto Basin assemblages. They see the "Pinto assemblages" as representing a development out of the Lake Mojave assemblages.

The Stahl site (Harrington 1957) has been cited as supporting the late date for Pinto material (Lanning 1963). Harrington's reasoning for a

1000–2000 B.C. date for the site, however, at times strains credibility. First, he argues that the site was occupied during a period of more effective moisture because of a now-dry streambed adjacent to the site and because the ground beneath the midden contained "many tree-holes and root holes, showing that a grove of trees had stood on the site of the village either while it was occupied or very shortly before. This we know because many of the holes contained village refuse which could not have occurred had the trees existed and died a long time before" (Harrington 1957:71). How the village refuse replaced the trees and roots is not discussed by Harrington, but it seems an improbable if not impossible interpretation of the submidden features. It seems more likely that they were extensive rodent burrows that had been filled with midden, indicating considerable mixing of the midden.

Harrington continues: "Another argument for a wetter climate is the presence of projectile points of Silver Lake and Lake Mohave types scattered among those of Pinto origin—90 of them among 497 Pinto points—indicating association or trade and a contemporary period" (1957:71). This association indicated a wetter period, we are told, because the Lake Mohave and Silver Lake points are associated with dry lakebeds in southeastern California and Nevada. The fact that the Lake Mohave and Silver Lake points are associated with lakes of Pleistocene age contradicts Harrington's argument.

Harrington dated the wet period at 1000–2000 B.C. during the "Little Pluvial" and not the "Great Pluvial" because the identifiable bone at Little Lake was all from surviving species. No extinct animals were represented. However, the modern fauna from Pleistocene deposits at Danger Cave and other sites in the Great Basin clearly indicates that the lack of Pleistocene fauna need not indicate a recent date. Finally, Harrington cites Shutler, Shutler, and Griffith's radiocarbon dates for the Stuart Rockshelter (Harrington 1957:72). The Stuart Rockshelter dates of 1920 ± 250 B.C. and 2100 ± 180 B.C. are associated with deposits that contained points identified as Pinto Shoulderless (Shutler *et al.* 1960). The three points, however, are very finely flaked and are almost certainly Humboldt Concave Base points.

The definition of the Pinto Basin Complex was based on material from the Mojave Desert, and it is this complex that must be dealt with chronologically. The radiocarbon dates on vaguely similar projectile points from the Great Basin are of little if any assistance in solving the chronological problems of the Pinto Basin Complex in the Mojave Desert.

The distinctive characteristics of the Pinto Basin Complex (Campbell and Campbell 1935) are the Pinto points in association with heavy-keeled scrapers, flat millingstones, and manos. Rogers (1939) described his Pinto–Gypsum complex as containing a range of tools similar to that described for the Pinto Basin. He noted, however, a paucity of flake scrapers and argued that manos and millingstones were not elements of the complex. He also maintained that the flat slab millingstones were not millingstones. He suggested, because of their highly polished and smooth surfaces, that they "may be platforms upon which fibrous leaves or skins were scraped. They are invariably associated with pulping planes" (Rogers 1939:52–53).

Susia (1964), in discussing Pinto material from surfaces sites at Tule Springs near Las Vegas, Nevada, also noted the presence of thin slabs with smooth, highly polished surfaces, large scrapers, and several varieties of Pinto points. The early Death Valley II assemblages (Hunt 1960:62–73; Wallace 1962a, 1977b:115–118) also appear to contain Pinto Basin artifacts: Pinto points, knives, scrapers and scraper-planes, and choppers are all present. Millingstones in any form, however, are absent.

Throughout most of the Mojave Desert, sites containing elements of the Pinto Basin Complex are small and usually limited to surface deposits (Rogers 1939). Their size and the amount of cultural debris suggest temporary and perhaps seasonal occupation by small groups. The Stahl site, in the northwestern Mojave Desert, is an exception to this pattern. The Stahl site has a midden 137 cm deep containing posthole patterns that appear to be the remains of houses. This site, however, contains small beaked gravers, narrow concave scrapers, and Silver Lake and Lake Mojave points, all of which are characteristic of the Lake Mojave Period. Small stemmed points and pottery of a much later occupation are also present. Furthermore, the deposits appear to be mixed by postdepositional disturbance, with late types of small stemmed points occurring in the same levels as Lake Mojave points. The Stahl site also contains Pinto points that exhibit the crude flaking typical of the Pinto points from the Pinto Basin and others that are pressure-flaked, resembling the flaking technology on similar points in the western Great Basin. The range of scrapers includes types apparently similar to those from the Pinto sites in the eastern Mojave Desert, but choppers are absent. The small, flat, highly polished slabs characteristic of the eastern Mojave Pinto sites are also absent, but manos and millingstones with circular basins are common. The Stahl site varies significantly from Pinto sites in the eastern Mojave. These differences may be caused by (1) mixing of earlier and later material, (2) seasonal occupation over a long period with heavier use and a different range of activities from the small temporary camps of the eastern Mojave, or (3) cultural divergence resulting from adaptation to different environmental conditions and cultural contacts.

The apparent lack of a technology for processing small hard seeds in Pinto sites in the eastern Mojave Desert suggests that a generalized hunting and gathering subsistence system, similar to that of the Lake Mojave Period, was practiced. That people could have successfully adapted to the extremely arid conditions of the Altithermal without a seed-grinding

technology seems unlikely, however. If the Pinto Complex lacks millingstones, then the argument that the Pinto Complex is associated with a
period of more effective moisture is given added weight. Wallace (1958,
1962a, 1977b) and others have correlated the Pinto Basin Complex with
the early portion of the Little Pluvial, which they date at 3000 B.C. to A.D.
1. Mehringer (1977:149) has shown that the Little Pluvial had a more
limited duration, beginning not earlier than 2000 B.C. (and perhaps as late
as 1000 B.C.) and ending at A.D. 1. Bettinger and Taylor (1974) and Warren
and Crabtree (1972) argue, based on dated assemblages, that other archaeological complexes date to this period. Therefore, it seems reasonable to
assign the Pinto Basin Complex to an earlier date. Mehringer (1977) has
suggested that an earlier period of more effective moisture occurred about
4500–3500 B.C. Moratto *et al.* (1978) also recognized a wet period north
and west of the Mojave Desert that began circa 5000 B.C. and ended circa
3500 B.C. This now seems to be the best chronological position in which
to place the Pinto Basin Complex.

It is postulated here that the Pinto Basin Complex evolved from the
hunting complexes of the Lake Mojave Period and that it represents a
small population dependent upon hunting and gathering, but lacking a
well-developed milling technology. As the Pleistocene lakes and rivers
dried up, the early hunting populations of the Lake Mojave Period adjusted to the arid conditions, perhaps by withdrawing to the margins of
the desert and concentrating about the few oases of the desert. The arid
conditions were a cause of environmental stress that limited the effectiveness of the early hunting subsistence system. The resulting adaptations remain unknown, but the tool assemblages underwent change that
resulted in the Pinto Basin Complex.

With the return of moister conditions, about 4500 B.C., the Pinto Basin
peoples reoccupied much of the lower Mojave Desert, attracted to the
shallow lakes, streams, and springs. They presumably followed their lifeway based on hunting large and small game, collecting vegetal foods, and
perhaps exploiting stream resources. The Pinto sites of the lower Mojave
Desert are small in area, lack midden, and generally appear to have been
temporary, seasonal camps of a highly mobile people. The small number
of these sites in conjunction with their apparent seasonal use and small
size suggest a small population, poorly adapted to the desert environment. With the return of more arid conditions, about 3500 B.C., they
probably again withdrew to the desert margins and oases, leaving much of
the region uninhabited until the end of the Pinto Period, about 2000 B.C.

*Gypsum Period (2000 B.C.–A.D. 500)*

The Gypsum Period is identified by the presence of Humboldt Concave Base, Gypsum Cave, Elko Eared, or Elko Corner-notched points, or

any combination of the four, and is dated between circa 2000 B.C. and A.D. 500. The initial date is based on the early occurrence of Elko points at Newberry Cave. Humboldt Concave Base points at the Stuart Rockshelter were also dated by radiocarbon at 1920 and 2100 B.C. (Shutler *et al.* 1960). Even earlier dates for Elko points at the O'Malley Shelter (Fowler *et al.* 1973) on the northeast edge of the Mojave Desert in Nevada have been reported. Other radiocarbon dates in the Mojave Desert that are applicable to the Gypsum Period are shown in Table 8.13. These three-point types appear to persist until after the time of Christ. Anasazi pottery is introduced in the eastern Mojave Desert about A.D. 500 (Shutler 1961), by which time the bow and arrow had essentially replaced the atlatl, as reflected in the reduced size of projectile points.

A few sites in the California deserts and adjacent Nevada and Arizona dating from this period have been excavated. These include Gypsum Cave (M. R. Harrington 1933), Newberry Cave (C. A. Davis 1981; Smith *et al.* 1957), Willow Beach (Schroeder 1961), Rose Spring (Lanning 1963), Ray, Baird, and Chapman caves (Hillebrand 1972, 1974; Panlaqui 1974), and Indian Hill Rockshelter (Wallace 1962a). Additional information is contained in the more general works of Rogers (1939), Wallace (1958, 1962a, 1977b; Wallace and Wallace 1978), Hunt (1960), and Shutler (1961), but data for this period are scanty and the definition of cultural units within this period remains a major problem.

The Gypsum Period incorporates or may be correlated with Bettinger and Taylor's (1974) Newberry Period; the Gypsum portion of Rogers' Pinto–Gypsum Complex (Heizer and Berger 1970; Rogers 1939); Early and

**TABLE 8.13**

**Radiocarbon-Dated Occurrences of Humboldt, Elko, and Gypsum Cave Points in the Mojave Desert**

| Site | Date | Projectile point types | References |
|------|------|------------------------|------------|
| Rose Spring | 950 ± 80 B.C. 290 ± 145 B.C. | Elko series | Clewlow, *et al.* (1970) |
| Newberry Cave | 1780–1020 B.C.[b] | Elko Eared Elko Corner-notched Gypsum Cave | C. A. Davis (1981:94) |
| Gypsum Cave | 450 ± 60 B.C. 950 ± 120 B.C. | Gypsum Cave | Heizer and Berger (1970) |
| Atlatl Rockshelter | 600 ± 120 B.C. | Gypsum Cave Elko Corner-notched Elko Eared | Warren (1982:23) |
| Ash Meadows (Barnett site) | 660 B.C.–A.D. 210[b] | Elko Eared Humboldt Concave-base Gypsum Cave | Muto *et al.* (1976) |

[a]Based on eight dates.
[b]Based on nine dates.

Middle Rose Spring (Clewlow *et al.* 1970; Lanning 1963); Amargosa I (Rogers 1939); Wallace's (1962a:176–177) Period III Amargosa; Hunt's (1960) Death Valley II, exclusive of the Pinto material; Hillebrand's (1972) Ray Phase; and Schroeder's (1961) Price Butte Phase at Willow Beach.

The assemblage of Gypsum Period sites, in addition to the diagnostic projectile points, include leaf-shaped points, rectangular-based knives, flake scrapers, T-shaped drills and occasional large scraper-planes, choppers, and hammerstones. Manos and millingstones became relatively common during this period and the mortar and pestle were introduced. Other artifacts include shaft smoothers, incised slate and sandstone tablets and pendants, fragments of drilled slate tubes (possibly pipes), *Haliotis* rings, beads and ornaments of central California "Middle Horizon" types, *Olivella* shell beads, and bone awls. At Newberry Cave (C. A. Davis 1981; Smith *et al.* 1957) perishable material, in apparent association with Elko and Gypsum Cave points, exhibits a wide range of items including an atlatl hook and dartshafts, foreshafts and butts, a feathered plume, sandals, S-twist cordage, a hearth for a fire drill, a sheep dung pendant, tortoise-shell bowls, and split twig figurines. The Newberry Cave material provides some indication of the kind of perishable material missing from the open sites of this period. Newberry Cave, however, is perhaps unique in that the materials may represent more ceremonial than mundane social and economic activities, a problem that is discussed below.

The Gypsum Period undoubtedly contains considerable variation through time and space that is not easily dealt with beacuse of the paucity of data. Changes in projectile-point forms and the addition of certain artifact types during this period are suggested but cannot be demonstrated at this time. Lanning (1963), Clewlow *et al.* (1970), Heizer and Berger (1970), Hester (1973), and Bettinger and Taylor (1974) all interpret Gypsum Period data in terms of the western Great Basin. These studies have dealt primarily with chronological problems and have emphasized the similarity in the projectile-point chronology of the two areas. Rogers (1939), Schroeder (1961), and Shutler (1961) interpret Gypsum Period sites in terms of southwestern relationships, noting the similarity of some projectile-point types, the occurrence of housepits along the eastern fringe of the Mojave Desert, and the introduction of southwestern pottery at the end of this period. These external influences, however, may not overshadow the continuity of cultural development in the California desert. Lanning (1963:268), Rogers (1939:72), and Hunt (1960:63), among others, argue for cultural continuity between the Pinto Period material and Gypsum Period material. Similarities in point forms and the use of the same sites, have at times made it difficult to distinguish between the material from these two periods, however.

Southwestern influence in the California deserts can be detected during Gypsum times. Although the physical evidence is limited primarily to split-twig figurines, the nature of these artifacts gives the influence some importance. Split-twig figurines are miniature animal figurines, constructed of a single long, thin willow branch, split down the middle, bent and folded so as to create a representation of an animal.

Split-twig figurines are reported from at least 16 sites in Arizona, Utah, Nevada, and California. Radiocarbon dates on figurines range in age from 2145 B.C. (Schroedl 1977:256) at Stantons Cave in the Grand Canyon to 1020 B.C. (C. A. Davis 1981) at Newberry Cave in California. Radiocarbon dates on material associated with the figurines at Cowboy Cave in southwestern Utah suggest that their occurrence continues as late as A.D. 455 (Schroedl 1977:261). The presence of Rose Spring projectile points in the same unit at Cowboy Cave corroborates this late date.

Schroedl (1977:263) placed the sites containing figurines into two groups. The first group consists of sites clustered in a small area of the upper Grand Canyon. These are relatively inaccessible caves and usually contain split twig figurines without any cultural associations. The figurines are most abundant in the Grand Canyon area and are found either in caches along the cave walls or scattered on the surface. Several of the figurines exhibit miniature cottonwood "spears" piercing the body. The second group contains sites from Arizona, California, Nevada, and Utah, which consist of caves that are generally accessible. In this group, the stick figurines are less abundant and are not found in caches, but are distributed throughout the deposits. They are never pierced with miniature spears and are found in association with some type of cultural inventory. Where found with diagnostic points, the most common association is with Gypsum Cave points.

Schroedl (1977:263) hypothesized "that the distinction between the two groups of sites results from a functional change over time in the use of the split-twig figurines." In the Grand Canyon group he inferred that the figurines were magico-religious objects used in a hunting ritual. In the second group, where split-twig figurines are found crushed, fragmented, and scattered throughout the midden debris of habitation areas, he suggested that the split-twig figurines perhaps functioned as "toys or playthings rather than ritual items." Schroedl thus sees the Grand Canyon group of sites as the "core area" for the development of split-twig figurines and the associated hunting ritual. As they spread out from this area, their function changed from a ritual object to a general social item.

The radiocarbon dates now available for the split-twig figurines from Newberry Cave (C. A. Davis 1981:94) are earlier than was the single date available to Schroedl. The more recent assayed dates suggest that the time differences between the Arizona and California figurines may be more apparent than real. The specialized nature of the artifact assemblage from Newberry Cave also has been interpreted as the result of ritual activities and not occupation (C. A. Davis 1981). The Newberry Cave data do not support Schroedl's hypothesis, but rather suggest that the ritual activities of Newberry Cave were repetitive and more complex than those represented by the split-twig figurines in the Grand Canyon area.

The pictographs of Newberry Cave most frequently depict some type of animal; both mountain sheep and rabbits may be represented (C. A. Davis 1981:89; Smith *et al.* 1957:156). The fashioning of split twig animal figurines, the painting of animals or symbols on the wall of the cave, and the use of such items as feathered plumes, quartz crystal wands, and a sheep dung pendant (amulet?) suggest a hunting ritual, perhaps to ensure success in the hunt and a plentiful supply of game. If a hunting ritual involving bighorn sheep is represented at Newberry Cave, then this ritual may be related to the hunting ritual represented by the elaborate petroglyphs of the Coso Range (Grant *et al.* 1968).

The Coso petroglyphs reflect a change in style through time that also illustrates a change from the use of the atlatl to the bow and arrow. On this basis it is possible to date the petroglyphs as probably beginning during the Gypsum Period and terminating in the following Saratoga Springs Period or later. The occurrence of the Coso petroglyphs during the Gypsum Period suggests the possible relationship to the presumed ritual associated with split twig figurines. Grant *et al.* (1968:114) interpreted the Coso Mountains as the heartland of hunting ritual that diffused eastward into southeastern Utah and northern Arizona (and also northward to the Columbia Plateau) and correlated this diffusion, at least in part, with the spread of Numic languages into the Great Basin. They note, however, that "the evidence of the rock drawings suggests that some migrations began at an early date. In southeastern Utah there are sheep with hoofs, men holding weighted atlatls very like Transitional Period Coso drawings. Men or ideas may have been moving eastward from the Coso region before AD 700" (Grant *et al.* 1968:114).

The Coso area was, on the basis of present knowledge, the area in which the most intense production of petroglyphs took place, and presumably is the area in which the associated rituals were most intensely practiced. That the Coso area was the center of development from which this ritual diffused is debatable, however. There is an apparent correspondence of dates between the earlier Coso-style petroglyphs and at least the late split-twig figurines in both the Mojave Desert and southeastern Utah. This suggests the possibility of a long-standing tradition of hunting ritual involving both split-twig figurines and petroglyphs.

It can be hypothesized that the split-twig figurines and associated hunting rituals originated in northern Arizona about 2200 B.C. and reached the central and western Mojave Desert a few hundred years later. The distribution of the split-twig figurines, from near Phoenix on the south to southeastern Utah on the north and from the upper Grand Canyon on the east to Newberry Cave on the west, suggests that split-twig figurines and associated rituals diffused as a magico-religious system across cultural boundaries. The hunting ritual associated with petroglyphs may have been another aspect of the same magico-religious system that reached its climax in the Coso Mountains, perhaps, as suggested by Grant *et al.* (1968:58), because of the depletion of the mountain sheep after the introduction of the bow and arrow.

Schroeder (1961:89–90, 97) and Rogers (1936:61–65) saw relationships between Rogers' (1939) Amargosa I and Basketmaker II that also suggest southwestern influence in the eastern Mojave. This influence may be tentatively dated at least as early as 250 B.C., based on the radiocarbon date for the Price Butte Phase at Willow Beach. The most diagnostic artifact is the Amargosa-type point, which is large, corner-notched, and often classified as Elko Corner-notched.

Wallace's (1977b:118–122) late phase of the Mesquite Flat Culture in Death Valley is correlated with Hunt's late Death Valley II and contains both Elko and Elko Corner-notched (Amargosa I) points, as well as mortars and pestles. On the eastern margin of the Mojave Desert in Nevada, preceramic, deep, circular housepits attributed to Basketmaker II are found containing similar projectile-point types and millingstones (Schroeder 1961:75–78, 96; Larson 1978). Schroeder (1961:95–96) derived these housepits from the west, but the occurrence of a corncob in one house (Larson 1978:16) further supports a southwest origin.

The occurrence of mortars and pestles on late Mesquite Flat and Death Valley II sites may be significant. Mortars and pestles (often of wood) were the tools used to process mesquite pods during the ethnographic period. They are found in close proximity to mesquite groves at Mesquite Flat, at one site on the Amargosa River, and at Corn Creek Dunes in southern Nevada where they are dated between 2080 and 3250 B.C. (Williams and Orlins 1963). This suggests that mesquite may have been first collected during the Gypsum Period.

Both the Corn Creek Dunes site and the late Mesquite Flat sites are relatively large and contain a wide range of artifacts, suggesting a permanent, seasonally occupied site where a variety of activities was undertaken. Wallace (1977b:121) also noted that the late Mesquite Flat people extended their food-gathering activities into the surrounding mountains, where small campsites are found containing projectile points typical of the late Mesquite Flat Phase. The reporting of these sites provides the earliest evidence of a seasonal round of economic activities.

The first clear evidence of contact with the California coast is found during the Gypsum Period. *Haliotis* and *Olivella* shell beads and ornaments are widespread, but not numerous, indicating some kind of limited trade relations that extended to the southern California coast.

The beginning of the Gypsum Period coincides with the beginning of the Little Pluvial about 2000 B.C. and continues into the succeeding arid period. The moister conditions present at the beginning of this period apparently allowed for more intensive occupation of the Mojave Desert. The archaeological assemblages of the Gypsum Period appear to be derived in part from the preceding Pinto Basin or similar complex(es). Tools were added to the assemblage as innovations or "borrowed" items or ideas. Millingstones and manos became relatively common, indicating the increased use of hard seeds, whereas the introduction of the mortar and pestle may indicate that the use of mesquite was introduced at this time. The bow and arrow were also introduced late in this period, making hunting more effective. The split-twig figurines and Coso petroglyphs suggest that adaptation was attempted through use of magico-religious practices.

The Gypsum Period was a time in which the human populations adapted to the arid desert. These adaptations included technological items, ritual activities, and increased socioeconomic ties through trade. As a result of these new adaptive means, the return to arid conditions at the end of the Little Pluvial had relatively little influence on the distribution of the populations of the late Gypsum Period.

### Saratoga Springs Period (A.D. 500–1200)

The Saratoga Springs Period corresponds to the time of Basketmaker III and Pueblo occupation along the lower Virgin River in southern Nevada, and is marked by strong regional developments. However, the same complex of artifacts, including Rose Spring and Eastgate projectile points, millingstones and manos, mortars and pestles, incised stones, and slate pendants, is found throughout the northwestern and northeastern Mojave Desert. To the south, the Hakataya influence begins during this period, extending across the Colorado Desert into the southern Mojave Desert and eventually to the eastern edge of Antelope Valley. The prehistoric culture of the Saratoga Springs Period can be divided into three, and possibly four, distinct regional developments: Northwestern Mojave, Eastern Mojave, Southern Desert, and possibly Antelope Valley (Figure 8.25).

In the Northwestern Mojave, the Saratoga Springs Period is marked only by the dominance of Rose Spring and Eastgate points over the earlier dart points of the Elko and Humboldt series. These small points apparently represent the use of the bow and arrow, which may be viewed simply as an addition of a technological device in a long line of such additions, and not as an indicator of major cultural changes. There does in fact appear to be a strong continuity with the Gypsum Period. The Coso rock art, which depicts the change from atlatl to bow and arrow, is evi-

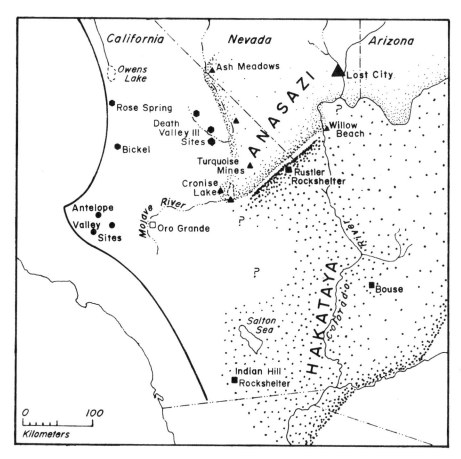

**Figure 8.25** Cultural boundaries during the Saratoga Springs Period (ca. A.D. 800–900). Black rectangles represent Hakataya sites with Lower Colorado Buff and Tizon Brown wares and Cottonwood Triangular points. White rectangles represent sites that have a predominance of Cottonwood Triangular points, but lack pottery. Black triangles represent sites with a predominance of Anasazi Gray Ware sherds. Black circles represent Antelope Valley village sites that appear to be receiving influence from the California coast. Black hexagons are sites without pottery and with a predominance of Rose Spring and Eastgate points.

dence of continuity in art style and magico-religious practices, whereas the sequence at Rose Spring (Lanning 1963) and Chapman Cave (Hillebrand 1972) depicts a gradual addition and deletion of artifact types without a period of rapid change to mark the beginning of the Saratoga Springs Period.

In the Eastern Mojave Desert, Anasazi interest in turquoise certainly had some influence in the Mojave Desert as far west as the Halloran Springs locality, where aboriginal turquoise mining was undertaken. Mining at that location included hundreds of small mines (Rogers 1929b) that most investigators assume were manned by the Anasazi during the initial phase of their operation. Rogers (1929b) reported an occasional turquoise chip as far south and west as Crucero and Cronise, where he listed two "Puebloan" sites just west of Crucero and one on the north shore of East Cronise Lake. Other sites along the Mojave trough where Anasazi pottery occurs include Halloran Springs (Rogers 1929b), the China Ranch (McKinney *et al.* 1971), and Ash Meadows (Hunt and Hunt 1964). These are habitation sites that suggest Anasazi occupation of the area. Rogers (1929b:12–13) states:

> There is no doubt that the Mohave Sink region had a scattered but permanent Puebloan population. Besides the East Cronise Lake site, several other widely separated sites in the south end of the sink produced dominant percentages of Puebloan type pottery; so though the region may never have had any large settlements, it certainly had many small sites and single houses scattered over a considerable area.

The degree to which the Anasazi occupied the Mojave Trough region is debatable. However, it is clear that mining operations were under way sometime between A.D. 500 and 700, since turquoise from the Halloran Springs mines has been identified from the Gila Butte Phase (A.D. 500–700) at Snaketown (Sigleo 1975:459–460).

Warren (1980a:51) has pointed out that if the miners were Anasazi they would have had to cross at least 240 km of desert to the nearest major pueblo. Therefore, a local support system based on local resources would have been necessary if they were to stay at the turquoise mines long enough to produce an appreciable quantity of turquoise.

In the Southern Desert region, the impetus for change appears to have derived from developments on the lower Colorado River. However, the cultural sequence on most of the lower Colorado River is unknown prior to about A.D. 800. The only cultural sequence on the lower Colorado River that extends back to before A.D. 1 is at Willow Beach. Willow Beach is located only 25 km downriver from Hoover Dam and is an area influenced by the Anasazi as well as by the Hakataya. Willow Beach is a small campsite that was reoccupied over many centuries, but many of the intermediate occupation levels produced small numbers of artifacts.

The first indications of Hakataya influence occur in the Roaring Rapids Phase dated before A.D. 750 on the basis of intrusive Basketmaker III pottery. Verde Gray and Cerbat Brown (Patayan) sherds also occur in these deposits as intrusive sherds. This is the phase during which small projectile points first occur in the form of crude "Rose Spring-like" points.

The final phase, Willow Beach, is dated at A.D. 900–1150 and is characterized by an abundance of Pyramid Gray pottery, a lower Colorado River ware, with intrusive sherds of Anasazi origin. The critical transition between the Gypsum and Saratoga Springs periods is not represented at Willow Beach. This transition is crucial to understanding the early Hakataya influence in the Southern Desert region, but only the scantest data are available. Consequently, the interpretations presented here are largely speculative.

The Hakataya influence in the Southern Desert region is seen in the Buff and Brown pottery and Cottonwood and Desert Side-notched projectile points. However, it appears that the Cottonwood Triangular point preceded the regular use of pottery throughout the Mojave River valley. Rogers (1945:175) identified the "nonceramic Yuman" Complex and dated it by "intrusive sherds" to the ninth century.

The Oro Grande Complex (Rector et al. 1979), from near Victorville, lacks both pottery and Desert Side-notched points but contains Cottonwood Triangular points, and is dated by radiocarbon at about A.D. 900–1100. These dates appear late but may indicate a time lag for the diffusion of pottery from the Colorado River. The Oro Grande site also contains shell beads from the California coast, a finding that suggests trade along the Mojave River route to the Colorado River. Trade with the southern California coast may well have been the impetus for the extension of Hakataya influence across the Mojave Desert.

Rogers (1945:174) proposed that during a period of "several centuries," when two permanent lakes formed in the Cronise Basin, the Mojave Sink was the "seat of the culture climax" that resulted, in part, from trade between the Colorado River and the southern California coast.

The initial date for the first Hakataya influence in the Mojave Desert remains unknown, but it appears that by A.D. 800–900 the Mojave Sink was being heavily influenced if not occupied by lower Colorado River peoples. The trade along the Mojave River extended Hakataya influence far to the west and essentially blocked all Anasazi influence west of the Cronise Basin and south of the New York and Providence mountains by about the beginning of the tenth century A.D. or earlier.

South of the Mojave River the influence of the Hakataya is seen in the occurrence of Cottonwood Triangular and Desert Side-notched points with Brown and Buff wares across the width of the Colorado Desert into the Peninsular Ranges by about A.D. 900 (May 1976). The Hakataya influence in the California deserts appears to have continued until well after the end of the Saratoga Springs Period.

In Antelope Valley and the western Mojave Desert, the Saratoga Springs Period can be identified in the archaeological data by the occurrence of Rose Spring points and associated radiocarbon dates. In Antelope Valley there is evidence of large village sites, containing deep middens and cemeteries, that are dated from 250 B.C. to A.D. 1650 (Sutton 1981:217).

The Antelope Valley village sites contain large quantities of southern California shell beads, as well as steatite items and other artifacts that derive from the coast. They also contain both Rose Spring and Cottonwood Triangular points. However, there is no discussion of cultural stratigraphy in the deep midden (Sutton 1980, 1981), nor is there discussion of changes in areal extent of the sites during their occupation.

It appears that Antelope Valley and perhaps adjacent areas were trading heavily with the coast and that Antelope Valley may have developed large villages as early as the Saratoga Springs Period. If this proves to be the case, then Antelope Valley may represent yet another divergent regional development during the Saratoga Springs and Protohistoric periods.

The occurrence of Cottonwood Triangular points and near absence of Desert Side-notched points (Sutton 1981:unpaginated) suggest that the Antelope Valley may have been influenced by the Hakataya as early as the late Saratoga Spring Period. However, the apparent lack of pottery in the large village sites suggests that Hakataya influence was negligible. Since trade between the coast and Antelope Valley villages was apparently well established, ties to the Mojave River trade route are suspected. However, the data reported from the large village sites are at present inadequate for evaluation of the extent or temporal placement of the suspected ties to the Mojave River trade route.

Cultural diversification with strong regional developments characterize the Saratoga Springs Period. Turquoise mining and long-distance trade networks appear to have attracted both the Anasazi and the Hakataya into the California deserts, whereas to the west, in Antelope Valley, trade with the coast may have stimulated the development of a more complex settlement–subsistence system with large permanent villages. Throughout much of the northwest Mojave Desert, however, the basic pattern established during the Gypsum Period continues, with little change through the Saratoga Springs Period.

### Protohistoric Period (A.D. 1200–Historic)

This period was termed Shoshonean by Warren (1980a:52) in his chronology for the Mojave Desert. However, the period marker, Desert Side-notched points, has a distribution throughout the California deserts and Sierra Nevada so that "Shoshonean" becomes misleading when applied to areas occupied by speakers of Yuman and other languages. Historic aboriginal peoples of the California deserts are quite clearly the descendants of the prehistoric peoples of this period, although some historic movements of peoples have occurred. Therefore, the term *Protohistoric* is a more appropriate name for this period than a linguistic or ethnic designation.

The regional cultural developments established during the Saratoga Springs Period continue with modifications. Three major cultural regions can be identified during the Protohistoric Period: the Southern Desert, Northern Mojave, and Antelope Valley (Figure 8.26).

In the Southern Desert region, Brown and Buff wares of western Arizona first appeared about A.D. 800 on the Lower Colorado River, and from there diffused westward across the California deserts by about A.D. 900 (May 1976). Apparently associated with the diffusion of this pottery, or perhaps somewhat later, are Desert Side-notched points. These points do not occur until after A.D. 1100 at Willow Beach and are not present at the Oro Grande site at circa A.D. 1100. However, in the Southern Desert region and apparently into western Arizona, they are found with Cotton-

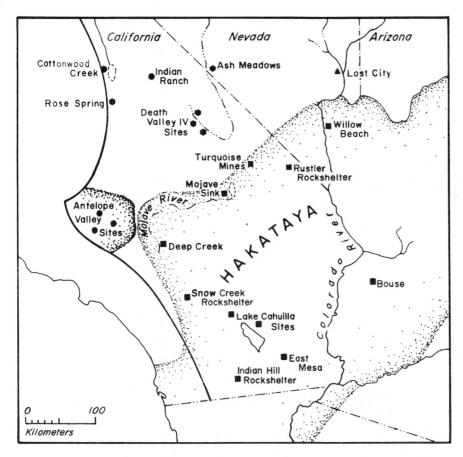

**Figure 8.26** Cultural boundaries during the Protohistoric Period (ca.A.D. 1300). Black rectangles represent Hakataya sites with Lower Colorado Buff and Tizon Brown wares. Black circles represent large villages in Antelope Valley receiving influences from the California Coast. Black hexagons represent sites with predominance of Owens Valley Brown and Paiute Utility wares. Black triangle represents the location of the Lost City site that had been abandoned by the Anasazi prior to this date.

wood Triangular points. These two forms dominate the projectile-point assemblages almost to the exclusion of other forms in the Colorado Desert and the southern Mojave Desert in late prehistoric times. The nature of this distribution argues for association of the Desert Side-notched points with the continued spread of Hakataya influences that occurred about A.D. 1150–1200.

During the Protohistoric Period, the Deep Creek site on the upper Mojave was occupied by a population using Colorado River pottery (including Red-on-Buff), Cottonwood Triangular points, and Desert Side-notched points. This same combination is found on sites down the length of the Mojave River, where they are associated with a rather elaborate artifact assemblage, including relatively abundant shell beads from the California coast, steatite shaft straighteners, and painted utilitarian items, such as millingstones. The apparent wealth of these sites probably is a result of the development of the important trade route along the Mojave River that was recorded during historic times.

Although the cultural assemblages of the Mojave River appear to have ties with the Yuman peoples of the Colorado River, there seems to be little doubt that these late sites along the Mojave River are the prehistoric remains of the Uto–Aztecan Serrano of the historic period. The reason that the Serrano appear to be more similar to the Yuman groups than their Uto–Aztecan neighbors to the north may be attributed to the Mojave River trade route that, for centuries, brought the Serrano in contact with the cultural developments of the lower Colorado River.

The trade along the Mojave River must have provided the middlemen of the region with opportunities to obtain relatively great amounts of wealth and to develop more complex socioeconomic and sociopolitical organizations. Housepit village sites are reported near the headwaters of the Mojave River (Smith 1963a) that suggest similarities to the large villages reported in the Antelope Valley (Sutton 1981). Regional differences between the villages of the Antelope Valley and the upper Mojave River are clearly marked by the apparent paucity of pottery in the Antelope Valley sites and the apparent abundance of Buff and Brown wares in the upper Mojave River villages. Although these two areas participated in trade networks between the desert and the coast, it appears that they were participants in different spheres of influence. In the Antelope Valley, a distinctive regional culture appears to have developed that had stronger ties with coastal peoples and were little influenced by the Hakataya developments along the Mojave River.

The sites in the Providence and New York mountains are clearly local expressions of the Hakataya cultural developments (J. T. Davis 1962; Donnan 1964; True *et al.* 1966) and represented the most northerly penetration during much of the Saratoga Springs Period. However, toward the end of Saratoga Springs, the Hakataya apparently moved far enough north to control the Halloran Springs turquoise mines, replacing the Anasazi.

The presence of the Hakataya south throughout the Colorado Desert and southern Mojave Desert is apparent in the consistent occurrence of Buff and Brown wares and Cottonwood Triangular and Desert Side-notched points. It is during this period that Lake Cahuilla receded and, if Wilke's interpretation is correct, the Hakataya peoples occupying the lakeshore moved west to the Peninsular Ranges, increasing the occupation density in areas such as Anza–Borrego and the higher elevations of Coachella Valley.

In the northwest Mojave Desert, the same general artifact assemblage continues from the Saratoga Springs Period into the Protohistoric Period with the addition of Desert Side-notched and Cottonwood Triangular points, Owens Valley Brown Ware and small steatite beads. This continuum can be seen in the Rose Spring sequence (Lanning 1963) and the Chapman I–II sequence of the Coso Mountains (Hillebrand 1972). Bettinger (1975, 1976, 1977a) attributes the beginning of regular piñon exploitation to this period, as shown by the appearance of camps in the piñon forests.

The Anasazi development in the eastern Mojave Desert is truncated about A.D. 1150 and its influence in the eastern Mojave Desert ends. The following Protohistoric Period is identified by the occurrence of Desert Side-notched points and coarse Brown Ware. Generally, the artifact assemblage is very similar to that found extending across the northern Mojave Desert to Owens Valley. This assemblage can be identified as relating directly to the historic Paiute. The cultural continuity of the Owens Valley and Coso Range extends back into the Gypsum Period, which suggests that the Protohistoric Complex of the eastern Mojave Desert derived from that region. Ethnobotanical and linguistic studies by C. Fowler (1972) support this interpretation. It appears, therefore, that the Paiute were moving into the eastern Mojave Desert at about A.D. 1100.

The cultural expressions of the northwest and eastern Mojave Desert that existed during the Saratoga Springs Period coalesced, forming a single cultural unit across the northern Mojave Desert. The area of the coalescence corresponds roughly to that of the Numic languages during the historic period. This northern Mojave region was apparently influenced during this period by the Hakataya, as seen in the coarse paddle-and-anvil Brown Ware and Cottonwood Triangular and Desert Side-notched points. This influence may have been short lived, however, as the Mojave River trade network apparently broke down. Rogers (1945) noted the decline of the occupation in the Mojave Sink, and Sutton (1981) noted the apparent abandonment of the large village sites in Antelope Valley late in the Protohistoric Period. The decline in trade postulated here may in fact be more apparent than real. However, there are two possible explanations for disruption in the trade route down the Mojave River: (1) the drying up of the lakes in Cronise Basin and (2) the movement of the Chemehuevi southward across the trade route in late Protohistoric times.

During the Protohistoric Period, the Hakataya geographic area included not only the Yumans but the Takic groups as far north as the Mojave River, whereas the Kitanemuk of the Antelope Valley seem to have developed along independent lines heavily influenced by the coastal cultures of southern California (Figure 8.27).

## Summary

The prehistoric occupation of the desert areas of California seems to reflect periods of cultural florescence and cultural decline as the early populations faced changing environmental and social conditions. The

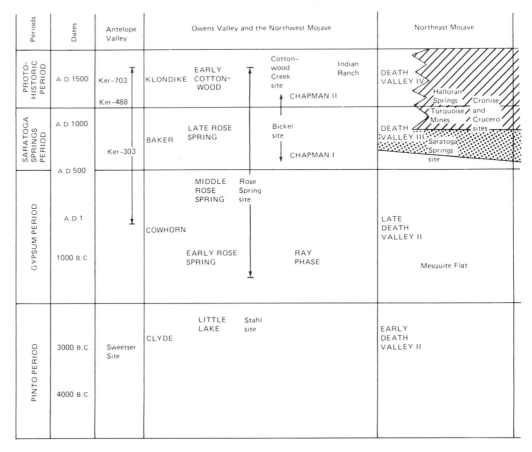

**Figure 8.27** Concordance of archaeological sequences in the Desert Region.

Pinto Period, an episode of dramatic environmental changes when traditionally important resources were drastically reduced, must have been a time when desert dwellers struggled, with only limited success, to adapt. Pinto Period materials are so limited that a hiatus is evident in the archaeological record for much of the low desert. The populations of the Mojave Desert, however, possessed diversified subsistence systems by the beginning of the Gypsum Period. This diversification of subsistence may have been derived from earlier and poorly documented subsistence adaptations made during the Pinto Period, or from adaptations made outside the California deserts. The distribution of split-twig figurines suggests a Southwest origin, whereas shell beads from Gypsum Period sites indicate contact with the California coast where milling equipment has an early date. Whatever its origin or origins, the diversified subsistence of the early Gypsum Period continued as a successful adaptation into the following periods of increasing aridity.

The Saratoga Springs Period is essentially a continuation of the Gyp-

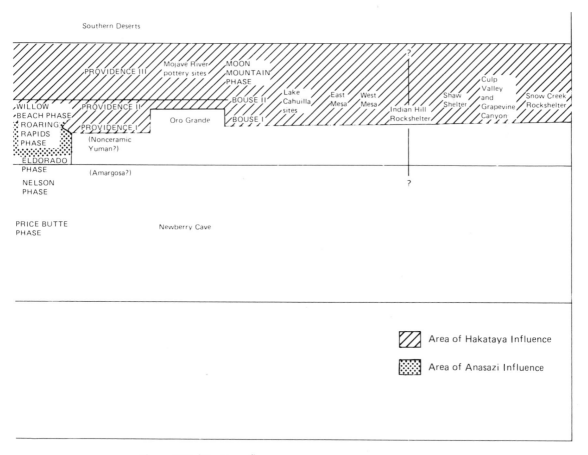

**Figure 8.27** (Continued)

sum Period subsistence adaptation throughout much of the California deserts. However, regional variations occur in (1) the eastern Mojave Desert as a result of Anasazi occupation in southern Nevada and exploitation of turquoise mines in the central Mojave; (2) Antelope Valley due to trade with the California coast; and (3) the southern Mojave and Colorado deserts, late in Saratoga Springs Period, due to the increasing Hakataya influence from the lower Colorado River Valley.

The Anasazi occupation was terminated throughout the eastern Mojave Desert, and the speakers of Numic languages moved eastward and replaced the Anasazi by the beginning of the Protohistoric Period. The Hakataya influence extends farther north, and Antelope Valley appears to undergo a localized cultural climax and decline. Throughout the Protohistoric Period the subsistence system was broad in scope, but based largely on technology that was present from the early Gypsum Period onward.

The subsistence technology from the early Gypsum Period to the end of the Protohistoric Period changed little, but the subsistence systems reflect the adaptation of this technology to changing environmental and social conditions. Diversified applications of this technology during periods of increasing aridity appear to have resulted in a wider range of food resources used and a shift in emphasis from hunting to collecting during the last 2000 years of California desert prehistory. The trade systems of the late periods probably influenced the subsistence system along the Mojave River and in Antelope Valley. Trade made it possible to move resources over relatively long distances and served as a buffer against shortages in local areas. Consequently, populations along such trade routes as the Mojave River could become more sedentary and could establish relatively large, permanent villages. Environmental changes and external influences on the trade systems were two major factors in shaping the late prehistory of the deserts.

The cultural chronology of the California desert region, presented in this chapter, differs significantly from that of Rogers' 1939 sequence. Numerous archaeologists have made significant contributions to California desert archaeology over the past four decades, so that most of the chronological and taxonomic problems that plagued early archaeologists have been solved. The culture history of the desert regions of California, as now understood, raises questions regarding cultural adaptation to changing physical and social environments. Questions such as, "What are the processes by which hunter–gatherers adapt to increasingly arid environments?" are replacing chronological and taxonomic queries. With these new research directions, the archaeology of the California desert region will contribute increasingly to the understanding of past cultures.

# 9. Northeastern California

Christopher Raven

In summertime they camped around in the hills and the valleys . . .
moving about in small groups . . . fishing, hunting, gathering crops of
roots and seeds, and practicing conscientiously a lot of good healthy
loafing. In the fall, when the nights were getting sharp and the
muledeer were turning red, all these wandering small families
returned home, converging . . . from the higher valleys and swales,
down the canyons, through the juniper . . . down to the sagebrush
flats, all trekking home to some wintering ground, at *Astaghiwa*
where there is a spring of hot water, at *Tapaslu* . . . at *Dalmo'ma*
where there are lots of wild turnips . . . there to dig themselves in for
the . . . snow and blizzards and days of calm with the sun shining
bright and the air cracking with frost.
*de Angulo (1979:194)*

Eastern escarpment of the Sierra Nevada looking west up Hot Creek, Mono County. (Photograph by Mary Hill; courtesy of Mary Hill.)

# Introduction

The northeastern corner of the state is California's best-kept secret. The population is sparse, the towns are few, and the major roads that cross it are generally going somewhere else. There is little to attract tourists save the annual deer hunt, and the region's chief exportable commodities (livestock and timber) are marginal when measured against the productivity of other areas. Even the pioneers who traversed it saw little reason to stop in the northeast on their way to Oregon along the Applegate Trail or, later, on their way to the promised riches of the central California gold fields. It was only after the excitement of the Gold Rush had waned that those who had once gone west retraced their steps to the east to settle down to the arduous business of making a living by ranching. Modoc County, for instance, was not settled until 1865, by which time most of the rest of the state could boast a reputation of commerce and regional enterprise.

It is not surprising that the northeast, as California's latecomer in so many respects, should be its least-known archaeological reserve. Few archaeologists have ventured to spend their time and slender funds within it, though many have recognized its potential significance as a contact zone between major cultural and natural areas. But precisely because development has been so slight, because the area has been little studied, and because the region's prehistoric inhabitants had lived there a long time, lured away neither by gold nor the 1862 Homestead Act, the region looms as the state's great untapped storehouse of undisturbed data on what people did in the past.

## Environment

The northern terminus of the Sierra hooks away from the main axis of the range to arc east–southeast in an ever dwindling chain of hills known as the Diamond Mountains. What Alistair Cooke called "the great granite fortress of the Sierra Nevada" stands here weakly buttressed against the geologically much more recent, and less well organized, wildness of northeastern California. And where geology has mapped a line, biology concurs; the Sierran granites erode to deep and complex soils that support a biomass of astonishing diversity, and the volcanic basalts of the northeast weather almost directly to clays, imposing upon all candidate plant and animal communities some formidable limitations. Because these attributes of the landscape and their biotic consequences figured importantly in patterns of prehistoric human behavior, it is worthwhile to get the environmental details straight before examining particulars of the archaeological record.

Northeastern California conveniently divides into three geomorphic provinces (Figure 1.2). At its western flank the Cascade Range, a geologically complex prominence of Pliocene to Recent vulcanism (Macdonald 1966), swings somewhat west of north in a line of volcanic cones and vents climaxing at Mt. Shasta (elevation, 4317 m), a feature visible from the crest of every minor range in the Northeast. The Cascades are moderately cool and moist (annual precipitation, 40–50 cm), hosting at the lower elevations a mixed oak and conifer woodland giving way in the higher ranges to dense coniferous forests composed chiefly of pine, fir, and cedar. The highest eminences (such as the peaks of Mt. Shasta and Mt. Lassen) stand well above the tree line. Drainage is chiefly to the south, via numerous sinuous tributaries of the Sacramento River or its principal branches, the Pit and the McCloud. Large standing bodies of water are rare.

East of the Cascades lies the volcanic tableland of the Modoc Plateau. Massive lava flows of Tertiary and Quaternary age (Macdonald 1966) alternate with broad, shallow basins drained, where at all, south by the Pit River (Figure 9.1) and its tributaries or north into Oregon. Because the clay-burdened, often alkaline soils receive only moderate annual precipitation (≈25–40 cm), vegetation is markedly less lush than in the Cascades; conifers are limited to modest patches on the higher elevations, generally replaced by western juniper over most of the area. The understory is dominated by varieties of sage. Several large basins hold major lakes (especially Klamath, Tule, Goose, and Eagle lakes), around which many aspects of prehistoric life centered.

The easternmost margin of California enters the geomorphic province of the Great Basin. Delineated in the north by the recently uplifted Warner Mountains (Russell 1927) and in the south by the vast Honey Lake Valley, an embayment of pluvial Lake Lahontan, the Basin consists of a mosaic of internal drainages separated by generally north–south-trending mountain ranges. Within this arid zone (annual precipitation, 10–40 cm), waters collect chiefly as snowpack on the higher mountains and run off quickly with the spring thaw to stand in often large but extraordinarily shallow catchments, most of which go dry by the end of an average summer. Trees are rare save for patches of juniper woodland, plant communities instead being dominated by the desert and mountain shrubs that have adapted to local conditions of aridity and alkaline soils.

**Figure 9.1** The gorge of Pit River near Big Bend in Madesiwi (Achumawi) territory, Shasta County. (Photograph by Clinton Blount.)

Historical land-use patterns have modified to varying degrees the natural ecological expressions of each of these areas, posing to archaeology a challenge to subtract the effects of the past 150 years in order to study correlations between environment and culture. The timber industry and modern practices of fire suppression have substantially altered the structure of plant communities in the Cascades and, to a lesser extent, on the Modoc Plateau, in turn affecting the numbers and species composition of dependent wildlife. In the Great Basin, a more fragile ecosystem has responded dramatically to pressures exerted by domestic livestock grazing, resulting in the attenuation of once-extensive grasslands and their replacement by tap-rooted shrubs, mainly sage and rabbitbrush (Corson 1977). Attrition of habitat, both through direct biotic devolution and from modern intrusion and predation, has rendered Basin wildlife patterns virtually unrecognizable when viewed from the perspective of their historic configurations at the dawn of white settlement.

All of this means that the now-classic exercise of environmental reconstruction takes as its point of departure in northeastern California a set of conditions that may bear little resemblance to those to which protohistoric peoples had adapted. The consequence of ignoring recent environmental changes would be to posit a suite of ecological circumstances under which aboriginal peoples never actually lived.

## Ethnographic Setting

The native peoples of northeastern California at the onset of the historic period reflect the linguistic and ethnic diversity so typical of the rest of the state. Nine relatively distinct ethnic groups, representing three major language stocks, fell within or impinged upon the area of concern (Figures 9.2 and 11.1).

To the west, the Cascade Range was dominated by speakers of Hokan languages, chiefly the Shastans (Shasta proper and the poorly known Okwanuchu) and the northernmost reach of the Yana. To the east, the Modoc Plateau exhibited greater diversity, being occupied mainly by the Achumawi and Atsugewi (belonging to the Palaihnihan family of Hokan) in its central range, but including at the north a major portion of the territory of the Modoc and, at the south, the northern fringe of the Maidu (Penutian stock). Along the eastern border of California ranged two groups of Northern Paiute, speakers of a Uto–Aztecan language with marked Great Basin affiliations, and, south of Honey Lake, the Washo, extending north from the Sierra, framed the mosaic with yet another outpost of Hokan speech (Heizer 1966a; Kroeber 1925; Shipley 1978). All these groups were hunter–gatherers whose subsistence and settlement systems were based upon the seasonal exploitation of plant and animal resources within their territory. To avoid repetition, and because some of these peoples were represented only marginally in northeastern California, we shall concentrate on the Shasta, the Modoc, the Pit River (Achumawi–Atsugewi), and the Northern Paiute.

The Shasta occupied a territory that, viewed against the background of the rest of northeastern California, seems especially provident. Along the rivers of the major valleys salmon, trout, and other fish could be taken, along with freshwater mussels. The higher country yielded hunters a

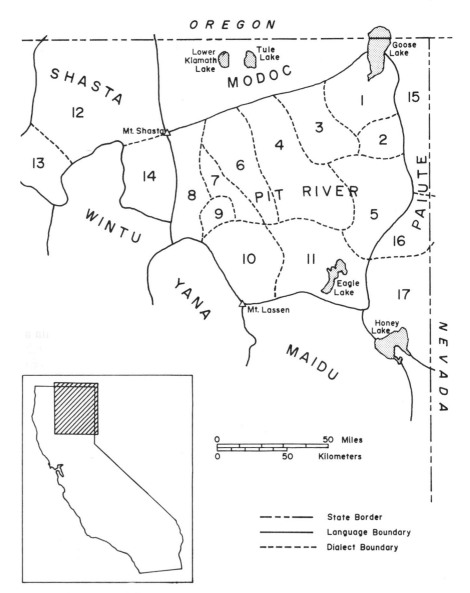

**Figure 9.2** Principal linguistic groups and band territories in northeastern California. Pit River: (1) Hewisidawi, (2) Kosalektawi, (3) Astiwawi, (4) Atwamsini, (5) Hammawi, (6) Achumawi, (7) Ilmawi, (8) Madesiwi, (9) Itsatawi, (10) Atsugewi, and (11) Aporigewi. Shasta: (12) Shasta, (13) New River Shasta, and (14) Okwanuchu. Paiute: (15) Gidutikadu, (16) Kamodokado, and (17) Wadatkuht. (Map drawn by Thad Van Bueren.)

variety of game, including the all-important deer as well as elk and bear, and all zones offered a host of rodents and other small mammals. Birds were also taken (Dixon 1907c; Silver 1978). For most of the Shasta the acorn was the principal plant food, augmented by locally abundant berries, roots, seeds, and pine nuts. The customary division of subsistence labor was observed; men hunted and fished, whereas women did most of the gathering. Both sexes might share in the acorn harvest.

The richness of the environment supported a fairly high population density, with occupation centered in a number of river-based villages. Dixon (1907c) estimated the average population of a village at about 40 persons. Each village invested the power of mediation in an apparently hereditary headman. Each of the four principal divisions of the Shasta also had a headman, implying at least an incipient higher level of political organization. That each village lay claim to a particular territory and that within these territories families or individuals could privately own favored hunting, fishing, and gathering places (Silver 1978) indicate a considerable geographic stability and continuity in subsistence and settlement patterns.

Villages contained semi-subterranean earth and board houses, rectangular in plan, which were often multifamily units. A larger assembly house dominated the center of large villages. Summer dwellings consisted of brush shelters or, during the time of the acorn harvest, of bark houses. Sweat houses and menstrual huts completed the roster of village architecture.

Technology was simple and characteristically Californian. The sinew-backed bow and obsidian-tipped arrow served for hunting, and the mortar or hopper–mortar and pestle were used for the preparation of acorns and roots. There was much work in obsidian to provide cutting and scraping edges. Basketry techniques were similar to those of the Yurok and Karok (Kroeber 1925), with the latter of whom, in fact, the Shasta often traded for baskets.

The Shasta traded with the Achumawi (for obsidian) and fought with the Modoc; their principal relations, however, were to the west with the Yurok, Karok, and Hupa, with whom they traded for subsistence goods (including acorns) and wealth items (such as shell beads) in exchange for such local items as obsidian and juniper beads (Silver 1978).

The Pit River peoples (Achumawi and Atsugewi) occupied the central portion of the Modoc Plateau, from the eastern flanks of the Cascades to the Warner Mountains (Figure 9.2). The peaks of Mt. Shasta and Mt. Lassen formed western boundary markers (Olmsted and Stewart 1978). Although the southwestern portion of their territory (especially along the lower drainages of the Pit River) offered a lushness comparable to that enjoyed by the Shasta, most of their land was high, relatively dry, shrubby, and snarled with juniper woodlands. Salmon, trout, freshwater mussels, and a variety of bottom-feeding fish were taken with nets and basketry traps from the Pit River and its principal tributaries, and the vast tracts of sage and juniper sustained deer, pronghorn, bighorn sheep, and small mammals. Waterfowl were of great importance, especially in the swamps along the drainage of the Pit. A wide variety of plant foods was collected; of particular importance was the *Epos,* a starchy, slightly sweet and storable root abundant in the spring on the rocky, loamy tablelands. The acorn was important in the western (downriver) reach.

The Achumawi were divided into nine bands, or "tribelets," the Atsugewi into two (Kniffen 1928; Merriam 1926). These groups each ranged within a given territory (Figure 9.2) and, although each interacted with other bands, dialectal differences suggest that the integrity of the band territories had respectable antiquity. With time, 11 mutually unintelligible languages might have emerged.

Within their territories, the various Pit River bands enjoyed access to a wide diversity of environmental zones, and settlement patterns were keyed to the exploitation of seasonally abundant resources. The ethnographic view that settlement was utterly river-dominated is contradicted by archaeology, and Kroeber's pronouncement (1925:305) that "the boundaries of Achomawi land are of little significance compared with an understanding of the narrow tracts actually dwelt in" recently has been demonstrated by S. Raven (1981a, 1981b) to be an artifact of past-century disruptions.

Winter villages consisted of groupings of semi-subterranean structures of pole, bark, shrub, and brush (Figure 9.3). Summer structures were less formal shelters of willow framework covered with tule mats (Bauman 1980). Villages served as multifamily bases from which to stage food-getting forays and at which to entertain visitors. Visiting between villages and even between bands was a favored event, and in promising years a village near the town of Likely was the site of a "big time," to which several groups came to join in the communal deer hunt. A village headman exhorted the populace to industriousness.

The sinew-backed bow and arrow, the mortar and pestle, and the mano and millingstone were principal implements of the food quest and food preparation. Obsidian, the preferred stone for flaking, was available to western groups at Glass Mountain and the Medicine Lake Highlands, and to eastern groups along the flanks of the Warner Mountains.

Trade relations were maintained with non-Pit groups to the west, with whom wealth and certain subsistence items were traded. The Paiute were disdained by most Pit bands, and the Modoc, who in the nineteenth century had acquired horses and embarked upon a campaign of slave raids, were generally feared. By the early decades of the twentieth century, most Pit River bands were adopting the trappings of Euroamerican culture (Figure 9.4).

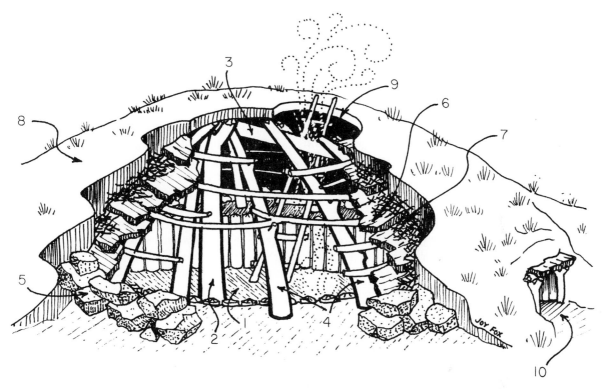

**Figure 9.3** Pit earth-lodge of northeastern California. Within this communal house, three to five families found shelter during 6 months of annual winter cold and wind in the high desert country of northeastern California. The semisubterranean structure, made mostly of juniper wood, lasted about 20 years before rotting. 1, hand-dug pit, approximately 1 m deep, 6 m long, and 4 m wide; 2, juniper log main post; 3, main ridge-log of juniper; 4, juniper log rafters; 5, lava rock parapet wall, used where digging was difficult; 6, cedar bark sheathing; 7, juniper needles; 8, earthen roof; 9, smoke hole and main entrance; 10, air-draft tunnel, also used as an entrance for small children and disabled elderly. (Drawing by Joy Fox; courtesy of Joy Fox.)

The Modoc, whose territory spanned the California–Oregon border (Figure 9.2), occupied the Klamath Lake, Tule Lake, and Clear Lake basins, reaching from Mt. Shasta in the southwest to Goose Lake on the east. The area was one of the best-watered in northeastern California, and the numerous lakes and streams encouraged an economy heavily reliant on aquatic resources. Fish were taken with a variety of hooks and specialized armaments, and waterfowl were netted. Plant gathering, too, had a lacustrine orientation; the *Wokas*, water-lily seeds, were a principal staple. *Epos* and camas were also economically important, and hunters took ungulates and small game. Settlement patterns included coalescence in winter villages and a spring-through-fall round of foraging based on local seasonal abundances (Ray 1963).

Much of the technology and architecture of the Modoc is comparable to that of the neighboring Pit River groups, though a specialized two-horned muller was used in the preparation of the *Wokas*. The focus on aquatic resources was aided by dugout canoes.

Many aspects of Modoc culture are poorly known; subsequent to the "Modoc War" of 1873, a military engagement with the U.S. Cavalry, most surviving Modoc were relocated to Seneca Springs on the Quapaw (Quahpah) Agency in Oklahoma.

Two groups of Northern Paiute (the Gidutikadu of Surprise Valley and the Wadatkut of Honey Lake, Secret Valley, and the southern Madeline Plains) occupied the Great Basin portion of northeastern California (Figure 9.2) (Kelly 1932b; Riddell 1960b). In the southernmost reach of their territory, along the base of the Diamond Mountains, the Paiute were able fairly intensively to exploit a local acorn harvest. Elsewhere, lacking such a rich and centralized resource, they followed a seasonal round of extensive foraging for a diverse food base.

Large, multifamily groups lived in winter villages, subsisting on stored foods and those animals (such as rabbits) that could be taken year-round in valley floor settings. During the spring, summer, and fall there

**Figure 9.4** Northeastern California Indians in transition, circa 1910. This photograph, from the vicinity of New Pine Creek, depicts an equestrian group in largely store-bought clothes. Note the "survivals" of traditional dress (e.g., eagle feathers second and third from left; pronghorn headdress fourth from left). (Photograph courtesy of Modoc County Museum.)

was a fractionization of group size, with family groups moving into high-er country to take roots (including camas), seeds (especially grass seeds such as Indian ricegrass and Great Basin wildrye), greens, and berries. Most animals save carnivores were hunted for food; pronghorn and rabbits were hunted communally.

Village composition was fluid, consisting in any winter of an assemblage of those foraging groups who in late fall found themselves in the vicinity (Kelly 1932b). The result was that personal contacts and family ties were maintained over long distances. Although band leadership focused on a headman whose succession was often hereditary, political organization appears to have been generally loose. Various kinds of power and authority were vested in those who displayed the appropriate aptitudes.

Paiute winter shelters consisted of single-family dwellings in the form of conical, mat-covered structures, 3–5 m in diameter, against which brush or grass was laid. The living floor might or might not be excavated (Riddell 1960b). Summer houses were more casual, often consisting only of roofless, brush windscreens. Technology consisted largely of the basic tools and methods employed by other California and Great Basin groups, with little by way of unique or specialized equipment.

## The Archaeological Record

The following summarizes the principal features of what is currently known about northeastern California archaeology. Because the kinds of questions that have been asked of the archaeological record have changed through time, and the kinds of answers they have yielded have differed significantly, it has seemed useful to phrase this discussion in terms of a number of historical themes which, on and off, have dominated inquiry into the region's past.

### Exploratory Archaeology

The first notice of archaeology in California's Northeast was delivered by J. Goldsborough Bruff, an adventurer and fortune seeker who had come west in the Gold Rush. In 1850, in the company of Peter Lassen, Bruff passed along the low gorge of Smoke Creek in Lassen County (a route that would eventually lead him to discover Honey Lake Valley), taking note of vast numbers of petroglyphs lining the walls of what he called the "Hieroglyphic Defile" (Bruff 1949) (see Figure 9.5). Recorded in his journal is a remarkably accurate sketch of one of the panels, which Clewlow

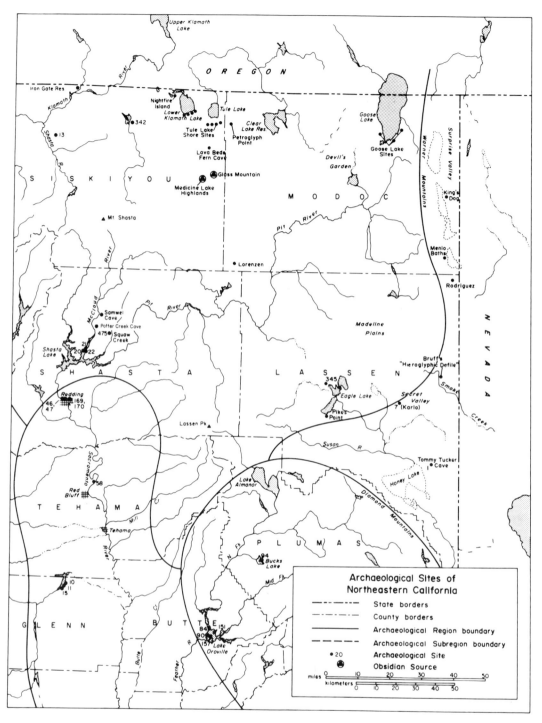

**Figure 9.5** Archaeological sites in northeastern California. (Map drawn by Allan Childres and Thad Van Bueren.)

(1978:619) regards as the "first record of prehistoric rock art in California." Nearly a century was to pass before such careful attention would again be paid to the archaeological record of the state's most remote corner.

Bruff's record was merely one entry in a catalogue of travels-among-wonders; the paradigm of inquiry asked simply, "what did you see along the way?" By the 1930s, however, when California archaeology had at least begun to pose some more sophisticated questions, it seemed desirable to accumulate data based somewhat less upon the principle of serendipity. The National Park Service provided the catalyst. Having begun to manage the newly created Lava Beds National Monument—site of the 1872–1873 conflict between the U.S. Cavalry and Captain Jack's band of Modoc Indians—the Park Service sponsored the first of several investigations into the prehistory of the area.

In 1935 D. H. Canfield and J. C. Couch undertook limited survey in the Lava Beds and made test excavations in Fern Cave (see Figure 9.5), a massive lava tube the mouth of which had served as a shelter in prehistory. Despite the shortcomings of a quick venture into the field with a research design based mainly upon curiosity, the authors tentatively were able to identify two sequential periods of occupation in the cave. The work was modest in scope, execution, and manner of reporting, and its importance was eclipsed within the decade by work performed outside of California.


## Chronology and Culture History

The research of Luther Cressman was to dominate northeastern California archaeology for at least 20 years. His work in the Guano Valley of southeastern Oregon (Cressman 1936) and in caves at Fort Rock, Paisley, Roaring Springs, and Catlow Valley (Cressman et al. 1940) established a regional chronology for the northern Great Basin that spanned the time from the Fluted-Point Tradition to the historic period. There was also some (arguable) evidence of the association of cultural remains with bones of extinct Pleistocene fauna. Much of Cressman's earliest material is typologically comparable to the assemblage of large stemmed projectile points, heavy basalt core tools, and chipped-stone "crescents" later incorporated by Bedwell (1970, 1973) into his Western Pluvial Lakes Tradition, thought to be an expression of early lacustrine adaptations between 9000 and 6000 B.C. Significant contributions to regional prehistory included the definition of the distinctive Catlow Twined basketry (of which Cressman took the center of diffusion to be southeastern Oregon) and recognition of the important role for both relative and absolute chronologies to be played by the Mount Mazama ash fall.

Although Catlow Twining has achieved something of the status of a horizon marker, Mazama ash has become, under ideal circumstances, a valuable stratigraphic index. The eruption of Mt. Mazama in south-central Oregon, which left the great caldera now occupied by Crater Lake, saw in addition to massive pumice flows the eolian deposition of petrographically identifiable ash (tephra) over a vast region of the Columbia Plateau and the northernmost reaches of California and the Great Basin (Williams 1942). Cressman originally estimated the date of the eruption to be between 8000 and 2000 B.C., and dated stratigraphically inferior materials accordingly; recent radiocarbon dating has fixed the principal episode of vulcanism at about 6900 years ago (J. O. Davis 1978; Kittleman 1973). The effects of the ash fall are still being debated; the deep deposits at Klamath Marsh (Mehringer *et al.* 1977) may have significantly altered water levels, and in the Fort Rock Basin of southern Oregon the eruption was coincident with the beginning of a 2000-year hiatus in human occupation (Bedwell 1973). This apparent abandonment, however, is probably related to the rigors of the Altithermal climatic episode, a hypothesized period of protracted warmth and aridity, to be discussed later. Grayson (1979) has concluded, for instance, that vertebrate faunal populations suffered no pronounced long-term effect from the Mazama event.

In 1940 Cressman brought his Great Basin perspective to northeastern California, with excavations at a number of locales in the Klamath Lake Basin. The intent of the Klamath Basin research, which was to become an early exemplar of interdisciplinary archaeology, was largely cultural–historical and stressed the discovery of areal patterns and their chronologies. Three cultural phases ("horizons") were defined for the Lower Klamath Lake vicinity (Cressman 1942). The earliest, designated The Narrows, was characterized by crude, plano-convex willow-leaf projectile points, fossilized bone foreshafts and beveled-edge knives, and the presence of manos. The evident association with extinct fauna, particularly mastodon, led Cressman to posit an age range of 8000–5500 B.C. for this horizon.

The Lairds Bay Horizon, with a suggested date of circa 2000 B.C. on the basis of Antevs' studies of lake bottom peat beds, saw a continuation of grinding stones as well as the introduction of large side-notched and corner-notched projectile points that today would be classified as Northern Side-notched and the Elko series.

The Modoc Horizon, characterized by assemblages equivalent to those observable in most local surface contexts and therefore taken by Cressman to represent the "historically modern" component of the Klamath Basin record, witnessed the reduction in size of projectile points (here, corner-notched and barbed), which has become recognized as the hallmark of the advent of the Rose Spring and Gunther series.

In an appendix to Cressman's report, Heizer (1942a) described materials taken from the south shore of Tule Lake and from caves at the nearby Petroglyph Point (Figure 9.6). The prevalence of small projectile points and shell beads of Pacific Coast origin indicated to Heizer that the assemblages fell late in the local sequence and were probably reflective of Modoc Indian occupation.

The value of Cressman's elegantly produced volume, elaborated when the Carnegie Institution was still in the business of sponsoring and publishing first-class archaeology, lay less in what it explained (and it sought, in anthropological terms, to explain very little) than in what it described. There was at once available an enormous body of data, meticulously described and superbly illustrated, against which materials from the Great Basin, the Plateau, and the Cascades might be compared. It was, for a long time, northeastern California's only venture into "big-time" archaeology.

The next 25 years saw largely a filling-in of the gaps in Cressman's programmatic synopsis of local prehistory. Surveys and excavations added details of place, time, and manner of life style, but with two notable exceptions (discussed below), they posed no new questions of the archaeological record. The intellectual climate of archaeology then was preoccupied with cataloging what lay on and in the ground, and theory-building was viewed as the somewhat frivolous enterprise of armchair practitioners who had never raised calluses from shovel and trowel (R. F. Heizer, personal communication, 1974).

Certainly, the record of archaeological research in the northeast displays throughout the 1940s, 1950s, and early 1960s a loving embrace of particularistic detail. In the first place, the Lava Beds and the Tule Lake vicinity (Figure 9.5) witnessed a frenzy of activity, much of which was bought under contract by the National Park Service. Squier and Grosscup (1952, 1954) documented surveys of the area in which they recorded 163 sites typed as rockshelters, "surface sites" (lithic scatters), rock art, and disposals of the dead. They observed that the southern shore of Tule Lake hosted most of their surface sites, and that rock art was most frequently found in cave–rockshelter associations. Subsequent survey by Squier, together with his excavation of three rockshelters and two open sites (Squier 1956), resulted in a subdivision of Cressman's (late) Modoc Horizon; the Indian Banks and Gillem Bluff phases appear to perpetuate some of the technological features and ecological orientations of the earlier Lairds Bay Horizon, being marked by large and medium-sized projectile points, stone mauls, and thin milling slabs. The subsequent Tule Lake Phase, however, which Squier (1956:2) took to reflect the material culture of the late prehistoric and protohistoric Modoc Indians, saw the introduction of small projectile points (including the Desert Side-notched type), the decline of thin millingstones, and the appearance of the slab hopper mortar.

**Figure 9.6** Petroglyph Point in Lava Beds National Monument, Modoc County. Remnants of shoreline sediments of prehistoric Tule Lake may be seen at the bottom of the lava cliff. (Photograph by Mary Hill.)

Additional survey in the Lava Beds–Tule Lake vicinity (Swartz 1961) and the excavation of Sis-101 on the Tule Lake shore (Swartz 1964) added to the roster of sites in the area and accumulated further detail on material culture, but the substance of these studies, including a proposed temporal sorting, made little advance toward understanding local prehistory. *Explanation* of the archaeological record had not been ventured.

Archaeology in the western portion of northeastern California, from the northern margin of the Sacramento Valley to the point where the Klamath River enters the state from Oregon, presents an even less well-articulated body of fact gathering. In part, this owes to the marginality of the area and to the complexity of its external relations; chronology-building, for instance, had to rely on sequences developed for the North Coast Ranges (Chapter 10), for central California (Chapter 5), for the Columbia River Plateau, and for the northern Great Basin. In even larger part, understanding has been inhibited by the limited goals and relentless preoccupations of the early stages of California research.

The initial forays were made at Potter Creek Cave (Figure 9.5) in Shasta County where, just after the turn of the twentieth century, the presence of apparent artifacts in a faunal assemblage containing bones of several extinct Rancholabrean species was taken as evidence of great antiquity (Krieger 1964; Putnam 1906; Sinclair 1904). Recent researches (detailed in Chapter 2), however, have shown the cultural materials in the deposit to be some 6000 years younger than the Rancholabrean animal bones (Payen and Taylor 1976).

Concerted investigation of the area's cultural history began in the early 1940s, influenced by a concern that was to manifest itself during more than two decades of local research design. Anticipating the inundation of the Sacramento–McCloud–Pit River confluences by the waters of Shasta Reservoir (Figure 9.5), University of California archaeologists undertook survey and very limited excavations to salvage something of the jeopardized record. While more will be said below about the limitations of reservoir archaeology in north-central California, the work at Lake Shasta was an inauspicious beginning. Sparsely funded and interrupted by the war effort, the 1941 and 1942 field seasons witnessed the recording of 37 archaeological sites and the minimal testing at 3 of them by a two-man crew, without vehicles! (Smith and Weymouth 1952a:1).

The manner of reconnaissance was not reported, but almost certainly it was extensive, intuitive, and preoccupied with habitation sites (house-pits were observed at 20 of the 37 recorded sites). A predominantly riparian orientation was noted in the site distribution, though one suspects also a riparian orientation in the survey. The most intensive occupation was noted along the lower McCloud River. River sites, terrace sites, and hill sites were distinguished, with a tendency for sites to be smaller and shallower as distance from the river increased. Excavated artifacts included numerous projectile points—especially small specimens that, under the designations Gunther Barbed and Desert Side-notched, eventually would be recognized as late time markers—as well as pestles and hopper mortars, and beads of shell, glass, and pine nuts. Thirty-seven burials were reported also in the course of this work.

Despite the limitations of their data, Smith and Weymouth (1952a: 30–31) concluded correctly that their excavated material was quite late, consonant with the ethnographic cultural inventory in the area. Similarly late specimens emerged from Sis-13 (Figure 9.5), a rockshelter near Yreka excavated in 1950 (Wallace and Taylor 1952). Small barbed (Gunther Barbed) projectile points again dominated the assemblage, although ground stone, unlike the Lake Shasta discoveries, consisted chiefly of the mano–millingstone complex. The deposit also contained assorted organic artifacts, including tule matting and Catlow Twined basketry. Wallace and Taylor concluded that the archaeological assemblage most resembled that of the Tule Lake sites, and that strong ethnographic correlates were to be found in the material culture of the Achumawi and Modoc.

In 1952 Adán Treganza proposed to the National Park Service a research program for data recovery from seven projected reservoir localities in central and north-central California, although work in the northern area was deferred until 1957 (Treganza 1958c). By that time C. Meighan

(1955a) had published his influential paper on the North Coast Ranges, in which he defined a late "Shasta Complex" (see Chapter 10), and Treganza's work in the Trinity and Whiskeytown Reservoir areas (Figure 10.4) served to confirm the presence of that complex in the hilly region north of the Sacramento Valley. (The Shasta Complex appears also at Sis-13 and at the Lake Shasta sites, discussed above.)

The 1957 season at Trinity Reservoir witnessed extensive earth-moving at three sites, and limited testing at another, of the 120 "village sites" that had been recorded during initial survey. Owing to the escalation of site destruction in the area, and to the inevitable shortness of time and money, some brusque techniques were employed; shovel broadcast was adopted as the standard means of artifact recovery except in complex features (with a screened control sample to monitor data loss), and at three sites bulldozers were used to peel away surface layers quickly since "of primary concern was the location of cemeteries" (Treganza 1958c:12). Although no cemeteries were found, various housepits and isolated burials were investigated. Treganza viewed the cultural inventory, which included apparently conical bark houses, pestles and hopper mortars, and small projectile points, to be late in time and characteristic (if in an impoverished way) of the Wintu who had occupied the area. The chief value of the report lies in Treganza's type definition of the Gunther Barbed projectile point, his discussion of its wide distribution, and his recognition of its probable value as a late prehistoric and historic time marker.

The philosophy, pace, and preoccupation of the 1957 Trinity Reservoir operation were perpetuated in the following years. In the second season at Trinity (Treganza 1959a), two village sites, a sweat house, and a dance house were investigated. The results of the season contributed little except some details of late prehistoric dance-house and sweat-house construction. In the Whiskeytown Reservoir area, excavations at two village sites were abandoned when no burials were found (Treganza and Heiksen 1960). Survey and excavation at Whiskeytown again supported continuity with ethnographic Wintu culture and reiterated the local prevalence of the Shasta Complex (although Treganza admonished that it probably consisted of recognizably discrete economic and sociopolitical elements). The largely homogeneous archaeological record in the area of the major reservoirs—Shasta, Trinity, and Whiskeytown—was believed to express a time depth not exceeding 900 years.

The "reservoir focus" in north-central California archaeology occurred at an unfortunate time in the development of research priorities in the state. That the work was cadenced in the feverish tempo of "crisis management" only in part explains its limitations. A preoccupation with cemeteries as the chief units of archaeological inquiry had been imported from central California, and the evaluation of the research potential of sites and even of entire regions depended largely upon detectable burial complexes.

More striking (and more chilling from later research perspectives) is the complacent manner in which some of the region's predictably richest archaeological zones were shaded in on the map, in confidence that all that *could* be learned *had* been learned. Treganza (1959a:28) states the view unequivocally:

> It is felt that there remains practically no archaeological data yet to be collected within the Trinity Reservoir area, save that [sic] data pertaining to individual burials. . . . Evidently all of the sites worth excavating have been excavated and *continued efforts in the region would almost undoubtedly result in an accumulation of quantitative data of little comparative value* [emphasis added].

In this R. F. Heizer, then doyen of California archaeologists, concurred, and the National Park Service expressed contentment (Treganza 1959a:*i–iii*).

The Whiskeytown vicinity was revisited in 1969–1971 by archaeologists from California State University, Chico, to salvage data from Sha-177, an open midden site in the lower Clear Creek drainage first recorded by Treganza (n.d.c). Limited testing produced a host of small, ostensibly late projectile points dominated by side-notched (including Desert Side-notched) and Gunther Barbed specimens. Water separation (flotation) techniques were employed to segregate plant macrofossils from a sample of the midden, leading the investigators to conclude summer occupancy from the abundance of manzanita berry seeds and the relative paucity of acorns (Johnson and Skjelstad 1974).

One of the most important sites in the area has been under excavation since 1970. S. E. Clewett (1974, 1977; Clewett and Sundahl 1983) has conducted investigations at Sha-475 on Squaw Creek (Figure 9.5), disclosing the region's single identified long-term cultural sequence. Supported by $^{14}$C dates (of which the oldest, at 6530 ± 300 B.P., dates an early episode of occupation at the site), Clewett has reconstructed a scenario of cultural change that he believes may extend to circa 8000 years ago.

The deepest deposits at Squaw Creek have yielded wide-stemmed projectile points apparently of the Borax Lake type (see Chapter 10). Millingstones were rare or absent before circa 5000 B.C., but from that date until circa 2000 B.C. they increased strikingly. Subsequent components are marked by a sharp decline in millingstones. The period 4000–0 B.C. saw the introduction of numerous projectile-point styles reminiscent of types defined for the North Coast Ranges, namely, Houx, Excelsior, and McKee (Baumhoff 1981b; see also Chapter 10), although there are both stylistic and temporal disparities. Large side-notched and small corner-notched (Rose Spring?) points appear at circa A.D. 1. The terminal deposits of the site exhibit the Gunther Barbed projectile points and hopper mortar of the Shasta Complex. Adequate comparisons and evaluation of the significance of the Squaw Creek finds must await further excavation, but Clewett's work already has posted landmarks in northeastern California's largest remaining chronological data gap.

The last major excavation along the western margin of our area of concern lay on the Klamath River just south of the Oregon border. The Iron Gate site (Figure 9.5), excavated in two seasons during 1960 (Leonhardy 1967), was a small, late prehistoric village. Radiocarbon determinations support a suggested occupancy from circa A.D. 1400 to 1600, and time-marker projectile points (especially Gunther Barbed and Desert Side-notched types) confirm this range. Excavation units were selected on the basis of the occurrence of housepits, with the result that one of the most substantive contributions of the research was the reconstruction of a conical, bark-covered pit house, 5–6 m in diameter, which, as Leonhardy noted, is atypical of the ethnographic (Shasta) traits observed along this segment of the Klamath River. Leonhardy concluded that the rectangular house, ethnographically characteristic of the area, must have been introduced sometime after A.D. 1500. Viewing the total assemblage, Iron Gate is expressive of a culture "transitional between central California and the Klamath Lakes–Columbia Plateau regions" (Leonhardy 1967:40), with particular California emphasis detected in house form and the hopper mortar complex.

Elsewhere in northeastern California chronological debates were being settled and the rudiments of regional culture histories were being sketched. Almost immediately upon formation of the California Archaeological Survey, F. A. Riddell began survey work in Lassen County, and in 1949 he and F. Fenenga published the first report on excavations in Tommy Tucker Cave (Las-1), a shelter on a high waterline of old Lake Lahontan (Fenenga and Riddell 1949) (Figure 9.5). These and subsequent excavations (Riddell 1956) identified the cave as a retreat of limited function, perhaps used for gambling or other time-passing activities. Its importance, however, in the decipherment of regional prehistory derived from the link that it established between the cultures defined by Cressman on the northern periphery of the Great Basin and those which had been detected in cave deposits in central Nevada. Riddell was able to point out numerous features of the assemblage that were characteristic of documented Great Basin ethnographic patterns, as well as specific details (such as projectile-point typology) congruent with materials from Lovelock Cave (Loud and Harrington 1929; Heizer 1951e), to the Late Phase of which he assigned the principal Tommy Tucker occupation (Figure 9.7).

There was, then, archaeological evidence for a western expression of Great Basin prehistoric cultures, alike but not identical, which appeared to accord well with the limits of the physiographic province as well as with the culture–area boundaries that Kroeber and Steward had drawn many years before on ethnographic grounds. Riddell returned to the problem in 1958 in a brief overview of research along the eastern border of California in which he noted the strong Basin orientation of much of eastern California co-occuring with pronounced interior California rela-

| Dates | Karlo/Honey Lake (Riddell 1960a, Theodoratus et al. 1979) | Surprise Valley (O'Connell 1971, 1975) | Eagle Lake (Pippin et al. 1979) | Nightfire Island (Grayson 1972) |
|---|---|---|---|---|
| | (Paiute) | (Paiute) | (Atsugewi) | (Modoc) |
| 1850 | | | | |
| 1500 | Amedee | Bidwell | Later Occupations | PHASE V |
| 1000 | Tommy Tucker | Alkali | | |
| 500 A.D. | | | Pikes Point | PHASE IV |
| 0 B.C. | | | | |
| 500 | | Emerson | | |
| 1000 | Karlo | | Aspen | PHASE III |
| 1500 | | Bare | Grove | |
| 2000 | | Creek | | |
| 2500 | | | | PHASE II |
| 3000 | Madeline | | | |
| 3500 | Dunes | Menlo | Eagle | PHASE I |
| 4000 | | | Lake | |
| 4500 | | | | |
| 5000 | | | | |

**Figure 9.7** Concordance of principal cultural sequences defined in northeastern California. Names of ethnographic groups in each locality are given in parentheses.

tions (expressed particularly in trade goods such as shell beads). Chronology was still sketchy, and the question of similarities and differences in adaptive strategies was still largely relegated to trait-list comparisons, but Riddell concluded (1958:46) that a temporal framework for understanding cultural affinities along the western periphery of the Great Basin was well within reach.

Reporting of excavations at the Karlo Site (Figure 9.5) in Secret Valley, Lassen County (Riddell 1960a), ushered the Basin portion of northeastern California into the mainstream of regional prehistory by providing a detailed body of substantive data that could be compared to the rapidly accumulating materials from both the Basin and interior California. The importance of the Karlo site was manifold: (1) it was the first major open site excavated in the Great Basin, thus complementing the record that had so far been "cave-dominated"; (2) it exhibited a deep, long sequence of occupation that contained among its large complement of projectile points virtually all the principal time markers which subsequent research in the Basin would define; (3) a large number of burials (42) was investigated, the grave goods of which allowed the definition of significant "units of contemporaneity"; (4) marine shell beads signaled datable relations with established interior California sequences; and (5) the deposits, although badly disturbed by rodents and vandals, preserved sufficient details to make possible a reconstruction of domestic architectural features and a sketch of a faunal assemblage the gross details of which later would be reiterated at scores of Great Basin sites.

The Karlo site occupied a slight rise above a broad plain (Secret Valley) composed chiefly of Tertiary and Quaternary lake sediments. The site rested near a spring-fed perennial stream, which was doubtless the chief factor in conditioning its placement. Sustaining a substantial midden deposit (maximum depth, 122 cm), it probably comes as close as any excavated site in the Great Basin to being comfortably regarded as a "village."

Of the large assemblage of artifacts recovered, 601 items were projectile points. Although the report appeared before several of the key Great Basin typological definitions had been made, it is possible to recognize the presence of the Northern Side-notched, Pinto, Humboldt, Elko, Rose Spring–Eastgate, and Desert Side-notched types (Figure 9.8). On comparative typological grounds, Riddell postulated a temporal equivalence between his Karlo Period (2000–0 B.C.) and the Early and Transitional phases of Lovelock Cave (Figure 9.7). The supposed beginning date of the Karlo occupation was given added weight by the occurrence of shell beads (particularly *Olivella* and *Haliotis*) of types that, in central California, are characteristic of the "Early Horizon" and the early portion of the "Middle Horizon."

Animal bones from the Karlo site demonstrated throughout the sequence a marked preoccupation with rabbits and small mammals on the part of the prehistoric hunters. Ungulates were taken during the entire range of occupation and appear to have figured importantly (Riddell 1960a:78), although for the most part the fragmentary remains were not assigned specifically to antelope, elk, deer, or mountain sheep, all of which were present in the identified fraction.

Patterns of postholes detected in the subsoil allowed the reconstruction of three domestic structures, circular in outline and all measuring ≈3 m in diameter. Although Riddell admitted that they might have been constructed during the Late Period of the site (A.D. 0–700), he suggested that they more likely had sprung from the Karlo Period, thereby introducing into the record a category of feature that previously had gone virtually unexplored in the Great Basin. Unfortunately, the subtle and confused stratigraphy at Karlo prevented the examination of the living surfaces themselves, and the excavation techniques employed (arbitrary 30-cm levels, shoveled through a 9-mm mesh) precluded any significant sorting of materials into house–unit associations.

Burials and cremations occurred intermixed throughout the deposits. Again, the stratigraphic vagueness of the site, together with the complication that several interments were apparently intrusive into older ones, reduced the clarity with which grave-lot associations could be defined and inhibited their placement into a convincing sequence. Nonetheless, categories of grave goods were recognized to include varieties of shell beads, projectile points of virtually every type defined for the site, ground-stone milling and pounding implements, and a wide range of bone, flaked-stone, and ground-stone tools. The burial complex at Karlo, then, emerged as directly reflective of the material culture of a large segment of the Great Basin sequence as it might be defined from cache, residential, and task-specific contexts, and underscored the absence of a (detectable) complex ceremonialism surrounding interment.

Some 80 km northeast of Secret Valley and the Karlo site lies Surprise Valley (Figure 9.5), a large pluvial lake bed that, although it spans the California–Nevada border, falls entirely within the Great Basin physiographic province and culture area. In 1966 O'Connell initiated a long-term program of site survey and excavation that was to establish for the first time within our area of concern a firm local chronology (Figure 9.7) that not only could be tied to the details of material culture, but (because of the way questions had been posed early in the research) could also address issues of human adaptation, social organization, and cultural ecology, and thereby ultimately lead to a tentative outline of the prehistoric subsistence–settlement systems operative over the past 6500 years. These anthropological questions are treated in a subsequent section; here we examine the chronological ordering of the assemblages.

From excavations at three major Surprise Valley occupation sites— Rodriguez in Lassen County, an ethnographic winter village identified by Kelly (1932b), and the Menlo Baths and Kings Dog sites, both of which are hot springs mounds located in Modoc County (Figure 9.5)—as well as from his survey data, O'Connell proposed a five-phase sequence (Figure 9.7). The time markers of this sequence consist chiefly of projectile points (Figure 9.8), but the sequence displays significant changes in many other cultural attributes through time (O'Connell 1971a, 1975; O'Connell and Ambro 1968).

The Menlo Phase (4500–2500 B.C.) is characterized by Northern Side-notched projectile points (the "Madeline Dunes" points of Riddell's Karlo Period) as well as by broad, lanceolate knives, T-shaped drills, distinctive stone pendants, manos and millingstones, mortars with V-shaped depressions and pointed pestles, and antler wedges. Large, semisubterranean

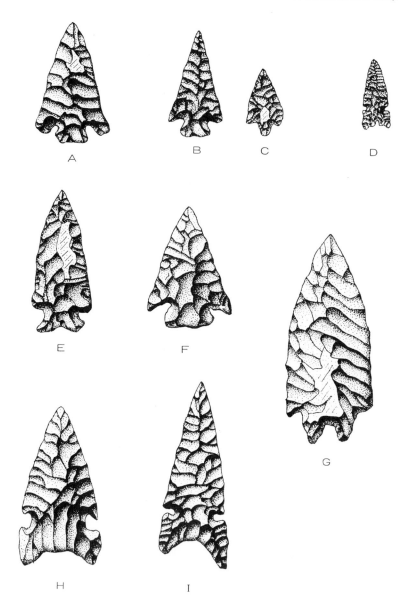

**Figure 9.8** Time-marker projectile points from Surprise Valley and adjacent localities: A, Eastgate; B, Rose Spring Corner-notched; C, Rose Spring Contracting-stem; D, Desert Side-notched; E, Elko Eared; F, Elko Corner-notched; G, Bare Creek (Pinto) Eared; H,I, Northern Side-notched. (Drawing by Christopher Raven.)

earth lodges were defined by living surfaces and posthole patterns (Figure 9.9) and are included in the phase on the basis of stratigraphy, artifact associations, and radiocarbon assays (6400 and 5975–6175 B.P.). The faunal assemblage of the Menlo Phase displays a strong orientation toward the hunting of sheep, bison, antelope, and deer, with less reliance on rabbits and other small game. O'Connell (1971a:262) finds the Menlo Phase to be less typical of Great Basin patterns recognized south and east of Surprise Valley than it is of the northern Great Basin–southern Columbia Plateau pattern at the same period.

The succeeding Bare Creek Phase (2500–1000 B.C.), bolstered by a radiocarbon date of 900 B.C. (O'Connell and Hayward 1972:38), is marked particularly by the prevalence of "Bare Creek" projectile points, apparently a local variant of the Pinto Series (Hester 1973; Hester and Heizer 1973). Also characteristic of the phase are Humboldt Concave Base projectile points, rounded, triangular knives, key-shaped drills, notched scrapers, and a continuation of the mano–millingstone complex. Bare Creek domestic structures consist of smaller, circular brush-covered shelters and windscreens, signaling a major departure from Menlo Phase practices. Also, the associated faunal assemblage implies reduced hunt-

**Figure 9.9** Excavation of Feature 28 at the King's Dog site (Mod-204), Modoc County, showing the oldest known (Menlo Phase) house floor in Surprise Valley. Feature 1—an Alkalai Phase house floor—is visible in the sidewall at rear. (Photograph by James F. O'Connell; courtesy of James F. O'Connell.)

ing of big game, with a concomitant rise in the importance of rabbits and small mammals and the first appearance in the sequence of significant numbers of waterfowl.

The technological and subsistence orientations of the Bare Creek Phase (Figure 9.7) generally persist through the ensuing Emerson Phase (1000 B.C.–A.D. 500), although the assemblage manifests the local appearance and floruit of the Elko series of projectile points (Figure 9.8), a ubiquitous style that has proved to be a useful time marker throughout much of the Great Basin (O'Connell 1967), and the persistence of Humboldt points. A radiocarbon date of 200 ± 100 B.C. applies to this phase. Although house forms do not undergo demonstrable changes from the preceding phase, there is a continuation of the trend for faunal assemblages to evidence less concern with ungulates and a growing preoccupation with small game and waterfowl. Bison disappear from the meat diet at this time and are not seen again in Surprise Valley.

The Alkali Phase (A.D. 500–1500; Figure 9.7) is marked by the introduction of Rose Spring and Eastgate projectile points (Figure 9.8), the appearance of which is widely believed to be coincident with the technological innovation of the bow and arrow. Further time markers include O'Connell's Surprise Valley and Alkali types, both probably local variants of the Rose Spring series (Hester and Heizer 1973), leaf-shaped knives, tubular pipes, and stone balls. House forms and the faunal assemblage largely replicate the patterns of the preceding stage, although an intensification in the taking of waterfowl may be noted. Two radiocarbon dates on associated materials secure the temporal placement of the phase.

O'Connell's final Surprise Valley phase, Bidwell (A.D. 1500 to the historic period), was not disclosed in excavations but was inferred from the presence in surface contexts and in private collections of great numbers of Desert Side-notched and Cottonwood projectile points, which are late to protohistoric time markers in the Great Basin. Owing to the comparability of the Alkali Phase assemblage and the ethnographically recorded material culture of the Surprise Valley Paiute, O'Connell proposed that the nonprojectile aspects of the Bidwell Phase would be similar to both.

The Surprise Valley sequence still stands as the exemplar of phase marking in northeastern California. Not only are the temporal ranges of several diagnostic artifacts defined but, more important, as we shall see later, the data were subjected to scrutiny for the purpose of anthropological problem-solving.

The only remaining theater of long-term archaeological research in the northeast is the Goose Lake basin (Figure 9.5). Hughes began working there in 1969, and has devoted virtually every field season since to further exploration. Lying between the Warner Mountains and the eastern reach of the Modoc Plateau, and encompassing the northernmost drainage of the Pit River, the Goose Lake vicinity hosts one of the lushest environments in our area of concern. The lake itself offers about 95 km of shoreline, centered on a drainage system embracing over 1535 km². Early notice was taken of the archaeological richness of the area by the assembly of formidable private collections, which included Lind Coulee type projectile points and mineralized bone artifacts (Riddell 1973; Theodoratus et al. 1979).

Hughes's work within the basin, although largely unpublished (Hughes 1972a,b, 1973, 1974, 1976, 1977), consists of site surveys and excavations around the southern extremity of the lake. His research purpose involved the definition of a locally applicable chronological framework, the delineation of adaptive patterns and their changes through time, the formulation of models of intergroup social relationships, and a correlation of archaeological and historical linguistic reconstructions of population dynamics. So far, his work has best served the interests of chronology.

On the basis of his surveys and various limited excavations, Hughes has posited a 6000-year sequence not strikingly dissimilar in most of its phases to the Surprise Valley sequence. The chief interpretive innovation that he offers is the identification of the Gunther Barbed projectile-point type (Figure 10.5b) as a cultural marker of the Achumawi (Pit River) peoples, to be distinguished from the coeval and regionally abundant Desert Side-notched type which he sees as an expression of late (protohistoric) Northern Paiute culture. The weight of the argument resides in its potential ability to delineate prehistoric ethnic boundaries; still unproven, it can only tantalize us with its possibilities.

Sporadic research has begun to define a chronology and to sketch some details of the local cultural history of the Eagle Lake basin (Figure 9.5). Following Riddell's recording of several sites known to local collectors, Corson and Smith (1979) reported the results of a stratified, random sample of 10% of the basin surface; 102 newly recorded sites were discovered, with the not surprising result that major occupation sites clustered significantly along the lake margin. Test excavations performed by Wohlgemuth (1978) at Las-345 recovered specimens probably relatable to the Pinto and Elko series of projectile points (Figure 9.8), whereas work by Friedman (1976, 1977a) at the south end of the lake sketched the details of a research program that was to result in a strong chronological framework for the basin.

Friedman's preliminary testing and evaluation prompted further research by the Desert Research Institute into the culture history of the Pikes Point site (Figure 9.5), a large surface and subsurface assemblage arrayed along the sandy beach of the southern Eagle Lake shoreline. Based on stratigraphy and eight radiocarbon dates, a four-phase chronology (Figure 9.7) was developed; the dates, as Pippin et al. (1979:143) pointed out in their report on the excavations, "more than double the chronometric data for the southern Modoc Plateau."

The Eagle Lake Phase, thought to date before 2500 B.C., marks a period during which the Pikes Point site was under water. Pippin attributes artifacts in the upper level to mixing of the deposit subsequent to its emergence. Northern Side-notched and Parman (Great Basin Stemmed) projectile points nonetheless signal the probability that humans were in the area during this period.

The falling of Eagle Lake water levels ushered in the Aspen Grove Phase (ca. 2500–0 B.C.). Characteristic artifacts include Sierra Stemmed-triangular and Martis Contracting-stem projectile points, multifunctional bifaces, and a milling complex of cobble manos and slab and block millingstones. Pippin infers a pattern of seasonal exploitation by hunter–gatherers.

The Pikes Point Phase (ca. A.D. 0–1000) saw little change in the functional categories of artifacts, but stylistic innovations include Rose Spring and Gunther Barbed projectile points, shaped manos, and bifacial millingstones. No significant changes in subsistence orientation were detected, nor was there indication of departure from seasonal occupancy.

The Later Occupations (A.D. 1000–Contact) at Pikes Point, reflected in the surface assemblage, do not differ significantly from the assemblage of the preceding phase. Cottonwood Leaf-shaped projectile points are the only useful (though equivocal) time markers of the phase, from which the anticipated and characteristically protohistoric Desert Side-notched points are surprisingly absent. Pippin *et al.* suggest (1979:79) that this might reflect disuse of the site after circa A.D. 1500, when the type became prevalent in northern California, but this may be overinterpretation; the site occupies a popular campground and beachfront that are frequented in the summer, and the surface assemblage has been subject to many hazards. Moreover, O'Connell and Ambro (1968) failed to recover Desert Side-notched points from the Rodriquez site in Surprise Valley despite the fact that it was an ethnographically recorded winter village resting atop an apparently unbroken 6000-year occupation.

The Eagle Lake work constitutes, to date, the last major contribution to sequence building in northeastern California. Some of the other questions asked of the archaeological record, and their anthropological implications, will be discussed later, but for the moment we should attend the degree to which the overall shape of the past has been temporalized. Cultural sequences (particularly, sequences of material culture) have been defined for the Klamath Lake–Tule Lake basins and (to a degree) for the adjacent Lava Beds, the Goose Lake basin, and the upper drainage of the Pit River, Surprise Valley, Honey Lake Valley, Secret Valley, and the Eagle Lake basin. Not surprisingly, research of the sort necessary to establish chronologies has been basin- and valley-dominated. Focusing on the richest lacustrine and riparian settings, archaeologists have selected for excavation those sites that most convincingly promised long sequences, complex features, and abundant artifact assemblages. It would, in fact, have been ill advised to do otherwise until a regional chronological framework had been sketched and the gross details of cultural change outlined. It means, however, that several large and ostensibly important segments of the landscape still are known only from surface reconnaissance, and their prehistory is inferred from afar (i.e., from the valley floor). Cases in point are the Warner Mountains between Surprise Valley and Goose Lake and the Devils Garden, a vast volcanic tableland lying between Goose Lake and the Tule Lake basin. Although such areas are not likely to alter much of our thinking about regional sequences, delineation of their time frames would allow much greater interpretive flexibility when, as is often the case today, we are interested in settlement patterns or land-use models and must be guided in our chronologic work by the stratigraphic column of a site that may be functionally and ecologically irrelevant to the analysis. Clearly, much remains to be done.

## Problem-Oriented Archaeology

If much of the preceding section reads like a catalog, it is because much of the archaeology so far performed in northeastern California has had cataloging as its chief inspiration. There have, however, been a number of instances in which the decision to excavate a site has been preceded by the phrasing of specific questions in order to resolve identified problems in understanding. When that has happened, the results almost always have been exciting.

One such early exercise was the excavation of the Lorenzen site (Figure 9.5), an occupation deposit in Little Hot Springs Valley, Modoc County, where Baumhoff and Olmsted (1963, 1964) sought to explore the separation of the Achumawi and Atsugewi languages of the Hokan stock through the correlation of archaeological and glottochronological data. Having established a minimum time depth of 31 to 35 centuries of linguistic separation, presumably marking the era when Achumawi and Atsugewi began their divergence from the parent language, they examined the sequence at the Lorenzen site to see whether there were significant discontinuities relatable to a population shift. Although the site exhibited a long sequence, marked by projectile points of the Cascade, Northern Side-notched, Borax Lake, Gunther Barbed, and Desert Side-notched types, and articulated by three radiocarbon dates ranging from 510 to 3310 B.P., there were no indications that the continuity of occupation had been broken. It was concluded, therefore, that the Pit River peoples had occupied their ethnographic territory for perhaps 3000 to 4000 years.

Noting, however, cultural similarities between the older Lorenzen material and the "Early Millingstone Horizon" in central California, and recalling the major discontinuity in the central California sequence at the end of the "Early Horizon," Baumhoff and Olmstead developed a model to account for the pattern observed at Lorenzen vis-à-vis the Valley. The model addressed the old notion of an early occupation of central California by speakers of Hokan languages, who subsequently were displaced and dispersed by the intrusion of Penutians. Lent venerability by having come originally from Kroeber (1923), the idea offered a comfortable explanation for the relative geographic distributions of Penutian and Hokan languages (see Chapter 11) and was further supported by lexicostatistics. Since the Lorenzen site seemed to display a continuous development from a base fundamentally similar to the "Early Horizon" pattern, which seemed to indicate that its occupants had been ancestral to the ethnographic Pit River groups, Baumhoff and Olmstead suggested that the "Early Horizon" expressed the Hokan presence in central California and the "Middle Horizon" the advent of Penutians. The early occupation of the Lorenzen site represented displaced Hokans who had adapted their valley pattern of hard seed grinding with the mano and millingstone complex to the resources of their new territory, never undergoing the major ecological shift to an acorn economy (and to the mortar and pestle complex) so characteristic of the Penutian occupancy of the foothills.

Some details of this model have run into difficulty in the wake of more recent work and reevaluation of early central Californian patterns, and there has been some juggling of the complexes thought most likely to represent the Hokan substratum, but the model's northeastern (receiving) end has not been substantively challenged. Kowta (1975b) has devised an elegant set of predictions against which variants of the hypothesis might be tested (most prescribing what would be anticipated in valley and foothill archaeology if the hypothesized events actually transpired), but there has been scant work in northeastern California directly relatable to the problem. A critical review by Jerald Johnson (n.d.) promised to assess the tenability of current views and to clarify what needs to be done to test them.

Another problem of long-term concern has been the reconstruction of past environments, along with the elucidation of the effects of detectable prehistoric environmental changes on the cultural ecosystems that experienced them. Nowhere has the debate raged more hotly or resulted in such explicit testing as it has in the Great Basin, and that portion of the Basin which encroaches into northeastern California has been the focus of some of the most incisive thinking on the issue.

The essentials of the debate pivot around an influential paper published by Ernst Antevs in 1948. Simply put, Antevs postulated, on the basis of a variety of evidence, chiefly geological, that the post-Pleistocene (or "Neothermal") climate of western North America could be understood in terms of a tripartite sequence of temperature and moisture regimes. The Anathermal phase (7000–5000 B.C.) was believed to have been characterized by somewhat moister, cooler conditions than obtain today. The subsequent Altithermal phase (5000–2000 B.C.) saw the gradual warming and drying trend of the Anathermal reach a climax in conditions significantly warmer and more arid than those now present. During this period, the pluvial lakes of the Great Basin evidently dried up, and Basin biotic communities took on a desert character reflecting the more xeric conditions. With the onset of the Medithermal Phase (2000 B.C. to the present) an essentially modern regime emerged, and some of the Altithermal's effects on groundwaters and biotic communities were reversed.

The fecundity of Antevs' model for generating ideas and stimulating a problem orientation in archaeological research has probably been more important, particularly in the Great Basin, than has its approach to accuracy. In the first place, archaeologists have been motivated to seek in pollen cores, sediment columns, and floral–faunal assemblages confirmation or denial of Antevs' sequence. The result has been a far closer scrutiny of paleoenvironments than might have emerged without a model to embrace or one at which to take potshots. In the second place, and more to the point, on the general premise that cultural patterns share a fundamental relationship to the environments in which they are manifested, archaeologists have looked for evidence of prehistoric culture change for which the Neothermal climatic sequence might offer an explanatory model. In northeastern California, two major programs of research have addressed the problem and both have suggested that, at least in the Great Basin, Antevs' model is an oversimplification.

First, excavations at Nightfire Island (Figure 9.5) along the shoreline of Lower Klamath Lake yielded a long sequence (ca. 6000 years) in which faunal evidence cast doubt on the local severity, and even the significance, of the Altithermal. L. Johnson's investigations (1969b) found the site to be a deeply stratified occupation deposit (with a maximum depth of 3 m) holding a rich assemblage of materials. Hunting, butchering, hide preparation, and woodworking tools are present, as are grinding implements, burials, and domestic structures. Although most of the research has not yet been published, Grayson's (1972, 1976) analysis of the faunal remains has substantially influenced thinking on the universality of the Antevs model.

Grayson (1972:3) delineates an occupation sequence for Nightfire Island, bolstered by some 20 radiocarbon dates (Figure 9.7): Phase I (4000–3000 B.C.) is marked by leaf-shaped and large (Northern) side-notched projectile points; Phase II (3000–2250 B.C.) by both large side-notched and large corner-notched (Elko?) points, mullers, and antler wedges; Phase III (2250–0 B.C.) by a relative increase in large corner-notched points; Phase IV (A.D. 0–1000) by small corner-notched and stemmed points that resemble those of the Rose Spring series; and Phase V (A.D. 1000–1400) by Gunther Barbed points. The projectile-point sequence poses few inconsistencies with those defined elsewhere in the northern Great Basin, except for the uncommonly early appearance of large corner-notched points (see, for example, the Surprise Valley sequence and Chapter 8).

Grayson's faunal sequence, however, suggests that patterns of animal exploitation were quite stable throughout the sequence and, in some instances, directly contradicted what would be anticipated had Antevs' scenario actually been played out in the Klamath Basin. Specifically, the predominance of deep-diving birds in the waterfowl assemblage of every phase clearly indicates that the lake had never dried up, as Cressman (1956) had proposed might have been the case. Moreover, the abundance of waterfowl who feed by diving in deep water was in fact most pronounced in the early phases at Nightfire Island (i.e., 4000–2250 B.C.), corresponding closely to the supposed era of the Altithermal when aquatic resources should have been most marginal. It would appear that the long, hot drought had little effect on environment or culture in the Klamath Basin.

A second test of the regional applicability of Antevs' climatic sequence constituted a major thrust of O'Connell's program of research in Surprise Valley, the chronological framework of which has been discussed already. During the several years of the Surprise Valley work, O'Connell and his colleagues had paid close attention to the ecological zonation of the valley and its hinterlands, had conducted surveys to test the frequency and kinds of sites occurring in various environmental settings, had excavated in several major occupation sites giving particular scrutiny to faunal sequences and domestic structures, and had attempted to the extent possible to correlate survey results with the cultural sequences forthcoming from the excavations (O'Connell 1971a; O'Connell and Ambro 1968; O'Connell and Ericson 1974). Among the goals of the research was to identify the degree to which the *implications* of the Antevs model (rather than the model itself) were relevant to the understanding of Surprise Valley prehistory (i.e., the exercise approached the question of past ecological adaptations more through the medium of the archaeological record than through direct paleoenvironmental reconstructions).

It will be recalled that O'Connell's first Surprise Valley phase (Menlo, 4000–2500 B.C.), which corresponds closely to the hypothesized term of the Altithermal, displayed residence in large, semisubterranean earth lodges (Figure 9.9) and a hunting pattern dominated by taking ungulates. During this period, lowland occupation sites exhibit the full range of functional categories of artifacts, whereas "upland temporary camps" display a single-minded focus on hunting and butchering. O'Connell and Hayward (1972:34–35) proposed that lowland occupation sites were inhabited at least from late fall to early spring and, owing to the abundance of plant-food processing equipment and the richness of the summertime valley-floor habitat, probably had a year-round resident population. During the spring, summer, and early fall, however, the uplands were exploited by hunting parties who took the big game not available on the valley floor during those months.

The significant changes detectable in the next and all succeeding Surprise Valley phases (i.e., the sequence after ca. 2500 B.C.) suggest a shift in subsistence orientation, the kind and magnitude of which challenge the Antevs model by seemingly reversing the direction of change that it would predict. The faunal assemblages of these later, presumably Medithermal, phases show a marked decline in the hunting of ungulates and a concomitant rise in the importance of rabbits, small rodents, and waterfowl. O'Connell and Hayward (1972:36) suggested that lowland occupation sites continued to be inhabited year-round (arguing from the presence of hibernating rodents and summer waterfowl, as well as juvenile rabbits, in the faunal assemblage), with exploitation of the uplands, as before, focusing on ungulates. However, the authors point out that, of the possible explanations for the shift in hunting emphasis, a warming, drying trend leading to an attrition of grasslands and the proliferation of more xerophytic plant communities would occur at the expense of ungulate populations by reducing winter forage. Such a change might force a shift to a concentration on meat sources, which previously had played a lesser role (it would, incidentally, favor rabbit populations, which thrive in more open, shrubbier habitats).

The shift to smaller domestic structures attending the later phases is perhaps explained by the restructured subsistence base; ungulates are most effectively taken by communal hunting efforts, but a more diversified food base may have encouraged a smaller group composition for some tasks while allowing occasional mutual efforts between groups (O'Connell and Hayward 1972:37).

The Altithermal–Medithermal climatic sequence, then, fails in Surprise Valley (as it fails in the Klamath Basin) to explain observed changes in human ecological adaptations. That it has worked usefully elsewhere in the Great Basin (e.g., Baumhoff and Heizer 1965; Layton 1972; Swanson 1966) argues that the concept cannot be jettisoned, but that its universality is probably better discarded in favor of a set of more regionally specific climatic sequences.

Another subtler and more far reaching question was addressed in the

Surprise Valley work, and it was one upon which the local effects of environmental change bore heavily. Jesse Jennings had maintained that the cultural sequence in the eastern Great Basin, and especially from Danger Cave, supported a model of long-term ecological and cultural stability in which climatic change had wrought little modification of the environment, and that there had been as a result little change in subsistence orientation, settlement pattern, social organization, and population over the several millennia that the Basin had been occupied. The "Desert Culture" (Jennings 1964; Jennings and Norbeck 1955) was modeled on ethnographic patterns observed by Steward (1938), which characterized populations as small, dispersed, and mobile, geared to the seasonal exploitation of a scattered and highly diversified resource base. The model has had many adherents as well as many detractors, the latter of which have often pointed to regional patterns of intensification (e.g., Heizer and Napton 1970) or have argued for evidence of environmental and cultural changes keyed to the phases of the Neothermal sequence. However, O'Connell and Hayward suggest that, although not reflecting the Antevs scheme, the Surprise Valley data lead to the conclusion that "one can no longer maintain that the general pattern of man–environment relationships in the Great Basin remains constant throughout the Holocene, nor can one argue that these relationships are homologous with those described by Steward except in the most abstract sense" (1972:38).

## Public Archaeology: Adverse and Beneficial Impacts

Since the passage of the National Environmental Policy Act (NEPA) in 1969, and especially since the mid-1970s when implementation of the NEPA began significantly to incorporate archaeological concerns into most federal land management and planning efforts, there has come about an astonishing change in the complexion of knowledge about the archaeology of northeastern California. In that all new data may usefully serve science, the results of the change have been salutary; in that the reasons for which and the manner in which data are collected may significantly affect their usefulness, the results often have been less than desirable.

On the one hand, the flow of data has come to flood tide. This has, of course, happened throughout the state, but the contrast is most dramatic in the northeast, where so little prior work had been done. In the interests of land-use planning, federal agencies have sponsored large-scale surveys, frequently based on stratified, random sampling schemes, to characterize the kinds. numbers, and distribution of archaeological sites. "Sensitivity maps" depicting relative site densities often have been a goal of these efforts. Thus, parameters of site location have been defined for the Lava Beds and Medicine Lake vicinities (Fox and Hardesty 1972; Hardesty and Fox 1974), for the Upper Pit River Valley (USDI–USDA 1977), for the eastern Honey Lake Valley (USDI 1978), for the Eagle Lake Basin (Corson and Smith 1979), and for Surprise Valley, the Madeline Plains, and Secret Valley (USDI 1979, 1980, 1981) (Figure 9.5). The list is by no means complete, because much remains unpublished, new surveys are under way, and several reports are in preparation. Moreover, hundreds of smaller-scale surveys and project-specific reconnaissances have been performed by the Forest Service, Park Service, and Bureau of Land Management, most of which will come no closer to publication than being filed in the archives for future reference. The immediate result of all this work has been to expand enormously the catalog of known sites. In fact, more sites have been recorded in northeastern California in the past 5 years than in the preceding 50.

On the other hand, the accumulation of so vast a data base has outpaced our abilities to synthesize it or to pose the new questions that it might most usefully answer. To an extent, this shortcoming has been and is being tempered by the production of a number of regional overviews (e.g., Friedman 1977b; Jensen 1979; McDonald 1979; Theodoratus *et al.* 1979; Wirth Associates 1981: see also Minor *et al.* 1979 and Thompson *et al.* 1979 for overviews of adjacent regions that utilize northeastern California data), but the bulk of each year's data increment quickly eclipses the currency of such studies.

Also, the reports of important new excavations risk going unheard because of the monotone language of cultural resource management and the small circulation of these reports. A minor highway salvage operation in Butte Valley north of Macdoel (and about 20 km southwest of Klamath Lake) potentially set the use of site Sis-342 between 10,500 and 7500 B.P. (Jensen and Farber 1982) and significantly expanded the known range of the Stemmed-Point Tradition (Bryan 1980). Fastidious fieldwork and nice attention to source-specific obsidian hydration readings enhanced the credibility of the work but, for its importance to be felt, and for it to affect the general view of prehistory in the area, it must be disseminated beyond the theater of contracting agency and compliance review offices.

More serious for the advance of archaeology in the northeast is the degree to which the response to historic preservation mandates has deflected the thrust of research away from those fundamental problems that, elsewhere in the state, have long been under scrutiny. As we have seen, for instance, in most parts of northeastern California cultural chronologies have barely been outlined and, in many cases, must rest on data from a single site. Reconstructions of cultural ecology, adaptive patterning, and social organization and the explanation of prehistoric cultural change have barely been ventured. This severely inhibits what can be done with the annual accumulation of more than 1000 new site forms, as we still lack a broad interpretive framework into which they might be integrated.

Public archaeology, too, is not doing very much to improve the situation. In some instances, the effort has served only to bring fragile resources to the attention of those who will use them badly (Figure 9.10). Further, by virtue of investing top priority in the mitigation of impacts, public agencies may accomplish their goal of legally required data preservation while at the same time promoting research that is premature. However excellent such work may be, it will always suffer from coming at the wrong time; the law is no anthropologist, and it can dare illogic with impunity. A case in point is the excavation of the Pikes Point site at Eagle Lake, discussed above. Pippin's examplary work there and his admirable descriptive and analytical report (Pippin *et al.* 1979) clearly will establish the standard for Eagle Lake research over the next several years, but his site-specific chronology and ecological reconstructions are based on data gathered from a site of low artifact yield and one of apparently only secondary importance to its prehistoric inhabitants. The work was

**Figure 9.10** Looting of archaeological sites remains a major cause of data loss in northeastern California, and indeed throughout the entire state. Law enforcement and cultural resource management programs have slowed the rate of destruction on public lands, but better education is needed to acquaint other land owners with the value of cultural properties and the need to conserve them.

well-funded because the site lay in the path of proposed development, whereas a dozen or more other, potentially much more pivotal sites along the shore of Eagle Lake must continue to repose until they too are threatened. In the meantime, increasing numbers of archaeologists will be directed by the availability of funding to work on sites selected not by anthropological problem-orientation but by the exigencies of keeping public agencies out of trouble.

## Conclusions and Prospectus

It has been demonstrated that northeastern California has had a period of human occupancy extending over at least the past 6000 years. Furtive glimpses of the "Western Pluvial Lakes Tradition," although less well documented, suggest that the actual range may be projected back to anywhere between 8000 and 11,000 B.P. And there is no reason (either environmental or cultural) to expect that the archaeological record might not be pushed back to embrace the Paleoindian traditions (see Chapters 2 and 3).

Despite the paucity of attention that has been paid to the area, the rudiments of a chronological sequence have been sketched and several major points of articulation have been recognized that may serve to outline, augment, or refine the sequences in those portions of the region so far studied only a little or not at all. The Surprise Valley sequence (Figure 9.7) appears to be the fullest in a developmental sense (i.e., it contains the fewest gaps and reflects something more than a succession of time-marker artifacts), but useful starts have been made in the basins of Eagle Lake and Goose Lake, and in Secret Valley and Honey Lake Valley. The Klamath Lake Basin research (especially that at Nightfire Island), when fully published, promises to expand the cultural–historical perspective with solid comparative data like those obtained in the Surprise Valley work.

Although research in the area has seldom achieved the intensity of sustained effort that other parts of the state have enjoyed, northeastern California has entered the mainstream of anthropological archaeology by serving some of the major preoccupations of the discipline. The Lorenzen site sparked a simple but innovative inquiry into the ethnic affiliation of a cultural complex. The Klamath Lake Basin was the site of one of the pioneering efforts in interdisciplinary research, the results of which still influence thinking about the structure of lacustrine orientations. Archaeological research with an ethnographic perspective has recognized on the Modoc Plateau (and around the Klamath Lake Basin) an intensification of focus on single resources such as the *Wokas* and *Epos*. And in Surprise Valley there has been detected at circa 1000 B.C. a diversification of exploitative patterns, where a preoccupation with the hunting of ungulates gradually gave way to a more eclectic pattern. That the last was perhaps a capitulation to the results of climatic change tests some of the current assumptions on the relationship of environment and culture and challenges one model of post-Pleistocene climate that has dominated our thinking about the landscape of the past for more than 3 decades.

Of course, much remains to be done to render the archaeological record from northeastern California acceptable as an understood and agreed-upon cultural–historical panorama, and much more research must preface our even beginning to realize its potential as an arena for the testing of models of cultural change and for anthropological theory-building. Rock art, for instance, has been little studied but much described (Gates 1980; Heizer and Baumhoff 1962; Heizer and Clewlow 1973; Steward 1929), even though the area may eventually emerge as one of the state's more provident storehouses of such data (Figure 9.11). We can identify a suite of topics and directions toward which future research might profitably be aimed.

First, and although it is an old problem, a regional chronology must be established that clearly integrates all of the locally recognized sequences. Although there is a high degree of comparability in the time-marker artifacts that have served the interests of sequence-building in most of the area, there has not yet emerged a sequence of nonprojectile artifact types applicable beyond the most immediately local sphere. That such sequences have proved definable in the Klamath Basin and Surprise Valley suggests that wider time-sensitive typologies are feasible.

Second, the structure of subsistence–settlement systems remains undefined for most of the area. Excavations *coordinated with* site surveys will be required if we are to begin to understand the human geography of the area, and if the results are to be integrated with ethnographic land-use models. For example, the models generated by the Surprise Valley research might profitably be tested in Honey Lake Valley, where there is comparable antiquity, an equally full documentation of ethnographic patterns, close ethnic relations in the recent period, and an ecological structure with differences specific enough (e.g., the acorn crop on the south side of the valley) that their effects upon the archaeological record might be predicted.

Third, the area holds the potential for making significant contributions to anthropological and archaeological theory. As a case in point, the southeastern Cascades and the central portion of the Modoc Plateau offer an excellent field in which to test models of incipient ethnicity (and, for that matter, to test the readability of ethnicity in the archaeological record). It will be recalled that the nine Achumawi bands or "tribelets" occupied discrete territories and apparently had been distinct from one

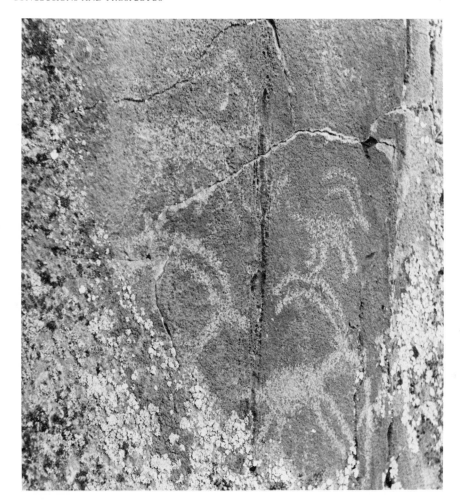

**Figure 9.11** Rock art panel from Fitzhugh Creek, Hammawi territory (cf. Figure 9.2). Bighorn sheep (now locally extinct) are depicted, possibly confronted by a hunter, lower right. (Photograph by Gerald R. Gates. Used with permission of the Modoc County Historical Society.)

another for long enough that marked dialectal differences had invaded their speech. The band territories are mapped with a fairly high degree of confidence, and the ethnic separateness of the bands is insisted upon by modern informants. Archaeologically, then, we might look for differences in economic orientation, technology, settlement plan, village composition, house form, or trade relations coincident with territorial boundaries. Whether observed differences were seen as the cause or the result of ethnic differences would depend upon the theoretical perspective brought to bear, and especially upon the operational definition of "ethnicity."

# 10. The North Coastal Region

David A. Fredrickson

Two young men in particular, a young chief and his brother, from a
neighboring village on the Trinity, were taller than the majority of
whites, superbly formed, and very noble in feature. The superiority,
however, was especially manifested in the women, many of whom
were exceedingly pretty; having large almond-shaped eyes, sometimes
of a hazel color, and with the red showing through the cheeks.

*Gibb (1851:42)*

Row of three Karok houses at *Waxek*. (Photograph by A. L. Kroeber, ca. 1901; courtesy of the R. H. Lowie Museum of
Anthropology, University of California, Berkeley.)

# Introduction

The rugged, mountainous North Coastal region, which extends along the Pacific Coast from the Oregon border to within a few kilometers of San Francisco Bay, can be divided into three major archaeological zones: the Northwest Coast subregion, the Eel River subregion, and the Russian River subregion (Figure 10.1). Each of these zones, far from being uniform, exhibits considerable natural and cultural diversity, with coastal, riverine, and montane valley environments and great variety of its people. The native inhabitants of the North Coastal region spoke at least 33 dialects of languages representing an unusually large number of language stocks or families: Athapascan, Algic, Hokan, Yukian, and Penutian (Shipley 1978). The region has been long inhabited, the Borax Lake and Mostin sites in Lake County showing dates in excess of 8000 B.C. (Kaufman 1980;

**Figure 10.1** Oak woodland and grassland environment characteristic of the interior valleys and foothills of northern California. Shown is a portion of the North Coast Ranges in central Mendocino County. (Photograph by Nelson Thompson.)

Meighan and Haynes 1970). Linguistic evidence, together with ethnographic and anthropometric observations, suggests that the Yukians may have been the most ancient inhabitants of the region (and perhaps of California), with members of other language stocks arriving in subsequent migrations (see Chapter 11).

The North Coastal region is predominantly (but not entirely) rough, mountainous country, and in many ways it illustrates the cultural stability and conservatism that seem to characterize remote mountainous areas elsewhere in the world. Running counter to this conservative tendency, however, the ethnographic, linguistic, and archaeological records suggest a succession of population movements, the spread of outside influences, and the development of many distinctive cultural styles.

## Environment

### Northwest Coast Subregion

Along much of California's Northwest Coast, mountains covered with redwood forest rise immediately from the sea. The redwood forest is kept comparatively moist by its proximity to the ocean and by summer fogs that contribute up to 25 cm of moisture per year (Major 1977). Temperatures are relatively mild throughout the year. In contrast, the coniferous forest of the interior, dominated by fir species, is subject to greater extremes with very high summer and low winter temperatures (Figure 10.1). Inland elevations are significantly greater than those of the coast, with ridge crests reaching 1525 to 2150 m and the highest peaks approaching 2750 m. Snowfall at these higher inland elevations makes these mountains generally inaccessible during the winter season. Several rivers drain the area, creating large and small valleys that cut through the rugged inland and coastal mountains.

The people of this area differed significantly from those of the Eel River and Russian River subregions to the south, having much in common with the so-called Northwest Coast culture area of Oregon, Washington, and British Columbia. Kroeber (1939) referred to the subregion as the Lower Klamath subarea of the Northwest Coast culture area. Highly dependent upon fish resources, the people of the Northwest Coast of California settled most heavily along the lagoons and river outlets of the Pacific shore, as well as along the banks of major rivers, most notably the Klamath and Trinity (Figure 10.2). They seem to have used mountainous areas largely for seasonal procurement of acorns, game, basketry materials, and other resources and for religious purposes rather than for habitation (Kroeber 1925).

**Figure 10.2** Coastal strand environment of northern California. (Photograph by Nelson Thompson.)

### Eel River Subregion

Within the Eel River subregion (Figures 1 and 10.4), elevations up to 1200 m are common, but there are few peaks with elevations greater than 1800 m. While sharing many characteristics with the Northwest Coast, there are also significant differences. The coniferous forest extends southward into the higher elevations of the relatively high and dry interior, and the redwood forest continues along the relatively moist coastal strip. However, lagoons and estuaries are generally absent, and the ocean shoreline is more rugged with tall, steep mountains frequently rising directly from narrow, rocky ocean beaches, making the coast far less habitable than the coastal zone just to the north.

The south-central interior of the Eel River subregion lies beyond the reach of summer fog and is subject to summer drought. The dominant plants of this area have evolved a variety of protective measures, such as thick, waxy cuticles on their leaves, to reduce water loss under drought conditions. Referred to as sclerophyll communities, the plants may occur as (1) forests of large oaks with grass ground-cover, (2) woodlands of dispersed oaks and other trees with plants such as grass or chaparral dominating the ground surface, or (3) chaparral in scattered areas mixed chiefly with woodland and grass (Cooper 1922; Shelford 1963).

Although the northward-flowing Eel River, from which the subregion obtains its name, becomes enormously swollen during the rainy season, the absence of continuous snowmelt during the summer reduces the water volume considerably with many smaller tributaries and other streams being reduced to a trickle or drying up completely. Anadromous fish resources continue to be important, but they do not occur as abundantly as farther north, resulting in a more diversified economy that drew heavily from the sclerophyll communities for both plant and associated animal resources. Settlements were usually in the lineal river valleys with seasonal base camps often established at higher elevations as populations dispersed to obtain seasonally available foods.

### Russian River Subregion

The Russian River subregion in the southern North Coast Ranges is similar to adjoining portions of the Eel River subregion in terms of terrain, climate, and vegetation, but differs in having even lower elevations, a somewhat milder climate, and broader valleys (Figure 10.3). Particularly outstanding are the Clear Lake basin in Lake County and the Laguna de Santa Rosa in Sonoma County. Clear Lake, the largest freshwater body situated entirely within the borders of California, dates well back into the Pleistocene and provided the indigenous peoples with abundant year-round lake and marsh resources, which complemented the already rich and diverse resources of the sclerophyll communities. Nestled between the two eastern arms of Clear Lake is Borax Lake, near which are both the ancient Borax Lake archaeological site and the Borax Lake obsidian flow, an important source for this valued commodity. Immediately south of Clear Lake's main body are the Mostin sites and the Mt. Konocti obsidian flows (Figure 6.4).

The Laguna de Santa Rosa, in the southernmost portion of the Russian River subregion, is another locality that in prehistoric times provided extensive marsh resources. Several miles directly east of the Laguna is the Anadel obsidian source, while, yet farther east, beyond the Russian River watershed, is the Napa Glass Mountain obsidian flow, which dominated obsidian trade in central California during the last two millennia of the prehistoric period. Another locality of interest in this subregion is the geothermal field of northeastern Sonoma County and adjoining portions of Lake, Mendocino, and Napa counties (Figure 6.4). Located in rugged chaparral country that seems unproductive and forbidding to the uninitiated, hot springs and fumeroles attracted prehistoric peoples for their

**Figure 10.3** Conifer forest characteristic of coastal areas and mid- to higher-elevation areas of northern California. Shown is a portion of the North Coast Ranges in Lake County. (Photograph by Nelson Thompson.)

curative and religious powers. Today the geothermal field is being tapped to generate electricity for the northern California power grid.

Environmental data from the North Coast Ranges suggest significant changes in both climate and vegetation over the past 10,000 years. A general post-Pleistocene warming trend that peaked between 4000 and 2800 years ago, followed by a cooling trend that continued to the present, is evidenced by analyses of the relative amounts of oak and conifer pollen (Sims 1976) and of the growth rate of tule perch based upon fish scales (Casteel *et al.* 1977), both data sets generated from sediment cores recovered from the floor of Clear Lake. Other minor climatic fluctuations appear to have occurred as well (Casteel and Beaver 1978). Although pine dominated the early (and cooler) portion of this time period, oak dominated the latter portion (Sims 1976).

Pollen samples from Tule and Barley lakes, two small landslide lakes north of Clear Lake within the Mendocino National Forest, have provided evidence for climatic shifts parallel to those identified at Clear Lake (West 1980, 1981). In general, pine and other conifers increase in abundance with elevation, whereas oak decreases. Shifts in proportions of oak and conifer pollen at Tule and Barley lakes suggest that mid-Holocene temperatures may have been warmer by 2.1° C, with a resulting upward shift of approximately 350 m in the elevation at which various proportions of oak and conifer are found. A cooling trend began approximately 2700 years ago (West 1981). An increase in the abundance of oaks, most notably at the higher elevations, would undoubtedly have influenced human use of the area, but details of this effect have not yet been worked out.

## Native Cultures

At the time of European contact, the northwest coast of California was occupied by speakers of at least 11 dialects representing 3 major linguistic groupings: the Algic superfamily, the Athapascan family, and the unproven Hokan stock (Figure 11.1). The Yurok, an Algic group, resided along the lower 75 km of the Klamath River and southward from the river mouth along the Pacific Coast to Trinidad Head where Yurok territory adjoined that of the Wiyot. Although the Wiyot were also Algic, the historical separation of Wiyot and Yurok occurred in the remote past, well before the entry of either into California (Shipley 1978; Whistler 1979a).

The Tolowa, an Athapascan group, extended along the coastal strip southward from Smith River to below Crescent City where Yurok territory began. The Athapascan Hupa lived along the lower course of the Trinity River down to its confluence with the Klamath where Yurok land began. The 10-km-long Hoopa Valley formed the center of the Hupa homeland. The Chilula, with only slight dialect differentiation from Hupa, occupied the lower reaches of Redwood Creek, except for the coastal portion claimed by the Yurok. The upper portion of Redwood Creek, as well as an interior portion of Mad River, was controlled by the Whilkut, another close relative of Hupa (Figure 11.1).

The Karok, speaking an isolate language assigned to the Hokan stock, resided along the upper Klamath from its confluence with the Trinity to the Seiad Valley above Happy Camp. The remaining northern California groups placed in the Hokan stock also were located in the interior. The Chimariko resided on the Trinity upriver from the Hupa, whereas the Konomihu and New River Shasta, both members of the Shastan family, held territories on the Salmon River, a Klamath tributary. The inclusion of these latter groups in the Northwest Coast subregion is arbitrary; they could equally well be included in the Cascade portion of the Northeast region.

Sustained Euro-American contact did not begin until the mid-1800s and, although ravages of disease and depredations by the invading settlers resulted in a high mortality rate among the native peoples and massive disruption of their traditional cultures, including virtual extinction of some of the smaller communities, a large and vital indigenous population still resides in the area.

Although small groups, such as the Chilula, resided along the ridges and small streams of the interior, most of the native peoples of the area were concentrated at coastal and riverine locations, where effective use of abundant marine mammal and fish resources allowed the growth of relatively large sedentary and socially complex communities. One of the most-intensively studied groups in the area was the Yurok, numbering approximately 3000. Yurok communities, clusters of redwood plank houses, were situated along both the Klamath River and the Pacific Coast (Kroeber 1925; Pilling 1978). In a study drawing together environmental variables and subsistence remains found in North Coastal archaeological sites, W. R. Hildebrandt (1981) identified the Yurok as following the pursuer, as contrasted with the searcher, strategy in hunting game (MacArthur 1972). Searchers exploit a wide range of prey dispersed over an extensive area, whereas pursuers seek specialized resources, predictable in their occurrences at particular times and places. Thus, annual runs of salmon, summer appearances of surf fish, and seasonal visits of sea lion and fur seal contributed to the perfecting of a sophisticated pursuer hunting technology, including the manufacture and use of dugout canoes of redwood, both small ones for river travel and large ones up to 12 m (40 ft) in length and 3 m (10 ft) in beam for ocean use (Gould 1968). The large canoe, employed only by the Yurok and Tolowa, appears to have been associated with the hunting of sea mammals at offshore rookeries and resting locations. The coastal strip south of the Yurok generally lacked offshore outcrops suitable for sea mammal use, and the oceangoing canoe was absent (Hildebrandt 1981). For all groups, abundant acorns and game contributed significantly to subsistence.

Although Yurok society lacked formal chiefs, the social classes of commoner and aristocrat were sharply differentiated (Pilling 1978). Adjoining villages were grouped into several districts, with high-ranking men within each district meeting from time to time to mediate disputes or to arrange details of ceremonies (Pilling 1978). Within villages, wealthy men had influence over others to whom they provided assistance and protection (Kroeber 1925). The Yurok shared with their neighbors a strong concern for wealth as well as an elaborate system of fines and penalties for personal insult and injury (Kroeber 1925).

Farther to the south, within the Eel River subregion, the searcher strategy gained in importance as the subsistence base became more diversified and dispersed within the increasingly sclerophyll environment. Athapascan groups occupied the northern portion of the subregion, whereas Yukian groups resided in the south. Except for the Mattole and the Sinkyone, who had ocean frontage, the Athapascans of this area tended to occupy interior riverbanks. Each village community generally held a territory defined by a drainage area. The Nongatl were situated for the most part within the watershed of the Van Duzen River, while to the south the Lassik occupied a portion of the Eel River proper (Elsasser 1978b; Kroeber 1925). South of the Lassik were the Wailaki, who occupied most of the Eel River watershed as well as much of its North Fork. The Wailaki and a final Athapascan group, the Cahto of the Eel River's upper South Fork, both had physical characteristics that link them not with their linguistic relatives but with Yukian peoples immediately to the south (Gifford 1926a). The two groups may have been descendants of more ancient residents who adopted the language of the more recently arriving Athapascans.

Yukians of the Eel River subregion include the Coast Yuki of the Pacific shore between Usal Creek and Cleone, the Huchnom of the South Eel River, and the Yuki proper whose territory included much of the upper Eel River watershed, including Round Valley, a major physiographic feature of eastern Mendocino County (Kroeber 1925; V. Miller 1978). As with the Northwest Coast subregion, intensive contact with Euro-American peoples did not occur until the mid-1800s. Again, although introduced diseases and violent excesses of intrusive settlers devastated both the native population and the indigenous cultures (Miller 1970), a significant body of descendants of the original populace still resides in the area with identity largely intact.

The cultures of this subregion, especially those in the northern portion, were strongly influenced by their Northwest Coast neighbors, with central California impulses felt as well, the latter being most evident to the south. Nonetheless, the adaptations of the local communities were distinctive in their own right and together gave coherency to the area. The largest corporate group was the tribelet, presided over by a local chief or headman. Each tribelet possessed a small territory, usually definable in terms of drainages. Each tribelet generally had a principal settlement, usually a ceremonial center, and several minor settlements, some of which, as among the Yuki, were occupied by only a single family. The rugged, mountainous terrain was deceptively rich in resources, both those which were widely dispersed, such as berries, seeds, and herbs, and those which periodically aggregate, such as salmon, lamprey, and surf fish. Members of a typical tribelet followed an annual four-season cycle that took them into all portions of their territory, often involving shifts in their social organization as their hunting mode shifted from searcher to pursuer and back again (Tamez 1978).

Along the coast among the Mattole and Sinkyone, fall was the most intensive season for food procurement since surf fish and salmon runs came hard upon one another, sea mammals were available, and acorns were ripening in the hills. It was necessary to obtain a surplus of food during the fall in order to have adequate stores for the winter season, when travel was difficult due to heavy rains and swollen streams and hunting and collecting were generally unproductive. The Mattole annually constructed a weir at the mouth of the Mattole River, an activity that required the cooperative effort of all males in the local group. Among both Mattole and Sinkyone, for a period of about 2 months during the fish runs, the entire village cooperated, camping near the stream, with men fishing while women transported, cleaned, smoked, and stored the fish.

After the fall fish run was over, people lived mainly on stored food supplies while residing above flood level in their streamside villages. By February or March, clover and other greens were gathered and steelhead were fished as they came back down the streams. About the end of May, small family groups adopted the searcher strategy as they scattered into the hills to hunt and forage for abundant but dispersed foods.

By early September, sea birds feeding upon surf fish beyond the breakers indicated that the smelt were gathering to spawn on the sandy beaches. People camped on the beaches, along with relatives and friends from inland, "even those of other speeches and tribes" (Kroeber and Barrett 1960:46). Massive quantities of fish were netted and sun-dried for future use. It was now that the pursuer strategy began anew as the coordinated labor of many effectively exploited the resources (Fredrickson 1975a).

In the interior, groups such as the Yuki and Wailaki followed a similar round, depending heavily upon stored foods in the winter while residing in their winter villages; collecting fresh greens and other foods in the early spring; moving to the uplands in late spring to gather berries and seeds, hunt deer, elk, and small game, and fish for summer steelhead; and in the fall gathering abundant acorns, hunting, and fishing while preparing food resources for winter storage. In the winter the Yuki lived in relatively large villages located on valley margins, dispersing in the spring as individual families or small groups of families, but the Wailaki lived in small winter villages situated along narrow, steep-sided streams and coalesced into larger groups at higher elevations after the winter snows melted (Roberts 1980).

Peoples of the Russian River subregion to the south shared many of the life-style features outlined above, but, because of broader valleys and often more concentrated resources, sedentism was more common and population aggregates often larger. The area was home to the speakers of six of the seven Pomo languages, as well as to speakers of Lake Miwok and Wappo. Speakers of the seventh Pomoan language, Northeastern Pomo, were situated in the Central Valley region (Figure 11.1). The Lake Miwok and Wappo were situated in the southeastern portion of the subregion, with the former located immediately south of the eastern arms of

Clear Lake and the latter residing to the south and west of Mt. St. Helena (Figure 11.1). Although descendants of the indigenous population still reside in the area, their numbers have been much reduced as a result of imported diseases, the aggressive actions of intruding settlers, and the effects of missionization.

Throughout the Russian River subregion, the primary sociopolitical unit was the tribelet. Among speakers of the Pomoan languages, there were more than 30 such tribelets (Kroeber 1962b), each nominally under the authority of a chief. Tribelets varied in size, ranging from fewer than 50 persons in less productive areas to as many as 1000 and 1500 for the Central Pomo village communities of *Yokaya* and *Shokowa*, respectively, on the Russian River (McLendon and Oswalt 1978). These large communities appear to have had a much more complex social and political organization than smaller ones. *Shokowa*, for example, is reported to have had 2 primary chiefs and 20 assembly-house chiefs and assistant chiefs (McLendon and Oswalt 1978). Houses were of several types, including communal residences that lodged up to 20 or 30 persons, sweat houses, and large assembly and dance houses.

Although food resources were generally similar to those of the Eel River subregion to the north, Clear Lake and the Laguna de Santa Rosa (around each of which resided relatively large and dense populations) provided abundant fish, waterfowl, and marsh resources in addition to the usual array of foods found in the sclerophyll setting.

The Pomo are particularly noted for the fine craftsmanship and artistry of their basketry (Barrett 1908c; Kroeber 1909a), an art that continues to be practiced to the present day. Also of interest are the clamshell and magnesite bead manufacture industries, which were near monopolies of groups within the Russian River subregion. Beads of these materials had standardized values, which increased with their distance from the source and were highly prized and widely used throughout central California.

# The Northwest Coast Subregion: Archaeology

K. W. Whistler (1979a), a linguist with considerable archaeological sophistication, has provided a hypothetical reconstruction of cultural sequences in the Northwest Coast subregion. Whistler (1979a:24) proposed that the area was first occupied by ancestors of the Karok who lived inland and depended upon hunting and gathering strategies, thus underutilizing the abundant riverine and coastal resources of the region. Archaeological evidence for this early, nonriverine, nonmaritime way of life

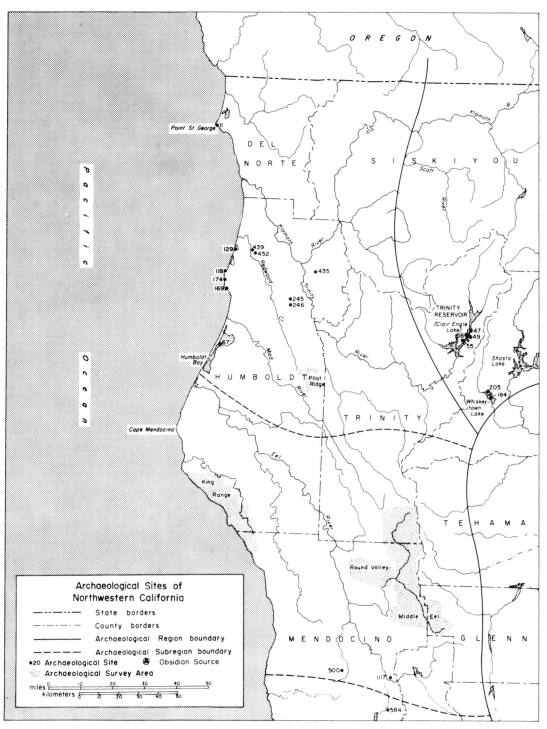

**Figure 10.4** Archaeological sites of northwestern California. (Map drawn by Allan Childers and Thad Van Bueren.)

has been found on the coast only within the lower component of the Point St. George site (DNo-11) north of Crescent City (Gould 1966a) (Figure 10.4). Whether this component, dated by radiocarbon to 310 B.C. (Gould 1972), can be attributed to the Karok is not known. In the interior, however, numerous ridgetop and high-elevation sites recently have been identified as containing distinctive assemblages that might have originated from this period. At least modest antiquity has been proposed for many of these sites, but recovery of only scanty materials and unsatisfactory dating have delayed an understanding of their cultural and temporal contexts. On the whole, relatively little work has been done on these interior sites. Until recently, virtually all archaeological investigations focused upon the coastal strip, where interest was aroused long ago by published accounts of local shell mounds and antiquities (MacLean 1884; Mason 1889), and where early excavations unearthed dramatic materials (Loud 1918). The coastal mounds, however, date from a later period, and it is in the interior that evidence of earlier adaptations should be sought (Whistler 1979a:24).

In Whistler's (1979a) reconstruction the Karok had relatively undisputed control of the area until Wiyot entry about A.D. 900. The Wiyot (as well as the later-arriving Yurok) may have derived from the Columbia River Plateau, entering northwestern California via the Deschutes River Valley and the Klamath River. Based on limited linguistic evidence, it seems likely that the Karok and Wiyot were direct neighbors at first (Bauman and Silver 1975). Since the Wiyot are presumed to have settled in the coastal strip, an area little used by the Karok, their entry would have entailed relatively little stress upon Karok lifeways.

Although the Yurok may have entered the region along with their linguistic relatives, the Wiyot, Whistler (1979a) suggested that their entry occurred about A.D. 1100, 200 years after the arrival of the Wiyot. The Yurok settled the lower stretches of the Klamath River and from there spread along the coast, possibly displacing the Wiyot (Whistler 1979a:24–25). They apparently brought with them a fishing and woodworking technology highly suitable for their new riverine home (Whistler 1979a) and, presumably, the technology for preserving and storing fish resources (Schalk 1977; see also McDonald 1979). The Karok adopted the technology of their new neighbors, shifting from their diversified interior lifeways to the specialized riverine adaptation, heavily dependent upon salmon, that marked their ethnographic culture.

It can be speculated that the Yurok developed the large oceangoing canoe, which probably was based upon the smaller riverine counterpart and benefited from the large-size logs provided by the redwood forest, out of their desire to exploit sea mammal rookeries located at such a distance from shore that regular use of smaller craft would not have proved feasible (Gould 1968; see also Kroeber 1925:126ff.). The spread of Yurok settlements along the Pacific shore may well be associated with an effective technology for marine mammal exploitation, including the taking of game from offshore rookeries (Hildebrandt 1981). It would have been at this time that the Yurok would have displaced or assimilated the Wiyot.

Archaeologically, the settlement of the region by Wiyot and Yurok is marked by the emergence and development of the so-called Gunther Pattern: assemblages of harpoon points, woodworking tools, *Dentalium* shells, and other distinctive artifacts of these coastal and riverine cultures (Figure 10.6). Evidence suggests that the new technologies, which allowed people to harvest salmon and other riverine and maritime resources, were quickly adopted by indigenous groups (such as the Karok) and by subsequently entering Athapascan groups, most notably the Hupa. As might be expected, the singular cultural style was considerably diluted among interior communities whose territories lacked major streams.

According to Whistler (1979a), the next wave of immigrants to the region were members of the Athapascan language family, ancestors of the Tolowa, Hupa, Chilula, and Whilkut. Athapascan entry may have occurred as late as A.D. 1300, with their route taking them along the eastern side of the Oregon coast ranges southward into the Siskiyou Mountains and hence into the North Coast Ranges (Baumhoff 1958a). It is presumed that the ancestors of the California Athapascans were at all times adapted to and utilized interior forested environments, and that their movement into and settling in California involved no essential changes in their habitat. Although it has yet to be determined whether the Athapascans brought with them an artifact assemblage appropriate for their presumably forested habitat, J. A. Bennyhoff (personal communication, 1982) has proposed that they introduced the toggle harpoon and the sinew-backed bow. Superiority of the latter over the self bow could have contributed to their penetration of previously occupied territory.

## The Gunther Pattern

Although avocational collectors did some digging in coastal sites around the turn of the twentieth century, the first systematic investigation reported was L. L. Loud's (1918) reconnaissance of Humboldt Bay and the lower reaches of the Mad and Eel rivers (Figure 10.4), during which 172 sites were recorded. Loud, who was associated with the University of California's Anthropology Museum in San Francisco, also excavated a trench in Hum-67, the former Wiyot village of *Tolowot* on Gunther Island in Humboldt Bay. Wiyot had resided at the site until 1860 when one night, under cover of darkness, a group of American settlers slipped into the village and brutally massacred many of its sleeping inhabitants (Moratto 1973a:46).

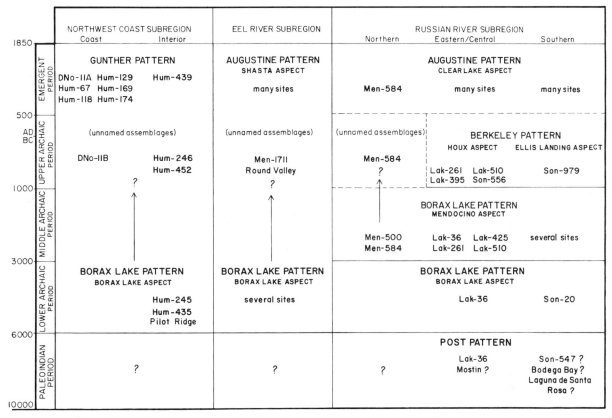

**Figure 10.5** Cultural sequence within North Coastal California.

Loud's excavation at Hum-67 yielded an extensive inventory of artifacts, now attributable to the Gunther Pattern (Figures 10.5 and 10.6), which reflected strong influences from the greater Northwest Coast culture area to the north. Such artifacts included *Dentalium* shells, bone and antler harpoon points, and various woodworking tools such as adzes, wedges, and mauls. Of special interest were ceremonial obsidian bifaces and well-made ground-stone zoomorphs. Six dorsally extended burials and 16 stratigraphically lower cremations were also unearthed. The cremations were later identified by R. F. Heizer and A. B. Elsasser (1964) as probable examples of preinterment grave-pit burning associated with the destruction of property at death.

Based on the depositional history of the mound as evidenced by midden size, stratigraphy, surface vegetation, and similarity of archaeological specimens to ethnographic ones, Loud (1918:350) suggested a maximum age of 1500 years for the site. Although within reason, this estimate proved somewhat greater than the $^{14}$C date of 1050 ± 200 B.P. (M-938)

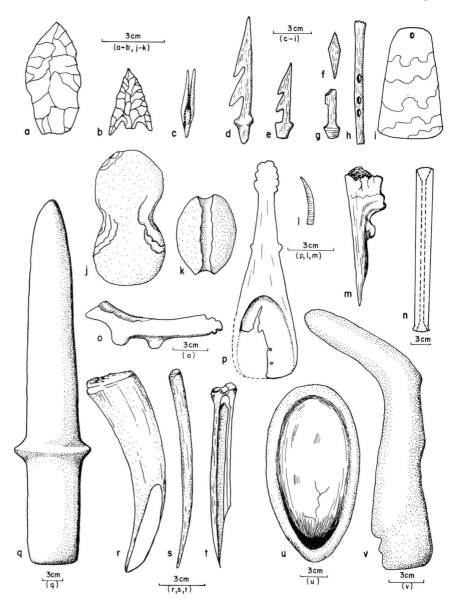

**Figure 10.6** Artifacts representative of the Gunther Pattern, northwestern California. a, chert biface; b, Gunther barbed projectile point; c, bone toggle-harpoon spur; d,e, bone simple-harpoon points; f, bone toggle-harpoon tip; g, bone toggle-harpoon spur; h, bird-bone flute; i, *Haliotis* ornament; j, k, stone net sinkers; l, *Dentalium* shell bead; m, ulna awl; n, steatite pipe; o, ground-stone zoomorph; p, antler spoon; q, ground-stone flanged pestle; r, antler wedge; s, bone flaking tool; t, bone awl; u, steatite bowl; v, stone adze handle. (Drawing by Nelson Thompson.)

obtained from peat collected from the base of the midden (Elsasser and Heizer 1966:2).

Large-scale digging was done at Hum-67 over a period of about 30 years by H. H. Stuart, a Eureka dentist. Beginning prior to 1920, Stuart dug up approximately 382 graves. When University of California archaeologists examined his materials in 1948, however, they found that many specimens had been sold, traded, or given away, and that records were available for only 142 grave lots. Among items found by Stuart at Hum-67 were red and black obsidian bifaces, Gunther Barbed arrow points, stone mauls, flanged and offset pestles, grooved and notched net weights, steatite vessels, zoomorphs, baked-clay figurines, and shell ornaments, as well as a variety of antler and bone wedges, chisels, harpoons, hairpins, and head scratchers (Heizer and Elsasser 1964).

The findings of Loud and Stuart allow some general interpretations. First, since no evidence of culture change was apparent from analysis of Stuart's data (Heizer and Elsasser 1964), the inference is that the site was occupied throughout its history by Wiyot and their direct ancestors.

Second, the association of zoomorphs and large obsidian bifaces with graves in all levels of the midden suggests that a wealth emphasis figured prominently throughout the span of Hum-67's occupation. R. E. Hughes (1978) recently provided evidence for continuities in the exchange and social-ranking spheres of Wiyot society at Hum-67 for at least 600 years. X-ray fluorescence analysis showed that during this period virtually all obsidian for arrow points, presumably utilitarian objects, came from the Medicine Lake Highlands source about 280 km to the east, whereas obsidian for the large bifaces, presumably valued ceremonial items, was acquired from the Warner Mountains and other quarries in northwestern Nevada and southern Oregon more than 400 km distant from Hum-67 (Hughes 1982). The maintenance of such exchange patterns and wealth emphasis during a span of 600 years or more strengthens the case for social continuity at Gunther Island throughout this interval. Hughes's findings also suggest that the system of social ranking implied by differential distribution of bifaces within the cemetery may well have entered in the subregion as a fully developed system, especially since evidence for *in situ* development is lacking.

Finally, it is notable that numerous distinctive zoomorphs (Figure 10.6, item o) were discovered at Hum-67, and others have been found elsewhere in Yurok territory; zoomorphs of this type are virtually absent in central and southern California. They have been discovered, however, in Siskiyou and Trinity counties, in several Oregon localities along the John Day, Deschutes, and lower Columbia River watersheds, and from Puget Sound northward to Vancouver (Loud 1918). When more is known of these distinctive artifacts, they may prove useful in tracing the southward movement of ancestral Algic peoples into California.

Hum-67 was situated in historic Wiyot territory, but several sites within Coast Yurok territory and probably utilized by them have also been investigated. These include Hum-118, an intensively used seasonal camp at Patricks Point; Hum-169, the historic Yurok village of *Tsurai* on Trinidad Bay; and Hum-129, the historic Yurok village of *Tsahpek*[w] at Stone Lagoon (Figure 10.4). Hum-174, a small ceremonial site on an offshore rock near Patricks Point, was also investigated. Except for Hum-174, presumed to have been used in conjunction with Hum-118, all sites contained both prehistoric and historic assemblages attributable to the Gunther Pattern. None contained identifiable earlier components. In Tolowa territory one Gunther Pattern site, DNo-11, the village of *Taiga'n*, has been excavated. DNo-11 also contained an earlier, non-Gunther component.

In 1948 a University of California team supervised by R. F. Heizer began investigations at Hum-118 at Patricks Point, excavating approximately 80% of the 4.25-m-deep shell midden. Four cultural components were revealed, for the most part marked by additions to or deletions from the assemblage. Earliest occupation of the site began about 600 years ago, judging from $^{14}$C ages of $640 \pm 90$ (GX-0181) and $545 \pm 115$ (GX-0182) years obtained from charcoal excavated by A. B. Elsasser in 1964 from its lowest levels.

Of particular note at Hum-118 was the nonmortuary occurrence of zoomorphs and well-made obsidian bifaces, with bifaces, five in number, occurring only in miniature form, and with seven of nine zoomorphs appearing as miniatures. Miniaturization of these distinctive artifact types suggests ritual rather than utilitarian functions for them (Elsasser and Heizer 1966:57).

Also of interest was the discovery of both large and small harpoons as well as large and small chipped-stone projectile points believed to have been used as harpoon tips. Bennyhoff (1950:299) has attributed differences in harpoons to their use in hunting animals of different sizes, with the large implements used for sea mammals and the small ones employed for salmon and other small game. Although analysis of midden occurrences of artifacts shows additions to and absences from the inventory through certain depths, Elsasser and Heizer (1966:56) remarked, "Only the simple harpoons show variation through time," and suggested further that the "typological variations may represent an amazingly quickened and sustained interest in sea lion hunting" and, it may be added, in the hunting of salmon and other small game.

Harpoons are characterized by having a head that, when it penetrates the prey, detaches from the shaft but remains connected to it by a retrieving line. Bennyhoff (1950:310), who conducted an extensive analysis of the northwestern California harpoon technology, identified area-wide shifts in the method of line attachment, first recognized at Hum-118. The line was attached to the earliest harpoon form at Hum-118 by shoulders carved out at its basal end (referred to as "bilateral line shoulder"), whereas in later specimens the line was held by protuberances that extended from each side near the base (referred to as "bilateral line guard") (Figure 10.6). An even later shift was to the use of a single protuberance for line attachment ("unilateral line guard"). Whether these shifts in the method of line attachment increased the effectiveness of the weapon or were only a matter of stylistic variation has not been determined.

Elsasser and Heizer (1966:56–57) concluded that much of what is now referred to as the Gunther Pattern had already been established by the time that Hum-118 was first occupied. Although Hum-67 evidently was occupied somewhat earlier than Hum-118, their artifact inventories differ only in a few details, and the respective lifeways were probably quite similar except for differing emphases upon sea mammal hunting.

In 1949 University of California researchers again focused upon northwestern California, investigating what appeared to be a Yurok ceremonial site, Hum-174, on an offshore rock near Patricks Point. Surface investigations and minor excavation led to the conclusion that 1000 or more partial and complete sea-lion skulls occurred on the small island. Because no other type of bone, such as mandibles, vertebrae, or long bones, was found, it was inferred that Hum-174 had functioned as a ritual site for the disposal of sea lion crania (Heizer 1951c).

Also in 1949, the University of California team investigated noncemetery portions of Hum-169, the Yurok village of *Tsurai* on Trinidad Bay. Using historical research to augment their analysis of 3000 Gunther Pattern artifacts recovered from the site, Heizer and Mills (1952) defined a four-period sequence: (1) Prehistoric, A.D. 1620(?)–1775; (2) Discovery and Exploration, A.D. 1775–1800; (3) Exploitation and the Fur Trade, A.D. 1800–1849; and (4) Decline and Fall: The American Invasion, A.D. 1850–1916. Like Hum-67, *Tsurai* gave every indication of being an important permanent village. Comparison shows the lower cultural deposits at Hum-169 to be similar to the intermediate levels at Patricks Point. This suggests, of course, that Tsurai was settled at a later date, probably about A.D. 1620 (Elsasser and Heizer 1966). The site was evidently a major Yurok village for at least three centuries prior to its abandonment in A.D. 1916.

As part of a site stabilization project in 1970, M. J. Moratto of San Francisco State University undertook extensive screening of looters' backdirt and also made detailed observations of surface features at Hum-129, the historic village of *Tsahpek$^w$* at Stone Lagoon. Nearly 1000 artifacts were recovered from this Gunther Pattern site, including objects of native manufacture, Euro-American goods, and Euro-American materials with native modifications (e.g., projectile points of green bottle glass). Analysis of the remains of five structures, two of which were still standing, allowed the tracing of accretional changes in native house forms as a result of Euro-American influences. Other data on historical period acculturation processes also were generated (Moratto 1970e, 1971e).

Work was again undertaken at *Tsahpek*$^w$ in 1976 and 1978 by Sonoma State University crews under the supervision of D. A. Fredrickson. The work, conducted under permits granted by the California Department of Parks and Recreation, was initiated at the request of the Northwest Indian Cemetery Protective Association (NICPA), an Indian organization dedicated to the protection and preservation of Indian cemeteries and grave sites. The major purposes of the NICPA-initiated work were protective in nature, since vandalism and erosion threatened the site (Milburn *et al.* 1979:2). The excavations were restricted to the portion of the site that Moratto had earlier identified as its prehistoric component. The known cemetery portion of the site was avoided.

Faunal remains from Hum-129 indicated that the site residents had been highly adapted to and dependent upon the procurement of marine mammals. Local Yurok consultants, who recalled visiting the site as children when it was still in use, pointed out Redding Rock, several miles out to sea, as an important location for the taking of sea mammals (Hewes 1947; Hildebrandt 1981). Based upon the artifact inventory, especially the impressively large number of notched net sinkers and information supplied by the Yurok consultants, there was also a heavy reliance upon lagoon resources, including fish and waterfowl, both of which were taken with nets weighted with sinkers. A $^{14}$C date of 1860 ± 120 B.P. (UCR-884) obtained from a charcoal lens at a depth of 60–70 cm in the 2-m-deep site must be viewed with caution, since its unexpectedly old date may reflect the use of redwood heartwood for house construction or some other purpose and thus not accurately date the site itself. Other dates obtained from the site were 215 ± 100 (UCR-883) and 1490 ± 100 (UCR-885) B.P.

The final Gunther Pattern site located on the coast from which a significant scientific sample was obtained is DNo-11, the principal Tolowa village of *Taiga'n*, located on Point St. George north of Crescent City (Figure 10.4). In 1964 R. A. Gould of the University of California carried out investigations at this very large site, which extends for nearly a kilometer along coastal bluffs. Integrating accounts of Tolowa consultants with his analysis of excavated data, Gould (1966a) identified three activity loci at DNo-11: (1) a habitation area; (2) a cemetery pointed out by Indian consultants but not excavated; and (3) a place where flint was chipped and where sea mammals, fish, and shellfish were processed prior to being brought to the residential area. Gould also identified an earlier, apparently non-Gunther Pattern component at DNo-11, which is discussed more fully below.

As indicated by faunal remains, the ocean harvest was supplemented by elk, deer, black bear, raccoon, and other small game. Tolowa consultants also described a seasonal round of subsistence activities in addition to those evidenced at DNo-11. From early to late fall, foraging parties fished for smelt at a favored place on the beach about 8 km north of the site, then shifted camp inland about 15 km to Mill Creek for the acorn harvest and salmon run, finally returning to the village at Point St. George with food stores for the winter (Gould 1966a,b). Noting that no clear evidence of historic era contacts were present and aware of Tolowa traditions to the effect that Point St. George had been swept by a lethal disease, Gould (1966a) suggested that the site may have been depopulated, possibly by a cholera epidemic, at some time during the nineteenth century before acculturative effects were felt.

A significant contribution of the DNo-11 work was the 1972 discovery by Gould and D. E. Crabtree that thermal shattering was extensively used in the stone-flaking technology of northwestern California. The predominant materials were chert and agate obtained locally as beach cobbles. Controlled flaking of such hard, rounded cobbles is notoriously difficult. Gould (1976:143) proposed that agate and chert cobbles may have been gathered by Indians either for the express purpose of lithic reduction or for use with the stone boiling technique. Regardless, pieces suitable for flaking were then selected from heat-crazed and shattered fragments. Such lithic reduction by fire was used not only at Point St. George but widely throughout northwestern California.

The earlier component at DNo-11, Point St. George I, seems to reflect intermittent camping by people whose chief economic venture at the site was the collecting and knapping of chert. Apart from a flint-knapping workshop structure made partly of whale bone, Point St. George I contained little evidence of habitation. Seafood remains were scanty and there was no indication of acorn processing. Bone tools, woodworking tools, and fishing tackle were not found. Gould (1966a:87–88) suggested that the component may represent the first human settlement on this portion of the California coast, or that it was a campsite utilized by people who came from the interior to exploit the abundant chert in the vicinity. Point St. George I was dated by charcoal from a cluster of hearths near the base of the deposit to 2260 ± 210 B.P. (I-4006), the earliest radiocarbon date yet recorded for any northwestern California site (Gould 1972). Applying Whistler's (1979a) hypothetical reconstruction, the $^{14}$C date suggests that Point St. George I may well represent limited ancestral Karok use of the Pacific shore.

## Interior Archaeology

Implementation of historic preservation and environmental protection laws gained momentum during the 1970s and brought about a major upsurge in archaeological activity throughout the nation; North Coastal

California was no exception. Attention shifted from particular sites or localities that were deemed important on archaeological grounds to specific parcels at which impacts were anticipated or which were being inventoried for archaeological resources for other regulatory reasons. In the North Coastal region, thousands of acres under both private and government ownership were subject to archaeological survey, significantly increasing the number of recorded prehistoric sites, especially in the mountainous interior zone that earlier had been examined only sporadically. Examples of surveys within the Northwest Coast subregion, which included significant portions of interior lands, are those of Redwood National Park in Humboldt and Del Norte counties ($\approx$15,000 acres; 60 sites) (Bickel 1979; Moratto 1973a); Hoopa Valley Indian Reservation, both the valley floor ($\approx$2000 acres; 18 sites) (Offerman *et al.* 1976) and mountainous portions ($\approx$3500 acres; 1 site) (Milburn and Fredrickson 1979; Origer *et al.* 1976; Stradford and Fredrickson 1978); and ridge crests and slopes of the eastern headwaters of Redwood Creek (1620 acres; 21 sites, including 8 petroglyph clusters) (Flynn and Roop 1976).

One rather surprising finding of these surveys was that interior sites were located not only along the rivers where late period population was most heavily concentrated, but also at high elevations, especially along major ridge systems. In 1976, H. Wylie reported surveys on Pilot Ridge to the south of the Hoopa Reservation in Six Rivers National Forest, where a large series of sites was recorded that contained wide-stem, indented-base projectile points, similar to ones found at the classic Borax Lake site in Lake County, as well as chipped-stone cutting and scraping tools and milling implements (Figure 10.7). Larger wide-stem points may have served as knives or to tip thrusting spears, whereas smaller specimens may have been used with the dart and atlatl. A site with a similar surface assemblage, Hum-435, was recorded on Hostler Ridge, east of Hoopa Valley (Milburn and Fredrickson 1979), and yet another site, Hum-245, was recorded on nearby Pine Ridge (Roberts 1975). These interior, ridge-top sites, attributable to the Borax Lake Pattern (discussed below), were believed to document early occupation of the northern interior and contained wide-stem, indented-base projectile points, chert flaking debris, and millingstones and manos (Milburn and Fredrickson 1979:26).

Excavations at Hum-245 (Figure 10.4) cast some doubt upon the cross-dating assumption that the wide-stem point necessarily indicated considerable antiquity. T. L. Jackson (1977; see also Flynn and Roop 1975) "guessed" that Hum-245 did not predate 500 B.C., basing his estimate at least in part on hydration rim measurements of obsidian material from the site. If Jackson's guess is correct, it would suggest persistence of the wide-stem point tradition and its accompanying lithic assemblage over a period of several thousand years into relatively late times. Although Jack-

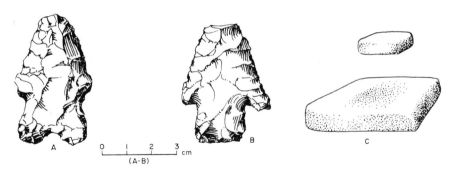

**Figure 10.7** Artifacts representative of the Borax Lake Aspect of the Borax Lake Pattern. A, chert wide-stem projectile point with bifurcated base; B, obsidian wide-stem projectile point; C, millingstone and mano. (Design by Nelson Thompson; drawing by Rusty Rossman.)

son's guess-date has not been widely accepted, since age estimates based upon nondiagnostic obsidian objects were extended to include nonobsidian tools, dating of the wide-stem point tradition in the northern interior will remain equivocal until more convincing data are obtained in support of either alternative. Also lacking are data that would allow evaluation of alternative hypotheses that sites with the wide-stem assemblage represent ancestral Karok (or other Hokan-related group) or are indicative of a relatively early Yukian substratum.

Jackson (1977) also investigated Hum-246 (Figure 10.4), a second site on Pine Ridge near Hum-245. Again basing his estimate at least in part on obsidian hydration results, Jackson guessed that the site was no older than A.D. 500, with occasional occupation into late prehistoric and early historic times in a manner consonant with ethnographic Chilula settlement patterns.

Other recent work in the interior includes test excavations by A. King and P. McW. Bickel (1980) at two sites, Hum-439 and Hum-452, within Redwood National Park (Figure 10.4). Hum-439 yielded projectile points similar to ones from the Gunther Pattern coastal sites discussed above. In contrast to the coastal sites, however, Hum-439 contained much obsidian. Although the site undoubtedly can be attributed to the late period, and may have cultural ties with Hum-246, it is not known whether it was used by coastal peoples, such as the Yurok or Wiyot, during seasonal trips to the interior or by interior peoples, such as the Chilula, who had no coastal frontage.

On the other hand, Hum-452 showed few similarities to coastal sites, instead sharing general characteristics in its chipped-stone assemblage with other interior sites such as Hum-246. Although insufficient data were recovered to assign contemporaneity of Hum-452 with other interior sites, there is no reason to doubt that it predates Hum-439 and may precede the appearance of the Gunther Pattern in the subregion. The hypothesis of ancestral Karok use of Hum-452 remains unverified.

Additional surveys and test excavations have been conducted within both coastal and interior portions of the Northwest Coast subregion, and the resulting data have been generally congruous with the data discussed above. Worthy of note, however, is the work of J. L. and K. K. Chartkoff (1975) along the upper Klamath River within historic Karok territory. The Chartkoffs studied environmental variables associated with 160 late period prehistoric habitation sites located along the river and found that site placement and high population density were positively related to ease of access to anadromous fish. Physiographic factors including rugged and precipitous terrain acted to limit settlement, whereas stable river features, including falls, rapids, and the mouths of large tributaries where the abundance and reliability of fish were greater than elsewhere, served to encourage settlement. It was also found that the most-densely populated portion of Karok territory, as judged on the basis of archaeological data, was the confluence of the Salmon River with the Klamath, not the downstream portion of their territory as suggested earlier on theoretical grounds (Baumhoff 1963).

## The Eel River Subregion: Archaeology

Until the advent of environmental protection and historical preservation legislation, little archaeological work had been done within the Eel River subregion (Figures 1 and 10.4). The earliest scientific work was that of E. W. Gifford (1965), who briefly tested the Coast Yuki village of *Lilem* while conducting ethnographic studies during the late 1920s. Gifford's investigation yielded limited data on molluscan remains pertinent to both dietary practices and shell artifact manufacture. His findings were compatible with statements of living consultants that the only type of shell bead formerly made by the Coast Yuki was the spire-ground *Olivella* shell. The only other early work of any consequence, done for the most part during the 1940s, was an extensive archaeological survey including minor test excavations, within historical territory of the Yuki proper, centering on Round Valley, as well as Hull's, Eden, and Williams valleys (Treganza *et al.* 1950). The work of Treganza and his associates, mostly under the auspices of the University of California, resulted in the recording of some 380 sites in an area of less than 250 km². The report includes an analysis of the site distribution pattern, which shows, among other trends, numerous sites lining the edges of the several valleys sur-

veyed. The work is of particular interest for its foreshadowing of settlement pattern studies that recently have received considerable attention
in the Eel River subregion.

## Culture Chronology

It is generally agreed on linguistic grounds that temporal priority
within the Eel River subregion can be assigned to ancestral speakers of
the Yuki language, who probably once had a more widespread distribution, extending northward to meet ancestral speakers of Karok or other
Hokan-related languages along a border as yet undefined, and extending
southward possibly to near San Francisco Bay (Elmendorf, in press; Whistler 1980b). Yukian continuity within the Eel River subregion may have
persisted until it was interrupted by Athapascan entry from the north,
possibly as late as A.D. 1300 (Whistler 1979a). Considerable interaction
must have attended Athapascan entry as evidenced by the fact that certain communities of the distinctive Yuki physical type, the Cahto and
Wailaki, apparently adopted the languages of the Athapascan immigrants
(Gifford 1926a). It is hypothesized here that the ethnographic territory
held by the three speakers of the Yuki language within the Eel River
subregion, the Yuki, Huchnom, and Coast Yuki (Figure 11.1), was continuously occupied by Yuki speakers and their ancestors throughout the
entire period represented by the known archaeological sequence.

The first archaeological sequence to apply to the Eel River subregion
was proposed by C. W. Meighan (1955a), who identified a series of six
archaeological complexes in the North Coast Ranges. Four of the six are
pertinent to the Eel River territory: the contemporaneous, late period
Shasta and Clear Lake complexes and the earlier Mendocino and Borax
Lake complexes. Although Meighan's complexes have been revised and
largely replaced, his work remains important as the foundation upon
which subsequent refinements were built.

To understand the special problems and complexities of archaeological investigation in the Eel River subregion, it might be best to begin the
discussion not with the more ancient periods, represented by few sites
and meager information, but with the ethnographic period. The archaeological expression of the ethnographic cultures of the Eel River subregion, and of their direct antecedents, is known as the Shasta Aspect of
the Augustine Pattern. It is marked by considerable economic and technological diversity, a diversity that derives from the great environmental
variability of the sclerophyll setting. Baumhoff (1978:20) has characterized the North Coast Ranges, within which is located the Eel River
subregion, as "probably California's richest area environmentally," linking its richness to a variety of vegetation types and the abundance of

rainfall. Throughout the subregion, the response to the environmental variability was the development of seasonal rounds tailored to the territory of the individual tribelet. Social organization of the tribelet, as well as its extractive technology, would shift throughout the year according to the changing demands of the annual cycle (Cohen 1968:44). Thus, for example, the entire tribelet might be together during a period of the winter, split into small family groups for acorn-gathering, into groups of men for deer-hunting, or groups of women for the gathering of basketry materials. For this reason, contemporaneous archaeological sites in different environments often exhibit contrasting and incomplete assemblages, hampering systematic comparisons and hindering the definition of an assemblage characteristic of the entire area.

Progress in identifying key archaeological elements has been slow also due to the lack of large-scale excavation at major village sites. To date, although numerous sites within the subregion have been tested minimally, large-scale excavations, similar to those conducted on the large coastal sites to the north, have not been carried out. Perhaps as a response to the inherent nature of the archaeological record, much attention has been focused upon the understanding of the ways in which one site differs from another, especially as the variability relates to environmental differences and the seasonal round. Even in this sphere, however, progress has been slow because of difficulties encountered in dating site assemblages and because of poor preservation of organic materials, in large part a function of the generally acidic soils of the area.

Meighan (1955a) identified key elements of the Shasta Complex, now known as the Shasta Aspect of the Augustine Pattern, largely upon the basis of collections made by Treganza *et al.* (1950) in Yuki and Wintun territories (see Chapter 5), as well as upon museum collections and ethnographic data. Meighan recognized the Shasta Aspect as showing influences from both northwestern and central California, with particularly strong affiliations with the Redding District of the northern Sacramento Valley (Elsasser 1978b). Included as elements of the Shasta Aspect are the basket hopper mortar; the Gunther Barbed arrow point; large, thin chert bifaces; spindle-shaped and phallic charmstones; and pine nut and spire-lopped *Olivella* beads (Figure 10.8).

Generally speaking, the Shasta Aspect was characteristic of the Athabascan and Yukian peoples of the Eel River subregion, whereas the Clear Lake Aspect of the Augustine Pattern marked Pomoan communities. But, in truth, actual dividing lines were not at all that rigid. For example, the Yuki-speaking Huchnom were known to share many Pomo traits (Kroeber 1925; Foster 1944), including ones identified as being part of the Clear Lake Aspect (Childress and Chartkoff 1966). Elements characteristic of the Clear Lake Aspect include slab mortar employed with a basket hopper, the small corner-notched arrow point, clamshell disk and

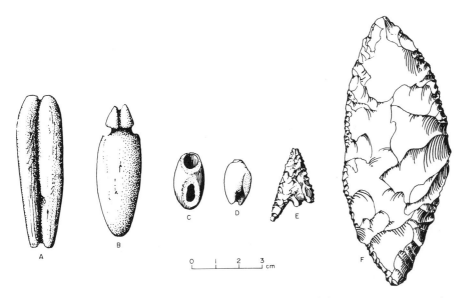

**Figure 10.8** Artifacts representative of the Shasta Aspect of the Augustine Pattern. A, stone spindle-shaped charmstone; B, stone phallic-shaped charmstone; C, pine-nut bead; D, spire-lopped *Olivella* bead; E, Gunther barbed projectile point; F, chert biface. (Design by Nelson Thompson; drawing by Rusty Rossman.)

magnesite beads, disk and whole-shell *Olivella* beads, and perforated charmstones of several shapes (Figure 10.9). The Clear Lake Aspect extended northward to meet the Shasta Aspect at about Willits in Mendocino County.

As for the more ancient periods, Fredrickson (1973, 1974a) has placed the earliest occupation of the North Coast Ranges within the Paleoindian Period (ca. 10,000–6,000 B.C.) (Figure 10.5). This period is represented by the provisional Post Pattern, which is documented only at the Borax Lake site (Harrington 1948a; Meighan and Haynes 1970) and possibly at the Mostin site (Kaufman 1980), both in Lake County in the Clear Lake basin. As already mentioned, both of these sites have been dated at over 10,000 years B.P. (see Chapter 3). Material remains include fluted points (which would imply the use of dart and atlatl) plus chipped-stone crescents, which may have served as transverse projectile points (Figures 3.4 and 10.10). Milling is postulated to have been absent or poorly developed. The inferred economic basis of the Post Pattern was generalized hunting and collecting around a lakeshore environment.

Moving into the Lower Archaic Period (6000–3000 B.C.), Fredrickson (1973, 1974a) redefined Meighan's (1955a) Mendocino and Borax Lake complexes, both of which employed the millingstone and mano, and included them as late and early manifestations, respectively, of the long-

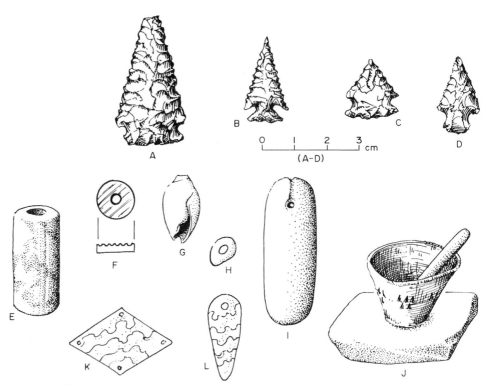

**Figure 10.9** Artifacts representative of the Clear Lake Aspect of the Augustine Pattern. A–D, obsidian corner-notched projectile points; E, magnesite cylinder; F, clamshell disk bead; G, spire-lopped *Olivella* bead; H, *Olivella* Saddle bead; I, perforated charmstone; J, hopper mortar and pestle; K,L, *Haliotis* ornaments. (Design by Nelson Thompson; drawing by Rusty Rossman.)

lasting Borax Lake Pattern. Under current terminology the redefined Mendocino and Borax Lake complexes become the Mendocino and Borax Lake aspects of the Borax Lake Pattern. The Borax Lake Pattern was organized around both hunting and seed collecting with a technology that was apparently well-adapted to the diversity of the sclerophyll communities. It extended from the Lower Archaic Period (6000–3000 B.C.) through the Middle Archaic Period (ca. 3000–1000 B.C.) and in some localities into the Upper Archaic (1000 B.C.–A.D. 500) and possibly a few centuries into the Emergent (A.D. 500–1850). Fredrickson (1973:112–116) based his revised regional sequence for the North Coast Ranges on the concept of the culture pattern, which could extend over one or more regions and could be isolated without reference to temporal context (see Chapter 5). Employing a modified version of the Willey and Phillips (1958) sequence of cultural-developmental stages, Fredrickson identified five major periods relevant to central California and the North Coast Ranges. Characteristic patterns for each period were subsequently defined.

Borax Lake Aspect sites of the Lower Archaic Period's Borax Lake Pattern are marked by wide-stem projectile points as well as the milling-stone and mano. Until recently it was believed that, during the Middle Archaic Period that followed, there was a general replacement of wide-stem points by concave-base and stemless forms. However, findings of Jackson (1977) at Hum-245, discussed above, and other distributional data, suggest that although the point replacement occurred in the Russian River subregion it may not have occurred farther north. It can be hypothesized that such differential replacement may be related to early Pomoan domination of the Russian River subregion and Yukian domination of the Eel River subregion and other localities to the north.

The Middle Archaic witnessed not only the introduction of the concave-base point but also the addition of the bowl mortar, without loss of the millingstone, part of the assemblage that marks the Mendocino Aspect of the Borax Lake Pattern (Figure 10.11). The acceptance of the bowl mortar may represent additional economic diversification through the adoption of more effective acorn-processing techniques. As with the concave-base point, the bowl mortar may not have made substantial inroads into Yukian-dominated Eel River localities, for reasons as yet unexplored.

During the following Upper Archaic Period, the Mendocino Aspect was replaced in the southern portions of the Russian River subregion by the intrusive Houx Aspect of the Berkeley Pattern (Figure 10.5). The Houx Aspect was marked by complete replacement of millingstones by mortars and pestles, and the replacement of concave-base projectile points with shouldered lanceolate and contracting-stem forms (Figure 10.12). Fredrickson (1973, 1974) described the Houx Aspect as a coalescent pattern containing elements of both the Borax Lake and Berkeley patterns. He further suggested that its appearance in the southern Clear Lake basin could represent initial entry of the Lake Miwok.

The Emergent Period, the final one in Fredrickson's scheme, was de-

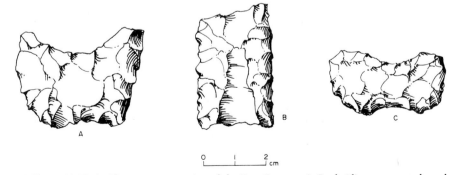

**Figure 10.10** Artifacts representative of the Post Pattern. A,C, obsidian crescent-shaped projectile points or tools; B, obsidian fluted, concave-base projectile point fragment (see also Figure 3.4). (Design by Nelson Thompson; drawing by Rusty Rossman.)

fined as a nonagricultural period equivalent to the Formative Stage of Willey and Phillips (1958). In the Eel River subregion, the Emergent was represented by the Shasta Aspect discussed above, whereas in the Russian River subregion it was represented by the Clear Lake Aspect. In both subregions interaction with the cultures of the Sacramento Valley, the Delta, and the San Francisco Bay regions, where the late period Augustine Pattern was flowering, strongly affected the native cultures.

As applied to the Eel River subregion, Fredrickson's model reveals gaps in knowledge as well as differences in the sequence of patterns. On the positive side, the cultural sequence begins with the Borax Lake Aspect, characterized by the wide-stem, indented-base point as well as the millingstone and mano (Figure 10.7), and culminates with the Shasta Aspect, marked by Gunther Barbed points and the hopper mortar (Figure 10.7). The replacement of the wide-stem point by the concave-base form has not been documented, and, indeed, it appears likely that the wide-stem point and associated milling equipment may have persisted, with some stylistic variation, throughout much if not the whole of the Archaic Period. The millingstone and mano also have been recovered from contexts lacking the wide-stem point. Concave-base points are occasionally found, but in late contexts and of a form similar to those that occur along the coast in the Northwest Coast subregion. The bowl mortar has been found sporadically within the Eel River subregion, but no sure assessment of its role or history can yet be made. Although the Houx Aspect of the Clear Lake basin is absent, the occurrence of small shouldered lanceolate points in Round Valley (G. White 1980) and other eastern portions of the Eel River subregion (Kuhn and Hughes 1981) opens the possibility for

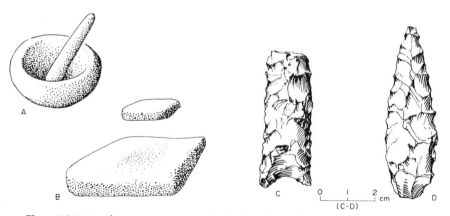

**Figure 10.11** Artifacts representative of the Mendocino Aspect of the Borax Lake Pattern. A, bowl mortar and pestle; B, millingstone and mano; C, chert nonfluted, concave-base projectile point; D, chert leaf-shaped projectile point. (Design by Nelson Thompson; drawing by Rusty Rossman.)

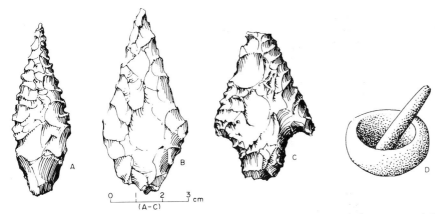

**Figure 10.12** Artifacts representative of the Houx Aspect of the Berkeley Pattern. A,B, obsidian shouldered, lanceolate projectile points; C, obsidian contracting-stem projectile point; D, bowl mortar and pestle. (Design by Nelson Thompson; drawing by Rusty Rossman.)

their entry into the vicinity from the east rather than from the south, at a time as yet unknown, but probably prior to the emergence of the Shasta Aspect. Finally, no archaeological assemblage has yet been identified that conceivably could mark the arrival of the Athapascans about 650 years ago. Although numerous surveys have been conducted throughout the Eel River subregion, resulting in the discovery of hundreds of sites in a wide range of environmental contexts, and small-scale subsurface testing has been carried out at more than three dozen sites, the archaeological sequence for any one locality, let alone the entire subregion, has yet to be worked out.

*Settlement Pattern Studies*

The advent of legally mandated inventories of archaeological resources has profoundly influenced research within the Eel River subregion. Two areas in particular have received extensive survey coverage: (1) the territories of the Mattole and Sinkyone along the coast, and (2) holdings of the Yuki in the interior (Figure 11.1). The coastal studies were conducted for the most part under the auspices of the U.S. Bureau of Land Management as part of its management plan for the 54,000-acre King Range National Conservation Area in southwestern Humboldt and northwestern Mendocino counties (Fredrickson 1975a; Levulett 1976, 1978) (Figure 10.4). Two of the interior studies in Yuki territory were conducted in conjunction with reservoir planning by R. L. Edwards (1966) and T. F. King (1966), respectively, of San Francisco State University for the National Park Service. A third, similar study in Huchnom territory was reported by J. Childress and J. L. Chartkoff (1966) of the University of California. Two additional studies of major importance in Yuki territory were the Middle Eel Planning Unit Archaeological Survey conducted by T. L. Jackson (1976) for the U.S. Forest Service, and the Cultural Resource Survey of the Round Valley Indian Reservation conducted by a team from Sonoma State University for the National Park Service (Stewart and Fredrickson, Eds. 1980) (Figure 10.4). The latter survey also included some Wailaki lands.

Along the Pacific edge of the King Range, Fredrickson (1975a) observed 53 sites along a 45-km stretch of shoreline that generally fell into four major clusters. He proposed that the four groupings may reflect tribelet organization and territoriality as well as land-use patterns. Levulett (1976) initiated subsurface investigations at several of the coastal sites, concluding that they represented seasonal camps utilized during spring and summer months and estimating that aboriginal settlement of the area occurred no earlier than 1000 years ago. In the interior drainages and on the mountain ridges of the King Range, Levulett (1976, 1978) recorded 25 prehistoric sites, virtually all of which appeared to reflect summer and fall hunting and gathering activities. On the basis of respective artifact inventories, including interior occurrences of millingstone and mano, the interior sites appeared to represent greater time depth than the coastal sites.

While early research in Yuki territory, including the reservoir studies, focused on large valleys or drainage basins, more recent surveys have included higher elevations as well. Thus, sites representing each phase of the annual round and in a wide range of environmental settings have been identified. Jackson's (1976) study of 260,000 acres in the Mendocino National Forest, although biased toward areas defined as sensitive, resulted in the discovery of 206 sites ranging in elevation from 460 to 2310 m. The complete survey of 17,500 acres within the Round Valley Indian Reservation (Stewart and Fredrickson, Eds. 1980) resulted in the recording of 368 sites ranging in elevation from 183 to 1628 m. Both forest and reservation studies yielded data on a previously unrecognized, high site density in mountainous areas. Although dating of the high-elevation sites is poorly understood, it is generally agreed that earliest occupation represents the Borax Lake Aspect of the Lower Archaic Period and may well date back as long ago as 6500 years when a somewhat warmer climatic regime began, lasting perhaps 4000 years (West 1980, 1981), expanding significantly the times of year during which high-elevation areas could have been utilized.

Considerable knowledge has accrued regarding site types in this mountainous region (e.g., Jackson 1976; Roberts 1980) and several predictive models have been formulated (e.g., Fredrickson 1975a; T. King 1974a; Tamez 1978). Although understanding of intersite variation associated with environmental features has grown, the absence of a reliable means of temporally ordering the hundreds of recorded sites has frustrated efforts to study changes in land use and demography over time, and has made it difficult to define even late period land-use patterns without recourse to the ethnographic record.

Culturally stratified sites, which offer the best opportunity to observe at least portions of a local cultural sequence, have rarely been tested in the Eel River subregion (e.g., G. White 1980), and time-sensitive artifacts, which at best in the Eel River area measure quite large time intervals, do not occur at all sites. Materials with potential for radiometric dating generally are absent from sites or poorly preserved. Although obsidian hydration data from Eel River sites have received considerable attention and have yielded good results, they are best employed as a relative dating technique. Since obsidian was a rare and valued resource not native to the Eel River vicinity, ideal number requirements for a sample frequently are impossible to obtain.

Despite such limitations, progress in understanding cultural processes over time in the mountainous Eel River subregion has been made. For example, one of the first models proposed for understanding changes in settlement patterns over time was T. F. King's (1974a) analysis of the Borax Lake Pattern subsistence and settlement pattern at high elevations. Employing excavation data from two Mendocino National Forest sites in eastern Yuki territory, King hypothesized contrasting patterns of land use and settlement between earlier (i.e., Borax Lake Aspect) and later (i.e., Shasta Aspect) occupation. T. F. King (1974a) predicted that earlier sites at high elevations would be relatively small but would evidence a wide range of subsistence activities, a pattern he deduced would reflect the activities of small, transient family groups, each moving as a group throughout summer and winter territories. With the emergence of a semisedentary residence pattern associated with permanent winter villages in lowland areas, King hypothesized that late period high-altitude sites would be limited to processing sites and small, temporary camps established for task-specific, and probably sex-differentiated, resource procurement.

King's argument was subsequently questioned by Jackson (1976), because of its failure to recognize that late period communities, such as those among the Wailkai, also moved to upland areas as complete family units. Nonetheless, support for other elements of King's model has come recently from the study of Men-1711, another Mendocino National Forest site in the uplands of eastern Yuki territory (Kuhn and Hughes 1981). The Kuhn and Hughes study is also one of the first to make use of recently available paleoclimatic data, reviewed above.

Kuhn and Hughes, on the basis of detailed surface observations and limited subsurface excavation, identified two components at Men-1711: a widely dispersed Borax Lake Aspect component, and a smaller, more concentrated late component, probably predating the Shasta Aspect. Using obsidian hydration results in support of cross-dating by means of the wide-stem Borax Lake projectile point, the Borax Lake component was placed within the period of warmer temperatures, which may have peaked about 5000 years ago. Assuming increases in oak and other seed plant productivity for the site catchment during this period of use, Kuhn and Hughes related the diverse artifact inventory (which included the wide-stem points) to a series of brief site visits during which a variety of subsistence and technological activities were carried out.

In contrast, later, pre-Shasta occupation was evidently the result of "one or more intensive occupational episodes" (Kuhn and Hughes 1981:129). For the most part, later artifacts appeared to have been oriented toward the procurement and processing of faunal resources, although a fairly wide range of other activities evidently was represented as well. Although the later component could have been deposited either by a task-specific, sex-differentiated group or by an entire family unit representing both sexes and their respective subsistence activities, the earlier component is comparable with the model proposed by King for Borax Lake occupation of high-altitude sites.

The use of obsidian within the Eel River subregion is worthy of comment. Since obsidian was not available from local sources, any obsidian utilized in the area must have been obtained by means of exchange with neighboring groups or through expedition to the source. Of the four obsidian sources within the North Coast Ranges, the Borax Lake and Mount Konocti flows are relatively close to Eel River localities, whereas the Napa, Anadel, and northern (e.g., Medicine Lake Highlands) sources are considerably more distant (Jackson 1974a) (Figures 6.4 and 10.4).

Although only preliminary data are available, and those only from Yuki territory, it appears that the Yuki obsidian procurement pattern contrasted with that of the Northwest Coast subregion. In the Northwest Coast, obsidian from northern sources, especially Medicine Lake Highlands, dominated (Hughes 1978; Jackson 1977). In Yuki territory, obsidian from the Borax Lake source dominated, with the Medicine Lake (and Mount Konocti) source represented by only minor amounts. An exception to Borax Lake dominance occurs in the northeasternmost portion of Yuki territory, where obsidian from Medicine Lake Highlands constituted 70% of the sample from two sites and Borax Lake obsidian contributed the remainder. It remains to be seen which obsidian procurement pattern will be represented in the remaining portions of the Eel River subregion.

Findings such as these indicate that, although the principle of least effort can explain in gross terms the distribution of obsidian in archaeological sites in that it predicts use of obsidian from a particular source as a function of geographic distance from that source (Ericson 1977b), it does not offer a satisfactory explanation for the details of observed distributions. As discussed earlier, Hughes (1978) has shown that, in the Northwest Coast of California, differential use of obsidian from different flows is associated with differences between utilitarian and ceremonial items, with the latter manufactured from sources more distant than those from which the former were made.

It is likely that physical characteristics of different obsidians, related to both workability and function, were also factors in its use. For example, according to Loeb (1926), the Clear Lake Pomo differentiated between Borax Lake obsidian, used in the manufacture of arrow points, and Mount Konocti obsidian, generally used for the manufacture of knives and razors. The small amounts of Konocti obsidian found to date in the Eel River subregion may be associated with such a functional difference. Locally available alternatives for the manufacture of items best made of Konocti obsidian may have had qualities equal or superior to those of the Konocti material, thus discouraging its entry into the obsidian procurement system.

## The Russian River Subregion: Archaeology

### Early Investigations

Extensive surveys of the southern portion of the Russian River subregion (Figures 1 and 6.4) began as early as 1903 when Jesse Peter, a naturalist affiliated with Santa Rosa Junior College, began 30 years of site recording, including much of the Sonoma County portion of the subregion within his purview. Peter was the first to survey extensively interior Sonoma County, recording scores of sites discovered in the northern and eastern segments of the Santa Rosa Plain. Unusual for this early period, Peter examined some upland areas and recorded flake scatters as well as large midden deposits (Stewart 1982). Peter worked jointly at times with L. L. Loud of the University of California (Loud and Peter 1920).

In 1921 Peter directed a group of high school students in the testing of Son-84 in eastern Sonoma County near the Anadel obsidian source (Figure 6.4). A trench and several test pits were excavated more than a meter deep to the bottom of the cultural deposit, yielding marine clamshell, obsidian flakes, and the remains of a hearth. Several mortars were found in an adjacent streambed. Peter concluded that Son-84 had been a temporary camp or food procurement site. The site was again tested in 1978, more than 50 years later, by a Sonoma State University team, yielding materials similar to those unearthed by Peter and which prompted the suggestion that the site was used seasonally over a long span of time during the Emergent Period (Adams and Fredrickson 1978).

As part of his extensive survey of the San Francisco Bay Region in 1907, N. C. Nelson (1909a) of the University of California recorded coastal sites within Southwestern Pomo territory from the Russian River southward. Between 1911 and 1913 Peter (1923) followed the same path, augmenting Nelson's records.

In Napa County, avocationalist D. T. Davis made surface collections from numerous sites within Wappo territory, and he undertook to record carefully excavations at several sites. Of special note was the contribution of Davis' data to the synthesis of Napa region archaeology, carried out in the late 1940s by University of California students under the direction of R. F. Heizer (Heizer, Ed. 1953). Also noteworthy was Davis' work at Nap-1 on the west bank of Napa River near Oakville (Figure 6.4). Davis collected intermittently from the surface of the site for 25 years and cooperated with student teams from the University of California who, in 1936 and 1937, made sporadic weekend investigations of the upper levels of the site. University of California students conducted additional test excavations at the site a decade later, digging two trenches to a depth of 229 cm (90 inches) and observing evidence of both physical and cultural stratification. Seven cremations, all but one containing grave goods, and painted stone tablets, which have come to typify the Napa District, were recorded in the friable midden of the upper 102 cm (40 inches), and the compacted deeper component yielded seven flexed burials. J. A. Bennyhoff (n.d.) recently analyzed the Nap-1 collection, identifying seven components beginning with the early Berkeley Pattern.

Although a group from Sacramento Junior College tested several sites in the vicinity of Clear Lake during the winter of 1934–1935, recording several burials and a variety of historic period artifacts (Neitz *et al.* n.d.), the most significant early work in Lake County was that of M. R. Harrington of the Southwest Museum, who excavated extensively Lak-36, the Borax Lake site, and tested two other sites (Harrington 1938a,b, 1943, 1948a,c,d) (Figure 6.4). The Borax Lake site is discussed briefly in Chapter 3 with reference to the occurrence of fluted points and chipped-stone crescentics, which link the site to the early Fluted-Point Tradition, believed to date to circa 12,000 B.P.

Harrington's findings at Lak-36 created controversy when they were announced, and the 1948 publication reporting his work at the site did little to clarify the issue. Because he could detect no stratigraphic change in the site, which contained cultural materials to a depth of about 2 m, Harrington (1948a) suggested that the entire artifact-bearing deposit was laid down within perhaps a few centuries. In addition, he assigned generic names to many of the projectile-point forms unearthed at the site: names such as Folsom, Pinto Basin, Silver Lake, Gypsum Cave, and Lake

Mohave points, employing their temporal affiliations elsewhere (not well understood at the time of his work) to date the Borax Lake site at about 10,000 B.P. Harrington also extended or modified idealized point types to include specimens with only superficial resemblances, for example, creating a "Folsomoid" category and attributing to it antiquity equivalent to the true Folsom points found elsewhere in the western United States. Finally, he linked generic point types and their extensions to different prehistoric groups and interpreted their presence as indicative of visits to the site by several groups who came there to make use of nearby obsidian quarries, "leaving their 'calling cards' in the form of characteristic implements" (Harrington 1948a:118).

It was not until the obsidian hydration and geological studies of C. W. Meighan and C. V. Haynes (1970) confirmed antiquity for the site and the disputed artifacts that controversy dissipated. Although the work of Meighan and Haynes supported Harrington's contention of great age for the site, it ruled out the suggestion that the site was formed during a span of only a few centuries. Instead, their findings demonstrated three major periods of site use, extending over a period of many thousands of years (Figure 10.5). The earliest period represented at Lak-36 has an estimated age of up to 12,000 B.P. with fluted points and crescents (Figures 3.4 and 10.10) linked with this time depth on the basis of obsidian hydration results.

The second period apparently followed a break in occupation and was estimated to have spanned the period between 6000 and 8000 B.P. Major use of the site occurred at this time and the characteristic Borax Lake Wide-stem point appeared for the first time (Figure 10.7). Although direct associations were lacking, Meighan and Haynes (1970) suggested that millingstones and manos were a part of the assemblage at this time. Fredrickson (1973, 1974a) later assigned these materials to the Early Borax Lake Pattern, here referred to as the Borax Lake Aspect of the Borax Lake Pattern, accepting the Meighan and Haynes age assignment.

The third period at Lak-36, with an apparent age of 3000–5000 B.P., was marked by concave-base points without fluting and by stemmed points (Figure 10.11). Millingstones and manos were suggested as a continuing part of the assemblage. Based on age estimates by Meighan and Haynes (1970:1220), who linked this period of use to the "Middle Horizon" of central California and suggested that the Mendocino Complex (Meighan 1955a) developed out of it, Fredrickson (1973, 1974a) assigned the Lak-36 assemblage at this time interval to the Late Borax Lake Pattern, here referred to as the Mendocino Aspect of the Borax Lake Pattern. Fredrickson mustered additional support for this dating from obsidian hydration results and radiocarbon dates from several sites elsewhere in the North Coast Ranges.

The proposed linkage of the Borax Lake Pattern's concave-base point tradition to central California's "Middle Horizon" should be viewed with caution, considering the later dating now generally attributed to that horizon (Elsasser 1978b; Ragir 1972) and in view of the Berkeley Pattern (Middle Horizon) affiliations of the Houx Aspect, which is stratigraphically later than Borax Lake nonfluted concave-base points at Lak-261, just a few kilometers south of Lak-36. Taking into account new evidence that has come to light since 1974, the possibility must be kept open that the two traditions of the Borax Lake Pattern, namely, the wide-stem (Borax Lake Aspect) and concave-base (Mendocino Aspect) point traditions, may have had different termination dates, as well as different beginning dates, in different portions of the North Coast Ranges. In the north, for example, the wide-stem tradition of the Borax Lake Aspect may have persisted into relatively late times, possibly to 500 B.C. or later if Jackson (1977) is correct with his age estimate of Hum-245. Persistence of the wide-stem tradition, and of millingstone and mano without the wide-stem point, perhaps may be associated with Yukian continuity in the north, as well as attributed to its effectiveness in exploiting the food resources of this area.

### Language and Archaeological Assemblages

Although more than 1000 archaeological surveys have been carried out in the Russian River subregion, and more than 100 sites tested by excavation, vast areas are virtually unknown archaeologically. A considerable amount is known about general trends, however, and linguistic reconstructions have offered assistance in understanding the prehistoric complexity implied by linguistic diversity. Although Fredrickson's proposed cultural sequence, described above in the Eel River section of this chapter, is applicable to the Russian River subregion, information generated since its original formulation militates against its being imposed as a simple unilineal model.

For example, although Berkeley Pattern influences can be identified throughout Sonoma, Napa, and southern Lake counties, the influences are experienced differently in different districts. In southern Sonoma and Napa counties, Berkeley Pattern manifestations are similar to those of the Bay Area generally, whereas in southern Lake County these manifestations appear as the Houx Aspect, merging earlier Borax Lake Pattern traits with newly introduced Berkeley Pattern attributes. Farther north in northern Lake and Mendocino counties, a pattern equivalent to Berkeley at the same time depth has yet to be defined.

When the geographic distributions of various assemblages are plotted on maps, they sometimes seem to correspond with certain ethnographic territories. Although it must be understood that there is no necessary linkage between ethnographic or linguistic groupings and particular assemblages, it should also be understood that such correlations may indeed occur. When changes in archaeological assemblages occur at the same time as do postulated linguistic changes, the relationship between the two phenomena should be explored. The major shortcoming is that archaeologists and linguists often pool their respective data in such a way that neither data set can serve as an independent test for the other. Nonetheless, the product of such interaction may be demonstrated as valid if it can be measured against still other data sets, including approximately dated paleoenvironmental reconstructions. The following discussion, making use of both linguistic and archaeological data, is offered with these strictures in mind.

As mentioned before, the Yukians are thought to have been the earliest human inhabitants of the North Coast Ranges. Just when the ancestors of the historic Pomo groups entered the area is not known. However, suggestions have been made that the appearance of millingstone cultures in northern California in the Lower Archaic Period may be correlated with the entry of peoples speaking languages affiliated with the Hokan stock (e.g., Baumhoff and Olmsted 1963). In the North Coast Ranges, Whistler (1980b) linked the Borax Lake Aspect of the Borax Lake Pattern (marked by wide-stem projectile points and millingstones; Figure 10.7) to the "Pre-Proto-Pomoan," who he believes entered the Clear Lake area from the east or northeast, perhaps about 5000 B.C., as part of a northward movement by Hokan peoples from southern California. It is suggested here that the newly introduced milling equipment made possible more effective utilization of the acorn, but by processes unlike those employed during the ethnographic period.

The northern movement of Hokan peoples may have been a response to environmental stress resulting from the warmer and less moist climates and the shrinking of the western pluvial lakes. At the time depth suggested by Whistler, a warming trend was also beginning in the North Coast Ranges (West 1981), but with results dramatically different from those to the south. As temperatures rose, oaks and other lower-elevation plants of the sclerophyll communities migrated upslope, replacing conifer forest with oak woodland and effectively increasing the carrying capacity of the area with respect to human communities. For the present, this reconstruction must remain conjecture, since it has not yet been demonstrated that increases in the spread of oaks occurred over a significantly large area.

Although Whistler's overall proposal has merit, his attribution of the wide-stem point to ancestral Pomo must be qualified. The Borax Lake Aspect assemblage is found north of Lake County in both Mendocino and Humboldt counties, well beyond territories assumed ever to have been occupied by Pomoans, but comfortably within lands attributed to early

Yukians. Whereas ancestral Pomoans may have introduced the assemblage, ancestral Yuki, or possibly ancestral Karok, were probably responsible for its spread. Since wide-stem points, apparently related to the Borax Lake Aspect, have also been found in Shasta County (Clewett 1977), it is reasonable to presume that there may have been more than one route of entry for the early millingstone complex and the wide-stem point into northern California, introduced by more than one Hokan group.

Although the Russian River Valley was at one time proposed as being the area where the Pomoans originally settled (Kroeber 1925:222; Webb 1971), many linguists today consider Clear Lake the more likely choice (Halpern 1964; Oswalt 1964). That the Pomo had ancient ties with the sclerophyll communities of the North Coast Ranges is suggested by Whistler's (1980b:9) remark, after reconstructing Pomoan plant terms, that "the overall pattern implies that the Pomo have occupied the California foothill oak woodland for a long time, with access to chaparral and marsh communities."

After settling in the Clear Lake region, Pomoan groups are thought to have radiated out toward the Russian River Valley, the probable homeland for the western group of Pomoan languages (Whistler 1980b) (see Chapter 11). Although satisfactory dating of this expansion has not yet been accomplished, it is believed to have occurred sometime after 3000 B.C. (Whistler 1980b), possibly near the peak of the warming trend identified by West (1981) and conceivably a response to population growth associated with the increasing productivity of once-marginal lands. The radiation of the western group of Pomoan languages into their ethnographic territories may have occurred as late as 500 B.C. (Elmendorf, in press), and possibly earlier, at the end of the warming trend and at the approximate start of the cooling trend that continued to the present (Sims 1976).

The radiation of ancestral western Pomoan peoples from the upper Russian River valley into their ethnographic territories probably occurred during the Middle Archaic Period, and may well have been marked by the Mendocino Aspect. This aspect, distinguished by continued use of millingslab and handstone as well as by the occurrence of nonfluted concave-base and lanceolate projectile points, appears archaeologically to have had its origin in the Clear Lake basin. It later spread throughout lands controlled ethnographically by Pomoan communities as well as into lands in the southern North Coast Ranges held ethnographically by non-Pomoan groups (White *et al.* 1981).

Since the Mendocino Aspect assemblage does not appear to have spread to any significant extent northward into ethnographic Yukian territory, it is reasonable to accept Whistler's (1980b) assignment of it to Pomoan proper. However, it is unlikely that Meighan's (1955a) Mendocino Complex represents an ancestral Yukian assemblage, as also suggested by Whistler (1980b:17). As pointed out earlier, Fredrickson (1973) subsumed the Mendocino Complex within the late Borax Lake Pattern on the basis of artifactual similarities (e.g., concave-base and lanceolate points occurring with the millingstone and mano) and a continuous geographic distribution.

At the time of the projected Pre-Proto-Pomoan entry into the Clear Lake basin, it is likely that the entire North Coast Ranges from San Francisco Bay northward into the Klamath Mountains was occupied by ancestral Proto-Yukians, although it is also possible that Proto-Karok may have been in the northern part of the area. The movement of ancestral western Pomoans into the upper Russian River Valley in all probability initiated a split between ancestral Yukian to the north and ancestral Wappo to the south. As the western Pomoans were expanding into their ethnographic territories, events in the San Francisco Bay area may well have placed additional pressures on the Wappo.

It is generally agreed that by about 3500 B.P. the Utians (ancestral Miwok and Costanoan) held the lands surrounding San Francisco Bay, initiating the lifeways known as the Berkeley Pattern. Perhaps 3000 years ago, the Miwokan branch began to expand north and east. The northern Miwokan movement, occurring about 2500 B.P., may well be represented by elements of the Houx Aspect of the Berkeley Pattern, which have been identified in Marin, Napa, Sonoma, and southern Lake counties (Fredrickson 1973; Whistler 1980b). As Miwok groups moved north and east, and Pomo groups moved south and west, it is likely that Wappo communities were being absorbed or displaced into continually shrinking territories, finally establishing themselves at the beginning of the Augustine Pattern in the Napa Valley and neighboring portions of Sonoma and Lake counties in the area that for the most part constituted their ethnographic territory.

## Local Sequences

In light of the foregoing discussion, it can be seen that different areas within the Russian River subregion will show significant variations in their cultural sequences. Localities to the west of Clear Lake basin may be expected to exhibit assemblages reflective of early and long-lasting Yukian habitation, followed by relatively recent Pomo occupation. Cultural changes evident in local cultural sequences should reflect this shift, and should also reflect impulses from other regions in the form of new ideas and technologies. Cultural change in response to environmental shifts may also be evident. Finally, change as a result of internal feedback processes, influenced by external factors, may also contribute to the cultural sequence. Closer to San Francisco Bay, in the Napa District, for example, greater complexity may be expected, for not only were all of the above processes operating, but quite probably there have been numerous population shifts as well, from Proto-Yukian to Hokan to Miwokan to Wappo.

### Napa District

Initial discussion of the cultural sequence for the Napa District was published in 1953, at which time it was concluded that its prehistory was "intimately related to the known culture succession of the lower Sacramento Valley region to the east" (Heizer, Ed. 1953:306). What are now called the Berkeley and Augustine patterns were represented, but there was no evidence of the Windmiller Pattern. Instead, reference was made to an inadequately studied phase predating Berkeley, and it was remarked that "the North Coast Ranges and lower Sacramento Valley regions were occupied, before Middle Horizon times, by populations differing rather markedly in cultural equipment" (Heizer, Ed. 1953:306).

Drawing heavily upon burial data from Napa District sites, employing stratigraphic analysis, and relying extensively upon cross-dating of artifacts known elsewhere in central California, Bennyhoff (n.d.) has identified a series of 11 named chronological phases for Napa that extend from protohistoric times back to perhaps 5000 B.C. Despite the fact that the Napa District is the best understood of any within the Russian River subregion because its nearness to Berkeley allowed its convenient use by University of California field classes (Heizer, Ed. 1953:225), Bennyhoff considers his framework tentative because many of the phases are scantily represented (Figure 10.13).

The Hultman Phase, believed to be the oldest in the Napa District, is represented by the assemblage at Nap-131 (Figure 6.4) in the upper Napa Valley, which contains millingstones, concave-base and lanceolate projectile points, and an array of other chipped-stone tool forms (Fredrickson 1961b; Meighan 1953b). Although he assigned the phase to the Mendocino Aspect, Bennyhoff (n.d.) attributed to it a date of 5000–3000 B.C. Fredrickson (1973:207–208), reasoning on the basis of obsidian hydration results, suggested an age of 3000–1000 B.C. for the assemblage. Although Bennyhoff (n.d.) favors a Hokan assignment for the phase, Proto-Yukian affiliation can also be argued.

An assemblage of heavy core tools, millingstones, and manos found to the east on the drought-exposed shoreline of artificial Lake Berryessa, and estimated to date between 6000 and 3000 B.C. (True *et al.* 1979), may represent a related, upland variant of either the Hultman Phase or the following Bale Phase. Also in this category are basalt tools and flakes from Nap-129 (Figure 6.4), near Nap-131, which are believed to have eroded out of soil buried beneath a late period occupation deposit (Meighan 1953b). Basalt core tools also have been recovered from the deepest levels of Nap-15, in the lower Napa Valley, where at a depth of about 2 m they were associated with three $^{14}$C dates of 3340 ± 75 B.P. (UGa-3411), 3485 ± 70 B.P. (UGa-2769), and 3605 ± 100 B.P. (UCR-1138) (Stradford and Schwaderer 1981). Nap-15 also yielded manos but no millingstones.

The Bale Phase, as well as the subsequent Rutherford Phase, is believed to be contemporaneous with the Windmiller Pattern of the lower Sacramento Valley, but shows influence by the lower Berkeley Pattern of the larger San Francisco Bay area (presumably a Utian influence) in the form of mortars and pestles, an emphasis on spear and dart points, and flexed burials, all found in the deepest levels of Nap-32. The later Rutherford Phase adds a more elaborate bone tool assemblage, stone cobbles stained with red ochre, and shouldered lanceolate points. Bennyhoff (n.d.) considered that the Bale Phase at Nap-32 represented sporadic use of the site, whereas Rutherford represented seasonal occupation. Although the question is in doubt, it is possible that Rutherford represents early Miwokan use of the Napa area.

The Kolb Phase, well represented at Nap-32, is believed to be an expression of the Houx Aspect of the Berkeley Pattern, indicative of Miwokan occupation. Dated to the transition between Windmiller and Berkeley patterns in the lower Sacramento Valley, the Kolb assemblage contains shouldered lanceolate points, an array of bone artifacts, and several types of *Olivella* beads, including a beveled form also found in a related assemblage in southern Lake County (Fredrickson 1973; White and Fredrickson 1981). The beveled *Olivella* beads date the transition between the Windmiller and Berkeley patterns in the Sacramento Valley and are believed to mark the entry there of ancestral Plains Miwok.

The Goddard Phase, embodied in an incomplete assemblage from the lower levels of Nap-1 and Nap-261, was identified on the basis of saucer and split-drilled *Olivella* beads associated with flexed burials. The beads date the phase to the beginning portion of the Berkeley Pattern in the Sacramento Valley.

Few data are available for the next several phases, which have been identified primarily by means of cross-dating limited assemblages. The River Glen Phase of the middle portion of the Berkeley Pattern was identified at Nap-261 by the occurrence of Saddle *Olivella* beads, distinctive charmstones, and supporting obsidian hydration rim measurements. The Yount Phase, indicative of the terminal Berkeley Pattern, is represented only by four steatite earspools from Nap-1. The Bridge Phase, found at both Nap-1 and Nap-32, marks early Phase 1 of the Augustine Pattern and is believed to be indicative of Wappo entry into the area. Circular *Haliotis* ornaments with scored incisions along the edges and thin rectangular *Olivella* beads identify the phase. Middle Phase 1 and the Oakville Phase are evidenced at Nap-1, Nap-129, and Nap-348 by serrated arrow points with straight or slightly expanding stems, collared stone pipes, steatite ring beads, rectangular *Olivella* beads, and several bone tool forms, including deer scapula grass cutters. Key markers of the subsequent *Davis* Phase, assigned to late Phase 1 of Augustine, are small serrated arrow points with corner notching or expanding stems. The protohistoric Lyman Phase occurs throughout the Napa area and contains the diagnostic clamshell disk bead complex.

---

**Figure 10.13** Cultural sequence in the Napa District: significant artifact types. (Based upon data provided by J. Bennyhoff. Relative scale attempted for related groups; position of specimens shown within facies has no chronological significance; approximate length or diameter of artifacts is provided in caption where available.) 1, *Olivella* lipped bead; 2, magnesite disk bead; 3, magnesite cylinder; 4,5, *Haliotis* ornaments, 2.9 cm; 6, steatite pipe, 2.8 cm; 7, decorated stone tablet (hatched area is painted red), 6.2 cm; 8, obsidian corner-notched arrow points, 5.1 cm; 9,10, incised bone-tube fragments; 11,12, clamshell disk beads; 13, *Olivella* thin rectangle bead (pendant); 14, magnesite disk bead with drilled decoration; 15, magnesite disk bead; 16, magnesite cylinder with drilled decoration; 17, slate pendant, 6.4 cm; 18, steatite hourglass bead, 7 mm (average length); 19, steatite tubular bead, 1.1 cm; 20, steatite disk, 1.5 cm; 21, *Haliotis* ornament, 3 cm; 22, *Haliotis* ornament, 2.2 cm; 23, *Haliotis* ornament, 4.7 cm; 24, *Haliotis* ornament, 2.7 cm; 25, *Haliotis* ornament, 3.3 cm; 26, *Haliotis* ornament; 27, steatite pipe, 41.8 cm; 28, ulna flaker, 9 cm (average length); 29, decorated stone tablet (hatched area is painted red), 2.54 cm; 30, obsidian corner-notched projectile point, 3.9 cm; 31, obsidian projectile point, 5.4 cm; 32, obsidian drill, 4.4 cm; 33, incised bone-tube fragment; 34, hopper mortar and pestle; 35, obsidian serrated, corner-notched projectile point. 4.7 cm; 36, obsidian stemmed projectile points with square serrations, 3 cm; 37, obsidian corner-notched projectile point with square serrations, 3.3 cm; 38, obsidian biface, 9 cm; 39, keeled obsidian tool, 6 cm; 40, obsidian knife, 5.7 cm; 41, steatite ring bead; 42, steatite pipe fragment; 43, obsidian expanding-stem projectile point, 2.2 cm; 44, obsidian corner-notched projectile point with square serrations, 5.6 cm; 45, obsidian serrated projectile point, 5.4 cm; 46, metapodial awl (Type A1bII); 47, bird-bone whistle; 48, despined scapula grass cutter; 49, ulna matting tool; 50, metapodial beamer; 51, *Olivella* thin rectangle bead; 52, *Haliotis* pendant with scored decoration, 4.35 cm; 53, steatite ear plug, 2.85 cm (average diameter); 54, *Olivella* square saddle bead; 55, obsidian bangle; 56, obsidian biface; 57, obsidian burin-faceted biface fragment; 58, scapula-saw fragment; 59, bone needle, 8.8 cm; 60, charmstone, 6.7 cm; 61, charmstone, 6.1 cm; 62, *Olivella* split-drilled bead; 63, *Olivella* saucer bead; 64, mica ornament; 65, bear claw; 66, bone bead; 67, obsidian projectile point, 3.1 cm; 68, obsidian drill, 5.2 cm; 69, metapodial awl (Type A1bI); 70, metapodial awl (Type A1bII); 71, bone-knife fragment; 72, deer-bone splint, 5.98 cm; 73, plummet charmstone, 9.9 cm (average length); 74, ulna fiber tool, 12 cm (average length); 75, beveled *Olivella* bead; 76, *Olivella* ring bead; 77, *Olivella* oval saddle bead; 78,79, *Haliotis* ornaments; 80, *Haliotis* ornament with punctate decoration, 9.3 cm; 81, *Haliotis* ornament, 6.7 cm; 82, incised bone; 83, bowl mortar and pestle; 84, decorated sandstone slab (hatched area is painted red), 15.24 cm; 85, obsidian shouldered projectile point, 6.5 cm; 86, cannon-bone awl; 87, ulna awl; 88, perforated deer-bone splint; 89, bipointed bone pin; 90, quartz crystals; 91, obsidian projectile point, 3.1 cm; 92, obsidian drill, 6.7 cm; 93, Ulna flaker, 9 cm (average length); 94, bone-punch fragment; 95, chert chopper; 96, obsidian drill, 5.5 cm; 97, keeled obsidian tool, 6.4 cm; 98, obsidian biface, 10.4 cm; 99, obsidian projectile point, 5.9 cm; 100, obsidian projectile point, 5.7 cm; 101, obsidian projectile point, 5.4 cm; 102, milling slab and handstone.

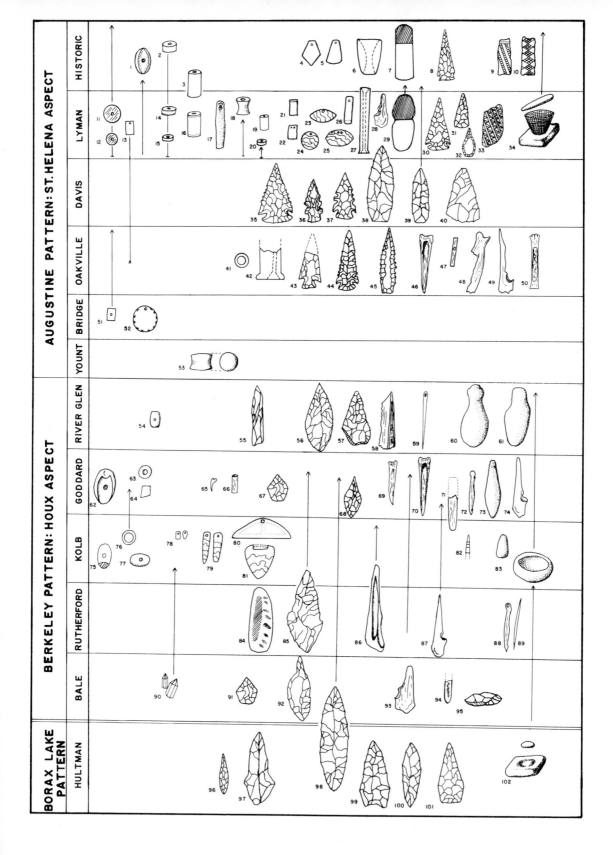

Sonoma District

Although numerous small-scale excavations have been conducted within the Russian River portion of the Sonoma District, excavation of stratified sites with contrasting assemblages has been rare. For the most part, the temporal assessment of sites and site assemblages has been dependent upon cross-dating of temporally diagnostic artifact forms, mostly projectile points. Recently, however, the obsidian hydration method has successfully duplicated the results of cross-dating in temporally ordering a group of sites and artifacts in the vicinity of the Laguna de Santa Rosa (Origer and Wickstrom 1981) and holds promise for accurate relative dating of site assemblages that lack temporally diagnostic artifact forms. Excavations currently under way at deeply stratified sites within the Warm Springs Dam project area in north central Sonoma County also hold promise to clarify the prehistory of the district. To date, although influences of San Francisco Bay are expressed, especially during the later periods, major affiliation with patterns of the North Coast Ranges is clearly evident.

Tantalizing but unsubstantiated evidence for the Post Pattern (dated ca. 10,000–6000 B.C.) comes from the recovery of two chalcedony effigy crescentic fragments from Son-977 (Figure 6.4) from the Laguna area (Origer and Fredrickson 1980:21) (Figure 10.14) and a similar, complete specimen in a private collection from the Bodega vicinity. Since the Laguna shared environmental characteristics with the Clear Lake area, the Laguna discoveries are compatible with the postulated lacustrine orientation of the Post Pattern.

Possibly representing nonlacustrine activities of Post Pattern peoples are materials found in the basal component of Son-547 at Warm Springs Creek (Figure 6.4). In their preliminary study of the archaeology of the Warm Springs Dam project area, M. A. Baumhoff and R. I. Orlins (1979)

A

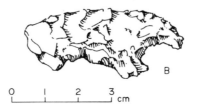

B

0    1    2    3   cm

**Figure 10.14** Chert crescentic objects from the Laguna de Santa Rosa, Sonoma County. (Drawing by Rusty Rossman.)

tentatively attributed to the Post Pattern the unusually high proportion of obsidian waste found in the lower levels of the site, which was followed by the usual pattern of predominant chert eventually being replaced by obsidian. Baumhoff and Orlins speculated that the materials might derive from a free-ranging, pretribelet social grouping. Also identified within the Warm Springs Dam project area were large, percussion-flaked tools and flakes of chert and jasper within water-deposited gravels of Yorty Creek. Although no ties to the Post Pattern could be recognized, stratigraphic evidence contributed to placement of the materials in "some pre-5000 B.C. limbo" (Baumhoff and Orlins 1979:102).

Evidence of the Borax Lake Aspect (dated ca. 6000–3000 B.C.) has occurred but rarely within the Sonoma District. Although occurrences of the diagnostic wide-stem point were reported from the vicinity of Occidental several years ago (Meighan 1955a:26), their occurrence elsewhere has been sporadic and poorly documented. Recently, however, large wide-stem points were recovered from Son-20 in the city of Santa Rosa (Wickstrom and Fredrickson 1982). Artifacts of Anadel obsidian yielded hydration measurements in excess of 6 μm, readings compatible with the postulated antiquity of the Borax Lake Aspect. In addition, several sites attributed to the Borax Lake Aspect have been identified in the Warm Springs area (Baumhoff and Orlins 1979). Although millingstones and manos now have been found at numerous sites within the Sonoma District, extending from the coast to the mountainous interior, they often occur either without other temporally diagnostic artifacts or with the concave-base point indicative of the Mendocino Aspect (Figure 10.15).

Although firm dating for the end of the Borax Lake Pattern is lacking, it is believed to have been replaced by the Houx Aspect of the Berkeley Pattern (possibly representing Miwokan influence) about 500 B.C. Whether the millingstone and mano persisted into Houx Aspect times is not known with certainty, although this would not be unexpected since Houx is conceived of as a merging of Berkeley and Borax Lake traits. At Son-556 in the Warm Springs project area, the occurrence of millingstones within a Houx Aspect assemblage dated after 500 B.C. is supported by both stratigraphy and radiocarbon dates (Baumhoff 1980a), although site mixing and reuse of materials discarded by earlier site occupants cannot be ruled out. The Warm Springs evidence, as well as other findings in the mountainous northern interiors of Sonoma and Napa counties, suggests that the milling toolkit may have been retained in upland areas for some time after its replacement in the valleys, a circumstance not incompatible with the seed resources of the interior and the projected function of the millingstone toolkit (Fredrickson 1979a).

The Berkeley Pattern is represented in the Sonoma District by both the Houx Aspect and a variant of the Ellis Landing Aspect of San Francisco Bay, with its strong bayside adaptation. Since the Ellis Landing variant

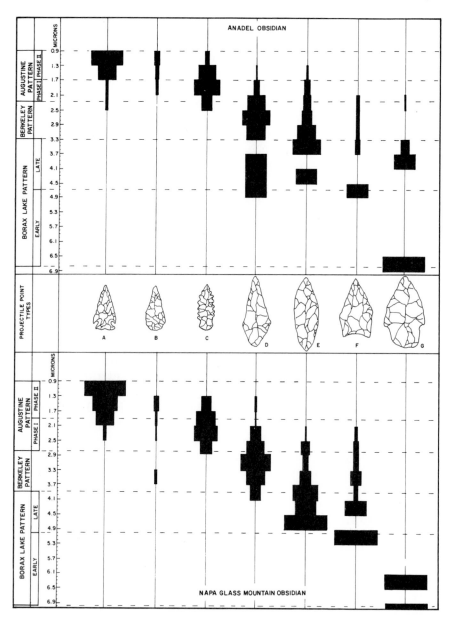

**Figure 10.15** Projectile points characteristic of the Sonoma District. A, corner-notched; B, round-base (preform); C, serrated, stemmed; D, shouldered, lanceolate; E, lanceolate; F, concave-base; G, wide-stemmed. The two sets of graphs (one for the Anadel obsidian source, the other for the Napa Glass Mountain source) show relative proportions for each projectile point category within each 0.4 µm interval. The shape of the distribution of any one category is referred to as a *battleship curve*. (Data source: Origer 1982; drawing by Nelson Thompson.)

has been recognized only at sites in the southernmost part of the district (e.g., at Son-979 on the Laguna) and at Houx sites in the northern portion (e.g., at Son-556 in the Warm Springs project area; Figure 6.4), the relationship between the two aspects is not yet known.

The repeated observation that projectile points are considerably more numerous than milling implements within Houx components, and probably represent a hunting emphasis, contrasts with observations of Upper Berkeley Pattern components on San Francisco Bay. Although it is not yet known whether the Houx hunting emphasis was related to environmental circumstance or to an adaptation with different historical roots, evidence from The Geysers in northeastern Sonoma County suggests that different historical roots associated with ethnicity could conceivably be involved.

Although an intensive survey of more than 26,250 ha (64,000 ac) at The Geysers has resulted in the recording of hundreds of sites, the vast majority appear to have either Clear Lake Aspect or, to a lesser extent, Mendocino Aspect affiliation. No site clearly identifiable with Houx has yet been found, although such sites are known only a few kilometers away in Lake County and in the adjacent Warm Springs area of Sonoma County (Eisenman and Fredrickson 1980). On the basis of contrasting patterns of obsidian utilization, marked by significant overrepresentation of Napa obsidian within Geysers sites, Eisenman and Fredrickson inferred that the Sonoma County portion of The Geysers had been occupied continuously by the Wappo for at least 2500 years. If Houx was associated with Miwokan entry into Lake County (Fredrickson 1973) and with Miwokan or Pomoan occupation of Warm Springs, its absence within Wappo lands at The Geysers would be at least partially explained.

The Clear Lake Aspect of the Augustine Pattern, including both Phase 1 and Phase 2 components, is represented within the Sonoma District by numerous sites throughout the area. However, no evidence has come to view suggesting that the strong ceremonial orientation of Phase 1 in the Delta (Bennyhoff 1977a; Fredrickson 1974b) carried over into the Sonoma District. Influences from the Delta and Bay appear to be accretional, building upon earlier adaptations. However, Baumhoff's (1980a) interpretation of the archaeology of the 5870 ha (14,500 ac) Warm Springs Dam project area, based upon inferred population shifts and consistent changes in chert and obsidian débitage ratios, deserves special mention.

Baumhoff assumed entry of a single Pomo tribelet into the Warm Springs area during the time of the Borax Lake Aspect. Earlier occupants were Yukian, assumed to have had a wide-ranging, pretribelet social organization. Initial Pomo occupation was characterized by a large winter village and several smaller satellite hamlets. During the time of the Mendocino Aspect, formalized exchange relationships were established and the flaked-stone industry expanded and diversified. Also at this time religion and industry were focused at one-family sites, at each of which resided exchange specialists, religious practitioners, or artisans. During the time of the Houx Aspect, for which Baumhoff offers a termination date of A.D. 1200, the tribelet experienced a cultural florescence, and the numerous petroglyphs on upper Dry Creek may have been made then. At the time of the Clear Lake Aspect (Baumhoff's Late Houx), this way of life ended and the population shifted to a single large village.

Baumhoff (1980) suggested that this shift announced the introduction of the Kuksu religion, which transformed native Pomo religion and realigned society into the ethnographic pattern with the large winter village as the ceremonial center. As Baumhoff considers that Kuksu was introduced by the Patwin of Penutian stock, the change in social organization could represent "Penutianization" of native Hokan culture (Baumhoff 1980).

Although the Patwin may have introduced Kuksu to the Pomo, Bennyhoff (1977a) suggested that Kuksu roots go back prior to Patwin entry at least to late Berkeley Pattern times and that the ceremonial system of Augustine Pattern's Phase 1 represents the spread of early Kuksu throughout central California (Fredrickson 1974b). However, since no archaeological evidence for the Phase 1 ceremonial system has yet been found in the Sonoma District, Baumhoff's reconstruction is not controverted.

Representing Phase 2, evidence of clamshell disk and *Olivella* bead manufacture has been unearthed at several sites in the vicinity of the Laguna, including Son-455 (Figure 6.4) south of Santa Rosa, signaling the significant entry of the protohistoric residents of the Sonoma District into the central California exchange system documented in the ethnographic record (J. Davis 1961).

### Mendocino and Lake Counties

The portion of Mendocino County within the Russian River subregion, including the coastal drainage system as well as the Russian River watershed, is little known archaeologically, being represented by only a small handful of investigations. The landmark investigation continues to be the 1951 excavations at Men-500 (Figure 6.4) in north-central Mendocino County where the Mendocino Complex (the Mendocino Aspect of the Late Borax Lake Pattern) was first recognized (Meighan 1955a). Work at the 1.2-m-deep site, carried out by the University of California Archaeological Survey under the supervision of C. W. Meighan, revealed a relatively shallow upper component containing protohistoric and historic materials, assigned to a local variant of the Clear Lake Complex, and a deeper component yielding Mendocino Complex materials. As already mentioned, Meighan (1955a) utilized information from the site to develop the first regional chronology for the North Coast Ranges.

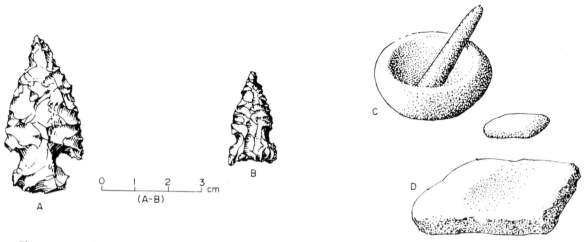

**Figure 10.16** Characteristic implements of the Mendocino Aspect of the Borax Lake Pattern, Men-500. A, chert corner-notched projectile point; B, chert side-notched projectile point; C, bowl mortar and pestle; D, millingstone and mano. (Design by Nelson Thompson; drawing by Rusty Rossman.)

Distinctive elements of the Mendocino Complex as defined by Meighan were large lanceolate, concave-base, and side-notched projectile points and the co-occurrence of bowl mortars and pestles with milling-stones and manos (Figure 10.16). Although Meighan (1955a) suggested that the Mendocino Complex was a northern phenomenon that possibly extended into the mountains of Humboldt and Trinity counties, subsequent work has shown its distribution to be predominantly southern with the characteristic assemblage occurring at sites throughout the Russian River subregion. Similarities between the assemblages of Men-500 and Lak-261 and other sites in Lake and Mendocino counties, including Lak-36, the classic Borax Lake site, led Fredrickson (1973) to assign the Mendocino Complex to the Borax Lake Pattern. This assignment is compatible with Meighan's (1955a:28) suggestion that the Mendocino Complex was an outgrowth of the Borax Lake Complex as it was then defined.

Another excavated site in Mendocino County, where materials similar to those from Men-500 were recovered, is Men-584, located on Cold Creek to the east of Ukiah. The Clear Lake and Mendocino aspects were both represented, as was a third, intermediate assemblage with large, expanding-stem and shouldered lanceolate projectile points (Soule 1975) (Figure 10.17). No other assemblages have been recognized in the Russian River portion of Mendocino County, although an avocational archaeologist has reported the large Borax Lake wide-stem points from Sherwood Valley (Donald Branscomb, personal communication, 1977).

Although the southern portion of the Clear Lake basin is relatively well known archaeologically, the northern part, and northern Lake County generally, is poorly represented. Excavated sites have yielded either Clear Lake or Mendocino Aspect materials (T. King 1975a; Moratto 1973c; Parker 1977) or little that is temporally diagnostic (A. King and Fredrickson 1978). The Upper Lake area is of particular interest because of the surprisingly low frequency of obsidian occurring on sites in the vicinity, considering the nearness of both the Borax Lake and Konocti obsidian flows (T. Jackson 1973).

The southern Clear Lake basin has the longest cultural sequence of any comparable area in the North Coast Ranges (Figure 10.5). The earliest occupation is that of the Post Pattern (ca. 10,000–6000 B.C.), represented only by materials at Lak-36 (Meighan and Haynes 1970), with a possible proto-Archaic variant at the Mostin site north of Kelseyville (Kaufman 1980). Mostin pentagonal points (Figure 10.18) and obsidian hydration rim readings suggestive of considerable antiquity also have been recovered from Lak-589 on Anderson Marsh at Lower Lake (Kaufman 1980).

The Borax Lake Aspect (ca. 6000–3000 B.C.) has been found through excavation only at Lak-36 (Meighan and Haynes 1970), although surface assemblages that include the distinctive wide-stem point have been recorded in the rolling lands south of Mount Konocti.

The Mendocino Aspect (ca. 3000–500 B.C.) is well represented in the southern Clear Lake basin, with components at excavated sites Lak-36 (Meighan and Haynes 1970), Lak-261 (Fredrickson 1973), Lak-425 (R. King 1975b), and Lak-510 (White and Fredrickson 1981).

The Houx Aspect (ca. 500 B.C.–A.D. 500?) has been identified at three excavated sites, Lak-261 (Fredrickson 1973), Lak-395 (Werner 1980), and Lak-510 (White and Fredrickson 1981), all within territory of the ethnographic Lake Miwok.

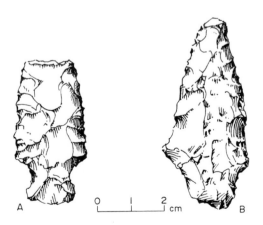

**Figure 10.17** Projectile points from an assemblage intermediate between the Mendocino Aspect and Clear Lake Aspect, Lak-584. A, chert expanding-stem lanceolate projectile point; B, chert shouldered lanceolate projectile point. (Drawing by Rusty Rossman.)

0   1   2   3
cm

**Figure 10.18** Mostin pentagonal projectile point, Lak-380. (Drawing by Rusty Rossman.)

The final archaeological pattern, the Clear Lake Aspect of the Augustine Pattern (ca. A.D. 500?–1850), has been recorded at numerous sites within the southern Clear Lake basin.

## Summary

Although the general outline of the prehistory of California's North Coastal region is fairly well understood, there are significant irregularities in the amount and quality of information available for key places and times. Little is known of Paleoindian occupation other than the tantalizing fluted points and crescents at the Borax Lake site, which obsidian hydration, cross-dating, and geology identified as legitimate representatives of early occupation, perhaps as far back as 12,000 B.P. The flaked-stone effigy crescents at the Laguna de Santa Rosa, and reportedly at Bodega Bay, although undatable at present, permit speculation that localities anywhere in the region that were favorably endowed with marsh or lacustrine resources may have been made use of by these early residents.

Whether the Mostin materials on Kelsey Creek, which appear equally old, are directly related to the Post Pattern cannot be determined at present. However, the occurrence of what otherwise appears to be an early Archaic adaptation is puzzling, to say the least. Recovery of Mostin-style pentagonal points and compatible obsidian hydration results from the Anderson Marsh vicinity at the southeastern end of Clear Lake give added legitimacy to inferences of an early Archaic adaptation. The Borax Lake and Mostin finds, either together or separately, may represent what

Whistler (1980b) referred to as Pre-Proto-Yukian, or may be the only remnants left of a language community long vanished from California.

The Borax Lake Aspect, with its wide-stem projectile points and millingstones, may have been built upon an earlier substratum, with the milling equipment possibly added by contacts with speakers of ancestral Hokan languages, moving northward from southern California or elsewhere. Although the Mendocino Aspect, with its concave-base and lanceolate points, evidently follows the early manifestation at the Borax Lake site, the observations that the wide-stem tradition has a northern distribution and the concave-base tradition a southern one, and that both traditions may persist in certain of their respective localities throughout the entire Archaic period, give rise to the conjecture that the wide-stem tradition was carried by ancestral Yukian or Yukian-influenced communities, whereas the concave-base tradition was an element of Pomoan or Pomoan-influenced communities.

The apparent persistence of the traditions within their respective territories not only speaks well of their adaptive value in providing subsistence benefits, but also hints that influences from populations and technologies external to the region were not overly strong or long-sustained, possibly because of the relative inaccessibility of the mountainous habitats in which the two traditions flourished. It is becoming more evident that a uniform set of dates for transitions between cultural assemblages may not be appropriate for the North Coastal region. Several factors argue for this caution: (1) the Borax Lake Pattern in both early and late manifestations was evidently well-suited for exploitation of the resources of the area; (2) external influences came more or less separately, not necessarily at identical times, from the north, east, and south; and (3) external influences appeared to weaken somewhat as they penetrated into the interior, leaving more remote areas with a strong core of traditional culture. Although climatic changes involving shifts of existing plant species up and down slopes, depending upon prevailing climatic regimes, may have been associated with some of the observed cultural shifts, climatic effects would not necessarily require changes in technology. Indeed, although changes in land use would be probable as a result of postulated vegetation shifts, the principle of seasonal dispersal of village communities alternating with aggregation would have provided sufficient flexibility so that settlement pattern and social organization need change only with respect to timing.

The appearance about 2500 B.P. of the Berkeley Pattern's Houx Aspect throughout the southern portion of the Russian River subregion, including the ethnographic territory of the Lake Miwok immediately south of Lower Lake, may well represent Miwokan influence. The limited geographic spread of the Houx assemblage (e.g., shouldered lanceolate points, burin-faceted projectile points, a reworked biface industry, bowl mortars and pestles, and split-beveled *Olivella* beads) supports this interpretation. As yet, no evidence of significant cultural change at that time depth, and nothing resembling the Houx assemblage, has been found beyond northern Sonoma and southern Lake counties.

The Emergent Period cultures of the North Coastal region were represented by two major cultural traditions, the Gunther Pattern in the north and the Augustine Pattern to the south.

The Gunther Pattern was a specialized riverine and coastal adaptation that evidently was brought into the area beginning about 1000 B.P. by ancestral Wiyot and Yurok, the latter of whom probably entered with a well-developed fishing and woodworking technology. The Karok, probably already established in the area with a diversified hunting–gathering economy, which in all probability included use of riverine resources as well as those of the higher elevations, shifted to the specialized riverine adaptation, as did the Hupa, who entered the area perhaps 650 B.P. with an economy adapted to interior forested environments.

Although the Emergent Period culture patterns of the nonriverine interior of the Northwest Coast subregion have not yet been subject to substantial archaeological investigation, the Shasta Aspect of the Augustine Pattern, an effective blend of northwestern and central California elements, characterized the ethnographic territories of both Athapascan and Yukian peoples of the Eel River subregion to the south.

The pursuer strategy required by the Northwest Coast adaptation—that of seeking specialized resources predictable in their occurrences at particular times and places—was heavily dependent upon the biological, geological, and hydrological characteristics of the area (Hildebrandt 1981). To the south, where the biophysical characteristics, such as offshore sea mammal rookeries, were not conducive to a year-round pursuer orientation, the pursuer strategy was alternated with or replaced by a searcher one, that of exploiting a wide range of prey dispersed over an extensive area. It is evident that the settlement patterns of local groups in the Eel River subregion were heavily dependent upon the interplay of resource availability, terrain, and technology, with all groups following more or less individualized seasonal rounds that required cyclical shifts in social organization.

The Augustine Pattern, discussed more fully in Chapter 5, representing a fusion of introduced elements with those of the older Berkeley Pattern, and linked to the southern spread of Wintuan peoples into the Sacramento Valley, was expressed in the Russian River subregion by its Clear Lake Aspect. Although cyclical seasonal rounds also characterized Russin River groups to some extent, it is probable that environmental factors were mediated to some extent by the increasing role of exchange in stabilizing resource availability, as evidenced by obsidian exchange patterns and the clamshell disk bead complex and supported by the ethnographic record.

## Summary and Conclusions

With one or two significant exceptions, the bulk of the important archaeological work conducted in the North Coastal region through the 1950s was carried out under the auspices of the University of California, Berkeley. An explicit strategy of Berkeley researchers, expressed by R. K. Beardsley (1954), consisted of the following elements: (1) deliberate investigation of small, single-component sites in order to isolate unmixed manifestations of each culture; (2) investigation of large, stratified sites in order to define the cultural sequence; (3) the treatment of each human burial, including associated artifacts and other attributes, as an analytic unit; and (4) the recognition of beads and ornaments and other stylistic details as sensitive indicators of temporal variation.

This methodologically sound strategy proved effective for a number of years, but, since the late 1960s, has not been applicable to the practice of archaeology in the North Coastal region. A number of different reasons account for this:

1. Systematic excavation in search of cemeteries was no longer appropriate, as archaeologists at last were forced to take heed of the concerns of Native Americans regarding proper treatment for their dead.
2. The nature of archaeological investigation itself shifted from large-scale excavation to large-scale, intensive survey and relatively small-scale test excavation. This, of course, was a function of environmental protection and historical preservation legislation.
3. In the North Coast Ranges, specifically, soil conditions were not conducive to the preservation of bone and shell, so beads and other perishables, which were important for their stylistic variations, were generally absent.
4. When excavation did occur, sites were selected on the basis of management rather than traditional research needs.
5. Theoretical and methodological developments associated with the so-called New Archaeology of the 1960s prompted a questioning of traditional problems and approaches and stimulated the emergence of additional problems and approaches.

Given these conditions and both the constraints and advantages that accrued from the shift in strategy implied by the foregoing factors, archaeologists working in the North Coastal region generally (but not exclusively) have addressed themselves to the following research domains: (1) space–time relationships, including typological studies and development of alternative dating techniques, focusing in particular upon the obsidian hydration method; (2) settlement–subsistence patterns, including problems of site typologies, predictive modeling, and environmental interaction; (3) paleoclimatic reconstructions, based for the most part on pollen data; (4) interaction and exchange systems, focusing particularly upon obsidian; (5) technological–demographic relationships, including problems of population growth and dispersal as well as utilization of marginal areas; and (6) sociocultural identity of prehistoric populations, tying in especially hypotheses based upon linguistic affiliations of ethnographic groups and historical linguistics.

It is emphasized that the items just listed are not an all-inclusive compilation of research directions, but merely a listing of what appear to be dominant research trends. Implementation of the "new strategy" has broken much new ground and has begun to make comprehensible the prehistory of a complex and previously little-known region.

# 11. Linguistic Prehistory

There are three main ways in which linguistics can illuminate
prehistory: (a) by establishing facts concerning the common origin
and subsequent divergence of languages, implying the earlier unity
and subsequent separations of peoples; (b) by discovering diffused
features (of phonetics, structure, or vocabulary) among languages,
which bear evidence of prehistoric culture contacts; and (c) by
reconstructing the vocabulary of old stages of languages in order to
bring out suggestions of the physical environment and content of
prehistoric cultures.
*Swadesh (1959b:20)*

Wintu dancers. (Photograph by C. H. Merriam; courtesy of the R. H. Lowie
Museum of Anthropology, University of California, Berkeley.)

# Introduction

California was the Babel of ancient America. The Indians of California accounted for about 20% of the nearly 500 separate languages spoken in America north of Mexico in A.D. 1492. In many ways the linguistic features of aboriginal California were more complex than those of any other area of equal size on earth, possibly excepting coastal New Guinea. There were in preconquest California no fewer than 23 language families and isolate languages, together accounting for some 90 distinct languages (Figure 11.1), further differentiated into a large but unknowable number of dialects. For analytic purposes, the patchwork of ethnic and linguistic units in early protohistoric California may be viewed as the end result of prehistoric cultural and linguistic developments. Accordingly, interpretations of archaeological data must take into account linguistic, as well as environmental and cultural, events, conditions, and processes.

The purpose of this chapter is to advance a model to show how California's linguistic mosaic might have developed, that is, to represent the area's linguistic prehistory. Both archaeological and linguistic information will be used to reconstruct the nature and age of key language shifts and to examine their possible causes. The data of historical linguistics indicate something of the cultural relationships and events that might have occurred, or must have occurred, in the past. Linguistic reconstructions thus identify specific possibilities and probabilities to be tested independently against the archaeological record.

What follows is a general summary of California's linguistic prehistory. This reconstruction embodies current linguistic and archaeological information, but it does not purport to be God's Truth. Rather, presented here is a working model, subject to verification and change as more and better data are brought to bear.

## Linguistic Models

One may assume that most California dialects and some languages and families evolved more or less in place as a result of the isolation and differentiation of ancestral languages. In addition, many incursions by speakers of distinct languages must have occurred to account for the numerous unrelated or distantly related stocks, families, and isolate languages in California. To the extent that yet other groups may have entered and later left the area, or entered and subsequently lost their linguistic identities, the number of migrations must be raised. The diversity of languages implies that repeated population shifts should be evinced in the archaeological record.

Clearly, no simple model can represent California's tangled linguistic prehistory. J. Goss has opined that "migrations of people speaking different languages in western North America for the past 10,000 years should probably be characterized as a diverse complexity of successive fission and fusion of linguistic communities" (1977:50). Accordingly, any model of linguistic prehistory must be wrong, at least in detail, because all models simplify and cannot represent the full array of possible variables. The idea is to work out the most elegant simulation to fit available information.

One problem in historical linguistic model building is that some languages may have vanished in prehistory (Lamb 1962). Thus, one may expect to find archaeological remains that cannot be linked to any known historic or predecessor language. Another problem is that language and culture are not always connected. Nearly identical cultures were shared, for example, by the protohistoric Karok (Hokan stock), Yurok (Algic superfamily), and Hupa–Chilula (Athapascan family) of northwestern California (Bright 1957, 1978; Goddard 1903; Kroeber 1925; Pilling 1978). Cultural resemblance does not perforce imply linguistic unity.

Although it is possible that certain stocks or families began in California with a single migration, it is well to remember that families as such probably never moved en bloc. In some cases two or more languages of a given family may have entered California separately and at different times, whereas other families doubtless evolved within California as a result of isolation and differentiation over a span of time. The dynamic unit is not the stock or family, but the language or dialect, and even these do not "migrate"; they spread by various means, such as the movement of their speakers, borrowing, and assimilation. A linguistic prehistory must account for the spread of *languages*, some of which may have been ancestral to later dialect groups, languages, families, or even stocks.

Other realities confound the prehistorian. People not only entered California but they sometimes left as well, taking their languages with them and leaving archaeological traces behind. Moreover, ethnic territories shifted frequently in California (Heizer 1962c; Kroeber 1959b); over the centuries, particular groups may have moved repeatedly. Finally, at any point in time language boundaries were rather arbitrary or indefinite, tending to merge gradually, especially between peoples with strong social

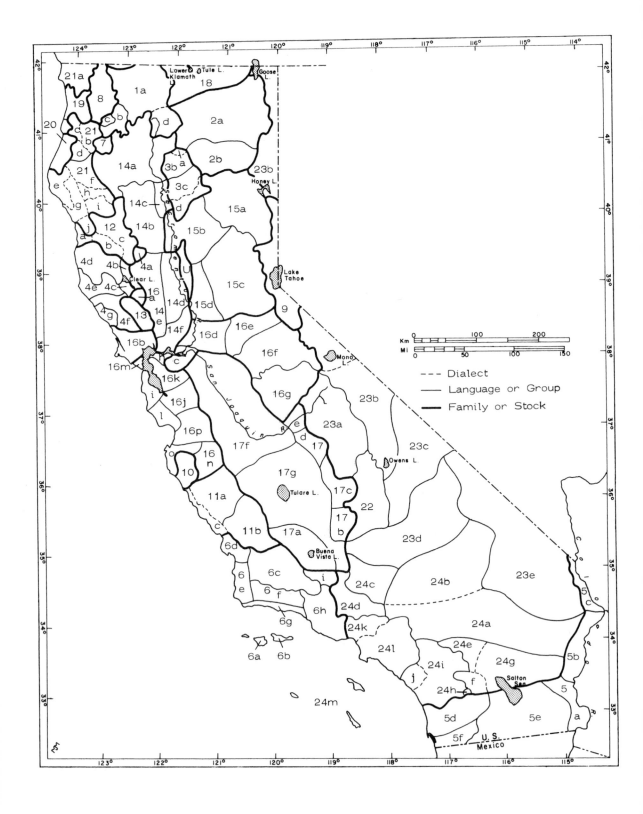

**Figure 11.1** Classification of California Indian languages.*

## HOKAN STOCK

**1. Shastan Family:** (a) Shasta language (4)†; (b) New River Shasta language (1); (c) Konomihu language (1); (d) Okwanuchu language (1).

**2. Palaihnihan Family:** (a) Achumawi (Pit River) language or group (9); (b) Atsugewi (Hat Creek) language (2).

**3. Yanan Family,** *Northern Yana language* (2): (a) Northern Yana dialect; (b) Central Yana dialect. *Southern Yana language* (2): (c) Southern Yana dialect; (d) Yahi dialect.

**4. Pomoan Family:** (a) Northeastern Pomo language (1); (b) Eastern Pomo language (2); (c) Southeastern Pomo language (1). *Western Pomo group:* (d) Northern Pomo language (1). *Southern Pomo subgroup:* (e) Central Pomo language (2); (f) Southern Pomo language (?); (g) Southwestern (Kashaya) Pomo language (1).

**5. Yuman Family,** *Colorado River group:* (a) Yuma (Quechan or Kwtsaan) language (1); (b) Maricopa (Halchidoma) language (1); (c) Mojave language (1). *California group:* (d) Northern Diegueño (Ipai) language (4). *Southern Diegueño subgroup:* (e) Southern Diegueño (Tiipay) language (1); (f) Kumeyaay language (1).

**6. Chumashan Family,** *Island Chumash group:* (a) Roseño Chumash language (1); (b) Cruzeño Chumash language (1). (c) Cuyama (Chumash language?) (1); (d) Northern (Obispeño) Chumash language (1). *Central Chumash group:* (e) Purisimeño Chumash language (1); (f) Ynezeño Chumash language (1); (g) Barbareño Chumash language (1); (h) Ventureño Chumash language (1); (i) Emigdiano Chumash language (1).

**Other Hokan Languages:** 7. Chimariko language (1); 8. Karok language (1); 9. Washo language (3); 10. Esselen language (Hokan?) (1); 11. Salinan language (or family?) (2?): (a) Antoniano dialect or language; (b) Migueleño dialect or language; (c) Playano dialect (doubtful).

## YUKIAN STOCK (OR FAMILY)

**12. Yuki language** (3): (a) Coast Yuki dialect; (b) Huchnom dialect; (c) (Interior) Yuki dialect. 13. **Wappo language** (4?).

## PENUTIAN STOCK‡

**14. Wintuan Family,** *Northern Wintun branch:* (a) Wintu language (3); (b) Hill Nomlaki language; (c) River Nomlaki language. *Patwin branch:* (d) River Patwin language (2); (e) Hill Patwin language (4); (f) Southern Patwin (Suisun) language (1).

**15. Maiduan Family:** (a) Maidu (Northeastern Maidu) language; (b) Konkow (Northwestern Maidu) language (2?). Nisenan language (7): (c) Hill Nisenan dialect group; (d) Valley Nisenan dialect group.

**16. Utian Family, Miwokan subfamily,** *Western division:* (a) Lake Miwok language (1); (b) Coast Miwok language (2). *Eastern division:* (c) Saclan (Bay Miwok) language (1); (d) Plains Miwok language (1); (e) Northern Sierra Miwok language (1); (f) Central Sierra Miwok language (2); (g) Southern Sierra Miwok language (2). **Costanoan (Ohlonean) subfamily:** (h) Karkin (Carquinez) Costanoan language (1); *Northern division:* (i) Ramaytush (San Francisco) Costanoan language (1); (j) Tamyen (Santa Clara) Costanoan language (1); (k) Chochenyo (East Bay) Costanoan language (1); (l) Awaswas (Santa Cruz) Costanoan language (1); (m) Southern Marin Costanoan (existence uncertain). *Southern division:* (n) Chalon (Soledad) Costanoan language (1); (o) Rumsen (San Carlos) Costanoan language (1); (p) Mutsun (San Juan Bautista) Costanoan language (1).

**17. Yokutsan Family,** *Foothill division:* (a) Buena Vista Yokuts language or group (3); (b) Poso Creek Yokuts language or group (2); (c) Tule–Kaweah Yokuts language or group (5); (d) Kings River Yokuts language or group (5); (e) Northern Hill Yokuts language or group (5–15).

*Valley division*: (f) Northern Valley Yokuts language or group (4); (g) Southern Valley Yokuts language or group (5).

**Isolate Penutian Language:** (18) Klamath-Modoc language (2).

## ALGIC SUPERFAMILY

**19. Yurok language** (2); 20. **Wiyot language** (1).

## 21. ATHAPASCAN FAMILY

**Oregon group:** (a) Tolowa language (1).

**California group,** Hupa–Chilula language (3): (b) Hupa dialect; (c) Chilula dialect; (d) Whilkut dialect. (e) Mattole language (2).

**Wailaki language or subgroup** (5): (f) Nongatl dialect; (g) Sinkyone dialect; (h) Lassik dialect; (i) Wailaki dialect; (j) Cahto dialect or language.

## UTO-AZTECAN FAMILY

22. **Tübatulabal (Kern River) language** (3).

23. **Numic Subfamily,** *Western group*: (a) Mono (Monachi) language (1); (b) Northern Paiute–Bannock (Paviotso) language (2). *Central group*: (c) Panamint (Koso) language (1). *Southern group*: (d) Kawaiisu language (1); (e) Chemehuevi language (1).

24. **Takic Subfamily,** *Serran group*: Serrano language (2): (a) Serrano dialect; (b) Möhineyam (Vanyume) dialect; (c) Kitanemuk language (1). (d) *Tataviam* (Alliklik) language ? (Uto-Aztecan ?). *Cupan group*: Cahuilla language (3): (e) Pass Cahuilla dialect; (f) Mountain Cahuilla dialect; (g) Desert Cahuilla dialect; (h) Cupeño language (1). Luiseño–Juaneño language (2): (i) Luiseño dialect; (j) Juaneño dialect. *Gabrielino–Fernandeño group*: (k) Fernandeño language or dialect; (l) Gabrielino language or dialect; (m) Nicoleño language or dialect.

---

*Compiled from Bennyhoff 1977a; Heizer, Ed. 1978; Kroeber 1925, 1932; Shipley 1978; Whistler 1977b, 1979a. (Map by the author.)

†Number of dialects.

‡Genetic status uncertain.

U = unclaimed land.

ties. As examples, the Northern Hill Yokuts and Southern Sierra Miwok often intermarried and lived in mixed villages near their common border (Broadbent 1964), and at least one Clear Lake Pomo village was occupied by speakers of Hill Patwin and five Pomo languages (Gifford 1926b). Such variables, coupled with the loss of countless archaeological sites in recent years, preclude our knowing "the details of migrations, fissions, and fusions of prehistoric linguistic communities" (Goss 1977:51). Even so, careful analyses of available data may permit testable inferences about population movements and language spreads in California prehistory.

Because the following discussion makes reference to glottochronology, a few words about this method are in order. "Glottochronology is the study of rate of change in language, and the use of the rate for historical inference, especially for the estimation of time depths and the use of such time depths to provide a pattern of internal relationships within a language family" (Hymes 1960:4). The method and its limiations have been summarized by Gudschinsky (1964) and Hymes (1960). Glottochronological dates are expressed in minimum centuries: speakers of the compared languages "must have been separated for at least the number of years cited to allow for the observed amount of lexical change" (Hopkins 1965:55). The true age of language divergence is thus assumed to be somewhat older than the glottochronological date. Although such dates admittedly are imprecise, they may serve as a *rough* index of the *relative* age and sequence of linguistic events.

## California's Native Languages

This overview aims to describe the aboriginal languages of California and to discuss their spatial and genetic relationships in terms of prehistory. Linguistic concepts are defined in the Glossary. The classification and historic distribution of the languages appear as Figure 11.1.

The ≈90 protohistoric Indian languages of California fall within six apparently unrelated stocks, superfamilies, or families (Figure 11.1 and Table 11.1). Of these, the Hokan and Penutian stocks incorporate most (≈67) of the languages. The Algic superfamily along with the Athapascan and Uto-Aztecan families belong to stocks with their greatest numbers of languages elsewhere in North America. Not definitely related to any other known grouping is the enigmatic Yukian stock, or family (Shipley 1978).

### Hokan Stock

Hokan was first defined by Dixon and Kroeber (1919) on the basis of lexical comparisons, and its reality as a genetic construct was generally

**TABLE 11.1**

**Summary of Linguistic Units in Native California**[a]

| Stock or superfamily | Families | Isolate language | Total languages | Dialects |
|---|---|---|---|---|
| Hokan | 6? | 5? | 34? | 57? |
| Yukian | | 2 | 2 | 7? |
| Penutian | 4? | 1 | 33? | 72–82? |
| Algic | | 2 | 2 | 3 |
| | Athapascan | | 4–5 | 11? |
| | Uto-Aztecan | 1 | 15? | 22? |
| | 12? | 11? | | |
| Totals | 23? | | ≈90? | ≥182? |

[a]Compiled from Kroeber (1925), Shipley (1978), and Whistler (1977a,b).

accepted for half a century. However, because the relationships among some languages ascribed to Hokan have not been confirmed, it seems best to view this stock as an unverified hypothesis (Shipley 1978). California Hokan is thought to include five isolate languages and six language families (Figure 11.1).

With the possible exception of Yukian, Hokan seems to be the oldest known California stock. Many years ago Kroeber (1925:222) called attention to structural differences among Hokan languages and to their dispersion in five blocks or clusters near California's borders (Figure 11.2), concluding that "a long history must separate them." As compared with Penutian, "the interrelationships of the Hokan languages lie much deeper in time, a fact paralleled by their geographical discontinuity" (Shipley 1978:85). The broken chain of Hokan islands around the margins of California presumably includes the relic areas surviving from an ancient, continuous distribution (Goss 1977; Hopkins 1965; Taylor 1961).

Similarly, the number of Hokan language families (6?) and isolate languages (5?) indicates great time depth in California. Karok is one such isolate that, despite intensive work, has not been proved to be related to any other Hokan language (Whistler 1979a). The same holds true for Washo, Salinan, and Chimariko; their Hokan roots are so deep that specific ties with other Hokan languages are difficult to establish. Esselen may or may not be Hokan. Its link with Hokan, suggested by a few lexical resemblances, is so weak that it may just as well prove to be the lone remnant of an extinct language family (Shipley 1978:81).

Two other lines of evidence have been adduced to support the notion of great antiquity for Hokan in California. First, a correlation of ethnographic traits by "tribe" (language group) indicated to Klimek (1935:61) and Kroeber (1935:7) that Hokan was related to the oldest identifiable "culture stratum" in California. Second, glottochronological dates of the separation of Hokan languages (e.g., 55 minimum centuries for Washo–Yana) tend to be older than those of other California stocks (cf. Baumhoff and Olmsted 1963; Kroeber 1955; Swadesh 1964). These dates are suspect, however, because cognate status is uncertain in the case of such interfamily or family-isolate comparisons. But even without the glottochronological dates, linguistic geography and internal differentiation attest to great time depth for the Hokan stock in California. Archaeological evidence bearing on Hokan prehistory will be taken up later in this chapter.

### Yukian Stock

The Yukian stock, or family, is not clearly related to any other language unit (Kroeber 1911b, 1925). Linguists have found similarities be-

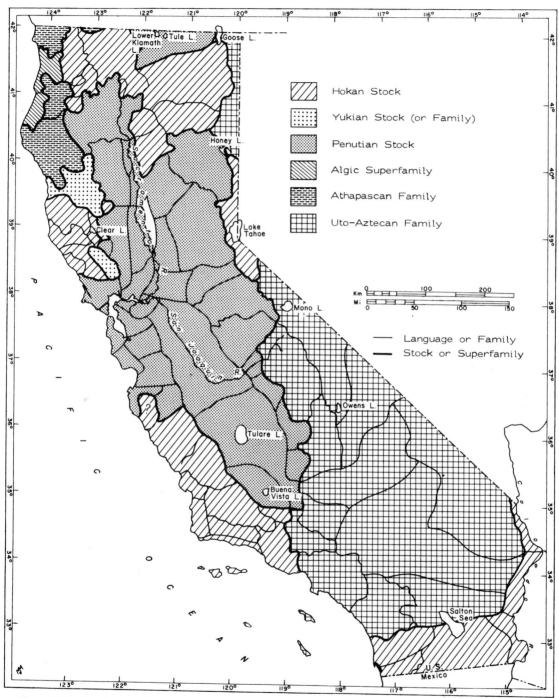

**Figure 11.2** Distribution of language stocks and families in California, circa A.D. 1750. (After Kroeber 1925 and Shipley 1978; map by the author.)

tween Yukian and Athapascan (Radin 1919), Siouan–Yuchi (Elmendorf 1963, 1964), and Hokan (Oswalt 1978; Swadesh 1964). Dixon and Kroeber (1919) noted that Yukian structure is rather surprisingly like that of Penutian languages, a view supported by Shipley's (1957) discovery of lexical resemblances. Wenger (1973) cites phonological and grammatical data as further evidence of a possible Yukian–Penutian connection. Still, the case for a Penutian link is far from compelling. Yukian remains an isolate. Ultimately, it may prove to be affiliated with one of the known stocks, or it may represent an otherwise vanished language group older in California than Hokan (Shipley 1978:82).

Yukian includes only two languages, Wappo and Yuki (Figure 11.1). The Yuki held the upper Eel River country and a bit of ocean frontage in the North Coast Ranges (Foster 1944; V. Miller 1979). The Wappo homeland extended from upper Napa Valley, through the hills near Mt. St. Helena, to Alexander Valley on the Russian River. There was also a small Wappo enclave (*Lile?ek*) on lower Cole Creek bordering Clear Lake (Barrett 1908a; Sawyer 1978).

Yuki and Wappo grammars differ greatly, and their few lexical cognates suggest a divergence on the order of ≈3000 years ago (Elmendorf 1968). It is possible that Yuki and Wappo entered northern California separately, or that an older Yukian continuum was broken up by a Pomoan spread. Alternatively, a Yukian group may have moved southward to become the Wappo (Sawyer 1978). A problem with all of these scenarios is that the short, relatively narrow-headed Yuki are distinct physically from the taller Wappo (cf. Gifford 1926a; Whitehead 1968). Although it is possible that a Yukian language ancestral to Wappo came to be spoken in the Napa Valley and Russian River areas by Indians not physically related to the Yuki (Sawyer 1978:258), it seems more likely that the ancestral Wappo were separated from their Yukian kin by Pomoan expansion and that they subsequently lost their biologic distinctiveness through centuries of intermarriage with neighboring peoples.


*Penutian Stock*


As used here, Penutian is an expeditious grouping of four language families (Wintuan, Maiduan, Yokutsan, and Utian) and one isolate language (Klamath–Modoc). More than 60 years of linguistic research have left the "Penutian hypothesis" unconfirmed; that is, the genetic status of Penutian as a stock is open to question (C. Callaghan, personal communication, 1982). The close, intrafamilial connection between Miwokan and Costanoan within the Utian family has been established, but relationships, if any, among the "Pen" languages are far from clear. Of the three groups assigned by Kroeber (1925) to "Pen," Maiduan and Wintuan perhaps may prove distantly related, but Yokutsan has resisted any such linkage. Linguistically, one may argue for separate migrations into California of groups ancestral to the Utian, Maiduan, Wintuan, and Yokutsan peoples.

Similarly, linguistic research has failed to establish avowed distant relationships between California Penutian and the Chinook, Tsimshian, Coos, Takelma, and Sahaptin languages of the Pacific Northwest (cf. Spencer, Jennings, *et al.* 1977). This is not to say that such a connection has been disproved—only that it has not been demonstrated. In the present context, therefore, Penutian is used only as a convenient heuristic device and not as a genetic or historic construct.

The exact number of California Penutian languages (roughly 27 to 38?) is uncertain. Yokutsan, for instance, encompassed some 40 to 60 tribelets, each with its own dialect; there may have been 2 languages or 12. Similarly, the Miwokan and Costanoan subfamilies of Utian include approximately 16 languages. Regardless of the precise number of languages, Penutian internal diversity (if Penutian were a stock) would indicate a time depth second only to Hokan among the major California stocks.

In A.D. 1750 speakers of Penutian tongues occupied nearly half of California (Figure 11.2). Their aggregate territory coincided largely with the Central Valley and bordering hill country, the chief exceptions being the reach of Klamath–Modoc into northeastern California and the Utian territory along the central coast (Figure 11.1). Two aspects of Penutian geography are striking. One is its mass or density, seen as a solid block of about 30 contiguous languages in the California heartland. The other is its spatial relationship to the peripheral Hokan islands (Figure 11.2). This distribution is probably the result of incursions by Penutians and their spread throughout the Central Valley, fragmenting and leaving in marginal areas the older continuum of Hokan languages.

Kroeber (1955:102) cited glottochronological evidence of an "explosive disruption" of the California Hokan languages $\approx$35 to 40 minimum centuries ago—possibly the result of a Penutian entry. Although these dates are equivocal, the linguistic diversity and geography of Penutian show that it is old in California and that it expanded after Hokan languages were established widely in the area. The Penutian block occupied nuclear California—its central coast and Valley. To the extent that language and culture may be related, Penutian was the most typically "Californian" of any stock.

## Algic Superfamily

The distant but clear affiliation of the Yurok and Wiyot languages was recognized long ago by their inclusion in a separate "Ritwan family".

(Dixon and Kroeber 1913). Sapir (1913) was the first to relate these languages to the Algonquian family. Although this classification was later disputed, Haas (1958) ultimately proved that Sapir was correct. Yurok and Wiyot are related, albeit remotely, to the Algonquian languages of the Great Plains and Northeast (e.g., Blackfoot, Menomini, Arapaho, and Ojibwa–Ottawa–Algonkin–Salteaux).

Algonquian, Yurok, and Wiyot are three branches of a very old Algic stock once located somewhere in north-central North America (Alberta?). Algic seems to have split into Algonquian and Yurok–Wiyot 4000 or more years ago (Whistler 1979a). Glottochronology would have ancestral Yurok–Wiyot leaving their pre-Algonquian kin roughly 51 to 61 minimum centuries ago, and diverging from one another about 23 minimum centuries ago (Swadesh 1959a). Subsequently, ancient Yurok and Wiyot arrived in northwestern California as distinct languages. Since they did not diverge from one another in place, they clearly represent two entries from the north and east (Shipley 1978:82). One explanation for the rather unlikely proximity of Yurok and Wiyot in California would be "parallel migrational responses by two similar but separate groups at different times to similar geographic and ecologic pressures and/or opportunities" (Whistler 1979a:17). On linguistic and archaeological grounds, Whistler (1979a) proposed that speakers of the Algic languages arrived in California from the Columbia Plateau at circa A.D. 900 (Wiyot) and circa A.D. 1100 (Yurok).

*Athapascan Family*

The Athapascan Family is represented in California by four languages: Tolowa, Hupa–Chilula, Mattole, and Wailaki (Figure 11.1). Of these, Tolowa is the southernmost of the Oregon (Rogue River) group and does not resemble the other three languages as much as they do each other. The California (and Oregon) Athapascan tongues are related to Navajo and Apachean of the Southwest and to certain languages of Alaska and Canada (Hoijer 1960; Hymes 1957).

Athapascan is a widespread family, more diversified in the north than in the south, but with less internal differentiation than Hokan, Penutian, or Algic. This suggests a northern (Alaskan?) origin and a recent spread of the family southward (Whistler 1979a). Glottochronology places Athapascan internal diversification at no more than $\approx 2400 \pm 500$ years ago (Krauss 1973). The Athapascans may have been among the latest arrivals in California, as the internal divergence of the southern Athapascan branches in only about 10 minimum centuries (Hoijer 1956; Hymes 1957; Kroeber 1959a). Linguistic evidence indicates that Athapascans entered California at circa A.D. 1250–1350 (Whistler 1979a).

Dixon and Kroeber (1919) described the California Athapascan languages as being remarkably conservative, even though their speakers were prone to cultural borrowing. The Athapascan groups were in California long enough to become nearly assimilated culturally, yet their languages seem not to have been influenced either structurally or lexically by their neighbors. Indeed, it appears that Athapascan was spreading until recently at the expense of older languages (Kroeber 1959c). One factor might have been asymmetric bilingualism, whereby Athapascan speech was adopted as a "prestige language" by peoples who chose to speak it rather than their own former language (Whistler 1979a). The Wailaki and Cahto, for instance, were Yukian in physical type and culture but Athapascan in language (Gifford 1926a). Possible mechanisms by which the Athapascans moved southward through country already occupied, at least in part, by speakers of Hokan, Algic, and Yukian languages are explored later in this chapter.

## Uto-Aztecan Family

The Uto-Aztecan family in California includes one isolate language (Tübatulabal) and two subfamilies (Numic and Takic), which form a continuum with the languages of the Great Basin (Figures 11.1 and 11.2). The California–Great Basin Uto-Aztecan languages are related to the Nahua, Papago, Hopic, and other families in Mexico and western North America. There were eight contiguous Takic languages in the arid lands of southern California from the ocean to the Yuman boundary near the Colorado River. The Numic languages were spoken over a vast area of the intermontane West; except for Washo, all Great Basin languages were Numic (Kroeber 1909b, 1925). Tübatulabal was an isolate language in the upper Kern River country of the southern Sierra Nevada (Figure 11.1).

The origins and age of Uto-Aztecan remain to be worked out. Linguistic geography and degree of internal differentiation suggest that Uto-Aztecan is younger than Hokan, Penutian, or Algic. Glottochronology indicates roughly 50 minimum centuries of Uto-Aztecan time depth (Figure 11.3). It seems probable that Uto-Aztecan began to diversify in California after Hokan and Penutian were present but before all of the Penutian languages achieved their late prehistoric distribution. On present evidence, Uto-Aztecans first entered California earlier than circa 2000 B.C. As outlined below, their subsequent prehistory in this area must have been fairly complicated.

Michael J. P. Nichols has advanced a model of diachronic cultural changes and relationships to account for the linguistic geography, internal reconstruction, and external reconstruction (borrowings) of "Old California Uto-Aztecan." Briefly, Nichols (1981:18) interprets the linguistic data

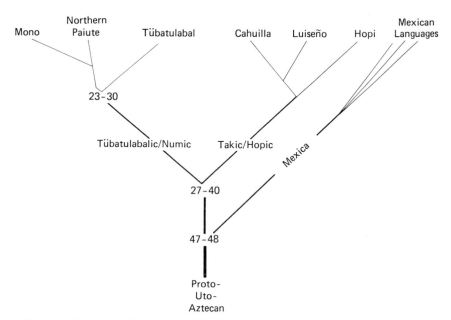

**Figure 11.3** Relationships among selected Uto-Aztecan language groups expressed in minimum centuries of separation, as calculated by glottochronology. (Compiled from Hale 1958; Swadesh 1954–1955, 1964.)

to mean that (1) early Proto-Uto-Aztecan (PUA) or pre-PUA long ago occupied the "northern edge of Old California," where it was in contact with several Old Oregon groups, Proto-Utian, and Proto-Maiduan; (2) subsequent PUA dialect differentiation must have occurred in some part of central California during a time of contact with Proto-Pomo, Northern Hokan, and possibly Proto-Chumash and early Yokuts; (3) initial Southern Uto-Aztecan first diverged from PUA after a period of direct contact with Eastern Miwok, Washo, and Maiduan, and then left the Old California area; (4) initial Northern Uto-Aztecan occupied the southern Sierra Nevada and southern San Joaquin Valley during a time of evident contact with Esselen, Yokuts, Eastern Miwok, and Obispeño Chumash; (5) Northern Uto-Aztecan began its dispersal into the Great Basin from southeastern California; and (6), finally, the Western Numic group spread northward along the east side of the Sierra, resuming Uto-Aztecan contact with Washo, Maiduan, Achumawi–Atsugewi, Klamath, and Sahaptin.

Any model of Uto-Aztecan prehistory must account for the sequence and nature of contacts that gave rise to borrowings into Uto-Aztecan languages as well as influence by Uto-Aztecan on neighboring languages. For example, the clear mutual influence of Northern Uto-Aztecan and Obispeño Chumash probably reflects Uto-Aztecan occupation of the San Joaquin Valley rather than Chumash movement to the fringe of some

Uto-Aztecan homeland farther east. When the sequence of linguistic borrowings is considered, along with linguistic geography and internal patterns, the number of reconstructions of prehistory is limited. In this case, a California center of Uto-Aztecan diversification and dispersion would seem to explain more than a center in the Great Basin or elsewhere.

## Prehistoric Language Shifts

Because available data permit only a tentative reconstruction of population movements and language spreads, the following model must be viewed as largely hypothetical. Arbitrary periods of time comprise the framework for this prehistory. The model advanced here extends beyond California to trace the spread of languages in larger areas of the West. California was neither an island nor a cul de sac, and its linguistic configurations can be understood only with reference to a larger sweep of prehistory.

### 10,000–6000 B.C.

This early Holocene period was characterized by warming, generally moist climates and by pluvial lakes in western lowlands (see Chapters 2 and 3). Before circa 10,000 B.C., California was occupied by speakers of languages unknown and probably unknowable. Similarly, some languages spoken between circa 10,000 and 6000 B.C. may have vanished without discernible linguistic trace. Still, one may suggest possible scenarios of linguistic change during this ancient period.

As discussed in Chapter 2, there were possibly two migration routes into subglacial America around 10,000 B.C.—the first through a midcontinental ice-free corridor and the second along the Pacific coast. As a guess, languages ancestral to Hokan, Siouan, and Algic might have originated inland, whereas Yukian, Penutian, Salishan, and Wakashan perhaps developed in the Pacific Northwest from coastal antecedents. This is not to say that each stock necessarily represents a separate migration, for it seems likely that at least some stocks evolved after 10,000 B.C. as a result of the geographic spread and internal differentiation of older speech communities.

Taylor (1961) proposed that Hokan groups were the first to settle in California, and Hopkins (1965) cited both archaeological and linguistic evidence that the Hokan dispersion occurred well before 10,000 years ago. Consistent with these views, it is suggested here that pre-Hokan languages may have been associated with the Western Fluted Point Tradition. It is further proposed that the development of the Western Pluvial Lakes Tradition (WPLT) and its regional variants may correspond to the emergence and initial differentiation of Hokan.

The WPLT encompasses a series of technically related yet regionally distinctive cultures seemingly derived from a common ancestral tradition. Hokan linguistic evidence—the degree of diversity within the stock, number of isolate languages, linguistic geography, and glottochronology—indicates for this stock a time depth in western North America consistent with the 8000- to 11,000-year age of the WPLT, a plausible connection in light of apparent archaeological continuities for more than 8000 years in parts of southwestern California where Hokan languages were spoken until historic times (see Chapter 4). Also, the nearly exclusive presence of Hokan languages in Baja California attests to the great antiquity of the stock in that area. In the future it may be possible to relate specific variants of the WPLT to early Hokan divisions. For the present, one may only speculate about such linkages (Figure 11.4).

Pre-Yukian peoples may have entered the North Coast Ranges in terminal Pleistocene or early Holocene times, possibly as part of a southward migration along the coast. If, as a conjecture, pre-Yukian activities are represented by the "pre-Archaic" lower component at the Mostin sites (Lak-380/381), then ancestral Yukian groups may have occupied the North Coast Ranges as early as 9500–9000 B.C. (see Chapters 3 and 10). This time depth is compatible with Yukian linguistic geography, the precedence of Yukian over Pomoan in the North Coast Ranges (Basgall 1982), and the apparent association of Yukian peoples with the spread of the Borax Lake Pattern.

### 6000–4000 B.C.

Global warming increased the rate of glacial melting, resulting in a sea-level rise from approximately −40 to −5 m during this period. Warm temperatures (the Altithermal) and reduced winter precipitation brought desert conditions to many areas of the American West. In the Great Basin and Mojave Desert pluvial lakes were vastly reduced in number and extent during this climatic interval. The replacement of woodlands by xeric plants in the Chihuahuan, Sonoran, and Mojave deserts evidently was a rapid, widespread, and synchronous event around 6000 B.C. Climatic effects were registered initially in the south and later in the north, as

**Figure 11.4** Hypothetical distribution of language groupings in western North America, circa 8000–6000 B.C. (1) Proto-Yukian; (2) Pre-Esselen; (3) Pre-Salinan; (4) Proto-Yuman; (5) Pre-Palaihnihan; (6) Pre-Karok; (7) Pre-Uto-Aztecan; (8) Pre-Penutian. (Map by the author.)

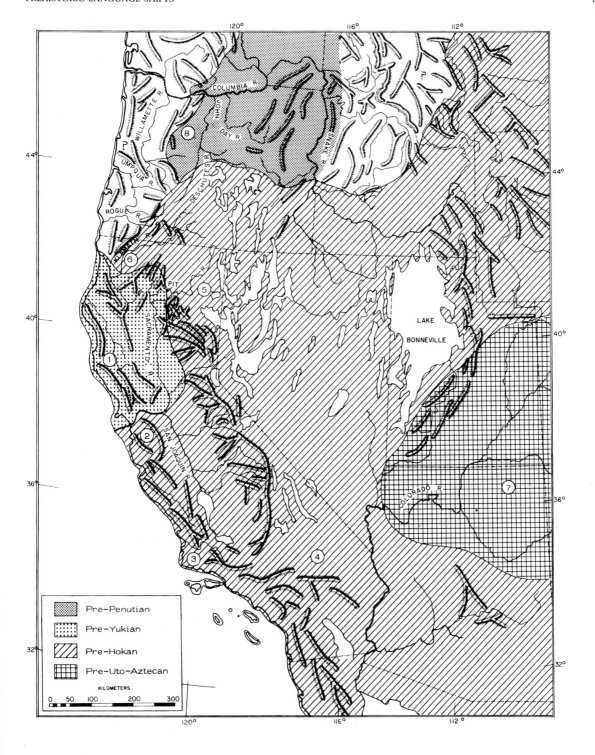

woodland species retreated northward, occupied higher elevations, and disappeared from the lowlands, whereas desert species increased (Van Devender and Spaulding 1979:706).

Warmer, drier climates and the decline of pluvial lakes would have triggered pronounced cultural adjustments in the Far West. Certain arid lands were abandoned, whereas other areas may have become increasingly productive as early Altithermal marshes replaced former deep lakes. In the main, however, human populations would have become smaller and more dispersed as favorable habitats were reduced. This implies that previously widespread dialect areas would have fissioned into relatively isolated language communities, especially in the deserts.

It is probable that, by circa 6000 B.C., pre-Uto-Aztecan was a distinct speech community in the Colorado Plateau country of the Southwest. The early Oshara Tradition (Irwin-Williams 1973) may represent the entry of pre-Uto-Aztecans into the Four Corners region and the beginning of a long sequence leading to some of the Anasazi cultures. Meanwhile, ancestral Penutian may have been a separate entity somewhere on the Columbia Plateau or in the northwestern Great Basin. It is likely that the ancient predecessors of the California Penutian groups were riverine and/or lacustrine in economic orientation, as judged by their later riverine and wetland adaptations in California.

Between 6000 and 4000 B.C., speakers of Hokan languages probably held nearly all of cismontane California. Pre-Karok, Shastan, and Palaihnihan groups may have occupied far northern California and parts of southern Oregon during this period. On linguistic grounds, Karok must be older in northwestern California than the Algic or Athapascan languages (Whistler 1979a), and the linguistic isolation of Karok suggests that it diverged long ago from its Hokan relatives. Similarly, Shastan and Palaihnihan are clearly older in northern California than the neighboring Wintu, Klamath–Modoc, or Paiute. So little is known of local cultural manifestations dated to the 6000–4000 B.C. interval, however, that the antiquity and relationships among these groups in far northern California will remain conjectural until more archaeological data are available.

Along the crestal zone and eastern side of the Sierra Nevada, occupation before circa 4000 B.C. is seen archaeologically in the Spooner Complex and related expressions marked by Pinto and Humboldt series projectile points. These cultural materials at high elevations may reflect the initial settlement of the Sierra by Hokan peoples, among them the pre-Washo, abandoning parts of the western Great Basin during especially warm–dry climatic intervals (see Chapter 8).

W. Taylor (1961) proposed that, soon after 7000 B.C., Hokan groups used (but did not necessarily originate) millingstones and other "Desert Culture" implements. Since Hokan peoples evidently were in the regions where deserts appeared very early, a case can be made for them bringing the millingstone technology into California. The advent of millingstone cultures in southeastern California may reflect actual population movements from the Great Basin. However, in southwestern California the appearance of millingstones between circa 6400 and 5500 B.C., establishing the Encinitas Tradition, probably resulted more from diffusion than from new migrations to the coast. The Encinitas Tradition seems to have developed mainly *in situ* from earlier coastal antecedents, although the adoption of millingstone industries may have been stimulated by the westward movement of desert peoples (presumably also speaking Hokan languages). In San Diego County, True (1966) found a significant archaeological continuity between the Encinitas Tradition (including the La Jolla Complex) and the protohistoric Diegueño (Cuyamaca Complex), but a cultural break separating Encinitas from Luiseño (San Luis Rey Complex) components. Hence, the Encinitas Tradition, and more generally the distribution of early millingstone complexes in California, appears related to Hokan developments.

It is proposed here that early Encinitas Tradition peoples occupied the northern Channel Islands by 5000 to 6000 B.C. or earlier; this is seen in the "Early Dune Dweller" components on Santa Rosa Island and related Early Period manifestations on the other islands. Farther north, the Salinan and Esselen are seen as descendants of early Hokan settlers in the South Coast Ranges. Given archaeological evidence for (Hokan?) occupation of the Santa Clara Valley and central coast as early as circa 8000 B.C. (see Chapter 6), pre-Esselen and pre-Salinan possibly emerged as separate, internally diversified language groupings by circa 4000–6000 B.C., or earlier.

Linguistic geography and glottochronological dates suggest that ancestral Pomoan and Yanan peoples may have diverged from their more southerly Hokan (Cochimí–Yuman) congeners and established themselves in northern California as early as 6000 B.C. Their spread in the Sacramento Valley and bordering uplands, archaeologically recognized by the first appearance of millingstones, possibly involved the displacement or assimilation of some older Hokan and Yukian groups.

The principal exception to exclusive Hokan control of California before 4000 B.C. would have been the Yukian enclave in the North Coast Ranges. The Borax Lake Aspect, including millingstones possibly introduced by Hokan groups, is thought to have spread through much of the Yukian territory after circa 6000 B.C.


*4000–2000 B.C.*

Climatically, this was the arid mid-Altithermal period in the Great Basin and California lowlands. Bristlecone pines in the White Mountains

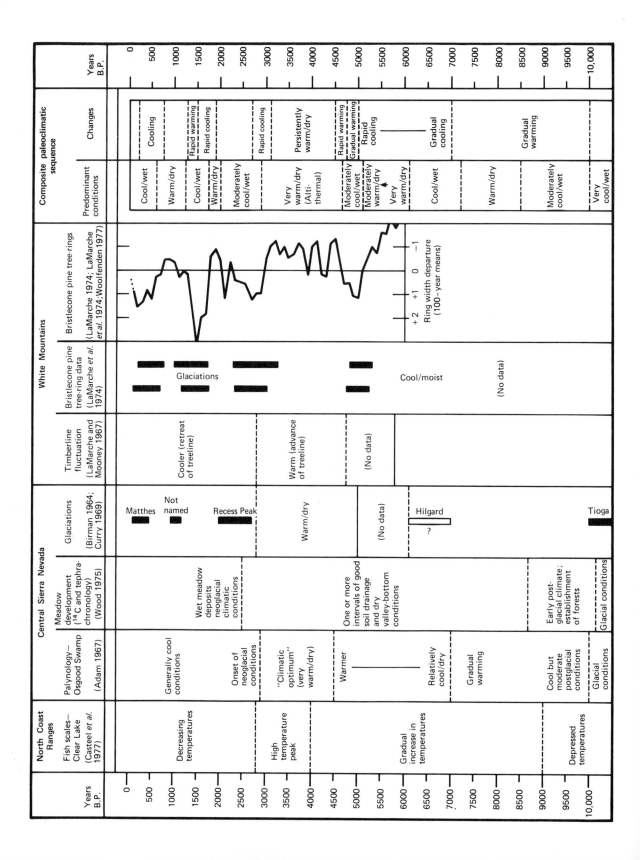

record (1) high summer temperatures from before 3400 B.C. until circa 2000–1000 B.C., when summers began to cool, and (2) less than normal precipitation from circa 4000 to 1000 B.C., except for a moist reversal between circa 3100 and 2600 B.C. (La Marche 1973; La Marche and Mooney 1967; LaMarche et al. 1974). In general, climates were very warm–dry from circa 4000 until 3100 B.C., cool–moist between 3100 and 2600 B.C., and variously warm–moist or warm–dry thereafter until 2100 B.C. (Figure 11.5) (Moratto et al. 1978). As part of a sustained global warming, the Altithermal was the Holocene interval of highest temperatures in the western United States. Sea levels rose from approximately −5 to +3 m during this period; twice, during the warm episodes beginning circa 4000 and 2600 B.C., oceans stood about 3 m higher than current mean sea level. Pluvial lakes vanished from the Great Basin, and desert conditions prevailed as far north as the Snake River Plain of southern Idaho. Diminished precipitation resulted in desiccation of the southern San Joaquin Valley and the advance of xeric vegetation in lowland southern California. Even coastal regions were affected by the persistent warming, as exemplified by the Santa Barbara Basin, where pollen studies indicate a trend toward warmer–drier climates culminating circa 3700 B.C. with chaparral and coastal sage scrub replacing Asteraceae and oak associations (Heusser 1978).

## Uto–Aztecan Stock

Many language shifts evidently occurred in the Far West during this mid-Altithermal period. It seems likely that Proto-Uto-Aztecan (PUA) or pre-PUA began to diversify roughly 5000 years ago (Figure 11.3), but opinions about the origins of this stock are far from unified. Taylor (1961:77) proposed that Uto-Aztecans had moved southward from the northern Rockies and across the Great Basin sometime earlier than 3000 B.C. An alternative view would have early Uto-Aztecans moving southward from the northern Great Basin in two branches, one skirting the Rockies and the other along the eastern side of the Sierra Nevada (Hopkins 1965:48–56). It has even been suggested that PUA was in the Great Basin considerably before 3000 B.C., and that complex but unknown events brought about its later diversification (Goss 1977).

Studies of lexical items and other linguistic features indicate further that the "pre-Californian" PUA homeland probably was in the uplands of northern Arizona or New Mexico (Jett 1977; Romney 1957; Swadesh 1964). In this regard, C. Fowler (1972:110–111) has postulated that Uto-Aztecans, including the predecessors of the Numic, Takic, Hopic, and Tübatulabalic peoples, entered southeastern California from Arizona, via

Figure 11.5 Reconstruction of Holocene climates in California. (After Moratto et al. 1978:Figure 1; courtesy of the *Journal of California and Great Basin Anthropology*.)

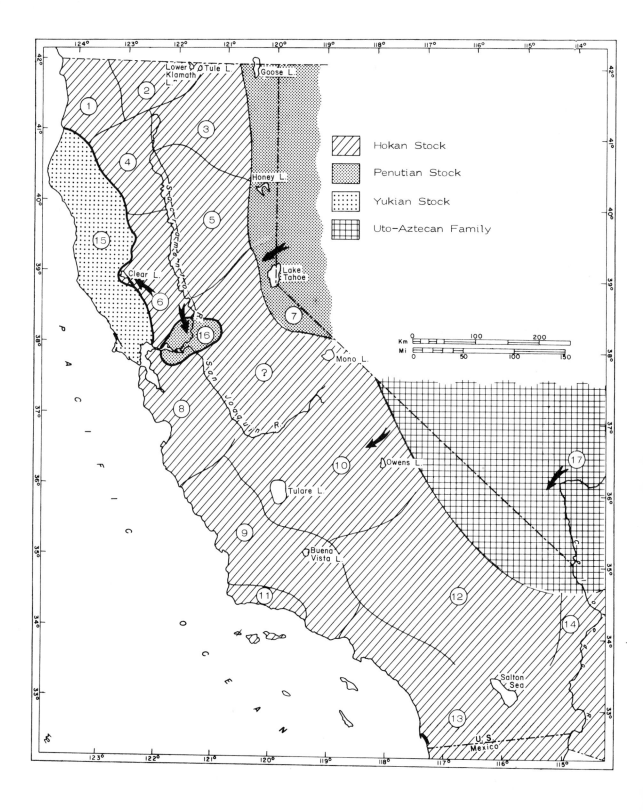

the Gila and Colorado River drainages, approximately 5000 years ago. Building upon Fowler's model, it is proposed here that by circa 4000–3000 B.C. a PUA speech community extended from northern Arizona, across southwestern Nevada, into eastern California (Figure 11.6). Archaeologically, this distribution would associate with Pinto Period components of the eastern Sierra, southwestern Great Basin, and northern Mojave Desert (Figure 4; see also Chapter 8). This reconstruction is consistent with Nichols's (1981) requirement for early contacts between PUA and early Penutian groups. Speakers of PUA, Proto-Utian, and Proto-Maiduan languages could have influenced one another in the western Great Basin between circa 3000 and 2000 B.C.

## Hokan Stock

As in earlier times, California probably was largely a Hokan province between 4000 and 2000 B.C. (Figure 11.6). Linguistic data suggest that lands east and south of San Francisco Bay were held by early Esselen peoples (Beeler 1977). It is possible that the BART, Sunnyvale, and "Stanford Man II" skeletons, the dune midden at SCr-7, the Santa Theresa Complex in the Santa Clara Valley area, and the sites identified with the Sur Pattern in the Monterey Bay area may be related to Esselen occupation. Similarly, the Coast Ranges south of Monterey Bay presumably were held by Proto-Salinan peoples.

Farther south, in the Santa Barbara Channel zone, the late Early Period transition from Encinitas to Campbell Tradition is thought to reflect the continuity of Hokan populations and the gradual evolution of a maritime economy. Since the Campbell Tradition ultimately gave rise to the Chumash Tradition (see Chapter 4), it seems likely that Campbell culture was borne by speakers of a language ancestral to Chumashan.

Northern California also was predominantly Hokan territory prior to 2000 B.C. By that time geographic isolation and population movements, including shifts triggered by Altithermal conditions in the Great Basin, would have brought about diversification within the Hokan stock. Proto-Shastan, -Pomoan, -Yanan, and -Palaihnihan may have emerged by 2000 B.C. as distinct units in northern California. In this regard, reconstructed Proto-Pomoan plant and fish terms strongly point to a Pomo homeland near Clear Lake (Levy 1979; McLendon 1973; Whistler 1980b). A westward Proto-Pomoan thrust into the Clear Lake vicinity at circa 3000 B.C.

---

**Figure 11.6** Hypothetical distribution of language groupings in and near California, circa 4000–2000 B.C. (1) Ancient Karok; (2) Proto-Shastan; (3) Proto-Palaihnihan; (4) ancient Chimariko; (5) Proto-Yanan; (6) Proto-Pomoan; (7) unknown (Hokan?) language; (8) ancient Esselen; (9) Proto-Salinan; (10) unknown (Penutian?) language(s); (11) Proto-Chumashan; (12) unknown (Hokan?) language(s); (13) Proto-Yuman; (14) Colorado River group of Proto-Yuman; (15) Yukian; (16) pre-Utian; (17) Uto-Aztecan languages. (Map by the author.)

may be recognized archaeologically as the Mendocino Aspect of the Borax Lake Pattern (see Chapter 10).

### Penutian Stock

At circa 2500 B.C. a Utian population (ancestral to Miwok–Costanoan) is thought to have entered the lower Sacramento Valley. Linguistic geography and archaeological continuities through time suggest that the advent of the Utian speech community in central California may relate to the early Windmiller Pattern (see Chapter 5). The oldest known Windmiller component, found at SJo-68 in the Delta locality (Figure 6.4), has been dated to circa 2400 B.C. This reconstruction agrees with an estimated Utian time depth of 40 to 45 minimum centuries, based upon linguistic data (C. Callaghan, personal communication, 1982).

As for Windmiller origins, Ragir (1972) proposed that the strongest ties were with Altithermal cultures of the Columbia Plateau. This is evidenced not only by the riverine–marshland orientation of the Windmiller Pattern, but also by extended burials, red ochre and quartz crystals in graves, charmstones, and projectile point types common to both. Also notable, however, are many similarities between Windmiller and the Lovelock Culture, dated circa 2700 B.C.–A.D. 500 at Lovelock Cave, in northwestern Nevada (Heizer and Napton 1970; Loud and Harrington 1929). Among the Windmiller (and Berkeley) Pattern traits shared with the Lovelock Culture are marshland adaptation; large foliate and triangular-stemmed projectile points; slate rods; an extensive bone industry with similar types of awls, scapula saws or grass cutters, bone tubes, atlatl spurs, spatulate objects, and style of punctate decoration; stubby, distinctive stone pipes; longitudinally split horn and antler tools; specific basketry techniques; and shell ornaments of California origin.

Citing such similarities, as well as the evident discontinuity between Lovelock and later Great Basin cultures associated with Uto-Aztecan languages, E. M. Hattori (1982:208) proposed that speakers of Penutian languages were responsible for the Lovelock Culture and that "relatively strong ties [existed] between Great Basin and California Penutian speaking groups." Hattori makes a good case for the occupation of northwestern Nevada by Penutian groups during Lovelock times. Accordingly, the pre-California origins of the Windmiller people might have been as easily in the northwestern Great Basin as in the southern Columbia Plateau region. Indeed, the two propositions are not necessarily mutually exclusive; before circa 2500 B.C., pre-Utian peoples may have occupied an area at the juncture of the Great Basin and Plateau provinces.

### 2000 B.C.–A.D. 1

This was a time of important environmental changes. Bristlecone pine studies show that Altithermal conditions persisted until circa 1100 B.C., with an especially warm period from circa 1600 until 1200 B.C. (Figure 11.5). A cool–moist episode between circa 1100 and 200 B.C. signaled the onset of the Medithermal climatic interval (LaMarche 1974; LaMarche *et al.* 1974). Cooler temperatures led to a Neoglacial age in the Sierra, seen in the development of wet meadows and in the Recess Peak glaciation of circa 600 to 200 B.C. (Birman 1964; Curry 1968, 1969, 1971; Wood 1975).

The Medithermal brought to some desert areas "improved" conditions: increased precipitation, cooler temperatures, retreat of xeric vegetation, greater availability of water, and more large animals. Some playas once again filled with lakes or marshes. At Little Lake in the Owens Valley, for example, the pollen record shows that a shallow lake replaced a salt grass meadow at about 1000 B.C. (Mehringer and Sheppard 1978:153). In other parts of California, Medithermal climatic changes affected local environments diversely. Although sea levels were high (Figure 6.2) and coastal erosion was intensive, San Francisco Bay and its rich marshlands were achieving their maximum extent. Inland, after circa 1000 B.C., increased precipitation resulted in seasonal flooding and extensive alluviation of Valley lowlands; the filling of Tulare and Buena Vista lakes; creation of additional sloughs and marshes; and, in the foothills, depression of the lower oak woodland border.

### Penutian Stock

Utian populations and languages spread and diversified during this period. In the Stockton and Cosumnes Districts the Windmiller Pattern may attest to early Utian, but not necessarily pre-Miwok–Costanoan, settlement. Between 2000 and 500 B.C. ancient Utians seem to have occupied not only the Delta and mid-Valley riparian and marshland zones, but also the hill country to the east and west. Windmiller components have been reported from Cache Creek (J. Johnson 1971a), the lower Calaveras River (J. Johnson 1967), Bear Creek (Olsen and Wilson 1964), and the central Sierran mortuary caves (see Chapter 7).

Soon after 2000 B.C., Utians are thought to have expanded westward. An early Windmiller salient into the east Bay area would have brought the Utians into contact with older Hokan and, north of Carquinez Straits, Yukian populations adapted to the hill and valley environments of the Coast Ranges. It is suggested that the emergence of the Berkeley Pattern represents a fusion of older Hokan (mostly Esselen?) and intrusive Utian cultural elements in the Bay area. Established local hunting and gathering practices (including acorn use) would have been adopted by the Utians, whose own emphasis on wetland exploitation would have been retained and adapted to the extensive marshlands then developing along the shore of the San Francisco Bay estuarine system. The ultimate success of the Utians in the Bay area, however, may have resulted as much from their complex social organization as from their particular subsistence strategies (see Chapter 6).

Linguistic data point to an interior origin for Proto-Miwok/Costanoan. Many Coast Miwok and Costanoan terms for plants and animals peculiar to coastal ecosystems are patent borrowings. Also, the diffusion of lexical items into Costanoan from Esselen and into Coast Miwok from Wappo show the primacy of Esselen and Wappo in the coastal zone (Levy 1978c:2–3).

The Proto-Costanoan homeland probably was located in the east Bay area. Costanoan internal classification and the retention of some phonological traits by Karkin alone strongly points to Costanoan origins in the Carquinez Straits vicinity (Levy 1979:8). In the San Ramon Valley, CCo-308C may attest to Proto-Costanoan occupation at circa 2000 B.C. or earlier (see Chapter 6). The Berkeley facies or lower component at the West Berkeley site (Ala-307), $^{14}$C-dated to 1910 ± 450 B.C., may signal the arrival of early Costanoans in the bayshore zone of the Alameda District. By circa 1500 B.C., Costanoans occupied most of the east shore of San Francisco Bay, presumably displacing or assimilating older Esselen groups as they advanced.

The spread of the Berkeley Pattern around San Francisco Bay after circa 1500 B.C. is marked by population growth, increased reliance on Bay shore resources, the establishment of large settlements, and the appearance of many distinctive stylistic and economic traits (see Bickel 1976) distinguishing Bay cultures from those of the Valley.

The University Village site in southern San Mateo County may record the Utian spread approximately 3200 years ago. To the extent that the University Village Complex may characterize an Early Bay Culture (Gerow with Force 1968), the latter probably reflects both Proto-Costanoan expansion and the adoption of Berkeley Pattern traits by older Hokan (Esselen?) populations. Comparing archaeological and human skeletal data, Gerow (1968, 1974b) concluded that cultural and biological differences between the lower Sacramento Valley and the southern California coast were greater and more fundamental at an early time, and that the Valley and coastal traditions gradually converged through time. Gerow argued convincingly that two main traditions existed in California for at least 4000 years. Windmiller (and, by extension to the Bay, Berkeley Pattern) marks the arrival of Penutians and the beginning of one tradition; the other relates to early coastal cultures and Hokan languages.

It is proposed that a pre-Yokutsan population entered central California after the Proto-Miwok and Proto-Costanoans had begun to spread in the Bay area. Several lines of evidence argue for Yokutsan being later than Utian in this area: (1) Yokutsan, with 2 to 12 languages, is less diverse internally than Utian, which includes 16 languages; (2) lexicostatistics allow >15 centuries for Yokutsan, but >25 centuries for the Miwokan division into eastern and western branches and even longer for Utian internal differentiation (Levy 1978b, 1979); and (3) Yokutsan ethnogeography is less complex than that of the Utians, encompassing only one large, contiguous area with two environmental zones (foothill and valley), as compared with the more extensive and varied Utian lands ranging from the seashore to the Sierran crest.

As a guess, pre-Yokutsan peoples may have settled in the Delta and northern San Joaquin Valley between circa 1500 and 1000 B.C. A northern origin may be indicated by distant linguistic connections to Chinook–Tsimshian and Coos–Takelma. This interpretation is supported by research showing that Yokuts string baskets and plain twined baskets are nearly identical to specimens from Roaring Springs Cave, Oregon, dated as early as circa 2000 B.C. (Dawson 1978a). It is possible that Yokutsan, as well as Wintuan and Maiduan, was derived from a widespread "pre-Pen" (Penutian) speech community in the northwestern Great Basin and southern Columbia Plateau. Once in the mid–Central Valley, the pre-Yokutsan culture may have incorporated many late Windmiller traits before spreading southward into the San Joaquin Valley and central Sierran foothills in circa 1000–500 B.C. Intermarriage between the Yokutsan and Delta Utian populations also may have occurred during this interval.

Although Utian peoples seem to have been established in the Alameda, Diablo, and Solano Districts between circa 2000 and 1000 B.C., the Utian radiation in central California was most intensive somewhat later. Numerous $^{14}$C-dated components trace this spread of the Berkeley Pattern (Figure 6.16 and Table 6.4). Lexicostatistical data suggest that the western and eastern Miwokan divisions separated more than 25 centuries ago (Levy 1978b:398). The spread of ancestral Western Miwok into the north Bay area after 1350 B.C. is recorded archaeologically in Berkeley Pattern components at Pacheco Valle, Miller Creek, De Silva Island, and Tiburon in Marin County (Figure 6.16). Similarly, after circa 500 B.C., predecessors of the Lake Miwok may be linked to the northward spread of the Houx Aspect into Lake County (see Chapter 10).

The western Miwokan spread would have displaced Yukians (early Wappo) in the north Bay area. The fact that the Western Miwok borrowed Wappo terms for redwood and black oak (Levy 1978c) shows that the Wappo were already in the southern North Coast Ranges when the Miwok arrived some 3300 years ago. The later northward expansion of ancestral Lake Miwok and displacement of older (Proto-Pomoan?) groups in the Napa Valley are evinced by the replacement of Borax Lake Pattern (Hultman Phase) materials by those of the Houx Aspect, Berkeley Pattern, at Nap-131 (Bennyhoff 1977b).

The early Miwok and Costanoans seem to have spread rapidly and widely in several directions. Between circa 500 and 100 B.C., ancestral Coast and Lake Miwok moved west and north, Plains Miwok pushed eastward, and Costanoans expanded south to Monterey Bay (Figure 11.7).

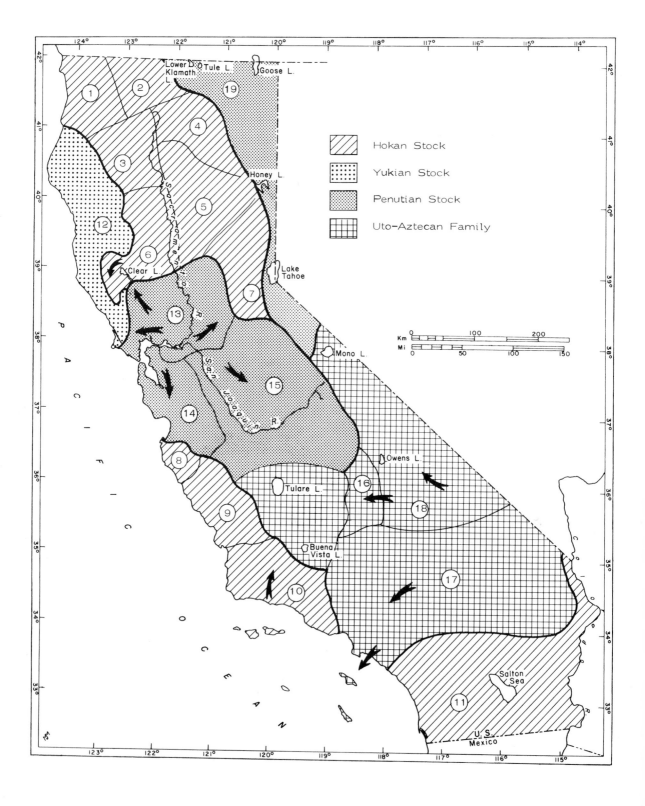

| | |
|---|---|
| ▨ | Hokan Stock |
| ⣿ | Yukian Stock |
| ▦ | Penutian Stock |
| ▦ | Uto-Aztecan Family |

In the mid-Central Valley, the displacement of the Windmiller Pattern by the Berkeley Pattern after circa 500 B.C. (Figure 5.7) may attest to an eastern spread of Miwokan peoples and cultural influences into an older Utian and Yokutsan domain. Coevally, Yokutsan expanded into the central Sierra and San Joaquin Valley. Yokutsan occupation of the central Sierra, beginning circa 500 B.C., is represented by the Crane Flat Phase in Yosemite National Park and by the Chowchilla Phase at Buchanan Reservoir. The "Middle Horizon" components at Tranquillity, Buena Vista Lake, and Los Banos (Pacheco A Complex) also may reflect Yokutsan occupation, although this ascription is especially tenuous.

It is notable that the extent of the early Utian radiation seems to match the distribution of marshlands. Most Utian settlements before circa 200 B.C. were situated on the margins of the best wetland environments in the Delta, Napa Valley, and San Joaquin Valley, as well as on the San Francisco Bay shore and central coast. A later emphasis on acorn use coincides with the intensified occupation of foothill oak woodland zones throughout central California. The success of the Utians may have been a result of their economic specialization coupled with a relatively complex social organization and dense populations, as compared with the less numerous and relatively generalized hunter–gatherers whom they supplanted. That is, social and economic strategies rather than force of arms may have conferred upon the Utians a selective advantage, allowing them to replace older populations and cultures in central California.

Regarding other Penutian developments before circa A.D. 1, the possibility of a Wintuan entry into northern California is suggested by a glottochronological age of 25 minimum centuries based upon Wintuan internal divergence (Levy 1979:22). Archaeological data, however, do not seem to confirm such an early Wintuan entry, possibly indicating that linguistic differentiation began before Wintuan peoples arrived in California or that material evidence of a Wintuan incursion 2000 or more years ago remains to be discovered.

## Hokan Stock

Ancient Pomoans are thought to have assimilated or displaced Yukians as they spread from the Clear Lake vicinity into the Russian River country, and ultimately to the coast, after circa 1000 B.C. Archaeologically, the

---

**Figure 11.7** Hypothetical distribution of language groupings in California, circa 2000 B.C.–A.D. 1. (1) Ancestral Karok; (2) Proto-Shastan; (3) ancestral Chimariko; (4) Proto-Palaihnihan; (5) Proto-Yanan; (6) Proto-Pomoan; (7) unknown (Hokan?) language(s); (8) Esselen remnant language; (9) Proto-Salinan; (10) Proto-Chumashan; (11) Yuman languages; (12) Yukian and, to the south, ancestral Wappo; (13) Proto-Miwokan; (14) Proto-Costanoan; (15) unknown Utian language(s); (16) ancestral Tübatulabal; (17) Takic dialect area; (18) Numic dialect area; (19) languages of the "pen" branch of Penutian. (Map by the author.)

Mendocino Aspect of the Borax Lake Pattern marks the western expansion of Pomoan territory (see Chapter 10). The extension of Pomo dominions to the coast would have isolated the ancestral Wappo from their more northerly Yukian kin.

An archaeological case of Yukian displacement by Pomoans may be recorded in the Warm Springs Dam vicinity of Sonoma County (Figure 6.4), where the (Yukian?) Skaggs Phase was replaced at circa 500 B.C. by Dry Creek Phase components with a high content of obsidian, mostly from Clear Lake sources, and other indications of Pomoan occupation (Basgall 1982; Baumhoff 1980a, 1981a). M. E. Basgall has suggested that an acorn-based economy may have figured importantly in the Pomo expansion:

> If Pomoans brought with them a processor strategy focused on the acorn, as the archaeological and perhaps linguistic data suggest, such an adaptation provided a significant selective advantage over their predecessors. By all accounts preceding populations, Yukian or otherwise, possessed a more mobile, less dense population and a more archaic adaptation. (Basgall 1982:16)

Similarly, Esselen territory was greatly reduced as a result of Costanoan expansion. By circa A.D. 1, the Esselen apparently had been limited to a small enclave south of Monterey Bay (Figure 11.7). Archaeologically, these developments are seen in the replacement of the older "Sur Pattern" (Esselen?) by the "Monterey Pattern" (Costanoan?) between circa 500 B.C. and A.D. 1 from Monterey Bay northward, and in the cultural continuity from "Sur Pattern" antecedents after A.D. 1 in the area south of Monterey Bay (Breschini and Haversat 1980).

Farther south, the Chumashan groups seem to have expanded both along the coast and inland as far as the edge of the southern San Joaquin Valley (Figure 11.7). The extent of the Campbell Tradition indicates that Chumashan peoples were widely established in their ethnographic homeland earlier than 2000 years ago.

In northwestern California, Point St. George was occupied, at least intermittently, as early as 310 B.C. (Gould 1966a, 1972). The Point St. George I and II components are discontinuous culturally, and only the latter can be related to Tolowa (Athapascan) settlement of the coast. Point St. George I may reflect periodic visits by the Karok at a time before the Athapascan incursion. Karok has a strong inland orientation and was probably derived from very early Hokan antecedents in northern California.

As for other Hokan languages, an archaeological sequence at the Lorenzen site (Mod-1) convinced Baumhoff and Olmsted (1963) that the Palaihnihan family had been in place for no less than 3300 years. This would agree with a glottochronological date of 31–35 minimum centuries for the differentiation of Palaihnihan into Achumawi and Atsugewi. It is not clear, however, whether the archaeological sequence at Mod-1—including projectile points ranging from Cascade through Madeline Side-notched, Borax Lake, Gunther Barbed, and Desert Side-notched types—really denotes cultural continuity. An age of >31–35 centuries for Palaihnihan internal diversity seems reasonable, but the evidence for this at Mod-1 is not compelling.

Baumhoff's work in Yana territory at Kingsley Cave (1955) and Payne Cave (1957) showed that the Yana had been present locally for a long interval of time, perhaps as long as the 3000 to 4000 years estimated by Kroeber (1955) on the basis of linguistic data. Farther south in the Sierra Nevada, the Martis Complex possibly represents ancient Penutian (pre-Maiduan?) occupation after circa 2000 B.C. (see Chapter 7).

## Uto–Aztecan Family

Uto–Aztecans seem to have entered the Mojave Desert from the east roughly 5000 years ago. Their later spread and diversification may have been stimulated by environmental changes that invited the settlement of desert lands that had been less attractive during earlier, drier climatic episodes. The Uto-Aztecan expansion in California after circa 2000 B.C. coincides with the Gypsum Period (see Chapter 8) or Newberry Period (Bettinger and Taylor 1974), recognized by millingstones, projectile points of the Humboldt, Gypsum, and Elko series, and by other traits introduced from the Southwest.

Glottochronological dates—for example, the 27–40 minimum centuries separating Luiseño and Tübatulabal (Figure 11.3)—suggest that Takic and Numic–Tübatulabalic diverged on the order of 3000 to 4500 years ago. Numic and Tübatulabalic are more closely related to each other than either is to other branches of Uto-Aztecan. By circa 1500 B.C. Numic and Tübatulabalic were becoming distinct; by 1000 B.C. the two had separated and Tübatulabal people evidently were present in the upper Kern River Plateau area that they were to occupy for the next three millennia. As early as 1200 B.C. the Tübatulabal (Canebrake Phase) can be distinguished archaeologically from the neighboring Numic groups (Newberry Phase) in terms of settlement patterns, rock-art styles, choice of lithic materials, and milling equipment (McGuire and Garfinkel 1976, 1980). It is assumed that other Uto-Aztecan or Hokan occupation of the Sierra Nevada foothills may have limited the Tübatulabal to the upper Kern River and prevented their spread farther down the western slope.

Uto-Aztecan internal and external reconstructions convinced Nichols (1981) that Northern Uto-Aztecan (Numic) peoples must have occupied parts of the southern San Joaquin Valley at some time prior to their dispersion into the Great Basin. A Numic homeland in the southern Valley and adjacent foothills, during a time after the Numic–Takic separation of circa 1500 B.C., would have allowed contacts—as evidenced by linguistic borrowings—between Numic peoples and the Esselen, Yokuts, Eastern Miwok, and Chumash.

Perhaps as early as 1500-1000 B.C. the Takic branch of Uto-Aztecan began to spread westward across the Mojave Desert and northward into the Tehachapi Mountains. An alternative possibility is that Uto-Aztecan populations entered the San Joaquin Valley as early as 3000–2000 B.C., and that the Takic branch later diverged and moved southward across the Tehachapis. As for the timetable of Takic expansion into southwestern California, Kowta (1969:50) proposed dates of circa 1000 B.C. for the entry of "Shoshoneans" in the Los Angeles Basin and 700 B.C. for their appearance on the southern Channel Islands. This chronology is consistent with archaeological evidence that the ancestral Gabrielino, Tataviam, and Northern Serrano—all Takic groups—had occupied their respective territories by the end of the Early Period, that is, circa 1500–1200 B.C. (see Chapter 4). The western salient of Takic peoples would have displaced Hokan groups on the southern coast, separating the Yuman and Chumashan blocks (Figure 11.7). In the north, Takic settlers ancestral to the Gabrielino seem to have borrowed heavily from the Chumash, adopting a maritime economy. That linguistic exchange occurred also is evinced by Uto-Aztecan features in Chumashan languages.

### A.D. 1–1000

A rapid, intensive shift from previously cool–moist climates to warm–dry conditions after circa A.D. 400 coincided with population movements, changes in settlement patterns, economic adjustments, disruption of exchange systems, and other cultural changes in many parts of California (Moratto *et al.* 1978). This was a time when much of California's ethnogeography took form.

### Penutian Stock

The progenitors of the Sierra Miwok may have diverged from the Plains Miwok as early as 2000 years ago and settled in the foothills and mountains between the American and Calaveras rivers (Figure 11.8). Manifestations of the Berkeley Pattern, such as the "Middle Horizon"

**Figure 11.8** Hypothetical distribution of language groupings in California, circa A.D. 1–1000. (1) Ancient Wiyot; (2) Proto-Wintuan, ancestral Wintu; (3) Proto-Wintuan, ancestral Patwin; (4) Proto-Maiduan; (5) speech communities of the eastern branch of Miwokan; (6) Pomoan; (7) Wappo; (8) Yokutsan; (9) Numic speech communities; (10) Takic speech communities; (11) early Tübatulabal; (12) Hokan (Yuman) languages in area occupied sparsely or intermittently.

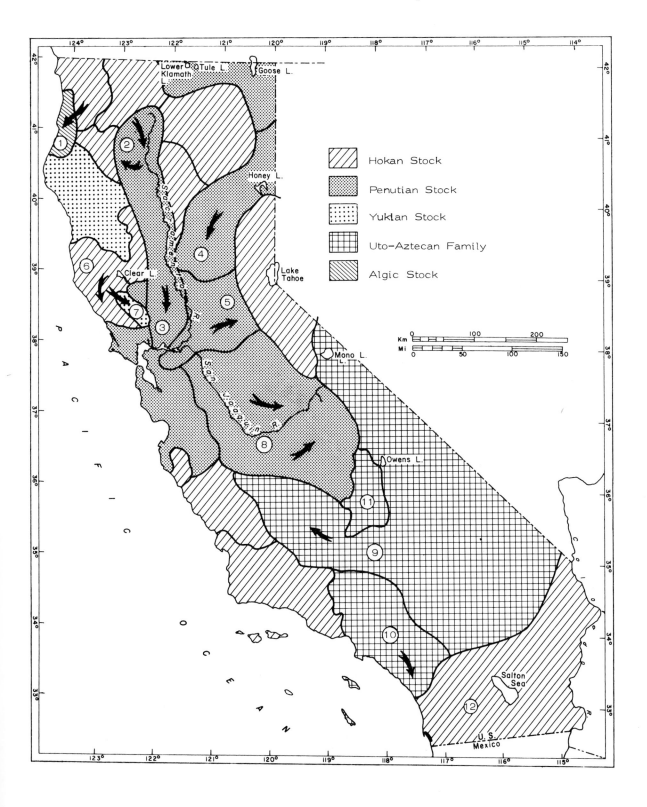

components at Camanche Reservoir, may be associated with Miwok expansion into the Sierra. Seasonal movements by the Miwok from the Valley to higher elevations may have preceded their first permanent occupation of the mountains. Lexicostatistical data imply a separation of Sierra and Plains Miwok >2000 years ago, whereas the internal time depth of Sierra Miwok is only >800 years (Levy 1978b:389), suggesting that the dispersion of Central and Southern Sierra Miwok from their northern homeland did not occur until later.

Ancestral Maiduans probably began to expand their northern Sierran territory by A.D. 1–200. Minimal linguistic divergence in Maiduan argues for a single, fairly late entry. Maiduan lexical sets for plants show irregularity, innovation, and borrowing—evidence of a recent arrival from a non-Californian homeland, probably in northwestern Nevada (Whistler 1978). Desiccation may have forced the Proto-Maiduans to abandon lands in the arid western Great Basin in favor of the mesic northern Sierra. In any event, their arrival in California perhaps would have displaced some Washo and Yana. Using various archaeological traits to distinguish Hokan and Penutian occupations, J. Johnson (1981) has shown that the Yana–Maidu boundary has been stable since circa A.D. 300–500. The Sierra Miwok also might have lost some ground as the Maiduans spread southward. The Bidwell Complex (Ritter 1970a,b) may reflect the Maiduan advance in the Oroville locality at circa A.D. 600–700. The Bidwell–Sweetwater–Oroville sequence seems to be culturally antecedent to the Maidu, whereas the older Mesilla Complex (ca. 1000 B.C.) is quite different and may relate to earlier Hokan activity in the northern Sierra.

The ancient Wintuans likely entered the upper Sacramento Valley between circa A.D. 1 and 500. By circa A.D. 700 or earlier, ancestral Patwin had arrived in the lower Sacramento Valley, followed by Hill Patwin expansion up the drainages toward Clear Lake (Whistler 1980b). Bennyhoff (1977b) has proposed that the Patwin expansion may have resulted in the southward displacement of Bay Miwok into the Diablo District (Figure 11.8). The Patwin also may have assimilated some Miwok and Pomo, as the Lake Miwok and Northeastern Pomo appear to be remnant groups left by Patwin expansion. Patwin borrowed much of its vocabulary for important central California plants (e.g., digger pine, live oak, buckeye, manzanita, and incense cedar) from Miwok, arguing for Patwin origin outside of central California and arrival after the Miwok were in place (Whistler 1977a).

Following the Patwin settlement of the southwestern Sacramento Valley, Wintu speakers from the vicinity of Cottonwood Creek apparently began to settle the upper Sacramento and Trinity River drainages ≈1100–1000 years ago (Whistler 1980a). Bauman (cited in Whistler 1979a) has shown that many Trinity and Hayfork Wintu place-names were originally Chimariko, an indication that the Wintu entered the

Trinity River country and supplanted the older Hokan group only recently. Farther east, the Yana seem to have retreated from the Sacramento Valley in the face of Wintu expansion (J. Johnson 1981). At about the same time as the Wintu radiation, the Nomlaki began to push westward from the Valley into Coast Range lands formerly held by Yukian and possibly Hokan groups.

The Wintuans almost certainly entered California from the north, as some of their cultural traits show contact with Algic peoples (Bennyhoff . 1977b). Based upon reconstructed Wintuan plant and animal terms, Whistler (1977a) concluded that the Proto-Wintuan language developed either in interior northwestern California (middle Klamath River area) or in southwest Oregon, with the upper Rogue River being the most likely Wintuan homeland. The evidence further points to a primary contact between the Patwin entering California and a Miwok group of prior occupancy (Whistler 1977a). Archaeologically, the Wintuan incursion coincides with the beginning of the Augustine Pattern in central California. Wintuan migrants probably contributed to this pattern such traits as the bow and arrow, harpoons, flanged stone pipes, and preinterment grave-pit burning. In this regard, the Shasta Aspect in the Redding District and the Sandhill Facies in the Colusa District probably relate to the advent of Wintuans.

Cultural elaboration and a wide distribution in the San Joaquin Valley and adjacent parts of the Sierra Nevada characterized the Yokuts during the favorable climatic interval before A.D. 400. The Yokuts of this period are recognized archaeologically in the Stockton District (e.g., at French Camp Slough), in the south-central Sierra Nevada by the Chowchilla and Crane Flat Phases, and on the Kaweah River by the Greasy Creek Phase. The appearance of the Meganos Aspect in the Diablo District at circa A.D. 1 possibly also marks a Yokutsan incursion (Bennyhoff 1977b).

Faced with a rapid desiccation of their lowland environment after circa A.D. 400, the Yokuts may have abandoned marginal foothill and Valley areas and congregated near reliable water sources at higher elevations, along principal streams, and near Delta waterways. A shrinking of Yokuts territory and populations during the first millennium A.D. would account for the time depth of only 15 centuries (Levy 1979:22) calculated for the Yokutsan family on the basis of internal differentiation. In this regard, Whistler (1978:1–2) reasons that, after circa A.D. 400,

> The Yokuts population may have collapsed to the point where it may have become a smaller, more choesive speech community than before. When Yokuts again expanded as the climate improved, that period of a small, restricted speech community would have been the starting point for a new period of diversification. Other remnant Yokuts groups may have been assimilated with other groups (Miwok, Salinan, Chumash, or Uto-Aztecan) during the period of collapse and subsequent expansion. The linguistic result of such a scheme would be a prehistoric "bot-

tleneck"—and any linguistic reconstruction would be valid only as far as that period of homogenization.

Archaeological evidence for this episode of cultural disruption and population coalescence after circa A.D. 400 includes abandonment of many Valley sites, cessation of trans-Valley trade, the apparent hiatus between the Crane Flat and Mariposa Phases in Yosemite National Park, and the Raymond Phase quasi-abandonment of the Sierran foothills. It seems likely that Yokutsan populations during this period were concentrated along the San Joaquin River and its major tributaries.

### Algic Stock

It is generally agreed that the Algic and Athapascan languages are more recent than Karok in northwestern California (Moratto 1973:1–8). To account for this, Whistler (1979a:25) proposed that the Wiyot entered California from the north circa A.D. 900 and occupied the lower Klamath River and adjacent coast. Later (ca. A.D. 1100?), the Yurok, also from the north, moved down the Klamath and displaced the Wiyot to the vicinity of Humboldt Bay. Finally, Athapascans from coastal Oregon moved south circa A.D. 1300, perhaps traveling in the hill country inland from the Algic enclaves, and spread to the coast along sparsely occupied streams. This linguistic succession and its archaeological manifestations are shown in Table 11.2.

Much of Whistler's model seems reasonable. First, there can be little doubt that the Algic groups came from the north (perhaps by way of the Deschutes River), given the remarkable likeness of their assemblages to those of the mid-Columbia River country (Table 11.3). Next, the apparent linguistic distance between Yurok and Wiyot implies separate movements into California rather than *in situ* divergence. Moreover, Bauman and Silver (1975) have adduced linguistic data to show that Wiyot and Karok were once in direct contact and that subsequently both Yurok and Hupa–Chilula intervened between them. To this evidence one may add

**TABLE 11.2**

**Concordance of Linguistic and Archaeological Successions in Northwestern California**[a]

| Linguistic group | Date | Archaeological expression |
|---|---|---|
| Oregon Athapascan, California Athapascan } | ca. A.D. 1300 | Point St. George II |
| Ancestral Yurok | { ca. A.D. 1300 <br> ca. A.D. 1100 | *Tsahpek^w*, Patricks Point, *Tsurai*, etc. |
| Ancestral Wiyot | ca. A.D. 900 | Lower Gunther Island |
| Ancestral Karok | Old | Point St. George I |

[a]After Whistler (1979a:23).

**TABLE 11.3**

Archaeological Traits Found in Northwestern California and along the Mid-Columbia River[a]

| | |
|---|---|
| Gunther Barbed arrowpoints | Stone adze handles |
| Ovate "salmon knives" of flint | Stone fish-clubs |
| Large "ceremonial blades" (bifaces) | Arrowshaft abraders |
| Simple harpoon tips of bone | Long pestles of flanged and off-set types |
| Zooform clubs ("slave killers") | Incised-bone head scratchers |
| C-shaped fishhooks of bone or shell | Incised baked-clay figurines, anthropomorphic |
| Notched-pebble net sinkers | Elongate cobble choppers |
| Girdled-stone net sinkers | Collared smoking pipes |
| Flanged mauls of distinctive form | Steatite vessels |
| Several types of antler wedges | Grave-pit burning |

[a]Compiled from Cressman (1960), Elsasser (1965), Heizer and Elsasser (1964), Loud (1918), and Strong (1959a,b).

that the Patricks Point site, historically Yurok, figures in Wiyot myths and probably was once in Wiyot territory. Finally, the Tolowa borrowing of Yurok terms for some marine animals would indicate the primacy of the Yurok on the coast (Whistler 1979a). To account for the unlikely Yurok–Wiyot proximity, Whistler (1979a:17) refers to "parallel migrational responses by two similar but separate groups at different times to similar geographic and ecological pressures and/or opportunities."

For the present, any scheme of linguistic prehistory in northwestern California must be somewhat sketchy because so little archaeological work has been done in the area. Still, Whistler's model reasonably integrates available linguistic and archaeological data, except that some chronological fine tuning may be needed. For example, the high degree of littoral specialization manifest in lower Hum-67, a presumed Wiyot component, on Gunther Island would imply either that the Wiyot had lived elsewhere on the seashore earlier than their initial occupation of Hum-67 at circa A.D. 1000 or that they had quickly borrowed subsistence practices from older, littoral-adapted peoples near Humboldt Bay. One possibility is that the Wiyot settled along the coast circa A.D. 800 or 900 and borrowed the subsistence practices of older Yukian populations. Site Hum-68, thought to reflect pre-Wiyot use of Gunther Island, may have been a Yukian coastal settlement before circa A.D. 800. The Yurok evidently did not reach the shore until circa A.D. 1100, but they may have lived along the Klamath River for some time before moving to the coast.

With the Algic groups came such traits as a woodworking technology, riverine fishing specialization, wealth consciousness, and distinctive artifact types (Figure 10.5) to initiate the Gunther Pattern of late prehistoric northwestern California (see Chapter 10).

### Yukian Stock

The Wappo, identified with the St. Helena Aspect of the Augustine Pattern, seem to have replaced earlier Western Miwok (Houx Aspect of the Berkeley Pattern) occupants of the Napa Valley soon after A.D. 500. This Wappo shift most likely was a result of displacement caused by Pomo expansion into the lower Russian River drainage and adjacent coastal areas (Basgall 1982; Bennyhoff 1977c). The northward expansion of Northern Pomo at about the same time would have further reduced Yuki territory and separated it from that of the Wappo (Whistler 1980b). Finally, Wappo settlement of the Napa Valley would have completed the separation of Coast and Lake Miwok (Figure 11.8).

### Hokan Stock

With a few notable exceptions, the California Hokans continued to lose ground after circa A.D. 1. The Karok, for example, relinquished coastal and lower Klamath River portions of their territory to the Algic settlers. Likewise, the Wintu appropriated Shastan, Chimariko, Palaihnihan, and Yanan lands in the upper Sacramento Valley and bordering uplands. The Palaihnihan and Yanan homelands were further reduced by Maiduan expansion. Whether the Maidu also acquired some Washo territory is unclear. The Washo, archaeologically known as the Kings Beach Complex, are thought to have spread in the Lake Tahoe vicinity after circa A.D. 500—about the same time as the Maiduan expansion. It is possible that the Washo entered eastern California from the western Great Basin in order to seek more favorable environments during the "Little Altithermal." If so, both would have supplanted older, presumably Hokan, populations in the northern Sierra.

Pomoan geography, as known in early historic times, had taken form by the end of this period. The Clear Lake Aspect of the Augustine Pattern records the emergence of complex Pomo societies in the Clear Lake area after circa A.D. 500. Comparable, largely synchronous, archaeological developments also can be traced in the Pomo domains farther west and south (Baumhoff 1980a,b).

In the southern deserts, Hakataya influence—notably the bow and arrow and Buff and Brown pottery—spread westward across the Colorado Desert and into the southern Mojave Desert after circa A.D. 500 (see Chapter 8). This appears to have been a case of diffusion rather than population replacement in an area long occupied by Hokans. Similarly, the persistence of "Yuman" traits as far west as the coast would imply a continuity of Hokan populations across far southern California, even allowing for intervals of local abandonment.

## Uto-Aztecan Family

During this period Uto-Aztecans came to occupy diverse environmental zones, particularly after circa A.D. 400 when climatic shifts made some desert areas uninhabitable. In the northeastern Mojave Desert, the basic cultural patterns established during the earlier Gypsum Period continued with little change, throughout the Saratoga Springs Period (A.D. 500–1200), suggesting that Uto-Aztecans continued to occupy this area. Uto-Aztecan groups also appear to have occupied Owens Valley (late Cowhorn and Baker Phases), the southern high Sierra (late Canebrake and Sawtooth Phases), the southern San Joaquin Valley between circa A.D. 400 and 1100 (no local phases have been named), and possibly far northeastern California (Alkalai Phase in Surprise Valley).

## A.D. *1000–1850*

Much of lowland California was inhabited only sparsely or intermittently during the warm–dry climatic interval before circa A.D. 1430. "Improved" (relatively cool–moist) conditions between circa A.D. 1430 and 1850 coincided with population growth and cultural elaboration (as seen, for example, in the late Augustine Pattern) in many regions. Population shifts and language spreads during this period brought California's ethnogeography to its early historic configuration.

## Uto-Aztecan Family

One of the most striking aspects of linguistic geography in the western U.S. is the extensive distribution of contiguous Uto-Aztecan languages and dialects, particularly in the Great Basin where, except for Washo, all of the enthnographic groups spoke Ut ɔ-Aztecan languages. The large sweep and minimal diversity of these lan ʒuages attest to their recent spread.

Lamb (1962) and Goss (1968) have inferred from linguistic diversity and "center of gravity" (apparent center of linguistic dispersion) that the origin and differentiation of Northern Uto-Aztecan were in southeastern California. Hopkins (1965) proposed that speakers of Numic languages began to spread into the Great Basin from southeastern California approximately 1000 years ago. He reasoned that the retreat of agriculturalists from the southern Great Basin as a consequence of desiccation would have permitted at least some Numic desert dwellers to occupy new lands. More importantly, however, the specialized seed-processing economy of the Numic peoples, along with their generalized hunting and gathering skills, may have conferred upon them a selective advantage in competition with older (Prenumic) Great Basin societies.

In this regard, Bettinger and Baumhoff (1982) have proposed certain

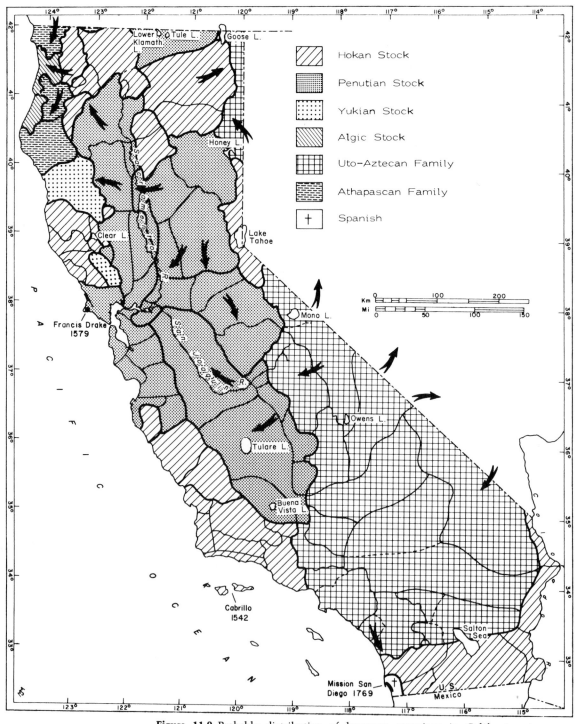

**Figure 11.9** Probable distribution of language groupings in California, circa A.D. 1000–1769. (Map by the author.)

social and cultural mechanisms by which the Numic expansion into the Great Basin might have occurred. The Prenumic occupants of this area are characterized as "travellers" who followed a low cost economic strategy "in which a good deal of time was spent finding and capturing large game and monitoring large resource areas for productive stands of high-ranked plant resources. This strategy is low in cost because it minimizes use of low-ranked resources" (Bettinger and Baumhoff 1982:497). Prenumic societies were distinguished also by low population densities and relatively high male:female sex ratios. By contrast, Numic hunter–gatherers were "processors", spending relatively "less time . . . in travel and relatively more time in the collection and processing of grass and other hard seeds within more restricted areas. This strategy is high in cost because it is reliant on low-ranked resources, i.e., those requiring extensive processing" (Bettinger and Baumhoff 1982:497). Numic societies featured *relatively* high population densities, by Great Basin standards, and low male:female sex ratios. Because of their processor strategy and higher population densities, the Numic peoples would have been able to spread at the expense of the lower density populations of Prenumic travellers.

Archaeologically, the Numic spread is marked by small, Desert Side-notched and Cottonwood Triangular arrow points, millingstones and manos, and simple coiled and scraped pottery. The Numic cultural inventory also features twined, paddle-shaped seed beaters and triangular winnowing trays. A different seed processing technology is inferred for the Prenumic societies, who used horn sickles and coiled parching/winnowing trays of Southwestern types. Bettinger and Baumhoff (1982) suggest that Prenumic groups were largely responsible for the elaborate rock art so widespread in the Great Basin, and that the later Numic peoples defaced or obliterated some of this art with their own scratched motifs, red pigment, or milling slicks.

Bettinger (1977a, 1978a) has shown that, by circa 1000 B.P., a well-developed processor strategy—almost certainly related to Numic populations—marked by attenuated travel, reduced dependence on large game, and increased reliance on seed plants, was established in Owens Valley. Soon thereafter, Numic groups began their spread into the Great Basin—a movement possibly stimulated by warming climates and reduced resources in Owens Valley. One may propose that the ancestral Western Numic (Mono–Paviotso) began to move northward along the east side of the cordillera by circa A.D. 1000–1200. At about the same time, or possibly 1 or 2 centuries later, the Monachi would have diverged from their Numic kin and crossed the Sierra to acquire sparsely occupied Yokuts lands on the western slope (Figure 11.9). Between circa A.D. 1200 and 1300, Southern Numic (Kawaiisu–Ute) peoples fanned out toward the east, contacting the Anasazi by circa A.D. 1300 as shown by the association of Southern Paiute and Anasazi pottery in the southern Great Basin. Thereafter the Central Numic (Panamint–Shoshone) radiation toward the northeast had begun by circa A.D. 1300–1500 (Figure 11.9). Finally, as a separate development, the Chemehuevi are thought to have diverged from the Virgin River Paiute and entered southeastern California less than 400 years ago.

This reconstruction is supported by glottochronological dates of Uto-Aztecan internal divergence, the timing of climatic episodes, and linguistic geography (Hopkins 1965:48). Further evidence of the Numic radiation into the Great Basin from its southwestern margin (Owens Valley area?) beginning around A.D. 1000 takes the form of dated Cottonwood Triangular and Desert Side-notched points and Paiute–Shoshone pottery. At stratified sites in the eastern Great Basin "this distinctive pottery is associated with Anasazi and/or Fremont ceramics, supporting the hypothesis that competition with Numic speaking [sic] groups was partially responsible for the disappearance of the Fremont culture" (Madsen 1975:82). In California, Wallace (1962a) assigned a basal date of circa A.D. 1000 to the Paiute–Shoshone pottery in Death Valley, and an initial date of circa A.D. 1300 is indicated for Owens Valley Brown Ware (Lanning 1963; Riddell and Riddell 1956). A further indicator of Numic expansion is that the Shoshone had borrowed certain Yokuts basketry techniques by circa A.D. 1200 (Bennyhoff 1977b), suggesting either an early Monachi arrival on the western slope of the Sierra or continued sporadic use of the San Joaquin Valley by Shoshoneans.

### Athapascan Family

Athapascans from western Oregon began to settle northwestern California approximately 700 to 800 years ago. Between circa A.D. 1200 and 1300 the predecessors of the Mattole and Wailaki became established on the coast, perhaps as far south as the Mattole River. The Hupa–Chilula may have entered California at about the same time, settling in or near Hoopa Valley. Linguistic geography and patterns of lexical borrowing, as well as degree of linguistic separation from other Athapascan languages, indicate that the Tolowa–Tututni did not arrive in California until after the Algic populations were more or less in place, that is, later than circa A.D. 1200 and possibly as late as A.D. 1300. Archaeologically, Tolowa presence is marked by the Point St. George II Phase near Crescent City.

Especially in the north, the Athapascans seem to have occupied lands that were underutilized previously, and at least some of them appear to have advanced by settling areas only sparsely inhabited. However, the more southerly Athapascan languages—Cahto and Wailaki—in recent times were expanding into presumably well-occupied Yukian territory. The Cahto and Wailaki were in fact Yukian people physically and culturally, who seem to have adopted Athapascan speech as a "prestige language" (Bennyhoff 1977b; Whistler 1979a).

## Penutian Stock

Several Penutian groups acquired new territory during late prehistoric times. After circa A.D. 1000, the Patwin spread westward from the Valley, displacing Pomoan and Miwokan peoples along the eastern front of the North Coast Ranges. Similarly, the Nomlaki moved westward at the expense of the Yuki; a glottochronological date of >500 years for Proto-Nomlaki would place this movement at circa A.D. 1500. Subsequently, between circa A.D. 1500 and 1850, the Wintu completed their northward thrust into the mountainous upper Sacramento–Trinity River country, acquiring lands from the Chimariko and Shasta. Archaeologically, this late prehistoric expansion of the Wintu and Nomlaki is identified with the Shasta Aspect of the Augustine Pattern. Linguistic data suggest that some of the more westerly Achumawi and Atsugewi also may have lost ground as the Wintu advanced. Simultaneously, however, "improved" environmental conditions may have allowed the Achumawi and Atsugewi to occupy (or reoccupy) the most easterly reaches of their territories.

After circa A.D. 1400, groups ancestral to the Central and Southern Sierra Miwok rapidly moved southward in the central Sierran foothills (Figure 11.9). Presumably displacing Yokuts enclaves as they advanced, the Sierra Miwok progressed as far south as the Fresno River by circa A.D. 1600. This Miwok radiation is seen archaeologically in the Horseshoe Bend Phase component at New Melones Reservoir and in the Mariposa and Madera phases farther south (see Chapter 7). Linguistically, the term for clamshell disk bead entered Sierra Miwok after its division into three languages (Levy 1978b), coinciding nicely with the A.D. 1450–1850 span of the "clam disk bead horizon" in central California.

The cause of the Sierra Miwok expansion is not well understood, but perhaps involved improved environmental conditions in the foothills after circa A.D. 1400 and the reduction of Yokuts populations in the Sierra during the millennium after A.D. 400. Another factor may have been pressure from the Nisenan. Linguistically, the divergence of Proto–Chico/Konkow and Proto-Nisenan is set at ≈600 years (Levy 1979:22), suggesting Maiduan population spread at circa A.D. 1300–1400. The late prehistoric expansion of the Nisenan can be identified archaeologically with Pla-101A (Spring Garden Ravine) at Auburn Reservoir and related components in the lower American River drainage.

Coeval with the Nisenan and Miwok spreads, Yokuts populations once again occupied Valley lands as water and water-dependent resources became more plentiful. Proto–Valley Yokuts are given a linguistic time depth of approximately six centuries (Levy 1979:22). By circa A.D. 1600–

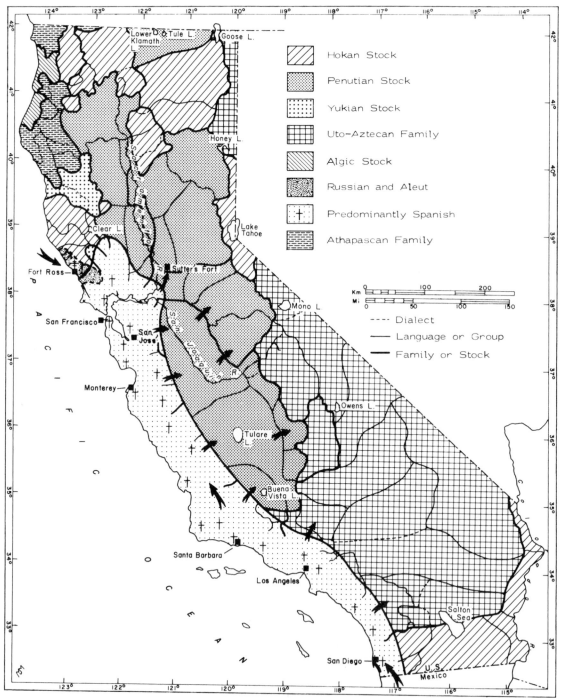

**Figure 11.10** Probable distribution of language groupings in California, circa A.D. 1770–1848. No attempt has been made to show the mixed and ever-changing distribution of native languages within the zone of direct mission influence. (Map by the author.)

1700 the Yokuts held virtually the entire San Joaquin Valley (Figure 11.9). Archaeological evidence of this rapid and widespread Yokuts dispersion is found widely from the Panoche Complex west of Los Banos to the late period cemeteries near Buena Vista Lake. Continuous occupation of the south-central and southern Sierra Nevada foothills by the Yokuts is recorded at such late prehistoric sites as Slick Rock Village (Tul-10) and China Diggings (Mad-173), respectively at Terminus and Hidden reservoirs (see Chapter 7).

## Historic Transformations

By circa A.D. 1750, California ethnogeography was essentially as depicted in Figure 11.1. Thereafter, the explosive spread of foreign populations, diseases, economic patterns, material traits, and languages was to change massively and nearly extinguish native sociocultural systems and languages (Castillo 1978). The first wave of foreign influence and domination came with the Spanish who, during the half century after A.D. 1769, established missions, pueblos, and presidios along the coast between San Diego and Sonoma (Figure 11.10). The purpose of this effort was to colonize Alta California. That goal was not achieved in the long term. The Spanish colonial enterprise, however, did manage to devastate Indian cultures and reduce populations in the coastal zone from an estimated 72,000 in A.D. 1770 to 18,000 in A.D. 1830—a net loss of 54,000 people (S. Cook 1943a, 1943b, 1978).

The impacts of missionization were far-reaching. Coastal peoples often fled to the interior, so that growing numbers of refugees were to be found, often residing with the local Miwok and Yokuts, in the Sierran foothills and Valley, especially after circa A.D. 1800. Simultaneously, the Spanish mounted numerous expeditions to interior California in order to capture apostates and to punish those who had given them succor (S. Cook 1960, 1962). The result was that, along with the projection of military power, Spanish livestock and material goods found their way into the Valley and Sierra long before non-Indians settled those regions. These contacts, however, did not affect the interior peoples nearly as much as did the introduced diseases, particularly the epidemic of 1833, which killed an estimated 75% of the Valley Indians (S. Cook 1955b).

The most devastating wave of foreign impacts was swept into California by the Gold Rush and attendant influx of Euro-American populations. During the single decade of A.D. 1845–1855, the Indian population of California was reduced from approximately 150,000 to 50,000; by A.D. 1900, the number had fallen to 20,000—less than 7% of the estimated preconquest level of 310,000 (S. F. Cook 1978).

This desolation was accomplished by a ruthless flood of miners and farmers who annihilated the natives without mercy or compensation. The direct causes of death

were disease, the bullet, exposure, and acute starvation. The more remote causes
were insane passion for gold, abiding hatred for the Red man, and complete lack of
any legal control. (S. F. Cook 1978:93)

Together, these and later historic episodes of colonization and conquest abruptly terminated the systems of Indian cultures and languages
that had been developing in California over a span of 150 centuries or
more.

# Appendix 1: Common and Scientific Names of Plants and Animals

### Plants*

Agave. See Mescal.

Alkali heath (*Frankenia grandifolia*)

Allocarya (*Allocarya* sp.)

Amaranth (*Amaranthus* sp.)

Amole. See Soap root.

Antelope bush (*Purshia tridentata*)

Arrowhead (*Sagittaria latifolia*)

Arrowweed (*Pluchea sericea*)

Aspen (*Populus tremuloides*)

Bear brush (*Garrya fremontii*)

Bear grass (*Xerophyllum tenax*)

Beavertail cactus (*Opuntia basilaris*)

Big tree (*Sequoiadendron giganteum*)

Bitterbrush. See Antelope bush.

Blackberry (*Rubus vitifolius*)

Black bush (*Coleogyne ramosissima*)

Black oak (*Quercus kelloggii*)

Blow-wives (*Achyrachaena mollis*)

Blue oak (*Quercus douglasii*)

Box elder (*Acer negundo*)

Bristlecone pine (*Pinus longaeva*)

Broadleaf maple (*Acer macrophyllum*)

Brodiaea (*Brodiaea* sp.)

Buckeye (*Aesculus californica*)

Bush chinquapin (*Castanopsis sempervirens*)

Button bush, Button willow (*Cephalanthus occidentalis*)

California bay (*Umbellularia californica*)

California coffeeberry (*Rhamnus californica*)

California holly. See Toyon.

California laurel. See California bay.

California poppy (*Escholtzia californica*)

Camas (*Cammasia quamash* or *C. leichtlinii*)

Canyon oak (*Quercus chrysolepis*)

Cattail (*Typha latifolia*)

Ceanothus (*Ceanothus* sp.)

Century plant. See Mescal.

Chamise (*Adenostoma fasiculatum*)

Chia (*Salvia columbariae*)

Cholla (*Opuntia* spp.)

Christmas berry. See Toyon.

Clover (*Trifolium* sp.)

Coast hemlock (*Tsuga heterophylla*)

Coast live oak (*Quercus agrifolia*)

Coffeeberry. See California coffeeberry.

Common bean (*Phaseolus vulgaris*)

Corn (*Zea mays*)

Cottonwood (*Populus fremontii*)

Coulter pine (*Pinus coulteri*)

*After Balls (1962); Byers (1967); Barbour and Major (1977); and Munz (1959).

575

Creosote bush (*Larrea tridentata* or *L. divaricata*)

Death-camas (*Zigadenus venenosus*)

Deer brush (*Ceanothus integerrimus*)

Deer grass (*Muhlenbergia ringens*)

Desert ironwood (*Olney tesota*)

Desert sage (*Salvia dorrii*)

Digger pine (*Pinus sabiniana*)

Dogbane (*Apocynum* sp.)

Douglas fir (*Pseudotsuga menziesii*)

Dove weed. See Turkey mullein.

Elderberry (*Sambucus* spp.)

Engelmann oak (*Quercus engelmannii*)

Epos (*Perideridia gairdneri*)

Eryngium (*Eryngium vaseyi*)

Fairy lantern. See Mariposa lily.

Fiddle neck (*Phacelia tanacetifolia*)

Flannel bush (*Fremontia californica*)

Foxtail pine (*Pinus balfouriana*)

Gilia (*Gilia* sp.)

Gourd (*Lagenaria* sp.)

Grand fir (*Abies grandis*)

Greasewood. See Antelope bush.

Great Basin wild rye (*Elymus cinereus*)

Green manzanita (*Arctostaphylos patula*)

Grindelia (*Grindelia* sp.)

Hairgrass (*Deschampsia* sp.)

Hazelnut (*Corylus cornuta*)

Horehound (*Marrubium vulgare*)

Horse-tail rush (*Equisetum* sp.)

Huckleberry (*Vaccinium* sp.)

Huckleberry oak (*Quercus vaccinifolia*)

Incense cedar (*Libocedrus decurrens*)

Indian hemp (*Apocynum cannabinum*)

Indian onion (*Brodiaea* spp.)

Indian potato (*Carum gairdneri*)

Indian ricegrass (*Oryzopsis hymenoides*)

Indian tobacco. See Tobacco.

Interior live oak (*Quercus wislizenii*)

Ipos. See Epos.

Iris (*Iris* spp.)

Jeffrey pine (*Pinus jeffreyi*)

Jimson weed (*Datura meteloides, D. stramonium*)

Johnny tuck (*Orthocarpus erianthus*)

Joshua tree (*Yucca brevifolia*)

Juniper (*Juniperus* spp.)

Kit-kit-dizze (*Chamaebatia foliolosa*)

Lace pod (*Thysanocarpus curvipes*)

Layia (*Layia* sp.)

Lemmon's willow (*Salix lemmoni*)

Lodgepole pine (*Pinus murrayana*)

Madia (*Madia* sp.)

Madrone or Madroño (*Arbutus californica*)

Maize (*Zea mays*)

Manzanita (*Arctostaphylos* spp.)

Mariposa lily (*Calochortus* spp.)

Maul oak. See Canyon oak.

Mescal (*Agave* spp.)

Mesquite (*Prosopis juliflora, P. pubescens*)

Milkweed (*Asclepias fascicularis*)

Mimetanthe (*Mimetanthe* sp.)

Monterey pine (*Pinus radiata*)

Mormon tea (*Ephedra* spp.)

Mountain hemlock (*Tsuga mertensiana*)

Mountain mahogany (*Cercocarpus betuloides*)
Mullein (*Verbascum* sp.)
Navarretia (*Navarretia* sp.)
Nitrophilia (*Nitrophilia* sp.)
Nutmeg (*Torreya californica*)
Oak (*Quercus* spp.)
Oregon ash (*Fraxinus oregona*)
Oregon oak (*Quercus garryana*)
Our Lord's candle (*Yucca whipplei*)
Palo verde (*Cercidium floridum*)
Pepperwood. See California bay.
Piñon or Pinyon pine (*Pinus monophylla*)
Poison oak (*Toxicodendron diversilobum*)
Ponderosa pine (*Pinus ponderosa*)
Prickley pear (*Opuntia occidentalis*)
Rabbit brush (*Chrysothamnus nauseosus*)
Red alder (*Alnus oregona*)
Redberry (*Rhamnus crocea*)
Redbud (*Cercis occidentalis*)
Red fir (*Abies magnifica*)
Redwood (*Sequoia sempervirens*)
Roble. See Valley oak.
Sagebrush (*Artemesia* spp.)
Saguaro or Sahuaro (*Cereus giganteus*)
Saltbush (*Atriplex cordulata* or *A. californica*)
Salt grass (*Distichlis spicata*)
Screwbean. See Mesquite (*P. pubescens*)
Sea blite (*Swaeda californica*)
Sequoia. See Big tree.
Shrub oak (*Quercus dumosa*)
Sierra plum (*Prunus subcordata*)
Silver pine (*Pinus monticola*)
Soap plant (*Chenopodium californicum*)

Soap root (*Chlorogalum pomeridianum*)
Spanish bayonet (*Yucca baccata*)
Spear grass (*Stipa pulchra*)
Squawbush (*Rhus trilobata*)
Storksbill (*Erodium botrys*)
Sugar pine (*Pinus lambertiana*)
Sunflower (*Wyethia longicaulis*)
Sycamore (*Platanus racemosa*)
Tanbark oak (*Lithocarpus densiflora*)
Tarweed (*Hemizonia* sp. or *Madia* sp.)
Tansy mustard (*Descurania pinnata*)
Tideland spruce (*Picea stichensis*)
Tobacco (*Nicotiana* spp.)
Toloache. See Jimson weed.
Tomcat clover (*Trifolium tridentatum*)
Toyon (*Heteromeles arbutifolia*)
Tule (*Scirpus lacustris*)
Tule potato. See Arrowhead.
Tuna (*Opuntia ficus-indica*)
Turkey mullein (*Eremocarpus setigerus*)
Utah juniper (*Juniperus utahensis* or *J. osteosperma*)
Valley oak (*Quercus lobata*)
Wappato. See Arrowhead.
Western hemlock (*Tsuga heterophylla*)
White alder (*Alnus rhombifolia*)
Whitebark pine (*Pinus albicaulis*)
White fir (*Abies concolor*)
Wild grape (*Vitis californica*)
Wild oats (*Avena fatua*)
Wild onion (*Allium* spp.)
Wild rose (*Rosa californica*)
Willow (*Salix* spp.)
Wokas (*Nymphaea polysepala*)
Yellow pine. See Ponderosa pine.

Yerba del pescado. See Turkey mullein.

Yerba mansa (*Anemopsis californica*)

Yerba santa (*Eriodictyon californicum*)

Yucca (*Yucca* spp., esp. *Y. whipplei*)

## Mollusks*

Bay mussel (*Mytilus edulis*)

Bay oyster (*Ostrea lurida*)

Bent-nosed clam (*Macoma nasuta*)

Black abalone (*Haliotis cracherodii*)

Black turban snail (*Tegula funebralis*)

California mussel (*Mytilus californianus*)

Freshwater clam (*Anodonta nuttalliana*)

Freshwater mussel (*Margaritifera margaritifera*)

Gaper, Horseneck clam (*Tresus nuttalli*)

Glycymeris (*Glycymeris migueliana* or *G. subobsoleta*)

Green abalone (*Haliotis fulgens*)

Heart cockle (*Clinocardium nuttalli*)

Horn (snail) shell (*Cerithidea californica*)

Moon snail (*Polinices lewisi*)

Olive snail (*Olivella biplicata* or *O. baetica*)

Razor clam (*Siliqua patula*)

Red abalone (*Haliotis rufescens*)

River mussel (*Anodonta oregonensis*)

Rock cockle (*Protothaca staminea*)

Rock oyster (*Hinnites giganteus*)

Sand clam (*Macoma secta*)

Speckled chione (*Aequipecten circularis*)

Washington clam (*Saxidomus nuttalli*)

Wavy chione (*Chione undatella*)

## Fishes**

Bat ray (*Mylobatis californica*)

Blackperch (*Embiotoca jacksoni*)

Black rockfish (*Sebastodes melanops*)

Brown smoothhound shark (*Mustelus henlei*)

Cabezon (*Scorpaenichthys marmoratus*)

California barracuda (*Syphyraena argentea*)

California halibut (*Paralichthys californicus*)

California roach (*Hesperoleucus symmetricus*)

China rockfish (*Sebastes nebulosus*)

Chinook salmon, king salmon (*Oncorhynchus tshawytscha*)

Delta smelt (*Hypomesus transpacificus*)

Green sturgeon (*Acipenser medirostris*)

Hitch (*Lavinia exilicauda*)

Jacksmelt (*Atherinopsis californiensis*)

Leopard shark (*Triakis semifasciata*)

Ling-cod (*Ophiodon elongatus*)

* After Ricketts and Calvin (1962).
** After Fitch (1967, 1969, 1972, 1975); Follett (1957, 1968, 1974, 1975a,b); and Moyle (1976).

Longfin smelt (*Spirinchus thaleichthys*)
Northern anchovy (*Engraulis mordax*)
Pacific halibut (*Hippoglossus stenolepsis*)
Pacific herring (*Clupea pallasii*)
Pacific lamprey (*Lampetra tridentata*)
Pacific mackerel (*Pneumatophorus japonicus*)
Pacific sardine (*Sardinops caeruleus*)
Pile perch (*Damalichthys vacca*)
Plainfin midshipman (*Porichthys notatus*)
Rainbow trout (*Salmo gairdneri*)
Redtail surfperch (*Amphistichus rhodoterus*)
Rock prickleback (*Xiphister mucosus*)
Rubberlip seaperch (*Rhacochilus toxotes*)
Sacramento squawfish (*Ptychocheilus grandis*)
Sacramento sucker (*Catostomus occidentalis*)
Shiner perch (*Cymatogaster aggregata*)
Silver salmon (*Oncorhynchus kisutch*)
Soupfin shark (*Galeorhinus zyopterus*)
Speckled dace (*Rhinichthys osculus*)
Spiny dogfish (*Squalus acanthias*)
Staghorn sculpin (*Leptocottus armatus*)
Starry flounder (*Platichthys stellatus*)

Thicktail chub (*Gila crassicauda*)
Thresher shark (*Alopias vulpinus*)
Top smelt (*Atherinops affinis*)
Tule perch (*Hysterocarpus traski*)
Turkey-red rockfish (*Sebastodes ruberrimus*)
Vermilion rockfish (*Sebastodes miniatus*)
Yellowtail (*Seriola dorsalis*)
Walleye surfperch (*Hyperprosopon argenteum*)
White seabass (*Cynoscion nobilis*)
White sturgeon (*Acipenser transmontanus*)
Wolf eel (*Anarrhichthys ocellatus*)

## Reptiles*

Desert tortoise (*Gopherus agassizii*)
Pacific freshwater turtle, Pond turtle (*Clemmys marmorata*)
Pacific rattlesnake (*Crotalus viridis*)

## Birds**

Bald eagle (*Haliaetus leucocephalus*)
Band-tailed pigeon (*Columba fasciata*)
Black-crowned heron (*Nycticorax nycticorax*)
Brant (*Branta* sp.)
Brown pelican (*Pelecanus occidentalis*)

*After Savage (1959) and Verner and Boss (1980).
**After Howard and Miller (1939) and Peterson (1969).

California condor (*Gymnogyps californianus*)

California woodpecker (*Melanerpes formicivorous*)

Canada goose (*Branta canadensis*)

Coot, Mudhen (*Fulica americana*)

Cormorant (*Phalacrocorax* sp.)

Flightless scoter (*Chendytes lawi*)†

Great blue heron (*Ardea herodias*)

Mourning dove (*Zenaidura macroura*)

Murre (*Uria troille*)

Red-shafted flicker (*Colaptes cafer*)

Sagehen (*Centrocercus urophasianus*)

Sandhill crane (*Grus canadensis*)

Snow goose (*Chen hyperborea*)

Teratornis (giant condor) (*Teratornis merriami*)†

Trumpeter swan (*Olor buccinator*)

Valley quail (*Lophortyx californica*)

Whistling swan (*Olor columbianus*)

White-faced glossy ibis (*Plegadis guarauna*)

White pelican (*Pelecanus erythrorhynchus*)


### Mammals*

Allen chipmunk (*Eutamias townsendi*)

Antelope. See Pronghorn.

Badger (*Taxidea taxus*)

Bay porpoise (*Phocaena vomerina*)

Beaver (*Castor canadensis*)

Bighorn sheep (*Ovis canadensis*)

Bison (*Bison bison*) (extinct in California)

Black bear (*Ursus americanus*)

Black-tailed deer. See Mule deer.

Black-tailed hare, Jackrabbit (*Lepus californicus*)

Bobcat (*Lynx rufus*)

Brush rabbit (*Sylvilagus bachmani*)

California lion (*Panthera atrox*)†

California sea lion (*Zalophus californicus*)

Canadian elk (*Cervus canadensis*)

Columbian mammoth (*Mammuthus columbi*)†

Common dolphin (*Delphinus bairdi*)

Cottontail (*Sylvilagus audubonii* or *S. nuttallii*)

Coyote (*Canis latrans*)

Dire wolf (*Canis dirus*)†

Dwarf mammoth, island mammoth. See Jefferson's mammoth.†

Four-horned antelope (*Breameryx minor*)†

Giant short-faced bear. See Short-faced bear.†

Gray fox (*Urocyon cineroargenteus*)

Grizzly bear (*Ursus arctos*) (extinct in California)

Guadalupe fur seal (*Arctocephalus townsendi*)

---

†Extinct species.
*After Ingles (1965); Kurtén and Anderson (1980); and Verner and Boss (1980).

Harbor seal (*Phoca vitulina*)

Horse (*Equus* sp.)† (reintroduced in 1769)

Jackrabbit. See Black-tailed hare.

Jefferson's mammoth (*Mammuthus jeffersonii*)†

Kangaroo rat (*Dipodomys* sp.)

Kit fox (*Vulpes macrotis*)

Lowland mink (*Mustela vison*)

Marmot (*Marmota flaviventris*)

Mountain coyote (*Canis latrans*)

Mountain lion (*Felis concolor*)

Mountain sheep (*Ovis canadensis*)

Mule deer, Black-tailed deer (*Odocoileus hemionus*)

Mylodont ground sloth (*Paramylodon harlani*)†

North American cheetah (*Acinonyx trumani*)†

Northern elephant seal (*Mirounga angustirostris*)

Northern fur seal (*Callorhinus ursinus*)

Pronghorn, Antelope (*Antilocapra americana*)

Raccoon (*Procyon lotor*)

River otter (*Lutra canadensis*)

Saber-toothed cat (*Smilodon californicus*)†

Sea otter (*Enhydra lutris*)

Shasta ground sloth (*Nothrotherium shastense*)†

Short-faced bear, Giant short-faced bear (*Arctodus simus*)†

Shrub-ox (*Euceratherium collinum*)†

Sierran ground sloth (*Megalony sierrensis*)†

Spotted skunk (*Spilogale putorius*)

Steller (or Steller's) sea lion (*Eumetopias jubata*)

Striped skunk (*Mephitis mephitis*)

Tapir (*Tapirus* sp.) (extinct in California)

Tule elk (*Cervus elaphus*)

Valley coyote (*Canis ochropus*)

Varying hare, snowshoe hare (*Lepus americanus*)

Western horse (*Equus occidentalis*)†

Weasel (*Mustela frenata*)

White-tailed jackrabbit (*Lepus townsendi*)

Wolf (*Canis lupus*) (extinct in California)

Wolverine (*Gulo luscus*)

Wood rat (*Neotoma lepida*)

†Extinct species.

# Appendix 2: County Abbreviations Used in Site Designations

| | | | | | |
|---|---|---|---|---|---|
| Ala | — | Alameda | Ora | — | Orange |
| Alp | — | Alpine | Pla | — | Placer |
| Ama | — | Amador | Plu | — | Plumas |
| But | — | Butte | Riv | — | Riverside |
| Cal | — | Calaveras | Sac | — | Sacramento |
| Col | — | Colusa | SBn | — | San Benito |
| CCo | — | Contra Costa | SBr | — | San Bernardino |
| DNo | — | Del Norte | SDi | — | San Diego |
| Eld | — | Eldorado | SFr | — | San Francisco |
| Fre | — | Fresno | SJo | — | San Joaquin |
| Gle | — | Glenn | SLO | — | San Luis Obispo |
| Hum | — | Humboldt | SMa | — | San Mateo |
| Imp | — | Imperial | SBa | — | Santa Barbara |
| Iny | — | Inyo | SCl | — | Santa Clara |
| Ker | — | Kern | SCr | — | Santa Cruz |
| Kin | — | Kings | Sha | — | Shasta |
| Lak | — | Lake | Sie | — | Sierra |
| Las | — | Lassen | Sis | — | Siskiyou |
| LAn | — | Los Angeles | Sol | — | Solano |
| Mad | — | Madera | Son | — | Sonoma |
| Mrn | — | Marin | Sta | — | Stanislaus |
| Mrp | — | Mariposa | Sut | — | Sutter |
| Men | — | Mendocino | Teh | — | Tehama |
| Mer | — | Merced | Tri | — | Trinity |
| Mod | — | Modoc | Tul | — | Tulare |
| Mno | — | Mono | Tuo | — | Tuolumne |
| Mnt | — | Monterey | Ven | — | Ventura |
| Nap | — | Napa | Yol | — | Yolo |
| Nev | — | Nevada | Yub | — | Yuba |

# Glossary

*Acheulian:* Named after the French town of St. Acheul, Old World lithic assemblages typified by hand axes; dated circa 1,000,000 to 60,000 B.P. in Africa, Europe, and southwest Asia.

*Adaptation:* Cultural mechanisms by which a society relates successfully to its effective environment.

*Alluvial fan:* A fan-shaped deposit of alluvium.

*Alluvium:* Sediments (gravel, sand, silt, etc.) deposited by a stream.

*Altithermal:* A warm, dry climate period during the mid-Holocene, dated circa 8000–2900 B.P.

*Amino-acid (racemization) dating:* An experimental method for determining the age of organic material based on the rate of amino-acid conversion (racemization) from L- to D-isomers. L-isomers occur in the proteins of living tissue. After death, over time, some of the L forms gradually are converted to D-isomers. Dating is accomplished by measuring the D:L ratio (which increases with age) in a given fossil.

*Anathermal:* The earliest Holocene climatic age, dated circa 11,000 to 8000 B.P., in western North America; a cool, moist postglacial period that became progressively warmer.

*Anthropology:* The scientific study of human cultures and physical traits; includes archaeology, ethnology, linguistics, biological anthropology, and other subdisciplines.

*Archaeology:* The branch of anthropology devoted to the scientific study of past cultures through their material remains. Archaeology seeks to describe and explain the nature and evolution of cultural systems.

*Arrastra:* A drag-stone mill for pulverizing mineral ore. Heavy, rough stones, turned within a circular enclosure by water power or animals, ground auriferous quartz during the Gold Rush.

*Arroyo:* A usually dry gully.

*Artifact:* Any product of human cultural activity; more specifically, any tools, weapons, artworks, etc., found in archaeological contexts.

*Aspartic-acid dating:* See *Amino-acid dating.*

*Aspect:* (1) The exposure or direction of a slope; e.g., that part of a hill sloping southward would be its south aspect. (2) In California, a grouping of similar or related facies or phases.

*Asphaltum:* Tar or bitumen naturally occurring at the surface. The Indians used it as an adhesive, for caulking, as a mastic for appliqué work, and for joining parts of a composite artifact.

*Assemblage:* The complete inventory of artifacts from a single, defined archaeological unit (such as a stratum or component).

*Atlatl:* An Aztec term for spear-thrower; a wooden device with a handle at one end and at the other a hook or spur that fits into a concavity at the proximal end of a dart (light throwing spear) shaft. The atlatl increases missile velocity by improving leverage during the cast. Atlatls were probably used in California from earlier than 10,000 B.P. until their gradual replacement by the bow and arrow after circa 1500 B.P. (see Hester *et al.* 1974).

*Auriferous:* Gold-bearing (ore); in the Sierra Nevada, most auriferous gravels are from 40 to 70 million years old.

*Band:* A small, loosely organized social group composed of several families.

*Barb:* A sharp projection on a harpoon, arrow point, etc., designed to impede removal of the weapon point from its target.

*Basalt:* A dense, fine-grained, tough extrusive igneous rock; a common material in California lava flows. Indians chipped basalt into knives, points, scrapers, and other implements.

*Base:* The proximal end of a knife or projectile point; bases may be concave, straight, convex, etc.

*Batholith:* An intrusive igneous rock mass, usually granitic, extending over an area larger than 100 km². The Sierra Nevada is an uplifted batholith.

*Bedrock milling station:* An outcrop of bedrock containing one or more mortar cups, milling slicks (bedrock "metates"), gyratory mills, or other features related to food grinding or crushing.

*Bedrock mortar:* A mortar cup in a bedrock outcrop.

*Biface:* Any stone artifact worked (flaked) on both the obverse and reverse faces. Most projectile points are bifaces.

*Bipolar flaking:* A distinctive type of percussion flaking in which a blow is struck against the top of a pebble or core resting on a hard "anvil" stone; this causes simultaneous flaking from both ends and results in flakes and flake scars peculiar to the method.

*Blade:* (1) A narrow, parallel-sided stone flake, struck from a prepared core; usually more than twice as long as wide. (2) The distal or "body" part of a projectile point or knife. (3) An exceptionally large biface.

*B.P.:* Before Present; by convention, before A.D. 1950.

*Breccia:* Angular rock and/or bone fragments naturally cemented together.

*Budding:* The movement of a group (often a family or lineage) to a new settlement away from the "parent" community; usually a result of excessive population at the older settlement.

*Burial:* Human remains disposed of by interment. Burials may be *simple* (containing the remains of one person) or *complex* (containing the remains of two or more individuals), *primary* (including the remains as originally interred) or *secondary* (where a reinterment follows a temporary disposal elsewhere).

*Burial orientation:* The direction or alignment of the body at the time of interment, specifically the direction toward which the head is positioned.

*Burin:* A small flaked-stone tool with a chisel-like cutting edge formed by snapping or retouching a blade or flake. Burins were often used to work bone, antler, ivory, or wood.

*$^{14}C$ (dating):* See *Carbon-14 dating.*

*Cairn:* A pile of rocks, daub, millingstones, and so forth; often used to cover a burial or protect valuables.

*Calcite:* A calcareous precipitate ($CaCO_3$) that may form stalactites or dripstone in caves. California Indians made ornaments and charmstones of calcite.

*Carbon-14 (radiocarbon or $^{14}C$) dating:* A method for determining the age of organic material by measuring the extent to which the radioactive isotope carbon-14 ($^{14}C$) has decayed into stable nitrogen-14 ($^{14}N$), comparing the observed $^{14}C$ fraction with the known half-life of 5568 ± 30 years (Michels 1973).

*Catchment:* The area around a settlment that can be exploited efficiently in the course of a day's work; usually an area within 1 or 2 hours' walk from a settlement. The best catchments incorporate both abundant and varied resources.

*Chalcedony:* A hard, light-colored, waxy-lustered rock composed of microscopic (cryptocrystalline) quartz. Knives, drills, projectile points, and so forth, were often made of chalcedony.

*Charmstone:* An elongate ground- and often polished-stone artifact, normally 5–20 cm in length, fashioned in a spindle, ovoid, phallic, plumb bob, or other shape; may be grooved or plain, perforate or imperforate; often found with burials. The prominence of charmstones in marshy regions has been noted. Their function as hunting charms, bolas stones, shamanistic gear, and so forth, is uncertain.

*Chellean:* Named after the French village of Chelles, an obsolescent term for Old World hand-axe industries.

*Chert:* A flintlike rock composed of chalcedony with variable amounts of clay and other impurities; commonly selected as a raw material for flaked-stone tools.

*Chiefdom:* A form of social organization in which (1) individual status is, at least partly, ascribed on the basis of heredity, and (2) political authority is vested in a chief who is typically responsible for redistributing goods and services within the community and for maintaining political and economic ties with outside groups.

*Chopper:* A large, often crude pebble, cobble, or core tool percussion-flaked to form an axe-like cutting edge along part of its margin; used for diverse chopping and cleaving work.

*Clactonian:* An assemblage of large flake tools without hand axes from southern England, assigned to the Holstein Interglacial age of circa 200,000 years ago.

*Clovis point:* A concave-base, lanceolate projectile point and/or knife, 4–12 cm long, with characteristic bifacial flutes extending about half the length of the artifact; most are ≈12,000–11,000 years old.

*Collagen:* A fibrous protein and the main organic component of bone. Collagen is the bone fraction most reliable for $^{14}$C dating.

*Comal:* A shallow, relatively flat griddle or frying pan made of steatite or baked clay.

*Complex:* A patterned grouping of similar artifact assemblages from two or more sites, presumed to represent an archaeological culture.

*Component:* A site or stratum within a site representing the activities of one cultural group during a relatively brief interval of time. (An exception would be a component resulting from the interaction of two or more groups at a single site.) Similar or related components within a locality or region comprise a phase.

*Coprolite:* Ancient, desiccated excrement.

*Core:* A cobble or smaller rock from which flakes or blades are removed; the core may be used as a tool as well as a source of flakes.

*Cremation:* Disposal of the dead by burning; a feature consisting of ash and small pieces of burned human bones and teeth.

*Cross-dating:* Inferring the age of one artifact by comparison with an artifact of the same type previously dated elsewhere.

*Cultigen:* A plant species being cultivated.

*Culture:* (1) The nonbiological and socially transmitted system of concepts, institutions, behavior, and materials by which a society adapts to its effective natural and human environment. (2) Similar or related assemblages of approximately the same age from a single locality or district, thought to represent the activities of one social group.

*Culture history:* The archaeological sequence of cultural activity through time, within a defined geographic space or relating to a particular group.

*Dart:* A projectile resembling a large arrow, normally 1.5–3.0 m long, designed to be cast with the aid of an atlatl.

*Datum point:* A reference point on an archaeological site from which measurements are taken and to which all finds are related by way of horizontal and vertical mapping.

*Daub:* Mud or clay packed onto a framework of poles and sticks as a construction method in semi-arid and desert regions; hardened daub sometimes preserves the impressions of the structural framework.

*Débitage:* Lithic refuse or debris produced during flaked-stone tool manufacture.

*Demography:* The study of human populations with particular reference to their size, density, composition, and distribution.

*Dendrochronology:* Dating by reference to tree rings and their distinctive ring-width patterns through time.

*Dental hypoplasia:* Defects, such as pits and grooves, of the dental crown enamel resulting from disruption of tooth development; thought to be caused by disease and malnutrition.

*Desert pavement:* A pavement-like veneer of rocks and/or pebbles on a flat desert surface. The desert pavement is created and sustained by the alternate wetting and drying of the uppermost soil horizon, a process that causes small stones to "float" to the surface.

*Desert varnish:* A dark, manganese- and iron-rich coating on exposed rock surfaces in dry regions. Associated with the dark layer is an orange coating that develops in contact with soil on the bottom of desert pavement stones. Clay minerals comprise more than 70% of the varnish. Desert varnish may hold potential for relative age dating.

*Dialect:* The variety of a language spoken by all members of a speech community; languages may include many, mutually intelligible dialects.

*Diffusion:* The transmission of concepts or artifacts from one cultural setting to another without population movement; the principal mechanism by which a culture acquires new traits.

*District:* "The geographic space, normally larger than a locality but smaller than a region, which exhibits a significant degree of total cultural conformity among its constituent components. The district is the basic spatial unit of analysis in that phases, the basic temporal units, are coterminous with district boundaries. Only one phase exists in one district at any one time" (Fredrickson 1973:95). In late prehistoric and early protohistoric times, districts largely coincided with language territories in California.

*Dolichocephalic:* Having a head width less than 75% of the head length, that is, having a cephalic index below 75; "long-headed."

*Ecotone:* The juncture between two biotic communities (e.g., grassland and forest). Ecotones offer more biotic diversity than "pure" communities because they contain species from both (or all) of the communities at the interface—the "edge effect." Ecotones were ideal places for aboriginal settlement because they afforded optimum resource exploitation.

*Egalitarian society:* A society in which all persons have equal access to resources. In an egalitarian society, status, wealth, and prestige are acquired through individual effort rather than by birthright.

*Eolian deposit:* Sediments (silt, sand, etc.) deposited by wind action.

*Ethnography:* The direct anthropological study of living human groups or the study of recent, historically documented groups.

*Eustacy:* Worldwide sea level fluctuations caused by the melting or accumulation of continental glaciers.

*Exogamy:* Marriage outside of any designated social unit.

*Facies:* A group of closely related components; phase.

*Feature:* A large, complex artifact or part of a site such as a hearth, cairn, housepit, rock alignment, or activity area.

*Flexed burial:* A human interment in the fetal position, that is, with the legs and arms bent and drawn toward the ribs.

*Fluted point:* A projectile point or knife distinguished by a longitudinal channel (flute) flaked upward from the base on one or both sides.

*Foliate:* Leaf-shaped, as applied to flaked-stone artifacts; having a form like that of a willow leaf.

*Folsom point:* A concave-base, lanceolate projectile point 2–7 cm long, with broad flutes extending nearly the full length on both sides. Most Folsom points appear to be 10,000–11,000 years old.

*Foramen magnum:* The large aperture at the base of the skull (in the occipital bone) through which the spinal cord passes.

*Glabella:* A flattened triangular area between the two superciliary ridges (brow ridges) on a human skull.

*Glottochronology (lexicostatistics):* A method based on the statistical comparison of word lists from two genetically related languages, which calculates the elapsed time since the languages diverged and became separate (see Gudschinsky 1964).

*Gyratory mill:* A mortar-like milling device in which foods or other products are ground by the rotation of a pestle and its abrasion against the inner wall of the mill.

*Hammerstone:* Usually a hard, tough, fist-sized rock used as a hammer to work flint, drive wedges, break shells, splinter bones, etc. Hammerstones in central and southern California tend not to be shaped except by battering while in use.

*Harris lines:* Transverse lines in long bones, detectable in radiographs, thought to be the result of temporary disruption of growth caused by disease or malnutrition.

*Hearth:* A feature containing ash, charcoal, burned rock, or other evidence of a fire kindled by people.

*Hematite (ochre):* An earthy iron oxide ($Fe_2O_3$), usually red to brown in color, used by the Indians in graves and as a pigment.

*Historic:* Refers to human activities recorded in writing, on film or tape, or by other formal documentary means. In each of California's regions, the historic period began with the advent of written records.

*Holocene (Recent):* The post-Pleistocene geologic epoch characterized by fluctuating but generally moderate climates and modern faunal assemblages; dated circa 11,000 B.P. to the present.

*Hopper mortar:* A mortar consisting of a stone base upon which rested a sturdy, conical basketry hopper without a bottom. The hopper was either glued to the base with asphaltum or pressed against it during milling; a pestle completed the device.

*Horizon:* A primarily spatial continuity represented by cultural traits and assemblages whose nature and mode of occurrence permit the assumption of a broad and rapid spread (Willey and Phillips 1958:32).

*House floor:* Compacted earth, post molds, hearths, and/or other associated features representing the floor of a structure.

*Housepit:* A depression of any shape representing the former location of a partly subsurface (semisubterranean) structure.

*Ideotechnic:* Ideotechnic artifacts are those that function primarily in the ideological realm (Binford 1962); ceremonial objects or special grave goods are ideotechnic artifacts.

*Innominate bones:* The bones of the pelvis.

*In situ:* In place; applied to archaeological remains found in their original, undisturbed location or position.

*Intaglio:* A design or motif cut, scraped, or gouged into some medium; a negative design as contrasted with relief work. Petroglyphs and the motifs made by removing stones from the desert floor are examples of intaglio art.

*Isostacy:* "Rebound" or alternate raising or lowering of land surfaces relative to sea level, brought about by fluctuations in the mass of continental glaciers.

*Knapping:* Manufacturing stone tools by controlled flaking.

*Lacustrine:* Related to a lake.

*Lacustrine deposits:* Sediments accumulated in a lake.

*Language:* A group of one or more mutually intelligible dialects.

*Language family:* A group of two or more languages that developed from a single ancestral language; the latter is called the proto-language for that family (Whistler 1979a).

*Language isolate:* A language that has not been determined to be genetically related to any other language or languages, even though it may be related distantly to some larger linguistic family (Whistler 1979a).

*Language stock:* A grouping of languages or language families that are suspected, but not proven, to be genetically related (Whistler 1979a).

*Lexicostatistics:* See *Glottochronology.*

*Lichenometry:* The study of lichen growth rates to determine the minimum age of the rock surface to which the lichen adheres; lichenometry may have potential value for dating petroglyphs, and it has realized applications in the dating of glacial moraines.

*Locality:* A geographical space small enough to permit the assumption of "complete" cultural homogeneity at any given time (Willey and Phillips 1958). In California, the locality corresponds to the area occupied by a few closely related tribelets. Several related localities may comprise a district.

*Lower Paleolithic:* The stage of Old World prehistory characterized in part by simple core and pebble tools with rare use of flakes and no "refined" artifacts; often associated with *Homo erectus* and other pre-Neanderthal hominids. Lower Paleolithic technologies persisted until 100,000 to 80,000 years ago in many parts of Europe and Africa.

*Macroband:* A temporary aggregation of two or more bands, united briefly (e.g., seasonally) for a common purpose such as game drives.

*Magnesite:* A metamorphic rock ($MgCO_3$) apparently known aboriginally only in Lake County. Chunks of this rock were baked, changing the color from white to rich brown or coral red, and fashioned into beads and cylinders of great value to the Indians.

*Mano:* From the Spanish *la mano* ("hand"), a loaf-shaped handstone used for grinding seeds, pigments, and so forth, on a metate or millingstone.

*Matrix:* The archaeological deposit surrounding an artifact or feature.

*Maul:* A heavy, shaped-stone hammer, usually made to be gripped rather than hafted; used to drive wedges or stakes and for other tasks.

*Medithermal:* The third climatic age of the Holocene epoch, dated circa 2900 B.P. until the present; a period characterized by moderate precipitation and moderate temperatures in the western United States.

*Metate:* From the Aztec *metatl*, a stone slab upon which corn and other grains are milled with a mano (worked with a push–pull motion). Metates of Mexican influence are usually rectangular slabs of vesicular basalt with three legs. (Compare with millingstone.)

*Midden:* A deposit marking a former habitation site and containing such materials as discarded artifacts, bone and shell, food refuse, charcoal, ash, rock, human remains, structural remnants, and other cultural leavings.

*Millingstone:* An amorphous or roughly shaped stone slab upon which seeds and other plant products are ground with the aid of a mano. The milling basin of the slab may be ovoid to round, depending on the elliptical or rotary motion of the handstone. (Compare with metate.)

*Miocene:* The middle epoch of the Cenozoic, approximately 26 to 5 million years ago.

*Moiety:* One of two basic, complementary divisions of a tribe; membership in a moiety is inherited from one parent.

*Moraine:* Rocky debris deposited by a glacier.

*Mortar:* A stone or wooden bowl-like artifact in which seeds, berries, meat, and other products are ground or pulverized with a pestle. Mortars occur in bedrock outcrops and as portable items.

*Neoglacial:* The most recent episode of montane glaciation in the Far West, dated circa 600 to 50 B.P.

*Nightstick fracture:* Fracture of the forearm (radius or ulna) caused by the blow of a club; usually received when the victim parries a blow intended for the head.

*Obsidian:* Natural volcanic glass. This was the premier material for chipped-stone artifacts in California, where it was obtained from no less than 25 separate sources.

*Obsidian hydration dating:* A method for determining the age of obsidian artifacts or déibitage by measuring the thickness of a specimen's hydration rim (layer of water penetration) and comparing the rim depth with the established hydration rate for the particular climatic–geographic area (effective hydration temperature) and type of obsidian.

*Ochre:* See *Hematite.*

*Olla:* A globular clay or stone vessel with a small mouth, often used as a water container.

*Paleolithic:* The Old Stone Age of the Eastern Hemisphere; a cultural stage typified by stone cobble, core, flake, and, ultimately, blade tools.

*Paleopathology:* The study of ancient diseases.

*Paleosol:* An ancient soil remnant; fossil soil.

*Palynology:* The study of fossil pollen for the purpose of reconstructing past vegetation distributions and climatic conditions.

*Paste:* The basic clay element of pottery.

*Patrilineality:* Reckoning descent through the paternal line.

*Patrilocality:* The residence pattern of married couples living with or near the husband's father.

*Pattern:* An adaptive mode extending across one or more regions, characterized by particular technological skills and devices, by particular economic modes (including participation in trade networks and practices regarding wealth), and by particular mortuary and ceremonial practices. The pattern is a cultural unit lacking temporal implications (Fredrickson 1973:7–8).

*Percussion-flaking:* The manufacture of stone artifacts by removing flakes with blows struck by a stone, antler, or bone "hammer."

*Pestle:* An elongate, often cylindrical stone or wooden artifact used to pulverize food products and other stuff in a mortar.

*Petroglyph:* A design or motif pecked or scratched into a rock surface; usually unpainted rock art.

*Phase:* A distinctive archaeological unit representing a fairly brief interval of time within a locality or region. A phase may be a single component at one side or a prolonged occupation of numerous related sites (Willey and Phillips 1958).

*Pictograph:* A design or motif painted on a rock surface; painted rock art.

*Playa:* A dry lake bed or floor of a desert basin lacking external drainage.

*Pleistocene:* A late Cenozoic geologic epoch characterized by fluctuating, generally cool climates—often accompanied by glaciation—and distinctive faunal assemblages; dated from 3 million years ago until circa 11,000 B.P.

*Pliocene:* The late Cenozoic geologic epoch following the Miocene and preceding the Pleistocene; dated from circa 5 million until 3 million years ago.

*Pluton:* A mass of igneous rock intruded as a magma into older material. Plutons having surface areas larger than about 100 km² are known as batholiths (q.v.).

*Pluvial lake:* A lake formed during a pluvial period; in this book, the term refers specifically to late Pleistocene and early Holocene lakes of western North America.

*Pluvial period:* A time of increased rainfall and/or decreased evaporation in nonglaciated areas, often coeval with periods of ice buildup elsewhere.

*Post mold:* An earthen feature representing the *in situ* butt of a post used in any form of construction.

*Prehistory:* The archaeological record of nonliterate cultures; the cultural past before the advent of written records.

*Preinterment burning:* The partial or complete burning of artifacts in a grave prior to the burial of human remains. Often the body was placed in the grave while the fire was still burning.

*Presidio:* A Spanish or Mexican fortification garrisoned by soldiers protecting civilian colonial outposts such as missions and pueblos.

*Pressure-flaking:* The manufacture of stone artifacts by removing flakes with pressure applied with a bone, antler, or metal knapping tool.

*Projectile point:* A sharp tip (usually stone) affixed to the business end of a spear, lance, dart, or arrow.

*Proto-language:* The ancestral language from which two or more languages in a family were derived.

*Pueblo:* A Spanish or Mexican hamlet or town.

*Quaternary:* The youngest period of geologic time, composed of the Pleistocene and Holocene epochs. The Quaternary Period follows the Tertiary and includes the most recent 3 million years of the Cenozoic era.

*Ramada:* A structure, often without walls, consisting of a relatively flat roof or sunshade supported by posts.

*Rancho:* A Spanish or Mexican ranch, particularly one of the vast holdings acquired by land grant during the 1830s and 1840s.

*Region:* An archaeological spatial unit smaller than an area and larger than a locality or district; the region usually includes several localities and/or districts. General, but not complete, cultural homogeneity is found within a region at a given time.

*Retouch:* The removal by pressure- or percussion-flaking of small chips from the working edge of a stone tool in order to sharpen it or alter the edge shape.

*Rockshelter:* A shallow cave or rock overhang, normally wider than it is deep, providing shelter from the elements.

*Scarp:* A line of cliffs produced by erosion or faulting, such as the steep eastern wall of the Sierra Nevada.

*Scraper:* Any of the myriad tool forms used chiefly for such scraping tasks as stripping bark, planing wood, removing scarf skin from hides, etc. Flakes and blades, less often cores, served as scrapers; in California scrapers of bone are uncommon.

*Seriation:* The ordering or arrangement of items in a series according to their degree of similarity to one another; seriation may give chronologic order.

*Serrate:* Having sawlike teeth along the edge(s).

*Shaped mortar:* A portable stone mortar with the exterior wall and rim shaped by pecking or grinding.

*Sherd:* A broken piece of pottery; potsherd.

*Sierra:* Spanish for "mountain range." Sierra Nevada means "Snowy Range."

*Site:* The location of past cultural activity; a defined space with more or less continuous archaeological evidence.

*Slip:* A mixture of fine clay and water applied to the surface of pottery.

*Sociotechnic:* Sociotechnic artifacts are those having their primary function in the social sphere of a cultural system (Binford 1962).

*Stage:* An integrative archaeological concept representing broad patterns of technology, economy, demography, and social organization shared by cultures within a region or area (Willey and Phillips 1958).

*Steatite (soapstone):* Hydrous magnesium silicate ($H_2Mg_3Si_4O_{12}$); a very soft and easily carved metamorphic rock valued by the Indians as a raw material for bowls, beads, and artwork. Its ability to withstand heat without cracking made steatite an ideal material for cooking vessels, tobacco pipes, and so forth.

*Sterile:* Devoid of any archaeological evidence; noncultural (as applied to strata or deposits).

*Stratigraphy:* The study of cultural and natural strata or layers in archaeological and geological deposits, particularly with the aim of determining the relative age of strata.

*Stratum:* A layer of material deposited by cultural or geological processes.

*Strigil:* A long, curved bladelike implement, such as a polished mammal rib, used as a sweat scraper.

*Tang:* A projection or stem intended to facilitate hafting an artifact such as a projectile point or knife.

*Technomic:* Technomic artifacts are those designed to cope directly with the physical environment (Binford 1962); weapons and food-processing implements are technomic artifacts.

*Tephra:* Volcanic ash. Ash fall from a single eruption may be used to show the contemporaneity of deposits at different sites.

*Tephrachronology:* Dating archaeological or geological deposits by reference to volcanic ash found therein.

*Tertiary:* The period of geologic time encompassing the Paleocene to

Pliocene epochs of the Cenozoic era. The Tertiary period lasted from 70 million until 3 million years ago.

*Thermoluminescence dating:* Thermoluminescence (TL) is the emission of light from crystalline solids, including ceramics, when heated. Over time, radioactive impurities cause ionization within ceramic materials. When the ceramic is heated (as in a laboratory) electrons and other charge carriers are released, their excess voltage appearing to sensitive instruments as light, measurable in photons. The amount of light emitted varies in proportion to the age of the ceramic, thus providing a basis for dating (Michels 1972).

*Tioga:* The last stage of Pleistocene glaciation in the Sierra Nevada, dated circa 30,000–10,000 B.P.

*Tradition:* A way of life or consistent patterning of technology, subsistence practices, and ecological adaptation that persists through a relatively long interval of time.

*Trait:* Any definable element or feature of culture suitable for comparative purposes.

*Tribelet:* The basic, autonomous, self-governing, and independent sociopolitical group in aboriginal California; an aggregation of several villages under the authority of a single chief (Kroeber 1925).

*Tufa:* Calcium carbonate ($CaCO_3$) deposited in limestone caves or as incrustations around calcareous water sources; also called dripstone or travertine.

*Wattle and daub:* A type of construction characterized by the plastering of a thick layer of mud or clay (daub) over a framework of poles or sticks (wattle).

# References

Abrams, D.
  1968     Salvage investigations at the Little Pico site: 4-SLO-175. In N. N. Leonard, III, *Archaeological salvage of the Pico Creek and Little Pico Creek sites.* Sacramento: Report to the California Department of Parks and Recreation.

Adam, D. P.
  1967     Late-Pleistocene and Recent palynology in the central Sierra Nevada, California. In E. J. Cushing and H. E. Wright, Jr., eds., *Quaternary paleoecology:*275–301. New Haven: Yale University Press.
  1974     Palynological applications of principal component and cluster analyses. Washington, D.C.: *United States Geological Survey, Journal of Research* **2**(6):727–741.

Adams, D. B.
  1979     The cheetah: Native American. *Science* **205**(4411):1155–1158.

Adams, J. C., and D. A. Fredrickson
  1978     An archaeological investigation of CA-Son-84, Santa Rosa, Sonoma County, California. Manuscript No. S-1163. Rohnert Park: Anthropological Studies Center, Sonoma State University.

Adovasio, J. M., J. D. Gunn, J. Donahue, R. Stuckenrath, J. Guilday, and K. Lord
  1979     Meadowcroft Rockshelter—retrospect 1977: Part 1. *North American Archaeologist* **1**(1):3–44.

Aginsky, B. W.
  1943     Culture element distributions, XXIV: Central Sierra. Berkeley: *University of California Anthropological Records* **8**(4).

Aikens, C. M.
  1970     Hogup Cave. Salt Lake City: *University of Utah Anthropological Papers* 93.
  1975a    *Earliest human occupation west of the Rockies.* Dallas: Paper presented at the 40th Annual Meeting of the Society for American Archaeology.
  1975b    Personal communication (to Michael J. Moratto) regarding California archaeology. Eugene: University of Oregon.
  1976     Current research, California/Great Basin. *American Antiquity* **41**(4):560–561.
  1977     Interdisciplinary models and Great Basin prehistory: A comment on current orientations. Reno: *Desert Research Institute Publications in the Social Sciences* 12:211–213.
  1978     The Far West. In J. D. Jennings, ed., *Ancient Native Americans:*131–181. San Francisco: Freeman.

Aker, R.
  1978     *Sir Francis Drake at Drakes Bay.* Palo Alto: Drake Navigators Guild.

Aker, R., and E. Von der Porten
  1979     *Rediscovering Portus Novae Albionis: Francis Drake's California harbor.* Palo Alto: Drake Navigators Guild.

Allen, J. D.
  1951     Snell's Cave in Tuolumne County. Stanford: *Monthly Report of the Stanford Grotto, National Speleological Society* 2(2).

Amsden, C. A.
  1935     The Pinto Basin artifacts. Los Angeles: *Southwest Museum Papers* 9:33–51.
  1937     The Lake Mohave artifacts. In E. W. C. Campbell, W. H. Campbell, E. Antevs, C. A. Amsden, J. A. Barbieri, and F. A. Bode, The archeology of Pleistocene Lake Mohave: A symposium. Los Angeles: *Southwest Museum Papers* 11:51–98.

Anderson, E. N., Jr.
1978     A revised, annotated bibliography of the Chumash and their predecessors. Socorro: *Ballena Press Anthropological Papers* 11.

Andrews, S. B.
1977a    Analyzing pictographs—communication and terminology. *Kern County Archaeological Society Journal* **1**:29–32.
1977b    Pictographs of the Tübatulabal. *Kern County Archaeological Society Journal* **1**:33–42.

Angel, J. L.
1966     Early skeletons from Tranquillity, California. Washington, D.C.: *Smithsonian Contributions to Anthropology* 2(1):1–19.

Anonymous
1873     Note regarding the discovery of fossil mammoth teeth on Santa Rosa Island. San Francisco: *California Academy of Sciences, Proceedings* **5**:152.
1891     Colorado Desert. *San Francisco Chronicle*, June 30:2.
1938     Where the vanished Yokuts buried their dead. *Standard Oil Bulletin*, February.
1975     "Sunnyvale Girl" discovery and dating. Northridge: *Society for California Archaeology Newsletter* 9(5–6):15.
1977a    Earlier Americans. *Scientific American* **236**(6):61–62.
1977b    Early man confirmed in North America 40,000 years ago. Washington, D.C.: *Science News* **111**(13):196.
1978     40,000 years in North America: Stone tools trace humans. Escondido: *Times Advocate*, March 6:A–6.
1981a    Awl in a day's work. Turlock: Department of Anthropology, California State College, Stanislaus, *Bedrock Bulletin* **6**(1):6.
1981b    *Moaning Cavern*. Vallecito: Leaflet for visitors published by the owners of Moaning Cavern.
1982     Scotts Valley outrage. *Society for California Archaeology Newsletter* **16**(1):5–6.

Antevs, E.
1937     Age of the Lake Mojave Culture. In E. W. C. Campbell, W. H. Campbell, E. Antevs, C. A. Amsden, J. A. Barbieri, and F. A. Bode, The archeology of Pleistocene Lake Mojave: A Symposium. Los Angeles: *Southwest Museum Papers* 11:45–50.
1938     Postpluvial climatic variations in the Southwest. *Bulletin of the American Meteorological Society* **19**:190–193.
1940     Age of artifacts below peat bed in Lower Klamath Lake, California. Washington, D.C.: *Carnegie Institution of Washington, Year Book* 39:307–309.
1948     Climatic changes and pre-white man. Salt Lake City: *University of Utah Bulletin* 38(20):168–191.
1952     Climatic history and the antiquity of man in California. Berkeley: *University of California Archaeological Survey Reports* 16:23–31.
1953a    Age of the Farmington Complex stone artifacts. Berkeley: *University of California Archaeological Survey Manuscripts* 167.
1953b    On division of the last 20,000 years. Berkeley: *University of California Archaeological Survey Reports* 22:5–8.
1953c    The Postpluvial or Neothermal. Berkeley: *University of California Archaeological Survey Reports* 22:9–23.
1955     Geologic-climatic dating in the West. *American Antiquity* **20**(4):317–335.

Archaeological Consulting and Research Services (ACRS)
1975     *Final report: Archaeological reconnaissance of the Fiberboard Exchange—the Basin.* San Francisco: Report to the U.S. Forest Service, California Region.
1977     *Report of the Bear Compartment archaeological reconnaissance.* San Francisco: Report to the U.S. Forest Service, California Region.

Arguelles, M. R., with M. J. Moratto
  1982   *Overview of cultural resources, Kern and Pixley National Wildlife Refuges, California.* Portland: Report to the U.S. Fish and Wildlife Service.
Arnold, A. B.
  1957   Archaeological investigations on Federal lands in Martis Valley, California. Manuscript. Sacramento: Department of Anthropology, California State University, Sacramento.
Aschmann, H. H.
  1958   Great Basin climates in relation to human occupance. Berkeley: *University of California Archaeological Survey Reports* 42:23–40.
Asturias, M.
  1971   A brief account of archaeology at 4-SMa-110. San Francisco: *Treganza Anthropology Museum Papers* 8:49–55.
Atwater, B. F., and C. W. Hedel
  1976   Distribution of seed plants with respect to tide levels and water salinity in the natural tidal marshes of the northern San Francisco Bay estuary. Menlo Park: *United States Geological Survey, Open-File Reports* 76–389.
Atwater, B. F., E. J. Helley, and C. W. Hedel
  1977   Late Quaternary depositional history, Holocene sea level changes, and vertical crustal movement, southern San Francisco Bay, California. Washington, D.C.: *United States Geological Survey, Professional Papers* 1014.
Avery, B. P.
  1873   Chips from an Indian workshop. *Overland Monthly* 2(6):489–493. (Reprinted.
  (1953)   Berkeley: *University of California Archaeological Survey Reports* 21:31–36.
Axelrod, D. I.
  1967a   Geologic history of the California insular flora. In R. N. Philbrick, ed., *Proceedings of the Symposium on the Biology of the California Islands*:267–315. Santa Barbara: Santa Barbara Botanic Garden.
  1967b   Quaternary extinctions of large mammals. Berkeley: *University of California Publications in Geological Sciences* 74:1–42.
Ayala, J.
  1775   Letter dated November 9, 1775, to His Excellency, Antonio María Bucareli. In J.
  (1971)   Galvin, ed., *The first Spanish entry into San Francisco Bay, 1775*:91–92. San Francisco: John Howell Books.
Ayres, W. O.
  1882   The ancient man of Calaveras. *American Naturalist* **16**:845–854.
Bada, J. L., and P. M. Helfman
  1975   Amino acid racemization dating of fossil bones. *World Archaeology* **7**:160–173.
Bada, J. L., and P. M. Masters
  1978   The antiquity of human beings in the Americas: Evidence derived from amino acid racemization dating of PaleoIndian skeletons. Fullerton: *Society for California Archaeology, Occasional Papers in Method and Theory in California Archaeology* 2:15–24.
Bada, J. L., R. A. Schroeder, and G. F. Carter
  1974   New evidence for the antiquity of man in North America deduced from aspartic acid racemization. *Science* **184**:791–793.
Bailey, E. H., ed.
  1966   Geology of northern California. Sacramento: *California Division of Mines and Geology Bulletin* 190.
Baker, S. M.
  1978   *Report on the Fort Mason archaeological test excavations.* San Francisco: Report to the National Park Service.

Baldwin, M. A.

1971a  *Cultural continuity from Chumash to Salina_ Indians in California.* M.A. thesis. San Diego: Department of Anthropology, San Diego State University.

1971b  Archaeological evidence of cultural continuity from Chumash to Salinan Indians in California. San Luis Obispo: *San Luis Obispo County Archaeological Society Occasional Papers* 6.

Balls, E. K.

1962  *Early uses of California plants.* Berkeley: University of California Press.

Barbour, M. G., and J. Major, eds.

1977  *Terrestrial vegetation of California.* New York: Wiley.

Barker, J. P., and S. H. Schlanger

1974  *An archaeological survey of Segments D and E of the proposed Kaiparowitz transmission line route.* Rosemead: Report to Southern California Edison Company.

Barker, M., E. Burton, and W. M. Childers

1973  A preliminary report on a burial excavated in the Yuha Desert of Imperial County, California. Manuscript. Riverside: Bureau of Land Management.

Barrett, S. A.

1903  A new Moquelumnan territory in California. *American Anthropologist* **5**:730.

1908a  The ethnogeography of the Pomo and neighboring Indians. Berkeley: *University of California Publications in American Archaeology and Ethnology* **6**(1):1–332.

1908b  The geography and dialects of the Miwok Indians. Berkeley: *University of California Publications in American Archaeology and Ethnology* **6**(2):333–368.

1908c  Pomo Indian basketry. Berkeley: *University of California Publications in American Archaeology and Ethnology* **7**(3):134–309.

1908d  Totemism among the Miwok Indians. *Journal of American Folklore* **21**:237.

1917  The Washo Indians. Milwaukee: *Bulletin of the Public Museum of the City of Milwaukee* **2**(1).

1919  Myths of the Southern Sierra Miwok. Berkeley: *University of California Publications in American Archaeology and Ethnology* 16(1):1–28.

1952  Material aspects of Pomo culture. Milwaukee: *Bulletin of the Public Museum of the City of Milwaukee* **20**(1–2):1–508.

Barrett, S. A., and E. W. Gifford

1933  Miwok material culture. Milwaukee: *Bulletin of the Public Museum of the City of Milwaukee* **2**(4).

Basgall, M. E.

1982  Archaeology and linguistics: Pomoan prehistory as viewed from northern Sonoma County, California. *Journal of California and Great Basin Anthropology* **4**(2):3–22.

Bateman, P. C.

1974  Model for the origin of Sierran granites. *California Geology* **27**(1):3–5.

Bateman, P. C., and C. Wahrhaftig

1966  Geology of the Sierra Nevada. San Francisco: *California Division of Mines and Geology Bulletin* **190:** 107–172.

Bauman, J.

1980  *Introduction to Pit River language and culture.* Anchorage: National Bilingual Materials Development Center, University of Alaska.

Bauman, J., and S. K. Silver

1975  *An areal survey of phonological processes in northern California languages.* San Francisco: Paper presented at the Annual Meeting of the American Anthropological Association.

Baumhoff, M. A.

1953  Carbonized basketry from the Thomas site. Berkeley: *University of California Archaeological Survey Reports* 19:9–11.

1955    Excavation of site Teh-1 (Kingsley Cave). Berkeley: *University of California Archaeological Survey Reports* 30:40–73.

1957a   An introduction to Yana archaeology. Berkeley: *University of California Archaeological Survey Reports* 40:1–61.

1957b   Catlow twine from central California. Berkeley: *University of California Archaeological Survey Reports* 38:1–5.

1958a   California Athabascan groups. Berkeley: *University of California Anthropological Records* 16(5):157–233.

1958b   Ecological determinants of population. Berkeley: *University of California Archaeological Survey Reports* 41:34–41.

1963    Ecological determinants of aboriginal California populations. Berkeley: *University of California Publications in American Archaeology and Ethnology* **49**(2):155–236.

1978    Environmental background. In R. F. Heizer, vol. ed., *Handbook of North American Indians, Vol. 8: California:*16–24. Washington, D.C.: Smithsonian Institution.

1980a   The evolution of Pomo society. *The Journal of California and Great Basin Anthropology* **2**(2):175–182.

1980b   *Warm Springs cultural resources study revised research design, investigation of prehistoric archaeological sites.* Rohnert Park: Anthropological Studies Center, Sonoma State University.

1981a   *Evolution of Pomo society.* Rohnert Park: Paper presented at the 1981 Hokan–Penutian conference at Sonoma State University, Rohnert Park.

1981b   Appendix A: North Coast Range point types. In *Cultural resource overview for the Mendocino National Forest and East Lake Planning Unit, BLM, California, Vol. 1: Ethnography and prehistory.* Willows: Report to the Mendocino National Forest.

Baumhoff, M. A., and J. S. Byrne
1959    Desert Side-notched points as a time marker in California. Berkeley: *University of California Archaeological Survey Reports* 48:32–65.

Baumhoff, M. A., and A. B. Elsasser
1956    Summary of archaeological survey and excavation in California. Berkeley: *University of California Archaeological Survey Reports* 33:1–27.

Baumhoff, M. A., and R. F. Heizer
1965    Postglacial climate and archaeology in the Desert West. In H. E. Wright, Jr., and D. C. Frey, eds., *The Quaternary of the United States:*697–707. Princeton: Princeton University Press.

Baumhoff, M. A., and J. J. Johnson
1969    Archaeological investigations at the Lorenzen site (Mod-250), Little Hot Springs Valley, Modoc County, California. Manuscript. Sacramento: Department of Anthropology, California State University, Sacramento.

Baumhoff, M. A., and D. L. Olmsted
1963    Palaihnihan: Radiocarbon support for glottochronology. *American Anthropologist* **65**(2):278–284.

1964    Notes on Palaihnihan culture history: Glottochronology and archaeology. Berkeley: *University of California Publications in Linguistics* 34:1–12.

Baumhoff, M. A., and R. I. Orlins
1979    An archaeological assay on Dry Creek, Sonoma County, California. Berkeley: *Contributions of the University of California Archaeological Research Facility* 40.

Baumler, M., and S. Carpenter
1982    *Archaeological investigations at El Portal.* Tucson: Western Archeological and Conservation Center, National Park Service.

Beals, R. L.
1933    Ethnology of the Nisenan. Berkeley: *University of California Publications in American Archaeology and Ethnology* **31**(6):335–410.

Beals, R. L., and J. A. Hester
1960    A new ecological typology of the California Indians. Philadelphia: *Acts of the International Congress of Anthropological and Ethnological Sciences* **5**:411–419.

Bean, L. J.
1960    The Wanakik Cahuilla. Los Angeles: *The Masterkey* **34**(3):111–120.
1972    *Mukat's people: The Cahuilla Indians of southern California.* Berkeley: University of California Press.
1976    Social organization in native California. In L. J. Bean and T. C. Blackburn, eds., *Native Californians: A theoretical retrospective:*99–123. Ramona: Ballena Press.
1978    Cahuilla. In R. F. Heizer, vol. ed., *Handbook of North American Indians, Vol. 8: California:*575–587. Washington, D.C.: Smithsonian Institution.

Bean, L. J., and T. F. King, eds.
1974    ?*Antap:* California Indian political and economic organization. Ramona: *Ballena Press Anthropological Papers* 2.

Bean, L. J., and H. W. Lawton
1973    Some explanations for the rise of cultural complexity in native California with comments on proto-agriculture and agriculture. Ramona: *Ballena Press Anthropological Papers* 1:i–xlvii.

Bean, L. J., and K. S. Saubel
1963    Cahuilla ethnobotanical notes: The aboriginal use of mesquite and screwbean. Los Angeles: *University of California, Los Angeles, Archaeological Survey Annual Report, 1962–1963:*51–75.
1972    *Temalpakh: Cahuilla Indian knowledge and use of plants.* Banning: Malki Museum Press.

Bean, L. J., and F. C. Shipek
1978    Luiseño. In R. F. Heizer, vol. ed., *Handbook of North American Indians, Vol. 8: California:*550–563. Washington, D.C.: Smithsonian Institution.

Bean, L. J., and C. R. Smith
1978a   Gabrielino. In R. F. Heizer, vol. ed., *Handbook of North American Indians, Vol. 8: California:*538–549. Washington, D.C.: Smithsonian Institution.
1978b   Serrano. In R. F. Heizer, vol. ed., *Handbook of North American Indians, Vol. 8: California:*570–574. Washington, D.C.: Smithsonian Institution.

Beardsley, R. K.
1942    Preliminary report on the excavation of the McClure site, CA-Mrn-266. Berkeley: *University of California Archaeological Survey Manuscripts* 116.
1946a   Miscellaneous notes and artifact distributions in San Francisco and Drakes Bay sites. *Berkeley: University of California Archaeological Survey Manuscripts* 48.
1946b   The Monterey Custom House flag pole: Archaeological findings. *California Historical Society Quarterly* **25**(3):204–218.
1948    Cultural sequences in central California archaeology. *American Antiquity* **14**(1):1–28.
1954    Temporal and areal relationships in central California archaeology. Berkeley: *University of California Archaeological Survey Reports* 24, 25.

Beardsley, R. K., and J. A. Bennyhoff
1952    Excavation notes for site CA-Sac-168, 1952. Berkeley: *University of California Archaeological Survey Manuscripts* 253.

Beatty, M. E.
1933    More Indian caves discovered. Yosemite National Park: *Yosemite Nature Notes* 12:7–8.

Beatty, W. C., R. L. Becker, and M. Crist
　1978　*Archaeological investigations of Squaw Leap for the Kerckhoff report, Fresno County.* San Francisco: Report to the Pacific Gas and Electric Company.
Beck, J. L.
　1970a　*The Fluted Point Tradition in the Far West.* Asilomar: Paper presented at the Annual Meeting of the Society for California Archaeology and the Southwestern Anthropological Association.
　1970b　Turtle-bone artifacts from Pinnacle Point Cave (4-Tuo-272), Tuolumne County, California. Davis: *University of California, Center for Archaeological Research at Davis, Publications* 2:1–8.
　1971　A chipped stone crescent from Tracy Lake, California. Los Angeles: *The Masterkey* **45**(4):154–156.
Beck, W. A., and Y. D. Haase
　1974　*Historical atlas of California.* Norman: University of Oklahoma Press.
Becker, G. F.
　1891　Antiquities from under Tuolumne Table Mountain in California. *Bulletin of the Geological Society of America* **2**:189–200.
Bedwell, S. F.
　1970　*Prehistory and environment of the pluvial Fork Rock Lake area of south-central Oregon.* Ph.D. dissertation. Eugene: Department of Anthropology, University of Oregon.
　1973　*Fort Rock Basin: Prehistory and environment.* Eugene: University of Oregon Books.
Beeler, M. S.
　1955　Saclan. *International Journal of American Linguistics* **21**:201–209.
　1959　Saclan once more. *International Journal of American Linguistics* **25**:67–68.
　1972　An extension of San Francisco Bay Costanoan? *International Journal of American Linguistics* **38**:49–54.
　1977　The sources for Esselen. Berkeley: *Proceedings of the Third Annual Meeting of the Berkeley Linguistics Society.*
　1978　Esselen. Banning: *Journal of California Anthropology Papers in Linguistics.*
Begole, R. S.
　1973　An archaeological survey in the Anza-Borrego Desert State Park: 1973 preliminary report. *Pacific Coast Archaeological Society Quarterly* **9**(2):27–55.
　1974　Archaeological phenomena in the California desert. *Pacific Coast Archaeological Society Quarterly* **10**(2):51–70.
Belous, R. E.
　1953　The central California chronological sequence reexamined. *American Antiquity* **18**(4):341–353.
Benedict, R.
　1924　A brief sketch of Serrano culture. *American Anthropologist* **26**:368–369.
Bennyhoff, J. A.
　1950　Californian fish spears and harpoons. Berkeley: *University of California Anthropological Records* **9**(4):295–337.
　1952　*An archaeological survey of selected areas of Yosemite National Park.* Report to the National Park Service, San Francisco. Berkeley: University of California.
　1953a　High altitude occupation in the Yosemite National Park region. Berkeley: *University of California Archaeological Survey Reports* 21:32–33.
　1953b　*Preliminary report on archaeological investigations in Yosemite National Park, September, 1953.* Report to the National Park Service, San Francisco. Berkeley: University of California.
　1956　An appraisal of the archaeological resources of Yosemite National Park, Berkeley: *University of California Archaeological Survey Reports* 34.
　1958　The Desert West: A trial correlation of cultures and chronology. Berkeley: *Uni-*

*versity of California Archaeological Survey Reports* 42:98–112.

1968    *A Delta intrusion to the Bay in the late Middle Period in central California.* San Diego: Paper presented at the Annual Meeting of the Society for California Archaeology and the Southwestern Anthropological Association.

1977a    Ethnogeography of the Plains Miwok. Davis: *University of California, Center for Archaeological Research at Davis, Publications* 5.

1977b    Linguistics in California prehistory. San Francisco: Lecture delivered in the Department of Anthropology, San Francisco State University.

1977c    *The Napa District and Wappo prehistory.* Davis: Paper presented at the Symposium on the Archaeology of the North Coast Ranges.

n.d.    The Napa District and Wappo prehistory. Manuscript in possession of the author.

Bennyhoff, J. A., and D. A. Fredrickson
1967    A typology of shell and stone beads from central California. Manuscript. Sacramento: Cultural Resources Section, State Department of Parks and Recreation.

1969    A proposed integrative taxonomy for central California archaeology. Manuscript. Rohnert Part: Department of Anthropology, Sonoma State University.

Bennyhoff, J. A., and R. F. Heizer
1958    Cross dating Great Basin sites by California shell beads. Berkeley: *University of California Archaeological Survey Reports* 42:60–92.

Berger, R.
1975    Advances and results in radiocarbon dating: Early Man in America. *World Archaeology* 7(2):174–184.

1979    An isotopic and magnetic study of the Calico site. In W. C. Schuiling, ed., *Pleistocene man at Calico* (2nd edition):31–34. Redlands: San Bernardino County Museum Association.

1982    The Wooley Mammoth Site, Santa Rosa Island, California. In J. E. Ericson, R. E. Taylor, and R. Berger, eds., Peopling of the New World:163–170. Los Altos: *Ballena Press Anthropological Papers* 23.

Berger, R., A. G. Horney, and W. F. Libby
1964    Radiocarbon dating of bone and shell from their organic components. *Science* **144**:999–1001.

Berger, R., and P. C. Orr
1966    The fire areas on Santa Rosa Island, California, II. *Proceedings of the National Academy of Sciences* **56**(6):1678–1682.

Berger, R., R. Protsch, R. Reynolds, C. Rozaire, and J. R. Sackett
1971    New radiocarbon dates based on bone collagen of California Paleoindians. Berkeley: *Contributions of the University of California Archaeological Research Facility* 12:43–49.

Berryman, L., and A. B. Elsasser
1966    *Terminus Reservoir.* Sacramento: United States Army Corps of Engineers, Sacramento District.

Bettinger, R. L.
1971    World views and archaeological investigation in interior southern California. Los Angeles: *University of California, Los Angeles, Archaeological Survey Annual Report, 1970–1971*:185–196.

1975    *The surface archaeology of Owens Valley, eastern California: Prehistoric man–land relationships in the Great Basin.* Ph.D. dissertation. Riverside: Department of Anthropology, University of California.

1976    The development of piñon exploitation in central eastern California. *The Journal of California Anthropology* **3**(1):81–95.

1977a    Aboriginal human ecology in Owens Valley: Prehistoric change in the Great Basin. *American Antiquity* **42**(1):3–17.

1977b    The surface archaeology of the Long Valley Caldera, Mono County, California. Riverside: *University of California Archaeological Research Unit Monographs* 1:1–77.

1978a    Alternative adaptive strategies in the prehistoric Great Basin. *Journal of Anthropological Research* **34**:27–46.

1978b    Alternative adaptive strategies: Reply to Lyneis. *The Journal of California Anthropology* **5**(2):292–296.

1978c    Humboldt Basal-notched bifaces as time markers in the western Great Basin. *Tebiwa* **10**:1–7.

1979a    Curation, statistics, and settlement studies: A reply to Munday and Lincoln. *American Antiquity* **44**(2):352–359.

1979b    Multivariate statistical analysis of a regional subsistence-settlement model for Owens Valley. *American Antiquity* **44**(3):455–470.

1980    Obsidian hydration dates for Owens Valley settlement categories. *Journal of California and Great Basin Anthropology* **2**(2):286–292.

1981a    Settlement data and subsistence systems. *American Antiquity* **46**(3):640–643.

1981b    Sampling and statistical inference in Owens Valley. *American Antiquity* **46**(3):656–660.

Bettinger, R. L., and M. A. Baumhoff
1982    The Numic spread: Great Basin cultures in competition. *American Antiquity* **47**(3):485–503.

Bettinger, R. L., and T. F. King
1971    Interaction and political organization: A theoretical framework for archaeology in Owens Valley, California. Los Angeles: *University of California, Los Angeles, Archaeological Survey Annual Report, 1970–1971*:137–152.

Bettinger, R. L., and R. E. Taylor
1974    Suggested revisions in archaeological sequences of the Great Basin and interior southern California. Reno: *Nevada Archaeological Survey Research Papers* 5:1–26.

Bickel, P. McW.
1974    *Toward a prehistory of the San Francisco Bay area.* Riverside: Paper presented at the Annual Meeting of the Society for California Archaeology.

1976    *Toward a prehistory of the San Francisco Bay area: The archaeology of sites Ala-328, Ala-12, and Ala-13.* Ph.D. dissertation. Cambridge: Department of Anthropology, Harvard University.

1978a    Changing sea levels along the California coast: Anthropological implications. *The Journal of California Anthropology* **5**(1):6–20.

1978b    Corrections to sea level article. *The Journal of California Anthropology* **5**(2):296–297.

1979    *A study of cultural resources in Redwood National Park.* Denver: Report to the National Park Service.

1981    San Francisco Bay archaeology: Sites Ala-328, Ala-13, and Ala-12. Berkeley: *Contributions of the University of California Archaeological Research Facility* 43.

Bickel, P. McW., T. L. Jackson, and T. F. King
1973    *Rising sea levels along the California coast: A preliminary consideration of some possible archaeological consequences.* San Francisco: Paper presented at the 38th Annual Meeting of the Society for American Archaeology.

Binford, L. R.
1962    Archaeology as anthropology. *American Antiquity* **28**(2):217–225.

1968    Archaeological perspectives. In S. R. Binford and L. R. Binford, eds., *New Perspectives in Archaeology*:5–32. Chicago: Aldine.

1980    Willow smoke and dogs' tails: Hunter–gatherer settlement systems and archaeological site formation. *American Antiquity* **45**(1):4–20.

Bingaman, J. W.
1966    *The Ahwahneechees.* Lodi: End-Kian.

Bingham, J. C.
1978    Archaeological test excavations within Border Field State Park, San Diego County. Sacramento: *State Department of Parks and Recreation, California Archaeological Reports* 16.

Birkeland, P. W., R. M. Burke, and J. C. Yount
1976    Preliminary comments on late Cenozoic glaciations in the Sierra Nevada. In W. C. Mahaney, ed., *Quaternary Stratigraphy of North America:*282–295. New York: Dowden, Hutchingson, and Ross.

Birman, J. H.
1964    Glacial geology across the crest of the Sierra Nevada, California. *Geological Society of America Special Paper* 75.

Bischoff, J. L., W. M. Childers, R. Protsch, and R. J. Shlemon
1979    Reply to Payen *et al.*, II. *American Antiquity* **44**(3):599.

Bischoff, J. L., W. M. Childers, and R. M. Shlemon
1978    Comments on the Pleistocene age assignment and associations of a human burial from the Yuha Desert. California: A rebuttal. *American Antiquity* **43**(4):747–749.

Bischoff, J. L., R. Merriam, W. M. Childers, and R. Protsch
1976    Antiquity of man in America indicated by radiometric dates on the Yuha burial site. *Nature* **261**:128–129.

Bischoff, J. L., and R. J. Rosenbauer
1981    Uranium series dating of human skeletal remains from the Del Mar and Sunnyvale sites, California. *Science* **213**(4511):1003–1005.

Bischoff, J. L., R. J. Shlemon, T. L. Ku, R. D. Simpson, R. J. Rosenbauer, and F. E. Budinger, Jr.
1981    Uranium-series and soils-geomorphic dating of the Calico archaeological site, California. *Geology* **9**:576–582.

Blackburn, T. C.
1974    *Chumash oral traditions: A cultural analysis.* Ph.D. dissertation. Los Angeles: Department of Anthropology, University of California.

Blackburn, T. C., and L. J. Bean
1978    Kitanemuk. In R. F. Heizer, vol. ed., *Handbook of North American Indians, Vol. 8: California:*564–569. Washington, D.C.: Smithsonian Institution.

Blackwelder, E., and E. W. Ellsworth
1936    Pleistocene lakes of the Afton Basin, California. *American Journal of Science* **31**(186):453–463.

Blake, W. P.
1868    Notice of a human skull found at a depth of 250 feet below surface near Columbia, Tuolumne County. San Francisco: *Proceedings of the California Academy of Sciences* **3**:291.
1899    The Pliocene skull of California and flint implements of Table Mountain. *Journal of Geology* **7**:631–637.

Boas, F.
1929    Classification of American Indian languages. *Language* **5**:1–7.

Bolton, H. E.
1931    In the south San Joaquin ahead of Garcés. San Francisco: *California Historical Quarterly* **10**:211–219.

Bolton, H. E., ed.
1911    Expedition to San Francisco Bay in 1770: Diary of Pedro Fages. *Academy of Pacific Coast History Publications* **2**(3):141–159.

Borden, C. E.
  1969   New evidence on the early peopling of the New World. Chicago: *Encyclopaedia Britannica Book of the Year, 1969*:101–104.
  1979   Peopling and early cultures of the Pacific Northwest. *Science* **203**(4384):963–971.

Boscana, G.
  1933   *Chinigchinich.* Santa Ana: Fine Arts Press.

Bowen, O. E., Jr., and R. A. Crippen, Jr.
  1948   Geologic maps and notes along Highway 49. San Francisco: *California Division of Mines Bulletin* **141**:35–86.

Bowen, W. J.
  1947   Queen of the Malibu. *The Californian* **3**(6):20–22, 62–64.

Bowers, D.
  1976   A surface survey of Las Flores Ranch (*Guapiabit*). Los Angeles: *Archaeological Survey Association of Southern California Occasional Papers* 9.

Bowers, S.
  1878   History and antiquities of Santa Rosa Island. Washington, D.C.: *Smithsonian Institution Annual Report for 1877*:316–320.
  1883   Fish-hooks from southern California. *Science* **1**(20):575. (Reprinted. Berkeley:
  (1963)  *University of California Archaeological Survey Reports* 59:71–72).
  1884   Relics in Ventura County, California. *Science* **3**:373–374.
  1885a  Relics in a cave. Honolulu: *Pacific Science Monthly* **1**:45–47.
  1885b  A report on a cave in the San Martín Mountains. Honolulu: *Pacific Science Monthly* **4**:1.
  1887   Aboriginal fishhooks. San Diego: *West American Scientist* **3**(32):243–245.

Brainerd, G. W.
  1953   A re-examination of the dating evidence for the Lake Mojave artifact assemblage. *American Antiquity* **18**(3):270–271.

Breschini, G. S.
  1972a  Archaeological investigations at Mnt-436—the Kodani site. *Carmel: Monterey County Archaeological Society Quarterly* **1**(4).
  1972b  *The Indians of Monterey County.* Carmel: Monterey County Archaeological Society.
  1973   Excavations at the Church Creek Rockshelter, Mnt-44. Carmel: *Monterey County Archaeological Society Quarterly* **2**(1).
  1978   The physical anthropology of the Holiday Inn site (CA-SCl-128. In J. C. Winter, ed., *Archaeological investigations at CA-SCl-128: The Holiday Inn site:* 35–68. San José: Report to the City of San José, Redevelopment Agency.
  1981   *Models of central California prehistory.* Bakersfield: Paper presented at the Annual Meeting of the Society for California Archaeology.

Breschini, G. S., and T. Haversat
  1978   *The Monterey County archaeological resources project.* Salinas: Published by the authors.
  1979   Archaeological overview of the central coast counties. Manuscript. Aptos: Department of Human Sciences, Cabrillo College.
  1980   Preliminary archaeological report and archaeological management recommendations for CA-Mnt-170, on Pescadero Point, Monterey County, California. Manuscript. Aptos: Archaeological Regional Research Center, Cabrillo College.
  1982   California radiocarbon dates. Manuscript (computer printout), dated January 13, 1982. Salinas: Archaeological Consulting.

Bright, M.
  1965   California radiocarbon dates. Los Angeles: *University of California, Los Angeles, Archaelogical Survey Annual Report, 1964–1965*:367–375.

Bright, W.
  1952a   Linguistic innovations in Karok. *International Journal of American Linguistics* **18**:53–62.
  1952b   Some place names on the Klamath River. *Western Folklore* **11**:121–122.
  1957    The Karok language. Berkeley: *University of California Publications in Linguistics* 13.
  1978    Karok. In R. F. Heizer, vol. ed., *Handbook of North American Indians, Vol. 8: California*:180–189. Washington, D.C.: Smithsonian Institution.
Bright, W., and M. Bright
  1969    Archaeology and linguistics in prehistoric southern California. Honolulu: *University of Hawaii Working Papers in Linguistics* 1(10):1–26. (Reprinted in *Essays by William Bright*. Stanford: Stanford University Press.)
  (1976)
Broadbent, S. M.
  1951a   Field notes from site CA-Mnt-101. Berkeley: *University of California Archaeological Survey Manuscripts* 125.
  1951b   Field notes from Mnt-107, Berwick Park, Pacific Grove. Manuscript. Pacific Grove: Pacific Grove Museum.
  1964    The Southern Sierra Miwok language. Berkeley: *University of California Publications in Linguistics* 38.
  1972    The Rumsen of Monterey: An ethnography from historical sources. Berkeley: *Contributions of the University of California Archaeological Research Facility* 14:45–94.
Broadbent, S., and C. Callaghan
  1960    Comparative Miwok: A preliminary survey. *International Journal of American Linguistics* **26**:301–316.
Broadbent, S. M., and H. Pitkin
  1964    A comparison of Miwok and Wintun. Berkeley: *University of California Publications in Linguistics* 34:19–45.
Broecker, W. S., E. A. Olson, and P. C. Orr
  1960    Radiocarbon measurements and annual rings in cave formations. *Nature* **185**:93–94.
Brooks, R. H.
  1975    Birds (from Ala-307). Berkeley: *Contributions of the University of California Archaeological Research Facility* 29:107–114.
Brooks, R. H., D. O. Larson, J. King, and K. Olson
  1977    *Phase 1 and 2 archaeological research in Imperial Valley.* Yuma: Report to the U.S. Bureau of Reclamation.
Brooks, S. T., B. L. Conrey, and K. A. Dixon
  1965    A deeply buried human skull and recent stratigraphy at the present mouth of the San Gabriel River, Seal Beach, California. Los Angeles: *Bulletin of the Southern California Academy of Sciences* **64**(4):229–241.
Brooks, S. T., and W. D. Hohenthal
  1963    Archaeological defective palate crania from California. *American Journal of Physical Anthropology* **21**(1):25–32.
Brown, A. K.
  1967    The aboriginal population of the Santa Barbara Channel. Berkeley: *University of California Archaeological Survey Reports* 69.
Brown, J. A., ed.
  1971    Approaches to the social dimensions of mortuary practices. Washington, D.C.: *Society for American Archaeology Memoirs* 25.
Bruff, J. G.
  1949    *Gold Rush: The journals, drawings, and other papers of J. Goldsborough Bruff,*

*April 2, 1849 to July 20, 1851,* G. W. Read and R. Gaines, eds. New York: Columbia University Press.

Brusa, B. W.
1975    *Salinan Indians of California and their neighbors.* Healdsburg: Naturegraph.

Bryan, A. L.
1965    Paleo-American prehistory. Pocatello: *Occasional Papers of the Idaho State University Museum* 16.
1979    A preliminary look at the evidence for a standardized tool technology at Calico. In W. C. Schuiling, ed., *Pleistocene man at Calico* (2nd edition): 75–79. Redlands: San Bernardino County Museum Association.
1980    The stemmed point tradition: An early technological tradition in western North America. In L. Harten, C. N. Warren, and D. Tuohy, eds., *Anthropological papers in memory of Earl H. Swanson:* 77–107. Pocatello: Special publication of the Idaho State University Museum of Natural History.

Bryson, R. A., D. A. Barreis, and W. M. Wendland
1970    The character of late glacial and post-glacial climatic changes. In W. Dort, Jr., and J. K. Jones, Jr., eds., Pleistocene and Recent environments of the central Great Plains. Lawrence: *University of Kansas, Department of Geology Special Publications* 3:53–74.

Buckley, J., and E. Willis
1970    Point Saint George I, California. *Radiocarbon* **12**(1).

Budinger, F. E., Jr.
1981    Evidence for Pleistocene man in America: The Calico early man site, Yermo, California. Yermo: *Friends of the Calico Early Man Site, Inc., Occasional Papers* 1.

Bull, C. S.
1977    *Archaeology and linguistics, coastal southern California.* M.A. thesis. San Diego: Department of Anthropology, San Diego State University.

Bunnell, L. H.
1911    *Discovery of the Yosemite and the Indian War of 1851.* Los Angeles: G. W. Gerlicher (originally published 1880).

Burnett, E.
1944    Inlaid stone and bone artifacts from southern California. *Contributions of the Museum of the American Indian, Heye Foundation* 13.

Burr, B. L.
1968    50,000 years ago. *Desert Magazine,* December:8–11.

Busby, C. I.
1975    A mammalian faunal analysis of CA-Ala-307. Berkeley: *Contributions of the University of California Archaeological Research Facility* 29:99–106.

Butler, R. B.
1961    The Old Cordilleran Culture in the Pacific Northwest. Pocatello: *Occasional Papers of the Idaho State College Museum* 5.

Byers, D. S., ed.
1967    *The prehistory of the Tehuacan Valley,* Vol. 1: *Environment and subsistence.* Austin: University of Texas Press.

Callaghan, C. A.
1958a    California Penutian: History and bibliography. *International Journal of American Linguistics* **24**(3):189–194.
1958b    Notes on Lake Miwok numerals. *International Journal of American Linguistics* **24**:247.
1977    The homeland of the Proto-Miwok. Manuscript. Berkeley: Department of Linguistics, University of California.

Campbell, E. W. C.
  1931    An archaeological survey of the Twenty-nine Palms region. Los Angeles: *Southwest Museum Papers* 7:1–93.
  1936    Archaeological problems in the southern California deserts. *American Antiquity* **1**(4):295–300.
  1949    Two ancient archaeological sites in the Great Basin. *Science* **109**:340.
Campbell, E. W. C., and W. H. Campbell
  1935    The Pinto Basin site: An ancient aboriginal camping ground in the California desert. Los Angeles: *Southwest Museum Papers* 9:1–51.
Campbell, E. W. C., W. H. Campbell, E. Antevs, C. E. Amsden, J. A. Barbieri, and F. D. Bode
  1937    The archaeology of Pleistocene Lake Mohave. Los Angeles: *Southwest Museum Papers* 11.
Canby, T. Y.
  1979    The search for the first Americans. *National Geographic* **156**(3):330–363.
Canfield, D. H., and J. C. Couch
  1936    *Report of preliminary archaeological reconnaissance, Lava Beds National Monument, November 18–December 14, 1935.* Washington, D.C.: Report to the National Park Service.
Carson, J. H.
  1852    *Early recollections of the mines, and a description of the Great Tulare Valley.* Stockton: *San Joaquin Republican.*
Carter, G. F.
  1941    Archaeological notes on a midden at Point Sal. *American Antiquity* **6**(3):214–226.
  1949    Evidence for Pleistocene man at La Jolla, California. New York: *Transactions of the New York Academy of Sciences,* Ser. 2, **2**(7):254–257.
  1950    Evidence for Pleistocene man in southern California. New York: *The Geographical Review* **40**(1):84–102.
  1951    Man in America: A criticism of scientific thought. *The Scientific Monthly* **73**(5):297–307.
  1952    Interglacial artifacts from the San Diego area. Albuquerque: *Southwestern Journal of Anthropology* **8**(4):444–456.
  1953    On submarine archaeology about San Diego. Los Angeles: *The Masterkey* **29**(1):21–27.
  1954a   An interglacial site from San Diego, California. Los Angeles: *The Masterkey* **28**(5):165–174.
  1954b   More evidence for interglacial man in America. London: *New World Antiquity* **8**:1–4.
  1955    Early man in America. London: *New World Antiquity* **2**(1):8–9.
  1957    *Pleistocene man at San Diego.* Baltimore: Johns Hopkins Press.
  1959a   Man, time, and change in the Far Southwest. Washington, D.C.: *Annals of the Association of American Geographers* **49**:8–30.
  1959b   Pleistocene man at San Diego, a reply. *American Antiquity* **24**(3):319–321.
  1975    Field guide—San Diego. Manuscript. San Diego: Friends of the Pleistocene.
  1980    *Earlier than you think: A personal view of man in America.* College Station: Texas A and M University Press.
Carter, G. F., and H. L. Minshall
  1976    *The Texas Street and related sites: Supporting evidence and recent new discoveries.* San Diego: Paper presented at the Annual Meeting of the Society for California Archaeology.
Cartier, R. R.
  1979a   *Archaeological recovery program: Cal/Trans 01-Mon-65.8, site CA-MNT-185,*

*Soberanes Creek.* Sacramento: Report to the California Department of Transportation.

1979b    Lower Archaic culture in Santa Clara County. *Society for California Archaeology Newsletter* **13**(5–6):5.

1979c    San José radiocarbon dates. *Society for California Archaeology Newsletter* **13**(4):3.

1980     *Early cultures and rock features of the Santa Theresa Hills: CA-SCl-64, CA-SCl-106, and CA-SCl-341.* San José: Report to the Santa Clara Valley Water District.

1982     Current research. *American Antiquity* **47**(1):229.

Casteel, R. W.

1970     Distribution of the native freshwater fish fauna of California. Davis: *University of California, Center for Archaeological Research at Davis, Publications* 2:9–26.

1972a    A key, based on scales, to the families of native California freshwater fishes. San Francisco: *Proceedings of the California Academy of Sciences* **39**:75–86.

1972b    *The use of fish remains in archaeology with special reference to the native freshwater and anadromous fishes of California.* Ph.D. dissertation. Davis: Department of Anthropology, University of California.

1974     On the remains of fish scales from archaeological sites. *American Antiquity* **39**:557–581.

1976     *Fish remains in archaeology.* New York: Academic Press.

Casteel, R. W., D. P. Adam, and J. D. Sims

1975     Fish remains from Core 7, Clear Lake, Lake County, California. Menlo Park: *United States Geological Survey Open-File Report* 75–173.

1977     Late-Pleistocene and Holocene remains of *Hysterocarpus traski* (tule perch) from Clear Lake, California, and inferred Holocene temperature fluctuations. *Quaternary Research* **7**:133–143.

Casteel, R. W., and C. K. Beaver

1978     Inferred Holocene temperature changes in the North Coast Ranges of California. *Northwest Scientist* **52**(4):337–342.

Castillo, E. D.

1978     The impact of Euro-American exploration and settlement. In R. F. Heizer, vol. ed., *Handbook of North American Indians,* Vol. 8: *California:*99–127. Washington, D.C.: Smithsonian Institution.

Caughey, J. W.

1961     *California.* Englewood Cliffs: Prentice-Hall.

Chagnon, N.

1970     Ecological and adaptive aspects of California shell money. Los Angeles: *University of California, Los Angeles, Archaeological Survey Annual Report, 1969–1970:*1–25.

Chartkoff, J. L.

1970     *Ecosystems, breeding populations, and terminal Pleistocene extinctions.* San Diego: Paper presented at the Annual Meeting of the American Anthropological Association.

Chartkoff, J. L., and K. K. Chartkoff

1972     Klamath River project reports 1–8. Manuscript. East Lansing: Department of Anthropology, Michigan State University.

1975     Late-period settlement of the middle Klamath River of northwest California. *American Antiquity* **40**(2):172–179.

1981     *Test excavations at three prehistoric sites in Stanislaus National Forest, Tuolumne County.* Sonora: Report to the Stanislaus National Forest.

Chartkoff, J. L., and J. Childress
  1966    An archaeological survey of tbe proposed Paskenta-Newville Reservoir in Glenn and Tehama Counties, northern California. San Francisco: Report to the National Park Service.

Chavez, D.
  1976    The archaeology of 4-Mrn-170: A Marin County shellmound. M.A. thesis. San Francisco: Department of Anthropology, San Francisco State University.

Childers, W. M.
  1974    Preliminary report on the Yuha burial, California. *Anthropological Journal of Canada* **12**(1):2–9.
  1977    Ridge-back tools of the Colorado Desert. *American Antiquity* **42**(2):242–248.

Childers, W. M., and H. L. Minshall
  1980    Evidence of early man exposed at Yuha Pinto Wash. *American Antiquity* **45**(2):297–308.

Childress, J., and J. L. Chartkoff
  1966    An archaeological survey of the English Ridge Reservoir in Lake and Mendocino Counties, California. San Francisco: Report to the National Park Service.

Childress, J. G., and E. W. Ritter
  1967    An archaeological survey of the proposed Auburn and Sugar Pine Reservoirs in El Dorado and Placer Counties. San Francisco: Report to the National Park Service.

Chrétien, C. D.
  1945    Culture element distributions, XXV: Reliability of statistical procedures and results. Berkeley: *University of California Anthropological Records* **8**(5):469–490.

Clark, D. L.
  1964    Archaeological chronology in California and the obsidian hydration method, Part 1. Los Angeles: *University of California, Los Angeles, Archaeological Survey Annual Report, 1963–1964:139–238*.

Clark, G.
  1904    Indians of the Yosemite Valley and vicinity: Their history, customs, and traditions. San Francisco: H. S. Crocker.

Clark, G. H.
  1929    Sacramento-San Joaquin salmon (Oncorhynchus tschawytscha) fishery of California. Sacramento: *California Department of Fish and Game, Fish Bulletin* 17.

Clements, T.
  1938    Age of the Los Angeles Man deposits. *American Journal of Science* **36**:137–141.
  1979    The geology of the Yermo fan. In W. C. Schuiling, ed., *Pleistocene man at Calico* (2nd edition):21–30. Redlands: San Bernardino County Museum Association.

Clements, T., and L. Clements
  1953    Evidence of Pleistocene man in Death Valley, California. *Geological Society of America Bulletin* **64**:1189–1204.

Clewett, S. E.
  1974    Squaw Creek: A multi-component Early Archaic site in Shasta County. Manuscript. Redding: Department of Anthropology, Shasta College.
  1977    CA-Sha-475: An interim report on Squaw Creek # 1, a complex stratified site in the southern Klamath Mountains. Paper presented at the Symposium on the Archaeology of the North Coast Ranges, California. Davis, May 14, 1977.

Clewett, S. E., and E. Sundahl
  1983    Archaeological excavations at Squaw Creek, Shasta County, California. Redding: Shasta College Archaeology Laboratory.

Clewlow, C. W., Jr.
  1967    Time and space relations of some Great Basin projectile point types. Berkeley:

*University of California Archaeological Survey Reports* 70:141–149.

1968a    Projectile points from Lovelock Cave, Nevada. Berkeley: *University of California Archaeological Survey Reports* 71:89–116.

1968b    Surface archaeology of the Black Rock Desert, Nevada. Berkeley: *University of California Archaeological Survey Reports* 73:1–94.

1978    Prehistoric rock art. In R. F. Heizer, vol. ed., *Handbook of North American Indians, Vol. 8: California*: 619–625. Washington, D.C.: Smithsonian Institution.

Clewlow, C. W., Jr., R. F. Heizer, and R. Berger
1970    An assessment of radiocarbon dates for the Rose Spring site (CA-Iny-372), Inyo County, California. Berkeley: *Contributions of the University of California Archaeological Research Facility* 7:19–25.

Clewlow, C. W., Jr., and H. F. Wells
1981    Radiocarbon dates from CA-Mrn-152. *Journal of California and Great Basin Anthropology* 3(1):143–144.

Clewlow, C. W., Jr., H. F. Wells, and A. G. Pastron, eds.
1978    The archaeology of Oak Park, Ventura County, California, Vols. 1–2. Los Angeles: *University of California, Los Angeles, Institute of Archaeology, Monographs* 5.

Clewlow, C. W., Jr., and D. S. Whitley, eds.
1979    The archaeology of Oak Park, Ventura County, California, Vol. 3. Los Angeles: *University of California, Los Angeles, Institute of Archaeology, Monographs* 11.

Cliff, F.
1929    Prehistoric Golgotha of the Mother Lode. *Oakland Tribune*, May 23:3.

Clough, H. F.
1976    Cultural resources evaluation of the Lamont Meadow and Morris Peak segments of the Pacific Crest Trail. Manuscript. Bakersfield: Bureau of Land Management.

Coberly, M. B.
1973    The archaeology of the Ryan mound, site Ala-329, a central California coastal village site. Greeley: *University of Northern Colorado, Museum of Anthropology Occasional Publications in Anthropology, Archaeology Series* 4.

Cohen, Y. A.
1968    Culture as adaptation. In Y. A. Cohen, ed., *Man in adaptation: The cultural present*:40–60. Chicago: Aldine.

Cole, D. M.
1968    *Archaeological excavations in Area 6 of Site 35-GM-9, the Wildcat Canyon site.* San Francisco: Report to the National Park Service.

Colton, H. S.
1939    Prehistoric culture units and their relationships in northern Arizona. Flagstaff: *Museum of Northern Arizona Bulletin* 17.

1945    The Patayan problem in the Colorado River Valley. *Southwestern Journal of Anthropology* 1(1):114–121.

Conover, K.
1972    *Archaeological sampling in Namu: A problem in settlement reconstruction.* Ph.D. dissertation. Boulder: Department of Anthropology, University of Colorado.

Conrotto, E. L.
1973    *Miwok means people.* Fresno: Valley.

Contreras, E.
1957    An extraordinary central California burial in Marin County. Berkeley: *University of California Archaeological Survey Reports* 38:29–33.

Cook, R. A.
1977    *Preliminary report: Archaeological test excavations at SDi-4558, 4562, and 4562A.* Sacramento: California Department of Transportation.

1978    *Final report: Archaeological test excavations in Moosa Canyon, San Diego County, California.* Sacramento: California Department of Transportation.

Cook, S. F.
1940    Population trends among the California mission Indians: Berkeley: *Ibero-Americana* 17.
1943a   The conflict between the California Indian and white civilization, I: The Indian versus the Spanish mission. Berkeley: *Ibero-Americana* 21.
1943b   The conflict between the California Indian and white civilization, II: The physical and demographic reaction of the non-mission Indians in colonial and provincial California. Berkeley: *Ibero-Americana* 22.
1943c   The conflict between the California Indian and white civilization, III: The American invasion, 1848–1870. Berkeley: *Ibero-Americana* 23.
1946    A reconsideration of shell mounds with respect to population and nutrition. *American Antiquity* **12**(1):50–53.
1950    Physical analysis as a method for investigating prehistoric habitation sites. Berkeley: *University of California Archaeological Survey Reports* 7:2–5.
1951    The fossilization of human bone: Calcium, phosphate, and carbonate. Berkeley: *University of California Publications in American Archaeology and Ethnology* **40**(6):263–280.
1955a   The aboriginal population of the San Joaquin Valley, California. Berkeley: *University of California Anthropological Records* **16**(2):31–74.
1955b   The epidemic of 1830–1833 in California and Oregon. Berkeley: *University of California Publications in American Archaeology and Ethnology* **43**(3):303–326.
1956    The aboriginal population of the north coast of California. Berkeley: *University of California Anthropological Records* **16**(3):1–130.
1960    Colonial expeditions to the interior of California: Central Valley, 1800–1820. Berkeley: *University of California Anthropological Records* **16**(6):239–292.
1962    Expeditions to the interior of California: Central Valley, 1820–1840. Berkeley: *University of California Anthropological Records* **20**(5):151–213.
1964    The aboriginal population of Upper California. Mexico City: *Actas y Memorias, XXXV Congreso Internacional de Americanistas, México, 1962* 3:397–403.
1968    The destruction of the California Indian. Berkeley: *California Alumni Monthly* **79**:14–19.
1970    The California Indian and Anglo-American culture. In C. Wollenberg, ed., *Ethnic Conflict in California History*:23–42. Los Angeles: Tinnon–Brown.
1974a   The Esselen: Language and culture. Carmel: *Monterey County Archaeological Society Quarterly* **3**(3):1–10.
1974b   The Esselen: Territory, villages. and population. Carmel: *Monterey County Archaeological Society Quarterly* **3**(2):1–12.
1976    *The population of the California Indians, 1769–1970.* Berkeley: University of California Press.
1978    Historical demography. In R. F. Heizer, vol. ed., *Handbook of North American Indians, Vol. 8:California:* 91–98. Washington, D.C.: Smithsonian Institution.

Cook, S. F., and A. B. Elsasser
1956    Burials in the sand mounds of the Delta region of the Sacramento–San Joaquin River system. Berkeley: *University of California Archaeological Survey Reports* 35:26–46.

Cook, S. F., and R. F. Heizer
1949    The archaeology of central California: A comparative analysis of human bone from nine sites. Berkeley: *University of California Anthropological Records* **12**(2).
1951    The physical analysis of nine Indian mounds in the lower Sacramento Valley.

Berkeley: *University of California Publications in American Archaeology and Ethnology* **40**(7):281–312.

1952    Fluorine and other chemical tests of some North American human and fossil bones. *American Journal of Physical Anthropology* **10**:289–304.

1962    Chemical and physical analysis of the Hotchkiss site (CCo-138). Berkeley: *University of California Archaeological Survey Reports* 57:1–24.

1965    The quantitative approach to the relation between populations and settlement size. Berkeley: *University of California Archaeological Survey Reports* 64:1–97.

1968    Relationships among houses, settlement areas, and population in aboriginal California. In K. C. Chang, ed., *Settlement Archaeology:*79–116. Palo Alto: National Press.

1973    Amador-3: The study of a dry cave deposit. In R. F. Heizer and T. R. Hester, *The archaeology of Bamert Cave, Amador County, California:*45–50. Berkeley: University of California Archaeological Research Facility.

Cook, S. F., and A. E. Treganza

1947    The quantitative investigation of aboriginal sites: Comparative physical and chemical analysis of two California Indian mounds. *American Antiquity* **13**(2):135–141.

1948    The quantitative investigation of aboriginal sites: Complete excavation with physical and archaelogical analysis of a single mound. *American Antiquity* **13**(3):287–297.

1950    The quantitative investigation of Indian mounds with special reference to the relation of the physical components to the probable material culture. Berkeley: *University of California Publications in American Archaeology and Ethnology* **40**(5):223–261.

Coombs, G. B.

1979a    The archeology of the northeast Mojave Desert. Riverside: *Bureau of Land Management, California Area, Cultural Resource Publications, Archeology.*

1979b    The archeology of the western Mojave (Desert). Riverside: *Bureau of Land Management, California Area, Cultural Resource Publications, Archeology.*

Cooper, W. S.

1922    The broad-sclerophyll vegetation of California: An ecological study of the chaparral and its related communities. Washington, D.C.: *The Carnegie Institution of Washington, Publications* 319.

Corbett, J. W.

1973    Late Pleistocene extinctions. *Science* **180**:905.

Cope, E. D.

1891    The California cave bear. *The American Naturalist* **25**:997–999.

Corson, C.

1977    *Some environmental parameters of prehistoric site locations in the northwestern Great Basin.* San Diego: Paper presented at the Annual Meeting of the Society for California Archaeology.

n.d.    The desert countryside in the wake of the beasts: Observations on the quality of environmental data in the northern Great Basin. In R. Berger and C. W. Clewlow, Jr., eds., *Perspectives in American Archaeology.* (In press.)

Corson, C., and G. Smith

1979    Preliminary assessment of cultural resources in the Eagle Lake Basin, Lassen County, California. *Eagle Lake Master Plan* 11. Sacramento: *Report to Raymond* Vail and Associates.

Cowan, R. A., C. W. Clewlow, Jr., C. H. Yonge, and J. F. O'Connell

1975    The unusual burial of a bear and child from the Sacramento Delta. *The Journal of New World Archaeology* **1**(2):25–30.

Cowan, R. A., and K. Wallof
  1974   *Field work and artifact analysis: Southern California Edison No. 2 Control-Casa Diablo 115 kv transmission line.* Rosemead: Report to Southern California Edison Company.

Crabtree, R. H.
  1981   Archaeology. In E. von Till Warren, R. H. Crabtree, C. N. Warren, M. Knack, and R. McCarty, eds., A cultural resources overview of the Colorado Desert Planning Units: 25–54. Riverside: *U.S. Bureau of Land Management, Cultural Resources Publications, Anthropology–History.*

Crabtree, R. H., C. N. Warren, and D. L. True
  1963   Archaeological investigations at Batiquitos Lagoon, San Diego County, California. Los Angeles: *University of California, Los Angeles, Archaeological Survey Annual Report, 1962–1963:*319–349.

Craig, S., and M. Roeder
  1978   Appendix IV: Fish and sea mammal remains from CA-Mnt-298. In W. Roop and K. Flynn, *Heritage on the half-shell: Excavation at Mnt-298:*462–490. Novato: Archaeological Resource Service.

Cressman, L. S.
  1936   Archaeological survey of the Guano Valley region of southeastern Oregon. Eugene: *University of Oregon Monographs, Studies in Anthropology* 1:1–48.
  1942   Archaeological researches in the northern Great Basin. Washington, D.C.: *Carnegie Institution of Washington Publications* 538.
  1956   Klamath prehistory. Philadelphia: *Transactions of the American Philosophical Society* **46**(4).
  1960   Cultural sequences at The Dalles, Oregon: A contribution to Pacific Northwest prehistory. Philadelphia: *Transactions of the American Philosophical Society* **50**(10).
  1968   Early man in western North America: Perspectives and prospects. Portales: *Eastern New Mexico University Contributions in Anthropology* **1**(4):78–87.
  1977   *Prehistory of the Far West: Homes of vanished peoples.* Salt Lake City: University of Utah Press.

Cressman, L. S., H. Williams, and A. D. Krieger
  1940   Early man in Oregon. Eugene: *University of Oregon Monographs, Studies in Anthropology* 3.

Crew, H.
  1970   Preliminary report: 4-Pla-36. In E. W. Ritter, ed., *Archaeological investigations in the Auburn Reservoir area, Phase II–III:*275–280. San Francisco: Report to the National Park Service.
  1981   Comments on the lithic assemblages from CA-Sac-370 and 379. In A. S. Peak, *Archaeological investigations of CA-Sac-370 and CA-Sac-379: The Rancho Murieta Early Man sites in eastern Sacramento County:*135–137. Sacramento: Ann S. Peak and Associates.

Croasdale, R.
  1973   A.V.A.S. surveys. *Antelope Valley Archaeological Survey Newsletter* **2**(12):2–3.

Curry, R. R.
  1968   *Quaternary climatic and glacial history of the Sierra Nevada, California.* Ph.D. dissertation. Berkeley: Department of Geology, University of California.
  1969   Holocene climatic and glacial history of the central Sierra Nevada, California. *Geological Society of American Special Papers* **123**:1–47.
  1971   Glacial and Pleistocene history of the Mammoth Lakes Sierra, California—a geologic guidebook. Missoula: *University of Montana, Department of Geology, Geological Series Publications* 11.

Curtice, C. G.
1961    *Cultural and physical evidence of prehistoric peoples of Sacramento County.* M.A. thesis. Sacramento: Department of Anthropology, Sacramento State University.

Curtis, E. S.
1907–   *The North American Indian.* Norwood: Privately printed.
1930

Curtis, F.
1960    Some Santa Cruz Island artifacts. Los Angeles: *The Masterkey* **34**(2):62–65.
1964    Description of artifacts (from Glen Annie Canyon site, SBa-142). Los Angeles: *University of California, Los Angeles, Archaeological Survey Annual Report, 1963–1964*:441–452.
1965    An archaeologist on San Miguel Island. Los Angeles: *Museum Alliance Quarterly* **3**(4):4–9.

Cutter, D. C.
1950    *Spanish exploration of California's Central Valley.* Ph.D. dissertation. Berkeley: Department of History, University of California.

Dall, W. H.
1899    The Calaveras skull. Philadelphia: *Proceedings of the Academy of Natural Sciences of Philadelphia, 1899*:2–4.

Damon, P. E., C. W. Ferguson, A. Long, and E. I. Wallick
1974    Dendrochronologic calibration of the radiocarbon time scale. *American Antiquity* **39**(2):350–366.

Danehy, E. A.
1951    The Cave of the Catacombs and its archaeological history. Stanford: *Monthly Report of the Stanford Grotto, National Speleological Society* **2**(3):14–23.

Daugherty, R. D.
1956    The archaeology of the Lind Coulee site, Washington. Philadelphia: *Proceedings of the American Philosophical Society* **100**(3):223–278.
1962    The Intermontane Western Tradition. *American Antiquity* **28**(2):144–150.

Davis, C. A.
1981    *Newberry Cave: An Elko religious site in San Bernardino County, California.* M.A. thesis. Riverside: Department of Anthropology, University of California.

Davis, C. A., and G. A. Smith
1981    *Newberry Cave.* Redlands: San Bernardino County Museum Association.

Davis, E. L.
1961    The Mono Craters petroglyphs, California. *American Antiquity* **27**(2):236–339.
1963    The Desert Culture of the western Great Basin: A lifeway of seasonal transhumance. *American Antiquity* **29**(2):202–212.
1964    An archaeological survey of the Mono Lake Basin and excavation of two rock-shelters, Mono County, California. Los Angeles: *University of California Archaeological Survey Annual Report, 1963–1964*:251–392.
1965    An ethnography of the Kuzedika Paiute of Mono Lake, California. Salt Lake City: *University of Utah Anthropological Papers* **75**:1–56.
1967    Man and water at Pleistocene Lake Mojave. *American Antiquity* **32**(3):345–353.
1968a   A rare find: A fluted point in process. San Diego: *Museum of Man News Bulletin,* April–May.
1968b   Early man in the Mojave Desert. Portales: *Eastern New Mexico University Contributions in Anthropology* **1**(4):42–47.
1970    Archaeology of the north basin of Panamint Valley, Inyo County, California. Carson City: *Nevada State Museum Anthropological Papers* **15**:83–141.
1973a   People of the Old Stone Age at China Lake. Manuscript. San Diego: Great Basin Foundation.

1973b    The Hord site: A Paleo-Indian camp. Costa Mesa: *Pacific Coast Archaeological Society Quarterly* **9**(2):1–26.

1974a    Field work on the Naval missile impact ranges, China Lake: 1969–1974. Manuscript. San Diego: Great Basin Foundation.

1974b    Paleo-Indian land use patterns at China Lake, California. Costa Mesa: *Pacific Coast Archaeological Society Quarterly* **10**(2):1–16.

1975     The "exposed archaeology" of China Lake, California. *American Antiquity* **40**(1):39–53.

Davis, E. L., ed.
1978     The ancient Californians: Rancholabrean hunters of the Mojave Lakes country. Los Angeles: *Natural History Museum of Los Angeles County, Science Series* 29.

Davis, E. L., C. W. Brott, and D. L. Weide
1969     The Western Lithic Co-Tradition. San Diego: *San Diego Museum Papers* 6.

Davis, E. L., and C. Panlaqui
1978     Chapters 1–5. In E. L. Davis, ed., The ancient Californians: Rancholabrean hunters of the Mojave Lakes country. Los Angeles: *Natural History Museum of Los Angeles County, Science Series* 29:4–152.

Davis, E. L., and R. Shutler, Jr.
1969     Recent discoveries of fluted points in California and Nevada. Carson City: *Nevada State Museum Anthropological Papers* 14:154–169.

Davis, G. H., J. H. Green, F. H. Olmstead, and D. W. Brown
1959     Ground water conditions and storage capacity in the San Joaquin Valley, California. Washington, D.C.: *U.S. Geological Survey Water Supply Paper* 1469.

Davis, J. O.
1978     Quaternary tephrachronology of the Lake Lahontan area, Nevada and California. Reno: *Nevada Archaeological Survey Research Papers* 7.

Davis, J. T.
1958     *The archaeology of three central Sierran sites.* San Francisco: Report to the National Park Service.

1960a    *The archaeology of site Fre-259, Kings Canyon National Park, California.* San Francisco: Report to the National Park Service.

1960b    The archaeology of the Fernandez site, a San Francisco Bay region shellmound. Berkeley: *University of California Archaeological Survey Reports* 49:11–53.

1961     Trade routes and economic exchange among the Indians of California. Berkeley: *University of California Archaeological Survey Reports* 54:1–71.

1962     The Rustler Rockshelter site (SBr-288), a culturally stratified site in the Mohave Desert, California. Berkeley: *University of California Archaeological Survey Reports* 57:25–65.

1963     Test excavations at site INY-372 conducted in 1961. In E. P. Lanning, Archaeology of the Rose Spring site, INY-372. Berkeley: *University of California Publications in American Archaeology and Ethnology* **49**(3):296–304.

Davis, J., and R. Elston
1972     New stratigraphic evidence of late Quaternary climatic change in northwestern Nevada. Reno: *Desert Research Institute Publications in the Social Sciences* 8:43–56.

Davis, J. T., and A. E. Treganza
1959     The Patterson mound: A comparative analysis of the archaeology of site Ala-328. Berkeley: *University of California Archaeological Survey Reports* 47:1–92.

Davis, W. A.
1967     Current research—Great Basin. *American Antiquity* **32**(2):281–282.

Dawson, L. E.
1978a   Personal communication to K. Whistler regarding similarities between Yokuts baskets and archaeological basketry from Oregon. Berkeley: R. H. Lowie Museum of Anthropology, University of California.
1978b   *Suggestions of Maidu prehistory from basketry evidence.* Yosemite National Park. Paper presented at the Annual Meeting of the Society for California Archaeology.

D'Azevedo, W. L., ed.
1963   The Washo Indians of California and Nevada. Salt Lake City: *University of Utah Anthropological Papers* 67.

de Angulo, J.
1979   Indians in overalls. In B. Callahan, ed., *A Jaime de Angulo reader:*187–246. Berkeley: Turtle Island.

de Angulo, J., and L. S. Freeland
1928   Miwok and Pomo myths. *Journal of American Folklore* **41:**232–252.
1930   The Achumawi language. *International Journal of American Linguistics* **6**(2):77–120.

de Cessac, J. F. A. L.
1951a   L. de Cessac's report on his activities in California. In R. F. Heizer, ed., The French scientific expedition to California, 1877–1879. Berkeley: *University of California Archaeological Survey Reports* 12:8–13.
1951b   Observations on the sculptured stone fetishes in animal form discovered on San Nicolas Island (California). N. E. Heizer, trans. Berkeley: *University of California Archaeological Survey Reports* 12:1–5.

Desgrandchamp, C. S.
1976   *Estuary exploitation in aboriginal California.* M.A. thesis. San Francisco: Department of Anthropology, San Francisco State University.

Dietz, S. A.
1976   *Echa Tamal: A study of Coast Miwok acculturation.* M.A. thesis. San Francisco: Department of Anthropology, San Francisco State University.

Dietz, S. A., and T. L. Jackson
198i   *Report of archaeological excavations at nineteen archaeological sites for the Stage I Pacific Grove–Monterey Consolidation Project of the Regional Sewerage System.* Santa Cruz: Archaeological Consulting and Research Services.

Divale, W., and M. Harris
1976   Population, warfare, and the Male Supremacist Complex. *American Anthropologist* **78**(3):521–538.
1978   On the misuse of statistics: A reply to Hirschfeld *et al. American Anthropologist* **80**(2):379–386.

Dixon, K. A.
1968   Cogged stones and other ceremonial cache artifacts in stratigraphic context at Ora-58, a site in the lower Santa Ana River drainage, Orange County. Costa Mesa: *Pacific Coast Archaeological Society Quarterly* **4**(3):57–65.
1970a   A brief report on radiocarbon and obsidian hydration measurements from Ora-58 (the Banning/Norris or Fairview Hospital site), Orange County, California. Costa Mesa: *Pacific Coast Archaeological Society Quarterly* **6**(4):61–68.
1970b   Archaeology and geology in the Calico Mountains: Results of the international conference on the Calico project. *The Informant* **1**(10):1–22. Long Beach: The Anthropology Club, California State University, Long Beach.
1975   New evidence for the most important archaeological discovery in Long Beach: The cogged stones and discs of Rancho Los Cerritos. Long Beach: *Los Fierros* **12**(2):20–31.

Dixon, R. B.
  1905a  The Northern Maidu. New York: *American Museum of Natural History Bulletin* **17**:119–346.
  1905b  The Shasta–Achomawi: A new linguistic stock with four new dialects. *American Anthropologist* **7**:213–217.
  1907a  Linguistic relationships within the Shasta–Achomawi stock. Quebec: *Acts of the 15th International Congress of Americanists* **2**:255–263.
  1907b  The Chimariko Indians and language. Berkeley: *University of California Publications in American Archaeology and Ethnology* **5**(5):293–380.
  1907c  The Shasta. New York: *Bulletin of the American Museum of Natural History* **17**:381–498.
  1911  Maidu: An illustrative sketch. In F. Boas, ed., Handbook of American Indian Languages. Washington, D.C.: *Bureau of American Ethnology Bulletin* **40**(1):679–734.
Dixon, R. B., and A. L. Kroeber
  1903  The native languages of California. *American Anthropologist* **5**(1):1–26.
  1912  Relationship of the Indian languages of California. *American Anthropologist* **14**(4):691–692.
  1913  New linguistic families in California. *American Anthropologist* **15**(4):647–655.
  1919  Linguistic families in California. Berkeley: *University of California Publications in American Archaeology and Ethnology* **16**(3):47–118.
Dobyns, H.
  1966  Estimating aboriginal American population: An appraisal of techniques with a new hemisphere estimate. *Current Anthropology* **7**(4):395–416.
Dodge, R. E.
  1914  California shellmounds. Washington, D.C.: *Records of the Past* **13**:120.
Donnan, C. B.
  1964  A suggested culture sequence for the Providence Mountains (eastern Mojave Desert). Los Angeles: *University of California, Los Angeles, Archaeologial Survey Annual Report, 1963–1964*:1–26.
Dotta, J. D.
  1967  The Gunther-barbed projectile point: A description and evaluation. Manuscript. San Francisco: Department of Anthropology, San Francisco State University.
Downs, J. F.
  1966  *The two worlds of the Washo.* New York: Holt, Rinehart, and Winston.
Downs, T., and G. J. Miller
  1971  Asphalt cemetery of the Ice Age. Chicago: *Encyclopaedia Britannica Yearbook of Science and the Future, 1972*:50–63.
Drake, R. J.
  1948  Archaeology investigations of the San Bruno shellmound, San Mateo County, California. Santa Fe: *El Palacio* **11**:317–323.
Driver, H. E.
  1936  Wappo ethnography. Berkeley: *University of California Publications in American Archaeology and Ethnology* **36**(3):179–219.
  1937  Culture element distribution, VI: Southern Sierra Nevada. Berkeley: *University of California Anthropological Records* **1**:53–154.
  1939  Culture element distributions, X: Northwest California. Berkeley: *University of California Anthropological Records* **1**(6):297–433.
  1961  *Indians of North America.* Chicago: University of Chicago Press.
Drover, C. E.
  1971  Three fired-clay figurines from 4-Ora-64, Orange County, California. Costa Mesa: *Pacific Coast Archaeological Society Quarterly* **7**(4):45–49.
  1975  Early ceramics from coastal southern California. *The Journal of California An-*

*thropology* **2**(1):101–107.

1978    Prehistoric ceramic objects from Santa Catalina Island. *The Journal of California Anthropology* **5**(1):78–83.

1979    *The late prehistoric human ecology of the northern Mohave Sink, San Bernardino County, California.* Ph.D. dissertation. Riverside: Department of Anthropology, University of California.

1980    The ethnohistory of turquoise mining in southeastern California. *Journal of California and Great Basin Anthropology* **2**(2):257–260.

Drover, C. E., R. E. Taylor, T. Cairns, and J. E. Ericson

1979    Thermoluminescence determinations on early ceramic materials from coastal southern California. *American Antiquity* **44**(2):285–295.

Drucker, P.

1937    The Tolowa and their southwest Oregon kin. Berkeley: *University of California Publications in American Archaeology and Ethnology* **36**(4):221–300.

1947    *Appraisal of the archeological resources of Isabella Reservoir, Kern County, California.* Washington, D.C.: West Coast Projects, River Basin Surveys, Smithsonian Institution.

1948a   *Appraisal of the archeological resources of Kelsey Creek Reservoir, Lake County, California.* Washington, D.C.: Pacific Coast Area, River Basin Surveys, Smithsonian Institution.

1948b   *Appraisal of the archeological resources of Monticello Reservoir area, Napa County, California.* Washington, D.C.: Pacific Coast Area, River Basin Surveys, Smithsonian Institution.

1948c   *Appraisal of the archeological resources of the Pine Flat Reservoir, Fresno County, California.* Washington, D.C.: Columbia Basin Project, River Basin Surveys, Smithsonian Institution.

1948d   *Appraisal of the archeological resources of Success Reservoir, Tulare County, California.* Washington, D.C.: Pacific Coast Area, River Basin Surveys, Smithsonian Institution.

1948e   *Appraisal of the archeological resources of Wilson Valley Reservoir, Lake County, California.* Washington, D.C.: Pacific Coast Area, River Basin Surveys, Smithsonian Institution.

1948f   *Archeological appraisal of Indian Valley Reservoir, Lake Co., Sly Park Reservoir, El Dorado County, and Dry Creek Reservoir, Sonoma County, California.* Washington, D.C.: Pacific Coast Area, River Basin Surveys, Smithsonian Institution.

1948g   *Preliminary appraisal of the archeological resources of Folsom Reservoir, Placer, El Dorado, and Sacramento Counties, California.* Washington, D.C.: Pacific Coast Area, River Basin Surveys, Smithsonian Institution.

Du Bois, C. A.

1935    Wintu ethnography. Berkeley: *University of California Publications in American Archaeology and Ethnology* **36**(1):1–148.

Dumond, D. E.

1980    The archaeology of Alaska and the peopling of America. *Science* **209**(29):984–991.

1982    Colonization of the American Arctic and the New World. *American Antiquity* **47**(4):885–895.

Durrenberger, R. W.

1965    *Patterns on the land: Geographical, historical, and political maps of California.* Palo Alto: National Press.

Duvall, J. G., and W. T. Venner

1979    A statistical analysis of the lithics from the Calico site (SBCM 1500A), California. *Journal of Field Archaeology* **6**(4):455–462.

Eardley, A. J., R. T. Shuey, V. Gvosdetsky, W. P. Nash, M. Dane Picard, D. C. Gray, and
G. J. Kukla
    1973    Lake cycles in the Bonneville Basin, Utah. *Geological Society of America Bul-
            letin* **84**:211–216.
Earle, T. K., and J. E. Ericson
    1977    *Exchange systems in prehistory.* New York: Academic Press.
Eberhart, H.
    1961    The cogged stones of southern California. *American Antiquity* **26**(3):361–370.
Edwards, H. A.
    1956    Notes on the archaeology of the northern Channel Islands. Los Angeles: *Archae-
            ological Survey Association of Southern California Newsletter* **3**:5–6.
Edwards, R. L.
    1966    *An archaeological survey of the Etsel-Franciscan Reservoir area, Mendocino
            County, California.* San Francisco: Report to the National Park Service.
    1967    Notes on the Aukum Reservoir survey, Amador County, California. Manu-
            script. Davis: Department of Anthropology, University of California.
    1968    *An archaeological survey of Point Reyes Peninsula and a settlement pattern
            hypothesis.* San Francisco: Report to the National Park Service, Western Region
            Office.
    1970    A settlement pattern hypothesis for the Coast Miwok based on an archaeologi-
            cal survey of Point Reyes Seashore. *San Francisco: Treganza Anthropology Mu-
            seum Papers* 6:105–114.
    1973    The Hartnell–Cabrillo College November 1972 archaeological field reconnais-
            sance: the Nacimiento River, Monterey County. Manuscript. Aptos: Depart-
            ment of Human Sciences, Cabrillo College.
    1975    *Prehistoric cultural resources at Hunter-Liggett Military Reservation.* Wash-
            ington, D.C.: Report to the Advisory Council on Historic Preservation.
Edwards, R. L., and M. E. Farley
    1974    An assessment of the cultural resources of the lower Pájaro River basin. Manu-
            script. Aptos: Archaeological Regional Research Center, Cabrillo College.
Edwards, R. L., P. Hickman, and G. Breschini
    1974    Assessment of the impact on cultural resources of the proposed San Clemente
            Dam, upper Carmel Valley, Monterey County, California. Manuscript. Aptos:
            Archaeological Regional Research Center, Cabrillo College.
Eisen, G.
    1898    Long lost mines of precious gems are found: The prehistoric turquoise mines of
            California and the ancient Indian workers. *The San Francisco Call*, March 18:6;
            March 27:17.
    1904    An account of the Indians of the Santa Barbara Islands in California. Prague:
            *Sitzungberichten der Koniglichen Bohemischen Gesellshaft der Wissen-
            schaften*, Klasse II: 1–30.
Eisenman, L., and D. A. Fredrickson
    1980    *Temporal seriation of Native American sites at The Geysers.* Redding: Paper
            presented at the Annual Meeting of the Society of California Archaeology.
Ellis, R. R., and R. H. Crabtree
    1974    *Archaeological impact statement on East Mesa, Area 1 and 2, Imperial Valley,
            California.* Boulder City: Report to the U.S. Bureau of Reclamation.
Elmendorf, W. W.
    1963    Yukian-Siouan lexical similarities. *International Journal of American Linguis-
            tics* **29**(4):300–309.
    1964    Item and set comparisons in Yuchi, Siouan, and Yukian. *International Journal
            of American Linguistics* **30**(4):328–340.

1968    Lexical and cultural change in Yukian. *Anthropological Linguistics* **10**(7):1–41.

1982    Features of Yukian pronomial structure. *Journal of California and Great Basin Anthropology, Papers in Linguistics.*

n.d.    Features of Yukian pronominal structure. *Journal of California and Great Basin Anthropology, Papers in Linguistics.* In press.

Elsasser, A. B.

1955    *Salvage archaeology at sites Nap-74 and Nap-93 in the Monticello Reservoir area, California.* San Francisco: Report to the National Park Service.

1958    Aboriginal use of restrictive Sierran environments. Berkeley. *University of California Archaeological Survey Reports* 41:27–33.

1959    *Archaeological survey of Sequoia-Kings Canyon National Parks.* San Francisco: Report to the National Park Service.

1960    The archaeology of the Sierra Nevada in California and Nevada. Berkeley: *University of California Archaeological Survey Reports* 51:1–93.

1962    *Indians of Sequoia and Kings Canyon National Parks.* Three Rivers: Sequoia Natural History Association.

1965    *The archaeology of the north coast of California.* Ph.D. dissertation. Berkeley: Department of Anthropology, University of California.

1966    Native occupation of the Terminus Reservoir region. In L. E. Berryman and A. B. Elsasser, *Terminus Reservoir:*7–29. Sacramento: Army Corps of Engineers.

1978a   Basketry. In R. F. Heizer. vol. ed , *Handbook of North American Indians, Vol. 8: California:*626–641. Washington, D.C.: Smithsonian Institution.

1978b   Development of regional prehistoric cultures. In R. F. Heizer, vol. ed., *Handbook of North American Indians, Vol. 8: California:*37–58. Washington, D.C.: Smithsonian Institution.

Elsasser, A. B., and R. F. Heizer

1963    The archaeology of Bowers Cave, Los Angeles County, California. Berkeley: *University of California Archaeological Survey Reports* 59:1–60.

1964    Archaeology of Hum-67, the Gunther Island site in Humboldt Bay, California. Berkeley: *University of California Archaeological Survey Reports* 62:5–122.

1966    Excavation of two northwestern California coastal sites. Berkeley: *University of California Archaeological Survey Reports* 67:1–149.

Elsasser, A. B., and E. R. Prince

1961    Eastgate Cave. Berkeley: *University of California Anthropological Records* **20**(4):139–149.

Elston, R.

1970    A test excavation at the Dangberg Hot Spring site (26-Do-1), Douglas County, Nevada. Reno: *Nevada Archaeological Survey Reporter* **1**(2):3–5.

1971    A contribution to Washo archaeology. Reno: *Nevada Archaeological Survey Research Papers* 2.

1972    *The Steamboat assemblage and its relationship to the Martis Complex.* Long Beach: Paper presented at the Annual Meeting of the Society for California Archaeology and the Southwestern Anthropological Association.

1974a   *An intensive archaeological investigation and evaluation of the Goodyear's Bar site (FS-05-17-53-15) in Sierra County, California.* Nevada City: Report to the Tahoe National Forest.

1974b   *Preliminary archaeological reconnaissance of Goodyear's Bar and Indian Valley, Sierra County, California.* Nevada City: Report to the Tahoe National Forest.

1976    *The structural analysis of lithic production systems.* Ph.D. dissertation. Pullman: Department of Anthropology, Washington State University.

Elston, R., and J. O. Davis
  1972    An archaeological investigation of the Steamboat Springs locality, Washoe
          County, Nevada. Reno: *Nevada Archaeological Survey Reporter* **6**(1):9–14.
Elston, R., J. O. Davis, A. Leventhal, and C. Covington
  1977    *The archaeology of the Tahoe Reach of the Truckee River.* Reno: Report to the
          Tahoe–Truckee Sanitation Agency.
Elston, R., J. O. Davis, and G. Townsend
  1976    *An intensive archaeological investigation of the Hawkins Land Exchange site
          (FS-05-17-57-33), 4-Nev-184.* Nevada City: Report to the Tahoe National Forest.
Elston, R., and D. Turner
  1968    An archaeological reconnaissance of the southern Truckee Meadows, Washoe
          County, Nevada. Manuscript. Reno: Nevada Archaeological Survey.
Emery, K.
  1960    *The sea off southern California.* New York: Wiley.
Enfield, R., and G. Enfield
  1964    Mammoth Creek Cave, Mono County, California. Los Angeles: *University of
          California, Los Angeles, Archaeological Survey Annual Report, 1963–1964:*
          393–424.
Ericson, J. E.
  1977a   Egalitarian exchange systems in California: A preliminary view. In T. K. Earle
          and J. E. Ericson, eds., *Exchange Systems in Prehistory:*109–126. New York:
          Academic Press.
  1977b   *Prehistoric exchange systems in California: The results of obsidian dating and
          tracing.* Ph.D. dissertation. Los Angeles: Department of Anthropology, Univer-
          sity of California.
  1978    Thermoluminescence measurements of fired clay from Feature 1, CA-Lak-741.
          In T. F. Weber, *Archaeological investigations at the Burns Valley sites, CA-
          Lak-741 and CA-Lak-742, Lake County, California:*192. Sacramento: Peak and
          Associates.
Ericson, J. E., and R. Berger
  1974    Late Pleistocene American obsidian tools. *Nature* **249**(5460):824–825.
Ernst, W. G.
  1979    California and plate tectonics. *California Geology* **32**(9):187–196.
Essene, F.
  1942    Culture element distributions, XXVI: Round Valley. Berkeley: *University of
          California Anthropological Records* **8**(1):1–97.
Estep, H. A.
  1933    The Indians of Pelican Island: Sites CA-Ker-59, CA-Ker-66, and CA-Ker-67.
          Berkeley: *University of California Archaeological Survey Manuscripts* 38.
Euler, R. C.
  1966    Southern Paiute ethnohistory. Salt Lake City: *University of Utah Anthropologi-
          cal Papers* 78.
Evans, R. K.
  1968    The Monterey Peninsula College sites (Mnt-371, 372, 373), preliminary report.
          Manuscript. Los Angeles: Department of Anthropology, University of
          California.
Fages, P.
  1972    *A historical, political, and natural description of California by Pedro Fages,*
  (1775)  *soldier of Spain,* H. I. Priestly, trans. Ramona: Ballena Press.
Fairbridge, R. W.
  1976    Shellfish-eating preceramic Indians in coastal Brazil. *Science* **191**(4225):353–359.
Farmer, M. F.
  1936    Tracing early man in western caves. *Hobbies* **40**:102–108.

Farquhar, F. P.
  1966    *History of the Sierra Nevada.* Berkeley and Los Angeles: University of California Press.

Faye, P.-L.
  1923    Notes on the Southern Maidu. Berkeley: *University of California Publications in American Archaeology and Ethnology* 20(3):35–53.

Fee, D. J.
  1980    An archaeological assessment of Sequoia-Kings Canyon National Parks, California. Manuscript. Tucson: National Park Service.

Fenenga, F. F.
  1940    A reply to "Folsom and Nepesta points." *American Antiquity* 6(1):78–79.
  1947a   Archaeology of Terminus Reservoir, Tulare County, California. Manuscript. Berkeley: University of California Archaeological Survey.
  1947b   *Preliminary survey of archaeological resources in the Isabella Reservoir, Kern County, California.* Washington, D.C.: Pacific Coast Area, River Basin Surveys, Smithsonian Institution.
  1948a   *Appraisal of the archaeological resources of Terminus Reservoir, Tulare County, California.* Washington, D.C.: Pacific Coast Area, River Basin Surveys, Smithsonian Institution.
  1948b   Work of the California Archaeological Survey at the Isabella Reservoir area, Kern County, California. Berkeley: *University of California Archaeological Survey Manuscripts* 24.
  1949    Methods of recording and present status of knowledge concerning petroglyphs in California. Berkeley: *University of California Archaeological Survey Reports* 3.
  1952    The archaeology of the Slick Rock Village, Tulare County, California. *American Antiquity* 17(4):339–347.
  1953    The weights of chipped stone points: A clue to their functions. *Southwestern Journal of Anthropology* 9(3):309–333.
  1973    *Archaeological work in the Hidden Valley Reservoir area, Madera County, California.* San Francisco: Report to the National Park Service.
  1975    *The post-contact archaeological sites on the Fresno and Chowchilla Rivers.* Santa Cruz: Paper presented at the Annual Meeting of the Society for California Archaeology.

Fenenga, F., and F. A. Riddell
  1949    Excavation of Tommy Tucker Cave, Lassen County, California. *American Antiquity* 14(3):203–214.

Ferguson, G. J., and W. F. Libby
  1962    UCLA radiocarbon dates I. *Radiocarbon* 4:109–114.

Fischer, G.
  1966    Archaeological investigations in the Camanche Reservoir area—1962, Amador and Calaveras Counties, California. Manuscript. Stanford: Department of Anthropology, Stanford University.

Fisher, E. M.
  1935    Shell deposits of the Monterey Peninsula. Berkeley: *University of California Archaeological Survey Manuscripts* 17.

Fitch, J. E.
  1967    Fish remains recovered from a Corona del Mar, California, Indian midden (Ora-190). Sacramento: *California Fish and Game* 53(3):185–191.
  1969    Fossil records of certain schooling fishes of the California current system. Sacramento: *California Marine Resources Commission Report* 13:71–80.
  1972    Fish remains, primarily otoliths, from a coastal Indian midden (SLO-2) at Diablo Cave, San Luis Obispo County, California. San Luis Obispo: *San Luis Obispo County Archaeological Society Papers* 7:101–120.

1975    Fish remains from a Chumash village site (Ven-87) at Ventura, California. Manuscript. Long Beach: California Department of Fish and Game.

Fitting, J., J. Costello, and H. Crew, compilers
n.d.    Cultural resources mitigation program, New Melones Lake project, Phase 1 draft report. La Jolla: Science Applications, Inc. Unpublished report to the Sacramento District, Corps of Engineers. La Jolla: Science Applications, Inc.

Fitzwater, R. J.
1962    Final report on two season's excavations at El Portal, Mariposa County, California. Los Angeles: *University of California, Los Angeles, Archaeological Survey Annual Report, 1961–1962:234–285.*

1968a   Excavations at Crane Flat, Yosemite National Park. Los Angeles: *University of California, Los Angeles, Archaeological Survey Annual Report, 1967–1968:276–302.*

1968b   Excavations at the Hodgdon Ranch site (Tuo-236). Los Angeles: *University of California, Los Angeles, Archaeological Survey Annual Report, 1967–1968:303–314.*

Fitzwater, R. J., and M. Van Vlissingen
1960    Preliminary report on an archaeological site at El Portal, California. Los Angeles: *University of California, Los Angeles, Archaeological Survey Annual Report, 1959–1960:155–200.*

Fladmark, K. R.
1979    Routes: Alternate migration corridors for Early Man in North America. *American Antiquity* **44**(1):55–69.

Flint, R. F.
1965    *Glacial and Quaternary geology.* New York: Wiley.

Flint, R. F., and W. A. Gale
1958    Stratigraphy and C-14 dates at Searles Lake, California. *American Journal of Science* **256**:689–714.

Flynn, K., and W. G. Roop
1975    *Archaeological testing of 4-Hum-245 and 4-Hum-246, Pine Ridge, Humboldt County, California.* Eureka: Report to Terra-Scan.

1976    *Preliminary archaeological reconnaissance and determination of zones of sensitivity of the Double B Ranch subdivision, northeastern Humboldt County, California.* Eureka: Report to Terra-Scan.

Follett, W. I.
1957    Fish remains from a shellmound in Marin County, California. *American Antiquity* **23**(1):68–71.

1968    Fish remains from Century Ranch site LAn-229, Los Angeles County, California. Los Angeles: *University of California, Los Angeles, Archaeological Survey Annual Report, 1968:132–143.*

1973    Fish remains from Bamert Cave, Amador County, California. In R. F. Heizer and T. R. Hester, *The Archaeology of Bamert Cave, Amador County, California:55–62.* Berkeley: University of California Archaeological Research Facility.

1974    Fish remains from the Shelter Hill site, Marin County, California. San Francisco: *Treganza Anthropology Museum Papers* 15:145–159.

1975a   Fish remains from the Stege mounds (CA-CCo-300 and CA-CCo-298), Richmond, Contra Costa County, California. Berkeley: *Contributions of the University of California Archaeological Research Facility* 29:123–128.

1975b   Fish remains from the West Berkeley shellmound (CA-Ala-307), Alameda County, California. Berkeley: *Contributions of the University of California Archaeological Research Facility* 29:71–98.

Foote, L.
    1964    Notes on Sta-133 near Patterson, California. Manuscript. Sacramento: California Department of Parks and Recreation.
Forbes, J. D.
    1969    *Native Americans of California and Nevada.* Healdsburg: Naturegraph.
Fortsch, D. E.
    1972    *A late Pleistocene vertebrate fauna from the northern Mojave Desert of California.* M.S. thesis. Los Angeles: Department of Geological Sciences, University of Southern California.
    1978    The Lake China Rancholabrean faunule. In E. L. Davis, ed., The ancient Californians: Rancholabrean hunters of the Mojave Lakes country. Los Angeles: *Natural History Museum of Los Angeles County, Science Series* 29:173–176.
Foster, G. M.
    1944    A summary of Yuki culture. Berkeley: *University of California Anthropological Records* 5(3):155–244.
Fowler, C. S.
    1972    Some ecological clues to proto-Numic homelands. Reno: *University of Nevada, Desert Research Institute Publications in the Social Sciences* 8:105–121.
Fowler, D. D., ed.
    1977    Models and Great Basin prehistory: A symposium. Reno: *University of Nevada, Desert Research Institute Publications in the Social Sciences* 12.
Fowler, D. D., D. B. Madsen, and M. Hattori
    1973    Prehistory of southeastern Nevada. Reno and Las Vegas: *Desert Research Institute Publications in the Social Sciences* 6.
Fox, S. J., and D. L. Hardesty
    1972    *A survey of archaeological resources in the Modoc and Shasta–Trinity National Forests, California.* San Francisco: Report to the Forest Service, Region Five.
Fredrickson, D. A.
    1949    *Appraisal of the archaeological resources of the New Melones Reservoir, Calaveras and Tuolumne Counties, California.* Washington, D.C.: Pacific Coast Area, River Basin Surveys, Smithsonian Institution.
    1961a   The archaeology of Lak-261, a stratified site near Lower Lake, California. Manuscript. Sacramento: California Department of Parks and Recreation.
    1961b   The archaeology of Nap-131, an early site in Napa County, California. Manuscript. Department of Anthropology, Sonoma State University.
    1962    *Archaeological investigations within construction site area of Unit No. 1 of Pacific Gas and Electric Company's Atomic Park, Sonoma County, California.* San Francisco: Report to Pacific Gas and Electric Company.
    1964a   Archaeological investigations near Alamo, Contra Costa County, California: CCo-308. Manuscript. Sacramento: California Department of Parks and Recreation.
    1964b   *Preliminary impression of the archaeology of Ker-116.* Sacramento: Report to the California Department of Parks and Recreation.
    1965a   *Buena Vista Lake: Thirty years after Wedel.* Los Angeles: Paper presented at the Annual Meeting of the Southwestern Anthropological Association.
    1965b   Recent excavations in the interior of Contra Costa County, California. Sacramento: *Sacramento Anthropological Society Papers* 3:18–25.
    1966    *CCo-308: The archaeology of a Middle Horizon site in interior Contra Costa County, California.* M.A. thesis. Davis: Department of Anthropology, University of California.
    1967    Additional C-14 dates for Water Resources investigations at Buena Vista Lake. San Francisco: *Society for California Archaeology Newsletter* 1(5):5.
    1968    Archaeological investigations at CCo-30 near Alamo, Contra Costa County,

California. Davis: *University of California, Center for Archaeological Research at Davis, Publications* 1.

1969  Technological change, population movement, environmental adaptation, and the emergence of trade: Inferences on culture change suggested by midden constituent analysis. Los Angeles: *University of California, Los Angeles, Archaeological Survey Annual Report, 1968–1969:*101–125.

1973  *Early cultures of the North Coast Ranges, California.* Ph.D. dissertation. Davis: Department of Anthropology, University of California.

1974a  Cultural diversity in early central California: A view from the North Coast Ranges. *The Journal of California Anthropology* **1**(1):41–54.

1974b  Social change in prehistory: A central California example. In L. J. Bean and T. F. King, eds., ?*Antap:* California Indian political and economic organization. Ramona: *Ballena Press Anthropological Papers* 2:57–73.

1975a  *An archaeological reconnaissance of the beach and marine terraces of the King Range National Conservation Area.* Ukiah: Report to the Bureau of Land Management.

1975b  Comments on dates from CCo-309, CCo-30, CCo-308. Manuscript. Davis: Distributed at a workshop on the archaeological chronology of the Delta subregion.

1977  *Prehistoric exchange systems in central California.* Sacramento: Paper presented at the Cosumnes River College Staff Development Symposium on the Archaeology of the Central Valley.

1979a  An archaeological survey of the Knoxville-Manhattan Mine area, Napa County, California. Manuscript No. S-1711. Rohnert Park: Anthropological Studies Center, Sonoma State University.

1979b  Recent archaeological studies by Sonoma State College in coastal northern California. In P. McW. Bickel, *A study of cultural resources in Redwood National Park:*148–159. Denver: Report to the National Park Service.

Fredrickson, D. A., and J. Grossman

1966  *Radiocarbon dating of an early site at Buena Vista Lake, California.* Reno: Paper presented at the Annual Meeting of the Society for American Archaeology.

1977  A San Dieguito component at Buena Vista Lake, California. *The Journal of California Anthropology* **4**(2):173–190.

Freeland, L. S.

1951  Language of the Sierra Miwok. *Indiana University Publications in Anthropology and Linguistics, Memoirs* 6.

Freeland, L. S., and S. Broadbent

1960  Central Sierra Miwok dictionary. Berkeley: *University of California Publications in Linguistics* 23:1–71.

Frémont, J. C.

1966   *Report of the exploring expedition to the Rocky Mountains.* Microfilm. Wash-
(1854)  ington, D.C.: Library of Congress.

Fried, M.

1967  *The evolution of political society.* New York: Random House.

Friedman, J. P.

1976  *Archaeological investigations at Aspen Grove Campground, Eagle Lake, Lassen County, California.* Susanville: Report to the Lassen National Forest.

1977a  *Archaeological investigations of Pikes Point, Eagle Lake, Lassen County, California.* Susanville: Report to the Lassen National Forest.

1977b  *Archaeological overview for the Mt. Dome and Timbered Crater regions, north central California.* Redding: Report to the Bureau of Land Management.

Frison, G. C.

1974  *The Casper site: A Hell Gap bison kill on the High Plains.* New York: Academic Press.

Fritts, H. C.
1965    Tree-ring evidence for climatic change in western North America. *Monthly Weather Review* **93**(7):421–443.

Fritz, J., and C. Smith
1978    *Archaeological overview of Pinnacles National Monument, San Benito County, California.* Tucson: Report to the National Park Service.

Fryxell, R., T. Bielicki, R. D. Daugherty, C. Gustafson, H. T. Irwin, and B. C. Keel
1968    Human skeletal materials and artifacts from sediments of Pinedale (Wisconsin) glacial age in southeastern Washington, United States. Tokyo: *Proceedings of the 8th International Congress of Anthropological and Ethnological Sciences, 1968: Ethnology and Archaeology* **3**:176–181.

Furlong, E. L.
1907    Reconnaissance of a recently discovered Quaternary cave deposit near Auburn, California. *Science* **25**:392–394.

Gage, R.
1969    *Summary of archaeological reconnaissance of the proposed New Melones Reservoir.* San Francisco: Report to the National Park Service.
1970    *Archaeological excavations in the New Melones Reservoir project: 1969 season,* W. E. Pritchard, ed. San Francisco: Report to the National Park Service.

Galdikas-Brindamour, B.
1970    Trade and subsistence at Mulholland: A site report on LAn-246. Los Angeles: *University of California, Los Angeles, Archaeological Survey Annual Report, 1970:*120–162.

Gallegos, D., ed.
1980    *Class II cultural resources inventory of the East Mesa and West Mesa regions, Imperial Valley, California,* Vol. 1. Riverside: Report to the U.S. Bureau of Land Management.

Galloway, J. P.
1976    *An analysis and comparison of burial data from CA-SMa-125.* M.A. thesis. San Francisco: Department of Anthropology, San Francisco State University.

Gallup, D. E.
1963    Archaeological survey of the lower Cache Creek area, Yolo County. Berkeley: *University of California Archaeological Survey Manuscripts* 330.

Galt, J. W.
1970    Calico conference. Riverside: *The Piltdown Newsletter* **2**(1):1–2.

Galvin, J.
1971    *The first Spanish entry into San Francisco Bay, 1775.* San Francisco: Howell Books.

Garcirodriguez de Montalvo
1508    Las sergas de esplandian. *Amadis de Gaula* 5 (157). Spain.

Garfinkel, A. P.
1980    A cultural resource management plan for the Fossil Falls/Little Lake locality. Bakersfield: *U.S. Bureau of Land Management, Cultural Resources Publications, Archaeology.*
1981    The identification of prehistoric aboriginal groups through the study of rock art. Manuscript: Sacramento: California Department of Transportation.

Garfinkel, A. P., and R. A. Cook
1979    Prehistoric change in central eastern California: The Sherwin Grade site. Sacramento: *California Department of Transportation Occasional Papers in Archaeology* 1.
1980    Radiocarbon dating of pinyon nut exploitation in eastern California. *Journal of California and Great Basin Anthropology* **2**(2):283–285.

Garfinkel, A. P., R. A. Schiffman, and K. R. McGuire, eds.
1980    Archaeological investigations in the southern Sierra Nevada: The Lamont
        Meadow and Morris Peak segments of the Pacific Crest Trail. Bakersfield: *U.S.*
        *Bureau of Land Management, Cultural Resources Publications, Archaeology.*

Garth, T. R.
1953    Atsugewi ethnography. Berkeley: *University of California Anthropological Re-*
        *cords* **14** (2):129–212.

Gates, G. R.
1980    A preliminary report on the prehistoric rock art of the Modoc National Forest.
        Alturas: *Journal of the Modoc County Historical Society* **2**:69–103.

Gaumer, D.
1968    Colloquia at University of California at Davis. *Society for California Archaeol-*
        *ogy Newsletter* **2**(2):14.

Gayton, A. H.
1929    Yokuts and Western Mono pottery making. Berkeley: *University of California*
        *Publications in American Archaeology and Ethnology* **24**(3):239–251.
1948a   Yokuts and Western Mono ethnography, I: Foothill Yokuts. Berkeley: *Univer-*
        *sity of California Anthropological Records* **10**(1):1–140.
1948b   Yokuts and Western Mono ethnography, II: Northern Foothill Yokuts and West-
        ern Mono. Berkeley: *University of California Anthropological Records*
        **10**(2):143–302.

Gehr, E. A., with L. Conton, D. Parrella, and J. Scott
1979    *Cultural resources survey and evaluation of Range 31 E, Tule Indian Reserva-*
        *tion.* Tucson: Report to the National Park Service.

Gerow, B. A.
1954    *The problem of culture sequences in central California archaeology.* Berkeley:
        Paper presented at the Annual Meeting of the American Association for the
        Advancement of Science.
1968    (with R. Force), *An analysis of the University Village Complex with a reap-*
        *praisal of central California archaeology.* Stanford: Stanford University Press.
1974a   Comments on Fredrickson's "Cultural diversity." *The Journal of California*
        *Anthropology* **1**(2):239–246.
1974b   Co-traditions and convergent trends in prehistoric California. San Luis Obispo:
        *San Luis Obispo County Archaeological Society Occasional Paper* **8**:1–58.

Gibb, G.
1851    *George Gibb's journal of Redick McKee's 1851 expedition through north-*
(1972)  *western California,* R. F. Heizer, ed. Berkeley: Archaeological Research Facility,
        University of California.

Gibson, R. O., A. Lönnberg, J. Morris, and W. G. Roop
1976    *Report on the excavations at Kirk Creek (4-Mnt-238), Monterey County, Cal-*
        *ifornia.* Sacramento: Report to the California Department of Transportation.

Gifford, E. W.
1913    Monterey County shell mounds. Berkeley: *University of California Archae-*
        *ological Survey Manuscripts* 22.
1961a   Composition of California shellmounds. Berkeley: *University of California*
        *Publications in American Archaeology and Ethnology* **12**(1):1–29.
1916b   Dichotomous social organization in south central California. Berkeley: *Univer-*
        *sity of California Publications in American Archaeology and Ethnology*
        **11**(5):291–296.
1926a   California anthropometry. Berkeley: *University of California Publications in*
        *American Archaeology and Ethnology* **22**(2):217–390.
1926b   Clear Lake Pomo society. Berkeley: *University of California Publications in*

*American Archaeology and Ethnology* **18**(2):287–390.

1926c    Miwok cults. Berkeley: *University of California Publications in American Archaeology and Ethnology* **18**(3):391–408.

1926d    Miwok lineages and the political unit in aboriginal California. *American Anthropologist* **28**:389–401.

1932     The Northfork Mono. Berkeley: *University of California Publications in American Archaeology and Ethnology* **31**(2):15–65.

1940     Californian bone artifacts. Berkeley: *University of California Anthropological Records* **3**(2).

1947     Californian shell artifacts. Berkeley: *University of California Anthropological Records* **9**(1).

1949     Diet and age of California shellmounds. *American Antiquity* **14**(3):223–224.

1955     Central Miwok ceremonies. Berkeley: *University of California Anthropological Records* **14**(4).

1965     The Coast Yuki. Sacramento: *Sacramento Anthropological Society Papers* 2:1–97.

Gifford, E. W., and W. E. Schenck

1926     Archaeology of the southern San Joaquin Valley. Berkeley: *University of California Publications in American Archaeology and Ethnology* **23**(1):1–122.

Gladwin, W., and H. Gladwin

1934     A method for designation of cultures and their variations. Globe: *Medallion Papers* 15.

Glassow, M. A.

1965     The Conejo rock shelter: An inalnd Chumash site in Ventura County. Los Angeles: *University of California, Los Angeles, Archaeological Survey Annual Report, 1964–1965*:19–80.

1977     *An archeological overview of the northern Channel Islands, California.* Tucson: Western Archeological Center, National Park Service.

1979     An evaluation of models of Ineseño Chumash subsistence and economics. *Journal of California and Great Basin Anthropology* **1**(1):155–161.

1980     Recent developments in the archaeology of the Channel Islands. In D. M. Power, ed., *The California Islands: Proceedings of a Multidisciplinary Symposium*:79–102. Santa Barbara: Santa Barbara Museum of Natural History.

Glassow, M. A., and J. D. Moore

1978     *Evaluation of cultural resources, Isabella Lake, California.* Report to the Army Corps of Engineers, Sacramento District. Santa Barbara: Social Process Research Institute, University of California.

Glassow, M. A., L. Spanne, and J. Quilter

1975     *Excavation of archaeological sites on Vandenberg Air Force Base, Santa Barbara County,* California. San Francisco: Report to the National Park Service.

Glennan, W. S.

1971a    *A glimpse at the prehistory of Antelope Valley—archaeological investigations at the Sweetser site (Ker-302).* Lancaster: Kern–Antelope Historical Society.

1971b    Concave-base lanceolate fluted points from California. Los Angeles: *The Masterkey* **45**(1):27–32.

1972     *The hypothesis of an ancient, pre-projectile point stage in American prehistory: Its application and validity in southern California.* Ph.D. dissertation. Los Angeles: Department of Anthropology, University of California, Los Angeles.

1976     The Manix Lake lithic industry: Early Lithic tradition or workshop refuse? Los Angeles: *The Journal of New World Archaeology* **1**(7):42–61.

n.d.     A Clovis point from California. Manuscript. Los Angeles: Department of Anthropology, University of California, Los Angeles.

Gobalet, K. W.

    1981    Analysis of fish remains from seven archaeological sites (CA-Mnt-110, 111, 112, 113, 114, 115, 116) located in Pacific Grove, Monterey County, California. In S. A. Dietz and T. L. Jackson, *Report of archaeological excavations at nineteen archaeological sites for the Stage I Pacific Grove-Monterey Consolidation Project of the Regional Sewerage System:* Appendix E (E1–E29). Santa Cruz: Archaeological Consulting and Research Services.

Goddard, P. E.

    1903    Life and culture of the Hupa. Berkeley: *University of California Publications in American Archaeology and Ethnology* **1**(1):1–88.

Godfrey, E.

    1941    Yosemite Indians. Yosemite National Park: *Yosemite Nature Notes* (special issue).

Goerke, E. B., and R. A. Cowan, with A. Ramenofsky and L. Spencer

    1983    The Pacheco site (Marin-152) and the Middle Horizon in Central California. *Journal of New World Archaeology* **6**(1):1–98.

Goldberg, S. K. (compiler)

    1983    Features. In M. J. Moratto *et al.*, New Melones archeological project, California: Indian sites 04-Cal-S-286, 04-Cal-S-347, and 04-Cal-S-461. *Final report of the New Melones Archeological Project* 4(2):413–468. Report to the National Park Service, Washington, D.C. Sonora: INFOTEC Development, Inc.

Goldberg, S., with M. J. Moratto

    1983    *Archaeological investigations at six sites on the Stanislaus National Forest, California.* Sonora: Report to the Stanislaus National Forest.

Goldschmidt, W.

    1951    Nomlaki ethnography. Berkeley: *University of California Publications in American Archaeology and Ethnology* **42**(4):303–443.

    1978    Nomlaki. In R. F. Heizer, vol. ed., *Handbook of North American Indians*, Vol. 8: *California*:341–349. Washington, D.C.: Smithsonian Institution.

Golla, V.

    1970    *Hupa grammar.* Ph.D. dissertation. Berkeley: Department of Linguistics, University of California.

Golomshtok, E. A.

    1921–    Monterey, Pacific Grove, and Salinas mounds. Berkeley: *University of Califor-*
    1922    *nia Archaeological Survey Manuscripts* 374.

Gonsalves, W. C.

    1955    Winslow Cave, a mortuary site in Calaveras County, California. Berkeley: *University of California Archaeological Survey Reports* 29:31–47.

Goodridge, J. D.

    1980    *California rainfall summary.* Sacramento: California Department of Water Resources.

Gordon, B. L.

    1974    *Monterey Bay area: Natural history and cultural imprints.* Pacific Grove: Boxwood.

Goss, J. A.

    1968    Culture historical inference from Utaztecan linguistic evidence. Pocatello: *Idaho State University Museum Occasional Papers* 22:1–42.

    1977    Linguistic tools for the Great Basin prehistorian. Reno: *Desert Research Institute Publications in the Social Sciences* **12**:49–70.

Gould, R. A.

    1963    Aboriginal California burial and cremation practices. Berkeley: *University of California Archaeological Survey Reports* 60:149–168.

    1964    Exploitative economics and culture change in central California. Berkeley: *Uni-*

*versity of California Archaeological Survey Reports* 62:123–163.

1966a Archaeology of the Point Saint George site and Tolowa prehistory. Berkeley: *University of California Publications in Anthropology* 4.

1966b The wealth quest among the Tolowa Indians of northwestern California. Philadelphia: *Proceedings of the American Philosophical Society* **110**(1):67–89.

1968 Seagoing canoes among the Indians of northwestern California. *Ethnohistory* **15**(1):11–42.

1972 A radiocarbon date from the Point St. George site, northwestern California. *Contributions of the University of California Archaeological Research Facility* 14:41–44.

1975 Ecology and adaptive response among the Tolowa Indians of northwestern California. *The Journal of California Anthropology* **2**(2):148–180.

1976 A case of heat treatment of lithic materials in aboriginal northwestern California. *The Journal of California Anthropology* **3**(1):142–144.

Graham, G. M.
1951 Ancient man in Hidden Valley, California. Los Angeles: *The Masterkey* **25**(3):79–82.

Grant, C.
1961 Ancient art in the wilderness. *Pacific Discovery* **14**:12–19.

1965 *The rock paintings of the Chumash.* Berkeley and Los Angeles: University of California Press.

1978a Chumash: Introduction. In R. F. Heizer, vol. ed., *Handbook of North American Indians, Vol. 8: California:* 505–508. Washington, D.C.: Smithsonian Institution.

1978b Eastern Coastal Chumash. In R. F. Heizer, vol. ed., *Handbook of North American Indians, Vol. 8: California:* 509–519. Washington, D.C.: Smithsonian Institution.

1978c Interior Chumash. In R. F. Heizer, vol. ed., *Handbook of North American Indians, Vol. 8: California:*530–534. Washington, D.C.: Smithsonian Institution.

1978d Island Chumash. In R. F. Heizer, vol. ed., *Handbook of North American Indians, Vol. 8: California:*524–529. Washington, D.C.: Smithsonian Institution.

Grant, C., J. W. Baird, and J. K. Pringle
1968 Rock drawings of the Coso Range, Inyo County, California. China Lake: *Maturango Museum Publications* 4.

Grayson, D. K.
1972 *The avian and mammalian remains from Nightfire Island.* Ph.D. dissertation. Eugene: Department of Anthropology, University of Oregon.

1976 The Nightfire Island avifauna and the Altithermal. In R. Elston, ed., Holocene environmental change in the Great Basin. Reno: *Nevada Archaeological Survey Research Papers* 6:73–103.

1977 Pleistocene avifaunas and the overkill hypothesis. *Science* **195**(4279):691–692.

1979 Mount Mazama, climatic change, and Fort Rock Basin archaeofaunas. In P. D. Sheets and D. K. Grayson, eds., *Volcanic activity and human ecology:* 427–457. New York: Academic Press.

Greengo, R. E.
1951 Molluscan species in California shell middens. Berkeley: *University of California Archaeological Survey Reports* 13:1–29.

1952 Shellfish foods of the California Indians. Berkeley: *Kroeber Anthropological Society Papers* 7:63–114.

1975 Shellfish (at Ala-307). Berkeley: *Contributions of the University of California Archaeological Research Facility* 29:65–69.

Greenwood, R. S.
1959 Early dwellers in Topanga Canyon. *Archaeology* **12**(4):271–277.

1969    The Browne site, early Milling Stone Horizon in southern California. *Memoirs of the Society for American Archaeology* 23.

1972    9000 years of prehistory at Diablo Canyon, San Luis Obispo County, California. San Luis Obispo: *San Luis Obispo County Archaeological Society Occasional Papers* 7:1–97.

1976    (assisted by V. Benté), *Evaluation of historical resources, New Melones project area*. Sacramento: Report to the U.S. Army Corps of Engineers, Sacramento District.

1977    (assisted by V. Benté), *Final evaluation of historic resources, New Melones Reservoir project*. Sacramento: Report to the U.S. Army Corps of Engineers, Sacramento District.

1978a   *Archaeological survey and investigation, Channel Islands National Monument*. Denver: Report to the National Park Service.

1978b   Obispeño and Purisimeño Chumash. In R. F. Heizer, vol. ed., *Handbook of North American Indians*, Vol. 8: *California*:520–523. Washington, D.C.: Smithsonian Institution.

Greenwood, R. S., with contributions by others

1982    New Melones archaeological project, California: Data recovery from historical sites. *Final report of the New Melones archaeological project* 5:1–351. Report to the National Park Service, Washington, D.C. Sonora: INFOTEC Development, Inc.

Greenwood, R. S., and R. O. Browne

1963    Preliminary survey of the Rancho Cañada Larga, Ventura County, California. Los Angeles: *University of California, Los Angeles, Archaeological Survey Annual Report, 1962–1963*:463–506.

1969    A coastal Chumash village: Excavation of *Shisholop*, Ventura County, California. Los Angeles: *Memoirs of the Southern California Academy of Sciences* 8.

Griffin, D. W.

1963    Prehistory of the southern Sierra Nevada. Los Angeles: *The Masterkey* **37**:49–57, 105–113.

Griffin, J. B.

1979    The origin and dispersion of the American Indians in North America. In W. S. Laughlin and A. B. Harper, eds., *The first Americans: Origins, affinities, and adaptations*:43–55. New York: Fischer.

Grinnell, J.

1935    A revised life zone map of California. Berkeley: *University of California Publications in Zoology* **40**:327–330.

Grosscup, G. L.

1954    *An archaeological survey of Yosemite National Park, 1954*. San Francisco: Report to the National Park Service.

Grossman, J. M.

1968    *Early cultural remains at Buena Vista Lake, California: Report on the 1965 season of field investigations*. Sacramento: Report to the California Department of Parks and Recreation.

Gudschinsky, S. C.

1964    The ABC's of lexicostatistics (glottochronology). In D. Hymes, ed., *Language in culture and society*:612–623. New York: Harper and Row.

Guilday, J. E.

1967    Differential extinctions during late Pleistocene and Recent times. In P. S. Martin and H. E. Wright, eds., *Pleistocene extinctions: The search for a cause*:121–140.

Guthrie, G.

1957    Southern Sierra Nevada archaeology. Los Angeles: *Archaeological Survey Association of Southern California Newsletter* **4**:1–2, 3–5.

Haag, W. G., and R. F. Heizer
1953     A dog burial from the Sacramento Valley. *American Antiquity* **18**(3):263–265.
Haas, M.
1958     Algonkian-Ritwan: The end of a controversy. *International Journal of American Linguistics* **24**(3):159–173.
1960     Some genetic affiliations of Algonkians. In S. Diamond, ed., *Culture in history: Essays in honor of Paul Radin:* 977–992. New York: Columbia University Press.
1966     Wiyot–Yurok–Algonkian and problems of comparative Algonkian. *International Journal of American Linguistics* **32**(2):101–107.
1967     Language and taxonomy in northwest California. *American Anthropologist* **69**(3–4):358–362.
1969     The prehistory of languages. *Janua Linguarum, Series Minor* 57. The Hague: Mouton.
1973     American Indian linguisitic prehistory. *Current trends in linguistics* 10A:677–712. The Hague: Mouton.
Hale, K.
1958     Internal diversity in Uto-Aztecan. *International Journal of American Linguistics* **24**(2):104–107.
1959     Internal diversity in Uto-Aztecan: II. *International Journal of American Linguistics* **25**(2):114–121.
1964     The sub-grouping of Uto-Aztecan languages: Lexical evidence for Sonora. *XXXV Congreso International de Americanistas, Actas y Memorias* **2**:511–518.
Hall, A. L.
1978     *Ethnohistorical studies of the Central Sierra Miwok, 1800–1900.* M.A. thesis. San Francisco: Department of Anthropology, San Francisco State University.
Hall, H. M.
1919     Life-zone indicators in California. San Francisco: *California Academy of Sciences, Proceedings* 9:37–67.
Hall, M. C.
1981     Land-use changes in Owens Valley prehistory: A matter of statistical inference. *American Antiquity* **46**(3):648–656.
Hall, M. C., and J. P. Barker
1975     *Background to the prehistory of the El Paso–Red Mountain desert region.* Riverside: Report to the U.S. Bureau of Land Management.
Halliday, W. R.
1959     *Adventure is underground.* New York: Harper.
Halpern, A. M.
1964     A report on a survey of Pomo languages. Berkeley: *University of California Publications in Linguistics* 34:88–93.
Hamilton, E. J.
1910     The cave man in California. *San Francisco Chronicle,* Oct. 2:3.
Hamilton, J.
1936     Indian shell mounds of San Mateo Creek and vicinity. Manuscript. San Mateo: Museum of San Mateo Historical Association.
Hammel, E. A.
1956     An unusual burial from Contra Costa County. Berkeley: *University of California Archaeological Survey Reports* 35:47–54.
Hammond, G. P.
1960     *The Larkin papers, Vol. 7, 1847–1848.* Berkeley and Los Angeles: University of California Press.
Hampson, R. P.
1979     A summary of archaeological activities in and near Redwood National Park. In

P. McW. Bickel, *A study of cultural resources in Redwood National Park*:177–184. Denver: Report to the National Park Service.

Hamy, E. T.
  1951    Hamy's report of the Pinart–de Cessac expedition. N. E. Heizer, trans. Berkeley: *University of California Archaeological Survey Reports* 13:6.

Hanks, H. E.
  1973    Preliminary archaeological evaluation of the Prince Exchange, Isabella Planning Unit. Manuscript. Bakersfield: Bureau of Land Management, Bakersfield District.

Hanks, H. G.
  1901    *The deep lying auriferous gravels and table mountains of California.* San Francisco: California Department of Mines.

Hansen, R., Sr.
  1970    *An application of systems analysis: Archaeology of Mrn-192.* M.A. thesis. San Francisco: Department of Anthropology, San Francisco State University.

Hansen, R., Sr., ed.
  1974    *Archaeological assessment of SMa-6.* San Mateo: Department of Anthropology, College of San Mateo.

Harden, E. W.
  1908    Indian pictographs in Pate Valley. *Sierra Club Bulletin* 6(4):258–259.

Hardesty, D. L., and S. Fox
  1974    Archaeological investigations in northern California. Reno: *Nevada Archaeological Survey Research Papers* 4.

Harding, M.
  1951    La Jollan culture. San Diego: El Museo 1(1):10–11; 31–38.

Hare, P. E.
  1974    Amino acid dating of bone—the influence of water. Washington, D.C.: *Carnegie Institution of Washington Yearbook* 73:576–581.

Harner, M. J.
  1953    Gravel pictographs of the lower Colorado River region. Berkeley: *University of California Archaeological Survey Reports* 20:1–29.

  1958    Lowland Patayan phases in the lower Colorado River Valley and Colorado Desert. Berkeley: *University of California Archaeological Survey Reports* 42:93–99.

Harper, K. Y., and G. M. Alder
  1972    Paleoclimatic inferences concerning the last 10,000 years from a resampling of Danger Cave, Utah. In D. D. Fowler, ed., Great Basin cultural ecology: A symposium. Reno: *Desert Research Institute Publications in the Social Sciences* 8:13–23.

Harradine, F.
  1953    Report on pedologic observations made at the "Capay Man" site in western Yolo County. Berkeley: *University of California Archaeological Survey Reports* 22:27.

Harrington, J. P.
  1918    Studies among the Indians of California. Washington, D.C.: *Smithsonian Miscellaneous Collections* 68:92–95.

  1923    Archaeological work in California. Washington, D.C.: *Smithsonian Miscellaneous Collections* 76(10):107–108.

  1927a    Archaeological and ethnological researches in California. Washington, D.C.: *Smithsonian Miscellaneous Collections* 78(7):232–237.

  1927b    Researches on the archaeology of southern California. Washington, D.C.: *Smithsonian Miscellaneous Collections* 78(1):106–111.

  1928    Exploration of the Burton Mound at Santa Barbara, California. Washington,

D.C.: *Smithsonian Institution, Bureau of American Ethnology Annual Reports* 44:23–168.

1933    Report of fieldwork on Indians of Monterey and San Benito Counties. Washington, D.C.: *Smithsonian Institution, Bureau of American Ethnology Annual Report for 1931–1932: 2–3.*

1942    Culture element distribution, XIX: Central California coast. Berkeley: *University of California Anthropological Records* 7(1):1–146.

Harrington, M. R.

1933    Gypsum Cave, Nevada. Los Angeles: *Southwest Museum Papers* 8.

1937    A stratified campsite near Boulder Dam. Los Angeles: *The Masterkey* **11**(3):16–89.

1938a    Early man at Borax Lake. Washington, D.C.: ·*Carnegie Institution of Washington News Service Bulletin, School Edition* **4**:259–261.

1938b    Folsom man in California. Los Angeles: *The Masterkey* **13**:133–137.

1938c    Pre-Folsom man in California. Los Angeles: *The Masterkey* **12**:173–175.

1938d    Recent excavations in California. Washington, D.C.: *Carnegie Institution of Washington, News Service Bulletin* **4**(31).

1943    A glimpse of Pomo archaeology. Los Angeles: *The Masterkey* **17**(1):9–12.

1945    Farewell to Borax Lake. Los Angeles: *The Masterkey* **19**:181–184.

1948a    An ancient site at Borax Lake, California. Los Angeles: *Southwest Museum Papers* 16:1–126.

1948b    A new Pinto site. Los Angeles: *The Masterkey* **22**:116–118.

1948c    Dollar Island. Los Angeles: *The Masterkey* **22**(5):154–156.

1948d    The Rattlesnake Island site. Los Angeles: *Southwest Museum Papers* 16:127–131.

1950    A storage cave near Walker Pass (Kern County). Los Angeles: *The Masterkey* **24**(3):89–90.

1957    A Pinto site at Little Lake, California. Los Angeles: *Southwest Museum Papers* 17.

Harrington, M. R., and R. D. Simpson

1961    Tule Springs, Nevada: With other evidence of Pleistocene man in North America. Los Angeles: *Southwest Museum Papers* 18.

Harris, E. F., and C. G. Turner, II

1974    SJo-68 dental morphology and its bearing on the "di-hybrid theory" of American Indian origins. Berkeley: *Contributions of the University of California Archaeological Research Facility* 22:1–46.

Harrison, W. M.

1964    *Prehistory of the Santa Barbara coast, California.* Ph.D. dissertation. Tucson: Department of Anthropology, University of Arizona.

1965    *Mikiw:* A coastal Chumash village. Los Angeles: *University of California, Los Angeles, Archaeological Survey Annual Report, 1964–1965:*91–178.

Harrison, W. M., and E. S. Harrison

1966    An archaeological sequence for the Hunting People of Santa Barbara, California. Los Angeles: *University of California, Los Angeles, Archaeological Survey Annual Report, 1965–1966:*1–89.

Hattori, E. M.

1982    *The archaeology of Falcon Hill, Winnemucca Lake, Washoe County, Nevada.* Ph.D. dissertation. Pullman: Department of Anthropology, Washington State University.

Haury, E. W.

1950    *The stratigraphy and archaeology of Ventana Cave, Arizona.* Tucson and Albuquerque: University of Arizona Press and University of New Mexico Press.

1959    Review of G. F. Carter, *Pleistocene man at San Diego. American Journal of Archaeology* **63**:116–117.

Hay, O. P.
1926    The geological age of Tuolumne Table Mountain. Washington, D.C.: *Journal of the Washington Academy of Sciences* **16**:358–361.

Hayden, J. D.
1966    Restoration of the San Dieguito type site to its proper place in the San Dieguito sequence. *American Antiquity* **31**(3):439–440.

Hayes, J. F., and D. A. Fredrickson
1978    *Description and analysis of historic and prehistoric artifacts from archaeological sites within Redwood National Park.* Crescent City: Report to the National Park Service.

Haynes, C. V., Jr.
1964    Fluted projectile points: Their age and dispersion. *Science* **145**(3639):1408–1413.

1969    A scientist disagrees . . . Chicago: *Encyclopaedia Britannica Yearbook of Science and the Future, 1970:76–77.*

1973    The Calico site: Artifacts or geofacts? *Science* **181**(4097):305–310.

1978    The geomorphology and geochronology of CA-Lak-741 and CA-Lak-742. In T. F. Weber, *Archaeological investigations at the Burns Valley sites, CA-Lak-741 and CA-Lak-742, Lake County, California:*190–191. Sacramento: Ann S. Peak and Associates.

Heady, H. F.
1977    Valley grassland. In M. G. Barbour and J. Major, eds., *Terrestrial vegetation of California:*491–514. New York: Wiley–Interscience.

Hedges, K.
1973    Rock art in southern California. *Pacific Coast Archaeological Society Quarterly* **9**(4):1–28.

Heizer, R. F.
1936    Notes and manuscript on the Miller Mound, site CA-Col-1. Berkeley: *University of California Archaeological Survey Manuscripts* 94.

1937a   Baked clay objects of the Lower Sacramento Valley, California. *American Antiquity* **3**(1):34–50.

1937b   Notes on the Drescher site, CA-Sac-109. Berkeley: *University of California Archaeological Survey Manuscripts* 64.

1938a   A Folsom-type point from the Sacramento Valley. Los Angeles: *The Masterkey* **12**(5):180–182.

1938b   The plank canoe of the Santa Barbara coast. Göteborg, Sweden: *Etnologiska Studier* **7**:193–237.

1939    Some Sacramento Valley–Santa Barbara archaeological relationships. Los Angeles: *The Masterkey* **13**(1):31–35.

1940a   Aboriginal use of bitumen by the California Indians. Sacramento: *California Division of Mines Bulletin* **118**:74.

1940b   A note on Folsom and Nepesta points. *American Antiquity* **6**(1):79–80.

1941a   Aboriginal trade between the Southwest and California. Los Angeles: *The Masterkey* **15**(5):185–188.

1941b   The direct historical approach in California archaeology. *American Antiquity* **7**(2):98–122.

1942a   Massacre Lake Cave, Tule Lake Cave, and shore sites. In L. S. Cressman, Archaeological researches in the northern Great Basin: 121–134. Washington, D.C.: *Carnegie Institution of Washington Publications* 538.

1942b   Walla Walla Indian expeditions to the Sacramento Valley, 1844–1847. San Francisco: *California Historical Society Quarterly* **21**(1):1–7.

1946    The occurrence and significance of Southwestern grooved axes in California. *American Antiquity* **11**(3):187–193.

1947    Francis Drake and the California Indians, 1579. Berkeley: *University of California Publications in American Archaeology and Ethnology* **42**(3):251–302.

1948a   A bibliography of ancient man in California. Berkeley: *University of California Archaeological Survey Reports* 2.

1948b   The California Archaeological Survey: Establishment, aims, and methods. Berkeley: *University of California Archaeological Survey Reports* 1:1–8.

1949    The archaeology of central California, I: The Early Horizon. Berkeley: *University of California Anthropological Records* **12**(1):1–84.

1950a   An unusual decorated steatite slab from northwestern California. *American Antiquity* **15**(3):252–254.

1950b   Archaeology of CCo-137, the "Concord Man" site. Berkeley: *University of California Archaeological Survey Reports* 9:15–20.

1950c   Observations on historic sites and archaeology in California. Berkeley: *University of California Archaeological Survey Reports* 9:1–5.

1950d   Observations on Early Man in California. Berkeley: *University of California Archaeological Survey Reports* 7:5–9.

1950e   The Stanford skull, a probable Early Man from Santa Clara County, California. Berkeley: *University of California Archaeological Survey Reports* 6:1–9.

1951a   A cave burial from Kern County, Ker-185. Berkeley: *University of California Archaeological Survey Reports* 10:29–37.

1951b   An assessment of certain Nevada, California, and Oregon radiocarbon dates. In F. Johnson, ed., Radiocarbon dating. Washington, D.C.: *Memoirs of the Society for American Archaeology* **8**:23–25.

1951c   A prehistoric Yurok ceremonial site (Hum-174). Berkeley: *University of California Archaeological Survey Reports* 11:1–4.

1951d   Indians of the San Francisco Bay area. San Francisco: *California Division of Mines Bulletin* **154**:39–56.

1951e   Preliminary report on the Leonard Rockshelter site, Pershing County, Nevada. *American Antiquity* **17**(2):89–98.

1952a   A review of problems in the antiquity of man in California. Berkeley: *University of California Archaeological Survey Reports* 16:3–17.

1952b   A survey of cave archaeology in California. Berkeley: *University of California Archaeological Survey Reports* 15:1–12.

1953    Sites attributed to Early Man in California. Berkeley: *University of California Archaeological Survey Reports* 22:1–4.

1958a   Prehistoric central California: A problem in historical-developmental classification. Berkeley: *University of California Archaeological Survey Reports* 41:19–26.

1958b   Radiocarbon dates from California of archaeological interest. Berkeley: *University of California Archaeological Survey Reports* 44:1–16.

1962a   Prefatory remarks to "The Rancho La Brea skull" by A. L. Kroeber. *American Antiquity* **27**(3):416.

1962b   *The Indians of California: A syllabus.* Berkeley: University of California, Extension Division.

1962c   Village shifts and tribal spreads in California prehistory. Los Angeles: *The Masterkey* **36**(2):60–67.

1964    The western coast of North America. In J. D. Jennings and E. Norbeck, eds., *Prehistoric man in the New World:*117–148. Chicago: University of Chicago Press.

1965    Problems of dating Lake Mojave artifacts. Los Angeles: *The Masterkey* **39**:125–134.

1966a    *Languages, territories and names of California Indian tribes.* Berkeley and Los Angeles: University of California Press.

1966b    Salvage and other archaeology. Los Angeles: *The Masterkey* **40**(2):54–60.

1970     Environment and culture: The Lake Mojave case. Los Angeles: *The Masterkey* **44**(2):68–72.

1972a    *California's oldest historical relic?* Berkeley: R. H. Lowie Museum of Anthropology.

1972b    *The eighteen unratified treaties of 1851–1852 between the California Indians and the United States Government.* Berkeley: University of California Archaeological Research Facility.

1973     Personal communication regarding the Fernandez site, as reported in Moratto 1973b:23–24.

1974a    *Elizabethan California.* Ramona: Ballena Press.

1974b    Studying the Windmiller Culture. In G. R. Willey, ed., *Archaeological researches in retrospect:*179–206. Cambridge: Winthrop.

1975     Some thoughts on California anthropology of the moment. Los Angeles: *The Journal of New World Archaeology* **1**(1):1–13.

1978a    Introduction. In R. F. Heizer, vol. ed., *Handbook of North American Indians, Vol. 8: California:*1–5. Washington, D.C.: Smithsonian Institution.

1978b    Trade and trails. In R. F. Heizer, vol. ed., *Handbook of North American Indians, Vol. 8: California:*690–693. Washington, D.C.: Smithsonian Institution.

Heizer, R. F., ed.

1951     The French scientific expedition to California, 1877–1879, by E. Hamy. Berkeley: *University of California Archaeological Survey Reports* 12:1–13.

1953     The archaeology of the Napa region. Berkeley: *University of California Anthropological Records* **12**(6):225–358.

1970     *An anthropological expedition of 1913 or get it through your head or yours for the revolution: Correspondence between A. L. Kroeber and L. L. Loud, July 12, 1913–October 31, 1913.* Berkeley: University of California Archaeological Research Facility.

1972     *George Gibb's journal of Redick McKee's expedition through northwestern California in 1851.* Berkeley: University of California Archaeological Research Facility.

1973     *Collected documents on the causes and events in the Bloody Island massacre of 1850.* Berkeley: University of California Archaeological Research Facility.

1974a    The Costanoan Indians. Cupertino: *De Anza College, Local History Series* 18.

1974b    *The destruction of the California Indians.* Santa Barbara and Salt Lake City: Peregrine Smith.

1974c    They were only Diggers: A collection of articles from California newspapers, 1851–1866, on Indian and white relations. Ramona: *Ballena Press Publications in Archaeology, Ethnology, and History* 1.

1978     *Handbook of North American Indians Vol. 8: California,* W. C. Sturtevant, gen. ed. Washington, D.C.: Smithsonian Institution.

Heizer, R. F., and A. F. Almquist

1971     *The other Californians: Prejudice and discrimination under Spain, Mexico, and the United States to 1920.* Berkeley and Los Angeles: University of California Press.

Heizer, R. F., and M. A. Baumhoff

1962     *Prehistoric rock art of Nevada and eastern California.* Berkeley and Los Angeles: University of California Press.

1970     Big game hunters in the Great Basin: A critical review of the evidence. Berkeley: *Contributions of the University of California Archaeological Research Facility* 7:1–2.

Heizer, R. F., and R. K. Beardsley
  1943    Fired clay figurines in central and northern California. *American Antiquity* **9**:199–207.
Heizer, R. F., and R. Berger
  1970    Radiocarbon age of the Gypsum Cave culture. Berkeley: *Contributions of the University of California Archaeological Research Facility* 7:13–18.
Heizer, R. F., and C. W. Clewlow, Jr.
  1973    *Prehistoric rock art of California.* Ramona: Ballena Press.
Heizer, R. F., and S. F. Cook
  1949    The archaeology of central California, a comparative analysis of human bone from nine sites. Berkeley: *University of California Anthropological Records* **12**(2):85–111.
  1952    Fluorine and other chemical tests of some North American human and fossil bones. *American Journal of Physical Anthropology* **10**(3):289–393.
  1953    "Capay Man", an ancient central California Indian burial. Berkeley: *University of California Archaeological Survey Reports* 22:24–26.
Heizer, R. F., and A. B. Elsasser
  1953    Some archaeological sites and cultures of the central Sierra Nevada. Berkeley: *University of California Archaeological Survey Reports* 12:1–42.
  1964    Archaeology of Hum-67, the Gunther Island site in Humboldt Bay, California. Berkeley: *University of California Archaeological Survey Reports* 62:1–122.
  1980    *The natural world of the California Indians.* Berkeley and Los Angeles: University of California Press.
Heizer, R. F., and A. B. Elsasser, eds.
  1956    Archaeological investigations on Santa Rosa Island in 1901 by Phillip Mills Jones. Berkeley: *University of California Anthropological Records* 17(2).
Heizer, R. F., and F. Fenenga
  1938    Archaeological notes on the Sandhill site (CA-Col-3). Berkeley: *University of California Archaeological Survey Manuscripts* 57.
  1939    Archaeological horizons in central California. *American Anthropologist* **41**(3):378–399.
Heizer, R. F., and T. R. Hester
  1973    *The archaeology of Bamert Cave, Amador County, California.* Berkeley: University of California Archaeology Research Facility.
  1978    Great Basin projectile points: Forms and chronology. Socorro: *Ballena Press Publications in Archaeology, Ethnology and History* 10.
Heizer, R. F., and G. W. Hewes
  1940    Animal ceremonialism in central California in light of archaeology. *American Anthropologist* **42**(4):587–603.
Heizer, R. F., and H. Kelley
  1962    Burins and bladelets in the Cessac collection from Santa Cruz Island, California. Philadelphia: *Proceedings of the American Philosophical Society* **106**(2):92–105.
Heizer, R. F., and A. D. Krieger
  1935–   Colusa County sites: Miller Mound (CA-Col-1), Sandhill Mound (CA-Col-2),
  1936    Howells Point Mound (CA-Col-3). Berkeley: *University of California Archaeological Survey Manuscripts* 383.
  1956    The archaeology of Humboldt Cave, Churchill County, Nevada. Berkeley: *University of California Publications in American Archaeology and Ethnology* **47**(1):1–190.
Heizer, R. F., and E. M. Lemert
  1947    Observations on archaeological sites in Topanga Canyon, California. Berkeley: *University of California Publications in American Archaeology and Ethnology* **44**(2):237–258.

Heizer, R. F., B. McKee, and L. Ristow
    1934    Excavation of the Herzog site, CA-Sac-27. Berkeley: *University of California Archaeological Survey Manuscripts* 60.

Heizer, R. F., and J. E. Mills
    1952    *The four ages of Tsurai: A documentary history of the Indian village on Trinidad Bay.* Berkeley and Los Angeles: University of California Press.

Heizer, R. F., and L. K. Napton
    1970    Archaeological investigations in Lovelock Cave, Nevada. Berkeley: *Contributions of the University of California Archaeological Research Facility* 10:1–86.

Heizer, R. F., and D. M. Pendergast
    1955    Additional data on fired clay human figurines from California. *American Antiquity* **21**(2):181–185.

Heizer, R. F., and R. J. Squier
    1953    Excavations at site Nap-32 in July, 1951. Berkeley: *University of California Anthropological Records* **12**(6):225–358.

Heizer, R. F., and A. E. Treganza
    1944    Mines and quarries of the Indians of California. Sacramento: *California Journal of Mines and Geology* **40**(3):291–359.
    n.d.    Archaeology of Bamert Cave. Manuscript. Berkeley: Department of Anthropology, University of California.

Heizer, R. F., and M. A. Whipple, eds.
    1951    *The California Indians: A source book.* Berkeley and Los Angeles: University of California Press.

Henn, W. G.
    1969    The archaeology of 4-Mad-158. San Francisco: *San Francisco State College Anthropology Museum, Occasional Papers* 5:1–30.
    1970    Faunal analysis of 4-Mrn-216, a seasonal site on Limantour Sandspit, Point Reyes National Seashore. San Francisco: *Treganza Anthropology Museum Papers* 6:195–210.
    1971    Excavations at 4-Tuo-279. San Francisco: *Treganza Anthropology Museum Papers* 9:45–65.

Henn, W. G., T. L. Jackson, and J. Schlocker
    1972    Buried human bones at the "BART" site, San Francisco, California. Sacramento: *California Geology* **25**(9):208–209.

Henn, W. G., and R. E. Schenk
    1970    An archaeological analysis of skeletal material excavated from the Civic Center of BART. San Francisco: *Society for California Archaeology, R. E. Schenk Memorial Archives of California Archaeology* 11.

Herring, A. K.
    1968    Surface collections from Ora-83, a cogged stone site at Bolsa Chica, Orange County, California. *Pacific Coast Archaeological Society Quarterly* **4**(3):3–37.

Hester, J. J.
    1960    Pleistocene extinction and radiocarbon dating. *American Antiquity* **23**(1):58–77.
    1967    The agency of man in animal extinctions. In P. S. Martin and H. E. Wright, eds., *Pleistocene extinctions: The search for a cause:*169–192. New Haven: Yale University Press.
    1972    *Blackwater Locality No. 1: A stratified Early Man site in eastern New Mexico.* Rancho de Taos: Fort Burgwin Research Center.
    1975    Paleoarchaeology of the Llano Estacado. In F. Wendorf and J. J. Hester, Late Pleistocene environments of the southern High Plains:247–256. Rancho de Taos: *Publication of the Fort Burgwin Research Center 9.*

Hester, T. R.
    1973    Chronological ordering of Great Basin prehistory. Berkeley: *Contributions of*

*the University of California Archaeological Research Facility* 17.

1978a    Esselen. In R. F. Heizer, vol. ed., *Handbook of North American Indians, Vol. 8: California*:496–499. Washington, D.C.: Smithsonian Institution.

1978b    Salinan. In R. F. Heizer, vol. ed., *Handbook of North American Indians, Vol. 8: California*:500–504. Washington, D.C.: Smithsonian Institution.

Hester, T. R., and R. F. Heizer

1973    *Review and discussion of Great Basin projectile points: Forms and chronology.* Berkeley: University of California Archaeological Research Facility.

Hester, T. R., and L. R. Jameson

1977    Evidence for the early occupation of the Washoe Lake Basin. Berkeley: *Contributions of the University of California Archaeological Research Facility* 35:17–22.

Hester, T. R., M. P. Mildner, and L. Spencer

1974    Great Basin atlatl studies. Ramona: *Ballena Press Publications in Archaeology, Ethnology, and History* 2:1–83.

Heusser, C. J.

1960    Late Pleistocene environments of North Pacific North America. New York: *American Geographical Society, Special Publications* 35.

Heusser, L.

1978    Pollen in Santa Barbara Basin, California: A 12,000-yr record. *Geographical Society of America Bulletin* **89**:673–678.

Hewes, G. W.

1941    Archaeological reconnaissance of the central San Joaquin Valley. *American Antiquity* **7**(2):123–133.

1942    Economic and geographical relations of aboriginal fishing in northern California. San Francisco: *California Fish and Game* **28**(2):103–110.

1943    Camel, horse, and bison associated with human burials and artifacts near Fresno, California. *Science* **97**(2579):328–329.

1946    Early man in California and the Tranquillity site. *American Antiquity* **11**(4):209–215.

1947    *Aboriginal use of fishery resources in northwestern North America.* Ph.D. dissertation. Berkeley: Department of Anthropology, University of California.

Heye, G. G.

1919    Certain aboriginal pottery from southern California. New York: *Indian Notes and Monographs* 7(1):3–48.

1921    Certain artifacts from San Miguel Island, California. New York: *Indian Notes and Monographs* 7(4).

1926    Stone objects from San Joaquin Valley, California. New York: *Indian Notes and Monographs* 3:107–111.

Hicks, F.

1961    Ecological aspects of aboriginal culture in the western Yuma area. Ph.D. dissertation. Los Angeles: Department of Anthropology, University of California.

Hildebrandt, W. R.

1981    *Native hunting adaptations on the North Coast of California.* Ph.D. dissertation. Davis: Department of Anthropology, University of California.

Hill, M.

1975    *Geology of the Sierra Nevada.* Berkeley and Los Angeles: University of California Press.

Hill, W. W.

1929    Monterey County sites, general. Berkeley: *University of California Archaeological Survey Manuscripts* 38.

Hillebrand, T. S.

1972    *The archaeology of the Coso locality of the Mojave region of California.* Ph.D.

dissertation. Santa Barbara: Department of Anthropology, University of California.

1974    The Baird site. China Lake: *Maturango Museum Monograph* 1:63–86.

Hillinger, C.

1958    *The California islands.* Los Angeles: Academy.

Hindes, M. G.

1959    A report of Indian sites and trails in the Huntington Lake region, California. Berkeley: *University of California Archaeological Survey Reports* 48:1–15.

1962    The archaeology of the Huntington Lake region in the southern Sierra Nevada, California. Berkeley: *University of California Archaeological Survey Reports* 58.

Hinkson, M.

1978    Karok. Paper presented at the Hokan–Yuman languages workshop, University of California, San Diego.

Hitchcock, C. H.

1870    The Calaveras skull. *Engineering and Mining Journal* 9:345–346.

Ho, T.-Y., L. F. Marcus, and R. Berger

1969    Radiocarbon dating of petroleum-impregnated bone from tar pits at Rancho La Brea, California. *Science* 164:1051–1052.

Hodge, W. F., ed.

1907–   Handbook of American Indians north of Mexico. Washington, D.C.: *Smithso-*
1910    *nian Institution, Bureau of American Ethnology Bulletin* 30(1–2).

1939    Picture writings in Pictograph Cañon, California. Los Angeles: *The Masterkey* 13(3):105–106.

Hoijer, H.

1956    The chronology of the Athapascan languages. *International Journal of American Linguistics* 22(4):219–232.

1960    Athabaskan languages of the Pacific Coast. In S. Diamond, ed., *Culture history: Essays in honor of Paul Radin:*960–976. New York: Columbia University Press.

Hole, F., and R. F. Heizer

1973    *An introduction to prehistoric archaeology* (third edition). New York: Holt, Rinehart and Winston.

Holland, F. R., Jr.

1962    Santa Rosa Island: An archaeological and historical study. *Journal of the West* 1(1):45–62.

1963    San Miguel Island: Its history and archaeology. *Journal of the West* 2(2):145–155.

Holland, R., and S. Jain

1977    Vernal pools. In M. G. Barbour and J. Major, eds., *Terrestrial vegetation of California:*515–533. New York: Wiley.

Holman, M. P.

1970    *An archaeological survey of the Southern California Edison Company right-of-way between the vicinity of Shaver Lake and Bakersfield.* Rosemead: Report to the Southern California Edison Company.

Holman, M. P., L. Barker, L. Reynolds, and J. Miller

1977    *The Sutro Baths sites: A preliminary archaeological investigation.* San Francisco: Report to the National Park Service.

Holmes, W. H.

1899    Preliminary review of the evidence relating to Auriferous Gravel Man in California. *American Anthroplogist* 1:107–121, 614–645.

1901    Review of the evidence relating to Auriferous Gravel Man in California. Washington, D.C.: *Smithsonian Institution, Report of the U.S. National Museum for 1899:* 419–472.

1902    Anthropological studies in California. Washington, D.C.: *Smithsonian Institution, Report of the U.S. National Museum for 1900:*155–187.

1912    Calaveras Man. Washington, D.C.: *Smithsonian Institution, Bureau of American Ethnology Bulletin* **30:**188.

1919    Handbook of aboriginal American antiquities. Washington, D.C.: *Smithsonian Institution, Bureau of American Ethnology Bulletin* **60.**

Holt, C.
1946    Shasta ethnography. Berkeley: *University of California Anthropological Records* **3**(3).

Hoover, R. L.
1971    *Some aspects of Santa Barbara Channel prehistory.* Ph.D. dissertation. Berkeley: Department of Anthropology, University of California.

1973    Chumash fishing equipment. San Diego: *San Diego Museum of Man Ethnic Technology Notes 9.*

Hopkins, D. M.
1967    *The Bering Land Bridge.* Stanford: Stanford University Press.

1979    Landscape and climate of Beringia during late Pleistocene and Holocene times. In W. S. Laughlin and A. B. Harper, eds., *The first Americans: Origins, affinities, and adaptations:*15–41. New York: Fischer.

Hopkins, N. A.
1965    Great Basin prehistory and Uto-Aztecan. *American Antiquity* **31**(1):48–60.

Howard, A. D.
1979    *Geologic history of Middle California.* Berkeley: University of California Press.

Howard, D. M.
1969    Archaeological investigations, Monterey–Big Sur area. San Francisco: *The Indian Historian* **2**(3):41–48.

1972    Excavations at Tes-haya: The Indian rancheria at Mission San Antonio de Padua (Mnt-100). Carmel: *Monterey County Archaeological Society Quarterly* **2**(1).

1973a    The archaeology of the Uriah Ray Rockshelter No. 1 (MNT-483). Carmel: *Monterey County Archaeological Society Quarterly* **2**(3):1–12.

1973b    The Gamboa site (Mnt-480)—an Esselen village, with a review of Esselen ethnography. Carmel: *Monterey County Archaeological Society Quarterly* **3**(1):1–11.

1974a    *Archaeology in Paradise: A survey of Monterey County archaeology.* Carmel: Antiquities Research Publications.

1974b    Big Sur archaeology at 4-Mnt-88. *Popular Archaeology* **3**(9–10):31–33, 36–37.

1974c    The Francis Doud site—Mnt-298. Pacific Grove: *Monterey County Archaeological Society Quarterly* **3**(4).

1974d    Radiocarbon dates from Monterey County. Carmel: *Monterey County Archaeological Society Quarterly* **3**(3).

1975    *Primitives in Paradise: The Monterey Peninsula Indians.* Carmel: Antiquities Research Publications.

1976    *Big Sur aracheology: A guide.* Carmel: Antiquities Research Publications.

Howard, D. M., and S. F. Cook
1971    The archaeology of the Hudson mound. Carmel: *Monterey County Archaeological Society Quarterly* **1**(1).

Howard, H.
1929    The avifauna of Emeryville shellmound. Berkeley: *University of California Publications in Zoology* **32:**301–394.

1960    Significance of Carbon-14 dates for Rancho La Brea. *Science* **131**(3402):712–714.

Howard, H., and A. H. Miller
1939    The avifauna associated with human remains at Rancho La Brea, California. Washington, D.C.: *Carnegie Institution of Washington, Publications* 514, *Paper* 3:39–48.

Hrdlička, Ales
  1906    Contributions to the physical anthropology of California. Berkeley: *University of California Publications in American Archaeology and Ethnology* 4(2):49–64.
  1907    Skeletal remains suggesting or attributed to Early Man in North America. Washington, D.C.: *Smithsonian Institution, Bureau of American Ethnology Bulletin* 33:21–28.
  1918    Catalogue of human crania in the United States National Museum collections: The Algonkin and related Iroquois; Calloan, Siouan, Salish and Sahaptin, Shoshonean, and Californian Indians. Washington, D.C.: *Smithsonian Institution, Proceedings of the U.S. National Museum* 69:1–127.
Hubbs, C. L.
  1967    A discussion of the geochronology and archaeology of the California islands. Santa Barbara: *Proceedings of the Symposium on the Biology of the California Islands*:337–341.
Hubbs, C., G. Bien, and H. Suess
  1960    La Jolla natural radiocarbon measurements. *American Journal of Science Radiocarbon Supplement* 2:197–223.
  1962    La Jolla natural radiocarbon measurements II. *Radiocarbon* 4:204–238.
  1965    La Jolla natural radiocarbon measurements IV. *Radiocarbon* 7:66–117.
Hudson, A. S.
  1873    On shellmounds in Oakland. San Francisco: *California Academy of Sciences, Proceedings* 5:302.
Hudson, D. T.
  1969    The archaeological investigations during 1935 and 1937 at Ora-237, Ora-238, and Ora-239, Santiago Canyon, Orange County, California. *Pacific Coast Archaeological Society Quarterly* 5(1):1–68.
  1976    Marine archaeology along the southern California coast. San Diego: *San Diego Museum Papers* 9.
Hudson, D. T., G. Lee, and K. Hedges
  1979    Solstic observations in Native California. *The Journal of California and Great Basin Anthropology* 1(1):38–63.
Hudson, D. T., J. Timbrook, and M. Rempe, eds. and annotators
  1978    *Tomol:* Chumash watercraft as described in the ethnographic notes of John P. Harrington. Socorro: *Ballena Press Anthropological Papers* 9.
Hudson, D. T., and E. Underhay
  1978    Crystals in the sky: An intellectual odyssey involving Chumash astronomy, cosmology, and rock art. Socorro: *Ballena Press Anthropological Papers* 10.
Hughes, R. E.
  1972a   *Archaeological research at Goose Lake, Modoc County, northeast California.* Salt Lake City: Paper presented at the Great Basin Anthropological Conference.
  1972b   *The Desert Side-notched projectile point: Radiocarbon dating and social process.* Sacramento: Paper presented at the Annual Meeting of the Society for California Archaeology.
  1973    *Archaeological reconnaissance: Renner land exchange and Cuppy Cave, Part II: Test excavation of Cuppy Cave (USFS-05-09-55-74), Modoc National Forest.* San Francisco: Report to the U.S. Forest Service, Region Five.
  1974    *Preliminary analysis of chipped stone debitage from a lowland occupation site in the Goose Lake Basin, northeast California.* Carson City: Paper presented at the Great Basin Anthropological Conference.
  1976    Test excavation of the Johnson Slough site (CA-Mod-428), Modoc County, California. Manuscript. Rohnert Park: On file at the Foundation for Educational Development, Sonoma State University.
  1977    *The archaeology of the Burrell site (CA-Mod-293), a lowland occupation site in*

*the Goose Lake Basin, northeast California.* Washington, D.C.: Report to the National Endowment for the Humanities.

1978   Aspects of prehistoric Wiyot exchange and social ranking. *The Journal of California Anthropology* **5**(1):53–66.

1982   Age and exploitation of obsidian from the Medicine Lake Highland, California. *Journal of Archaeological Science* **9**(2):173–185.

Humphreys, S. E.

1969   *The archaeology of New Bullards Bar.* San Francisco: Report to the National Park Service.

Hunt, A. P.

1960   Archaeology of the Death Valley salt pan, California. Salt Lake City: *University of Utah Anthropological Papers* 47.

Hunt, A. P., and C. B. Hunt

1964   Archaeology of the Ash Meadows Quadrangle, California and Nevada. Manuscript. On file, Death Valley National Monument.

Hymes, D. H.

1957   A note on Athapascan chronology. *International Journal of American Linguistics* **23**(4):291–297.

1960   Lexicostatistics so far. *Current Anthropology* **1**(1):3–44.

Ike, D., J. L. Bada, P. M. Masters, G. Kennedy, and J. C. Vogel

1979   Aspartic acid racemization and radiocarbon dating of an early Milling Stone Horizon burial in California. *American Antiquity* **44**(3):524–530.

Ingles, L. G.

1965   *Mammals of the Pacific states.* Stanford: Stanford University Press.

Irving, W. N.

1982   Pleistocene cultures in Old Crow Basin: Interim report. In J. E. Ericson, R. E. Taylor, and R. Berger, eds., Peopling of the New World:69–80. Los Altos: *Ballena Press Anthropological Papers* 23.

Irving, W. N., and C. R. Harington

1973   Upper Pleistocene radiocarbon-dated artefacts from the northern Yukon. *Science* **179**(4071):335–340.

Irwin, H. T.

1975   The Far West. In S. Gorenstein, ed., *North America:*133–164. New York: St. Martin's Press.

Irwin, W. P.

1960   Geologic reconnaissance of the northern Coast Ranges and Klamath Mountains, California, with a summary of mineral resources. San Francisco: *California Division of Mines and Geology Bulletin* **179.**

Irwin-Williams, C.

1973   The Oshara Tradition: Origins of Anasazi culture. Portales: *Eastern New Mexico University Contributions in Anthropology* **5**(1).

Jack, R. N., and I. S. E. Carmichael

1969   The chemical "fingerprinting" of acid volcanic rocks. Sacramento: *California Division of Mines and Geology, Short Contributions to California Geology, Special Report* 100:17–32.

Jackson, T. L.

1971   Determining the source of artifactual lithic material. San Francisco: *Treganza Anthropology Museum Papers* 9:167–180.

1972   X-ray fluorescence analysis of obsidian from 4-DNo-14. In M. J. Moratto, *Archaeological investigations in the Redwood National Park Region, California:* Appendix 1. San Francisco: Report to the National Park Service.

1973   Obsidian sources. San Francisco: *Treganza Anthropology Museum Papers* 11:46–57.

1974a     *The economics of obsidian in central California prehistory: Applications of X-ray fluorescence spectrography in archaeology.* M.A. thesis. San Francisco: Department of Anthropology, San Francisco State University.

1974b     San José Village: A northern Marin County site. San Rafael: *Miwok Archaeological Preserve of Marin, Papers* 1.

1975     *Metates in the sky, rocks in the head.* San Francisco: Report to the U.S. Forest Service, Region Five.

1976     *Report of the Middle Eel Planning Unit archaeological survey.* San Francisco: Report to the U.S. Forest Service, Region Five.

1977     *Hupa Mountain archaeological project: Report of salvage excavations at 4-Hum-245 and 4-Hum-246.* Ukiah: Report to U.S. Bureau of Land Management.

1979a     *Report of the Chawanakee Flats archaeological survey.* Fresno: Report to the Sierra National Forest.

1979b     RFP R5-04-79-05: Cultural resource survey of three timber sales, Sierra National Forest: Technical proposal. Manuscript. Santa Cruz: Archaeological Consulting and Research Services.

Jackson, T. L., and P. D. Schulz

1975     Typology, trade, and trace analysis: A test of local manufacture of Sacramento Valley obsidian tools. *Journal of New World Archaeology* 1(2):1–8.

Jacobsen, W. H., Jr.

1958     Washo and Karok: An approach to comparative Hokan. *International Journal of American Linguistics* 24(3):195–212.

Jaeger, E. C.

1965     *The California deserts.* Stanford: Stanford University Press.

Jansen, C.

1971     *The history and mystery of Moaning Cave.* Vallecito: Leaflet available at Moaning Cave.

Jenkins, O. P.

1941     Geomorphic provinces of California. San Francisco: *California Division of Mines Bulletin* 118(2):83–88.

1948     Geologic history of the Sierran gold belt. San Francisco: *California Division of Mines Bulletin* 141:23–30.

1973     Pleistocene Lake San Benito. *California Geology* 26(7):151–163.

Jenkins, O. P., ed.

1951     Geologic guidebook of the San Francisco Bay counties. San Francisco: *California Division of Mines Bulletin* **154.**

Jennings, C. H., and P. Kisling

1971     Archaeological resources of the Mineral King. San Francisco: *Society for California Archaeology, R. E. Schenk Memorial Archives of California Archaeology* 29.

Jennings, J. D.

1957     Danger Cave. Salt Lake City: *University of Utah Anthropological Papers* 27.

1964     The Desert West. In J. D. Jennings and E. Norbeck, eds., *Prehistoric man in the New World:* 149–174. Chicago: University of Chicago Press.

1974     *Prehistory of North America* (2nd ed.). New York: McGraw–Hill.

1978     Origins. In J. D. Jennings, ed., *Ancient Native Americans:* 1–41. San Francisco: Freeman.

Jennings, J. D., and E. Norbeck

1955     Great Basin prehistory: A review. *American Antiquity* 21(1):1–11.

Jennings, J. D., and E. Norbeck, eds.

1964     *Prehistoric man in the New World.* Chicago: University of Chicago Press.

Jensen, P. M.

1970     Notes on the archaeology of the Sutter Buttes, California. Davis: *University of California, Center for Archaeological Research at Davis, Publications* 2:29–64.

1979     *An anthropological overview and cultural resources inventory of the northern*

*Sacramento Valley and southern Cascade Range.* Redding: Report to the U.S. Bureau of Land Management.

Jensen, P. M., and A. Farber
  1982 *Archaeological data recovery program at CA-Sis-342 on 02-Sis-97 P.M. 41.5 to 42.3, Department of Transportation, Redding, California.* Sacramento: Report to the California Department of Transportation.

Jepson, W. L.
  1925 *A manual of the flowering plants of California.* Berkeley and Los Angeles: University of California Press.

Jertberg, P. M.
  1978 *A qualitative and quantitative analysis of relationships of the eccentric crescent and its value as an indicator of culture change.* M.A. thesis. Fullerton: Department of Anthropology, California State University.

Jett, S. C.
  1977 Comment on Goss' "Linguistic tools for the Great Basin prehistorian." Reno: *Desert Research Institute Publications in the Social Sciences* **12**:71–78.

Jewell, D. P.
  1964 Archaeology of the Oroville Dam spillway. Sacramento: *Department of Parks and Recreation Archaeological Reports* 10(1).

Jewell, D. P., and J. S. Clemmer
  1958 Archaeological salvage excavations of sites CA-Sut-21 and CA-Sut-22 on the Feather River Levee near Nicolaus, California. Berkeley: *University of California Archaeological Survey Manuscripts* 259.

Johnson, D. L.
  1977a The California Ice-age refugium and the Rancholabrean extinction problem. Seattle: *Quaternary Research* **8**:149–153.
  1977b The late Quaternary climate of coastal California: Evidence for an Ice Age refugium. Seattle: *Quaternary Research* **8**:154–179.

Johnson, E.
  1940 The serrated points of central California. *American Antiquity* **6**(2):167–169.

Johnson, F., and J. P. Miller
  1958 Review of G. F. Carter, *Pleistocene Man at San Diego. American Antiquity* **24**(2):206–210.

Johnson, J. J.
  1966 A preliminary survey of the archaeological resources of lower Mill Creek. Manuscript. Davis: Department of Anthropology, University of California.
  1967 The archaeology of the Camanche Reservoir locality, California. Sacramento: *Sacramento Anthropological Society Papers* 6.
  1970a Archaeological investigations at the Applegate site (4-Ama-56). Davis: *University of California, Center for Archaeological Research at Davis, Publications* 2:65–144.
  1970b *Archaeological investigations at the Keeler site (Teh-300).* Manuscript. Sacramento: Department of Anthropology, California State University, Sacramento.
  1971a Personal communication regarding the French Camp Slough site, SJo-91. Sacramento: California State University, Sacramento.
  1971b Preliminary report on the French Camp Slough site, SJo-91. Manuscript. Sacramento: Department of Anthropology, California State University, Sacramento.
  1974 *An archaeological reconnaissance of the Pit 1 Project.* San Francisco: Report to the Pacific Gas and Electric Company.
  1975 *Archaeological investigations in and around Lassen National Park.* Tucson: Report to the National Park Service.
  1977 *Exploding myths in Central Valley archaeology: An overall update.* Paper presented at the Cosumnes River College staff development symposium on the archaeology of the Central Valley. November 5th. Sacramento.

1981    *Cultural conservatism and population movements: Hokan and Penutian interaction.* Rohnert Park: Paper presented at the 1981 Hokan–Penutian Conference, Sonoma State University.

Johnson, J. J., ed., with C. Assad, G. Greenway, B. Poswall, W. Soule, W. Wiant, K. Wilson, H. Keesling, J. Wood, D. Sumner, and P. Morgan
1976    *Archaeological investigations at the Blodgett site (CA-Sac-267), Sloughhouse locality, California.* San Francisco: Report to the National Park Service.

Johnson, J. J., and R. J. Johnson
1969    *Archaeological reconnaissance of the Pit 3, 4, and 5, and Battle Creek Projects.* San Francisco: Report to the Pacific Gas and Electric Company.

Johnson, J. J., and D. J. Theodoratus, eds.
1978    *Cultural resources of the Marysville Lake, California Project (Parks Bar site), Yuba and Nevada Counties, California.* Sacramento: Report to the U.S. Army Corps of Engineers, Sacramento District.

Johnson, K. L.
1966    Site LAn-2: A late manifestation of the Topanga Complex in southern California prehistory. Berkeley: *University of California Anthropological Records* 23:1–36.
1975    *Archaeological evaluation of site FS-05-11-54-8, Plumas National Forest, Butte County, California.* San Francisco: Report to the U.S. Forest Service.

Johnson, K. L., and L. S. Skjelstad
1974    *The salvage archaeology of site 4-Sha-177, Whiskeytown National Recreation Area, Shasta County, California.* San Francisco: Report to the National Park Service.

Johnson, L., Jr.
1969a   Obsidian hydration rate for the Klamath Basin of California and Oregon. *Science* **165**:1354–1355.
1969b   The Klamath Basin archaeological project. Manuscript. Eugene: Research proposal submitted to the Museum of Natural History, University of Oregon.

Johnson, P. J.
1973a   *Archaeological survey: Hat Creek and Hamilton Branch Projects.* San Francisco: Report to Pacific Gas and Electric Company.
1973b   *The New Melones Reservoir archaeological project, Calaveras and Tuolumne Counties, California: Phase IV.* Tucson: Report to the National Park Service.
1978    Patwin. In R. F. Heizer, vol. ed., *Handbook of North American Indians, Vol. 8: California*:350–360. Washington, D.C.: Smithsonian Institution.

Johnston, R. L.
1937    An Indian village site near the Mariposa Grove. Yosemite National Park: *Yosemite Nature Notes* 16:6.

Johnston, V. R.
1970    The ecology of fire. *Audubon* **72**:76–81, 85–119.

Jones, J.
1969    *An archaeological survey of Southern California Edison's Tule River Project, Tulare County, California.* Rosemead: Report to the Southern California Edison Company.

Jones, J., and T. F. King
1970    The archaeological reconnaissance of the Hungry Hollow Reservoir region, Tulare County, California. Manuscript. Los Angeles: Department of Anthropology, University of California, Los Angeles.

Jones, P. M.
1923    Mound excavation near Stockton. Berkeley: *University of California Publications in American Archaeology and Ethnology* **20**(7):113–122.
1956    Archaeological investigations on Santa Rosa Island in 1901 (ed. by R. F. Heizer

and A. B. Elsasser). Berkeley: *University of California Anthropological Records* **17**(2):201–280.

Journey, A. E.

1970    *An archaeological survey of Lassen Volcanic National Park, California.* M.A. thesis. Sacramento: Department of Anthropology, California State University, Sacramento.

1972    *An archaeological survey of Route 1 and vicinity of the park road in Lassen Volcanic National Park.* San Francisco: Report to the National Park Service.

Kaldenberg, R. L.

1976    *Paleo-technological change at Rancho Park North, San Diego County, California.* M.A. thesis. San Diego: Department of Anthropology, San Diego State University.

1980    Personal communication regarding the Rancho Park North site, San Diego County. Forest Falls: Mighty Fine Research, Inc.

Kaldenberg, R. L., and P. H. Ezell

1974    Results of the archaeological mitigation of Great Western sites A and C, located on the proposed Rancho Park North development. Manuscript. San Diego: Department of Anthropology, San Diego State University.

Kantor, J. R. K., ed.

1964    *Grimshaw's narrative.* Sacramento: Sacramento Book Collectors' Club Publication.

Kaufman, T. S.

1978a    CA-Lak-741, obsidian hydration dates. In T. F. Weber, *Archaeological investigations at the Burns Valley sites, CA-Lak-741 and CA-Lak-742, Lake County, California:* 177–179. Sacramento: Ann S. Peak and Associates.

1978b    Obsidian hydration analysis of artifacts from CA-Lak-742. In T. F. Weber, *Archaeological investigations at the Burns Valley sites, CA-Lak-741 and CA-Lak-742, Lake County, California:*193–196. Sacramento: Ann S. Peak and Associates.

1980    *Early prehistory of the Clear Lake area, Lake County, California.* Ph.D. dissertation. Los Angeles: Department of Anthropology, University of California, Los Angeles.

Kautz, R. R.

1972    Review of "The Dead at Tiburon" by Thomas F. King. *American Antiquity* **37**(4):558–559.

Keesling, H. S., and J. J. Johnson

1978    *Preliminary test excavations conducted at Nev-199, Truckee, California.* Sacramento: California Department of Transportation.

Kelly, I. T.

1932a    Ethnographic field notes on the Coast Miwok Indians. Manuscript. Berkeley: On file at the Bancroft Library, University of California.

1932b    Ethnography of the Surprise Valley Paiute. Berkeley: *University of California Publications in American Archaeology and Ethnology* **31**(3):67–210.

1934    Southern Paiute bands. *American Anthropologist* **36**:548–560.

1939    Southern Paiute shamanism. Berkeley: *University of California Anthropological Records* **2**(4).

1978    Coast Miwok. In R. F. Heizer, vol. ed., *Handbook of North American Indians, Vol. 8: California:* 414–425. Washington, D.C.: Smithsonian Institution.

Kelly, J. F.

1974    *China Diggings, CA-Mad-173: An archaeological site in the Upper Sonoran life zone of the Sierra Nevada.* M.A. thesis. Long Beach: Department of Anthropology, California State University, Long Beach.

Kemnitzer, L.
1968    A survey of archaeology in Contra Costa County. Davis: *University of California, Center for Archaeological Research at Davis, Publications* 1:173–183.

Kesseli, J. E.
1942    The climates of California according to the Köppen classification. *Geographical Review* **32**:476–480.

Kilgore, B. M., and D. Taylor
1979    Fire ecology of a Sequoia-mixed conifer forest. *Ecology* **60**(1):129–142.

King, A. G., and P. McW. Bickel
1980    *Resource evaluation at nine archaeological sites, Redwood Creek Basin, Redwood National Park, California.* Arcata: Report to Redwood National Park.

King, A., and D. A. Fredrickson
1978    *Archaeological test excavations at archaeological site CA-Lak-944, Middle Creek Campground, Upper Lake Ranger District, Mendocino National Forest.* Willows: Report to the U.S. Forest Service.

King, C. D.
1962    Excavations at Parker Mesa (LAn-215). Los Angeles: *University of California, Los Angeles, Archaeological Survey Annual Report, 1961–1962*:91–155.

1967    The Sweetwater Mesa site (LAn-267) and its place in southern California prehistory. Los Angeles: *University of California, Los Angeles, Archaeological Survey Annual Report, 1966–1967*:25–76.

1968    Excavations at Ala-342: A summary report. Manuscript. Sacramento: On file at the California Department of Parks and Recreation.

1969    Approximate 1760 Chumash village locations and populations (map). Los Angeles: *University of California, Los Angeles, Archaeological Survey Annual Report, 1968–1969*:3.

1971    Chumash inter-village economic exchange. San Francisco: *The Indian Historian* **4**(1):31–43.

1974    The explanation of differences and similarities among beads used in prehistoric and early historic California. In L. J. Bean and T. F. King, eds., *?Antap: California Indian political and economic organization.* Ramona: *Ballena Press Anthropological Papers* 2:75–92.

1976    Part I: Background to prehistoric resources of the East Mojave Planning Unit. In C. D. King and D. Casebier, *Background to historic and prehistoric resources of the east Mojave Desert region:*3–53. Riverside: U.S. Bureau of Land Management.

1978    Protohistoric and historic archaeology. In R. F. Heizer, vol. ed., *Handbook of North American Indians, Vol. 8: California:*58–68. Washington, D.C.: Smithsonian Institution.

1981    *The evolution of Chumash society: A comparative study of artifacts used in social system maintenance in the Santa Barbara Channel region before A.D. 1804.* Ph.D. dissertation. Davis: Department of Anthropology, University of California.

King, C. D., and T. C. Blackburn
1978    Tataviam. In R. F. Heizer, vol. ed., *Handbook of North American Indians, Vol. 8: California:*535–537. Washington, D.C.: Smithsonian Institution.

King, C. D., T. C. Blackburn, and E. Chandonet
1968    The archaeological investigation of three sites on the Century Ranch, western Los Angeles County, California. Los Angeles: *University of California, Los Angeles, Archaeological Survey Annual Report, 1967–1968*:12–107.

King, C. D., and D. G. Casebier
1976    *Background to historic and prehistoric resources of the east Mojave Desert region.* Riverside: U.S. Bureau of Land Management.

King, C. D., and L. B. King
  1973    General research design: Bay Area Archaeological Cooperative. In T. F. King and
          P. P. Hickman, *The Southern Santa Clara Valley: A general plan for archaeol-
          ogy:* Appendix 3. San Francisco: Treganza Anthropology Museum.
King, L. B.
  1969    The Medea Creek cemetery (LAn-243): An investigation of social organization
          from mortuary practices. Los Angeles: *University of California at Los Angeles,
          Archaeological Survey Annual Reports, 1968–1969:*23–68.
King, R. F.
  1975a   *Archaeological test excavations near Upper Lake, Lake County, California.*
          Sacramento: Report to the California Department of Transportation.
  1975b   *Archaeological test excavations near Laytonville, Mendocino County, Califor-
          nia.* Sacramento: Report to the California Department of Transportation,
          Sacramento.
King, R. F., and G. Berg
  1973    The Mostin site: A preliminary report on Lake County salvage operations.
          Manuscript: Rohnert Park: Department of Anthropology, Sonoma State
          University.
King, T. F.
  1966a   A cache of stone artifacts having musical properties, from Marin County, Cal-
          ifornia. *American Antiquity* **31**(5):739.
  1966b   *An archaeological survey of the Dos Rios Reservoir region, Mendocino County,
          California.* San Francisco: Report to the National Park Service.
  1967    Test excavation at Mrn-375, the Palo Marin site in Point Reyes National Sea-
          shore. San Francisco: *Society for California Archaeology, R. E. Schenk Memori-
          al Archives of California Archaeology* 17.
  1968    The archaeology of the Schwabacher site, 4-Mad-117. San Francisco: *San Fran-
          cisco State College, Anthropology Museum, Occasional Papers* 4(2):1–135.
  1969    Three little settlements: Initial investigation of small Mariposa Complex mid-
          dens at Buchanan Reservoir. San Francisco: *San Francisco State College, An-
          thropology Museum, Occasional Papers* 5:32–81.
  1970a   Archaeological problems and research in the Coast Miwok area. San Francisco:
          *Treganza Anthropology Museum Papers* 6:275–288.
  1970b   The dead at Tiburon. Petaluma: *Northwestern California Archaeological Soci-
          ety, Occasional Papers* 2.
  1971a   Rethinking "The dead at Tiburon." Manuscript. Riverside: Department of An-
          thropology, University of California.
  1971b   *Status ascription in the Bay Area Middle Horizon.* Sacramento: Paper presented
          at the Annual Meeting of the Society for California Archaeology.
  1972a   *An assessment of the potential impact of proposed improvements to U.S. High-
          way 199 on historic and prehistoric resources.* Sacramento: Report to the Cal-
          ifornia Department of Transportation.
  1972b   New views of California Indian societies. San Francisco: *The Indian Historian*
          5(4):12–17.
  1973a   A possible Paleoindian cemetery and village site in Lake County. Fullerton:
          *Society for California Archaeology Newsletter* **6:**1–2.
  1973b   *Patton Mill pasture: An archaeological investigation.* San Francisco: Report to
          the U.S. Forest Service.
  1973c   *The direct impact of the San Felipe Division facilities on archaeological re-
          sources.* Tucson: Report to the National Park Service.
  1973d   The last days of Zuma Creek. *Popular Archaeology* 7:8–13.
  1973e   Deciphering the dead at Tiburon. *Popular Archaeology* 2(9):24–31.
  1974a   *Manos on the mountain: Borax Lake Pattern high altitude settlement and*

*subsistence in the North Coast Ranges of California.* San Francisco: Report to the U.S. Forest Service.

1974b    *Suscol Village (4-Nap-15): An archaeological study for highway planning.* San Francisco: Report to the California Department of Transportation.

1974c    The evolution of status ascription around San Francisco Bay. In L. J. Bean and T. F. King, eds., ?*Antap: California Indian political and economic organization.* Ramona: *Ballena Press Anthropological Papers* 2:35–54.

1975     *Fifty years of archeology in the California desert: An Archaeological overview of Joshua Tree National Monument.* Tucson: National Park Service.

1976     *Political differentiation among hunter–gatherers: An archaeological test.* Ph.D. dissertation. Riverside: Department of Anthropology, University of California.

King, T. F., and P. P. Hickman

1973     *The southern Santa Clara Valley: A general plan for archaeology.* San Francisco: Treganza Anthropology Museum.

King, T. F., and W. Upson

1970     Protohistory on Limantour Sandspit: Archaeological Investigations at 4-Mrn-216 and 4-Mrn-298. San Francisco: *Treganza Anthropology Museum Papers* 6:116–194.

King, T. F., W. Upson, and R. Milner

1966     Archaeological investigations in the San Antonio Valley, Marin and Sonoma Counties, California. Petaluma: *Northwestern California Archaeological Society Occasional Papers* 1.

Kipps, J. A.

1981a    *An archaeological reconnaissance of Whiskey Ridge in the southern Sierra Nevada, California.* M.A. thesis. Tucson: Department of Anthropology, University of Arizona.

1981b    *The Dinkey Creek prehistoric testing program.* Fresno: Report to the Kings River Conservation District.

Kittleman, L. R.

1973     Mineralogy, correlation, and grain-size distributions of Mazama tephra and other postglacial pyroclastic layers, Pacific Northwest. *Geological Society of America Bulletin* **84**:2957–2980.

Klimek, S.

1935     Culture element distributions: The structure of California Indian cultures. Berkeley: *University of California Publications in American Archaeology and Ethnology* **37**(1):12–70.

Knack, M.

1981     Ethnography. In E. von Till Warren, R. H. Crabtree, C. N. Warren, M. Knack, and R. McCarty, A cultural resources overview of the Colorado Desert Planning Units:83–105. Riverside: *U.S. Bureau of Land Management, Cultural Resources Publications, Anthropology–History* (unnumbered).

Kniffen, F. B.

1928     Achomawi geography. Berkeley: *University of California Publications in American Archaeology and Ethnology* **23**(5):297–323.

1939     Pomo geography. Berkeley: *University of California Publications in American Archaeology and Ethnology* **36**(6):353–400.

Koerper, H.

1981     *Prehistoric subsistence and settlement in the Newport Bay area and environs, Orange County, California.* Ph.D. dissertation. Riverside: Department of Anthropology, University of California.

Kowta, M.

1969     The Sayles Complex: A late Milling Stone assemblage from Cajon Pass and the ecological implications of its scraper planes. Berkeley: *University of California Publications in Anthropology 6.*

1975a   *Quantitative inferences from the "lithic scatter" at 4-Plu-121, Chester, California: Report of the salvage archaeology of 4-Plu-121 and preliminary evaluation of 4-Plu-120, Plumas County, California.* Sacramento: Report to U.S. Army Corps of Engineers, Sacramento District.

1975b   Research design: Northeastern California. Manuscript. Chico: On file in the Department of Anthropology, California State University, Chico.

Kowta, M., and J. C. Hurst

1960   Site Ven-15: The Triunfo Rockshelter. Los Angeles: *University of California, Los Angeles, Archaeological Survey Annual Report, 1959–1960:*201–230.

Krantz, G. S.

1970   Human activities and megafaunal extinctions. *American Scientist* **58**(2):164–170.

1977   The populating of western North America. Fullerton: *Society for California Archaeology Occasional Papers in Method and Theory in California Archaeology* 1:1–64.

Krauss, M. E.

1973   Na-Dene. *Current trends in linguistics* 10B:903–978. The Hague: Mouton.

Krieger, A. D.

1935a   Correlations of archaeological data from the San Francisco Bay region—principal excavations, 1904–1935. Berkeley: *University of California Archaeological Survey Manuscripts* 144.

1935b   Notes and news—early man. *American Antiquity* **29**(1):100–101.

1958   Review of George F. Carter, *Pleistocene man at San Diego. American Anthropologist* **60**:974–978.

1959   Comment on George F. Carter, "Man, time and change in the far Southwest." *Association of American Geographers, Annals* **49**:31–33.

1962   The earliest cultures in the western United States. *American Antiquity* **28**(2):138–144.

1964   Early Man in the New World. In J. D. Jennings and E. Norbeck, eds., *Prehistoric man in the New World:*23–81. Chicago: University of Chicago Press.

Kroeber, A. L.

1904   The languages of the coast of California south of San Francisco. Berkeley: *University of California Publications in American Archaeology and Ethnology* **2**(2):29–80.

1906   The dialect divisions of the Moquelumnan family in relation to the internal differentiation of other linguistic families of California. *American Anthropologist* **8**:652–663.

1907a   The Washo language of east central California and Nevada. Berkeley: *University of California Publications in American Archaeology and Ethnology* **4**(5):251–317.

1907b   The Yokuts language of south central California. Berkeley: *University of California Publications in American Archaeology and Ethnology* **2**(5):165–377.

1909a   California basketry and the Pomo. *American Anthropologist* **11**:233–249.

1909b   Notes on the Shoshonean dialects of southern California. Berkeley: *University of California Publications in American Archaeology and Ethnology* **8**(5):235–269.

1909c   The archaeology of California. In *Anthropological essays presented to Frederic Ward Putnam in honor of his seventieth birthday, April 16, 1909, by his friends and associates:*1–42. New York: Stechert.

1910a   At the bedrock of history: Recent remarkable discovery of human bones over three hundred years old in the San Joaquin Valley of California. *Sunset*

25(3):255–260. (Reprinted, Berkeley: *University of California Archaeological Survey Reports* 11:5–10.)

1910b The Chumash and Costanoan languages. Berkeley: *University of California Publications in American Archaeology and Ethnology* 9:237–271.

1911a Shellmounds at San Francisco and San Mateo. *Records of the Past* 10:227–228.

1911b The languages of the coast of California north of San Francisco. Berkeley: *University of California Publications in American Archaeology and Ethnology* 9(3):273–435.

1915 Monerey Bay mounds, general. Berkeley: *University of California Archaeological Survey Manuscripts* 27.

1920 California culture provinces. Berkeley: *University of California Publications in American Archaeology and Ethnology* 17(2):151–170.

1923 The history of native cultures in California. Berkeley: *University of California Publications in American Archaeology and Ethnology* 20(8):125–142.

1925 Handbook of the Indians of California. Washington, D.C.: *Smithsonian Institution, Bureau of American Ethnology Bulletin* 78.

1929 The Valley Nisenan. Berkeley: *University of California Publications in American Archaeology and Ethnology* 24(4):253–290.

1932 The Patwin and their neighbors. Berkeley: *University of California Publications in American Archaeology and Ethnology* 29(4):253–423.

1935 Preface to S. Klimek's Culture element distributions: The structure of California Indian culture. Berkeley: *University of California Publications in American Archaeology and Ethnology* 37(1):1–11.

1936a Culture element distributions: III, Area and climax. Berkeley: *University of California Publications in American Archaeology and Ethnology* 37(3):101–116.

1936b Prospects in California prehistory. *American Antiquity* 2(2):108–116.

1938 Lodi man. *Science* 87(2250):137–138.

1939 Cultural and natural areas of native North America. Berkeley: *University of California Publications in American Archaeology and Ethnology* 38:1–240.

1954 The nature of land-holding groups in aboriginal California. Berkeley: *University of California Archaeological Survey Reports* 56:19–58.

1955 Linguistic time depth results so far and their meaning. *International Journal of American Linguistics* 21:91–104.

1959a Ethnographic interpretations, 8: Reflections and tests on Athabascan glottochronology. Berkeley: *University of California Publications in American Archaeology and Ethnology* 47(3):241–258.

1959b Ethnographic interpretations, 9: Recent ethnic spreads. Berkeley: *University of California Publications in American Archaeology and Ethnology* 47(3):259–281.

1959c Possible Athabascan influence on Yuki. *International Journal of American Linguistics* 25:59.

1959d Northern Yokuts. *Anthropological Linguistics* 1(8):1–19.

1962a The Rancho La Brea skull. *American Antiquity* 27(3):416–417.

1962b Two papers on the aboriginal ethnography of California. The nature of land holding groups in aboriginal California. Berkeley: *University of California Archaeological Survey Reports* 56:21–58.

1963 Yokuts dialect survey. Berkeley: *University of California Anthropological Records* 11(3):177–251.

Kroeber, A. L., and S. A. Barrett

1960 Fishing among the Indians of northwestern California. Berkeley: *University of California Anthropological Records* 21(1):1–210.

Kroeber, A. L., and M. J. Harner

1955 Mojave pottery. Berkeley: *University of California Anthropological Records* 16(1):1–30.

Kroeber, T., and R. F. Heizer
    1968    *Almost ancestors: The first Californians.* San Francisco: Sierra Club-Ballantine Books.
Küchler, A. W.
    1964    Potential natural vegetation of the conterminous United States. *American Geographical Society Special Publication* 36.
    1977    Map of the natural vegetation of California. In M. G. Barbour and J. Major, eds., *Terrestrial vegetation of California:* Separate. New York: Wiley.
Kuhn, S., and R. E. Hughes
    1981    *Archaeological test excavations in the Ives Timber Sale, Mendocino National Forest, California.* Willows: Report to the U.S. Forest Service.
Kurtén, B., and E. Anderson
    1980    *Pleistocene mammals of North America.* New York: Columbia University Press.
LaJeunesse, R. M.
    1972    *A morphological investigation of a prehistoric population from the southern Sierra Nevada of California.* M.A. thesis. San Francisco: Department of Anthropology, San Francisco State University.
LaJoie, K. R.
    1974    Personal communication regarding radiocarbon dates and the geology of site SCr-7. Menlo Park: U.S. Geological Survey.
LaJoie, K. R., E. Peterson, and B. A. Gerow
    1980    Amino acid bone dating: A feasibility study, south San Francisco Bay region, California. In P. E. Hare, ed., *Biochemistry of amino acids:*477–489. New York: Wiley.
LaMarche, V. C., Jr.
    1973    Holocene climatic variations inferred from treeline fluctuations in the White Mountains, California. *Quaternary Research* 3:632–660.
    1974    Paleoclimatic inferences from long tree-ring records. *Science* 183:1043–1048.
    1978    Tree-ring evidence of past climatic variability. *Nature* 276:334–338.
LaMarche, V. C., Jr., C. W. Ferguson, and W. B. Woolfenden
    1974    Holocene climatic correlations in the western United States: Tree ring and glacial evidence. *AMQUA Abstracts.*
LaMarche, V. C., Jr., and H. A. Mooney
    1967    Altithermal timberline advance in the western United States. *Nature* 213(5080):980–982.
Lamb, S. M.
    1958    Linguistic prehistory in the Great Basin. *International Journal of American Linguistics* 24(2):95–100.
    1962    Linguistic diversification and extinction in North America. Mexico, D. F.: *XXXV Congreso Internacional de Americanistas, Actas y Memorias* 3:457–464.
Landberg, L. C. W.
    1965    The Chumash Indians of southern California. Los Angeles: *Southwest Museum Papers* 19.
Langdon, M.
    1974    Comparative Hokan–Coahuiltecan studies: A survey and appraisal. *Janua Linguarum, Series Critics* 4. The Hague: Mouton.
Lanning, E. P.
    1963    The archaeology of the Rose Spring site (INY-372). Berkeley: *University of California Publications in American Archaeology and Ethnology* 49(3):237–336.
LaPena, F.
    1978    Wintu. In R. F. Heizer, vol. ed., *Handbook of North American Indians, Vol. 8: California:*324–340. Washington, D.C.: Smithsonian Institution.

Larson, D. O.
    1978    *A preliminary report on the excavations at Black Dog Mesa, Clark County,
            Nevada.* Las Vegas: Report to the Nevada Power Co.
Lathrap, D., and D. Shutler
    1955    An archaeological site in the high Sierra of California. *American Antiquity*
            **20**(3):226–240.
Latta, F. F.
    1977    *Handbook of the Yokuts Indians* (second ed., rev. and enlarged). Santa Cruz:
            Bear State Books.
Laughlin, W. S.
    1975    Aleuts: Ecosystem, Holocene history, and Siberian origin. *Science* **189**:507–515.
Laughlin, W. S., and S. I. Wolf
    1979    Introduction. In W. S. Laughlin and A. B. Harper, eds., *The first Americans:
            Origins, affinities, and adaptations:*1–11. New York: Fischer.
Lawton, H. W., and L. J. Bean
    1968    A preliminary reconstruction of aboriginal agricultural technology among the
            Cahuilla. San Francsico: *The Indian Historian* **1**(5):18–24, 29.
Layton, T. N.
    1970    *High Rock archaeology: An interpretation of the prehistory of the northwestern
            Great Basin.* Ph.D. dissertation. Cambridge: Department of Anthropology, Har-
            vard University.
    1972    A 12,000 year obsidian hydration record of occupation, abandonment and lithic
            change from the northwestern Great Basin. *Tebiwa* **15**(2):22–28.
    1979    Archaeology and paleo-ecology of pluvial Lake Parman, northwestern Great
            Basin. *Journal of New World Archaeology* **3**(3):41–56.
Leakey, L. S. B., R. D. Simpson, and T. Clements
    1968    Archaeological excavations in the Calico Mountains, California: Preliminary
            report. *Science* **160**:1022–1023.
    1969    Man in America: The Calico Mountains excavations. Chicago: *Encyclopaedia
            Britannica Yearbook of Science and the Future, 1970*:64–75, 77–79.
Leakey, L. S. B., R. D. Simpson, T. Clements, R. Berger, J. Witthoft, and participants of
the Calico Conference
    1972    *Pleistocene Man at Calico: A report on the International Conference on the
            Calico Mountains Excavations, San Bernardino County, California.* Redlands:
            San Bernardino County Museum.
Lee, G., and D. McCarthy
    1979    *Stanislaus River rock art.* Sacramento: Report to the U.S. Army Corps of En-
            gineers, Sacramento District.
Lee, P.
    1970    Fieldnotes on 1970 College of San Mateo excavations at SMa-12. Manuscript.
            San Mateo: Department of Anthropology, College of San Mateo.
Leonard, N. N., III
    1966    Ven-70 and its place in the Late Period of the western Santa Monica Mountains.
            Los Angeles: *University of California, Los Angeles, Archaeological Survey An-
            nual Report, 1965–1966*:215–242.
    1968    *Archaeological salvage of the Pico Creek and Little Pico Creek sites.* Sacramen-
            to: Report to the California Department of Parks and Recreation.
    1971    Natural and social environments of the Santa Monica Mountains (6000 B.C. to
            1800 A.D.). Los Angeles: *University of California, Los Angeles, Archaeological
            Survey Annual Report, 1970–1971*:97–135.
Leonard, N. N., III, and C. Drover
    1980    Prehistoric turquoise mining in the Halloran Springs District, San Bernardino
            County, California. *The Journal of California and Great Basin Anthropology*
            **2**(2):245–256.

Leonhardy, F.
    1967    The archaeology of a late prehistoric village in northwestern California. Eugene: *University of Oregon, Museum of Natural History Bulletin* 4.

Levulett, V. A.
    1976    *A second archaeological reconnaissance within the King Range Conservation Area.* Ukiah: Report to the U.S. Bureau of Land Management.
    1977    *A third archaeological reconnaissance within the King Range National Conservation Area.* Ukiah: Report to the U.S. Bureau of Land Management.

Levy, R.
    1978a   Costanoan. In R. F. Heizer, vol. ed., *Handbook of North American Indians, Vol. 8: California*:485–495. Washington, D.C.: Smithsonian Institution.
    1978b   Eastern Miwok. In R. F. Heizer, vol. ed., *Handbook of North American Indians, Vol. 8: California*:398–413. Washington, D.C.: Smithsonian Institution.
    1978c   *The linguistic prehistory of California: A processual view.* Tucson: Paper presented at the Annual Meeting of the Society for American Archaeology.
    1979    The linguistic prehistory of central California: Historical linguistics and culture process. Manuscript. Lexington: Department of Anthropology, University of Kentucky.

Lewis, H. T.
    1973    Patterns of Indian burning in California: Ecology and ethnohistory. Ramona: *Ballena Press Anthropological Papers* 1:1–101.

Lillard, J. B., R. F. Heizer, and F. Fenenga
    1939    An introduction to the archaeology of central California. Sacramento: *Sacramento Junior College, Department of Anthropology Bulletin* 2.

Lillard, J. B., and W. K. Purves
    1936    The archaeology of the Deer Creek–Cosumnes area, Sacramento Co., California. Sacramento: *Sacramento Junior College, Department of Anthropology Bulletin* 1.

Lindgren, W.
    1911    The Tertiary gravels of the Sierra Nevada. Washington, D.C.: *U.S. Geological Survey Professional Papers* 73.

Littlewood, R. A.
    1960    An analysis of skeletal material from the Zuma Creek site. Los Angeles: *University of California, Los Angeles, Archaeological Survey Annual Report, 1959–1960*:135–154.

Loeb, E.
    1926    Pomo folkways. Berkeley: *University of California Publications in American Archaeology and Ethnology* **19**(2):149–405.

Loomis, B. F.
    1958    *Lassen Volcano: A pictorial history.* Mineral: Loomis Museum Association and Lassen Volcanic National Park.

Lopatin, I. A.
    1940    Fossil man in the vicinity of Los Angeles, California. *Proceedings of the Sixth Pacific Science Congress* **4**:177–181.

Lorenzo, J. L.
    1970    *Cronología y la posición de Tlapacoya en la prehistoria americana.* Mexico, D. F.: Paper presented at the 35th Annual Meeting of the Society for American Archaeology.

Loud, L. L.
    1912    Half Moon Bay mounds. Berkeley: *University of California Archaeological Survey Manuscripts* 363.
    1915    Fieldnotes on excavations at the Princeton site, SMa-22. Berkeley: *University of California Archaeological Survey Manuscripts.*

1918    Ethnogeography and archaeology of the Wiyot territory. Berkeley: *University of California Publications in American Archaeology and Ethnology* **14**(3):221–437.

1924    The Stege mounds at Richmond, California. Berkeley: *University of California Publications in American Archaeology and Ethnology* **17**(6):355–372.

Loud, L. L., and M. R. Harrington
1929    Lovelock Cave. Berkeley: *University of California Publications in American Archaeology and Ethnology* **25**(1):1–183.

Loud, L. L., and J. Peter
1920    Sonoma Valley sites. Berkeley: *University of California Archaeological Survey Manuscripts* 373.

Lowie, R. H.
1939    Ethnographic notes on the Washo. Berkeley: *University of California Publications in American Archaeology and Ethnology* **36**(5):301–352.

Luomala, K.
1978    Tipai–Ipai. In R. F. Heizer, vol. ed., *Handbook of North American Indians, Vol. 8: California*: 592–609. Washington, D.C.: Smithsonian Institution.

Lyneis, M. M.
1978    On the correspondence between villages and wetlands in the Great Basin. *The Journal of California Anthropology* **5**(2):289–292.

Mabry, D. M., and D. J. Theodoratus
1961    An analysis of Ama-3, a rock shelter near Ione, California. Manuscript. Sacramento: Department of Anthropology, California State University, Sacramento.

McAlexander, M., and W. Upson
1969    *Gewachiu* (Fre-398). San Francisco: *San Francisco State College Anthropology Museum, Occasional Papers* 5(8):313–321.

MacArthur, R. H.
1972    *Geographical ecology.* New York: Harper and Row.

McBeath, J.
1966    *Archaeology of the Novato Bypass site.* Sacramento: Report to the California Department of Parks and Recreation.

McCown, B. E.
1955a   *Temeku:* A page from the history of the Luiseño Indians. Los Angeles: *Archaeological Survey Association of Southern California Papers* 3.

1955b   The Lake LeConte beach line survey. Los Angeles: *The Masterkey* 29(3):88–92.

1964    Excavation of Fallbrook site No. 7. Los Angeles: *Archaeological Survey Association of Southern California Papers* 6:61–84.

McCown, T. D.
1950    The Stanford skull: The physical characteristics. Berkeley: *University of California Archaeological Survey Reports* 6:10–19.

Macdonald, G. A.
1966    Geology of the Cascade Range and Modoc Plateau. San Francisco: *California Division of Mines and Geology Bulletin* **190**:65–96.

McDonald, J. A.
1979    *Cultural resource overview of the Klamath National Forest.* Yreka: Klamath National Forest.

McEachern, J. M.
1968    *Mortuary caves of the Mother Lode region of California.* M.A. thesis. Sacramento: Department of Anthropology, California State University, Sacramento.

McEachern, J. M., and M. A. Grady
1977    *New Melones cave inventory and evaluation study, preliminary report: Archaeological caves.* Dallas: Department of Anthropology, Southern Methodist University.

McGeein, D. J.
1950    Archaeological notes on the Deniz site, CA-Mer-3. Berkeley: *University of California Archaeological Survey Manuscripts* 81.

McGeein, D. J., and W. C. Mueller
1955    A shellmound in Marin County, California. *American Antiquity* **21**(1):52–62.

McGuire, K. R., and A. P. Garfinkel
1976    Comment on "The development of pinyon exploitation in central eastern California." *The Journal of California Anthropology* **3**(2):83–85.

1980    Archaeological investigations in the southern Sierra Nevada: The Bear Mountain segment of the Pacific Crest Trail. Bakersfield: *Bureau of Land Management, Cultural Resources Publications, Archaeology.*

McGuire, K. R., A. P. Garfinkel, and M. E. Basgall
1981    *Archaeological investigations in the El Paso Mountains of the western Mojave Desert: The Bickel and Last Chance sites (CA-Ker-250 and 261).* Riverside: Report to the U.S. Bureau of Land Management.

McHenry, H.
1968    Transverse lines in long bones of prehistoric California Indians. *American Journal of Physical Anthropology* **29**(1):1–18.

McHenry, H. M., and P. D. Schulz
1978    Harris lines, enamel hypoplasia, and subsistence in prehistoric central California. Socorro: *Balenna Press Publications in Archaeology, Ethnology, and History* **11**:35–50.

McKern, T. W.
1939    The Midwestern Taxonomic Method as an aid to archaeological culture study. *American Antiquity* **4**(4):301–313.

McKinney, A.
1968    Cogged stones in private collections. *Pacific Coast Archaeological Society Quarterly* **4**(3):39–56.

McKinney, A., D. Hafner, and J. Gothold
1971    A report on the China Ranch area. *Pacific Coast Archaeological Society Quarterly* **7**(2):1–48.

McKusick, M. B.
1959a   Introduction to Anacapa Island archaeology. Los Angeles: *University of California, Los Angeles, Archaeological Survey Annual Report, 1958–1959:*73–108.

1959b   Three cultural complexes on San Clemente Island, California. Los Angeles: *The Masterkey* **33**:22–25.

MacLean, J. J.
1884    Remarks on shellmounds near Cape Mendocino, Humboldt County. In C. Rau, ed., Prehistoric fishing in Europe and North America. Washington, D.C.: *Smithsonian Institution Contributions to Knowledge* **25**:254–256.

McLendon, S.
1973    Proto-Pomo. Berkeley: *University of California Publications in Linguistics* 71.

McLendon, S., and R. L. Oswalt
1978    Pomo: Introduction. In R. F. Hezier, vol. ed., *Handbook of North American Indians, Vol. 8: California:*274–288. Washington, D.C.: Smithsonian Institution.

McMillan, J. H.
1963    *The archaeological human ecology of the Mountain Meadows area in southwestern Lassen County, California.* M.A. thesis. Sacramento: Department of Anthropology, California State University, Sacramento.

MacNeish, R. S.
1972    Early Man in the Andes. In R. S. MacNeish, ed., *Early Man in America:*69–79. San Francisco: Freeman.

1979a   The early Man remains from Pikimachay Cave, Ayacucho Basin, highland Peru. In R. L. Humphrey and D. Stanford, eds., *Pre-Llano cultures of the Americas: Paradoxes and possibilities:*1–47. Washington, D.C.: The Anthropological Society of Washington.

1979b   Review of "The ancient Californians: Rancholabrean hunters of the Mojave Lakes country", by Emma Lou Davis. *American Antiquity* **44**(3):630–631.

Madsen, D. B.
1975   Dating Paiute-Shoshoni expansion in the Great Basin. *American Antiquity* **40**(1):82–86.

1981   The emperor's new clothes. *American Antiquity* **46**(3):637–640.

Major, J.
1977   California climate in relation to vegetation. In M. G. Barbour and J. Major, eds., *Terrestrial vegetation of California:*11–74. New York: Wiley.

Mallery, G.
1893   Picture writing of the American Indians. Washington, D.C.: *Smithsonian Institution, Bureau of American Ethnology Annual Report for 1888–89:*25–807.

Manners, R. A.
1974   Paiute Indians I, Southern Paiute and Chemehuevi: An ethnological report. New York: Garland.

Margolin, M.
1978   *The Ohlone way: Indian life in the San Francisco–Monterey Bay area.* Berkeley: Heyday Books.

Martin, P. S.
1958   Pleistocene ecology and biogeography of North America. In C. L. Hubbs, ed., *Zoogeography:*375–420. Washington, D.C.: American Association for the Advancement of Science.

1967   Prehistoric overkill. In P. S. Martin and H. E. Wright, eds., *Pleistocene extinctions: The search for a cause:*75–120. New Haven: Yale University Press.

1973   The discovery of America. *Science* **179**(4077):969–974.

1975   Paleolithic players on the American stage: Man's impact on the late Pleistocene megafauna. In J. D. Ives and R. G. Barry, eds., *Arctic and alpine environments:*669–700. London: Methuen.

Martin, P. S., G. I. Quimby, and D. Collier
1947   *Indians before Columbus.* Chicago: University of Chicago Press.

Martz, P.
1974   An analysis of the glass beads from CA-Mad-173. In J. L. Kelly, *China Diggings, CA-Mad-173: An archaeological site in the Upper Sonoran life zone of the Sierra Nevada:*337–348. M.A. thesis. Long Beach: Department of Anthropology, California State University, Long Beach.

1976   The Vandenberg Air Force Base project: A correlation of relative dates with radiocarbon dates. *Journal of New World Archaeology* **1**(7):1–40.

Mason, J. A.
1912   The ethnology of the Salinan Indians. Berkeley: *University of California Publications in American Archaeology and Ethnology* **10**(4):97–240.

Mason, O. T.
1889   The Ray collection from the Hupa Reservation. Washington, D.C.: *Smithsonian Institution, Annual Report for 1886:*205–239.

Matson, R. G.
1970   The pollen from Placer-101. In E. W. Ritter, ed., *Archaeological investigations in the Auburn Reservoir Area, Phase II–III:*282–289. San Francisco: Report to the National Park Service.

1972   Pollen from the Spring Garden Ravine site (4-Pla-101). Davis: *University of California, Center for Archaeological Research at Davis, Publications* 3: 24–27.

Matthes, F. E.
1930   Geologic history of the Yosemite Valley. Washington, D.C.: *U.S. Geological Survey Professional Papers* 160.
1950   *The incomparable valley: A geologic interpretation of the Yosemite.* Berkeley: University of California Press.

May, R. V.
1976   An early ceramic date threshhold in southern California. Los Angeles: *The Masterkey* **50**(3):103–107.

Mead, R., and J. Moss
1967   Report on the salvage of CCo-311. Manuscript. Berkeley: R. H. Lowie Museum of Anthropology.

Mehringer, P. J., Jr.
1967   Pollen analysis of the Tule Springs site area, Nevada. In H. M. Wormington and D. Ellis, eds., Pleistocene studies in southern Nevada. Carson City: *Nevada State Museum Anthropological Papers* 13:129–200.
1977   Great Basin late Quaternary environments. In D. Fowler, ed., Models and Great Basin prehistory: A symposium:113–168. Reno and Las Vegas: *Desert Research Institute Publications in the Social Sciences* 12.

Mehringer, P. J., Jr., E. Blinman, and K. L. Petersen
1977   Pollen influx and volcanic ash. *Science* **198**(4314):257–261.

Mehringer, P. J., Jr., W. P. Nash, and R. H. Fuller
1971   A Holocene volcanic ash from northwestern Utah. Salt Lake City: *Proceedings of the Utah Academy of Sciences, Arts and Letters* **48**(1):46–51.

Mehringer, P. J., Jr., and J. C. Sheppard
1978   Holocene history of Little Lake, Mojave Desert, California. In E. L. Davis, ed., The ancient Californians: Rancholabrean hunters of the Mojave Lakes country:153–166. Los Angeles: *Natural History Museum of Los Angeles County, Science Series* 29.

Mehringer, P. J., Jr., and C. N. Warren
1976   Marsh, dune, and archaeological chronology, Ash Meadows, Amargosa Desert, Nevada. In R. Elston, ed., Holocene environmental change in the Great Basin:120–151. Reno: *Nevada Archaeological Survey Research Papers* 8.

Meighan, C. W.
1950a   Excavations in sixteenth century shellmounds at Drakes Bay, Marin County. Berkeley: *University of California Archaeological Survey Reports* 9:27–32.
1950b   Report on the 1949 excavation of 16th century Indian shellmounds at Drakes Bay. Berkeley: *University of California Archaeological Survey Manuscripts* 79.
1953a   Acculturation in Californian awl forms. Berkeley: *Kroeber Anthropological Society Papers* 8 and 9:61–68.
1953b   Archaeology of sites Nap-129 and Nap-131. In R. F. Heizer, ed., The archaeology of the Napa region. Berkeley: *University of California Anthropological Records* **12**(6):315–317.
1953c   The Coville rock shelter, Inyo County, California. Berkeley: *University of California Anthropological Records* **12**(5):171–224.
1953d   Preliminary excavation at the Thomas site, Marin County. Berkeley: *University of California Archaeological Survey Reports* 19:1–8, 12–14.
1954   A late complex in southern California prehistory. *Southwestern Journal of Anthropology* **10**(2):215–227.
1955a   Archaeology of the North Coast Ranges. Berkeley: *University of California Archaeological Survey Reports* 30:1–39.
1955b   Excavation of Isabella Meadows Cave, Monterey County, California. Berkeley: *University of California Archaeological Survey Reports* 29:1–30.
1955c   Notes on the archaeology of Mono County. Berkeley: *University of California Archaeological Survey Reports* 28:6–28.

1959a   Archaeological resources of Borrego State Park. Los Angeles: *University of California, Los Angeles, Archaeological Survey Annual Report, 1958–1959;25–44.*

1959b   California cultures and the concept of an Archaic Stage. *American Antiquity* **24**(3):289–305.

1959c   The Little Harbor site, Catalina Island: An example of ecological interpretation in archaeology. *American Antiquity* **24**(4):383–405.

1961    The growth of archaeology in the West Coast and the Great Basin, 1935–1960. *American Antiquity* **27**(1):33–38.

1963    Pre-milling stone cultures. Carson City: *Nevada State Museum Anthropological Papers* 9:78–81.

1965    Pacific Coast archaeology. In H. E. Wright and D. C. Frey, eds., *The Quaternary of the United States:709–720.* Princeton: Princeton University Press.

1976    Two views of the Manix Lake lithic industry. *Journal of New World Archaeology* **1**(7):41.

Meighan, C. W., and H. Eberhart
1953    Archaeological resources of San Nicolas Island, California. *American Antiquity* **19**(2):109–125.

Meighan, C. W., F. J. Findlow, and S. P. DeAtley, eds.
1974    Obsidian dates I: A compendium of the obsidian determinations made at the UCLA obsidian hydration laboratory. Los Angeles: *University of California, Los Angeles, Archaeological Survey Monograph 3.*

Meighan, C. W., and C. V. Haynes
1968    New studies on the age of the Borax Lake site. Los Angeles: *The Masterkey* **42**(1):4–9.

1970    The Borax Lake site revisisted. *Science* **167**(3922):1213–1221.

Meighan, C. W., and R. F. Heizer
1952    Archaeological exploration of sixteenth century Indian mounds at Drakes Bay. *California Historical Society Quarterly* **31**(2):98–108.

Meighan, C. W., and F. A. Riddell
1972    The Maru cult of the Pomo Indians: A California Ghost Dance survival. Los Angeles: *Southwest Museum Papers* 23.

Melander, R., and C. Slaymaker
1969    *The salvage archaeology of 4-Mrn-168.* San Francisco: Department of Anthropology, San Francisco State University.

Meredith, H. C.
1899    Aboriginal art in obsidian. *Land of Sunshine* **11**:255–258.

1900    Archaeology in California: Central and northern California. In W. K. Moorehead, ed., *Prehistoric implements:258–294.* Cincinnati: Robert Clarke.

Merriam, C. H.
1898    Life zones and crop zones in the United States. Washington, D.C.: *U.S. Department of Agriculture, Biological Survey Bulletin* 10:1–79.

1902–   Mewuk (Sierra Miwok) and Miwok (Plains Miwok) tribes and villages. Manu-
1930    script. Berkeley: University of California, Bancroft Library, C. Hart Merriam Collection.

1907    Distribution and classification of the Mewan stock of California. *American Anthropologist* **9**:338–357.

1909    Ethnological evidence that the California cave skeletons are not recent. *Science* **29**:805–806.

1910    *The dawn of the world: Myths and wierd tales told by the Mewan Indians of California.* Cleveland: Clark.

1914    Distribution of Indian tribes in the southern Sierra and adjacent parts of the San Joaquin Valley, California. *Science* **19**(494):912–917.

1917    Indian village and camp sites in Yosemite Valley. San Francisco: *Sierra Club Bulletin* **10**:202–209.

1918    Review of the grizzly and big brown bears of North America (genus *Ursus*) . . . Washington, D.C.: *U.S. Department of Agriculture, Biological Survey, North American Fauna* 41:1–136.

1926    The classification and distribution of the Pit River Indian tribes of California. Washington, D.C.: *Smithsonian Institution Miscellaneous Contributions* **78**(3):1–52.

1955    *Studies of California Indians.* Berkeley and Los Angeles: University of California Press.

1957    The *hang-e* or ceremonial house of the Northern Miwok near Railroad Flat, Calaveras County, California. Berkeley: *University of California Archaeological Survey Reports* 38:34–35.

1967    Ethnographic notes on California Indian tribes, III: Central California Indian tribes. Berkeley: *University of California Archaeological Survey Reports* 68(3).

Merriam, J. C.

1906    Recent cave explorations in California. *American Anthropologist* **8**:221–228.

1909    Note on the occurrence of human remains in California caves. *Science* **30**:531–532.

1910    The true story of the Calaveras skull. *Sunset* February:153–158.

1914    Preliminary report on the discovery of human remains in an asphalt deposit at Rancho La Brea. *Science* **40**(1023):198–203.

Merriam, J. C., and associates

1938    Paleontology, Early Man, and historical geology. Washington, D.C.: *Carnegie Institution of Washington Year Book* 37:340–364,

Michels, J. W.

1964    The Snow Creek rock shelter site (Riv-210). Los Angeles: *University of California, Los Angeles, Archaeological Survey Annual Report, 1963–1964*:85–128.

1973    *Dating methods in archaeology.* New York: Seminar Press.

Michelson, T.

1914    Two alleged Algonquian languages of California. *American Anthropologist* **16**:361–367.

Milburn, J. W.

1977    *Report on 1977 excavations by Sonoma State College at* Tsahpek^w, 4-Hum-129. Rohnert Park: Paper presented at the Annual Data Sharing Meeting of the Society for California Anthropology.

Milburn, J. W., and D. A. Fredrickson

1979    *Final report: A cultural resources study of proposed timber sale areas on the Hoopa Valley Indian Reservation, Humboldt County, California.* Tucson: Report to the National Park Service.

Milburn, J. W., D. A. Fredrickson, M. Dreiss, L. Memichael, and W. Van Dusen

1979    *A preliminary report on the archaeology of CA-Hum-129.* Sacramento: Report to the California Department of Parks and Recreation.

Miller, G. J.

1969    Man and Smilodon: A preliminary report on their possible coexistence at Rancho La Brea. Los Angeles: *Los Angeles County Museum Contributions in Science* 163:1–8.

1979    Personal communication regarding Rancholabrean animal bones with possible artificial cuts from Rancho La Brea. El Centro: Imperial Valley College Museum.

Miller, V. P.

1970    *The Yuki: An ethnohistorical approach.* M.A. thesis. Davis: Department of Anthropology, University of California.

1978    Yuki, Huchnom, and Coast Yuki. In R. F. Heizer, ed., *Handbook of North American Indians, Vol. 8: California:*190–204. Washington, D.C.: Smithsonian Institution.

1979    *Ukomno'm:* The Yuki Indians of northern California. Socorro: *Ballena Press Anthropological Papers* 14.

Miller, W. R.
1966    Anthropological linguistics in the Great Basin. Reno: *Desert Research Institute, Technical Report Series* 1:75–111.

Milliman, J. D., and K. O. Emery
1968    Sea levels during the past 35,000 years. *Science* **162:**1121–1123.

Minor, R., S. D. Beckham, and K. A. Toepel
1979    Cultural resource overview of the BLM Lakeview District, south-central Oregon: Archaeology, ethnography, and history. Eugene: *University of Oregon Anthropological Papers* 16.

Minshall, H. L.
1976    *The broken stones: The case for Early Man in California.* La Jolla: Copley Books.

Mohr, A.
1948    The excavation of site CA-Sta-6. Berkeley: *University of California Archaeological Survey Manuscripts* 44.

Molarsky, M. G.
1976    Personal communication regarding artifacts from the Huntington Lake vicinity. Ross.

Moorehead, W. K., ed.
1900    *Prehistoric implements.* Cincinatti: Robert Clarke.

Moratto, M. J.
1968    A survey of the archaeological resources of the Buchanan Reservoir area, Madera County, California. San Francisco: *San Francisco State College, Occasional Papers in Anthropology* 4(1):1–121.

1969    The archaeology of the Jones site, 4-Mad-159. San Francisco: *San Francisco State College, Occasional Papers in Anthropology* 5(3):82–218.

1970a   A history of archaeological research at Point Reyes, California. San Francisco: *Treganza Anthropology Museum Papers* 6:97–104.

1970b   Buchanan archaeological project: Report of 1969 excavations. San Francisco: *Treganza Anthropology Museum Papers* 7:1–85.

1970c   California's vanishing past: Urban sprawl and the destruction of prehistory. In T. F. King, ed., *Death of the past:*1–6. Daly City: Society for California Archaeology.

1970d   Report of 1970 archaeological excavations at Buchanan Reservoir. San Francisco: *R. E. Schenk Memorial Archives of California Archaeology* 15.

1970e   *Tsahpekʷ:* An archaeological record of nineteenth century acculturation among the Yurok. San Francisco: *R. E. Schenk Memorial Archives of California Archaeology* 7.

1971a   A century of archaeology in east-central California. San Francisco: *Treganza Anthropology Museum Papers* 9:24–38.

1971b   *An archaeological survey of selected areas within Redwood National Park.* San Francisco: Report to the National Park Service.

1971c   *A proposed sequence of prehistoric cultural development in California.* Sacramento: Paper presented at the annual meeting of the Society for California Archaeology.

1971d   Archaeological investigations at 4-Tuo-300, Tuolumne County, California. San Francisco: *Treganza Anthropology Museum Papers* 9:78–111.

1971e   Archaeology and cross-cultural ethics in coastal northwest California. San Francisco: *R. E. Schenk Memorial Archives of California Archaeology* 28.

1971f   A study of prehistory in the Tuolumne River Valley, California. San Francisco: *Treganza Anthropology Museum Papers* 9.

1971g   Contributions to the archaeology of San Mateo County, California. San Francisco: *Treganza Anthropology Museum Papers* 8:1–85.

1972a  *Archaeological investigations in the Redwood National Park Region, California.* Tucson: Report to the National Park Service.

1972b  *A study of prehistory in the southern Sierra Nevada foothills, California.* Ph.D. dissertation. Eugene: Department of Anthropology, University of Oregon.

1972c  Chowchilla River prehistory. Madera: *Madera County Historian* **12**(2):1–6.

1972d  *Paleodemography in the western Sierra Nevada, California.* Miami: Paper presented at the annual meeting of the Society for American Archaeology.

1972e  Reviews of "Archaeolgoy of the Grayson site, Merced County, California" by W. H. Olsen and L. A. Payen, and "Archaeology of the Menjoulet site, Merced County, California" by W. E. Pritchard. *American Antiquity* **37**(4):556–558.

1973a  *A survey of cultural resources in and near Redwood National Park, California.* Tucson: Report to the National Park Service.

1973b  *The status of California archaeology.* Riverside and Los Angeles: Society for California Archaeology.

1973c  (with S. Van Dyke, S. Dietz, and T. Jackson) Sam Alley: Excavations at 4-Lak-305 near Upper Lake, California. San Francisco: *Treganza Anthropology Museum Papers* 11.

1974a  *An assessment of the cultural resources within Point Reyes National Seashore.* Tucson: Report to the National Park Service.

1974b  Archaeological and ethnohistorical sources for the San Francisco Bay area. *Treganza Anthropology Museum Papers* 13:1–101.

1974c  Notes on site SCr-7. Manuscript notes in the possession of the author.

1974d  A summary of archaeology in the northern San Francisco Bay area. San Francisco: *Treganza Anthropology Museum Papers* 15:17–56.

1976a  *Archaeological investigations of site 4-Cal-S-414, a rockshelter in Calaveras County, California.* Sacramento: Report to the U.S. Army Corps of Engineers, Sacramento District.

1976b  Further comments regarding the Shelter Hill site (4-Mrn-14), Mill Valley, California. *The Journal of California Anthropology* **3**(1):148.

1976c  *New Melones archaeological project—Stanislaus River, Calaveras and Tuolumne Counties, California: Phase VI.* San Francisco: Report to the National Park Service. (Also issued as *Conservation Archaeology Papers* 3[1–5]:1–570.)

1976d  *Tuolumne Wild and Scenic River study: Archaeology.* Sonora: Report to the Stanislaus National Forest.

1977a  *A review of the draft "Management plan for cultural resources for New Melones Lake Recreation Area" by Iroquois Research Institute.* San Francisco: Report to the National Park Service.

1977b  Research prospects: New Melones archaeological project. In M. B. Schiffer and G. J. Gumerman, eds., *Conservation archaeology: Models for cultural resources management studies:*401–411. New York: Academic Press.

1978  An archaeologial overview of Redwood National Park. Tucson: *National Park Service, Western Archeological Center, Publications in Anthropology* 8.

1980  Some archaeological research prospects in northwestern California. In P. Bickel and A. King, *Research design for the assessment and preservation of Redwood National Park archaeological resources:*116–123. Crescent City: Report to Redwood National Park.

1981a  An archaeological research design for Yosemite National Park, California. Tucson: *National Park Service, Western Archeological and Conservation Center, Publications in Anthropology* **19.**

1981b  (with contributions by others) *Mid-Sierran archaeology: A survey of 14 compartments in the Stanislaus National Forest, California.* Sonora: Report to the Stanislaus National Forest.

n.d.     Field notes regarding the 1970 excavation of site 4-Fre-444. Manuscript. San Francisco: Department of Anthropology, San Francisco State University.

Moratto, M. J., and M. R. Arguelles, with S. K. Goldberg and W. L. Singleton

1983     Site 04-Cal-S-286. In M. J. Moratto *et al.*, New Melones archeological project, California: Indian sites 04-Cal-S-286, 04-Cal-S-347, and 04-Cal-S-461. *Final report of the New Melones archaeological project* 4(1):7–108. Report to the National Park Service, Washington, D.C. Sonora: INFOTEC Development, Inc.

Moratto, M. J., M. R. Arguelles, S. K. Goldberg, S. O'Brien, L. M. Riley, and W. L. Singleton, with contributions by others

1983     New Melones archaeological project, California: Indian sites 04-Cal-S-286, 04-Cal-S-347, and 04-Cal-S-461. *Final report of the New Melones archaeological project* 4(1–3). Report to the National Park Service, Washington, D.C. Sonora: INFOTEC Development, Inc.

Moratto, M. J., and R. Heglar

1973     A deeply buried human skeleton from the U.S. Army Presidio, San Francisco. San Francisco: *R. E. Schenk Memorial Archives of California Archaeology* **38.**

Moratto, M. J., T. F. King, and W. B. Woolfenden

1978     Archaeology and California's climate. *The Journal of California Anthropology* **5**(2):147–161.

Moratto, M. J., and L. M. Riley

1980     *Balsam Meadow: Archaeological testing at six sites in eastern Fresno County, California.* Rosemead: Report to the Southern California Edison Company.

Moratto, M. J., L. M. Riley, and S. C. Wilson, eds.

1974     Shelter Hill: Archaeological investigations at 4-Mrn-14, Mill Valley, California. San Francisco: *Treganza Anthropology Museum Papers* 15 and *Miwok Archaeological Preserve of Marin, Papers* 2:1–166.

Morehead, M. T.

1975     *An archaeological survey of the Mineral King Road corridor.* Tucson: Report to the National Park Service.

Morejohn, G. V.

1974     Personal communication regarding bones of *Chendytes lawi* from site 4-SCr-7. San José: Department of Biology, San José State University.

Moriarty, J. R., III

1966     Cultural phase divisions suggested by typological change coordinated with stratigraphically controlled radiocarbon dating in San Diego. *The Anthropological Journal of Canada* **4**(4):20–30.

1967     Transitional pre-Desert phase in San Diego County, California. *Science* **155**(3762):553–556.

1968     The environmental variations of the Yuman cultural area of southern California. *Quarterly Bulletin of the Anthropological Association of Canada* **6**(2):2–29.

1969     The San Dieguito Complex: Suggested environmental and cultural relationships. *The Anthropological Journal of Canada* **7**(3):2–18.

Moriarty, J., and R. Broms

1971     The antiquity and inferred use of stone discoidals in the Southwest. *The Anthropological Journal of Canada* **9**(1):16–36.

Moriarty, J. R., and H. Minshall

1972     A new pre-Desert site discovered near Texas Street. *The Anthropological Journal of Canada* **10**(3):10–13.

Moriarty, J. R,, III, G. Shumway, and C. Warren

1959     Scripps Estates Site I (SDi-525): A preliminary report on an early site on the San Diego coast. Los Angeles: *University of California, Los Angeles, Archaeological Survey Annual Report, 1958–1959*:185–216.

Morlan, R. E.
  1980    Taphonomy and archaeology in the Upper Pleistocene of the northern Yukon Territory: A glimpse into the peopling of the New World. Ottawa: *Mercury Series, National Museum of Man, Archaeological Survey of Canada, Papers* 94.

Morrison, R. B.
  1965    Quaternary geology of the Great Basin. In H. E. Wright and D. C. Frey, eds., *The Quaternary of the United States:*265–284. Princeton: Princeton University Press.

Moseley, M., and G. A. Smith
  1962    Archaeological investigations of the Mojave River drainage. Redlands: *San Bernardino County Museum Association Quarterly* **9**:3.

Mosimann, J. E., and P. S. Martin
  1975    Simulating overkill by Paleoindians. *American Scientist* **63**:304–313.

Motz, L.
  1978    An archaeological survey of the proposed Collierville Transmission line. Manuscript. Sacramento: Department of Anthropology, California State University, Sacramento.

Moyle, P. B.
  1976    *Inland fishes of California.* Berkeley and Los Angeles: University of California Press.

Munday, F. C., and T. R. Lincoln
  1979    A comment on Bettinger: Problems in archaeological interpretation. *American Antiquity* **44**(2):345–351.

Mundy, W. J.
  1980    *Test excavation near Westcone.* Fresno: Report to the Sierra National Forest.

Munz, P. A.
  1959.    *A California flora.* Berkeley and Los Angeles: University of California Press.

Muñoz, J.
  1974    California Indians of the Fresno River Reservation: An initial report. Manuscript. Long Beach: Department of Anthropology, California State University, Long Beach.
  1975a    *The ethnocartography of the southern Sierra foothills and the Fresno Indian Reservation.* Santa Cruz: Paper presented at the Annual Meeting of the Society for California Archaeology.
  1975b    The Indian population of the Fresno River Reservation, 1850–1860. Manuscript. Long Beach: Department of Anthropology, California State University, Long Beach.

Muto, G. R., P. J. Mehringer, Jr., and C. N. Warren
  1976    A technological analysis of projectile points from a burial, Amargosa Desert, Nevada. *The Kiva* **41**:267–276.

Napton, L. K.
  1974a    *Archaeological research in Yosemite National Park, California: Review and evaluation of reconnaissance, survey, testing, and excavation.* Tucson: Report to the National Park Service.
  1974b    *Archaeological survey of the Ackerson Timber Sale tract, Stanislaus National Forest.* Sonora: Report to the Stanislaus National Forest.
  1974c    *Archaeological survey of the Granite Timber Sale tract, Stanislaus National Forest.* Sonora: Report to the Stanislaus National Forest.
  1974d    *Archaeological survey of the Jawbone Timber Sale tract, Stanislaus National Forest.* Sonora: Report to the Stanislaus National Forest.
  1974e    *Archaeological survey of the Monty Timber Sale tract, Stanislaus National Forest.* Sonora: Report to the Stanislaus National Forest.

1974f    *Archaeological survey of the Sourgrass Timber Sale tract, Stanislaus National Forest.* Sonora: Report to the Stanislaus National Forest.

1974g    *Archaeological survey of the Spring Timber Sale tract, Stanislaus National Forest.* Sonora: Report to the Stanislaus National Forest.

1978     *Archaeological overview of Yosemite National Park, California.* Tucson: Report to the Western Archaeological Center, National Park Service.

Napton, L. K., A. D. Albee, and E. A. Greathouse

1974a    *Archaeological survey in Kings Canyon-Sequoia National Park.* Tucson: Report to the Western Archeological Center, National Park Service.

1974b    *Archaeological survey in Yosemite National Park, California: Wawona (Parts 1–2).* Tucson: Report to the Western Archeological Center, National Park Service.

1974c    *Archaeological survey in Yosemite National Park, California: Yosemite Valley (Parts 1–2).* Tucson: Report to the Western Archeological Center, National Park Service.

Napton, L. K., and E. A. Greathouse

1976     Archaeological investigations in Yosemite National Park, California: Part 1, project summary, CSC/IAR 1976. Report to the Western Archeological and Conservation Center, National Park Service.

1982     *Cultural resource investigations, Stanislaus National Forest, California: Smoothwire archaeological site (05-16-52-284).* Sonora: Report to the Stanislaus National Forest.

Neasham, A.

1952     *A program of archaeological investigations at Drakes Bay.* San Francisco: Report to the National Park Service.

Neitz, G., R. Olsen, and J. Lillard

n.d.     Untitled notes regarding survey and testing by Sacramento Jr. College archaeologists at various sites near Clear Lake, November 21, 1934 to February 23, 1935. Sacramento: On file in the office of the State Archaeologist.

Nelson, N. C.

1907a    Original notes on Tehama–Red Bluff mounds. Berkeley: *University of California Archaeological Survey Manuscripts 350.*

1907b    San Francisco Bay mounds. Berkeley: *University of California Archaeological Survey Manuscripts 349.*

1909a    Shellmounds of the San Francisco Bay region. Berkeley: *University of California Publications in American Archaeology and Ethnology 7(4):309–356.*

1909b    Site survey, Russian River to Golden Gate mounds. Berkeley: *University of California Archaeological Survey Manuscripts 351.*

1910a    San Rafael mound # 86C. Berkeley: *University of California Archaeological Survey Manuscripts 354.*

1910b    Sausalito mound # 3. Berkeley: *University of California Archaeological Survey Manuscripts 353.*

1910c    The Ellis Landing shellmound. Berkeley: *University of California Publications in American Archaeology and Ethnology 7(5):357–426.*

1911     Greenbrae mound # 76. Berkeley: *University of California Archaeological Survey Manuscripts 358.*

1936     Notes on the Santa Barbara culture. In *Essays in honor of Alfred Louis Kroeber:199–209.* Berkeley: University of California Press.

Nevers, J. A.

1976     *Wa She Shu: A Washo tribal history.* Salt Lake City: University of Utah Press.

Newman, R. W.

1947     Notes on the excavation of the Richard site, CA-Sac-160. Berkeley: *University of California Archaeological Survey Manuscripts 13.*

1957     A comparative analysis of prehistoric skeletal remains from the lower Sacramento Valley. Berkeley: *University of California Archaeological Survey Reports* 39:1–66.

Newman, S.
1944     Yokuts language of California. New York: *Viking Fund Publications in Anthropology* 2.

Nichols, M. J. P.
1981     Old California Uto-Aztecan. *Survey of California and Other Indian Languages, Reports* 1:5–41.

Nissley, C.
1975     *Archaeological investigations at CA-Mer-27: Phase II.* Sacramento: Report to the U.S. Bureau of Reclamation.

Norwood, R. H., C. S. Bull, and R. Quinn
1980     A cultural resource overview of the Eureka, Saline, Panamint, and Darwin region, east central California. Riverside: *U.S. Bureau of Land Management, Cultural Resources Publications—Anthropology, History.*

Oakeshott, G. B.
1971     *California's changing landscapes: A guide to the geology of the state.* New York: McGraw Hill.

Oakley, K. P.
1963     Relative dating of Arlington Springs man. *Science* **141**:1172.

O'Brien, S.
1981     *Balsam Meadow II: Archaeological testing at three sites in eastern Fresno County, California.* Rosemead: Report to the Southern California Edison Company.

O'Brien, S., with M. J. Moratto
1983     Site 04-Cal-S-347. In M. J. Moratto *et al.*, New Melones archaeological project, California: Indian sites 04-Cal-S-286, 04-Cal-S-347, and 04-Cal-S-461. *Final report of the New Melones Archaeological Project* 4(1):109–154. Report to the National Park Service, Washington, D.C. Sonora: INFOTEC Development, Inc.

O'Connell, J. F.
1967     Elko-eared and Elko Corner-notched projectile points as time markers in the Great Basin. Berkeley: *University of California Archaeological Survey Reports* 70:129–140.

1971a    *The archaeology and cultural ecology of Surprise Valley, northeast California.* Ph.D. dissertation. Berkeley: Department of Anthropology, University of California.

1971b    Recent prehistoric environments in southeastern California. Los Angeles: *University of California, Los Angeles, Archaeological Survey Annual Report, 1971*:175–184.

1975     The prehistory of Surprise Valley. Ramona: *Ballena Press Anthropological Papers* 4:1–57.

O'Connell, J. F., and R. D. Ambro
1968     A preliminary report on the archaeology of the Rodriguez site (CA-Las-194), Lassen County, California. Berkeley: *University of California Archaeological Survey Reports* 73(2):95–194.

O'Connell, J. F., and J. E. Ericson
1974     Earth lodges to wikiups: A long sequence of domestic structures from the northern Great Basin. Reno: *Nevada Archaeological Survey Research Papers* 5:43–61.

O'Connell, J. F., and P. S. Hayward
1972     Altithermal and Medithermal human adaptations in Surprise Valley, northeast California. In D. D. Fowler, ed., Great Basin cultural ecology: A sym-

posium:25–42. Reno: *Desert Research Institute Publications in the Social Sciences* 8.

O'Connell, J. F., P. J. Wilke, T. F. King, and C. L. Mix, eds.
1974    Perris Reservoir archaeology: Late prehistoric demographic changes in southeastern California. Sacramento: *California Department of Parks and Recreation, Archaeological Reports* 14.

Odum, E. P.
1977    The emergence of ecology as a new integrative discipline. *Science* **195**(4284):1289–1293.

Offerman, J. K., T. M. Origer, and D. A. Fredrickson
1976    *An archaeological survey of Hoopa Valley, Hoopa Indian Reservation, Humboldt County, California.* Tucson: Report to the National Park Service.

Ogden, A.
1933    Russian sea otter and seal hunting on the California coast, 1803–1841. *California Historical Society Quarterly* **12**(3):217–239.
1941    *The California sea otter trade, 1784–1848.* Berkeley: University of California Press.

Oliphant, R.
1968    Further excavation of site 4-Ala-12. Manuscript. San Francisco: Department of Anthropology, San Francisco State University.
1971    The archaeology of 4-SMa-101. San Francisco: *Treganza Anthropology Museum Papers* 8:37–48.

Olmsted, D. L., and O. C. Stewart
1978    Achumawi. In R. F. Heizer, vol. ed., *Handbook of North American Indians, Vol. 8: California*:225–235. Washington, D.C.: Smithsonian Institution.

Olsen, W. H.
1963    *The comparative archaeology of the King Brown site (4-Sac-29).* M.A. thesis. Sacramento: Department of Anthropology, California State University, Sacramento.

Olsen, W. H., and L. A. Payen
1968    Archaeology of the Little Panoche Reservoir, Fresno County, California. Sacramento: *California Department of Parks and Recreation, Archaeological Reports* 11.
1969    Archaeology of the Grayson site, Merced County, California. Sacramento: *California Department of Parks and Recreation, Archaeological Reports* 12.

Olsen, W. H., L. A. Payen, and J. L. Beck
1966    *An archaeological survey of Pinnacles National Monument, San Benito County, California.* San Francisco: Report to the National Park Service.

Olsen, W. H., and F. A. Riddell
1962    Salvage of the Rio Oso site, Yuba County, California. Sacramento: *California Department of Parks and Recreation, Archaeological Reports* 6.
1963    The archaeology of the Western Pacific Railroad relocation, Oroville Project, Butte County, California. Sacramento: *California Department of Parks and Recreation, Archaeological Reports* 7.

Olsen, W. H., and N. Wilson
1964    The salvage archaeology of the Bear Creek site (SJo-112), a terminal central California Early Horizon site. Sacramento: *Sacramento Anthropological Society Papers* 1.

Olson, E. A., and W. S. Broecker
1961    Lamont natural radiocarbon measurements, VII. *Radiocarbon* **3**:141–175.

Olson, R. L.
1930    Chumash prehistory. Berkeley: *University of California Publications in American Archaeology and Ethnology* **28**(1):1–22.

Oman, P., with M. Moratto
  1982 New Melones archaeological project, California: Encoded archaeological site data. *Final report of the New Melones archaeological project* 10. Washington, D.C.: Report to the National Park Service.

Origer, T. M.
  1977 *Report on investigations by Sonoma State College at the Laguna de Santa Rosa.* Rohnert Park. Paper presented at the Northern California Data Sharing Meeting of the Society for California Archaeology.
  1982 *Temporal control in the southern North Coast Ranges of California: The application of obsidian hydration analysis.* M. A. thesis. San Francisco: Department of Anthropology, San Francisco State University.

Origer, T. M., and D. A. Fredrickson
  1980 *The Laguna archaeological research project, Sonoma County.* Santa Rosa: Report to the Public Works Department, City of Santa Rosa.

Origer, T. M., J. K. Offerman, and D. A. Fredrickson
  1976 *An archaeological survey of proposed timber sale areas on the Hoopa Valley Indian Reservation, California.* Tucson: Report to the National Park Service.

Origer, T. M., and B. Wickstrom
  1981 *The implications of obsidian hydration analysis in small-scale archaeologial studies.* Bakersfield: Paper presented at the Annual Meeting of the Society for California Archaeology.

Orlins, R. I.
  1971 *An archaeological survey of the Indian Valley Reservoir, Lake County, California.* San Francisco: Report to the National Park Service.
  1972 *Obsidian hydration analysis from Indian Valley, Lake County, California.* San Francisco: Report to the National Park Service.
  1977 *Cultural resources survey of fee lands for public access, lower Stanislaus River, California.* Sacramento: Report to U.S. Army Corps of Engineers, Sacramento District.

Orr, P. C.
  1942 The "Queen" of Mescalitan Island. *The Scientific Monthly* **54**:482–484.
  1943 Archaeology of Mescalitan Island and customs of the Canaliño. Santa Barbara: *Santa Barbara Museum of Natural History Occasional Papers* 5:1–61.
  1951a Ancient population centers of Santa Rosa Island. *American Antiquity* **16**(3):221–225.
  1951b Cave man hunt. *Museum talk* **26**:30–35.
  1952a Excavations in Moaning Cave. Santa Barbara: *Santa Barbara Museum of Natural History, Department of Anthropology Bulletin* 1.
  1952b Indian caves of Santa Rosa Island and their relation to antiquity. Stanford: *National Speleological Society, Monthly Report of the Stanford Grotto* 2(5):41–43.
  1952c Review of Santa Barbara Channel archaeology. *Southwestern Journal of Anthropology* **8**:211–226.
  1956a Dwarf mammoths and man on Santa Rosa Island. Salt Lake City: *University of Utah Anthropological Papers* 26:74–81.
  1956b Radiocarbon dates from Santa Rosa Island, I. Santa Barbara: *Santa Barbara Museum of Natural History, Department of Anthropology Bulletin* 2:1–9.
  1960a Late Pleistocene marine terraces on Santa Rosa Island. New York: *Bulletin of the Geological Society of America* **78**:1113–1119.
  1960b Radiocarbon dates from Santa Rosa Island, II. Santa Barbara: *Santa Barbara Museum of Natural History, Department of Anthropology Bulletin* **3**.
  1962a Arlington Spring man. *Science* **135**:219.
  1962b The Arlington site, Santa Rosa Island, California. *American Antiquity* **27**(3):417–419.

1964    Pleistocene chipped stone tool on Santa Rosa Island, California. *Science* **143**:243–244.

1968    *Prehistory of Santa Rosa Island.* Santa Barbara: Santa Barbara Museum of Natural History.

Orr, P. C., and R. Berger

1966    The fire areas on Santa Rosa Island, California. *Proceedings of the National Academy of Sciences* **56**(5):1409–1416.

Osborne, D.

1948    *Preliminary appraisal of the archaeological resources of Mariposa Reservoir, Mariposa County, California.* Washington, D.C.: Pacific Coast Area, River Basin Surveys, Smithsonian Institution.

Ostrovsky, R., and R. E. Schenk

1966    *An archaeological survey of the proposed Butler Valley Reservoir, Humboldt County, California.* San Francisco: Report to the National Park Service.

Oswalt, R. L.

1962    The internal relationships of the Pomo family of languages. *XXXV Congreso Internacional de Americanistas, Actas y Memorias* 3:413–427.

1964    A comparative study of two Pomo languages. Berkeley: *University of California Publications in Linguistics* 34:149–162.

1978    An exploration of the affinity of Wappo and some Hokan and Penutian languages. In J. Redden, ed., Proceddings of the 1978 Hokan languages workshop:56–71. Carbondale: *Southern Illinois University Department of Linguistics, Occasional Papers in Linguistics* 5.

Owen, R. C.

1964    Early Milling Stone Horizon (Oak Grove), Santa Barbara County, California: Radiocarbon dates. *American Antiquity* **30**(2):210–213.

1967    Assertions, assumptions, and Early Horizon (Oak Grove) settlement patterns in southern California: A rejoinder. *American Antiquity* **32**(2):236–241.

Owen, R. C., F. Curtis, and D. S. Miller

1964    The Glen Annie Canyon site, SBa-142, an Early Horizon coastal site of Santa Barbara County. Los Angeles: *University of California, Los Angeles, Archaeological Survey Annual Report, 1963–1964:429–517.*

Page, B. M.

1966    Geology of the Coast Ranges of California. Sacramento: *California Division of Mines and Geology Bulletin* **190**:255–276.

Palumbo, P. J.

1964    Archaeological investigation of Sol-30, California. Manuscript. Sacramento: California Department of Parks and Recreation.

1966    Dry Creek: An archaeology survey and site report. M.A. thesis. Sacramento: Department of Anthropology, California State University, Sacramento.

1967    The archaeology of 4-Ama-23. Sacramento: *Sacramento Anthropological Society Papers* 6(2).

Panlaqui, C.

1974    The Ray Cave site. China Lake: *Maturango Museum Monographs* **1**:1–62.

Parker, J. W.

1977    *Summary report on archaeological test excavations at CA-Lak-267 and CA-Lak-785 on 01-Lak-20 P.M. 16.8/18.1, Lucerne, Lake County, California.* Sacramento: Report to the California Department of Transportation.

Payen, L. A.

1959    Petroglyphs of Sacramento and adjoining counties, California. Berkeley: *University of California Archaeological Survey Reports* 48:66–92.

1964    "Pipe" artifacts from Sierra Nevada mortuary caves. Castro Valley: *Cave Notes* **6**(4):25–32.

1965    Preliminary report on the archaeological investigation of Pinnacle Point Cave,

Tuolumne County, California. Manuscript. Sacramento: Department of Anthropology, California State University, Sacramento.

1966    *Prehistoric rock art in the northern Sierra Nevada, California.* M.A. thesis. Sacramento: Department of Anthropology, California State University, Sacramento.

1968    A note on cupule sculptures in exogene caves from the Sierra Nevada, California. Castro Valley: *Caves and Karst* 10(4):33–39.

1970    A spearthrower (atlatl) from Potter Creek Cave, Shasta County, California. Davis: *University of California, Center for Archaeological Research at Davis, Publications* 2:157–170.

1973    *Crevis Creek: New light on the Farmington Complex.* San Francisco: Paper presented at the Annual Meeting of the Society for American Archaeology.

1974    *Archaeological survey of potential locations for the Helms Creek Storage Project construction camp sites.* San Francisco: Report to the Pacific Gas and Electric Company.

1978    Review of *The Broken Stones* by Herbert Minshall. *Journal of California Anthropology* 5(1):142–143.

1982    Artifacts or geofacts at Calico: Application of the Barnes Test. In J. E. Ericson, R. E. Taylor, and R. Berger, eds., Peopling of the New World:193–201. Los Altos: *Ballena Press Anthropological Papers* 23.

Payen, L. A., and D. S. Boloyan
1961    Archaeological excavations at Chilcoot Rockshleter, Plumas County, California. Sacramento: *California Division of Beaches and Parks, Archaeological Reports* 1:1–14.

1963    *Tcó-se:* An archaeological study of the bedrock mortar-petroglyph at Ama-14, near Volcano, California. Sacramento: *California Department of Parks and Recreation, Archaeological Reports* 8.

Payen, L. A., and J. J. Johnson
1965    Current cave research in the central Sierra Nevada mountains: A progress report. Sacramento: *Sacramento Anthropological Society Papers* 3:26–35.

Payen, L. A., and W. Olsen
1969    *Archaeological investigations in Stampede Reservoir, Sierra County, California.* San Francisco: Report to the National Park Service.

Payen, L. A., C. H. Rector, E. Ritter, R. E. Taylor, and J. E. Ericson
1978    Comments on the Pleistocene age assignment and associations of a human burial from the Yuha Desert, California. *American Antiquity* 43(3):448–453.

Payen, L. A., C. H. Rector, E. W. Ritter, and R. E. Taylor
1979    Reply to Bischoff, Childers, and Shlemon. *American Antiquity* 44(3):596–599.

Payen, L. A., L. R. Scott, and J. M. McEachern
1969    *Archaeological reconnaissance in the New Melones Reservoir, Calaveras and Tuolumne Counties, California: 1968 season.* San Francisco: Report to the National Park Service.

Payen, L. A., and R. E. Taylor
1976    Man and Pleistocene fauna at Potter Creek Cave, California. *Journal of California Anthropology* 3(1):51–58.

Peak, A. S.
1973    *New Melones Reservoir archaeological project, Calaveras and Tuolumne Counties, California: Phase III.* Tucson: Report to the National Park Service.

1976    *Buchanan Reservoir salvage project, Madera County, California: Archaeological Excavation.* Sacramento: Report to the U.S. Army Corps of Engineers, Sacramento District.

1981a    *Archaeological investigations: Cattle Timber sale, CA-Mad-448.* Fresno: Report to the Sierra National Forest.

1981b    *Archaeological investigations of CA-Sac-370 and CA-Sac-379, the Rancho*

*Murieta Early Man sites in eastern Sacramento County.* Sacramento: Ann S. Peak & Associates.

Peck, B. J., and D. M. Varner
    1977    *Archaeological investigations for the New Melones 230 KV transmission line, Tuolumne County.* San Francisco: Report to the Pacific Gas and Electric Company.

Peck, S. L.
    1953    Some pottery from the Sand Hills, Imperial County, California. Los Angeles: *Archaeological Survey Association of Southern California, Papers* 1.
    1955    An archaeological report on the excavation of a prehisotric site at Zuma Creek, Los Angeles County, California. Los Angeles: *Archaeological Survey Association of Southern California, Papers* 2.

Pendergast, D. M., and C. W. Meighan
    1959    The Greasy Creek site, Tulare County, California. Los Angeles: *University of California, Los Angeles, Archaeological Survey Annual Report, 1958–1959*:1–14.

Péron, R., E. Von der Porten, and W. F. Upson
    1973    *Excavations and site survey information from Point Reyes National Seashore.* Tucson: Report to the National Park Service.

Pestrong, R.
    1972    San Francisco Bay tidelands. *California Geology* **25**(2):27–40.

Peter, J.
    1923    Survey of Tomales Bay, Bodega Bay, and Sonoma County coast sites. Berkeley: *University of California Archaeological Survey Manuscripts* 436.

Peterson, R. T.
    1969    *A field guide to western birds.* Boston: Houghton Mifflin.

Phebus, G., Jr.
    1973    Contributions to Costanoan archaeology: Archaeological investigations at 4-Ala-330 and 4-SMa-22. San Francisco: *Treganza Anthropology Museum Papers* 12:1–75.

Pilling, A. R.
    1948a   Archaeological survey of northern Monterey County. Berkeley: *University of California Archaeological Survey Manuscripts* 106.
    1948b   The Vaqueros Province. Berkeley: *University of California Archaeological Survey Manuscripts.*
    1955    Relationships of prehistoric cultures of coastal Monterey County, California. Berkeley: *Kroeber Anthropological Society Papers* 12:70–87.
    1978    Yurok. In R. F. Heizer, vol. ed., *Handbook of North American Indians, Vol. 8: California*:137–154. Washington, D.C.: Smithsonian Institution.

Pilling, A. R., and R. K. Beardsley
    1948    Notes on various collections from Monterey County. Berkeley: *University of California Archaeological Survey Manuscripts* 26.

Pilling, A. R., and others
    n.d.    Notes on the archaeology of San Benito County. Berkeley: *University of California Archaeological Survey Manuscripts* 82.

Pippin, L. C., J. O. Davis, E. Budy, and R. Elston
    1979    Archaeological investigations at the Pikes Point site (4-Las-537), Eagle Lake, Lassen County, California. Reno: *Desert Research Institute, Social Sciences Center Publications* 72007.

Pohorecky, Z. S.
    1964    *Archaeology of the South Coast Ranges of California.* Ph.D. dissertation. Berkeley: Department of Anthropology, University of California.
    1976    Archaeology of the South Coast Ranges of California. Berkeley: *Contributions of the University of California Archaeological Research Facility* 34:1–235.

Powell, J. W.
    1891    Indian linguistic families of America north of Mexico. Washington, D.C.:
            *Smithsonian Institution, Bureau of American Ethnology Reports* 7:1–142.
Power, D. M., ed.
    1980    *The California Islands.* Santa Barbara: Santa Barbara Museum of Natural
            History.
Powers, S.
    1877    Tribes of California. Washington, D.C.: U.S. Department of the Interior, Geo-
    (1976)  graphical and Geological Survey of the Rocky Mountain Region, *Contributions
            to North American Ethnology, III.* (Reprinted 1976 as *Tribes of California.*
            Berkeley and Los Angeles: University of California Press.)
Presnall, C. C.
    1930a   Indian picture writing in Yosemite. Yosemite National Park: *Yosemite Nature
            Notes* **9**:94.
    1930b   Indian rancherias found. Yosemite National Park: *Yosemite Nature Notes*
            **9**:33–35.
Price, J. A.
    1962    *Washo economy.* M.A. thesis. Salt Lake City: Department of Anthropology,
            University of Utah.
Pritchard, W. E.
    1967    *The archaeology of lower Los Banos Creek.* M.A. thesis. Sacramento: Depart-
            ment of Anthropology, California State University, Sacramento.
    1968a   *Preliminary excavations at El Castillo, Presidio of Monterey, Monterey, Cal-
            ifornia.* Sacramento: Central California Archaeological Foundation.
    1968b   San Luis Forebay site (Mer-S119). Sacramento: California Department of Parks
            and Recreation.
    1970    Archaeology of the Menjoulet site, Merced County, California. Sacramento:
            *California Department of Parks and Recreation, Archaeological Reports* 13.
    n.d.    A comparative analysis of bead types from three mortuary caverns in the central
            Sierras of California. Manuscript. Sacramento: Department of Anthropology,
            California State University, Sacramento.
Protsch, R. R.
    1978    *Catalog of fossil hominids of North America.* New York and Stuttgart: Fischer.
Putnam, F. W.
    1906    Evidence of the work of man on objects from Quaternary caves in California.
            *American Anthropologist* **8**(2):229–235.
Rackerby, F.
    1964    *An appraisal of the archaeological resources of the Buchanan Reservoir project
            on the Chowchilla River, Madera County, California.* San Francisco: Report to
            the National Park Service.
    1965a   An archaeological survey of the Chowchilla River, Madera County, California.
            Los Angeles: *University of California, Los Angeles, Archaeological Survey An-
            nual Report, 1964–1965:303–322.*
    1965b   *The archaeology of the Middle Fork American River project, Placer County,
            California.* San Francisco: Report to the National Park Service.
    1967    The archaeological salvage of two San Francisco Bay shellmounds. San Francis-
            co: *Treganza Anthropology Museum Papers* 3(1):1–86.
Radin, P.
    1919    The genetic relationship of North American Indian languages. Berkeley: *Univer-
            sity of California Publications in American Archaeology and Ethnology*
            **14**(5):489–502.
Ragir, S. R.
    1972    The Early Horizon in central California prehistory. Berkeley: *Contributions of
            the University of California Archaeological Research Facility* 15.

Ransome, F. L.
   1899    Mother Lode district folio, California. Washington, D.C.: *U.S. Geological Survey, Geologic Atlas of the United States, Folio* 63.
Rantz, S. E.
   1969    Mean annual precipitation in the California region. *U.S. Geological Survey, Water Resource Division, Basic Data Compilation* 1020-01 (map).
Rasson, J.
   1966    Excavations at Ahwahnee, Yosemite National Park, California. Los Angeles: *University of California, Los Angeles, Archaeological Survey Annual Report, 1965–1966:*165–184.
Rathje, W. L., and M. B. Schiffer
   1982    *Archaeology.* New York: Harcourt Brace Jovanovich.
Raven, S.
   1981a   *The Devil, he walks behind you: Pit River use and avoidance of Devils Garden.* M.A. thesis. Sacramento: Department of Anthropology, California State University, Sacramento.
   1981b   *A cultural context for changing Pit River land use.* Bakersfield: Paper presented at the Annual Meeting of the Society for California Archaeology.
Ray, V. F.
   1942    Culture element distributions, XXII: Plateau. Berkeley: *University of California Anthropological Records* **8**(2).
   1963    *Primative pragmatists: The Modoc Indians of northern California.* Seattle: University of Washington Press.
Rector, C.
   1976    Rock art of the east Mojave Desert. In C. D. King and D. G. Casebier, Background to historic and prehistoric resources of the east Mojave Desert region:236–278. Riverside: *U.S. Bureau of Land Management, Cultural Resources Publications, Anthropology-History.*
   1979    Summary and conclusions. In C. Rector, J. D. Swenson, and P. J. Wilke, *Archaeological studies at Oro Grande,* Mojave Desert, California. Riverside: Report to the Victor Valley Wastewater Reclamation Authority.
Rector, C., J. D. Swenson, and P. J. Wilke
   1979    *Archaeological studies at Oro Grande, Mojave Desert, California.* Riverside: Report to the Victor Valley Wastewater Reclamation Authority.
Reichard, G. A.
   1926    Wiyot: An Indian language of northern California. *American Speech* **1**:654–658.
Reichlen, H., and R. F. Heizer
   1964    The scientific expedition of Leon de Cessac to California, 1877–1879. Berkeley: *University of California Archaeological Survey Reports* 61:9–23.
Reinman, F. M.
   1964    Maritime adaptation on San Nicolas Island, California: A preliminary and speculative evaluation. Los Angeles: *University of California, Los Angeles, Archaeological Survey Annual Report, 1963–1964:*47–77.
Reinman, F., D. L. True, and C. N. Warren
   1960    Archaeological remains from rock shelters near Coyote Mountain, Imperial County, California. Los Angeles: *University of California, Los Angeles, Archaeological Survey Annual Report, 1959–1960:*231–248.
Ricketts, E., and J. Calvin
   1962    *Between Pacific tides.* Stanford: Stanford University Press.
Riddell, F. A.
   1949    *Appraisal of the archaeological resources of Farmington Reservoir, Littlejohns Creek, San Joaquin and Stanislaus Counties, California.* Washington, D.C.: Smithsonian Institution, River Basin Surveys, Pacific Coast Area.

1951    The archaeology of site Ker-74. Berkeley: *University of California Archaeological Survey Reports* 10:1–28.

1956    Final report on the archaeology of Tommy Tucker Cave. Berkeley: *University of California Archaeological Survey Reports* 35.

1958    The eastern California border: Cultural and temporal affinities. Berkeley: *University of California Archaeological Survey Reports* 42:41–48.

1960a   The archaeology of the Karlo site (Las-7), California. Berkeley: *University of California Archaeological Survey Reports* 53.

1960b   Honey Lake Paiute ethnography. Carson City: *Nevada State Museum Anthropological Papers* 4.

1969a   *An archaeological reconnaissance of the Bucks Lake project, Plumas County, California.* San Francisco: Report to the Pacific Gas and Electric Company.

1969b   *Aspects of Miwok Indian culture.* Sacramento: Report to United States Land, Inc.

1969c   Pleistocene faunal remains associated with carbonaceous material. *American Antiquity* **34**(2):177–180.

1973    Fossilized California bone artifacts. Los Angeles: *The Masterkey* **47**(1):28–32.

1978    Maidu and Konkow. In R. F. Heizer, vol. ed., *Handbook of North American Indians, Vol. 8: California*:370–386. Washington, D.C.: Smithsonian Institution.

Riddell, F. A., and D. F. McGeein
1969    California atlatl spurs. *American Antiquity* **34**(4):474–478.

Riddell, F. A., and W. H. Olsen
1965    Archaeology of Mer-14, Merced County, California. Manuscript. Sacramento: California Department of Parks and Recreation.

1969    An Early Man site in the San Joaquin Valley. *American Antiquity* **34**(2):121–130.

Riddell, F. A., W. H. Olsen, and R. B. Hastings
1972    *Archaeological reconnaissance and study of the proposed Helms Creek project.* San Francisco: Report to the Pacific Gas and Electric Company.

Riddell, F. A., and W. E. Pritchard
1970    *A report on the archaeology of the Rainbow Point site (4-Plu-S94) at Bucks Lake, Plumas County, California.* San Francisco: Report to the Pacific Gas and Electric Company.

Riddell, F. A., and H. S. Riddell, Jr.
1940    Archaeological notes on site CA-Sac-28. Berkeley: *University of California Archaeological Survey Manuscripts* 34.

n.d.    Archaeology of the buried Strawberry site. Manuscript. Berkeley: Department of Anthropology, University of California.

Riddell, H. S., Jr.
1951    The archaeology of a Paiute village site in Owens Valley. Berkeley: *University of California Archaeological Survey Reports* 12:14–28.

Riddell, H. S., Jr., and F. A. Riddell
1956    The current status of archaeological investigations in Owens Valley, California. Berkeley: *University of California Archaeological Survey Reports* 33:28–33.

Riley, L. M.
1976    *An assessment of endangered archaeological sites at Point Reyes National Seashore.* San Francisco: Report to the National Park Service.

1979    *Shelter Hill: An analysis of faunal remains and artifacts from a Marin County shellmound (04-Mrn-14).* M.A. thesis. San Francisco: Department of Anthropology, San Francisco State University.

Rinehart, C. D., and N. K. Huber
1965    The Inyo Crater lakes—a blast in the past. *California Division of Mines and Geology, Mineral Information Service Bulletin* **18**(1):169–172.

Ringer, D.
  1971    *Environmental exploitation at a prehistoric Indian site (Ala-328) in Alameda County, California.* M.A. thesis. San Francisco: Department of Anthropology, San Francisco State University.

Ritter, E. W.
  1968    *Culture history of* Tie Wiah *(4-But-84), Oroville locality, California.* M.A. thesis. Davis: Department of Anthropology, University of California.
  1970a   Northern Sierra foothill archaeology: Culture history and culture process. Davis: *University of California, Center for Archaeological Research at Davis, Publications* 2:171–184.
  1970b   The archaeology of 4-Pla-101, the Spring Garden Ravine site. In E. W. Ritter, ed., *Archaeological investigations in the Auburn Reservoir area, Phase II–III*:270–538. San Francisco: Report to the National Park Service.
  1971    *Archaeological reconnaissance of the Folsom South Canal, Central Valley, California.* San Francisco: Report to the National Park Service.

Ritter, E. W., ed.
  1970    *Archaeological investigations in the Auburn Reservoir area, Phase II–III.* San Francisco: Report to the National Park Service.

Ritter, E. W., B. W. Hatoff, and L. A. Payen
  1976    Chronology of the Farmington Complex. *American Antiquity* **41**(3):334–341.

Ritter, E. W., and R. G. Matson
  1972    Form categories, cluster analysis, and multidimensional scaling: A case study of projectile points. *Southwestern Lore* **37**(4):102–116.

Ritter, E. W., and P. D. Schulz, eds.
  1972    Papers on Nisenan environment and subsistence. Davis: *University of California, Center for Archaeological Research at Davis, Publications* 3.

Ritter, E. W., P. D. Schulz, and R. Kautz, eds.
  1970    Papers on California and Great Basin prehistory. Davis: *University of California, Center for Archaeological Research at Davis, Publications* 2.

Roberts, P.
  1975    *Preliminary archaeological reconnaissance of the proposed Hupa Mountain Timber Sale, Humboldt County.* Ukiah: Report to the U.S. Bureau of Land Management.
  1980    Research design and analysis. In S. B. Stewart and D. A. Fredrickson, eds., *A cultural resources survey of the Round Valley Indian Reservation, Mendocino and Trinity Counties, California*:118–162. Tucson: Report to the National Park Service.

Robinson, E.
  1942    Shell fishhooks of the California coast. Honolulu: *Occasional Papers of the B. P. Bishop Museum* **17**(4):57–65.

Robinson: R. W.
  1977    The prehistory of the Antelope Valley, California: An overview. *Kern County Archaeological Society Journal* **1**:43–48.

Rogers, D. B.
  1929    *Prehistoric man of the Santa Barbara Coast.* Santa Barbara: Santa Barbara Museum of Natural History.

Rogers, M. J.
  1929a   Archaeological field work in North America during 1928, California. *American Anthropologist* **31**(3):341.
  1929b   Report on an archaeological reconnaissance in the Mojave sink region. San Diego: *San Diego Museum of Man Papers* 1.
  1929c   The stone art of the San Dieguito Plateau. *American Anthropologist* **31**(3):454–467.
  1936    Yuman pottery making. San Diego: *San Diego Museum of Man Papers* 2.

1938 Archaeological and geological investigations in an old channel of the San Dieguito Valley. Washington, D.C.: *Carnegie Institution of Washington, Yearbook* 37:344–345.

1939 Early lithic industries of the lower basin of the Colorado River and adjacent desert areas. San Diego: *San Diego Museum of Man Papers* 3.

1941 Aboriginal culture relations between southern California and the Southwest. San Diego: *San Diego Museum Bulletin* 5(3):1–6.

1945 An outline of Yuman prehistory. Albuquerque: *Southwestern Journal of Anthropology* 1(2):167–198.

1958 San Dieguito implements from the terraces of the Rincón–Patano and Rillito drainage system. *The Kiva* 24(1):1–23.

1966 *Ancient hunters of the Far West.* San Diego: Union–Tribune.

Romney, A. K.
1957 The genetic model and Uto-Aztecan time perspective. Seattle: *Davidson Journal of Anthropology* 3(2):35–41.

Rondeau, M. F.
1978 *The Sanguinetti quarry site.* Sacramento: Report to the California Department of Transportation.

Roop, W. G.
1976 *Adaptation on Ben Lomond Mountain.* M.A. thesis. San Francisco: Department of Anthropology, San Francisco State University.

1981 The archaeology of vernal pools: An example from Placer County. Manuscript. Novato: Archaeological Resource Service.

Roop, W. G., and L. Barker, with C. Detlefs
1977 *Cultural resource inventory of the Scotts Valley Wastewater Project service area.* Novato: Archaeological Resource Service.

Roop, W. G., with K. Flynn
1978 *Heritage on the half-shell: Excavations at Mnt-298.* Monterey: Report to the City of Monterey, Urban Renewal Agency.

Roop, W. G., C. Gerike, and K. Flynn
1981 *Request for determination of eligibility to the National Register of Historic Place for fourteen prehistoric cultural resources within the Guadalupe Corridor, northern Santa Clara Valley, California.* San José: Report to the Santa Clara County Transportation Agency.

Ross, L. A.
1969 *The Irvine Complex: A late prehistoric horizon archaeological complex for the Newport Bay area, California.* M.A. thesis. Pullman: Department of Anthropology, Washington State University.

1970 Ora-190: A descriptive report of a late prehistoric horizon site in Orange County, California. Costa Mesa: *Pacific Coast Archaeological Society Quarterly* 6(2–3):1–135.

Rostlund, E.
1952 Freshwater fish and fishing in native North America. Berkeley: *University of California Publications in Geography* 9.

Rozaire, C. E.
1959a Archaeological investigations at two sites on San Nicolas Island, California. Los Angeles: *The Masterkey* 33(4):129–152.

1959b Excavations at site AnI-8, Le Dreau Cove. Los Angeles: *University of California, Los Angeles, Archaeological Survey Annual Report, 1958–1959*:91–93.

1962a Archaeological site survey of Anacapa Island, May 26 to May 30, 1962. Manuscript. Los Angeles: Los Angeles County Museum of Natural History.

1962b Underwater finds at Dana Point. Los Angeles: *The Masterkey* 36(2):77–78.

1965 *Archaeological investigations on San Miguel Island.* San Francisco: Report to the National Park Service.

1967    Archaeological considerations regarding the southern California islands. In R. N. Philbrick, ed., *Proceedings of the Symposium on the Biology of the Channel Islands:327–336.* Santa Barbara: Santa Barbara Botanic Garden.

1978    *A report on the archaeological investigations of three California channel islands: Santa Barbara, Anacapa, and San Miguel.* San Francisco: Report to the National Park Service.

Ruby, J. W.
1961    Excavations at Zuma Mesa. Los Angeles: *University of California, Los Angeles, Archaeological Survey Annual Report, 1960–1961:190–232.*

1970    *Culture contact between aboriginal southern California and the Southwest.* Ph.D. dissertation. Los Angeles: Department of Anthropology, University of California.

Russell, R. J.
1927    The landforms of Surprise Valley, northwestern Great Basin. Berkeley: *University of California Publications in Geology 2:323–358.*

Salzman, S.
1977    *The valley of the South Fork of the Kern River: Cultural resource management proposal for the Long Canyon Village site.* Bakersfield: U.S. Bureau of Land Management.

Sample, L. L.
1950    Trade and trails in aboriginal California. Berkeley: *University of California Archaeological Survey Reports 8:1–30.*

Sanborn, A. A.
1964    *Archaeological site survey of Lamont Meadow Project 3080, Long Valley Project 3079, Chimney Creek Campground, Long Valley Campground.* Bakersfield: Report to the U.S. Bureau of Land Management.

Sapir, E.
1913    Wiyot and Yurok, Algonkin languages of California. *American Anthropologist* **15**(4):617–646.

1917    The position of Yana in the Hokan stock. Berkeley: *University of California Publications in American Archaeology and Ethnology* **13**(1):1–34.

1929    Central and North American Indian languages. London and New York: *Encyclopaedia Britannica,* 14th ed., 5:138–141.

Savage, J. M.
1959    *An illustrated key to the lizards, snakes, and turtles of the West.* San Martín: Naturegraph.

Sawyer, J. O.
1978    Wappo. In R. F. Hezier, vol. ed., *Handbook of North American Indians, Vol. 8: California:256–263.* Washington, D.C.: Smithsonian Institution.

Saxe, W. E.
1875    Observations on a shellmound at Laguna Creek, 6 miles north of Santa Cruz. San Francisco: *Proceedings of the California Academy of Sciences* **5:**157.

Schalk, R. F.
1977    The structure of anadronmous fish resources. In L. Binford, ed., *For theory building in archaeology:207–249.* New York: Academic Press.

Schroedl, A. R.
1977    The Grand Canyon figurine complex. *American Antiquity* **42**(2):254–265.

Shelford, V. E.
1963    *The ecology of North America.* Urbana: University of Illinois Press.

Schenck, W. E.
1926a    Historic aboriginal groups of the California Delta region. Berkeley: *University of California Publications in American Archaeology and Ethnology* **23**(2):123–146.

1926b    The Emeryville shellmound: Final report. Berkeley: *University of California Publications in American Archaeology and Ethnology* **23**(3):147–282.

Schenck, W. E., and E. J. Dawson
  1929   Archaeology of the northern San Joaquin Valley. Berkeley: *University of Califor-
         nia Publications in American Archaeology and Ethnology* **25**(4):289–413.
Schenk, R. E., ed.
  1970   Contributions to the archaeology of Point Reyes Peninsula: A compendium in
         honor of Adán E. Treganza. San Francisco: *Treganza Anthropology Museum
         Papers* 6.
Schiffman, R. A.
  1974   *Archaeological investigation of a Tübatulabal Indian hamlet site.* Porterville:
         Report to the Sequoia National Forest.
  1976   *Archaeological resources of the Lake Isabella region and adjacent lands under
         the jurisdiction of the United States Army Corps of Engineers.* Sacramento:
         Report to the U.S. Army Corps of Engineers, Sacramento District.
  1977   A possible Tübatulabal calendar. *Kern County Archaeological Society Journal*
         **1**:25–28.
Schiffman, R. A., and A. P. Garfinkel
  1981   Prehistory of Kern County: An overview. Bakersfield: *Bakersfield College Pub-
         lications in Archaeology* 1.
Schiffman, R. A., D. S. Whitley, A. P. Garfinkel, and S. B. Andrews, eds.
  1982   Pictographs of the Coso region: Analysis and interpretation of the Coso Painted
         style. Bakersfield: *Bakersfield College Publications in Archaeology* 2.
Schroeder, A. H.
  1952   A brief survey of the lower Colorado River, from Davis Dam to the international
         border. Manuscript. Sante Fe: National Park Service.
  1957   The Hakataya cultural tradition. *American Antiquity* **23**(2):176–178.
  1958   Lower Colorado Buff Ware, a descriptive revision. In H. S. Colton, ed., Pottery
         types of the Southwest. Flagstaff: *Museum of Northern Arizona Ceramic Series
         3D.*
  1961   The archaeological excavations at Willow Beach, Arizona, 1950. Salt Lake City:
         *University of Utah Anthropological Papers* 50.
  1979   Prehistory: Hakataya. In A. Ortiz, vol. ed., *Handbook of North American Indi-
         ans, Vol. 9: Southwest:*100–107. Washington, D.C.: Smithsonian Institution.
Schuiling, W. C., ed.
  1972   *Pleistocene man at Calico.* Bloomfield: San Bernardino County Museum
         Association.
  1979   *Pleistocene man at Calico* (2nd edition). Redlands: San Bernardino County Mu-
         seum Association.
Schulz, P. D.
  1970   Solar burial orienation and paleodemography in the central California Wind-
         miller tradition. Davis: *University of California, Center for Archaeological Re-
         search at Davis, Publications* 2:185–198.
  1975   Radiocarbon (C-14) dates—lower Sacramento–San Joaquin Valley. Davis: Un-
         published chart distributed at a workshop on the archaeological chronology of
         the Delta subregion.
Schulz, P. D., D. M. Abels, and E. W. Ritter
  1979   Archeology of the Jonson site (CA-Sac-65), Sacramento County, California. Sac-
         ramento: *California Department of Parks and Recreation, Archaeological Re-
         ports* 18.
Schulz, P. D., and E. W. Ritter
  1977   Archaeology of the Safflower site (CA-SJo-145). Manuscript. Sacramento: Cal-
         ifornia Department of Parks and Recreation.
Schumacher, P.
  1874   Some kjökkenmöddings and ancient graves of California. *Overland Monthly*
         **13**:297–302.

1875a    Ancient graves and shell heaps of California. Washington, D.C.: *Smithsonian Institution, Annual Report for 1874*:335–350.

1985b    Die Anfertigung der Angelhaken aus Muschelschalen bei den früheren Bewohnern der Inseln im Santa Barbara Kanal. Braunschweig: *Archiv für Anthropologie* **8**:223–224.

1875c    Etwas über Kjökkenmoddinge und die Funde in Alten Graben in Südcalifornien. Braunschweig: *Archiv für Anthropologie* **8**:217–221.

1875d    Some remains of a former people. San Francisco: *Overland Monthly* **15**:374–379.

1877a    Aboriginal settments of the Pacific Coast. New York: *Popular Science Monthly* **10**(1).

1877b    Researches in the Kjökkenmoddings and graves of a former population of the Santa Barbara Channel and the adjacent mainland. Washington, D.C.: *Bulletin of the United States Geological and Geographical Survey of the Territories* **3**:37–61.

1878a    Ancient olla manufactory on Santa Catalina Island, California. Philadelphia: *American Naturalist* **12**(9):629.

1878b    Die Gräber und Hinterlossenschaft Urvölker an der Kalifornischen Küste. Berlin: *Zeitschrift für Ethnologie* **10**:183–192.

1878c    The method of manufacture of several articles by the former Indians of southern California. Cambridge: *Peabody Museum Annual Report* **11**:258–268.

1880     Method of manufacture of pottery and baskets among the Indians of southern California. *Peabody Museum Annual Report* **12**(2):521–525.

Schuyler, R. L.
1978     Indian–Euro-American interaction: Archaeological evidence from non-Indian sites. In R. F. Heizer, vol. ed., *Handbook of North American Indians, Vol. 8: California*:69–79. Washington, D.C.: Smithsonian Institution.

Sellards, E. H.
1960     Some early stone artifact developments in North America. *Southwestern Journal of Anthropology* **16**:160–173.

Šercelj, A., and D. P. Adam
1975     A late Holocene pollen diagram from near Lake Tahoe, El Dorado County, California. *U.S. Geological Survey Journal of Research* **3**(6):737–745.

Service, E. R.
1962     *Primitive social organization: an evolutionary perspective.* New York: Random House.

Shangraw, C., and E. P. Von der Porten
1981     *The Drake and Cermeño expeditions' Chinese porcelains at Drakes Bay, California.* Santa Rosa and Palo Alto: Santa Rosa Junior College and Drake Navigators Guild.

Sharp, R. P.
1972     Pleistocene glaciation, Bridgeport Basin, California. *Geological Society of America Bulletin* **83**(8):2233–2260.

Sheets, P. D., ed.
1974     Mountain Rest archaeological project: Phases I and II. Manuscript. Fresno: Department of Anthropology, California State University, Fresno.

Shelford, V. E.
1963     *The ecology of North America.* Urbana: University of Illinois Press.

Shiner, J. L.
1949     A Fernandeño site in Simi Valley, California. Los Angeles: *The Masterkey* **23**(3):79–81.

Shipley, W.
1957     Some Yukian–Penutian lexical resemblances. *International Journal of American Linguistics* **23**(4):269–274.

1978     Native languages of California. In R. F. Heizer, vol. ed., *Handbook of North*

*American Indians, Vol. 8: California*:80–90. Washington, D.C.: Smithsonian Institution.

Shlemon, R. J.
1981 Letter, dated 11 August 1979, to Ann S. Peak regarding the estimated age of the Rancho Murieta sites. In A. S. Peak, ed., *Archaeological investigations of CA-Sac-370 and CA-Sac-379: The Rancho Murieta Early Man sites in eastern Sacramento County*:128. Sacramento: Ann S. Peak & Associates.

Short, H. W.
1970 The geology of Moaning Cave. *Bulletin of the National Speleological Society* **32**(2).

Shumway, G., C. L. Hubbs, and J. R. Moriarty
1961 Scripps Estates site, San Diego, California: A La Jolla site dated 5460 to 7370 years before present. *New York Academy of Sciences, Annals* **93**(3):37–132.

Shutler, R., Jr.
1961 Lost City, Pueblo Grande de Nevada. Carson City: *Nevada State Museum Anthropological Papers* 5.
1967 Cultural chronology in southern Nevada. Carson City: *Nevada State Museum Anthropological Papers* 13:303–308.
1968 The Great Basin Archaic. Portales: *Eastern New Mexico University Contributions in Anthropology* **1**(3):24–26.

Shutler, R., Jr., M. E. Shutler, and J. S. Griffith
1960 Stuart rockshelter: A stratified site in southern Nevada. Carson City: *Nevada State Mueseum Anthropological Papers* 3.

Sigleo, A. C.
1975 Turquoise mine and artifact correlation for Snaketown site, Arizona. *Science* **189**:459–460.

Silver, S.
1978 Shastan peoples. In R. F. Heizer, vol. ed., *Handbook of North American Indians, Vol. 8: California*:211–224. Washington, D.C.: Smithsonian Institution.

Simons, D. D.
1981 Bird and mammal remains from eight archaeological sites (CA-Mnt-107, 110, 111, 112, 113, 114, 115, 116) located in Pacific Grove, Monterey County, California. In S. A. Dietz and T. L. Jackson, *Report of archaeological excavations at nineteen archaeological sites for the Stage I Pacific Grove-Monterey Consolidation Project of the Regional Sewerage System:* Appendix D. Santa Cruz: Archaeological Consulting and Research Services.

Sims, J. D.
1976 Paleolimnology of Clear Lake, California, U.S.A. In S. Horie, *Paleolimnology of Lake Biwa and the Japanese Pleistocene* 4:658–702.

Simpson, R. D.
1947 A classic Folsom from Lake Mojave. Los Angeles: *The Masterkey* **21**(1):24–25.
1954 A friendly critic visits Texas Street. Los Angeles: *The Masterkey* **28**(5):174–176.
1956 An introduction to early western American prehistory. Los Angeles: *Southern California Academy of Sciences Bulletin* **55**(2):61–67.
1958 The Manix Lake archaeological survey. Los Angeles: *The Masterkey* **32**(1):4–10.
1960 Archaeological survey of the eastern Calico Mountains. Los Angeles: *The Masterkey* **34**(1):25–35.
1964 The archaeological survey of Pleistocene Manix Lake (an early lithic horizon). *Proceedings of the 35th International Congress of Americanists* **35**:5–9.
1965 An archaeological survey of Troy Lake, San Bernardino County: A preliminary report. *San Bernardino County Museum Association Quarterly* **12**(3).
1976 A commentary on W. Glennan's article. *Journal of New World Archaeology* **1**(7):63–66.
1977 *Calico Mountains archaeological project, progress report.* San Diego: Paper pre-

sented at the Annual Meeting of the American Ethnological Society and the Society for California Archaeology.

1980    The Calico Mountains site (oldest known Early Man site in America). *ASA Journal* **4**(2):8–25. Redlands: Archaeological Survey Association of Southern California.

Simpson, R. D., L. W. Patterson, and C. A. Singer

1981    *Early lithic technology of the Calico site, southern California.* Mexico City: Paper presented at the 10th International Congress of Prehistoric and Protohistoric Sciences.

Sinclair, W. J.

1904    The exploration of the Potter Creek Cave. Berkeley: *University of California Publications in American Archaeology and Ethnology* **2**:1–27.

1908a    Recent investigations bearing on the question of Neocene man in the auriferous gravels of Butte County, California. London: *Journal of the Royal Anthropological Institute of Great Britain and Ireland* **17**:332–337.

1908b    Recent investigations bearing on the question of the occurrence of Neocene man in the auriferous gravels of the Sierra Nevada. Berkeley: *University of California Publications in American Archaeology and Ethnology* **7**(2):107–131.

Singer, C. A.

1977    Abstract of "Classification and isolation of the Calico lithic industries." San Diego: *Abstracts* of papers presented at the Annual Meeting of the American Ethnological Society, Society for California Archaeology, and other organizations:109.

Singer, C. A., and J. Ericson

1977    Quarry analysis at Bodie Hills, Mono County, California: A case study. In T. K. Earle and J. E. Ericson, eds., *Exchange systems in prehistory*:171–190. New York: Academic Press.

Singleton, W. L.

1983    Flaked stone tools. In M. J. Moratto *et al.*, New Melones archaeological project, California: Indian sites 04-Cal-S-286, 04-Cal-S-347, and 04-Cal-S-461. *Final report of the New Melones archaeological project*, 4(2):127–364. Report to the National Park Service, Washington, D.C. Sonora: INFOTEC Development, Inc.

Skertchley, S. B. J.

1888    On the occurrence of stone mortars in the ancient (Pliocene?) river gravels of Butte County, California. London: *Journal of the Royal Anthropological Institute of Great Britain and Ireland* **17**:332–337.

Slaymaker, C. M.

1971    The Moccasin site, 4-Tuo-314. San Francisco: *Treganza Anthropology Museum Papers* 9:129–136.

1972    *Cry for Olompali.* Privately printed (no publisher or city given).

1974    *Fidemo, the twilight and before: A study of Coast Miwok political organization.* M.A. thesis. San Francisco: Department of Anthropology, San Francisco State University.

Smith, C. E., and W. D. Weymouth

1952a    Archaeology of the Shasta Dam area, California. Berkeley: *University of California Archaeological Survey Reports* 18:1–35, 43–49.

1952b    Excavations at Redding mound 1 (Sha-47) in 1935. Berkeley: *University of California Archaeological Survey Reports* 18:36–42.

Smith, C. R.

1978    Tübatulabal. In R. F. Heizer, vol. ed., *Handbook of North American Indians, Vol. 8: California*:437–445. Washington, D.C.: Smithsonian Institution.

Smith, G. A.

1950    *Prehistoric man of the San Bernardino Valley.* Redlands: San Bernardino County Historical Society.

1955    *A preliminary report of the archaeological survey of the Deep Creek site in San Bernardino County, California.* The Archaeological Survey Association of Southern California, and the San Bernardino County Historical Society and Museum Association.

1963a   *Archaeological survey of the Mojave River area and adjacent regions.* San Bernardino: San Bernardino County Museum Association.

1963b   Split-twig figurines from San Bernardino County, California. Los Angeles: *The Masterkey* **37**(3):86–90.

Smith, G. A., W. C. Schuiling, L. Martin, R. Sayles, and P. Jillson
1957    *The archaeology of Newberry Cave, San Bernardino County, California.* San Bernardino: San Bernardino County Museum Association.

Smith, J. E.
1958    Excavations in Mitchell's Caverns. Manuscript. Berkeley: Department of Anthropology, University of California.

Snyder, C. T., G. Hardman, and F. F. Zdenek
1964    Late Pleistocene lakes of the Great Basin. Washington, D.C.: *U.S. Geological Survey Miscellaneous Geologic Investigations* Map I-416.

Soil Conservation Service (SCS)
1960    *Soil classification: A comprehensive system, 7th approximation.* Washington, D.C.: U.S. Department of Agriculture, Soil Conservation Service. Government Printing Office.

Soule, W.
1975    *Archaeological investigations at Men-584, Mendocino County, California.* M.A. thesis. Sacramento: Department of Anthropology, California State University, Sacramento.

Spanne, L.
1975    Seasonal variability in the population of Barbareño Chumash villages: An explanatory model. San Luis Obispo: *San Luis Obispo County Archaeological Society Occasional Papers* 9:61–87.

Sparkman, P. S.
1908    Culture of the Luiseño Indians. Berkeley: *University of California Publications in American Archaeology and Ethnology* **8**(4):187–234.

Spencer, R., J. D. Jennings, *et al.*
1977    *The Native Americans* (2nd ed.). New York: Harper and Row.

Spier, L.
1923    Southern Diegueño customs. Berkeley: *University of California Publications in American Archaeology and Ethnology* **20**(16):297–358.

Spier, R. F. G.
1978a   Foothill Yokuts. In R. F. Heizer, vol. ed., *Handbook of North American Indians, Vol. 8: California*:471–484. Washington, D.C.: Smithsonian Institution.

1978b   Monache. In R. F. Heizer, vol. ed., *Handbook of North American Indians, Vol. 8: California*:426–436. Washington, D.C.: Smithsonian Institution.

Squier, R. J.
1956    Recent excavation and survey in northeastern California. Berkeley: *University of California Archaeological Survey Reports* 33:34–38.

Squier, R. J., and G. L. Grosscup
1952    *An archaeological survey of Lava Beds National Monument, California, 1952.* San Francisco: Report to the National Park Service.

1954    Preliminary report of archaeological excavations in lower Klamath Basin, California, 1954. Berkeley: *University of California Archaeological Survey Manuscripts* 183.

Stafford, J.
1973    A preliminary quantitative report on excavations by the University of California at Santa Cruz on the Bonny Doon or Brown site, CA-SCr-20, Santa Cruz County.

Manuscript: Santa Cruz: Department of Anthropology, University of California, Santa Cruz.

Stephenson, R. L.
1971    Thoughts on the Calico Mountains site. Columbia: *University of South Carolina, The Institute of Archaeology and Anthropology Notebook* 3:3–9.

Steward, J. H.
1929    Petroglyphs of California and adjoining states. Berkeley: *University of California Publications in American Archaeology and Ethnology* **24**(2):47–238.
1933    Ethnography of the Owens Valley Paiute. Berkeley: *University of California Publications in American Archaeology and Ethnology* **33**(3):233–438.
1935    *Indian tribes of the Sequoia National Park region.* Berkeley: National Park Service Field Division of Education.
1938    Basin–Plateau aboriginal sociopolitical groups. Washington, D.C.: *Smithsonian Institution, Bureau of American Ethnology Bulletin* **120.**

Stewart, O. C.
1939    The Northern Paiute bands. Berkeley: *University of California Anthropological Records* **2** (3).

Stewart, S.
1982    *Prehistoric overview, Northwest Region: California archaeological inventory, Volume 3: Napa and Sonoma counties.* Rohnert Park: Anthropological Studies Center, Sonoma State University.

Stewart, S., and D. A. Fredrickson, eds.
1980    *A cultural resources survey of the Round Valley Indian Reservation, Mendocino and Trinity Counties, California.* Tucson: Report to the National Park Service.

Stickel, E. G.
1980    Culture history: Chronology. In E. G. Stickel and L. J. Weinman-Roberts, An overview of the cultural resources of the Mojave Desert:45–58. Riverside: *U.S. Bureau of Land Management, Cultural Resources Publications, Anthropology–History* (unnumbered).

Stickel, E. G., J. McKenna, and H. Henry
1980    *Preliminary analysis of a 6 meter stratified site in Santa Clara County, California.* San Diego: Paper presented at the Annual Meeting of the Southwestern Anthropological Association.

Stock, C.
1918    The Pleistocene fauna of Hawver Cave. Berkeley: *University of California, Department of Geology Bulletin* 10.
1924    A recent discovery of ancient human remains in Los Angeles, California. *Science* **60**:2–5.
1930    Rancho La Brea: A record of Pleistocene life in California. Los Angeles: *Los Angeles County Museum of Natural History Science Series* 4.

Stock, C., and E. L. Furlong
1928    The Pleistocene elephants of Santa Rosa Island, California. *Science* **68**(1754):140–141.

Storer, T. I., and L. P. Tevis, Jr.
1955    *California grizzly.* Lincoln: University of Nebraska Press.

Storer, T. I., and R. Usinger
1970    *Sierra Nevada natural history.* Berkeley: University of California Press.

Stradford, R. A., and D. A. Fredrickson
1978    *An archaeological survey and cultural resource evaluation of proposed timber sale areas on the Hoopa Valley Indian Reservation, Humboldt County, California.* Tucson: Report to the National Park Service.

Stradford, R. A., and R. Schwaderer
1981    *Remembrance of things bypassed: Archaeological investigations at CA-*

*Nap-15/H, Napa County, California.* Sacramento: Report to the California Department of Transportation.

Strong, E.
1959a    *Stone age on the Columbia River.* Portland: Binfords & Mort.
1959b    *Wakemap mound and nearby sites on the Long Narrows of the Columbia River.* Portland: Binfords & Mort.
1969    *Stone Age in the Great Basin.* Portland: Binfords & Mort.

Strong, W. D.
1929    Aboriginal society in southern California. Berkeley: *University of California Publications in American Archaeology and Ethnology* **26**(1):1–358.

Suchey, J. M.
1975    *Biological distance of prehistoric central California populations derived from non-metric traits of the cranium.* Ph.D. dissertation. Riverside: Department of Anthropology, University of California.

Susia, M. L.
1964    Tule Springs archaeological surface survey. Carson City: *Nevada State Museum Anthropological Papers* 12.

Sutton, M. Q.
1978    A series of discoidals from northern San Diego County, California. *The Journal of California Anthropology* 5(2):266–270.
1980    Some aspects of Kitanemuk prehistory. *The Journal of California and Great Basin Anthroplogy* 2(2):214–225.
1981    Archaeology of the Antelope Valley, western Mojave Desert, California. Manuscript. In possession of the author.

Swadesh, M.
1954    Time depths of American linguistic groupings. *American Anthropologist* **56**(3):361–364.
1954–    Algunas fechas glotocronológicas importantes para la prehistoria nahua. *Revista*
1955    *Mexicana de Estudios Antropológicas* **14**(1):173–192.
1956    Problems of long range comparison in Penutian. *Language* **32**(1):17–41.
1959a    *Indian linguistic groups in Mexico.* Mexico, D. F.: Escuela Nacional de Antropología e Historia, Instituto Nacional de Antropología e Historia.
1959b    Linguistics as an instrument of prehistory. *Southwestern Journal of Anthropology* **15**(1):20–35.
1964    Linguistic overview. In J. D. Jennings and E. Norbeck, eds., *Prehistoric man in the New World:*527–556. Chicago: University of Chicago Press.

Swanson, E. H.
1966    The geographic foundations of the Desert Culture. Reno: *Desert Research Institute Publications in the Social Sciences and Humanities* **1**:137–146.
1968    Utaztecan prehistory. Pocatello: *Occasional Papers of the Idaho State University Museum* 22.

Swartz, B. K., Jr.
1961    *A preliminary archaeological survey along the proposed highway, Lava Beds National Monument, California.* San Francisco: Report to the National Park Service.
1963    Klamath Basin petroglyphs. Madison: *University of Wisconsin Archives of Archaeology* 21.
1964    *Archaeological investigations at Lava Beds National Monument, California.* Ph.D. dissertation. Tucson: Department of Anthropology, University of Arizona.

Swezey, S. L., and R. F. Heizer
1977    Ritual management of salmonid fish resources in California. *The Journal of California Anthropology* **4**(1):6–29.

Tainter, J. A.

1971    Hunter–gatherer territorial organization in the Santa Ynez Valley. *Pacific Coast Archaeological Society Quarterly* **7**(3):27–63.

1972    Simulation modeling of inland Chumash economic interaction. Los Angeles: *University of California, Los Angeles, Archaeological Survey Annual Report, 1972:79–106.*

1975    Hunter–gatherer territorial organization in the Santa Ynez Valley. Costa Mesa: *Pacific Coast Archaeological Society Quarterly* **11**(2):27–40.

Tamez, S.

1978    *An archaeological overview of portions of the North Coast Ranges of northwestern California.* Ukiah: Report to the U.S. Bureau of Land Management, Ukiah District.

Tartaglia, L. J.

1976    *Prehistoric maritime adaptations in southern California.* Ph.D. dissertation. Los Angeles: Department of Anthropology, University of California, Los Angeles.

Taylor, A. S.

1862    Indianology of California. San Francisco: *California Farmer and Journal of Useful Sciences,* May 16.

Taylor, R. E.

1975    Fluorine diffusion: A new dating method for chipped lithic material. *World Archaeology* **7**(2):125–135.

1982    Dating chipped lithics by fluorine profile measurements: Problems and potentials. In J. E. Ericson, R. E. Taylor, and R. Berger, eds., Peopling of the New World:285–298. Los Altos: *Ballena Press Anthropological Papers* 23.

Taylor, R. E., and L. A. Payen

1979    The role of archaeometry in American archaeology: Approaches to the evaluation of the antiquity of *Homo sapiens* in California. In M. B. Schiffer, ed., *Advances in Archaeological Method and Theory,* Vol. 2:239–283.

Taylor, W. W.

1961    Archaeology and language in western North America. *American Antiquity* **27**(1):71–81.

Teeter, K. V.

1964    The Wiyot language. Berkeley: *University of California Publications in Linguistics* 37.

Theodoratus, D. J., and J. Crain

1962    *Reconnaissance survey of Millerton Lake State Park.* Sacramento: Report to the California Departemnt of Parks and Recreation.

Theodoratus, D. J., F. A. Riddell, C. M. Blount, D. A. Bell, and M. E. Peters

1979    *Anthropological overview of a portion of Lassen and Modoc Counties.* Susanville: Report to the U.S. Bureau of Land Management.

Thieler, D.

1983    Gary Pahl at Mrn-17. *MAPOM News,* March, 1983 (n.p.). San Rafael: Miwok Archaeological Preserve of Marin.

Thomas, D. H.

1979    *Archaeology.* New York: Holt, Rinehart, and Winston.

Thompson, G., S. Wilke, and G. Lindeman

1979    *Cultural resource overview, Winema National Forest, Oregon.* Seattle: Shannon and Wilson.

Thomsen, H., and R. F. Heizer

1964    The archaeological potential of the Coast Yuki. Berkeley: *University of California Archaeological Survey Reports* 63:45–83.

Townsend, J. B.

1960    Two rock-shelters and a village site in Borrego State Park, Los Angeles: *Univer-*

*sity of California, Los Angeles, Archaeological Survey Annual Report, 1959–1960:249–275.*

Tozzer, A. M.

1900 Sierra Miwok field notes. Manuscript. Berkeley: University Archives, University of California.

"Trapper" (Col. J. W. Warner?)

n.d. Reminiscences of early life in California. (A clipping, probably from an early nineteenth century newspaper, in Hayes' Mission Book, Vol. 1, inserted between Documents 217 and 218, Bancroft Library, University of California), cf. Cook (1955b).

Treganza, A. E.

1942 An archaeological reconnaissance of northeastern Baja California and southeastern California. *American Antiquity* **8**:152–163.

1945 The ancient stone fish traps of the Coachella Valley, California. *American Antiquity* **10**(3):285–294.

1947a Notes on the San Dieguito lithic industry of southern California and northern Baja California. Berkeley: *University of California Publications in American Archaeology and Ethnology* **44**(2):253–255.

1947b Possibilities of an aboriginal practice of agriculture among the Southern Diegueño. *American Antiquity* **12**(3):169–173.

1950 *The Topanga Culture and southern California prehistory.* Ph.D. dissertation. Berkeley: Department of Anthropology, University of California.

1952 Archaeological investigations in the Farmington Reservoir area, Stanislaus County, California. Berkeley: *University of California Archaeological Survey Reports* **14**:1–37.

1953 *The archaeological resources of seven reservoir areas in central and northern California.* San Francisco: Report to the National Park Service.

1954 Salvage archaeology in the Nimbus and Redbank Reservoir areas, central California. Berkeley: *University of California Archaeological Survey Reports* **26**:1–39.

1955 *Salvage archaeology at sites Nap-74 and Nap-93 in the Monticello Reservoir area, California.* San Francisco: Report to the National Park Service.

1957 *The examination of Indian shellmounds within San Francisco Bay with reference to the possible 1579 landfall of Sir Francis Drake.* Vacaville: Reporter.

1958a Archaeological excavations in the Coyote Valley Reservoir area, Mendocino County, California. Manuscript. San Francisco: Department of Anthropology, San Francisco State University.

1958b An evaluation of the pre-Caucasian human resources of northwestern California. *Natural resources of northwestern California: History and archaeology supplement*:66–90. San Francisco: National Park Service.

1958c Salvage archaeology in the Trinity Reservoir area, northern California. Berkeley: *University of California Archaeological Survey Reports* **43**:1–38.

1958d The examination of Indian shellmounds within San Francisco Bay with reference to the possible 1579 landfall of Sir Francis Drake, second season. Manuscript. San Francisco: Department of Anthropology, San Francisco State University.

1959a Salvage archaeology in the Trinity Reservoir area—Field season 1958. Berkeley: *University of California Archaeological Survey Reports* **46**:1–32.

1959b Some new ideas in interpreting flake and core industries in California. Manuscript. Berkeley: Department of Anthropology, University of California.

1959c *The examination of Indian shellmounds in the Tomales and Drakes Bay areas with references to sixteenth century historic contacts.* Sacramento: Report to the California Department of Parks and Recreation.

1960a Archaeological investigations at Bolinas Bay, California. Manuscript. San Francisco: Department of Anthropology, San Francisco State University.

1960b    *Archaeological investigations in the San Luis Reservoir area, Merced County, California.* Sacramento: Report to the California Department of Parks and Recreation.

1962     *An archaeological survey of the aboriginal and early historic sites of Lassen Volcanic National Park, California.* San Francisco: Report to the National Park Service.

1964a    *Archaeological observations on the Kellogg Reservoir area, Contra Costa County, California.* San Francisco: Report to the National Park Service.

1964b    A review of California archaeology. Manuscript. San Francisco: Department of Anthropology, San Francisco State University.

1964c    An ethno-archaeological examination of Samwel Cave. Castro Valley: *Cave Studies* **12**:1–29.

1964d    *Warm Springs Dam project archaeological survey.* San Francisco: Report to the National Park Service.

1965a    *Archaeological problems in the north-central Sacramento Valley.* Berkeley: Paper presented at the Annual Meeting of the Kroeber Anthropological Society.

1965b    *Salvage archaeology in the Red Bluff-Redding areas of Shasta and Tehama Counties, California.* San Francisco: Report to the National Park Service.

1966a    Archaeological investigations in the Bolinas Bay area with reference to the 1579 landfall of Francis Drake. Manuscript. San Francisco: Department of Anthropology, San Francisco State University.

1966b    *Archaeological observations at Angel Island State Park.* Sacramento: Report to the California Department of Parks and Recreation.

n.d.a    A reconsideration of the data pertaining to the Borax Lake site. San Francisco: Society for California Archaeology, *R. E. Schenk Memorial Archives of California Archaeology* 9.

n.d.b    Early Man in southern California. Manuscript. San Francisco: Department of Anthropology, San Francisco State University.

n.d.c    *Salvage archaeology along Clear Creek and Cow Creek, Shasta County, California.* San Francisco: Report to the National Park Service.

Treganza, A. E., and A. Bierman
1958     The Topanga Culture: Final report on excavations, 1948. Berkeley: *University of California Anthropological Records* **20**(2):45–86.

Treganza, A. E., and S. F. Cook
1948     The quantitative investigation of aboriginal sites: Complete excavation with physical and archaeological analysis of a single mound. *American Antiquity* **13**(4):287–297.

1950     The quantiative investigation of aboriginal sites: With special reference to the relation of the physical components to the probable material culture. Berkeley: *University of California Publications in American Archaeology and Ethnology* **40**(5):223–262.

Treganza, A. E., and A. B. Elsasser
1955     *Salvage archaeology at sites Nap-74 and Nap-93 in the Monticello Reservoir area, California.* San Francisco: Report to the National Park Service.

Treganza, A. E., and M. H. Heiksen
1960     Salvage archaeology in the Whiskeytown Reservoir area and the Wintu Pumping Plant, Shasta County, California. San Francisco: *San Francisco State College Occasional Papers in Anthropology* 1.

1969     Salvage archaeology in the Black Butte area, Glenn County, California. San Francisco: *San Francisco State College, Anthropology Museum Occasional Papers* 2(1):1–54.

Treganza, A. E., and R. F. Heizer
1953     Additional data on the Farmington Complex, a stone implement assemblage of

probable early postglacial date from central California. Berkeley: *University of California Archaeological Survey Reports* 22:28–41.

Treganza, A. E., and T. F. King
1968    *Archaeological studies in Point Reyes National Seashore, 1959–1986.* San Francisco: Report to the National Park Service.

Treganza, A. E., and C. G. Malamud
1950    The Topanga Culture: First season's excavation of the Tank Site, 1947. Berkeley: *University of California Anthropological Records* 12(4):129–157.

Treganza, A. E., C. E. Smith, and W. D. Weymouth
1950    An archaeologial survey of the Yuki area. Berkeley: *University of California Anthropological Records* 12(3):113–124.

Treutlein, T.
1972    Fages as explorer, 1769–1772. *California Historical Quarterly* 51(4):338–356.

True, D. L.
1958    An early complex in San Diego County, California. *American Antiquity* 23(3):255–263.

1966    *Archaeological differentiation of Shoshonean and Yuman speaking groups in southern California.* Ph.D. dissertation. Los Angeles: Department of Anthropology, University of California, Los Angeles.

1970    Investigation of a late prehistoric complex in Cuyamaca Rancho State Park, San Diego County, California. Los Angeles: *University of California, Los Angeles, Archaeological Survey Monographs* 1.

1977    *Archaeological investigations in San Diego County, California: Preliminary report on sites SDi-4558, 4562, and 4562A.* Sacramento: Report to the California Department of Transportation.

1980    The Pauma Complex in northern San Diego County: 1978. *The Journal of New World Archaeology* 3(4):1–39.

True, D. L., M. A. Baumhoff, and J. E. Hellen
1979    Milling stone cultures in northern California: Berryessa I. *The Journal of California and Great Basin Anthropology* 1(1):124–154.

True, D. L., E. L. Davis, and E. L. Sterud
1966    Archaeological surveys in the New York Mountains region, San Bernardino County, California. Los Angeles: *University of California, Los Angeles, Archaeological Survey Annual Report, 1965–1966:*243–278.

True, D. L., C. W. Meighan, and H. Crew
1974    Archaeological investigations at Molpa, San Diego County, California. Berkeley: *University of California Publications in Anthropology* 11.

True, D. L., E. L. Sterud, and E. L. Davis
1967    An archaeological survey at Indian Ranch, Panamint Valley, California. Los Angeles: *University of California, Los Angeles, Archaeological Survey Annual Report, 1966–1967:*1–24.

Tuohy, D. R.
1968    Some Early Lithic sites in western Nevada. Portales: *Eastern New Mexico University Contributions in Anthropolcgy* 1(4):27–38.

1969    Breakage, burin facets, and the probable technological linkage among Lake Mojave, Silver Lake, and other varieties of Paleo-Indian projectile points in the Desert West. Carson City: *Nevada State Museum Anthropological Papers* 14:132–152.

1971    Review of *The Western Lithic Co-Tradition* by E. L. Davis, C. W. Brott, and D. L. Weide. *American Anthropologist* 73(2):417–418.

1974    A comparative study of late Paleo-Indian manifestations in the western Great Basin. Reno: *Nevada Archaeological Survey Research Papers* 5:91–116.

Tuohy, D. R., ed.
1978    Selected papers from the 14th Great Basin Anthropological Conference. Socorro: *Ballena Press Publications in Archaeology, Ethnology, and History* 11.

Tuthill, C., and A. A. Allanson
1954    Ocean-bottom artifacts. Los Angeles: *The Masterkey* 28(6):222–232.

Tyson, R.
1976    Personal communication, including photographs, regarding the *Olivella* sp. specimens found with human bones at site SDM W-2. Dated August 18, 1976. San Diego: Department of Anthropology, San Diego Museum of Man.

Uhle, M.
1907    The Emeryville shellmound. Berkeley: *University of California Publications in American Archaeology and Ethnology* 7(1):1–106.

USDI (United States Department of the Interior), Bureau of Land Management
1978    *Proposed geothermal leasing: Honey Lake Valley.* Final Environmental Assessment Record. Susanville: Bureau of Land Management.
1979    *Proposed livestock grazing management for the Tuledad/Home Camp Planning Unit.* Final Environmental Impact Statement. Susanville: Bureau of Land Management.
1980    *Proposed livestock grazing management for the Cowhead-Massacre Planning Unit.* Final Environmental Impact Statement. Susanville: Bureau of Land Management.
1981    *Proposed livestock grazing management for the Cal-Neva Planning Unit.* Draft Environmental Impact Statement. Susanville: Bureau of Land Management.

USDI-USDA
1977    *The upper Pit River area: Proposed geothermal leasing.* Final Environmental Analysis Record. Susanville and Alturas: U.S. Bureau of Land Management and U.S. Forest Service.

Upson, W.
1967    Excavations at Mrn-298W: 1966–1967 season. Manuscript. Santa Rosa: Department of Anthropology, Santa Rosa Junior College.
1968    Excavations at Mrn-298W: 1967–1968 season. Manuscript. Santa Rosa: Department of Anthropology, Santa Rosa Junior College.
1969    Excavations at 4-Mrn-298W, Fall 1968. Manuscript. Santa Rosa: Department of Anthropology, Santa Rosa Junior College.

Van Bueren, T.
1982    *Archaeological perspectives on Central Sierra Miwok culture change during the historic period.* M.A. thesis. San Francisco: Department of Anthropology, San Francisco State University.

Van Devender, T. R.
1977    Holocene woodlands in the southwestern deserts. *Science* 198:189–192.

Van Devender, T. R., and W. G. Spaulding
1979    Development of vegetation and climate in the southwestern United States. *Science* 204:701–710.

Van Dyke, S.
1971    The archaeology of 4-SMa-100. San Francisco: *Treganza Anthropology Museum Papers* 8:21–36.
1972    *Settlement patterning in prehistoric Marin County.* M.A. thesis. San Francisco: Department of Anthropology, San Francisco State University.

Van Valen, L.
1969    Late Pleistocene extinctions. *Proceedings of the North American Paleontological Convention,* E:469–485.

Van Valkenburgh, R.
1952    We found the lost cave of the San Martins. *Desert Magazine* 15:5–8.

Various Authors (sic)
    1958    Field notes from site CA-Yol-13 (summer field class, 1958). Berkeley: *University of California Archaeological Survey Manuscripts* 257.

Varner, D. M
    1976    *Archaeological excavations at Bass Lake Recreation Point site (FS # 05-15-57-20), Madera County.* San Francisco: Report to the U.S. Forest Service.

Varner, D. M., and W. C. Beatty, Jr.
    1980    *An archaeological investigation of cultural resources for the Balsam Meadow project, Fresno County, California.* Rosemead: Report to Southern California Edison Company.

Varner, D. M., and R. Bernal
    1976    *Archaeological investigations at Kerckhoff Reservoir, Madera County.* San Francisco: Report to the Pacific Gas and Electric Company.

Varner, D. M., and K. G. McCormick
    1977    *Archaeological investigations for the Kerckhoff hydroelectric project, Fresno County.* San Francisco: Report to Pacific Gas and Electric Company.

Varner, D. M., and D. R. Stuart
    1975    *A survey of archaeological and historical resources in the central Yokohl Valley, Tulare County, California.* Sacramento: Report to the U.S. Bureau of Reclamation.

Vayda, A.
    1966    Pomo trade feasts. *Humanités: Cahiers de l'Institut de Science Economique Appliquée.* (Reprinted 1967, in G. Dalton, ed., *Tribal and peasant economies:*484–500. Garden City: Natural History Press.)

Verner, J., and A. S. Boss (coordinators)
    1980    California wildlife and their habitats: Western Sierra Nevada. Berkeley: *U.S. Forest Service, Pacific Southwest Forest and Range Experiment Station, General Technical Report* PSW-37.

Voegelin, E. W.
    1938    Tübatulabal ethnography. Berkeley: *University of California Anthropological Records* **2**(1):1–84,

Von der Porten, E. P.
    1963    *Drakes Bay shell mound archaeology, 1951–1962.* Point Reyes: Drake Navigators Guild.
    1965    *Drake-Cermeño: An analysis of artifacts.* Point Reyes: Drake Navigators Guild.
    1970    The porcelains and terra cottas of Drakes Bay. San Francisco: *Treganza Anthropology Museum Papers* 6:223–256.
    1972    Drake and Cermeño in California: Sixteenth century Chinese porcelains. *Historical Archaeology* **4**:1–22.
    1976    *Two oriental porcelain sherds from Olompali, Marin County, California.* Point Reyes: Drake Navigators Guild.
    n.d.    (compiler) Field notes regarding Drake Navigators Guild and Santa Rosa Junior College Excavations at Point Reyes, 1957–1964. Santa Rosa: Notes in possession of compiler.

Von der Porten, E. P., and R. Péron (compilers)
    n.d.a    Field notes regarding Santa Rosa Junior College archaeological investigations at Point Reyes National Seashore, 1970–1973 seasons. Santa Rosa: Department of Anthropology, Santa Rosa Junior College.
    n.d.b    (with J. A. Rauschkolb, III), Archaeology in the Point Reyes National Seashore, 1973. Point Reyes: Drake Navigators Guild.

Von Endt, D. W., P. E. Hare, D. J. Ortner, and A. I. Stix
    1975    *Amino acid isomerization rates and their use in dating archaeological bone.*

Dallas: Paper presented at the Annual Meeting of the Society for American Archaeology.

Von Werlhof, J. C.

1960    *Archaeological investigations at Hospital Rock, Tulare County, California.* San Francisco: Report to the National Park Service.

1961a   *Aboriginal trails of the Kaweah Basin.* San Francisco: Report to the National Park Service.

1961b   *Archaeological investigations at Tul-145 (Cobble Lodge).* San Francisco: Report to the National Park Service.

1961c   *Revised report on test excavations at Buckeye Flat, Hospital Rock, and Potwisha Camp.* San Francisco: Report to the National Park Service.

1961d   *What we found at Hospital Rock.* San Francisco: Report to the National Park Service.

1965    Rock art of the Owens Valley, California. Berkeley: *University of California Archaeological Survey Reports* 65.

Von Werlhof, J. C., and S. Von Werlhof

1979    Archaeological examinations of the Magma site, East Mesa. Manuscript. El Centro: Imperial Valley College Museum.

Wahrhaftig, C., and J. H. Birman

1965    The Quaternary of the Pacific mountain system in California. In H. E. Wright, Jr., and D. G. Frey, eds., *The Quaternary of the United States:*299–340. Princeton: Princeton University Press.

Walker, E. F.

1935    A Yokuts cemetery at Elk Hills. Los Angeles: *The Masterkey* **9**:145–150.

1937    Sequence of prehistoric material culture at Malaga Cove. Los Angeles: *The Masterkey* **11**:210–214.

1947    *Excavation of a Yokuts Indian cemetery.* Bakersfield: Kern County Historical Society.

1951    Five prehistoric sites in Los Angeles County, California. Los Angeles: *Publications of the Frederick Webb Hodge Anniversary Publication Fund* 6:1–116.

Wallace, W. J.

1951a   The archaeological deposits in Moaning Cave, Calaveras County, California. Berkeley: *University of California Archaeological Survey Reports* 12.

1951b   The mortuary caves of Calaveras County, California. *Archaeology* **4**:199–203.

1954    The Little Sycamore site and early Milling Stone cultures in southern California. *American Antiquity* **20**(2):112–123.

1955a   A suggested chronology for southern California coastal archaeology. Albuquerque: *Southwestern Journal of Anthropology* **11**:214–230.

1955b   Early man in Death Valley. *Archaeology* **8**(2):88–92.

1958    Archaeological investigations in Death Valley National Monument. Berkeley: *University of California Archaeological Survey Reports* 42:7–22.

1962a   Prehistoric cultural development in the southern California deserts. *American Antiquity* **28**(2):172–180.

1962b   Archaeological sites in the mountain Palm Springs area, Anza–Borrego Desert State Park. In W. J. Wallace, Archaeological explorations in the southern section of Anza–Borrego Desert State Park. Sacramento: *California Department of Parks and Recreation, Archaeological Reports* 5.

1962c   Test excavations at BW-9, a late prehistoric site in Anza–Borrego Desert State Park. In W. J. Wallace, Archaeological explorations in the southern section of Anza–Borrego Desert State Park. Sacramento: *California Department of Parks and Recreation, Archaeological Reports* 5.

1962d   Prehistoric settlements in the Indian Gorge–Indian Valley district of

Anza–Borrego Desert State Park. In W. J. Wallace, Archaeological Explorations in the southern section of Anza–Borrego Desert State Park. Sacramento: *California Department of Parks and Recreation, Archaeological Reports* 5.

1964    An archaeological reconnaissance in Joshua Tree National Monument. *Journal of the West* **3**(1):90–101.

1966    Hollywood Riviera: An early Milling Stone Horizon site in Los Angeles County, California. *American Antiquity* **31**(3):422–427.

1968    *Archaeological resources of the Hidden Reservoir area, Madera County, California.* San Francisco: Report to the National Park Service.

1969    *Two archaeological sites in the Hidden Reservoir area, Madera County, California: Preliminary excavations.* San Francisco: Report to the National Park Service.

1970a   Archaeological investigations at Hidden Reservoir, Madera County, California. Los Angeles: *Archaeological Research Associates, Contributions to California Archaeology* 7:1–46.

1970b   Seasonal Indian campsites in the Lake Isabella area. Los Angeles: *The Masterkey* **44**(3):84–95.

1971    Indian use of California's rocks and minerals. *Journal of the West* **10**(1):35–52.

1977a   A half-century of Death Valley archaeology. *The Journal of California Anthropology* **4**(2):249–258.

1977b   *Death Valley National Monuments' prehistoric past: An archaeological overview.* Tucson: Report to the National Park Service.

1978a   Northern Valley Yokuts. In R. F. Heizer, vol. ed., *Handbook of North American Indians, Vol. 8: California:*462–470. Washington, D.C.: Smithsonian Institution.

1978b   Post-Pleistocene archaeology. In R. F. Heizer, vol. ed., *Handbook of North American Indians, Vol. 8: California:* 25–36. Washington, D.C.: Smithsonian Institution.

1978c   Southern Valley Yokuts. In R. F. Heizer, vol. ed., *Handbook of North American Indians, Vol. 8: California:* 448–461. Washington, D.C.: Smithsonian Institution.

Wallace, W. J., and R. J. Desautels

1960    An excavation at the Deep Tank-Squaw Tank site, Joshua Tree National Monument, California. Los Angeles: *Archaeological Research Associates, Contributions to California Archaeology* 4(2).

Wallace, W. J., A. P. Hunt, and J. P. Redwine

1959    An investigation of some stone mounds in Death Valley National Monument, California. Los Angeles: *Archaeological Research Associates, Contributions to California Archaeology* 3(1).

Wallace, W. J., and D. W. Lathrap

1952    An early implement assemblage from a limestone cavern in California. *American Antiquity* **18**(2):133–138.

1975    West Berkeley (CA-Ala-307): A culturally stratified shellmound on the east shore of San Francisco Bay. Berkeley: *Contributions of the University of California Archaeological Research Facility* 29.

Wallace, W., and E. Taylor

1952    Excavation of Sis-13, a rock shelter in Siskiyou County, California. Berkeley: *University of California Archaeological Survey Reports* 15.

1955    Archaeology of Wildrose Canyon, Death Valley National Monument. *American Antiquity* **20**(4):355–367.

1958    An archaeological reconnaissance in Bow Willow Canyon, Anza-Borrego Desert State Park. Los Angeles: *The Masterkey* **32**(5):155–166.

1959    A perceramic site at Saratoga Springs, Death Valley National Monument. Los Angeles: *Archaeological Research Associates, Contributions to California Archaeology* 3(2).

1960a   An archaeological survey of the Deep Tank-Squaw Tank district, Joshua Tree National Monument. Los Angeles: *Archaeological Research Associates, Contributions to California Archaeology* 4(1).

1960b   The surface archaeology of Indian Hill, Anza-Borrego Desert State Park. Los Angeles: *The Masterkey* 34(1):4–18.

Wallace, W. J., E. S. Taylor, and others
1956    The Little Sycamore shellmound, Ventura County, California. Los Angeles: *Archaeological Research Associates, Contributions to California Archaeology* 2.

Wallace, W. J., E. S. Taylor, and G. Kritzman
1962    Additional excavations at the Indian Hill Rockshelter, Anza–Borrego Desert State Park, California. In W. J. Wallace, Archaeological explorations in the southern section of Anza-Borrego Desert State Park. Sacramento: *California Department of Parks and Recreation, Archaeological Reports* 5.

Wallace, W. J., and E. Wallace
1978    *Ancient peoples and cultures of Death Valley National Monument.* Ramona: Acoma Books.

Walsh, J. McL.
1976    John Peabody Harrington: The man and his California Indian fieldnotes. Ramona: *Ballena Press Anthropological Papers* 6.

Warren, C. N.
1964    *Cultural change and continuity on the San Diego coast.* Ph.D. dissertation. Los Angeles: Department of Anthropology, University of California, Los Angeles.

1967a   The San Dieguito Complex: A review and hypothesis. *American Antiquity* 32(2):168–185.

1967b   The southern California Milling Stone Horizon: Some comments. *American Antiquity* 32(2):233–236.

1968    Cultural tradition and ecological adaptation on the southern California coast. In C. Irwin-Williams, ed., Archaic prehistory in the western United States. Portales: *Eastern New Mexico University Contributions in Anthropology* 1(3):1–14.

1970    Time and topography: Elizabeth W. C. Campbell's approach to the prehistory of the California desert. Los Angeles: *The Masterkey* 44(1):4–14.

1973    California. In J. E. Fitting, ed., *The development of North American archaeology*:212–249. Garden City: Anchor Books.

1980a   The Archaeology and archaeological resources of the Amargosa–Mojave Basin Planning Units. In C. N. Warren, M. Knack, and E. von Till Warren, A Cultural Resource Overview for the Amargosa–Mojave Basin Planning Units. Riverside: *U.S. Bureau of Land Management, Cultural Resources Publications, Anthropology–History* (unnumbered).

1980b   Pinto Points and problems in Mojave Desert archaeology. In L. B. Harten, C. N. Warren, D. R. Tuohy, eds., *Anthropological Papers in Memory of Earl H. Swanson, Jr.*, Pocatello: Special publication of the Idaho State Museum of Natural History: 67–76.

1982    *Prehistoric developments at Atlatl Rock.* Report to the Nevada Division of State Parks. Goleta: Institute for American Research.

Warren, C. N., ed.
1966    The San Dieguito type site: M. J. Rogers' 1938 excavation on the San Dieguito River. San Diego: *San Diego Museum Papers* 5:1–39.

Warren, C. N., and J. DeCosta
1964    Dating Lake Mojave artifacts and beaches. *American Antiquity* 30(2):206–209.

Warren, C. N., M. Knack, and E. von Till Warren
1980 A Cultural resource overview for the Amargosa–Mojave Basin Planning Units. Riverside: *U.S. Bureau of Land Management, Cultural Resources Publications, Anthropology–History* (unnumbered).

Warren, C. N., and H. T. Ore
1978 Approach and process of dating Lake Mojave artifacts. *The Journal of California Anthropology* 5(2):179–187.
1980a The archaeology and archaeological resources of the Amargosa–Mojave Basin Planning Units. In C. N. Warren, M. Knack, and E. von Till Warren, eds., A cultural resource overview for the Amargosa–Mojave Basin Planning Units:1–136. Riverside: *U.S. Bureau of Land Management, Cultural Resources Publications, Anthropology–History* (unnumbered).
1980b Pinto points and problems in Mojave Desert archaeology. In L. B. Harten, C. N. Warren, and D. R. Tuohy, *Anthropological papers in memory of Earl H. Swanson, Jr.:*67–76. Pocatello: Idaho State Museum of Natural History.

Warren, C. N., K. Bergin, D. Ferraro, and K. Olson
1978 *Archaeological excavations at the Valley of Fire.* Las Vegas: Report to the Nevada State Park System.

Warren, C. N., and R. H. Crabtree
1972 The prehistory of the southwestern Great Basin. Manuscript in press. *Handbook of North American Indians*, Vol. 11: *Great Basin.* Washington, D.C.: Smithsonian Institution.

Warren, C. N., and M. B. McKusick
1959 A burial complex from the southern San Joaquin Valley. Los Angeles: *University of California, Los Angeles, Archaeological Survey Annual Report, 1959:*17–26.

Warren, C. N., and M. G. Pavesic
1963 Shell midden analysis of site SDi-603 and ecological implications for cultural development of Batequitos Lagoon, San Diego County. Los Angeles: *University of California, Los Angeles, Archaeological Survey Annual Report, 1962–1963:*407–438.

Warren, C. N., and A. J. Ranere
1968 Outside Danger Cave: A view of Early Man in the Great Basin. Portales: *Eastern New Mexico University Contributions in Anthropology* 1(4):6–18.

Warren, C. N., and D. L. True
1961 The San Dieguito Complex and its place in California prehistory. Los Angeles: *University of California, Los Angeles, Archaeological Survey Annual Report, 1960–1961:*246–338.

Warren, C. N., D. L. True, and A. A. Eudey
1961 Early gathering complexes of western San Diego County: Results and interpretations of an archaeological survey. Los Angeles: *University of California, Los Angeles, Archaeological Survey Annual Report, 1960–1961:*1–106.

Warren, E. von Till, R. H. Crabtree, C. N. Warren, M. Knack, and R. McCarty
1980 *A cultural resources overview of the Colorado Desert Planning Units.* Riverside: Report to the U.S. Bureau of Land Management.

Watson, P. J., S. A. LeBlanc, and C. L. Redman
1971 *Explanation in Archaeology.* New York: Columbia University Press.

Webb, N. M.
1971 A statement of some phonological correspondences among the Pomo languages. *International Journal of American Linguistics, Memoirs* 26.

Weber, T. F.
1978 *Archaeological investigations at the Burns Valley sites, CA-Lak-741 and CA-Lak-742, Lake County, California.* Sacramento: Ann S. Peak and Associates.

Wedel, W. R.

    1935a    Archaeological notes on the Howell's Point site (CA-Col-2) and CA-Sha-47. Berkeley: *University of California Archaeological Survey Manuscripts* 18.

    1935b    Burial data on the Howells Point site (CA-Col-2). Berkeley: *University of California Archaeological Survey Manuscripts* 35.

    1935c    Field notes on the Howells Point mound, site CA-Col-2. Berkeley: *University of California Archaeological Survey Manuscripts* 111.

    1935d    Archaeological reconnaissance of Point Lobos Reserve. Manuscript. Berkeley: University of California, Bancroft Library.

    1941    Archaeological investigations at Buena Vista Lake, Kern County, California. Washington, D.C.: *Bureau of American Ethnology Bulletin* 130.

Weide, M. L.

    1968    *Cultural ecology of lakeside adaptation in the western Great Basin.* Ph.D. dissertation. Los Angeles: Department of Anthropology, University of California, Los Angeles.

    1976    A cultural sequence for the Yuha Desert. In P. J. Wilke, ed., Background to prehistory of the Yuha Desert region:81–94. Ramona: *Ballena Press Anthropological Papers* 5.

Welday, E. E., and J. W. Williams

    1975    Offshore surficial geology of California. Sacramento: *California Division of Mines and Geology Map Sheet* 26.

Wellman, K. F.

    1979    A quantitative analysis of superimpositions in rock art of the Coso Range, California. *American Antiquity* **44**(3):546–556.

Wells, P., and R. Berger

    1967    Late Pleistocene history of coniferous woodland in the Mojave Desert. *Science* 155:1640–1647.

Wendorf, M.

    1982    Early Man on Santa Rosa Island: A reassessment. *Leakey Foundation News* 22.

Wenger, P.

    1973    *Numerical taxonomy and linguistic classification: West Coast languages as a test case.* Ph.D. dissertation. Davis: Department of Anthropology, University of California.

Werner, R. H.

    1980    Archaeological investigations at CA-Lak-395, Detert Reservoir, Lake County, California. Manuscript. Rohnert Park: Anthropological Studies Center, Sonoma State University.

West, G. J.

    1979    The archaeology of Ven-100. Sacramento: *Department of Parks and Recreation, California Archaeological Reports* 17.

    1980    Pollen analysis of Tule Lake, Mendocino National Forest, California. *Archaeological investigations at three sites on Sanhedrin Mountain (CA-Lak-1112, 1113, CA-Men-1612), Mendocino National Forest, California:* Appendix 5. Willows: Report to the U.S. Forest Service.

    1981    Pollen analysis of sediments from Barley Lake, Mendocino National Forest, California. In J. M. Flaherty, *Archaeological investigations at Graves Cabin (CA-Men-1609, CA-Men-1614), Mendocino National Forest, California:* Appendix D. Willows: Report to the U.S. Forest Service.

Whalen, N. M.

    1976    An archaeological survey in southeastern Imperial County, California. Costa Mesa: *Pacific Coast Archaeological Society Quarterly* **12**(2):25–50.

Whalen, J.

    1967    A partial faunal analysis of Ala-12 and 13, two San Francisco Bay shellmounds. *Treganza Anthropology Museum Papers* 3(2):1–24.

Whistler, K. A.

1977a  Wintun prehistory: An interpretation based on plant and animal nomenclature. Berkeley: *Proceedings of the Third Annual Meeting of the Berkeley Linguistics Society:* 157–174.

1977b  Working draft of refined classification of California languages. Manuscript. In author's possession.

1978  Personal communication regarding central California linguistic prehistory. Berkeley: University of California.

1979a  Linguistic prehistory in the Northwest California culture area. In P. McW. Bickel, *A study of cultural resources in Redwood National Park:*11–26. Denver: Report to the National Park Service.

1979b  Personal communication regarding central California linguistic prehistory. Santa Barbara: University of California.

1980a  Personal communication regarding California linguistic prehistory. Sonora.

1980b  Pomo prehistory: A case for archaeological linguistics. Rohnert Park: *Sonoma State University, Anthropological Studies Center Manuscripts* S-2107.

1980c  Personal communication regarding the relative time depth and relationships among Penutian groups in California prehistory. Porterville.

White, C.

1980  Regional research design. In D. Gallegos, ed., *Class II cultural resources inventory of the East Mesa and West Mesa regions, Imperial Valley, California,* 1:183–187. Report to the U.S. Bureau of Land Management, Riverside. San Diego: WESTEC Services, Inc.

White, G.

1980  A history of archaeology in the Round Valley Indian Reservation area and the Round Valley Indian Reservation artifact collection. In S. B. Stewart and D. A. Fredrickson, eds., *A cultural resource survey of the Round Valley Indian Reservation, Mendocino and Trinity Counties, California:*88–100, 165–279. Tucson: Report to the National Park Service.

White, G., and D. A. Fredrickson

1981  *Archaeological investigations at CA-Lak-510, near Lower Lake, Lake County, California.* Sacramento: Report to the California Department of Transportation.

White, G., T. Jones, J. Roscoe, and L. Wiegel

1981  *Is the Borax Lake Complex? Or does the Borax Lake Pattern?* Bakersfield: Paper presented at the Annual Meeting of the Society for California Archaeology.

Whitehead, J. M.

1968  *The physcial anthropology of the Yuki Indians.* Ph.D. dissertation. Berkeley: Department of Anthropology, University of California.

Whitney, J. D.

1867  Notice of a human skull, recently taken from a shaft near Angels, Calaveras County. San Francisco: *Proceedings of the California Academy of Sciences* **3:**277–278.

1872  Cave in Calaveras County. Washington, D.C.: *Smithsonian Institution, Annual Report for 1867:*406–407.

1880  The auriferous gravels of the Sierra Nevada in California. Cambridge: *Memoirs of the Museum of Comparative Zoology of Harvard College* 3(1).

Whitney, S.

1979  *The Sierra Nevada.* San Francisco: Sierra Club Books.

Whittaker, J. C., with L. Huckell

1981  Archaeology in Yosemite National Park: The Wawona testing project. Tucson: *National Park Service Publications in Anthropology* 18.

Wickstrom, B.

1982  Archaeological investigations at CA-Son-20, Santa Rosa, Sonoma County, California. Rohnert Park: *Sonoma State University, Anthropological Studies Center Manuscripts* S-2870.

Wickstrom, B. P., and D. A. Fredrickson

    1982    *Archaeological investigations at CA-SON-20, Santa Rosa, Sonoma County, California.* Report prepared for Episcopal Homes Foundation, Santa Rosa.

Wieslander, A. E., and H. A. Jensen

    1946    Forest atlas, timber volumes, and vegetation types in California. Berkeley: *California Forest and Range Experiment Station, Forest Survey Releases* 4.

Wildesen, L.

    1969    Dos Palos (Mer-66). San Francisco: *Treganza Anthropology Museum Papers* 5(7):266–278.

Wilke, P. J.

    1971    Late prehistoric change in land use patterns at Perris Reservoir. Los Angeles: *University of California, Los Angeles, Archaeological Survey Annual Report, 1971*:155–164.

    1978a   Cairn burials of the California deserts. *American Antiquity* **43**(3):444–448.

    1978b   Late prehistoric human ecology at Lake Cahuilla, Coachella Valley, California. Berkeley: *Contributions of the University of California Archaeological Research Facility* 38.

Wilke, P. J., ed.

    1976    Background to prehistory of the Yuha Desert region. Ramona: *Ballena Press Anthropological Papers* 5.

Wilke, P. J., and D. N. Fain

    1974    An archaeological cucurbit from Coachella Valley. *The Journal of California Anthropology* **1**(1):110–114.

Wilke, P. J., and H. W. Lawton

    1975    Early observations on the cultural geography of Coachella Valley. Ramona: *Ballena Press Anthropological Papers* 3(1):1–43.

Wilke, P. J., T. W. Whitaker, and E. Hattori

    1977    Prehistoric squash (*Cucurbita pepo* L.) from the Salton Basin. *The Journal of California Anthropology* **4**(1):55–59.

Willey, G. R.

    1966    *An introduction to American archaeology, Vol. 1: North and Middle America.* Englewood Cliffs: Prentice-Hall.

Willey, G. R., and P. Phillips

    1958    *Method and theory in American archaeology.* Chicago: University of Chicago Press.

Willey, G. R., and J. A. Sabloff

    1974    *A history of American archaeology.* San Francisco: Freeman.

Williams, H.

    1942    The geology of Crater Lake National Park, Oregon, with a reconnaissance of the Cascade Range southward to Mount Shasta. Washington, D.C.: *Carnegie Institution of Washington Publications* 540.

Williams, P. A., and R. I. Orlins

    1963    The Corn Creek Dunes site in southern Nevada. Carson City: *Nevada State Museum Anthropological Papers* 10.

Wilson, N. L.

    1963    *The archaeology of the Loyalton Rock Shelter, Sierra County, California.* M.A. thesis. Sacramento: Department of Anthropology, California State University, Sacramento.

Wilson, N. L., and A. H. Towne

    1978    Nisenan. In R. F. Heizer, vol. ed., *Handbook of North American Indians, Vol. 8:*

*California*:387–397. Washington, D.C.: Smithsonian Institution.

Wilson, S. C.
  1970    Faunal analysis of 4-Mrn-298W: A perspective on 4-Mrn-216. San Francisco: *Treganza Anthropology Museum Papers* 6:211–222.

Winslow, C. F.
  1857    On human remains along with those of mastadon in the drift of California. Boston: *Proceedings of the Boston Society of Natural History* 6:278–279.

Winter, J. C.
  1977a   *Test excavations at four archaeological sites in the Almaden Valley.* San José: Report to the Santa Clara Valley Water District.
  1977b   The archaeological resources of Chesbro Reservoir. San José: *Society for California Archaeology, Occasional Papers in Cultural Resource Management* 1.
  1978a   *Archaeological investigations at CA-SCl-128, the Holiday Inn site.* San José: Report to the City of San José Redevelopment Agency.
  1978b   *Tamien: 6000 years in an American city.* San José: Report to the City of San José Redevelopment Agency.

Winterbourne, J. W.
  1938    Orange County anthropological project. Manuscript. Los Angeles: Southwest Museum.
  1968    Orange County California historical research project, report of Banning Estate
  (1935)  excavation (Norris property) (1935). Costa Mesa: *Pacific Coast Archaeological Society Quarterly* **4**(2):10–17.

Wirth Associates, Inc.
  1981    A cultural resource overview of the Bonneville Power Adminstration's proposed transmission line from Malin, Oregon, to Alturas, California. Bonneville Cultural Resources Group Report No. 100-19. Cheney: *Eastern Washington University, Reports in Archaeology and History.*

Witthoft, J.
  1979    Technology of the Calico site. In W. C. Schuiling, ed., *Pleistocene man at Calico* (2nd edition):47–53. Redlands: San Bernardino County Museum Association.

Wohlgemuth, E. N.
  1978    *Preliminary investigation and evaluation of CA-Las-345, Eagle Lake, Lassen County, California.* Susanville: Report to Lassen County Department of Public Works.

Wood, A. E.
  1930    Monterey Bay mounds, general. Berkeley: *University of California Archaeological Survey Manuscripts* 380.

Wood, S. H.
  1975    *Holocene stratigraphy and chronology of mountain meadows, Sierra Nevada, California.* Ph.D. dissertation. Pasadena: Department of Geology, California Institute of Technology.

Woodcock, W. E.
  1977    Personal communication regarding the provenience of a Clovisoid fluted point from Modoc County, California. San Francisco.

Woodward, A.
  1937    Atlatl dart foreshafts from the La Brea pits. Los Angeles: *Bulletin of the Southern California Academy of Sciences* **36**:41–60.

Woolfenden, W. B.
  1969    A study of Glenn-10: The Brownell Indian Cemetery. San Francisco: *Treganza Anthropology Museum Papers* 2(2):1–101.
  1970    *A study in historic sites archaeology.* M.A. thesis. San Francisco: Department of Anthropology, San Francisco State University.

Wormington, H. M.
    1959    Ancient man in North America (4th, rev. ed.). Denver: *Denver Natural History Museum Popular Series* 4.

Wren, D. G.
    1974    *Test excavation at China Peak Resort, Fresno County, California.* Fresno: Report to the Sierra National Forest.
    1976    *Two high Sierra sites, Fre-534 and Fre-535.* San Francisco: Report to the Pacific Gas and Electric Company.
    1978    *Archaeological investigations in the western Sierras (sic) and foothills of Fresno County, California.* San Francisco: Report to the Pacific Gas and Electric Company.

Wright, G. F.
    1891    Prehistoric man on the Pacific Coast. *Atlantic Monthly,* April:501–513.
    1892    Discussion of Becker's paper. *Bulletin of the Geological Society of America* **2**:200.

Wright, R. H.
    1971    Map showing locations of samples dated by radiocarbon methods in the San Francisco Bay region. Menlo Park: *U.S. Geological Survey Miscellaneous Field Studies Map* MF–317.

Wright, W. H., III
    1975    The Stanislaus River—A study in Sierra Nevada geology. *California Geology* **28**(1):3–10.

Wylie, H. G.
    1976    *Pilot Ridge survey: A graphic summary of Borax Lake points and other materials from the Six Rivers National Forest.* San Diego: Paper presented at the Annual Meeting of the Society for California Archaeology.

Yates, L. G.
    1875a    Localities of mounds in Alameda County, Washington Township. *Alameda County Independent,* June 26, July 3, July 10.
    1875b    The relics of the mound builders of California. *Alameda County Independent,* June 19.
    1889    Charmstones or "plummets" from California. Washington, D.C.: *Annual report of the Smithsonian Institution for 1886:296–305.*
    1902    Prehistoric California. Los Angeles: *Bulletin of the Southern California Academy of Sciences* 1(8):97–100.

# Author Index

# Subject Index